Canadian Economic History

BY

W.T. EASTERBROOK

AND

HUGH G.J. AITKEN

UNIVERSITY OF TORONTO PRESS
Toronto Buffalo London

© University of Toronto Press 1988
Toronto Buffalo London
Printed in Canada
ISBN 0–8020–6696–8 (paperback)

First published in 1956 by The Macmillan Company of Canada Limited.
Re-issued by Gage Publishing Limited in 1980. This edition has been photo-
graphically reproduced from the Gage (Macmillan) edition by permission of
Gage Educational Publishing Limited.

Reprinted 1958, 1961, 1963
(with corrections) 1965, 1967, 1968, 1969, 1970, 1975, 1978, 1979, 1981, 1984

Canadian Cataloguing in Publication Data

Easterbrook, W.T. (William Thomas), 1907–
Canadian economic history

Originally published: Toronto: Macmillan of
Canada, 1956.
Includes bibliographies and index.
ISBN 0–8020–6696–8

1. Canada – Economic conditions. I. Aitken,
Hugh G.J. II. Title

HC113.E22 1988   330.971   C88-095115-X

PREFACE

This book requires no extensive introduction. It is and purports to be nothing more than a straightforward presentation of the leading events and processes of Canadian economic history, selected and arranged in such a way that they will have meaning for the interested reader. The authors hope that it will prove a useful book: useful not only to Canadians but also to all those interested in the study of economic development.

Any work of historical inquiry must inevitably be selective. The point of view of the author influences not only the interpretation of events but also the selection of the events to be interpreted. The authors of this book share a common interest in economic organization, both on the level of the national economy and on that of the individual business unit. If this book has a central focus, it is on the part which business organizations, big and small, working in co-operation with government, have played in creating a national economy in Canada.

Partly for reasons of space, partly because we believe that extensive documentation is less appropriate in a textbook than in a research monograph, we have allowed ourselves the liberty of omitting footnotes. We trust that in this lapse from scholarly convention we shall have the indulgence of our professional colleagues. If authority is required for any statement of fact in the text, it will usually be found in the works listed as *Suggestions for Further Reading* at the end of each chapter. These works, needless to say, represent only a small fraction of the historical literature on which we have drawn for assistance. Our gratitude must be given, therefore, not so much to specific authors but rather to all those who have preceded us in the study of Canadian history.

To the friends and colleagues who have read parts or the whole of this book in manuscript and assisted us by their advice we owe special thanks. To Professor V. C. Fowke of the University of Saskatchewan, to Professor R. Craig McIvor of McMaster University, to Professor Reid Elliott, Victoria College, University of British Columbia, and to Professors V. W. Bladen, Karl Helleiner, A. W. Currie, W. C. Hood, A. E. Safarian, and J. H. Dales of the University of Toronto we are particularly grateful. The Committee administering the Rockefeller grant to the University of Toronto for study of the economic, political, and social development of Canada contributed toward the payment of typing expenses. The maps in this book were prepared by Captain C. C. J. Bond; to his skill and meticulous accuracy we would like to pay our respects. Miss Anne B. Hunter and Janice Aitken assisted in the reading of proof and the preparation of the index; for these indispensable services we are sincerely grateful. Responsibility for all statements made in the text, however, and for any errors it may contain, must rest solely with the authors.

W.T.E.
H.G.J.A.

Cambridge, England
Riverside, California
July, 1956

CONTENTS

PART II

ESCAPE FROM COLONIALISM

CONTENTS

CONTENTS

CONTENTS

PART III

TRANSCONTINENTAL ECONOMY

MAPS

PART I

STAPLES AND COLONIAL EXPANSION

CHAPTER I

THE EUROPEAN BACKGROUND

INTRODUCTION: EUROPEAN EXPANSION IN THE AMERICAS

OVER much of its course Canadian economic history may be fairly described as an extension of European economic and political influence in the northern part of North America. It is important to notice that this northern expansion was only one phase of European expansion into the Americas, and that development elsewhere in the New World helped to determine the direction and character of economic change in Canada. In other words, Canada cannot be studied in isolation from Europe or the rest of North America, since she did not, in any sense, develop separately from these areas. Our problem at the beginning is to set out those factors in European economic history which were most significant in Canada's early history, and, as our study proceeds, to note events in both Europe and the New World which help to explain how our economy changed and grew in the way it did. In doing so we shall have in mind the contributions of Europe as a market for our commodities, as a source of supply of man-power and capital, and as a centre of economic and political influence which established the pattern we find in our country's development.

It is not difficult to take account of the European nations which first actively engaged in trade and colonial activities in the New World, nor of the first important points of contact between Europe and the Americas. These nations were Portugal and Spain, France, Holland, England and Russia, and the first points of contact were in the Caribbean area, the North Atlantic regions, and points on the Pacific coast of South and North America. Of these nations, France and England played the most important roles in North American economic history. Of the others, Spain must be singled out even though her leaders concentrated their attention largely on areas to the south of what is now Canada. We need pay less attention to Holland, but this nation cannot be neglected entirely because of her great influence on European expansion in the seventeenth and eighteenth centuries. Portugal will be referred to very briefly, for although she appeared very early in the fisheries of the North Atlantic she left very little impression on the course of events in North America. In the North Pacific, Russian traders were active over a long period but

Russia becomes important only towards the end of the eighteenth century and discussion of her activities is left to a later period in our study.

PORTUGAL AND SPAIN

Although little Portugal engaged in the fisheries of the Grand Banks four hundred and fifty years ago and continues to be active today, she made no contacts of importance with North America. To the south, Brazil, which has been described as a monument to Portugal, attests to her once-great role as a colonizing nation, but absorption by Spain (1580-1640) lessened her importance in European affairs and it is to the greater power that we must turn. For a time Spain participated actively in the North Atlantic fisheries, her operations here reaching their peak in the period 1570 to 1580, only to decline rapidly after the destruction of the Spanish Armada in 1588. Yet her place as the leading nation over much of the sixteenth century, her great colonizing efforts in the Caribbean and in South America and her defensive policies in North America were matters of the greatest importance in the extension of European influence to the New World. She was leader in a century in which the modern world began to take shape. It was a century which witnessed an outburst of energy in economic and political expansion, in capital accumulation and in social and political revolutions comparable to that of the present day. These were exciting times and not the least interesting aspect of these was the great power of Spain at the beginning and her decline as the century drew to its close.

A true index of Spanish power was her sixteenth-century supremacy in the struggle among European nations for colonial empire. In 1493 the Pope had awarded the western part of the New World including the Americas (apart from most of Brazil) to Spain. The union of Aragon and Castile (with the marriage of Ferdinand and Isabella in 1469), the end of the struggle of Moslems and Christians in 1492, and such factors as a strong monarchy and favourable geographic locations were conditions which enabled Spain to exploit her monopoly position and she lost no time in taking advantage of her head start. There followed her occupation of the West Indies over the period from 1492 to 1519 which gave her a base for expansion to the mainland of the Americas. The Indies were important also for Spain's defence of her growing New World possessions and for control and regulation of her colonial trade. She moved from this key point to the Panama region, which in turn provided a base for expansion into Peru and the La Plata valley and north to the rich mines of Mexico. The southern part of North America, from California to Florida, was explored but lack of precious metals in this region spelled lack of interest in settlement. By the close of the century

4

this remarkable burst of colonizing and exploratory zeal had given Spain control of the territory south of the Rio Grande, while across the Pacific the Philippines had been added to round out this great New World empire.

Later expansion in the seventeenth and eighteenth centuries was designed less to acquire new territories than to protect the rich Spanish holdings in Central and South America. The appearance of the French in South Carolina, Florida and Texas led to Spanish moves to control these regions. In the Pacific signs of English interest and the appearance of the Russians to the north led to extensions of Spanish power up the Pacific coast of North America. The attacks of rivals on Spanish possessions were to result eventually in the loss of much of the West Indies and the southern parts of North America to England, France and Holland, but Spain's system of defensive salients enabled her to hold the heart of Spanish America well into the nineteenth century. The strength of Spanish institutions in Central and South America remained great long after her power in Europe had been broken and her monopoly of much of the New World had been destroyed.

It was toward the close of the sixteenth century that indications of weakness in Spain's position in Europe became apparent. The Dutch declared their independence of Spanish control in 1581, and seven years later the Spanish Armada was thrown back by England, a power whose aggressions against ports and treasure ships in the Spanish Main became increasingly difficult to contain. The end of Spanish invincibility was in sight, and in the seventeenth century both Portugal (1640) and the northern provinces of the Netherlands (1648) gained recognition of their independence of Spain. In the New World, Jamaica, Virginia, South Carolina and North Georgia were lost to the English, San Domingo to the French, and Curaçao to the Dutch, as Spanish retreat to intrenched positions in Central and South America continued. The reasons for this decline in Spanish power and prestige must be sought in the Old World and, since this decline was of the greatest consequence in European and North American history, its causes should be noted briefly even though there is still much controversy concerning their relative importance.

Much has been written about the effects of huge imports of New World treasure, silver and gold, on the Spanish economy. These began in 1503, reached their peak in the last decade of the sixteenth century, and continued in volume to the 1630's. This inflow of precious metals and a later resort to currency debasement led to a great rise in prices in Spain, a process which aided other nations seeking to sell their wares in the Spanish market in return for the precious metals they lacked. At the same time, inflation in Spain increased costs of production in Spanish industry and made it more difficult for Spain to compete with the other nations in world markets. There is not much question that in the end this weakened Spain's economy, at times to the point of collapse. And it is fair to say that the real beneficiaries of Spain's discoveries of New World riches were those nations who engaged in trade with her. Yet there were other elements in Spain's position which must be taken into account in any explanation of her failure to keep pace with the growing economic power of her rivals, even though little more than a summary of these can be given in these pages.

To begin with, although a semblance of political unity had been achieved early in Spanish history, there were serious but continuing obstacles to the welding together of the various regions in a strong national economy. Geographically the Iberian peninsula is broken into a number of sharply demarcated geographic divisions and no natural or common centre, such as London in England, is present to serve as a focus for national energies. Historically, in the centuries-long struggle with the Moors, important towns had received charters guaranteeing their independence, and their particularism proved to be very difficult to overcome in the national interest. These obstacles to a strongly unified state proved to be an increasingly serious handicap as stronger rivals emerged to challenge Spain's leadership. It was all the more serious because of Spain's almost constant involvement in religious and dynastic wars on the continent of Europe. These put a heavy strain on her man-power and finance, just at the time she was engaged in extensive New World ventures. It is significant that England, on the other hand, was clear of entanglements on the continent of Europe before turning to New World expansion of empire.

It was not for want of adventurous spirit that Spain failed to retain world leadership among nations. The clues to the failure must be sought rather in her inability to develop into a strong national state as Holland, England and France were developing at the time of her decline. This inability was reflected in the tight grip of medieval attitudes and institutions which withstood the impact of American silver and gold and the excitement of New World discoveries. The power of the Mercantile Guild, of the Mesta and its six-centuries-long control of Spain's great migratory sheep industry, and of the medieval Church stood opposed to the emergence of a modern state. As a consequence, New World expansion was much less a commercial operation than a transplantation of feudal institutions whose grip remains strong in South America to the present day. Close and elaborate regulation of shipping and transoceanic trade along medieval lines channelled the energies of merchants and traders in directions which permitted very little freedom in economic pursuits. Unlike the business men of Holland and England who were steadily gaining in influence over national policies, those of Spain never emerged from the shell of medieval corporate organization. In other words, Spain never became a mercantilist nation in the same sense that her rivals did, and

6

her inability or refusal to move into the orbit of Western European economic change must be closely linked with her failure to keep pace in economic terms with those who profited most by her weakness.

Spain's sixteenth-century greatness and the beginnings of decline in the 1630's have been stressed because they were of the greatest consequence to the course of international rivalries in North America. From this standpoint there were two aspects of Spain's magnificent failure to retain her leadership among European nations. In the first place, Spanish weakness gave her rivals the opportunity to move into her possessions in the West Indies and southern North America. Her attempts to develop tobacco and sugar plantations here as a means of strengthening her grip and conserving her precious metals through development of other lines of trade only led her rivals to do the same and it was the latter who used these commodities to build great systems of trade linking North America and Europe. In the seventeenth century the West Indies with their great sugar-producing potential became a key point in England's world network of trade and a great source of strength to France in her efforts to build an empire in this part of the world. If Spain had retained her monopoly of this region the whole course of North American economic history would have followed very different lines.

The same may be said of another aspect of Spanish decline. Her great imports of precious metals and their unfortunate impact on the Spanish economy led to the emergence of Spain as a great market or sponge for the imports of nations anxious to obtain some of her New World treasure. Since they had no direct access to these riches within their own empires, trade was looked to as a means to this end. By selling to Spain more than they bought from her, other nations acquired the precious metals they lacked. The fisheries of the North Atlantic have been described as the gold mines of England at this time and certainly the cod was a major commodity in the trade by which England and to some degree France drained Spain of a good part of her New World wealth. Both nations developed systems of three-cornered trade, with the Spanish market as the key point in the triangle. The decline of the Spanish fisheries, her weakness in agriculture and her Catholic population all contributed to the demand for the fishery products of the North Atlantic. The strategic place of Spain in our early economic history will become apparent when we turn to a survey of international rivalries in North America before 1763. Enough at this time to say that the mines of New Spain, like the fur trade of the French, were poor instruments for empire-building in the New World. They aroused the envy of other powers, yet provided no strong economic supports for defence against their attacks.

As Spain fell behind, other nations strove to capitalize on her growing weakness. And in the struggle for the trade and territories of the New World, it was the free-ranging maritime nations with strong navies who were best situated to take the lead. Holland, a nation which had co-operated with England to destroy Spain's monopoly of the New World, was the first to succeed Spain as a centre of aggressive expansion. For much of the seventeenth century she overshadowed England as a great naval power and Amsterdam appears at this time as the centre of world commerce and finance. Dutch merchant shipping seemed to be everywhere, trading and carrying a great array of the commodities of the Baltic, the Mediterranean and the New World more efficiently and cheaply than the shipping of any other nation. Amsterdam's greatness was based on the carriage and financing of foreign trade and her mastery in this respect was attained only by England in the eighteenth century. Led by a mercantile oligarchy which maintained its position by the gains of trade, Holland dominated the sea lanes of the world. Her East India Company promoted trade and colonies in the East and in Africa, and her West India Company spearheaded her ventures in North and South America. Dutch settlements appeared in Brazil, Guiana and the Caribbean, and to the north in the Hudson valley of North America. New Amsterdam was founded in 1614 by Amsterdam merchants, and Dutch settlers pushed along the Hudson, Connecticut and Delaware Rivers. Promising beginnings were made in the fur trade, and farming and settlement in New Amsterdam appeared to indicate a strong grip on this part of North America. Holland seemed destined to become as great a power in the Americas as she was in Europe.

Unfortunately for the Dutch there were serious elements of weakness in this great empire of trade. It is apparent that the primary interest was not in colonization and settlement, or the putting down of roots in the New World; the great merchants strongly preferred the quick returns of trade to the less exciting, slower and more uncertain profits of colonization. In this respect Holland lagged behind her great rivals, the English and the French, and her hold on her far-distant possessions was in most instances easily broken. Nor was her position in Europe as strong as it appeared to be in the first half of the seventeenth century. Her concentration on commerce and finance was so great as to check interest in the nation's industrial development. The merchants' point of view led to a strong tendency to emphasize large short-term profits, to glory in Holland's position as the great carrier and paymaster of Europe at the time when the early industrial revolutions of England and France were slowly transforming these economies into first-class industrial powers. It is true that Holland was not well endowed with the resources of this new industrialism, but it is doubtful whether in view of the strength of the mercantile point of view a better resource position would have greatly altered the character of her development. This was a matter of the greatest consequence, because the balance of power in Europe was shifting rapidly in favour of the strong industrial nation with its greater productivity in both peace and war. In short, Holland's leadership rested on an extremely narrow foundation and her failure to develop a strong industrial base largely accounts for her decline in the eighteenth century to the status of a second-class power.

Her vulnerability to attack by her rivals was exploited by England in the second half of the seventeenth century. This nation, seeking to break the grip of the Dutch on world trade, struck at the very bases of Dutch power, her carrying-trade and her shipping. In 1651 Parliament passed the most famous of the English Navigation Acts. This legislation underwent many changes before the Navigation Laws were repealed in the nineteenth century, but fundamentally this Act and its modifications set out a pattern of governmental regulation designed to produce an integrated system of trade linking overseas possessions with the mother country. At the beginning Holland was the obvious target for the English legislators. By eliminating the Dutch from England's expanding network of trade and retaining within the Empire the profits of shipping and trade in colonial products, England made it very difficult for her rival to continue as the world's great carrying nation. England's tactics alone do not account for Holland's decline, and too much has been made of this aspect of the Navigation Acts, but in striking at the roots of that nation's commercial structure they undoubtedly hastened her retreat from greatness. War helped too and the Second Dutch War (1664-7) saw Holland's naval power broken, her dominion on the continent of North America brought to an end. Nevertheless, there had been clear indications that Holland's reach had been greater than her economy could support and war made it apparent that hers was an over-extended position.

In North America, New Netherland, which separated the English colonies in New England from those in the south, was lost to Great Britain in 1664. The Dutch colony, faced with official indifference at home and the pressure of English settlers moving into its preserves, fell easily before the attack of a greater colonizing power. But in their short stay in this part of the world, the Dutch succeeded in demoralizing the French fur-trade system to the north and in leaving traces of their early occupancy in the Hudson valley which remain even today. Apart from isolated points still retained in the West Indies and South America, the Dutch ceased to play an active part in the Americas. They fared better in Europe, but as commercialism slowly gave way before the power of industrialism, theirs was to be a minor role in the new economic order that was beginning to emerge. Their earlier supremacy had forced botn England and France to move aggressively against her and her greatest contribution to developments in our part of the world lies in the pressure she exerted on these nations. England, in particular, partly in response to this pressure, forged a new empire of trade and colonies which was to give her world leadership. This, however, awaited the outcome of her struggle with an even more dangerous rival, the power of absolutist France.

FRANCE

France, like Spain, and unlike Holland, was a continental nation and it is highly important to keep in mind that expansion by continental nations follows lines and exhibits aims and motivations quite different from those characteristic of maritime nations. In these centuries the former faced numerous handicaps which their maritime rivals did not encounter. In the first place, it is much more difficult to bring about a strong unity in a sprawling continental area broken by geography into numerous regions. By contrast, the smaller and more compact maritime area, with its shorter distances between important centres and its greater ease of communications, is more easily welded into a strong state. This is a highly important matter in a world of political and economic rivalries in which state power must play a strategic role. Like Spain, France faced much more difficult problems in achieving a strongly unified state than did Holland or England.

In the second place, continental powers have long exposed borders to defend, a serious problem where wars are common and the threat of attack is seldom absent. This was only too true of Europe from the mid-sixteenth to the mid-seventeenth century, a period in which eight costly wars were fought and in which devastation was widespread. For France, historical and geographic influences ruled out any escape from these conflicts, and the effects were apparent in the character of her economic development and in the absolutist rule of the Bourbons with their administrative control over the economic life of the country. More fortunately situated areas could escape the heavy burdens and enormous expenses of land warfare; the sea warfare engaged in by maritime nations meant much less dislocation and damage to the nations involved. For France there was no escape from the heavy burdens present in maintaining national security on the continent and these burdens fell very heavily on the mercantile classes of this continental power.

Not only did France face serious obstacles to her dreams of a New World empire, but in economic terms she felt less strongly the need to engage in overseas expansion. As a continental nation she was more self-sufficient than a maritime power could be, and under less pressure to seek the gains of trade which the latter were forced to seek if they were to survive. Although the New World could be expected to provide commodities in short supply in her own domestic markets, in the main military and religious considerations overshadowed economic elements in French overseas expansion. Maritime trading nations, on the other hand, forced to live on the returns of their shipping and commerce, worked under great pressure to develop their New World holdings as key points in imperial structures of trade. In the more complex French system with its mixture of aims and objectives, no such single-minded pursuit of profits was apparent. As a consequence, French activities in North America and the Caribbean provide many points of contrast with those of her maritime rivals. Obstacles to the achievement of a strong and unified economy and heavy burdens of continental defence weakened France's competitive position and increased her reliance on military expansion, with the result that she never achieved the necessary economic strength to enable her to support her political and religious aspirations in the New World.

The mercantile classes which played so prominent a role in Dutch and English empire-building failed to obtain any corresponding freedom and power to influence national policy in France. Heavily taxed in the interests of defence, subordinate to military and ecclesiastical interests in a system of state absolutism, they fitted into, rather than dominated, the nation's course of development. This is not to say that French merchants were not aggressive in promoting their aims in Europe and North America but rather that they faced greater obstacles than their English counterparts in shaping policies to their own ends. That this was true of French enterprise in general was apparent in the condition of industry and agriculture in France in the sixteenth and seventeenth centuries.

Professor Nef has shown that in the period 1540-1640 French industrial progress lagged behind that of England. France remained the greater power, and her rate of economic progress over the first seven decades of the sixteenth century and after 1600 was respectable, but available statistics indicate that she failed to keep pace in key industries with her rival. Although the details of this failure cannot be given here, two important points should be noted. First, in contrast to England, state control and regulation of industry steadily increased to the point where a substantial part of French industrial enterprise was dependent on governmental support and privileges, much of it subject to direct governmental interference. Secondly, the strength of Crown, nobility, and clergy, the elements freest of tax burdens, ensured a strong demand for luxury or quality products in preference to quantity production more suited to the requirements of heavy industry. As a result the machinery of government was used to strengthen traditional forms of production which were losing ground in more economically progressive regions. Competitive weakness led French industrial enterprise to rely on the government for support and protection and to follow cautious, conservative policies at a time when a freer and more aggressive development was necessary if France was to retain her leadership. This retardation of French industry was a source of weakness in both the Old World and the New. In North America, for example, French fur-traders were seriously handicapped by their inability to supply cheap wares in quantity for their Indian allies, and here, as elsewhere, this weakness led to even heavier reliance on the state.

Similarly, in French agriculture, no reorganization of this basic industry along more productive lines comparable to that achieved in England's agricultural revolutions took place. The traditional small unit of production, the small farm of low productivity, resisted the pressures for more advanced techniques to meet market demands, and even after the French Revolution the peasant proprietor on his small holding remained the typical figure in French agriculture, a centre, with his fellows, of stability and resistance to change. Viewed in terms of its consequence for the French economy, the strength of tradition in French agriculture, like that in industry, was a source of serious weakness in a world in which economic power occupied a highly important place in international rivalries. The small farmer like the small artisan pursuing his small goals provided weak supports for a nation faced with the growing might of England. Low agricultural productivity also had its effect on French expansion in the New World. The weakness of her supply position enhanced the need for commodities for home consumption. The cod of the North Atlantic was viewed much less as an article of trade than as a valuable addition to the domestic diet, an addition all the more valuable because of religious considerations. As a result, the cod fisheries were of limited significance in the development of France's external trade. And they were of even less significance as a factor working in the direction of greater freedom from close state regulation of the nation's commerce, in sharp contrast with the pressure exerted in this direction by the fisheries of England.

In every avenue of France's economic life, in her commerce, industry and trade, the business man of France found himself hemmed in by regulations imposed by the authority of the state. A continental power, almost constantly engaged in destructive land warfare, evolved a political and social structure into which the enterpriser had to fit. His political weakness and lack of social prestige gave him small voice in national affairs. Merchants might be entrusted with the task of developing overseas territories, but the test of performance was set by the state. This authoritarian mode of expansion showed very little change over the period of French activity in North America, and conclusions as to its effects may be noted briefly at this point.

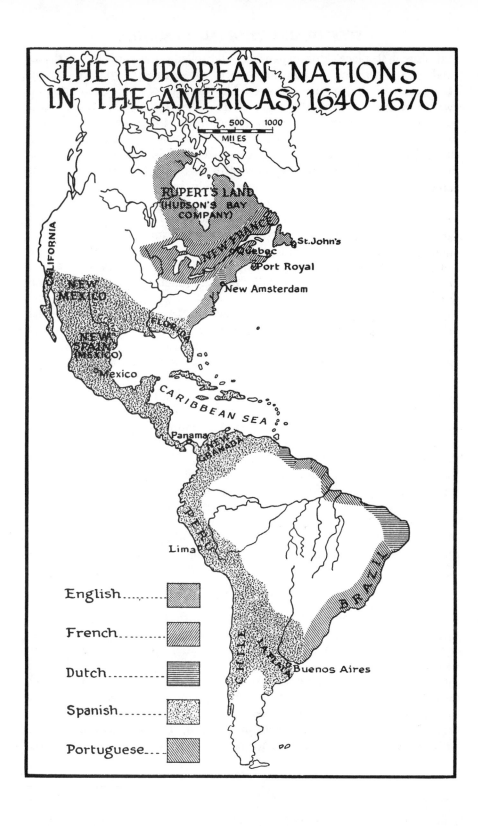

THE EUROPEAN NATIONS IN THE AMERICAS, 1640-1670

500   1000
MILES

RUPERT'S LAND
(HUDSON'S BAY
COMPANY)

NEW FRANCE

St. John's

Quebec

Port Royal

New Amsterdam

CALIFORNIA

NEW
MEXICO

FLORIDA

NEW
SPAIN
(MEXICO)

Mexico

CARIBBEAN SEA

Panama

NEW
GRANADA

PERU

Lima

BRAZIL

CHILE

LA PLATA

Buenos Aires

English

French

Dutch

Spanish

Portuguese

In the first place, this expansion, controlled in accordance with the needs of self-sufficiency, took the form of direct lines of contact between each area and the mother country. The fisheries of the North Atlantic, the fur of New France, the sugar of the West Indies, reflected the pull of a continental economy. At no time was there an effective linking together of these different parts of the system with each other. This could have resulted only from greater freedom in the development of new lines of trade and the presence of a more flexible, less rigid system of control. A better balanced, more closely integrated structure would have resulted, but this never materialized. Secondly, the French drive to New World empire was more spectacular than that of her rival, her early gains more impressive, because of the strength of state participation and the important part played by military force. But at the same time, this reliance on force was an indication of weakness rather than strength, for it reflected the inability of the French to compete effectively in economic terms.

In the third place, the French grip on the New World remained weak because it lacked the push of migrants from the Old World such as that provided by religious differences in seventeenth-century England; nor was there any strong pull since the effective demand for French manpower was light in both the fur trade and the sugar plantations. Further, and most serious in the end, naval power was the trump card of maritime nations and France's inability to keep on equal terms with the English in this respect was fatal. Open lines of communication were crucially important, and the naval superiority of England and later New England tipped the balance heavily against the French. This combination of factors forced France into ventures in which political aspirations far outstripped economic realities. Perhaps the most remarkable feature of her struggle for America was the skill and tenacity with which she hung on against great odds until the end in 1763. The forces which account for this final retreat must be sought mainly in the Old World where history and geography seemed to combine against her dreams of conquest in the New.

ENGLAND

The picture is very different when we turn to England. Geography in particular was exceedingly kind to this island power. Here there were few obstacles to the building of a unified nation, little need for big and expensive standing armies to defend her borders, and, in her phase of New World expansion, no involvement in the devastating wars of the continent. And if there were no obstacles imposed by geography to a strong national development, there were much stronger incentives to expand overseas. For, as a maritime nation, England was under the necessity of deriving a large part of her income from external trade;

self-sufficiency for her could mean only that of a balanced structure of trade linking many regions in a trading network of which the mother country was the natural centre. Maritime areas are forced to look outward and England was no exception. Only large continental areas may seek self-sufficiency within established borders. Favoured by freedom from obstacles to expansion and under considerable pressure to seek external markets and sources of trading supplies, England turned more or less inevitably to a policy of aggressive commercial exploitation of the resources of overseas areas. Furthermore, in an age when sea-power spelled success or failure in empire-building, the navy of this maritime nation was to play a decisive role in the outcome of international rivalries in Europe and the Americas.

To sum up at this point, England's physical environment made comparatively easy the early achievement of national unity, saved her from the continental wars of the sixteenth century, and provided the drive to external expansion. Moreover, geography gave her an excellent location on the world's trade routes and led to an early emphasis on control of the sea-lanes so vital to unbroken contacts with distant regions. Finally, her agricultural and mineral resources were sufficient to prevent the one-sided reliance on commerce and finance which had helped to spell ruin for her great maritime rival, the Holland of the eighteenth century.

In almost every respect, the business men of England seemed to be destined to lead their country to world leadership. Compared to other national units, theirs was a stable area in which to carry on trade and investment, free of the pressure for state control of economic life which prolonged and expensive wars exert and of the heavy taxation burdens which are the consequence of heavy expenditures for defence. And there were other elements in their favour which strengthened their hand against attempts by the English Crown to control the nation's economy in the interests of stability and established positions. First, the break with Rome and the dissolution of the monasteries resulted in the end in a transfer of much of the country's land resources from Church to merchants, members of the legal profession and economically-minded landowners. Secondly, a secular or long-run rise in prices beginning in the 1540's and extending well into the next century, stimulated enterprise as costs rose less slowly than prices, a situation highly favourable to satisfactory returns from market activities. In this respect, French enterprise benefited too, but the freer business men of England were more aggressive in exploiting their opportunities. Thirdly, as merchants and industrialists gained in wealth their greater economic power was reflected in their increasing political influence and great social prestige. This led to tensions as new forces in national life clashed with traditional forms opposed to the growing power of enterprisers and their demands for a stronger voice in national affairs.

This issue came to a head in the seventeenth century and there resulted one of the most important developments in English history, the supremacy of the English Parliament and its leadership in national affairs. For the business man of England, this was a matter of the greatest consequence; for him Parliament represented a great and permanent institution through which he could exert a continuing influence on national policies. No longer subject to the arbitrary whims and exactions of ruling monarchs he could look to this institution as a sounding-board responsive to the needs and pressures of rising economic interests which sought their place in the sun. There were now no serious obstacles to the growing freedom of enterprise, and a movement already well under way in this direction increased in momentum until it reached its peak in the nineteenth century. Shifts in the balance of economic and political power could now take place without serious threats to national stability. A combination of domestic tranquillity and naval power gave English enterprise the security essential to an unrestrained pursuit of gain in the nation's agriculture, industry and commerce.

The key role of the merchant in national life was reflected in national policies in which his wealth and welfare were closely identified with the wealth and welfare of the nation. Sir Walter Raleigh's remark (Nef, p.86) that "who rules the trade of the world rules the wealth of the world and consequently the world itself" sums up this philosophy. It is true that merchants were slow to shift away from monopoly positions in trade, shipping and plantations, but attacks on monopoly powers steadily increased as the nation's commerce grew. Centres of aggressive attack on England's old colonial system and its monopoly control hastened the move toward greater freedom in the conduct of the Empire's commerce. Unfortunately this shift came too late to save the first British Empire (its collapse is discussed in Chapters V and VI) but in the end the downfall of commercial monopoly was complete. Nevertheless, even as the struggle between monopoly and competition developed in the seventeenth and eighteenth centuries, English merchants succeeded in constructing a well-balanced, closely integrated system of trade linking the Old World with the New. It was a mutually reinforcing system in which each part contributed to the strength of the whole, and it was the outcome of a free and aggressive pursuit of the gains of trade backed by the naval power necessary to protect the country's shipping and commerce. Furthermore, it was a structure which only a maritime commercial nation could have built, for it grew out of the necessity of developing a multilateral commerce, one binding together many regions, in contrast to that of continental France. For the latter, emphasis on the home market and on direct lines of trade between the mother country and each of her possessions spelled a lack of that unity and cohesion in the whole system which was necessary to strength and permanence.

Back of England's rise to leadership in commerce were major changes in the industrial and agricultural sectors of the economy. The guild structure was becoming an increasingly antiquated form of enterprise, and, as such, an obstacle to more efficient and productive lines of development in industry. For the Crown, on the other hand, the guild had its uses as an instrument of state control over industry and as a means of maintaining a stability threatened by the growing power of those impatient of the old restraints. But in contrast with France, where the state strengthened and extended the guild system as a centre of economic control (a policy most efficiently followed by Colbert), in England attempts in this direction failed to stem the tide of change.

The Statute of Artificers (1563) may be taken as a definite turning-point in England's industrial policy. In this legislation, a comparatively broad and flexible system of national regulation marked the end of effective local intervention and control of much of the nation's industry. Its regulations relating to apprenticeship, wages, employment and working conditions were sufficiently broad and general to provide wide room for change. It is significant that even these regulations were much less rigidly enforced than were those of the French administration, and equally significant that the Statute applied only to industries in existence when it was passed; the great cotton industry of later times escaped from its regulations altogether. From the standpoint of industrial progress, there is irony in the fact that the French government's success in regulating the nation's industrial life was a highly important element in the country's failure to keep pace in industrial change, whereas the English government's failure to maintain watertight control of English industry helps to account for her rise as a great industrial power. The cotton industry which appears in both countries about 1670 provides a good illustration of this contrast; in France state restrictions effectively stunted the new industry and skilled workmen migrated elsewhere, whereas in England steps taken to save the old woollen trade from this rival were too halting and too late.

In this favourable climate of enterprise, England's industry, with the exception of iron production which experienced a setback after 1630, progressed rapidly over much of the sixteenth and seventeenth centuries. An enormous increase in the output of British coal (according to Professor Nef, a fourteen-fold increase between 1550 and 1680) provides an accurate index of the phenomenal rate of change in many branches of industry. Output in such industries as cloth and worsted manufactures, finished metal goods, shipbuilding, gunpowder, soap, glass and beer greatly increased. Unsolved problems in the smelting of iron checked this industry, but imports of pig and bar iron from Sweden and elsewhere helped to make good the deficiency until the late eighteenth century, when England's great coal resources were used in making iron in quantity.

Although England did not definitely take the lead in industry until the early nineteenth century, her extraordinary rate of progress in these earlier centuries in the mass production of cheap wares provided her with a very strong card to play in her struggle with France in North America. Here, cheap English manufactures gave the traders of the Hudson's Bay Company and of Albany to the south a competitive advantage which the French never overcame. It was an advantage which emerged directly from England's progress in the direction of a freer, more flexible and more highly productive industrial system at a time when industrial power was beginning to take on a new significance in international conflict.

This pattern of change, the increasing strength and freedom of enterprise in England's commerce and industry, was repeated in English agriculture, and in fact, extensive reorganization of agriculture was basic to England's industrial progress. In the sixteenth century, the growing needs of the native woollen textile industry led to an agricultural revolution in the course of which extensive tracts of land were turned over to sheep-farming. The inability of the Crown to protect the rights of small tenants who were turned off the land in large numbers reflected its weakness in coping with the growing strength of merchants and landed gentry with their interest in raw materials and in country industries. Consolidation of holdings, the turning of these into grass land, and enclosure of the commons were steps by which medieval agriculture organization was transformed in accordance with the growing market demand for wool. The movement reached its peak about the middle of the sixteenth century following the dissolution of the monasteries. Land was now becoming a form of capital investment, to be used as an instrument of material gain.

This process of reorganizing agriculture along commercial lines never slackened off completely in the seventeenth century, but it took a new form in the eighteenth. London's population had grown to 700,000 by 1750, and a growing population meant a growing market for agricultural produce. Further, the famous Corn Laws, in the protection they gave to agriculture from 1670 onwards, encouraged grain-growing as a matter of national policy. There was still plenty of unenclosed land left and, under the impact of market demands for grain and livestock products, a second wave of enclosures began. This was a highly complex process, but fundamentally it represented a shift to large tenant farms and to a systematic utilization of improvements in techniques of agricultural production. The end result was not only a vast improvement in agricultural productivity, but also a movement to greater concentration of control over agricultural land by large landowners.

In contrast with the French landed aristocracy, the great landlords of England, with their close contacts with commerce and industry, took an active part in enterprises important in the life and work of the nation. And these massive changes in agriculture in their turn released a large supply of man-power for employment in factories, so that in a very real sense the agricultural and industrial revolutions of England's eighteenth and nineteenth centuries went hand in hand. It is true that there was a heavy price to pay for all these changes. For some people the enclosures, early and late, with all their dislocation of settled ways meant much suffering and misery, but for many of these, life had always been hard, and the changes at least offered the prospect of better things to come. For the country as a whole, the process of agricultural reorganization represented a removal of obstacles to economic development and the building of a stronger and more prosperous nation.

Closely associated with this rise to greatness was the Bank of England, an institution established in 1694 and destined to become the centre of the world's monetary system. The pound sterling as the great international medium of exchange came to symbolize a leadership which came to an end only with the disastrous wars of the twentieth century. The great Bank rounded out an economic system in which progress in every phase of the nation's economic life provided the foundations for England's nineteenth-century supremacy in Europe and much of the New World.

MERCANTILISM AND COLONIAL EXPANSION

We may conclude this summary view of those factors in European economic history most significant to developments in our part of the world by reference to mercantilism, the prevailing economic philosophy of most European governments from the sixteenth to the eighteenth century. It is, unfortunately, a vague term and many different meanings have been attached to it. We can touch only its general features and note that in practice different states tended to emphasize different aspects of this philosophy. We may agree that the chief objective of mercantilist legislation was the power of the state. In achieving this objective, nations faced two sets of problems. In the first place, there were those problems associated with the establishment of a strong unity within the nation's own borders, the ending of local restrictions and regulations which presented obstacles to unification under a strong central government. Second, there was the problem of building a strong economy and in particular a thriving commerce and industry. These two lines of policy were closely linked in a programme aimed at making the state strong in a dangerous and warring world. In its economic aspect, a country's power was closely identified with its wealth, and the question became that of evolving techniques for increasing the wealth of the nation.

The most promising means to this end appeared to be that of foreign trade, the acquisition of treasure through the building up of favourable or active balances of trade with other nations, with the excess of exports over imports being paid in precious metals. Techniques of achieving this desirable end included the protection and support of domestic industries, prohibitions or at least restrictions on imports of foreign goods, and favourable trade treaties. Cheap supplies of raw materials for native industry and the immigration of skilled workers were encouraged; on the other hand, the entry of competing manufactured wares and emigration of those with skills and knowledge important to the nation were opposed. These were among the tactics adopted in what was essentially a form of economic warfare, with the state playing a central role in each campaign. Wage policies and control of quality of goods produced were other elements present in various systems of central planning. Colonial trade was looked on as a means of supporting these mercantilist designs and overseas expansion was favoured as a source of increasing the supply of experienced navigators and seamen. From the vantage-point of the twentieth century, it is easy to be critical of these measures of statesmanship, but the world of the mercantilist was a highly uncertain world, many of these policies were experimental in nature, and, in view of the problems faced and the inadequacies of many of the institutions and techniques of earlier days, the achievements of their designers compare favourably with those of the legislators of our own time.

Problems of interpretation emerge when we turn to individual nations, for mercantilism appears in a somewhat different guise in each national unit. It has been argued, for example, that Holland provides us with the only instance of pure mercantilism, i.e., the system of the merchant in contrast to the older system of landlordism. As pointed out earlier, this form of mercantilism had its limitations since it led to neglect of features of national economic life other than commerce. The German historian, Schmoller, on the other hand, in writing of Prussia has little to say about the merchant, but much about unification or the means whereby the different regions in a country were welded together in a strong national unity. In the final analysis, our conclusions must rest on ascertaining those elements in a nation which directed and assumed responsibility for the task of state-making. In Holland, as an extreme case, a mercantile oligarchy assumed this role. This was true of England too, but there is a difference; for in England merchants and landed gentry participated actively in every area of economic life, and mercantile leadership rested on a much broader and stronger base than in Holland. It is highly significant that this more adequate and comprehensive programme of state-making was closely identified with the growing freedom of enterprisers to shape national legislation in their own interests or to escape it altogether when new ventures beckoned. In the end it was this freedom that was to promote most effectively the national strength sought by all the powers.

In France, as has been shown, leadership rested not with the merchant, whether narrowly or broadly defined, but with the Crown and privileged groups who put their faith in state regulation and control in a close-knit system of national planning in which enterprisers were regarded as instruments of national progress. As such, they had little opportunity to innovate or to push into new lines of endeavour in which they made the primary decisions; a paternalistic state assumed this role and the result was a rigid, cumbersome, slow-moving structure in which there was comparatively little room for spontaneity in economic life. Spain presents an extreme case of this "controlled mercantilism"; the springs of economic progress dried up early in that once-great power.

In a real sense, these different variants of mercantilism underline the strength and limitations of the national powers engaging in a New World conflict. Overseas areas may be viewed as testing-grounds for rival systems and there is much in the early history of Canada to illustrate the severity of the test which faced the nations struggling for mastery in the Americas. It was a test which in some instances strengthened, in others weakened, the empires involved in this struggle. Spain's history bears witness to the debilitating effects of the loot or plunder of her richer American holdings, and France suffered from the heavy drain of overseas ventures on her European resources. In both empires, expansion overseas strengthened established traditional forms of control, and for the most part attempts to break loose of administrative controls were held closely in check.

England was more fortunate in that forces opposed to established interests were sufficiently strong to bring about significant modifications in the structure of empire trade, and a more aggressive and spontaneous development was the result. This in turn produced strains which hastened the collapse of the first British Empire, but British North America remained to play its part in a strong, imperial economy. A new nation, the United States, was to carry further the transformation of economic life along lines of increasing freedom from the type of regulation which had served the purpose of mercantilists in the era of state-making. We may agree that in this era, the sixteenth to the eighteenth century, the roots of change in America must be sought in Europe, but New World developments helped to shape the pattern of events. Consequently much of our economic history must be written in terms of a close interplay between changes in the Old World and the New. This interplay is, in fact, the central theme of this book, for ours is an international economy and must be studied from this point of view.

Canada's economy first emerged and grew in response to the demands of European metropolitan centres for its natural products. Fish, fur and lumber were to be the export staples which gave the new economy the larger part of its income and drew man-power and capital to exploit its abundant resources. Expansion of trade in these products gave rise to elaborate trading organizations, brought nations into conflict in the North Atlantic and North America and, last but not least, led to modifications in the commercial policies of Old World powers. As long as Canada remained simply a source of supplies for more economically advanced regions, the fundamentals of her economic growth may be sought in the physical characteristics of a very limited number of key staples, the techniques borrowed or developed for their exploitation, and the economic and political institutions which emerged to struggle with the problems of a staple-producing economy. Discovery of the rich re- sources of the Newfoundland fisheries more than four and a half centuries ago set in motion this complex process of interaction among geographic, technological and institutional factors. The early consequences of this discovery are the subject of the following chapter.

SUGGESTIONS FOR FURTHER READING

Bowden, W., M. Karpovitch, and A. P. Usher, *An Economic History of Europe since 1750* (New York, 1937), Chapters 4 and 5

Brebner, J. Bartlet, *North Atlantic Triangle: the Interplay of Canada, the United States and Great Britain* (Toronto and New Haven, 1945), Chapters III, IV and V

Heaton, Herbert, *Economic History of Europe* (New York, 1948), Chapters XII-XV

Heckscher, Eli, *Mercantilism* (Encyclopedia of Social Sciences. New York, 1933), Vols. 9-10, pp. 333-9

Helleiner, K. (ed.), *Readings in European Economic History* (Toronto, 1946), Chapters V and VII

Nef, John U., *Industry and Government in France and England* (American Philosophical Society Memoirs, No. 15, 1940)

Williamson, Harold F. (ed.), *Growth of the American Economy* (New York, 1953), Chapters II-III

Wright, Chester W., *Economic History of the United States* (New York, 1941), Chapter III

CHAPTER II

ECONOMIC BEGINNINGS: MARITIME AND CONTINENTAL

THE DISCOVERY OF THE NORTH ATLANTIC FISHERIES

To FIND a starting date for Canadian economic history is not as easy as it might appear. Nor is this difficulty confined to the history of Canada. No matter where we choose to break into the continuous stream of events which is history-as-it-happens, our selection is always more or less arbitrary. The best we can do is to pick out an event which seems to have marked a turning-point of some kind—one from which later developments can be shown to have stemmed more or less directly, even though the event we select is itself part of a continuous process.

One event which is often taken as representing the beginning of Canadian economic history is the voyage of John Cabot from Bristol to Newfoundland in 1497. Cabot himself was a citizen of Venice; his voyage of exploration, however, was backed by Henry VII of England and financed by merchants of Bristol. What Cabot was looking for, and what his backers expected him to find, was a short sea route to the Far East, an objective which had also inspired Columbus' voyage to the Bahamas and Cuba in 1492. At that time, we must remember, it was not realized that the whole continent of North and South America lay between Europe and Asia. Cabot did not discover his sea route to Asia; what he did find was Newfoundland and Cape Breton, which he mistook for part of the Asian mainland.

Cabot's discovery of part of what is now Canada was an episode in the great wave of expansion which, starting in the late fifteenth century and continuing throughout the sixteenth, carried the European nations across the Atlantic and gave them a foothold in the New World. The original objective of the first explorations was, as we have said, the discovery of a westward sea route to Asia by means of which the countries of western Europe could establish direct trade with the civilizations of Japan and China. An objective which was at first of secondary importance, but which rapidly became dominant as it came to be realized that the lands which had been discovered were not parts of Asia but a new continent, was the exploitation of the sources of wealth which the new lands contained. In pursuing this second objective Spain at an early date outdistanced all her European competitors, for Spain's explorations had led her to Central America where, in Peru and Mexico, there existed rich and sophisticated civilizations which on the one hand possessed large supplies of gold and silver and on the other were incapable of retaining them against Spain's superior military force. Of all the resources which the New World contained none was so much desired as gold and silver. To Spain, which had led the way in exploration and which had, almost by accident, established its foothold in the area where gold and silver were most easily to be obtained, fell the richest prizes which the New World had to offer.

To England Cabot's discoveries promised no such quick and easy rewards. If the backers of his expedition had correctly understood his findings, which they did not, they might well have been disappointed. The rugged and inhospitable shores of Newfoundland and Cape Breton harboured no wealthy civilizations such as Spain's explorers had found to the south. Minerals there were, to be sure, but it was to take four centuries of technological advance to make them available for commercial use. In Central America Spain could harvest riches by force of arms; organized plunder was sufficient to secure the resources which were sought. Farther to the north, in the area of the English explorations, wealth could be won only by development, immigration, and trade. In the region which Cabot had explored there was only one resource which, from a commercial point of view, promised to be immediately rewarding: fish.

Compared to gold and silver, dried fish was a humble and unexciting commodity. Nevertheless, it had several characteristics which made it by no means ill-suited to serve as the economic basis for commercial enterprise in the New World. As a basic item of diet, a fast-day food, and an important source of protein, it had a ready market throughout all of Catholic Europe. When suitably cured, either by drying in the sun or by means of salt, it did not deteriorate for a long period of time and was therefore well adapted to the slow transatlantic voyages of that day. Above all, fish could be obtained relatively easily and with little capital investment. Fishing-ships strong enough to make the voyage from Europe to the North Atlantic fishing-grounds were not so expensive that they could not be financed by a small group of partners, perhaps with the assistance of credit from a merchant, and a good catch (subject to the hazards of war and weather) was reasonably certain. Fish was, in a word, eminently well suited for long-distance trade; it was available in vast quantities with a minimum of fixed capital investment; and it could be obtained with the very loosest form of commercial organization— small units of enterprise, working independently of each other, able to shift their activities quickly from one area to another as self-advantage indicated, and free from reliance upon the direct government support and military protection which, in other areas, exploitation of the wealth of the New World required.

To say that John Cabot discovered the great fishing-grounds off Newfoundland, Labrador, and Nova Scotia would be an exaggeration. It seems very probable that at least some European fishing captains, moving north and west from the fishing-banks of the North Sea and the Irish coast to Iceland and beyond, always searching for a richer catch and less crowded waters, had already reached the fishing-grounds off the northeast coast of North America. If this is so it would help to explain why Cabot chose to sail in that direction and why the shrewd merchants of Bristol were confident enough of the feasibility of his venture that they were willing to invest their money in it. The Iceland fishing-grounds were quite familiar to English fishing captains in this period; it would have been strange indeed if some of them had not ranged as far as the Banks off Newfoundland, even though they chose not to announce the fact when they returned to their home ports. Cabot's voyage, on the other hand, was well publicized. Within a few months of his return the results of his venture were widely known. "They affirm," wrote one Italian from London to the Duke of Milan, "that the sea is covered with fish which are caught not merely with nets but with baskets, a stone being attached to make the basket sink in the water, and this I heard the said Master Zoanne [John] relate." After Cabot's voyage the wealth of the Newfoundland Banks was no longer a fishing captain's secret; it was public information.

The consequence was that by the early years of the sixteenth century fishing fleets from several European nations were sailing to the waters off Newfoundland and Cape Breton, fishing there, and returning to Europe with their catch. In earlier years English ships had been very active in the fishing-grounds off Iceland; now in ever-increasing numbers they began to fish off Newfoundland instead, a trend which was to continue for many years thereafter. But England was far from having the field to herself; French and Portuguese ships were among the first to fish in Newfoundland waters and from the beginning provided serious competition. By the end of the second decade of the sixteenth century a very active international fishery had developed. At first the ships seem to have stayed close to the shores of Newfoundland, the Gaspé, and Cape Breton, but by about 1540, with greater confidence and experience, they were reaching out to the Banks, which were then and still remain one of the richest fishing-grounds in the world.

The Banks are a group of underwater plateaux or marine tablelands, being in reality the higher portions of an extensive land mass which, formerly above sea-level, in some remote geological epoch subsided and became submerged beneath the sea, forming a kind of underwater shelf projecting from the mainland. The depth of water over the Banks varies between fifty and three hundred feet, sufficiently shallow to permit the growth of a large variety of marine life, particularly plankton, the minute organisms on which feed young cod, caplin, herring, and other small fish. The Arctic or Labrador Current and the Gulf Stream meet and mingle over the Banks, providing a variety of temperature and degree of salinity which helps to account for the variety of fish resources found there. There are four principal groups of Banks: the New England Banks, such as Georges and Browns; the Nova Scotia Banks, such as Sable and Banquereau; the Newfoundland Banks, particularly Grand, Pierre, and Green Banks, the largest of all; and Hamilton Inlet Bank off the coast of Labrador.

Here, on the Banks, the fishers of the sixteenth century found resources greatly in demand in Europe, in enormous quantities, easily accessible, and requiring fishing and curing techniques which had already been perfected in other areas. The exploitation of these resources provides the background for the intense national rivalries of the next century and a half in the North Atlantic area.

In these rivalries, a tremendous initial advantage lay with the French and Portuguese. Because of their climate, these nations could obtain large supplies of cheap solar salt, essential for the "green"-curing technique. Because of their Catholic populations, they were provided with a steady and predictable domestic demand for fish. The English, in contrast, had to import their salt and had a limited home market. They were therefore at a competitive disadvantage. The first half of the sixteenth century, in consequence, saw the Newfoundland fisheries dominated by the fleets of France and Portugal. Geographically, this period saw the fisheries extended from the coastal waters of Newfoundland to the Grand Banks, to the Banks of the south and west, and to the Gulf of St. Lawrence.

In the second half of the century, particularly after 1580, the English fisheries expanded rapidly and came into sharp conflict with the French and Spanish fleets. Legislation to encourage the English fisheries does not seem to have been very effective, but the defeat of the Armada in 1588 and the subsequent decline of the Spanish fisheries led to a noticeable extension of English activity in the Newfoundland and St. Lawrence areas. In 1580, too, Denmark finally succeeded in enforcing a licensing system in the Iceland fisheries; English fishers thereupon shifted more and more from the Iceland to the Newfoundland fishing-grounds, a shift which was accompanied by a decline of east-coast fishing-ports in England and the rise of the West Country ports in Devon and Cornwall, such as Plymouth, Barnstaple, Lyme, and Bideford. The story of the English fisheries in the North Atlantic after this point is largely the story of the activities of these and other West Country ports.

The English fisheries, however, still laboured under the handicap oi inadequate salt supplies. This difficulty was in part overcome by obtaining salt from Portuguese fishers, sometimes by purchase, sometimes in return for "protection". But a more important means of meeting the problem was by the use of a dry-curing technique, requiring less salt, by which the fish were laid out on rocks, beaches, or wooden stages, to be dried by the heat of the sun.

This development had important consequences. In the first place, the English fishers tended to concentrate in regions suitable for drying their catch and where salt could be obtained from the Portuguese, particularly in the Avalon peninsula of Newfoundland. Secondly, it made it necessary for the English fishers to establish at least semi-permanent bases on Newfoundland, where stages and harbours could be erected. These bases formed the nuclei of future settlements. And thirdly, the hard, dry cure was especially suitable for long-distance trade, particularly to the Mediterranean area after the decline of the Spanish fisheries. The export of dry-cured fish to Spain and the Mediterranean, first from the fishing-ports in England and later directly from Newfoundland, accentuated competition between the French and English fishers and at the same time brought the English West Country fishers into conflict with the great chartered companies which, working under the protection of a royal grant of monopoly, dominated England's external trade. The English fishers were prepared to trade with anyone; to the chartered companies this was a threat to their profits and to national security. For these reasons the development of the dry-curing technique was an innovation of the first importance.

English expansion in this period was not accompanied by a decline in the French fisheries. The concentration of the English fishers in the Avalon peninsula, however, was followed by a shift in the principal areas of French activity to more remote waters. French ships based on Bay of Biscay ports, such as Bordeaux, Bayonne, and La Rochelle, moved to fishing areas off the mainland such as the Canso Bank, while those based on the Channel ports tended to concentrate in the Gaspé and the Gulf of St. Lawrence. The French used the dry-curing technique, like the English, as well as the heavily salted green cure, the green fish being intended for the domestic markets at Paris and Rouen, the dried fish for the markets in Spain and the Mediterranean. French fishers, however, with cheaper supplies of salt and a larger home market than the English, preferred to salt all their catch on the Banks and bring it back to their home ports, where part of it would be dried. On the one hand this made it unnecessary for the French to establish bases in Newfoundland; but on the other it resulted in a poorer quality of cure. By the end of the century the English had established a permanent foothold in Newfoundland; the French, relying on their cheaper supplies of salt, had not.

The Portuguese fisheries in this period declined to a relatively minor position and after 1581, when Portugal was absorbed by Spain, suffered from the effects of English depredations. Spain, in turn, after a brief period of successful expansion between 1570 and 1580, proved unable to survive a series of English attacks on her fishing fleets in the following decade and after 1590 her ships were seldom seen on the Banks, except as whalers.

The decline of the Spanish fisheries had far-reaching consequences and cannot be explained solely in terms of English attacks and the defeat of the Armada, important though these certainly were. Inadequate support from the central government, concentration of interest upon her wealthy conquests to the south, and a prolonged period of inflation, all contributed to Spanish weakness in the North Atlantic, as did many other less obvious factors. Indirectly, however, Spain continued to play a very important role. The influx of precious metals from her possessions in Central and South America made the Spanish market a rich and attractive one, which her failure to maintain a competitive position in the North Atlantic fisheries opened to the exports of other nations. Green and dried cod exported to Spain enriched her most bitter rivals and made it possible for them to secure the specie from which Spain herself was unable to secure lasting profit.

NATIONAL AND INTERNATIONAL CONFLICTS IN THE FISHERIES

It is well to bear in mind that the early development of the North Atlantic fisheries took place in an atmosphere of intense international rivalry—a rivalry which from time to time erupted into war but which, even when nations were ostensibly at peace, aggravated and accentuated the inevitable frictions of economic competition. Conflict in the North Atlantic fisheries was part of a general European conflict, a reflection, so to speak, on what was then the outer margin of European economic expansion, of the struggle taking place at the centre.

By the first decades of the seventeenth century the lines of conflict between the French and English fisheries in the North Atlantic had become clear. France, like Spain and Portugal, concentrated at first mainly on salting down the fish for the demands of her large domestic metro-politan markets. Low agricultural productivity, the influence of religious beliefs on diet, and the emphasis on self-sufficiency characteristic of a large continental country combined to encourage concentration on the internal market and, for a time, neglect of foreign markets and the possibilities of the codfish as an article of international commerce. The English, in contrast, developed the dry cure at an early date and emphasized cod as an article of trade rather than merely a supplement

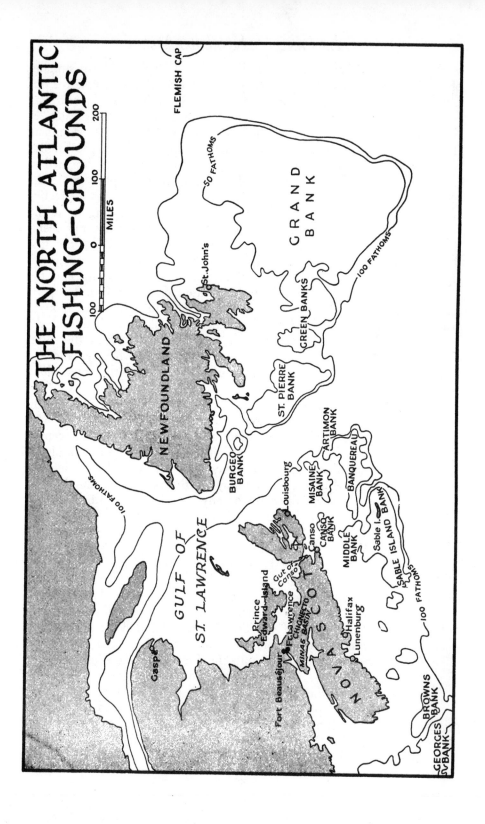

THE NORTH ATLANTIC FISHING-GROUNDS

to their domestic diet. The availability to the French of cheap supplies of high-quality solar salt was probably the chief factor responsible for this highly important difference in techniques. But other factors also had their effect. The English fishers found little outlet for their catch in their home market. The Dutch had at an early date come to dominate the English coastal fisheries and continued to supply much of the English market during the sixteenth century. Legislative enactments designed to help the Newfoundland fishers largely failed of their purpose, while the official designation of certain days of the week as fish days was ineffective in stimulating demand. Nor did the Reformation, implying as it did a decline in the observance of fast days, help matters. All these problems encouraged an interest in cod as an article of trade, and by the first decade of the seventeenth century a form of triangular trade had grown up between the English West Country ports, Newfoundland, and the Iberian peninsula. English fishing-ships based on West Country ports carried their catch directly from Newfoundland to Spain and brought back specie, wines, salt and other products to England. With this development the stage was set for prolonged conflict between the West Country ports, anxious to develop an expanding dry fishery, and the London chartered companies which sought to organize the trade along monopolistic lines.

The English and the French fisheries differed, however, not only in their techniques but also in another respect which had much to do with the final outcome: their organization and relationship to the central government. From the beginning the French fisheries were decentralized. In Europe her ships operated from many ports scattered along a lengthy coastline—those of Brittany, of the Bay of Biscay, and of the English Channel—without central direction or any attempt at co-ordination. In the New World the same decentralization was characteristic: French ships operated on the Banks, off Belle Isle, in the Gulf of St. Lawrence, and off the shores of what is now Nova Scotia, without any single principal area of concentration. Partly because of this dispersion of interest, the French North Atlantic fisheries were highly vulnerable to English attack and were never able to exercise effective influence upon the policies of their government. State aid, of course, was not entirely absent, but the divisive, competitive spirit of the fisheries made it difficult for them to make any impress upon the French state bureaucracy and its policies. The fisheries never fitted neatly into the French structure of trade; the fur trade, as we shall see, was much more congenial.

The contrast with the English fisheries is sharp at every point. The English fishing-ships operated from a relatively concentrated set of home bases—the West Country ports. The use of the dry cure compelled them to concentrate in the New World in certain rather limited areas where fish could be dried, stages erected, and a relatively permanent foothold on land secured. Greater co-ordination of policies and community of interests was the result on both sides of the Atlantic: in Newfoundland, exploitation of the defensive weakness of the French by calculated aggressiveness; in England, effective influence upon national policy through the agency of a parliamentary system which the French lacked.

But the English North Atlantic fisheries in this period were not only growing in size; they were also growing in national importance. "A successful attack on the Newfoundland fleet," said Sir Walter Raleigh, "would be the greatest misfortune that could befall England." Codfish provided the staple item of diet for the navy and for all ships sailing to hot climates. The fisheries themselves served as a training-ground for seamen and a reservoir of skilled man-power on which the navy could draw in time of war. The prosperity of important towns with considerable influence in Parliament depended upon profits from the fisheries and from the trade in cod. Most important of all, the expanding trade with Spain raised fundamental issues of national policy, not only because it represented commerce with a hostile power but also because it was an important means of acquiring specie, the foundation (or so it was believed) of national strength.

The typical instrument of English economic expansion overseas at the end of the sixteenth century was the chartered company. These corporations, endowed by the Crown with certain prescribed monopoly rights and possessing extensive influence in Parliament and at court, were created to serve as the spearheads of expansion in a period when the state itself was too weak or too disinterested to take the initiative. Already, however, they were encountering increasing hostility and competition, as the system of which they were the chief agents and beneficiaries gradually came to be superseded by newer theories of mercantilism, no less monopolistic in temper, but with the state playing a more active role in the furtherance of policies designed to serve the national interest. In accelerating the shift to these newer policies, the North Atlantic fisheries were to play an important part.

The growing importance of the cod fisheries, the substantial profits which could be derived from them, and the vital significance which was attached to the trade with Spain made it inevitable that attempts would be made to control and regulate the trade by the creation of chartered companies. Opposed to such a development were the West Country ports, asking only to be left alone to fish and trade with whom they pleased and bitterly resentful of any attempts at centralized control by the financial and commercial interests of London. The focus of this struggle in the Old World was Parliament; in the New, Newfoundland.

The designs of the corporate interests were very clear. They intended to develop permanent settlements in Newfoundland and encourage the growth of a resident fishery based on these settlements. Such a fishery would, they argued, provide cargoes for English shipping engaged in trade. This would strengthen the fisheries and the merchant marine, suppress foreign competition, reduce piracy, establish law and order in Newfoundland, make possible a longer fishing season, and create a valuable naval base in the event of hostilities with Spain or France. Incidentally, of course, it would produce handsome profits for those who controlled the settlements and the carrying-trade.

The carrying-trade and plantation interests had much in their favour. Not only did they possess considerable political influence but the increasing complexity of the fisheries themselves seemed to demand the intervention of some superior authority. The growth in the size and number of the English fishing-ships led to serious problems of allocating space for the erection of stages and the storage of equipment. Piracy was common, as was the stealing of boats, the wasteful use of scarce timber, the dumping of ballast into harbours, and similar abuses which the fishers themselves seemed powerless to prevent. Most important of all was the labour situation in the fisheries. The number of men taken out by ships to work at dry-fishing operations was in excess of the number required as crew, one contemporary estimate being that ten extra men were required for each ship. This extra personnel, whose only use was in Newfoundland, amounted to a large item of expense, and there was a strong incentive to reduce costs by leaving surplus labour in Newfoundland over the winter. This, of course, favoured the growth of permanent settlements, the very thing which the fishers themselves wished to avoid. At the same time, since the number of fish which the fishing-ships could catch in a season was usually in excess of the number they could carry to market in their own holds, by the early years of the seventeenth century several score of ships were sailing to Newfoundland each year solely to purchase, not catch, fish there for sale in the Spanish and other markets. These ships, which were known as sack ships (probably because they brought back to England dry—in French, *sec*—white wines from Spain and the Canaries), came to play an important part in the trade. Not only did they encourage an increase in the production of fish, but also, since they sailed from England without cargo and could offer very cheap freight rates, they tended to encourage immigration and settlement. Thus developments in the fisheries themselves, quite apart from any political influence of the plantation and carrying-trade interests, seemed to point to the growth of permanent settlement and a resident fishery in Newfoundland.

So it was that the development of the North Atlantic fisheries not only accentuated conflict between nations but also contributed to conflict between competing interests within each nation. In England this conflict had three aspects. In the first place there was the conflict between the great chartered companies, with their headquarters in London, and the

West Country fishing interests, whose main strength was centred in Bristol. The chartered companies stood for centralized control over England's foreign trade, while the fishing interests vigorously resisted any attempt to restrict their freedom to market their catch in any foreign country they chose. In the second place there was the conflict between Crown and Parliament. The chartered companies wielded their greatest influence at court and operated under a direct grant of monopoly from the King. In Parliament, on the other hand, the West Country interests could make their views heard more effectively. The regional conflict between London and the West Country, between the chartered companies and the fishing-ports, therefore contributed to the great constitutional struggle of the sixteenth and seventeenth centuries, with the fishing interests arguing against the King's right to grant exclusive privileges of monopoly. And in the third place there was the conflict between those who wished to encourage settlement and a *resident* fishery in Newfoundland, and those who wished to see the island remain merely a seasonal base for the English fishing-ships, with no permanent population of any sort. The chartered companies were strong supporters of the settlement policy, while the West Country ports were determined to resist it. These three lines of conflict, interacting with one another, were to shape English policy toward the fisheries and toward Newfoundland for the next two hundred years.

A plan for the development of Newfoundland had been worked out as early as 1578 by one Anthony Parkhurst, and in 1583 Sir Humphrey Gilbert had attempted to carry Parkhurst's plans into execution. The colony and government which he established quickly failed, however, largely because of his interference with the customary rights of the fishers, and the only permanent result of his expedition was to build up a tradition of West Country opposition to later ventures of the same sort.

During the reign of James I (1603-25), no less than six further attempts were made to colonize Newfoundland. All of them failed, partly because of the sheer inhospitability of the island and its lack of easily available resources save fish and lumber, but principally because of the hostility of the West Country fishers. The first and most determined of these attempts was made by a certain Mr. Guy, a merchant of Bristol, with whom were associated various distinguished and influential members of the aristocracy. These persons and their associates formed a joint stock company in 1608 and two years later received a charter under the title of the London and Bristol Company (also known as the Newfoundland Company). Ostensibly the purpose of the venturers was to trade; actually their intention was to establish a colony in Newfoundland and bring the fishery under their control. Guy was appointed governor of the colony and promptly proceeded to issue regulations for the control of the fisheries.

The fishers, not surprisingly, refused to recognize his authority, particularly his right to allocate space for drying fish. The custom had been that the first ship to reach a Newfoundland harbour at the start of the season had first choice in selecting drying-sites. Clearly, if settlers were to live in Newfoundland all year round, this system would no longer work. Hence arose the complaints of the fishers that the settlers took over the best sites and appropriated property which had been left from the previous season. And there were other complaints, some trivial, some serious. The root of the trouble was the refusal of the West Country fishers to accept the jurisdiction of a competing and vastly different type of organization.

Both sides resorted to violence, and both appealed to the mother country for justice. An investigator, Captain Richard Whitbourne, was sent out to investigate the situation, but as he had previously been employed by the Company he was inclined to take a somewhat one-sided view of the problem. Conflict continued for several years. In 1618 the Privy Council reviewed the complaints of both parties and tended, in its judgment, to favour the Company. But nothing tangible resulted, largely because no administrative machinery existed to enforce the Council's decisions. Strengthened by financial support from a group of Scottish merchants, the Company continued its efforts to establish a colony, and in 1620 again protested against the depredations of the fishers. The protest on this occasion was accompanied by a request that the Company should be explicitly authorized to enforce its jurisdiction over both English and foreign fishers and that armed vessels should be provided to make its authority effective. The Privy Council's decision again favoured the Company, perhaps partly because two of its distinguished members had recently purchased land in Newfoundland, but the authority requested was not granted.

The Company thereupon attempted to strengthen its position by selling large tracts of land to members of the English aristocracy, at least one of whom, Sir George Calvert, made a serious effort to come to terms with the fishers and establish a permanent settlement. But all these efforts came to nothing, and after 1628 the London and Bristol Company faded into obscurity. A similar fate befell other companies formed and settlements attempted in the following years. The net result of their efforts was prolonged litigation in England and the stranding in Newfoundland of a few unfortunate colonists whose descendants were a nuisance to the fishers for generations.

In essence, the whole issue rested on the companies' claim to ownership of land which the fishers could not do without. In political terms the struggle was between the Crown, which claimed the right to grant monopolies as part of the royal prerogative, and the House of Commons, in which the smaller industries and regional groups outside London, as well as those who were suspicious of royal absolutism, could exert effective influence. But the Crown's support in any event was seldom more than lukewarm and the settlement companies never succeeded in making good in practice their claim to jurisdiction over the fishing-sites, which was the crux of the matter.

It can hardly be said, however, that the West Country fishers had any very enlightened conception of freedom of trade. In a sense their attitude was more analogous to the localism of the medieval commercial town, with its distrust of feudal authority and hostility to centralized control. The opposition of the West Country fishers to settlement in Newfoundland was probably more backward-looking than progressive. Yet the results were clear: the beginning of the end of a colonial policy based on corporate monopolies and the turn to direct state regulation of foreign trade and colonization.

THE RISE OF NEW ENGLAND

In Newfoundland those who wished to encourage permanent settlement had run afoul of a long-established and highly aggressive vested interest —the West Country fishers—and they had been defeated. Elsewhere in North America, where no such hostile group existed, they had more success. In 1606 the first Virginia charter was issued, which in effect set up two companies: the Plymouth Company, which attempted to establish settlements on the Kennebec River in Maine; and the London Company, which in 1607 began a successful colonization venture on the James River in Virginia. The northern enterprise, representing interests centred in Plymouth, England, failed, and its settlement at Sagadahoc was soon abandoned. But the London Company, backed by leading merchants of the City of London some of whom were also connected with the East India Company, fared better, and its settlement at Jamestown became the first permanent English settlement in North America. In 1612 a new charter was obtained and the venture was reorganized as an English commercial company, using the joint stock device; actually it represented a union of the capital of London and the labour of the colonists. The Company went bankrupt in 1624, when Virginia became the first royal colony, but it was successful in attracting settlement and, with the expansion of tobacco cultivation and the growth of slavery, became an important market for the northern fisheries, especially for the poorer grades of fish.

In New England the first permanent settlements followed the chartering in 1620 of the New England Council, a company composed largely of landed gentry under the leadership of Sir Ferdinando Gorges. The charter of the Company granted wide monopolistic powers, including the right to charge fishermen a licence fee for the use of drying-sites. Opposition to the Company appeared at once from three principal groups: from members of Parliament in England who challenged the Crown's right to grant such powers; from the Virginia Company, which feared exclusion from the northern fishing-grounds; and from the West Country fishers.

The intention of the Council was to establish permanent settlements and a resident fishery in New England. Strongly feudalistic in outlook, the Council is most significant because of its attempts to encourage landed proprietorship. Partly because of the wide opposition it encountered and the growing resistance to the granting of monopoly powers under the royal prerogative, progress in actual colonization was slow, except for the establishment of Salem in 1628, and for a time it looked as if the story of Newfoundland was to be repeated in New England. But there were two new factors in the situation which combined to produce an entirely different result. One was the fact that the New England fisheries, unlike those of Newfoundland, had only recently been discovered and there had not been the same opportunity for a strong vested interest to develop. Despite the advantages of earlier and longer fishing seasons, only fifty West Country vessels were reported fishing in New England waters in 1624 and fifteen in 1637, whereas the Newfoundland fleet in these years usually numbered between 250 and 400. The New England Council, until its charter was surrendered in 1635, was considerably more successful in enforcing its territorial rights and in encouraging a resident fishery than the Newfoundland Company had been.

The second factor was Puritanism—which was especially strong in England's commercial middle class—and its effect on emigration. The Pilgrim Fathers originally emigrated to America under a grant received from the London Company and, when this arrangement proved inconvenient, bought out the English interests concerned. Well established by 1627, the colony was eventually absorbed by the Massachusetts Bay Company, which was chartered in 1629 with the financial support of a group of Puritan merchants who looked to the New World as a refuge from the policies of Charles I. Several other settlements in Maine and New Hampshire had a similar origin, while others developed as offshoots of the Massachusetts Bay colony, a continuous stream of immigration providing the drive for development and expansion. Ships brought settlers to New England, whereas to Newfoundland they brought ballast.

This emigration movement received support from landowners in England, but the principal force behind it was religious. Over 20,000 immigrants had arrived in America by 1640, and by this time settlement was sufficiently advanced for the colonists to develop their own resources, even when immigration slackened. With the West Indies providing a growing market, fisheries, shipbuilding, and agriculture were energetically developed. By the middle of the seventeenth century the New England settlements were providing highly effective competition in the North Atlantic fisheries, and the West Country ports found themselves faced with a new rival which in the end was to prove too powerful for them.

New England's early history was determined by free immigrants; dreams of a closely-regulated, well-disciplined plantation never materialized. The expansion of settlement, a resident fishery, and commercialism in New England under the protection of monopoly made the eventual decline of monopoly control inevitable. The diversity of resources and activities in the area made central control extremely difficult; it was from the first a maritime region, outward-looking, seeking export markets through freedom of trade very much like the more enterprising sections of England. Newfoundland provides a sharp contrast; it also was a maritime region, but in Newfoundland the fisheries had been the principal factor inhibiting settlement, whereas in New England settlement, trade, and a resident fishery mutually supported each other. The rise of New England meant an increase in the strength of entrepreneurial elements within the English trading system, and these aggressive new elements were in the end to force drastic readjustments and realignments in imperial policy.

While the early growth of New England was strongly conditioned by religious influences, the later drive was to come from expanding markets in the British and later the French West Indies, and eventually in the China trade. Particularly important, even before 1650, were the West Indies. Spain was partly responsible for this development. Anxious to conserve her resources of gold and silver, Spain attempted to encourage tobacco and sugar production in her colonies, intending to use these products, rather than specie, to pay for her imports. England countered this move by the development of the tobacco industry in Virginia and by encouraging the growth of tobacco and, later and more important, sugar cane in the British West Indies. By 1650 there were important tobacco and sugar industries within the British imperial system which not only served to reduce dependence on imports from Spain but also played a large part in the development of intercolonial trade.

The rise of the British West Indies was to have two very important consequences. In the first place it greatly stimulated the economic development of New England, providing a market for fish, lumber, and surplus agricultural produce and employment of ships and workers, not to mention the raw material—molasses—for one of New England's principal articles of trade: rum. And in the second place it contributed to the strength of the English plantation and carrying-trade interests, who found in the West Indies a new field for expansion along the old lines of regulation and control. These parallel and interacting developments were a guarantee of future disturbance, as the growing economic power of

New England came to contrast more and more sharply with her relative lack of political influence, as compared with the West Indies plantation interests, in the shaping of British colonial trade policy.

It would be difficult to exaggerate the importance of New England as a centre of activity and source of conflict in the North Atlantic during the next century. Up to 1650 it is possible to take the West Country ports as the focal point for the study of developments in the North Atlantic; after that date, New England emerges as the significant focus. For a time she was the key factor in Anglo-French rivalries and a vital element in the destruction of the French trading empire. At the same time she was in sharp conflict with competing elements within the British system—with the English fisheries in Newfoundland, where New England sought to encourage settlement as a basis for trade, and with the English plantation interests in the West Indies, where the struggle against monopoly control over trade reached its climax. After 1650 New England takes the place of the West Country fishers as the most effective force working against centralized control of colonial expansion. Thus we see in the North Atlantic, on a smaller scale, the pattern of change which was being worked out in England—the shifting balance of power as feudalism, based on land ownership, becomes weaker, and new entrepreneurial interests, based on the wealth acquired from trade, grow in strength. In France the opposition to the older forms of organization was much weaker and in the fur trade, as we shall see, the power of monopoly was to increase to a point where it was never seriously challenged.

THE CONTINENTAL FUR TRADE: GENERAL CHARACTERISTICS

In discussing the early history of the North Atlantic fisheries we have been dealing with a form of economic activity which was characterized by the presence of a great number of small units, relatively low investments of fixed capital, substantial freedom of entry, intense competition, and considerable geographical mobility. For these reasons the fisheries acted as a disruptive force, compelling changes in the older system of monopolistic trade and pointing the way to new patterns of national expansion. In contrast, the continental fur trade, beginning in the middle of the sixteenth century with rapid expansion continuing throughout the seventeenth, fitted neatly into the older pattern of centralized control and proved admirably adapted to close regulation along mercantilist lines. In the few brief periods when competition did break out, it appeared as a destructive force, leading to wasteful exploitation and demoralization of markets.

The fur trade was characteristically a continental activity, requiring large-scale organization for the conduct of trade over long distances by means of extensive transportation systems. It could be carried on successfully only by large enterprises with ample supplies of working capital and elaborate marketing connections. Overhead costs were high and, as in all industries with a similar cost structure, profitability depended upon the fullest possible utilization of equipment and man-power. In the fur trade the answer to all problems was expansion.

The fur trade, in its maturity, formed Canada's first transcontinental economic system, carrying the influence of Europe across the continent to the Pacific far in advance of settlement and the establishment of formal political control. Three factors in particular determined the pace of expansion. In the first place, the pressure of overhead costs made competition ruinous; the creation of monopoly control meant either the absorption of rivals, with the territory which they had exploited, or expansion into unexploited areas where competition could be avoided. Secondly, the character of the staple was such that constant expansion was necessary to maintain supplies. The beaver was easily trapped, particularly after the introduction of steel traps and the use of castoreum as bait, and the speed with which the animals were exterminated, especially when competitive trapping took place, made necessary a continual movement into new areas. Further, the furs most in demand—the so-called *castor gras*—were those which had been processed and worn by the Indians, so that the long guard hairs dropped out and the skins became supple. But these took time to produce and could be obtained only from tribes in the interior. The search for *castor gras* therefore necessitated constant movement westward. And in the third place the exchange of European goods for furs resulted in the rapid growth of an insatiable demand among the Indians for such products of European technology as fire-arms, metal tools, kettles, and rum. This demand added its weight to the speed of resource exploitation.

The character of the staple explains not only the speed of expansion but also its uneven tempo. Beaver fur in this period was used almost exclusively for the manufacture of hats, the large beaver hat being an expensive article and a symbol of wealth and rank. The demand for beaver fur, therefore, being dependent upon the demand for a high-priced luxury product, was highly inelastic. The market was narrow and vulnerable to the whims of fashion. Increases in supply brought catastrophic price falls rather than larger sales, while attempts to control prices led to protests from hat manufacturers and could result in a permanent shift of fashion away from beaver. A more unsatisfactory staple to serve as the permanent economic basis of a continental empire would be hard to find. Furthermore, the fur trade acted as a positive deterrent to immigration and settlement. The large fur-trade organizations, whether private or governmental, did everything they could to restrict settlement in fur-trading areas, realizing clearly that wherever agriculture took hold their monopoly over supply was at an end. The life of the *coureur de bois* or Indian trader offered excitement and the prospect of quick profits which attracted labour away from the unexciting toil of pioneer agriculture. And the ships from Europe which supplied the fur trade had little space for immigrants, carrying as they did heavy, bulky cargoes of European goods on the outward voyage and light, valuable cargoes of beaver fur on the homeward journey. Increases in settlement only served to accentuate this problem of unbalanced cargoes.

BEGINNINGS OF THE FUR TRADE

The French were the first nation to enter the North American fur trade. Competition in the cod fisheries in the first half of the sixteenth century pushed the French fishers into marginal areas. Unable to secure a foothold in Newfoundland, the French turned to sites on the mainland and came into contact with the Indians. By the 1530's, when Cartier explored the Gulf of St. Lawrence, a small-scale and sporadic trade in furs had already grown up as an offshoot of the fishing industry. Development was slow, however, partly because beaver fur was still little valued in Europe (the beaver hat had not yet come into fashion), and partly because the economy of the Huron-Iroquois Indians who then occupied the lower St. Lawrence was based on fishing and agriculture rather than hunting. Promising beginnings were made, however, in trade with the migratory Indians of the Saguenay region, the Algonquins and Montagnais, whose economic life was based on hunting and who had developed effective techniques for trapping beaver.

During the second half of the sixteenth century important changes took place. In Europe the wearing of beaver hats came into fashion and led to a strong demand for beaver fur. In North America the Iroquois Indians of the St. Lawrence valley were driven south of the St. Lawrence, in a prolonged series of inter-tribal wars, by the hunting Indians from the Saguenay, possibly with the aid of European commodities which these latter Indians had acquired in trade. The new demand for beaver fur arose, therefore, at a time when supply conditions also had been drastically changed. The principal route to the interior was now controlled by hunting Indians, highly skilled in trapping beaver and familiar with the best hunting-grounds. While the English continued to dominate the richer regions of the fisheries and the mainland to the south, French influence was pushed steadily inland along the St. Lawrence and the Ottawa in pursuit of the beaver. Once engaged in this trade, there could be no turning back, for it demanded continual expansion as a condition of survival.

The establishment of Quebec in 1608 may be taken as marking the beginning of French attempts to gain control of the entire St. Lawrence area. The rapidly increasing familiarity of traders with Indian culture and the growing demand for European goods among the Indians set the stage for rapid expansion. Trade was still hampered, however, by tribal conflicts between the Iroquois and the northern Indians, so that the St. Lawrence route to the interior remained extremely hazardous. French efforts were therefore directed toward opening up the Ottawa River-Georgian Bay route by means of alliances with the Algonquins, the Hurons, and other tribes who had access to the rich fur-bearing regions of the north. The older Saguenay route, which was considerably more difficult, was used in this period only when the Ottawa was closed by Iroquois attacks. French aid to the northern tribes in the form of fire-arms and metal implements was partially counterbalanced by the more ample food supplies possessed by the Iroquois, while considerable difficulty was experienced by the French in co-ordinating the policies of the migratory northern tribes to repel Iroquois attacks.

Penetration westward demanded not only protection from the Iroquois and the maintenance of a strong base at Quebec but also the development of a transport system and an adequate supply centre in the interior. A strategic position came to be occupied by certain semi-agricultural tribes such as the Hurons, who had access to adequate supplies of corn and used it, in combination with fish, as their staple diet when travelling long distances by canoe. These tribes came to play an indispensable role in the expansion of the trade from Quebec to the lower Lakes and Georgian Bay. Not only did they in part supply the food requirements of the northern hunting Indians; they also acted as middlemen, collecting furs over wide areas, transporting them to Quebec, exchanging them for European goods, and distributing these goods to hunting tribes in the interior. This trading system appears to have been well established by 1623. It had obvious advantages not only for the Hurons but also for the French since it enabled them to cut to the minimum the fixed costs of the trade.

The attempts of the Hurons to establish a monopoly position were bitterly resented by other tribes, particularly the Algonquins and Montagnais. The use of European weapons and improved hunting equipment led to a rapid exhaustion of beaver supplies in the areas around the St. Lawrence, so that tribes which had previously traded directly at Quebec found themselves forced to penetrate to more remote areas where they were largely dependent upon the Hurons for food and European goods. The Hurons, however, were successful not only in maintaining their position against these other tribes but also, to some extent, in restricting French attempts to establish more direct contact with the hunting tribes. By this time ships were being sent from France specifically for the fur trade; the increasing demand for beaver and the urgent necessity of obtaining large quantities of furs to provide return cargoes for these ships led the French into attempts to establish direct trade relations with the more distant tribes, particularly after the crushing defeat inflicted on the Hurons by the Iroquois in 1648. French traders and explorers had penetrated to Lakes Michigan and Superior by 1650, while the activities of Jesuit missionaries also contributed to the spread of French influence. The offer of assistance to one side or the other in inter-tribal wars was frequently instrumental in cementing alliances and increasing the supply of furs.

Attempts of this kind to accelerate the rate of exploitation, as well as the expenses involved in defence against the Iroquois, inevitably led to increases in the overhead costs of the trade and encouraged measures to restrict competition. The potential profitability of monopoly control was also accentuated by the peculiar nature of supply and demand conditions. The supply of furs brought down to Quebec by the Indians each year was highly inelastic; so was the supply of European goods shipped to Quebec for trade. Neither side was in a position to withhold supplies from the market from one year to the next. Under competitive conditions the supply of European goods tended to increase, so that the price of beaver rose and profits fell. Partly for this reason, but principally with a view to co-ordinating defensive strategy, the early years of the seventeenth century saw a series of attempts to establish monopoly control over the purchasing, shipping, and marketing of furs.

THE ESTABLISHMENT OF NEW FRANCE

The forces leading toward monopoly in the fur trade were paralleled and reinforced by French ambitions for a continental empire in North America. It should be noted that religious and political factors were considerably more important than economic motives in shaping French colonial policy. This was less true of most of the English ventures, which were aimed primarily at profits and capital accumulation through trade. The costs of dynastic struggles in Europe, however, the opposition of the French finance minister, Sully, to colonial ventures, and the rather erratic enthusiasms of the French king meant that, in the first half of the seventeenth century, the central government played a relatively passive role. Instead, the French looked to the well-tried device of the chartered company, and relied upon private venturers, operating under the protection of monopoly, to develop the fur trade and—much more important from the standpoint of national policy—to establish a permanent colony. In the first half of the seventeenth century, therefore, French policy in North America was executed and to a large degree determined by a series of corporate organizations, each of which attempted in the interests of profits to eliminate competition in the fur trade and at the same time, though with considerably less zeal, to encourage agriculture and settlement in the St. Lawrence lowlands.

Attempts to establish monopoly control in the fur trade had been recurrent ever since 1588, when the French king had granted a monopoly to two nephews of Cartier in compensation for certain sums owed them by the government. The readiness of the French Crown to make such grants was due in large part to a realization that as long as the fur trade was carried on as a seasonal business, with fleets sailing to the St. Lawrence each spring for trade but with no attempts to establish a permanent garrison or colony, the French position in North America had little prospect of permanence. The merchants of St. Malo, La Rochelle, and Rouen might indeed reap rich profits from such a seasonal trade, but they would not on their own initiative bring out settlers nor support a military establishment. Only a large company with guaranteed immunity from competition could hope to secure the financial backing necessary for such an undertaking. On the other hand, it was not easy to suppress competition. Merchants excluded from the monopoly were certain to protest violently and to make things as difficult as possible for their privileged rivals. And it was even more difficult to insure that the chartered companies carried out their obligations.

The monopoly granted to Cartier's nephews was revoked within four months as a result of strong protests from merchants and fishers excluded from the trade. A second monopoly granted eleven years later to Pierre Chauvin lasted only three years before it was cancelled on the grounds that the obligation to bring out colonists had been evaded. In 1603 a determined attempt was made, under the leadership of Pierre de Gua, Sieur de Monts, to form a company which would include all the larger merchants interested in the trade. A charter was obtained which granted a monopoly of the fur trade not only in the St. Lawrence but also in the Gaspé and Acadian peninsulas as far south as the fortieth parallel, while the company promised in return to take out sixty colonists each year. Capital was subscribed by merchants of St. Malo, La Rochelle, St. Jean-de-Luz, and Rouen, and in 1604 a fleet was sent out to trade and establish a colony at Ste. Croix at the mouth of the river St. John.

Some difficulty was encountered in enforcing the monopoly, especially in the coastal areas where the fishing-ships continued to trade with the Indians, but de Monts' company managed to secure a sizable portion of the trade and to make moderate profits. The colony established at Ste. Croix was transferred in 1605 to Port Royal (now Annapolis) and, in spite of the difficulty of attracting colonists, began to show signs of permanence. Unfortunately, the price of furs in this period rose considerably, perhaps partly because of the existence of the monopoly, and the powerful Hatters' Corporation of Paris lodged vigorous protests with the finance minister, Sully, who in any event had little liking for colonial ventures. The charter of the company, in consequence, was suddenly cancelled, although it had seven years still to run.

De Monts then decided to concentrate exclusively on the St. Lawrence. A direct appeal to the King secured for him a new monopoly grant for one year only, with no conditions as to colonization. Financial support was obtained from some of his former Rouen partners. In 1608 he sent out a fleet of three ships and, with Champlain's assistance, established a fort and trading-post at Quebec. His monopoly grant, however, was not extended.

For the next twelve years the trade was open to all comers, though de Monts and Champlain continued to maintain their establishment at Quebec and to take the major responsibility for exploration and defence against the Iroquois. Increasingly severe competition and the necessity for sharing the costs of defence led to the formation of informal agreements among competing traders and finally in 1612 to the formation of a large company, under Champlain's leadership, which was intended to include all the principal merchants engaged in the trade. This company obtained a monopoly grant of the fur trade from Quebec westward for twelve years; in 1613 the grant was extended to include Gaspé also. Capital was subscribed by merchants of Rouen and St. Malo.

Champlain's grant was cancelled in 1620 on the grounds that colonization had been neglected and little attention paid to the maintenance of the fort at Quebec. A new grant was made to the Caën brothers, Huguenot merchants of Rouen, who joined with Champlain's organization to form the United Company. This grant also was revoked in 1627, when the Company of New France was formed under the leadership of Cardinal Richelieu. Majority control of this new company was held in Paris, not Rouen or St. Malo, and it was clearly intended that the formation of this large and powerful organization would establish French dominion in North America on a permanent basis.

Unfortunately for these ambitious plans, the Company of New France lost almost all its capital as a result of the capture of its supply fleets by English privateers in 1628 and 1629. In consequence, the Company leased its monopoly rights to various subsidiary companies until 1642, when it resumed direct control. The increasing complexity of the trade, however, rendered centralized control from Paris clumsy and slow, and in 1645 monopoly rights were leased by a small group of influential settlers organized as the Company of Habitants. Large profits made by this Company were followed by agitation for freer trade in the interior and in 1647 trade with the Indians was thrown open to all settlers, although all furs had to be sold to the Company at prices fixed by the colonial government. Iroquois aggression from 1648 onward drove the Company of Habitants into bankruptcy and after a brief interlude under the Company of Normandy the French Crown assumed direct control in 1663.

The details of these successive grants are not very important. What is remarkable is the persistence with which the French government adhered to a form of colonial development which was clearly not adapted to the circumstances. To almost every one of the chartered companies monopoly control of the fur trade was granted on condition that settlers should be brought out from France to the new colony. These commitments were not carried out. Quebec was founded in 1608, but it was nine years before the first settler arrived and twenty before the first ox-plough was at work. As Champlain sourly remarked, the companies were more concerned with high dividends than with the encouragement of agriculture. It was, in fact, not to be expected that fur-trading companies should show any enthusiasm for the founding of permanent settlements. To bring settlers from France was an expensive business and an unproductive investment of the companies' capital. European agricultural techniques could not quickly be adapted to the new environment, and it was not easy to prevent settlers from engaging in the fur trade themselves and thus competing with the very organization which had brought them to the colony. In so far as agriculture could contribute directly to the fur trade it was encouraged, but the growth of settlement was painfully slow. The effects were evident in the strategic vulnerability of Quebec and in the failure of the French, at this time or later, to convert their colony on the St. Lawrence into a supply base for the North Atlantic fisheries.

INTERNATIONAL RIVALRIES

The slow development of the colony was due, however, not only to the disinterest of the chartered companies in the encouragement of agricultural settlement but also to the difficulty of defending the colony and its supply lines against the attacks of rival nations. Serious setbacks resulted from the outbreak of war with England in 1627. English naval power on the Atlantic, which remained a decisive factor in imperialistic rivalries in North America over the entire period to 1763, was utilized at this early stage against the French position on the St. Lawrence. In 1628 the Kirke brothers, with the help of other London merchants, secured letters of marque from the British government and prepared a small fleet which successfully intercepted and captured the convoy sent out by the Company of New France. The colony on the St. Lawrence, seriously weakened by this interruption in the flow of supplies from France and unable to provide its own food requirements, capitulated in the following year. For the next three years the fur trade of the St.

Lawrence was carried on by a British organization known as the Scottish and English Company, formed by the Kirke brothers and their associates with the assistance of Sir William Alexander. In 1632, however, the British king, Charles I, who was experiencing considerable financial embarrassment through Parliament's refusal to vote subsidies, returned Quebec to France in return for the payment of the remainder of his wife's dowry, his wife being the King of France's sister. The opportunity to consolidate English influence on the St. Lawrence was thereby lost. The ease with which Quebec had been taken, however, amply demonstrated the strategic weakness of the French position in the face of English sea-power and the failure of the fur-trading organizations to build up a self-sustaining colony.

Meanwhile serious difficulties were emerging in the fur trade itself. The establishment of a Dutch trading-post at the mouth of the Hudson River in 1614 marked the first serious threat to French control of the trade. New Amsterdam was far distant from the best fishing-grounds; it had, however, a magnificent harbour, free from ice during the winter months, and it stood at the entrance to one of the few natural water routes across the Appalachian mountains—the valleys of the Hudson and Mohawk Rivers. The prosperity of the Dutch settlement clearly depended upon making good use of these natural advantages by the development of trade with the interior. Trade with the interior in this period meant the fur trade and nothing else, since furs were the only commodities available to the Indians which had commercial value in Europe. Unfortunately, the fur resources of the Hudson valley were limited and of poor quality. The development of a fur trade based on New Amsterdam depended upon obtaining access to the rich fur areas of the north, or in other words the very areas which were already being exploited by the French. The entry of the Dutch into the fur trade, therefore, brought them into immediate conflict with the French, thus raising the curtain on the first act of a drama which has continued throughout Canadian history—the rivalry between the economy based on the Hudson River and that based on the St. Lawrence.

Just as the French depended upon the Hurons to serve as middlemen and distributors, so the Dutch came to depend upon the Iroquois who, being an agricultural tribe in a poor fur-producing area, could obtain high-quality furs and thereby the coveted European goods only by trade. Supplied by the Dutch with guns and ammunition, the Iroquois were in an excellent position to disrupt by attacks against the Hurons the transport system which the French had built up between Georgian Bay and Quebec via the Ottawa River. These attacks were highly effective and culminated in the virtual extermination and dispersal of the Hurons in the years 1649-50.

The disappearance of the Hurons meant the destruction of the French trading system in the interior. Small parties of Indians continued to visit Quebec by the circuitous Saguenay and St. Maurice routes, and French traders made strenuous efforts to induce the hunting tribes to trade only with the French. But the defeat of the Hurons not only disrupted the French transport system; it also meant the loss of the corn supplies on which the hunting Indians had relied and these supplies could not quickly be replaced. By the middle of the seventeenth century, therefore, the French fur trade on the St. Lawrence had practically come to a standstill. It was evident that, if the trade were to continue and the colony to survive, new resources and new techniques would have to be enlisted in the struggle against the Dutch and their Iroquois allies.

FUR-TRADING AND EMPIRE-BUILDING

Already, however, the St. Lawrence fur trade had developed certain characteristic features which were to persist in subsequent periods. The most obvious of these was the control of the trade by large monopolistic organizations. The cost structure of the industry, the necessity for effective lobbying with the home government, the problems raised by relations with the Indians, and the close connection between trade and empire-building, all contributed to making monopoly control a persistently recurring tendency. The very geography of the St. Lawrence valley seemed to point toward centralization. These monopolistic organizations, needless to say, were not immune from competition, but this competition was of a different type from that which, for example, characterized the fisheries. Competition in the fur trade was essentially competition between regions, particularly regions marked out by the drainage basins of large river systems. The most serious threat to the French position on the St. Lawrence was not the competition of interlopers from French fishing-ports but the competition from the Dutch on the Hudson River and also, in a later period, from the English on Hudson Bay. The survival and profitability of fur-trading organizations was therefore closely linked to the maintenance of political control by rival European nations over the few navigable waterways which provided access to the interior of the continent. Fur-trading and empire-building were inextricably tied together.

The fur trade was, in consequence, intrinsically well adapted to furthering the aims of French colonial expansion. The difficulty was in finding a form of organization which could carry on the trade effectively and at the same time promote the long-term designs of the French government. This the early chartered companies failed to do, and, up to 1650, no satisfactory means had been found of reconciling the interests of government and private business. This problem also was to be encountered in later years, not only during the French regime but also after the conquest. Since the fur trade provided the spearhead of westward expansion, no government could ignore its demands, particularly when expansion from other commercial centres threatened to outrun the spread of control from the St. Lawrence. On the other hand, the interests of the fur trade were not in all respects consistent with the growth of healthy and self-sustaining colonies nor with what were regarded as the best interests of the mother country. In particular, the concentration of energies and financial resources upon a single staple product—and one which was thoroughly unsuitable as a basis for permanent control— militated against attempts to build up a more diversified economy. This led to increasing difficulties in meeting the competitive threat of stronger economic areas to the south and to increasing reliance upon military and other state aid.

We may note, in conclusion, that the economic problems facing the French colonial administrators were strikingly similar to those faced later by their English successors and still later by the political and economic leaders of Canada in the period following Confederation. The emphasis on nation-building by the exploitation of a single staple with a highly uncertain income, combined with the enormous costs of continental penetration by road and river, canal and railway, has led Canada at times to the verge of national bankruptcy. The experience of the fur trade with cost-price relationships has been repeated for a whole range of staple products, including lumber and prairie wheat. Even without the danger of absorption by stronger national states, the problems of maintaining any sort of political or economic unity have often seemed almost insurmountable.

SUGGESTIONS FOR FURTHER READING

BASIC WORKS:

Biggar, Henry P., *The Early Trading Companies of New France* (Toronto, 1901)

Brebner, J. Bartlet, *The Explorers of North America, 1492-1806* (New York, 1955), pp. 88-122

Innis, Harold A., *The Fur Trade in Canada; an Introduction to Canadian Economic History* (New Haven, 1930), Chapter I and Chapter II, Sec. 1, pp. 1-19

Innis, Harold A., *The Cod Fisheries: the History of an International Economy* (Toronto and New Haven, 1940), Chapters I-IV, pp. 1-94

Judah, Charles B., Jr., *The North American Fisheries and British Policy to 1713* (Urbana, Illinois, 1933), Chapters I-IV, pp. 11-85

Lounsbury, R. G., *The British Fishery at Newfoundland, 1634-1763* (New Haven, 1934), Introduction and Chapters I-II, pp. 1-91

Rich, E. E., *The Hudson's Bay Company, 1670-1870* (London: The Hudson's Bay Record Society, 1958), Volume I, 1670-1763, pp. 1-60

SUPPLEMENTARY WORKS:

Andrews, C. M., *The Colonial Period of American History* (New Haven, 1938), Vol. I, Chapters I, II, III, and XV; Vol. IV, Chapters I, II, III, IV, and X

Beer, G. L., *The Origins of the British Colonial System, 1578-1660* (New York, 1908), Chapters I-III

Graham, Gerald S., *Empire of the North Atlantic: the Maritime Struggle for North America* (Toronto, 1950), Chapters I-III, pp. 3-57

Newbigin, Marion I., *Canada, the Great River, the Lands and the Men* (London, 1926), Chapters I-V, pp. 3-93

CHAPTER III

NORTH ATLANTIC RIVALRIES: 1650–1713

INTRODUCTION

IN CONTRAST to the continental fur trade, where monopoly control established itself at an early date, the North Atlantic in the period from 1650 to 1713 continued to be the scene of intensely competitive rivalries. Spain and Portugal now played only a minor role as active participants in the fisheries, though they retained their importance as markets. French fishermen established themselves with government support on the south coast of Newfoundland, in Cape Breton, and in the Gulf of St. Lawrence and offered serious competition to the English fishing fleets operating from ports in Devon and Cornwall. Despite the opposition of the English West Country fishing captains, permanent settlements developed in Newfoundland with the support of trading interests based on London, Bristol, and Boston. In the West Indies, with the expansion of slavery and sugar cultivation, new markets appeared for lumber, agricultural products, and the poorer grades of fish. The English West Country fishing fleets, exposed to increasingly severe competition from the French, from New England, and from the resident fishery in Newfoundland, entered upon a period of decline, while New England emerged as the focus of a flourishing fishery and a vigorous trading system.

Throughout the whole period wars, preparations for wars, and the treaties that ended wars profoundly influenced the working-out of economic tendencies. Wars between Britain and Holland and between Britain and France, which were in part caused by imperialistic and commercial rivalry on the North Atlantic, affected the control of strategic areas in North America and the West Indies, the security, profitability, and direction of trade, and the growth and decline of settlements. Britain was at war with the Dutch between 1652 and 1654, between 1664 and 1667, and between 1672 and 1674, and with the French between 1689 and 1697 and between 1701 and 1713. Control of the North Atlantic trade routes and fisheries, in consequence, depended very largely upon the outcome of power struggles between the nations of Europe and in particular upon the relative naval strength of the warring nations. Conversely, the need for large and efficient navies and for government revenues to finance wars meant that a new importance was attached to colonies as sources of raw materials and to the fisheries as sources of experienced seamen.

THE CARRYING-TRADE AND THE NAVIGATION ACTS

At the middle of the seventeenth century the Dutch dominated the maritime trade of the civilized world, possessing a superiority in merchant shipping over all other nations comparable to the superiority in manufacturing which Britain was to possess two centuries later. According to the estimate of the French statesman, Colbert, the merchant marine of the European nations at mid-century totalled approximately 20,000 vessels, and of these 80 per cent were Dutch. No nation could hope to establish secure overseas colonies so long as Holland possessed such preponderance in shipping. No nation could hope to build up the self-sufficient commercial empire which was the goal of mercantilist statecraft so long as the Dutch dominated the carrying-trade. The wars between Britain and Holland during the second half of the seventeenth century marked Britain's attempt to wrest control of the Atlantic trade routes away from the Dutch and to weld together into a single trading system of mutually complementary parts the mother country and her colonies in North America and the Caribbean. The expansion of British merchant and naval shipping was the first objective of this policy.

The legal instrument used by Britain to oust the Dutch from the carrying-trade took the form of a series of statutes known as the Navigation Acts, the general intent of which was (1) to confine the trade between the colonies and the mother country to British shipping; (2) to establish Britain as the entrepôt for all trade between Europe and the colonies; (3) to provide protected and exclusive markets in Britain for certain important colonial products; and (4) to reserve the market for manufactured goods in the colonies for British exporters.

Particularly important was an Act passed by the British Parliament in 1651. This Act had three principal provisions: (1) no goods grown or manufactured in Asia, Africa, or America were to be imported into Britain or the British colonies except in British ships (the term "British" in this context being understood as covering England, Ireland, Wales, Berwick-on-Tweed, the Channel Islands, and the colonies, but not Scotland until 1702); (2) no goods grown or manufactured in Europe were to be imported into Britain or the British colonies except in British ships or in ships belonging to the country where the goods were produced; and (3) no goods of foreign growth or manufacture were to be imported into Britain unless they were shipped directly from the country of origin. In 1660 the provisions of the statute of 1651 were re-enacted and certain new regulations were added. In addition to the three types of prohibition mentioned above, certain products of colonial origin were specified which were not to be exported from the British colonies except to England, Ireland, or some other English colony. These "enumerated commodities", as they were called, were originally sugar, tobacco, cotton-wool, indigo, and fustic and other dyeing woods. Other products were added in later years. In 1663 a further statute was passed which laid it down that commodities grown or manufactured in Europe could be exported to America only if they were first shipped to Britain, warehoused there, and then reshipped in British vessels for the colonies.

These statutes, with a mass of supplementary legislation, formed the basic economic framework of the first British Empire. Their fundamental assumption was that colonies existed for the benefit of the country which had founded them and that, in the words of the mercantilist writer, Sir Josiah Child, "all Colonies or Plantations do endamage their Mother-Kingdoms, whereof the Trades of such Plantations are not confined by severe laws . . . to the Mother-Kingdom." Aimed in the first instance against Holland, the Navigation Acts proved strikingly successful in excluding the Dutch from the British colonial trade, in stimulating development in the colonies along certain lines, and in encouraging the growth of British and colonial shipping. British merchant shipping in foreign trade doubled in tonnage between 1663 and 1688, while, under the protection of the Acts, a flourishing shipbuilding industry developed in New England.

The original "enumerated commodities" were all products of the southern colonies or of the West Indies: tobacco came from Virginia and Maryland, sugar and the other commodities mostly from Barbados and Jamaica. These were the areas in the New World which fitted most closely the mercantilist conception of the ideal colony, since they produced commodities which, in the absence of colonies, would have had to be purchased by the mother country from foreign nations. The northern colonies, in contrast, particularly New England, did not fit neatly into the mercantilist scheme of things. With the exception of furs and masts, the commodities they produced were not in demand in England. True, they imported most of their manufactured goods from the mother country, but to pay for these imports they had to engage in trade with the other colonies and directly with Europe and thus compete with the merchant marine of England. New England, in fact, was from the beginning an anomaly in the British colonial system, a centre of enterprise which could grow and flourish only by trade but which, by trading, consistently pressed against the confining regulations of the imperial economy. The Navigation Acts, a code of legislation designed to make England the focus and entrepôt of imperial trade, encouraged in New England the development of a trading community which increasingly found its interests diverging from those of the mother country.

THE NEWFOUNDLAND FISHERY

Newfoundland also occupied a somewhat anomalous position in the imperial system. In terms of mercantilist doctrine, the fisheries played a highly important role in increasing the strength of the nation, not only because they were a "nursery for seamen", but also because, since their product was sold almost entirely in foreign countries, they contributed largely to a favourable balance of trade. But was the island a "plantation", or was it merely a seasonal base for the North Atlantic fishing fleets? This was far from an academic question, for round it revolved the conflicting aims and policies of the West Country fishermen on the one hand and of the merchants of London on the other.

It was recognized at an early date that the island required special attention and could not be included under the general regulations of the Navigation Acts. Throughout the second half of the seventeenth century, therefore, the condition of the North Atlantic fisheries was continually before the attention of the British government and from time to time special regulations to promote the interests of the fisheries were issued. Salt for use in the fisheries was exempted from the statute of 1663 which required all imports to be laden and shipped in England; convoys were provided for the fishing fleets in time of war; and seamen employed in the fishery were occasionally exempted from impressment in the navy. Most important of all, until about 1680 the full weight of government authority was lent in support of attempts to suppress settlement and colonization in Newfoundland.

Despite such generally favourable treatment by the government, both under Cromwell's Protectorate and after the Restoration of the monarchy, the West Country fishing interests found the period after 1650 one of increasing difficulty. The disturbances of the Civil War and the Dutch Wars, together with the growing competition of the French, resulted in a marked decline in the size of the West Country fishing fleets and in the profitability of the trade. Tariffs excluded English fish from the French market, while access to the markets of Spain and Portugal was hindered by pirates, privateers, and enemy fleets. New England also emerged as a competitor.

In their appeals to the government for assistance, however, the West Country fishing captains put less emphasis on these factors as being responsible for their plight than they did upon the increase of settlement in Newfoundland and the activities of a new source of English competition: the byeboatkeepers. Byeboatkeeping was a method of carrying on the inshore fisheries by means of small boats. A merchant in England would hire a few fishermen and send them out to Newfoundland as passengers on the fishing-ships. Once on the island they would fish independently from temporary bases on the shore and sell their catch to any purchaser who offered, but most frequently to the "sack" or trading ships which plied between England, Newfoundland, and the European markets. Byeboatkeeping was, in brief, a sort of compromise between a resident fishery carried on by permanent settlers on the island and the methods of the West Country fishing-ships, which sailed to Newfoundland annually from bases in England. In good years it was highly profitable: there was little risk and the initial investment was small, since boats could be obtained cheaply and the fishing-ships were willing to carry passengers on the outward voyage at very low rates.

Byeboatkeeping was an activity which the West Country fishing captains could probably have suppressed without much difficulty, if they had been able to act in concert, for it was mainly as passengers on the fishing-ships that the byeboatkeepers reached Newfoundland. In this respect as in others, however, the divisive, individualistic nature of the industry prevented concerted action. To the individual fishing captain the passage money which he received for taking byeboatkeepers to the island was clear profit, and in consequence byeboatkeeping grew and flourished. This was a development highly welcome to the merchants of Bristol and London, since it meant that they could send their "sack" ships to Newfoundland, purchase all the fish they needed in a few days from the byeboatkeepers, and sail immediately for Europe, thus getting the best prices for their fish at the start of the season and increasing the rate of turnover of their capital. Many of the ordinary fishermen, too, preferred byeboatkeeping to serving as crew on the fishing-ships, since the work was considerably less arduous and since they could make their way without difficulty to New England if they wanted to, as for example to escape the attentions of the navy "press gangs" in England. The West Country fishing captains, however, vehemently opposed byeboatkeeping, asserting that it would encourage settlement on Newfoundland and inevitably tend to weaken the English fisheries, the principal reservoir of skilled man-power for the navy. If settlement and a resident fishery were allowed to become established, they warned, Newfoundland would soon go the way of New England, which carried on its own fishery and its own trade in competition with the mother country.

These arguments, conforming as they did to sound mercantilist doctrine, appealed strongly to the government authorities in England, and for more than thirty years after 1650 the regulations and statutes which were drawn up to govern the Newfoundland fisheries mirrored the interests of the West Country fishing-ports. In 1661, for example, Charles II reissued the Western Charter of 1634, which favoured the fishing-ships as against the settlers, and added to it a new regulation which prohibited the transportation to Newfoundland of persons who were neither settlers nor members of the crews of fishing-vessels. This measure was, of course, designed to suppress the byeboatkeepers. In 1663 Parliament passed an Act which provided that no tax should ever be levied on codfish caught by Englishmen at Newfoundland; since codfish was the only form of wealth available on the island, this statute effectively prevented for many years any attempt to establish a civil government. In 1671, under the terms of a new Western Charter which imposed even more stringent restrictions on the settlers, the inhabitants of the island were prohibited from cutting, burning, or destroying any trees useful for timber, from occupying any stages or other fishing facilities before the fishing fleet arrived from England, and—the most severe restriction of all—from erecting houses or other buildings within six miles of the shore. At the same time masters and owners of fishing-ships were prohibited from transporting to Newfoundland any persons other than members of their crews.

If rigorously carried out, these regulations would certainly have eliminated both the settlers and the byeboatkeepers. That this was the intention is clear from the instructions given to the naval commodore in the area, who was directed to encourage the settlers to leave the island and migrate to the West Indies. Fortunately for the settlers, the new regulations (re-enacted in 1675) were never put into effect in Newfoundland.

The merchants of London and the settlers on Newfoundland opposed this policy as strenuously as they could but for many years their protests were ineffective. To some extent government officials were handicapped by the lack of reliable information. There was no doubt that the Newfoundland fishery, as carried on from the West Country ports, had entered upon a period of decline, and the government tended to accept the explanation of this decline which the fishing captains themselves offered: the presence of settlers on the island and the activities of the byeboatkeepers and the sack ships. Not until the 1680's were there indications of a change in government policy.

This change followed upon the submission to the government of the first relatively impartial reports upon the situation in Newfoundland: the reports of the naval officers sent out to command the convoys which guarded the fishing fleets. In 1669, for example, Captain Robert Robinson of the Royal Navy, who had commanded the convoy during the second Dutch War, submitted a report to the Crown in which he strongly urged that a civil government should be established on the island. This, of course, would have implied government approval of permanent settlement. Sir John Berry, who commanded the convoy in 1675, reported that the proposed expulsion of the settlers was not advisable and would indeed be positively harmful to the fisheries if carried out. Many of the abuses of which the West Country fishermen complained, such as the destruction of stages and other fishing facilities, were, he stated, not the fault of the settlers but rather of the fishermen themselves, for the captains of the fishing-ships had found it profitable to destroy the stages at the end of the season and sell the wood to the sack ships as fuel. Berry also alleged that many of the fishing captains actually encouraged some of their men to remain in Newfoundland permanently in order to avoid the expense of bringing them back to England at the end of each season, and pointed out that the settlers, now some 1,600 in number, ordinarily produced about one-third of the total catch each year, so that they formed by no means an unimportant part of the industry. The general tenor of his analysis was supported by Sir William Poole, convoy commander in 1677.

These and other naval reports, combined with the steady political pressure of the London merchant capitalists, undermined the confidence which the government had earlier placed in the West Country fishing interests. By the 1680's it was coming to be suspected that the combination of permanent settlement, byeboatkeeping, and the sack ships provided, as far as the dry fishery was concerned, a more efficient method of carrying on the industry than the annual fishing fleets which sailed from ports in the West of England, and that the secular decline of the West Country fishery was due in part at least to the competition of a more effective type of economic organization. Of course many other factors were involved—the shrinkage of European markets, for example, congestion on the drying beaches in Newfoundland, and the competition of France and New England—and the West Country fishing-ports could make out a good case, in terms of mercantilist theory and the realities of English politics, for special consideration. But attempts to suppress settlement and byeboatkeeping had not in fact produced any improvement in the condition of the West Country fishing industry; on the contrary, according to contemporary estimates, the number of English ships fishing in Newfoundland waters had fallen from 300 in 1670 to 150 in 1675 and 97 in 1680, without any increase in the size of the average ship. The proportion of the total catch marketed by the settlers and byeboatkeepers during this period appears to have increased slightly, from about 27 per cent in 1675 to 33⅓ per cent in 1680, despite the fact that the resident fishermen were equally affected by marketing difficulties and in addition had to pay more for materials and provisions, most of which had to be imported. Meanwhile the French had established themselves on the south coast of Newfoundland and were developing a flourishing dry fishery under the protection of a local government and garrison, in addition to the green or Bank fishery in which they had never lost their supremacy.

In these circumstances the British government began to move away from its former policy of uncompromising hostility to settlement and in

1680 amended the Western Charter so as to permit settlers to remain in Newfoundland and to participate on equal terms in the fishery. This compromise, combined with a temporary revival of prosperity in the industry, appeared to satisfy all parties for the time being. The outbreak of war with France in 1689, however, again disturbed conditions in the fishery and brought a new flood of complaints from the merchants and from the West Country fishermen. The tenuousness of the British hold on the island and the vulnerability of the settlement and fishing-bases in the absence of a local government and garrison were sharply emphasized by a series of successful raids from the French fort at Placentia. This consideration probably contributed to the passing by the British Parliament of the Newfoundland Act in 1699.

The Newfoundland Act is sometimes regarded as having brought to a close the period of West Country control in Newfoundland, but actually it made very few departures from the charters of 1634, 1661, and 1676. Settlers and byeboatkeepers were, under the terms of the Act, allowed to participate in the fisheries and to keep their drying-stages if they had owned them before 1685, but no governor was appointed and the management of the fisheries was left in the hands of the West Country ship captains, subject to the general supervision of the naval commander. Apart from the official sanction given to the position of settlers and byeboatkeepers, the Newfoundland Act merely consolidated in a rigid statute the practices which had developed since the failure of the earlier attempts to suppress settlement.

During the years which elapsed between the passing of the Newfoundland Act and the beginning of the War of the Spanish Succession in 1701, conditions in Newfoundland showed little improvement. Since there was no civil government on the island, attempts to administer justice and prevent illegal trade were inevitably abortive. By this time New England had begun to take an active interest in Newfoundland, not so much as a fishing centre, but rather as a centre for trade. Though the reports which reached England were highly exaggerated, it seems clear that the Massachusetts merchants who brought supplies and provisions to Newfoundland did carry on a certain amount of smuggling on the side. The fishing-ships, which by special regulation were permitted to buy their salt in the markets of continental Europe and in Madeira and the Canary Islands, not infrequently purchased wines, brandy, and other European goods there as well, and then traded these supplies to the New England merchants who met them in Newfoundland. In the same way, a certain amount of sugar and tobacco—which, being enumerated commodities, should have been exported only to Britain—were brought to Newfoundland on the New England trading-ships and thence carried to foreign markets.

These practices were, of course, in contravention of the Navigation

Acts and, though the total volume of this illicit trade was probably small, at least before 1713, they were regarded by the Committee for Trade and Plantations in London as a grave violation of the colonial regulations. Unless such smuggling was suppressed it was feared that Newfoundland, with the aid and encouragement of the merchants of Boston, would become (as the Commissioners of the Customs expressed it in 1687) "a Magazine of all sorts of Goods brought thither directly from France, Holland, Scotland, Ireland and other places". It was alleged, too, that the Boston traders encouraged fishermen to leave Newfoundland and migrate to New England. Since one of the reasons why the fisheries were so highly esteemed in England was that they formed a source of skilled seamen for the navy, this was regarded as a very serious matter. But as long as the only persons in Newfoundland charged with enforcing the law were the naval commanders and the so-called "admirals" of the fishing fleets, little could be done to remedy the situation.

THE FRENCH FISHERY

A variety of factors combined to bring about the decline of the West Country fishery in the second half of the seventeenth century, but of fundamental importance was the expansion of the French fishery and of the New England carrying-trade. The French empire in North America around 1650 was rather similar in general structure to the English, but there were a number of important differences. Both countries had small settlements and a dry fishery in Newfoundland, and both had a group of rich sugar-producing islands in the West Indies. But whereas England enjoyed the benefit of a string of colonies on the Atlantic seaboard from Florida to northern Massachusetts, including after 1664 the former Dutch colony at the mouth of the Hudson River, the French had only their single continental colony on the St. Lawrence, together with a dubious claim to Nova Scotia and a small trading-post at the mouth of the Mississippi. The English, too, were relatively successful in welding together their possessions into a single trading system, largely because of the commercial expansion of New England under the shelter of the Navigation Acts. The French were unable to do this, partly because they lacked a counterpart to New England. In short, during the second half of the seventeenth century the English fisheries declined while their intercolonial carrying-trade expanded; the French fisheries expanded, but their intercolonial carrying-trade languished.

French settlements in the West Indies had been established in the first half of the century, beginning with a settlement on St. Christopher in 1625, and by 1655 the total French population in the islands had reached 15,000. After early experiments with tobacco, sugar production

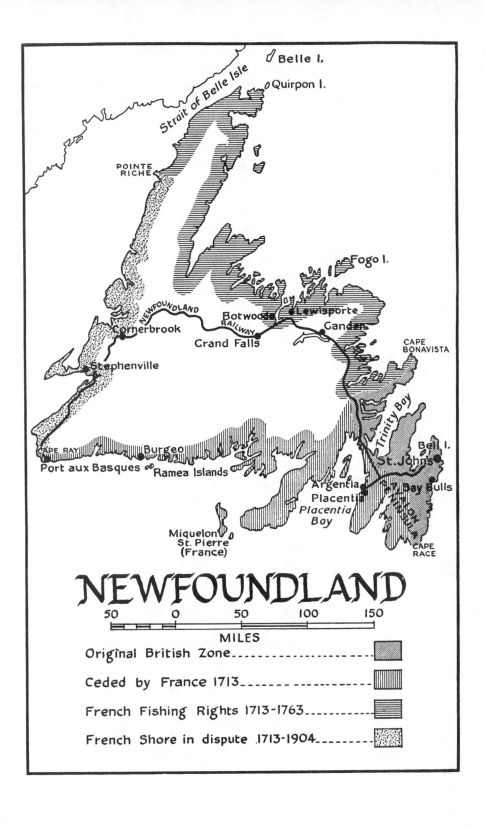

NEWFOUNDLAND

| 50 | 0 | 50 | 100 | 150 |

MILES

Original British Zone............................ ▨

Ceded by France 1713........................ ▨

French Fishing Rights 1713-1763.......... ▤

French Shore in dispute 1713-1904........ ▨

became the major industry and the slave population increased rapidly, reaching 12,000 in 1655. Every effort was made by the French government to support the sugar plantations, but from the first the problems of supplying the islands with the necessary imports of food and materials were acute. France sent out salt, pork and beef, flour, wines, staves, and other commodities, but these supplies were inadequate and expensive. Some nearer and more convenient source of supply was urgently needed, particularly for the low-grade dried fish which was a staple item in the diet of the slaves.

French commercial and colonial policy in this period was directed largely by Colbert, the famous mercantilist statesman, and under his guidance a series of very determined attempts were made to form trading connections between New France, Newfoundland, and the French West Indies, the objective of which was to build up a mutually reinforcing system of exchange which would benefit each area individually and render unnecessary any dependence upon the English colonies. The West Indies would export sugar to France and be supplied with foodstuffs, timber, and other commodities from Newfoundland and New France; these latter areas would in turn be supplied from France, besides trading with each other.

An important part of this general policy was the development of a dry fishery in Newfoundland. As we have already seen, the French had earlier concentrated their attention on the green or Bank fishery, producing a grade of cured fish which was well suited for the domestic market in France but less suited than the dry cure, in which the English specialized, for long-distance trade and sale in tropical areas. Expansion into the dry fishery was indispensable if the French fishery was to be built up as a source of supply for the West Indies. But to make such expansion possible it was necessary for the French to establish bases on Newfoundland, where the fish could be dried on beaches or on wooden "flakes". The English fishermen had already appropriated the best locations in the Avalon peninsula and on the east coast between Cape Bonavista and Cape Race. Consequently the French, when they moved into the dry fishery, established their bases on the south coast, between Cape Ray and Cape Race. To protect these scattered bases the French government in 1662 constructed a fort at Placentia where, in the following years, they maintained a permanent garrison and a small squadron of armed ships. A civil administration was set up and immigration was encouraged.

By the establishment of the fort at Placentia the French gave clear warning of their intention to enter the dry fishery in competition with the English and to claim sovereignty over part at least of Newfoundland. The English West Country fishermen, however, at first attached little importance to this new development. They regarded the English settlers and byeboatkeepers as the more important threat and were inclined to make light of the danger from the French for fear it would lead the British government to send out a governor and encourage settlement. In this they showed little foresight, for in the years which followed the expansion of the French fishery and the decline of the English went hand in hand.

In some respects the French bases on the south coast of the island were better suited for the dry fishery than the English bases on the Avalon peninsula. Placentia was free from field ice early in the spring, so that French ships could arrive in Newfoundland in February or March and leave in August, thus making deliveries in Europe before the English. In many places along the south shore the fish could be dried on the open beaches without the necessity of constructing wooden stages. In terms of organization, too, the French fishermen had certain advantages. They had good financial backing from the merchants of the Channel and Biscay ports and, unlike the English, did not need to mortgage their ships to pay the expenses of the annual voyage; in Newfoundland they were under the supervision of an established government which gave them a measure of security and prompt arbitration of disputes. The conflict between the settlers and the West Country ship captains which characterized the English fishery had no counterpart in the French. At the French bases property such as boats, buildings, and stages could safely be left unguarded from one season to the next, while settlers were given secure title to their holdings. There were, of course, squabbles over rights to the best drying-areas, and the taxes levied to pay the expenses of the local government were a source of complaints, but in general the French dry fishery was better organized, better managed, and better financed than the English. By 1678 it was estimated that the French had three hundred ships employed in the fishery; the English in 1680 had less than one hundred.

The French also continued active in the green fishery and in the less important dry-fishing areas of Nova Scotia (Acadia), Cape Breton, and the Gulf of St. Lawrence. Despite their successes in these fishing areas, however, the French position as a whole remained insecure. The course of events in Nova Scotia illustrates the fundamental weakness. On the Atlantic side of the peninsula there were only a few scattered settlements, which were hardly more than temporary fishing-stations. At Port Royal (Annapolis) there were about 360 settlers in 1670, and in the fertile marshlands of the Minas Basin and other outposts of settlement around the Bay of Fundy probably about one hundred more. Except for the nominal garrison maintained at Port Royal, the colony received little material aid from the French government and nothing was done to develop its potentialities either as a source of agricultural exports or as a base for the fisheries. Instead of becoming the keystone in the great arch of commerce which was to link Quebec, Newfoundland, and the French West Indies, the settlements at Port Royal and in the Minas Basin were allowed to remain in a state of primitive self-sufficiency. Such external trade as did exist was carried on largely with New England through the agency of the small ships from Boston which fished in Nova Scotian waters. In a commercial and naval sense the French settlements in Acadia came within the sphere of influence of Boston rather than of Placentia or Quebec. Highly vulnerable as they were to attack from the sea, they remained French only on the sufferance of the merchants and privateers of New England.

If the settlements in Acadia failed to contribute significantly to the consolidation of the French colonies, the settlements on the St. Lawrence were hardly more successful. The difficulty in New France did not lie in inadequate support from the home government; it lay rather in the slow development of agriculture. In most years the colony could hardly supply its own requirements, far less produce a surplus for export. This was largely a result of concentration on the fur trade and on military defence—tasks which left little man-power available for farming. In addition, even when commodities were available for export to the West Indies, serious difficulties were encountered in devising suitable shipping arrangements.

Unlike Boston and the other New England ports, the St. Lawrence was closed to shipping during the winter months because of ice. During the summer months of July, August, and September, on the other hand, the West Indies were highly dangerous for small sailing-ships because of hurricanes. A ship which left the St. Lawrence as soon as the river was free from ice (the end of April at the earliest) could barely reach the West Indies before the hurricane season began. Sailings from Quebec during the fall months were less hazardous, but likely to encounter many delays. Ordinarily no cargoes of sugar were available in the West Indies until the end of February. A ship which left the St. Lawrence in the late fall, just before the ice formed, would reach the West Indies about the end of December or early January. There it would have to wait idle for six or eight weeks before loading its cargo of sugar for France. With luck and good management it might be able to return to the St. Lawrence toward the end of summer, so that one round trip annually was the most it could make. Alternatively, it might leave Quebec in the late summer and arrive in the West Indies about the middle of October, in which case it might reach France in January and return to Quebec in the spring; but the late summer was the worst time for securing cargoes of dried fish in New France and October was not a good month to get a price for such a cargo in the West Indies.

In short, whatever arrangements were devised, the three-cornered voyage between New France, the West Indies, and France was slow and expensive. New England ships, in contrast, could make two voyages a year to the West Indies during the winter season and occupy themselves in the off-shore fisheries during the summer. New France, handicapped by distance and climate, could not compete with New England as a supply base for the West Indies. The situation might have been different if a shipping and trading centre had been developed in Nova Scotia or Cape Breton, but as we have seen this was not done.

Distance and climate, then, combined to prevent the French from consolidating their colonial empire in North America. This failure to achieve consolidation, combined with failure to achieve and hold command of the seas, was in the end to prove fatal, for it meant that the economic development of the various regions tended to drive them farther apart, not closer together. New France, for example, pushed its military and fur-trading influence far into the interior; partly for this reason, the colony failed to develop as a reliable supply base for the fisheries and the West Indies. The fisheries on the south shore of Newfoundland flourished while the competing English fisheries declined, but they concentrated on the European market where their high-grade product found a ready sale, rather than on the French islands in the Caribbean where the "refuse" grades were in demand. Even Placentia, the cornerstone of French power in Newfoundland, was dependent to some extent on New England for supplies. The French West Indies developed rapidly after 1660 as a cheaper and richer source of sugar than the British islands; but they obtained most of their supplies of fish, agricultural products, and timber from the British colonies, not from the French. The French empire, in short, developed centrifugally. Trading voyages between New France, Newfoundland, and the French West Indies were rare experiments; each area had far closer connections with Europe than with the other French colonies in North America. The British colonies, in contrast, were linked together by a complex network of trade. The Navigation Acts, which bound them commercially to England, formed merely the knot, as it were, which tied together the multiple threads of this network and prevented them from unravelling. The British colonial system in North America was characterized by a flourishing intercolonial trade; the French was not.

NEW ENGLAND AND THE WEST INDIES

Of fundamental importance in building up this British intercolonial trade was the expansion of the shipbuilding industry and of merchant shipping in New England. Unlike the southern colonies such as Virginia, Maryland, and the West Indies, which produced commodities greatly in demand in Britain, the New England colonies produced no staple which could profitably be marketed in Britain except small quantities of naval stores and furs. Consequently the northern colonies were much less valued in Britain than the staple-producing areas to the south, which provided the mother country with an ample supply of tropical products for home consumption and for export.

The passing of the Navigation Acts and the successful wars against Holland opened up for New England possibilities of development as a commercial and shipbuilding centre, and this opportunity was promptly seized. The necessary materials—timber, pitch, turpentine, and so on— were readily available; the fisheries of the Massachusetts coast and the Gulf of Maine served as an excellent training-ground for seamen; and the farms and forests of the coastal strip provided commodities which, even if they could not profitably be exported to Britain, were much in demand in the other colonies. In the second half of the seventeenth century the volume of shipping owned by New England merchants expanded rapidly, and the northern group of colonies—Massachusetts, Connecticut, Rhode Island and (after 1664) New York—established themselves as the shipping and trading centre of the British colonial empire in North America.

Since few of New England's products could profitably be exported to England, while most of her imports came from that country, there was a strong financial incentive for New England merchants to engage in the intercolonial carrying-trade in order to earn the sterling exchange with which to pay for their imports. Bills on London regularly sold for substantial premiums in Boston and to obtain these bills—or, what was equivalent, cargoes which could be shipped directly to Britain—the merchants of Salem, Boston, Providence and the other northern harbours consigned New England produce, principally timber, provisions, and dried fish, to any port on the Atlantic seaboard or in the Caribbean where a profitable sale could be expected. New England ships sailed to Newfoundland for bills on London; to the West Indies for sugar; to Virginia for tobacco; to Madeira and the Canaries for salt; and to West Africa for slaves.

None of New England's major products was on the enumerated list; there were no restrictions upon the export of fish, timber, rum, or provisions to any country. By far the greater part of New England's trade was completely legal. But there were exceptions, and as the commercial development of the region progressed, these exceptions became more and more conspicuous, both as grievances in New England when the British authorities tried to enforce the trade regulations and as grievances in Britain when New England evaded them. For example, it was not permissible for New England merchants to import goods directly from Europe; the laws of navigation laid it down that all goods except salt sent from European countries to the British colonies had first to be shipped to England. But it was not easy to enforce this regulation when New

England ships were sailing directly to European ports with cargoes of dried fish and when the profits of the voyage depended largely upon obtaining a return cargo. Nor was it easy to insure that such ships did not clandestinely export to Europe consignments of enumerated commodities which should by law have gone to Britain only. New England provisions, too, played an important part in supplying the Newfoundland fishery; but who was to prevent a few casks of French brandy or wine from finding their way, at the unpoliced fishing-stations of the island, into the possession of a Boston merchant? Who could disprove the bland assertion of a ship captain seized off the coast of Maine with a cargo of French brandy, who claimed that he "took it up floating in the sea"?

The volume of this smuggling trade is very difficult to estimate, since in the nature of the case it did not become a matter of official record. But the vigorous protests and active resistance which appeared in New England when attempts were made to suppress it suggest that it was not inconsiderable. It is not true that the Navigation Acts seriously retarded the development of the New England area. On the contrary, it was under the shelter of British commercial legislation that New England entered upon its commercial expansion. The point is, rather, that the remarkable commercial development which the Navigation Acts encouraged soon grew too vigorous and too aggressive to be contained within the bounds which the Navigation Acts laid down. It was for this reason that Sir Josiah Child called New England "the most prejudicial plantation to this Kingdom". New England ships competed with British ships in the carrying-trade; New England provisions competed with British provisions in the markets of Newfoundland and the West Indies; New England merchants continually violated the Navigation Acts. "In my opinion," Child continued, "there is nothing more prejudicial and in prospect more dangerous to any mother Kingdom than the increase of shipping in her colonies." In terms of mercantilist doctrine this was correct; but on the other hand New England contributed very largely to the economic integration of the British colonies in North America and thus strengthened the position of Britain in the New World as against France. By 1662 Boston alone had a commercial fleet of 300 vessels engaged in trade with Nova Scotia, Virginia, the West Indies, and Madeira. Without New England the British sugar plantations in the West Indies could hardly have survived. The smuggling trade reflected the impossibility of confining this vigorous and aggressive commercial centre within the statutory limits of mercantilist regulation.

The conflict which was inherent in the development of New England as a rival commercial centre within Britain's mercantilist empire showed itself most conspicuously in the issue of trade with the West Indies. British permanent settlement in this area dated from 1624, when a small colony had been established on the island of St. Christopher. With the decline of Spanish power in the Caribbean other islands came under British control and by 1642 St. Christopher, Barbados, Nevis, Montserrat, and Antigua were British. Jamaica was added in 1658. The French in the same period held Guadeloupe, Martinique, Tortuga, and part of St. Christopher, while the Spanish maintained possession of Cuba, Hispaniola (Haiti), Puerto Rico, and Trinidad, together with large sections of the mainland.

In the British islands, of which Barbados was for long the most important, the first staple export had been tobacco. After 1639, however, tobacco prices fell markedly because of increased production in the West Indies and elsewhere, and Barbados tobacco, which had a noticeably earthy taste, became almost unsalable in competition with exports from Virginia. With the assistance of Dutch merchants, who in this period practically monopolized the trade of the area, the richer and more enterprising settlers turned to the cultivation of sugar cane, and after about 1645 sugar and molasses replaced tobacco as the export staple.

One consequence of this was a revolutionary change in the pattern of land ownership. Tobacco had been grown in small plots and almost entirely by white labour. One estimate places the total white population of Barbados at 36,000 in 1645, and the population density at approximately 217 white persons per square mile. Sugar cultivation, in contrast, led to the development of large plantations worked with slave labour. The white population of the islands fell after 1645, while the Negro population increased rapidly. In 1640 there had been no more than a few hundred Negroes in Barbados; in 1645 there were 6,000, and in 1650 over 20,000. The change from tobacco to sugar led, therefore, to a great increase in the number of slaves, to the development of large plantations, and to the appearance of a small class of rich magnates, most of whom lived in England as absentee landlords. These West India plantation owners came to form a wealthy and highly influential pressure group in English politics.

With the spread of tea, coffee, and chocolate drinking in England, the demand for sugar increased steadily, and the islands of the West Indies came to occupy a position of very great importance in the British colonial empire. The demands of the sugar plantations for Negro labour encouraged an expansion in the slave trade from West Africa, which earlier had been largely in the hands of the Dutch and the Portuguese; to prevent the British islands from being entirely dependent upon foreign sources of supply, the Africa Company was chartered in 1660 and the Royal Africa Company in 1672, the objective of both organizations being to transport Negroes from West Africa to the West Indies under the protection of a charter of monopoly. By 1700, however, the slave trade was thrown open to all, and a kind of triangular trade developed, with British ships sailing from Liverpool with manufactured goods, exchanging them in West Africa for slaves, selling the slaves in the West Indies, and then returning to Britain with cargoes of sugar. Between 1672 and 1708 over 150,000 slaves were imported in this way by the British colonies in the West Indies.

New England also participated in the slave trade but played a more important role in relation to the West Indies as a customer and as a source of provisions. Dried fish was a major item in the diet of the slaves and was supplied almost exclusively by New England traders, who exported to the West Indies the "refuse" grades of fish from their own off-shore fisheries and from Newfoundland. Timber, horses, and beef also found a ready market in the sugar islands. As a customer, New England imported from the West Indies not only sugar but also large quantities of molasses which, distilled into rum, was sold to the Indians in the fur trade, to the English fishers and settlers in Newfoundland, and to the West African slave-traders, as well as being consumed locally. Rum distilled from West Indian molasses was, indeed, a ubiquitous item in all of New England's trade and was to play an important part in the commercial rivalry of the French and British empires.

When the Spaniards, in the early years of the sixteenth century, had first begun planting sugar cane on Hispaniola, they had regarded molasses as a useless by-product of the process of sugar manufacture. And it remained true in the second half of the seventeenth century, when the British and French sugar plantations went into production, that there was little demand for molasses in Europe. For the British West Indies, consequently, New England's willingness to accept molasses in part payment for provisions, slaves, and timber was a very great advantage indeed. By 1661 the New England provision trade had become so indispensable that a colonial writer called it "the key to the Indies without which Jamaica, Barbados and ye Charibby Islands are not able to subsist."

In the French West Indies the transition from tobacco to sugar occurred somewhat later than in the English and was considerably more gradual. But by 1660 the French islands also were important sugar producers and there were indications that, because of their better methods of cultivation and the less exhausted condition of their soil, they were likely to become cheaper producers than the English. In particular the French islands produced large quantities of molasses which they could not export to France. The production of rum was frowned upon within the French empire because it would compete with French domestic producers of wines and brandy. The French fur-traders, as we shall see later, were seriously handicapped in competition with the English because they had no rum of their own to offer in trade. Since the French West Indies, like all the Caribbean colonies, had to import quantities of provisions and lumber, there was a clear opportunity for New England merchants to carry on the same profitable trade with the French planters as they had with the English. And this they were not slow to do.

As long as the New England traders merely exported provisions and lumber to, and imported sugar and molasses from, the French West Indies they did not contravene the Navigation Acts. Particularly after 1700, however, the rapid development of trade between New England and the French islands led to protests from two quarters: the British sugar-planters, and the customs officials in the colonial ports. The planters complained because New England was assisting the development of a competing source of supply. If this was not contrary to the letter of the Navigation Acts, it was certainly contrary to their spirit. The governor of the Leeward Islands, for instance, warned the home government in 1701 that the French "begin to tred upon our heels in the sugar trade" and suggested, to remedy the situation, that a law be passed prohibiting the export of provisions and lumber from Ireland and the North American colonies to the French West Indies. By threatening in this way the interests of the British plantation owners, New England was incurring the hostility of a powerful vested interest with considerable influence in the British Parliament. The British customs officials in the colonial ports, for their part, found it very difficult to check the clandestine importation of European goods into the colonies in the ships that traded with the French islands. Like Newfoundland, the French West Indies came to play the part of a clearing-house through which New England colonists obtained European products in violation of the British commercial code. The continued inability of British customs officials to prevent such illicit trading was partly responsible for the annulment of the charter of Massachusetts and the assumption of direct government by the British Crown in 1684. But the economic forces at work were too deep-seated to be halted by a change in methods of administration, and the control of New England's trade continued to be a serious and intractable problem for the British government until the Revolution.

FRENCH AND BRITISH COLONIAL EXPANSION: SOME GENERAL CONSIDERATIONS

Involving as it does the conflicting interests and policies of several nations and of a variety of economically dissimilar areas, the history of the trade and fisheries of the North Atlantic after 1650 is inevitably rather complex, and it is important to keep in mind the general tendencies that were working themselves out. The story has two principal and interrelated themes: the rivalry of the nations of the Old World, particularly France and Britain, in colonial expansion, and the development within the New World of the centres of economic growth which were to form the nuclei of the Canadian and American nations of today. To tie these two themes together we have analysed the patterns of economic relationship that grew up between the various colonies established in North America and between them and Europe, particularly the relationships of trade through which the various areas—serving different markets, employing different technologies, and making use of different human and physical resources—maintained themselves and accumulated the reserves necessary for growth. The analysis of trade relationships has directed our attention to the policies followed by the various government authorities in their attempts to regulate trade, to the effectiveness with which these policies were carried out, and to the consequences, sometimes expected but more often unforeseen, for the regions involved.

England and Holland had been allies against Spain at the time of the Armada, but when, early in the seventeenth century, Spanish power in Europe and the New World began to wane, they became rivals. The decline of Spain left, as it were, a vacuum, particularly in the commerce of the Caribbean and South America, which other European nations hastened to fill. But Holland was much quicker off the mark than England. A small, compact, and remarkably homogeneous country, in whose political life the influence of the merchants was supreme, Holland was free from the internal dissensions and civil strife which retarded England's overseas expansion. By the middle of the seventeenth century the Dutch had become the world's great maritime carriers and Amsterdam the world's great entrepôt—the place to which cargoes of goods from all parts of the world were brought and from which they were sent to the markets of the other European nations.

The Dutch, though they were great traders, were not themselves great colonizers. In North America and the Caribbean they founded few colonies of their own, preferring the surer and quicker profit to be gained from the trade of the colonies which others had founded. England's Navigation Acts were designed to exploit this weakness. They were, in a literal sense, an act of economic warfare against the Dutch, a means of excluding them entirely from all trade between England and her colonies overseas. Their success was remarkable. What made this success possible was the great expansion in the English and colonial shipbuilding industry and in the number of ships which flew the British flag. No attempt to exclude the Dutch from the English carrying-trade could possibly have been effective if English merchant shipping had not been able to take over the functions which earlier had been performed by the Dutch.

Unlike England and Holland, France was primarily a continental power and her colonial policy was influenced more by the exigencies and distractions of continental defence in Europe than were the policies of either of her chief rivals. Although she had excellent harbours on both her Mediterranean and her Atlantic coasts, she also had extended frontiers on land which had to be defended by large armies and expensive fortifications, so that the attention given to overseas maritime expansion by the French Crown was at best sporadic. The French economy, too, with the exception of certain commodities such as fish, furs, sugar, and tobacco which were to prove important later, was very largely self-sufficient; economic life was organized around internal trade and the domestic market, rather than the export-import trade and foreign markets. And in addition, throughout the sixteenth century, religious strife and civil war prevented France from playing any significant part in the colonization of North America. Cartier's expedition to the St. Lawrence in 1534, for example, was not effectively followed up until Champlain's expeditions almost three-quarters of a century later. When Champlain made his first voyage to the West Indies in 1599, he did so in the employ of Spain, not of France. At the beginning of the seventeenth century France was almost non-existent as a maritime power. She had no colonies, little overseas commerce, and practically no navy.

During the first half of the seventeenth century, under the able guidance of Richelieu, the French navy was expanded and modernized, and partially successful attempts were made to establish permanent colonies in North America and the West Indies. The instrument of the chartered company was extensively used in these attempts, largely as a means of minimizing the direct financial burden upon the government while at the same time insuring—as far as a charter could insure—that certain objectives of state policy were achieved. As means of establishing strong and permanent colonies, these chartered companies left much to be desired; as means of building up France's external trade and her merchant marine they were even more disappointing. A colony established on the St. Lawrence, for example, gave employment to only a handful of ships, which shuttled back and forth each year between the colony and the mother country. A trading system of this type, carried on under an exclusive charter of monopoly and confined to a single unchanging route, was in sharp contrast to the flexible multilateral "venture" trade carried on by the Dutch and later by New England. Apart from the Newfoundland and Banks fisheries which were not under company control, the French merchant marine in the North Atlantic remained weak. One consequence of this was that the Dutch, when they were ousted from the English carrying-trade, concentrated their efforts on the French trade and offered very severe competition to French merchant ships. Colbert, the French mercantilist minister, was well aware of the insecurity which dependence on Dutch shipping meant for the French colonial empire and did his best to encourage shipbuilding in New France and at home. But until well into the eighteenth century much of the French colonial trade remained in the hands of the Dutch.

The expansion of shipbuilding and merchant shipping in New England, which was encouraged by the Navigation Acts and did much to make their success possible, introduced into the British colonial system in

North America an important integrative force which stimulated the development of colonial trade and the growth of the various areas of British settlement. But at the same time it introduced potentially disruptive tendencies into the system. A mercantilist empire had room for only one active centre of commerce: the mother country. The role of colonies, in theory, was a purely passive one: to serve as sources of raw materials. During the second half of the seventeenth century New England emerged as a competing active commercial centre whose interests increasingly diverged from those of the mother country. The southern colonies, such as Virginia and Maryland, were the termini for a "shuttle" trade with England and did not develop an active commerce of their own. New England, lacking an important exportable staple which would have linked her economy closely to the British market, could develop only by commerce and became the focus for increasingly complex networks of trade which tied together, in a commercial sense, the colonies of the Atlantic seaboard, Newfoundland, and the Caribbean. The commercial enterprise of the New England ports consolidated the British colonial empire in North America in a sense in which the French colonial empire was never consolidated. Illicit trade and the repressive measures adopted by the British colonial authorities to regulate New England's commerce reflected the difficulty of assimilating this competing commercial centre into a mercantilist empire.

The importance of New England as a base for supplies and ships became evident during the wars against France which marked the close of the seventeenth and the beginning of the eighteenth centuries. During the War of the League of Augsburg (1689-97) colonies and colonial commerce were not among the principal issues. Nevertheless New England, whose land frontier was dangerously exposed to attack by the French and their Indian allies and whose shipping was vulnerable to French privateers operating from Acadia, equipped two naval expeditions against Port Royal and one against Quebec. Poor leadership and bad organization, however, prevented these raids from having decisive effect and both Port Royal and Quebec were in French hands at the end of the war. The British settlements in Newfoundland, meanwhile, suffered severely from French attack and by 1697 the British foothold on the island had been reduced to Trinity and Conception Bays. The Treaty of Ryswick which ended the war effected no changes in sovereignty as far as North America was concerned.

During the War of the Spanish Succession (1701-13), in contrast, colonies and colonial trade were very much at stake. The cause of the war was nominally the attempt of Louis XIV of France to place his grandson on the Spanish throne; actually the war was fought to prevent France from taking over the trade of the Spanish colonial empire. England and Holland, formerly enemies and commercial rivals, joined with Austria to defeat this threat. In North America hostilities followed what was coming to be the traditional pattern: naval squadrons based on New England attacked Port Royal and Quebec; French raiders from Placentia harassed the English settlements on Newfoundland; and land forces from Massachusetts and the other New England colonies threatened Montreal. Port Royal was captured in 1709, but attacks on Quebec and Placentia failed. French defeats in Europe, however, more than compensated for the inconclusive results of the war in North America, and the Treaty of Utrecht, signed in 1713, decisively altered the alignment of European powers in North America. Under the terms of the treaty Nova Scotia (except Cape Breton) and the Hudson Bay region were ceded to Britain, together with St. Christopher in the West Indies. Newfoundland also became British territory and Placentia was evacuated, but the French were permitted to retain fishing rights on the northern and northeastern shores of the island between Cape Bonavista and Point Riche.

The Dutch, who had suffered as England's enemies in the latter half of the seventeenth century, suffered equally as England's allies in the first quarter of the eighteenth, and their strength declined markedly during the hostilities against France. Although retaining an important position in the carrying-trade, particularly in the Baltic and the North Sea, Holland was no longer a major participant in the struggle for colonial empire. The commerce of Spain was also hard hit, although her navy and merchant marine staged a brief but remarkable recovery in the second quarter of the century. Britain and France remained as the major opposing powers in North America.

The pattern of conflict which was to persist during the next half-century was already evident in 1713. Britain had emerged from the war richer and stronger than she had entered it. Her command of the seas seemed unassailable. Her position in Newfoundland, Nova Scotia, the Atlantic colonies, and the West Indies appeared secure. France, although she had lost her foothold in Newfoundland, retained her possessions in the West Indies and in New France, together with Cape Breton, the key to the St. Lawrence. Wars and dynastic struggles in Europe had done much to shape the structure and alignment of these rival colonial empires, but the conflict between them in North America was not merely a distant reflection of the shifting balance of power in Europe. On the North Atlantic, fisheries and trade continued to affect naval strength, the security of highly-valued sources of raw materials, and the prosperity of settlements. In the interior of the continent French expansion along the St. Lawrence and down the Mississippi threatened to encircle the Atlantic colonies, expose their undefended landward frontiers to hostile attack, and deprive them of access to the hinterland.

SUGGESTIONS FOR FURTHER READING

BASIC WORKS:

Innis, Harold A., *The Cod Fisheries: the History of an International Economy* (Toronto and New Haven, 1940) Chapter V, pp. 95-143

Judah, Charles B., Jr., *The North American Fisheries and British Policy to 1713* (Urbana, Illinois, 1933), Chapters V-VIII, pp. 86-176

Lounsbury, Ralph G., *The British Fishery at Newfoundland, 1634-1763* (New Haven, 1934), Chapters III-VII, pp. 92-244

SUPPLEMENTARY WORKS:

Beer, George L., *The Old Colonial System, 1660-1754* (New York, 1933), Part I, Vols. I and II

Brebner, J. Bartlet, *New England's Outpost: Acadia before the Conquest of Canada* (New York, 1927)

Dickerson, Oliver M., *The Navigation Acts and the American Revolution* (Philadelphia, 1951)

Harper, Lawrence A., *The English Navigation Laws* (New York, 1939)

Newton, Arthur P., *The European Nations in the West Indies, 1493-1688* (London, 1933)

Pitman, Frank W., *The Development of the British West Indies, 1700-1763* (New Haven, 1917)

CHAPTER IV

CONTINENTAL EXPANSION: 1650–1713

RECONSTRUCTION OF THE ST. LAWRENCE FUR TRADE

THE dispersion of the Hurons by Iroquois attack in 1649 and 1650 destroyed the trading system by which the French on the St. Lawrence had been enabled to secure supplies of furs from the tribes of the interior. The reconstruction of the trade demanded military protection against the Iroquois and the development of a transport system by which the French themselves could convey trade goods to remote tribes and carry back furs to Montreal and Quebec. The creation of this new trading system and its defence against attack were the principal tasks facing the French colony on the St. Lawrence during the second half of the seventeenth century.

The purpose of the Iroquois attack upon the Hurons around Georgian Bay had been to disrupt the flow of furs from the western tribes to Montreal and to divert this flow into the hands of the Iroquois themselves. By 1640 beaver supplies in what is now upper New York state were exhausted. Without beaver the Iroquois were unable to obtain from the Dutch on the Hudson River the European goods which were by now indispensable to them. The only sources from which beaver could be obtained were the western hunting tribes whose fur "exports" were at this time monopolized by the Hurons. Attempts to secure a portion of this trade by peaceful agreement with the French and the Hurons having failed, the Iroquois turned to violence, seeking to take over from the Hurons the profitable functions of middlemen and distributors. Access to fur supplies was a life or death matter for the Iroquois. Having grown accustomed to European tools, utensils, and fire-arms, they now could not do without them.

For a time it looked as if the Iroquois policy had achieved complete success. With the Huron trading empire destroyed, they sought peace with the French and a treaty was ratified in September, 1653. But they did not succeed in taking over the position in the fur trade formerly held by the Hurons, a fact for which their series of wars against the Eries, the Petuns, and other tribes to the north and west was at least partly responsible. Instead the Ottawas became the middlemen of the Montreal fur trade and a new trading system developed along the Ottawa River-Lake Nipissing-Georgian Bay route. In a sense, indeed, the dispersion of the Hurons and their allied tribes accelerated the spread of the

74

fur trade, for it scattered Indians familiar with European goods among remote tribes which had previously had little knowledge of them. Thus after 1650 we find the Ottawas penetrating as far as Lake Michigan and the north shore of Lake Superior in their search for furs, and trading there with tribes anxious to obtain European goods and to organize hunting expeditions on condition that the Ottawas promised to return each year.

For a few years after 1650 the St. Lawrence fur trade almost came to a standstill, but in 1654, after the peace was signed, large canoe fleets once again came down the Ottawa to Montreal, and while the truce with the Iroquois lasted the trade remained fairly prosperous. But the very failure of the Iroquois to capture the western trade was a guarantee of future trouble, and in 1657 the Ottawa River route was again closed by Iroquois attack. It was becoming clear, indeed, that the fur trade, and with it the French colony, could never hope for security until the Iroquois were subdued by superior military force.

To organize and finance a major military expedition against the Iroquois was beyond the ability of the Company of New France which, after the bankruptcy of the Company of the Inhabitants, had once again assumed responsibility for the colony. In 1663, therefore, the charter of this Company was revoked and the colony was taken under the direct supervision and care of the French king. This made it possible for a much more aggressive policy to be followed. In 1664 the colony and the fur trade were put under the charge of the newly formed Company of the West Indies, which was responsible for all of France's possessions in the New World, and shortly thereafter several companies of the famous Carignan-Salières regiment arrived at Quebec. Two punitive expeditions into Iroquois territory south of the St. Lawrence induced the Iroquois to sue for peace in 1667.

The subduing of the Iroquois was only the first, though the indispensable, step in the new policy of expansion and consolidation which the assumption of control by the Crown brought to New France. Local administration was placed in the capable hands of Jean Talon, the intendant or special representative of the King, while in France the King's chief minister, Colbert, gave the colony his powerful support. Symptomatic of the new era in the colony's history was the increase in immigration and population, and the greater attention given to agriculture, domestic manufacture, and shipbuilding. But the fur trade remained the principal source of wealth, the commercial backbone of the colony, and it was the fur trade which served as the spearhead of westward expansion.

With the Iroquois quiet, for the time being at least, the way was open for French explorers, traders, and priests to penetrate to the interior of the continent, not by the old Ottawa River route, but by the Great Lakes, and to extend their activities westward as far as Lake Superior and the head-waters of the Mississippi. While the Ottawas continued to play an important role as middlemen, the French after 1670 increasingly organized their own trading expeditions and made direct contact with the western tribes. The annual fairs at Montreal, Quebec, and Three Rivers declined in importance, and the focus of the trade moved west to such points of concentration as Green Bay, Michilimackinac, and Sault Ste. Marie, where French traders and Indian trappers met and bartered. The establishment of Fort Frontenac on Lake Ontario in 1673 and the construction of ships on Lake Erie and Lake Ontario in 1677-9 reflected the increasing importance of the Great Lakes route and the rapid expansion of French commercial and military influence. By 1680 the St. Lawrence fur trade had begun to assume the form which, with minor modifications, it was to retain until its disappearance in 1821; no longer depending upon Indian middlemen, the French had begun to organize their own transport and distributing system. The *coureur de bois* and the *voyageur* were coming to be the characteristic figures of the trade.

ORGANIZATION OF THE TRADE

The westward expansion of the trade brought changes in its organization and financing. Trading expeditions to the western tribes involved relatively heavy expenditures for consignments of trade goods imported from France and sent by canoe to the interior, and the turnover of capital was slow. Many of the smaller merchants were, in consequence, forced out of business, and by 1685 the concentration of the trade in the hands of a few large merchants at Quebec and Montreal was already exciting comment. But at the same time the success of a trading venture depended very largely upon the skill, experience, and resourcefulness of the individual trader in the interior. Consequently working arrangements between the merchant and financier at Montreal and the trader in the interior usually took the form of a partnership, rather than a wage contract, so that the risks and the profits were shared between the parties involved. These partnerships, formed for a stipulated period of years, remained characteristic of the St. Lawrence fur trade throughout its existence.

Westward expansion brought not only rising costs and slower turnover but also serious difficulties in marketing. The demand for furs was highly inelastic, so that increases in supply tended to result in a sharp fall in prices which could have disastrous results for the whole colony, since fur was the only important export. To solve this problem, attempts were made to fix official prices for furs and to restrict the number of traders by requiring each of them to secure a government licence.

Neither of these policies had much success. After the bankruptcy of the Company of the Inhabitants, monopoly rights in the fur trade were sold to a private merchant who held them until 1666, when they were transferred to the Company of the West Indies. Heavy expenditures for defence during the war against the Iroquois, combined with large increases in supplies of fur and a serious fall in prices when the war was concluded, plunged the Company heavily into debt, and its charter was revoked in 1674. Monopoly rights were then sold to another private merchant, but only on condition that he agreed to purchase at a fixed price all furs offered to him. This policy encouraged the traders to throw on the market large quantities of low-grade furs, particularly the *castor sec* obtained from the Indians of what is now northern Wisconsin. *Castor sec* was the term used for beaver fur which had not been worn by the Indians as robes and which still retained the guard hair. It was less valuable than the soft and supple *castor gras* and was used in much smaller quantities for hat-making, the usual proportions for hats being three parts of *castor gras* to one of *castor sec*. These large supplies of *castor sec* brought very poor prices in Europe and led to the adoption of a new policy in 1677, according to which the trader received a higher price for *castor gras* than for the poorer grades. But the possibilities of regulating supply by adjusting price differentials were very limited because of the repercussions upon relations with the Indians. Refusal to accept all the furs which the Indians had to offer threatened to weaken their allegiance to New France and to encourage the spread of English influence in the west.

A more direct attack upon the problem of supply was by restricting the number of traders in the interior. Such a policy had other advantages also. The fur trade was a serious drain on the man-power of the colony, attracting the most enterprising and ambitious men away from the unexciting but indispensable work of agriculture, while the sale of licences to traders offered the prospect of supplementing public revenues. Regulations to limit the number of men trading in the interior were first issued in 1673 and regularly reissued thereafter. In 1696 the drastic step was taken of prohibiting independent trading entirely and of confining the trade to certain specified posts where it could be carried on under military supervision. In general these licensing schemes proved ineffective. The regulations were very difficult to enforce, particularly since illegal traders, if outlawed by the French, were always sure of a ready market for their furs and experience at Albany, and many opportunities were open for abuse and evasion.

To summarize developments in this period, the French succeeded in rebuilding a trading system which gave them access to the rich fur-supply areas of the interior. With the assumption of state leadership and responsibility in 1663, effective measures were taken to defend the lines of supply and trade. Control of the Ottawa route was regained, while the construction of forts on Lake Ontario gave temporary military control of the lower Lakes and encouraged the beginnings of lake shipping.

French explorers penetrated to Lake Superior and the head-waters of the Mississippi and direct trading connections were made with the western tribes. Increases in supplies, particularly of the poorer furs from the region south of the upper Lakes, led to serious problems of marketing which proved insoluble by valorization and licensing schemes. The costs of the trade tended to rise, partly because of the lengthening of supply lines and partly because of the burden of military expenditures. Defence remained the major problem for the colony and the fur trade. Continuing difficulties with the Iroquois between 1684 and 1694 led to further heavy expenditures for defence and to a temporary return to the Ottawa River route.

THE ENGLISH FUR TRADE FROM NEW YORK AND HUDSON BAY

As long as the French held the St. Lawrence they controlled one major transport route to the interior of the continent. But it was by no means the only route. Separated by low heights of land from the drainage basin of the St. Lawrence were three other river systems: the Hudson-Mohawk system, flowing through what is now New York state; the system of rivers—the Nelson, the Hayes, the Severn, the Albany and others—flowing north and northeast into Hudson Bay; and the vast Mississippi system, including the Missouri, the Ohio, the Allegheny and other tributaries, flowing south to the Gulf of Mexico. The last-named of these was unexplored until the 1680's and thereafter remained under French control; but the other two river systems, each of which provided easy access to the interior, were not controlled by the French, and during the second half of the seventeenth century both were developed as transport routes to serve the needs of competing fur-trade organizations. Competition in the fur trade was fundamentally competition between drainage basins. The key to success was control of the low heights of land which separated one drainage basin from another. This was necessarily the case as long as the trade remained dependent upon water transportation.

The Dutch on the Hudson River had caused trouble for the French ever since the founding of New Amsterdam on Manhattan Island in 1624. The Dutch colony itself was weak, to be sure, and its development was held back by internal dissension and by very limited immigration from Holland, but it did provide an alternative market for furs, and it was the existence of this market that provided the Iroquois with the incentive and the means to break into the French trade. This competitive threat from the south became much more serious after 1664, when the Dutch colony fell into the hands of the English. The Hudson River route was now controlled by men whose aggressive designs upon the St. Lawrence colony were obvious. The English colonial merchants who supplanted the Dutch at New York and Albany were well aware of the profits to be gained from the fur trade and even less hesitant than their predecessors in selling fire-arms to the Iroquois, on whom they depended for supplies of fur. Backed by the English merchants, the Iroquois recovered swiftly from their defeats of 1665-6 and, as we have seen, continuously harassed the French lines of communication with the interior, particularly after 1683 when French penetration into the Illinois country south of Lake Michigan encroached upon fur-supply areas which previously had been monopolized by the Iroquois.

The alliance between the Albany traders and the Iroquois was as firm as the alliance between the French and the Hurons had been before 1650, and for the same reasons. The Iroquois depended upon Albany for the European goods which were now necessary for their survival, particularly guns and ammunition. These goods could be obtained only in exchange for furs, and to obtain these furs the Iroquois necessarily had to tap the same supply areas as did the French. Nor was it possible for the French to hope that they could compete with the Iroquois by peaceful means alone, for the Albany traders could offer better prices. The manufactured goods sold by the English traders were sometimes priced as low as one-half of the French prices, lower production costs in England and lower freight rates on the North Atlantic being responsible for the difference. And in addition the English could supply the Indians with rum from the West Indies, a cheap trading commodity which was much in demand among the Indians and which could not be obtained from the French, for French mercantilist regulations prohibited the use of rum in the fur trade, not so much because of its effects on the consumer but rather in the hope of increasing the demand for brandy. The Indians were not averse to brandy, but rum was cheaper.

The ability of the Albany traders to offer more suitable trade goods and better terms of exchange than the French was of very great importance in the long run, for it meant that it was not in the interests of the French to come to a permanently amicable agreement with the Iroquois, even if this had been possible. Purely commercial competition in terms of prices would have permitted the cost advantages of the Albany traders to exercise their full influence upon supply and would certainly have diverted large quantities of furs away from the St. Lawrence route to the Hudson River. Over the long run, therefore, French policy was directed toward excluding the Iroquois from the western trade, by force if necessary; but on the other hand it was not in French interests to destroy the Iroquois entirely, for it was fear of the Iroquois which kept the western tribes in alliance with the French and prevented them from turning to the cheaper markets at Albany and, after 1670, on Hudson Bay.

Concentration upon the immediate threat from the south may have blinded the French authorities to the possibility of an equally serious threat from the north. It was by this time coming to be recognized that the best furs were to be obtained from the country north and northwest of Lake Superior. The shortest route from this area to the sea was not by the Great Lakes and the St. Lawrence but by the rivers leading into Hudson Bay, and to certain of the more enterprising French traders in the interior the advantages of the northern route were becoming clear. Two of these traders, Médard Chouart, usually called des Groseilliers, and Pierre-Esprit Radisson, proposed an expedition by the Hudson Bay route in 1660, when they returned to Montreal after a very profitable trading venture in the country around Lake Superior, but they were given short shrift by the governor, partly because their last venture had infringed the official monopoly. Convinced of the soundness of the idea, Groseilliers then went to France in an attempt to enlist the support of the home government, but was unsuccessful. An attempt to sell his scheme to the French merchants at Cadiz also failed. Frustrated in his efforts to gain support from the officials and financiers of his own country, Groseilliers then turned to the English and in 1662 or thereabouts he and Radisson took their proposals to Boston. Here they met with a more favourable reception and, with the help of a group of Boston merchants, two expeditions to the Bay were actually fitted out. Neither reached the Bay, however, the first because the captain refused to venture among the icebergs, the second because one of the ships was wrecked. Groseilliers and Radisson then approached the English officials in New York, two of whom, Colonel George Cartwright and Colonel Richard Nicholls, the governor, expressed considerable interest and persuaded the two Frenchmen to go to England. There they landed in 1665, equipped with introductions to several persons with influence at court.

The favourable reaction which met Groseilliers and Radisson in Boston and New York and later in England contrasts sharply with the lack of interest, amounting almost to positive hostility, which they encountered in Montreal and France. The principal reason for this was, of course, that they were proposing to divert the fur trade away from the colony on the St. Lawrence, which was the key to the French empire in North America. Without the revenue provided by the fur trade the colony would certainly have withered and died. No doubt French influence among the Indians might have been maintained from Hudson Bay as easily as from the St. Lawrence, but trading-posts on the Bay would hardly have provided a suitable environment for settlement. The logic of the situation was clear: without the fur trade, New France could not survive; but New France was at this time the only permanent French settlement, except Acadia, on the mainland of North America, and it was essential to French imperial interests that it be maintained; therefore it was inconceivable that Frenchmen should be permitted to divert the trade away from the St. Lawrence.

No such considerations troubled the men whom Radisson and

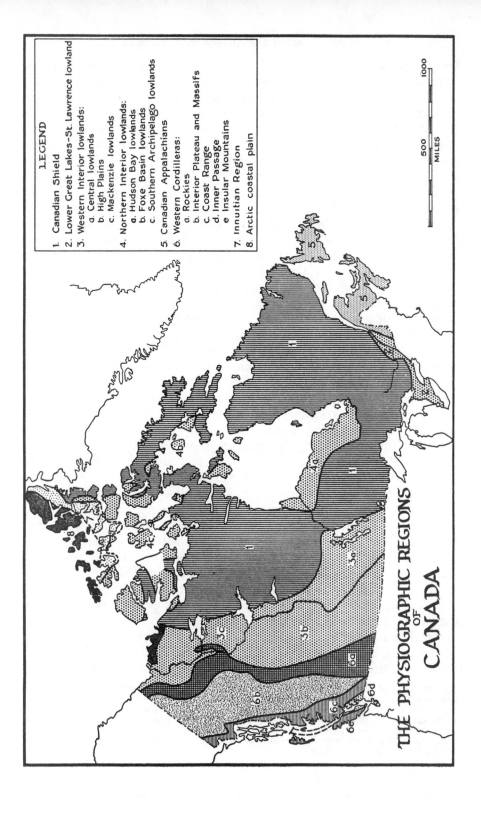

LEGEND

1. Canadian Shield
2. Lower Great Lakes–St. Lawrence lowland
3. Western Interior lowlands:
   a. Central lowlands
   b. High Plains
   c. Mackenzie lowlands
4. Northern Interior lowlands:
   a. Hudson Bay lowlands
   b. Foxe Basin lowlands
   c. Southern Archipelago lowlands
5. Canadian Appalachians
6. Western Cordilleras:
   a. Rockies
   b. Interior Plateau and Massifs
   c. Coast Range
   d. Inner Passage
   e. Insular Mountains
7. Innutian Region
8. Arctic coastal plain

500   1000

MILES

THE PHYSIOGRAPHIC REGIONS
OF
CANADA

Groseilliers met in England. If expectations of profit were of prime importance to the merchants and bankers of London, they were also not without a certain attractiveness to the aristocrats who busied themselves around the court of Charles II, and in both groups hopes for financial gain were reinforced by the aggressive spirit of Restoration imperialism—a desire to extend Britain's commerce, a curiosity about places still unknown, a zest for discovery and exploration—particularly, in this case, the search for a northwest passage to the Pacific. The proposal to send a trading expedition to Hudson Bay was laid directly before the King and met with his immediate support. The war with the Dutch and the plague that was raging in London prevented action being taken for a few years, but in 1668 two small ships, one of them borrowed from the navy, were sent to the Bay with miscellaneous cargoes of trade goods. One of these ships reached its destination safely, took possession of the land in the King's name, traded with the Indians, and returned to England in October, 1669. Meanwhile another ship had been sent out which explored the coast of the Bay west of Rupert River.

The results of these pioneer voyages were considered promising, and the syndicate of thirteen men who had backed the first ventures lost no time in seeking a royal charter which would enable them to form a company and obtain exclusive rights to the trade. This charter was obtained on May 2, 1670. It granted to the Company—usually known as the Hudson's Bay Company, but formally the "Company of Adventurers of England trading into Hudson's Bay"—the monopoly of all trade through Hudson Strait, together with exclusive possession of all the lands within the drainage basin of the Bay—a vast area which included the greater part of the present prairie provinces as well as the barren tundra of the north.* Prince Rupert, the King's cousin, was appointed first governor of the Company, and his private secretary, Sir James Hayes, was for many years the most active figure in its management. Of the other stockholders, several were influential aristocrats, others important financiers in the City of London. Most of them were closely connected with government and imperial policy in other capacities.

The Hudson's Bay Company, one of the longest-lived business organizations in all history, was a late-comer among the great English chartered companies. In terms of the general trend of English commercial organization and policy, it was distinctly a throw-back to an earlier era which was now moving into its last phases—an era when all of England's overseas commerce had been organized under great companies with exclusive

*The terms of the charter were not, in a geographic sense, very specific. The Company was granted ". . . the sole trade and commerce of all those seas, straits, bays, rivers, lakes, creeks and sounds, in whatsoever latitude they shall be, that lie within the entrance of the straits, commonly called Hudson's Straits, together with all the lands, countries and territories upon the coasts and confines of the seas, straits, bays, lakes, rivers, creeks and sounds aforesaid, which are not now actually possessed by any of our subjects, or by the subjects of any other Christian Prince or State."

privileges granted to them by the Crown. Nevertheless, the reasons why a chartered company was a particularly appropriate instrument in this case are quite clear. Small-scale ventures could not have been successful, for the risks were too great and the profits too uncertain. The French would certainly be hostile, the navigation of the Bay was unfamiliar and dangerous, and the possibility of losing one or even two ships in a single year was very real. Only a large organization with monopoly rights and access to adequate supplies of capital could hope to survive, establish itself on the Bay, and yield a profit. On the other hand it was not the kind of commitment in which the King or Parliament would wish to participate directly. The attractions of the Bay were almost entirely commercial. To be sure, there was the unfounded hope of finding a northwest passage and the possibility of stealing a march on the French, but Parliament was not likely to vote funds for such purposes. The King could, however, grant important privileges without consulting Parliament. The royal prerogative was sufficient to insure a monopoly of trade in the Bay and exclusive possession of the surrounding lands. These privileges involved neither the Crown nor Parliament in any expense, but they were solid assets to a company seeking support from private investors. Even with these advantages the risks were great; the original stockholders in the Hudson's Bay Company had to wait fourteen years before they received their first dividend.

The early policies of the Company reflected an awareness of these risks and a wish to keep to a minimum the extent of the fixed investment. Capital resources in the early years were very limited and the Company whenever possible borrowed ships from the navy or leased them from private owners. Emphasis was placed on rapid turnover of capital; ships were supposed to leave England and return within the year and not winter in the Bay. The shortness of the open season in the Bay meant quick unloading of cargoes and loading of furs, so that it was necessary to establish permanent bases—a step which was advisable in any case, if the Company was to make good by effective occupation its claim to the territory granted by the charter. These bases, the first of which were built at the estuaries of the rivers leading into James Bay, became important distributing points. Their maintenance was indispensable to the Company's trade, but at the same time they were highly vulnerable to attack, as the French were shortly to demonstrate.

Despite early difficulties, the Company had solid advantages in its favour. The drainage basin of the Bay gave those who controlled it a grip on the best fur preserve of the whole continent. In terms of transportation costs the advantages lay wholly on the side of the Bay route. While the French transport system required trans-shipment at Quebec and Montreal and further packing and repacking as the traders moved inland, the English could bring in supplies to the mouths of rivers which tapped at close range an enormous fur-bearing territory, much of it beyond the effective pull of the St. Lawrence. The French transport routes lay along the rim, as it were, of a great wheel; the English routes lay along the spokes. With a cheaper transport system and cheaper and more suitable trading commodities, the Company could attract Indian trappers and middlemen a long distance to its posts on the Bay and thus avoid the costs of working out its own distributing system in the interior.

THE FRENCH REACTION TO ENGLISH COMPETITION

The French on the St. Lawrence were now threatened by English competition on both flanks. Two lines of policy were adopted to neutralize the threat from the north. The first centred around military and naval attacks against the Company's posts on the Bay, while the second involved the construction of forts in the interior to cut off the supplies of furs which otherwise would go to the Company. Like the French at an earlier date, the Company at first relied exclusively upon Indian middle-men to bring furs down to the posts on the Bay and to distribute trade goods in the interior. In this case the function of middlemen was performed by the Crees. South of the Crees were the Assiniboines and the Sioux. The Sioux normally obtained goods from the French and sent their furs to Montreal, but the Assiniboines were allied to the Crees and sent their furs to the Bay. To extend the trade in French goods and to offset in part the pull of the Company's posts, the French attempted to form an alliance of the three tribes and to this end negotiated a peace treaty at the head of Lake Superior in 1679. To strengthen still further French influence among the marginal tribes—marginal in the sense that they could trade either with the Bay or with the French—posts were built north of Lake Superior, on Lake Nipigon, and in 1685 near the junction of the Kenogami and Albany Rivers.

These moves strengthened the French position in the disputed territory north of Lake Superior. Their purpose was to give the French control of the height of land which separated the drainage basin of Hudson Bay from the drainage basin of the Great Lakes. This was a limited objective; if achieved, it would neutralize the posts which the Company had established on the south shore of Hudson Bay and in James Bay, but it would not and could not neutralize posts established on the western shore of the Bay, and in particular the important post at York Factory on the Nelson River, which gave access to the vast territory drained by the Saskatchewan River, stretching as far west as the Rockies. To offset this threat, the French had two alternatives open to them: either to move into the Saskatchewan area themselves in direct competition with the English, or to destroy the Company's posts on the Bay. The latter alternative was tried first; the struggle for the Saskatchewan was not taken up until after 1713.

War between England and France was not officially declared until 1689, but pretexts for attacking the Company's posts before then were not hard to find. In 1683 the fort on the Nelson River was captured and destroyed. It was later rebuilt and reoccupied by the English, but the attacks continued and for the next fourteen years a succession of small-scale but bitter naval and military engagements was fought in and around the Bay. The details of the struggle are complex; forts were captured by one side, recaptured by the other, and then captured once again. On the whole the French had the advantage. By 1697, when the Treaty of Ryswick temporarily halted hostilities, the French had secured possession of all the Company's posts except Fort Albany, a minor post on James Bay. Despite the renewal of hostilities in 1702, they continued to hold these posts until the Treaty of Utrecht was signed in 1713. During the whole period from 1683 to 1713 the Company carried on its trade under very difficult conditions, its foothold on the Bay being reduced over most of the period to a single post. The French military effort, in short, achieved a large measure of success and competition from Hudson Bay was practically eliminated.

As in the case of the punitive expeditions against the Iroquois, these military measures seemed at the time to be very effective. But they were also very expensive and represented an additional burden of costs on an already costly trade. The St. Lawrence fur trade provided no sound base for such expenditures and there was little prospect that it ever would. The costs of defence had to be met out of revenues which were quite inadequate to support any such burden. In an economic sense, a very large investment was being made to preserve a relatively small income. Economic considerations, however, were not paramount; the French were fighting to maintain their hold on the continental hinterland and the fur trade was, from this point of view, merely the instrument of imperial ambition. Costs which were unwarranted from a commercial point of view were necessary as an investment in empire. Nevertheless, in New France, bouts of inflation early in the eighteenth century and a drastic revaluation of the currency in 1713 reflected the fact that the colony had invested more than it could afford on the basis of its current income.

The French reaction to competition from Hudson River and Hudson Bay also took the form of attempts to develop the fur trade in non-competitive areas. This involved further expansion into the interior, particularly south of the upper Lakes and into the drainage basin of the Mississippi. In 1658-62 Radisson and Groseilliers had explored Lake Huron and the upper part of Lake Michigan before turning their attention northward. Forts and trading-posts had been established in 1666 at Saint Esprit

(Ashland) on the southwestern shore of Lake Superior and in 1669 at St. François Xavier on Lake Michigan, at the mouth of the Fox River. From each of these points there was easy access, by rivers and short portages, to tributaries of the Mississippi, the St. Croix in the one case, the Wisconsin in the other. In 1669, too, La Salle, starting from Lake Ontario, had reached the Ohio River by following the Genesee and the Allegheny. By 1670 the stage was set for expansion into the Mississippi valley. In 1673 Jolliet and Marquette, using the Fox River portage, descended the Mississippi as far as its junction with the Arkansas and confirmed that it entered the Gulf of Mexico, instead of flowing to the Pacific as some had imagined. Nine years later La Salle finally reached the sea by the Mississippi route and claimed the whole drainage basin for France. The French empire in North America now extended, in name at least, from the St. Lawrence to the Gulf of Mexico.

French success in quelling competition from Hudson Bay and in extending the fur trade both north and south of the Great Lakes represented a considerable achievement in the face of very great difficulties. But at the same time it accentuated problems which were inherent in the situation and organization of the colony. A period of peace with the Iroquois had made possible the opening up of the Mississippi. After 1684, however, hostilities broke out once again and renewed expenditures were necessary to finance punitive expeditions and to construct or rebuild forts in the interior. French control of the Mississippi valley made it possible to develop an alternative route to the interior from bases on the Gulf of Mexico; but the Mississippi route, far from proving complementary to the St. Lawrence, increasingly became competitive with it. The southern furs which were exported by the Mississippi route were of poor quality and damaged the market in France, bringing low prices, a falling off in the demand for beaver hats, and increased use of substitute materials. Successes in the Hudson Bay region, too, brought difficulties in marketing. Before 1700, as we have already seen, the problem had been to restrict supplies of *castor sec* and increase supplies of the more valuable *castor gras*. After 1700 precisely the opposite problem had to be faced. Largely because of the opening up for French trade of the Hudson Bay drainage basin, the market was now flooded with supplies of *castor gras* and a complete reversal of policy became necessary, with ill effects upon French relations with the Indians.

The French had attempted to meet competition from Hudson Bay and Hudson River by adopting two complementary policies: expansion into new areas, and military attack upon the sources of competition. Both of these policies were costly, and both, to the extent that they were in fact successful in checking competition, resulted in large increases in the supply of furs. Beaver fur, however, was a luxury article; the demand for it in France was very limited. Increases in supply tended, therefore, to flood the market and depress prices. Since the revenue of the colony, apart from direct subsidies, was obtained almost entirely from receipts from the sale of furs, a slump in fur prices was a very serious matter. To the extent, therefore, that measures to check competition were successful, the financial difficulties of the colony tended to grow more, not less, acute. Inflation of the currency was the only apparent solution; but inflation, by raising the prices of French commodities used in the fur trade, made the competition of other sources of supply still more serious and rendered measures to check competition still more necessary. Only rigid control over supply, given the characteristic demand conditions to be faced, would have enabled the colony to achieve financial stability. But control over supply, difficult to achieve even within the French trading organization, was impossible as long as English traders, with cheaper commodities to sell, provided alternative markets.

THE DEVELOPMENT OF NEW FRANCE

If New France had been able to develop an export trade in some commodity other than fur, these financial difficulties would have been less serious. Had the colony possessed some other source of income it would have found it easier to bear the costs involved in defence and Indian alliances, and at the same time these costs would have been less necessary. Without the fur trade the French would certainly not have been able to explore the continental hinterland and bring it within their sphere of influence as rapidly as they did; but if a more diversified economic base had been developed on the St. Lawrence, the French empire in North America might well have proved better equipped to resist English expansion.

The French colonial authorities were not unaware of the importance of diversification and on many occasions exerted their influence to stimulate the development of other forms of economic activity. Considerable importance was attached to immigration, particularly after 1663. Shiploads of young women were sent out from France; demobilized soldiers were given grants of land; and government subsidies were provided to encourage marriage and large families. The results were evident in an increase in population, from about 3,000 in 1663 to 6,705 ten years later. This increase in numbers involved pressure on food supplies, for the expansion of agricultural production was held back by the rigorous climate, by the problems involved in adapting traditional agricultural techniques to an unfamiliar environment, and by the persistent loss of man-power to the fur trade. There were few years when the colony produced a surplus for export over and above its own immediate requirements; stocks of foodstuffs carried over from one year to the next were generally small, and grain had to be imported from France when the crops failed. Official encouragement was also given to the development of manufacturing. Jean Talon, the energetic intendant appointed in 1663, was instrumental in organizing ship-building on the River St. Charles near Quebec and in promoting the manufacture of potash and the building of the St. Maurice iron forges, besides attempting to encourage the production of flax and hemp.

These and other attempts to develop a more diversified economy in New France attained only limited success, and for this various factors were responsible. In the first place, the colony was too small to support extensive division of labour. Even with official support, the rate of immigration was by no means comparable to that of New England, for example. In the case of the English colonies, the desire of religious dissenters to live under their own form of church government and ritual had been an important factor in increasing immigration; there was no counterpart to this in the case of New France, where the Catholic Church held undisputed sway. High birth rates, to be sure, contributed largely to population increase, but could not compensate for the relatively low rate of immigration compared to the English colonies. Secondly, manufacturing development in New France was retarded by the scarcity and high cost of skilled labour and of capital. This was, of course, a retarding factor in all colonial economies, and it is difficult to say whether it was more of a handicap to New France than it was to the English colonies. But in New France the fur trade drained both capital and labour away from other employments to a degree which was not paralleled in the English possessions. And thirdly, the economic life of New France was organized along very traditionalistic, almost medieval, lines. The colony as a whole was burdened by the cost of supporting a large civil, military, and ecclesiastical bureaucracy, and almost every aspect of social life was subject to detailed regulation. Agriculture and land settlement took place within the semi-feudal framework of the seigneurial system, while manufacture and trade were regulated in a manner reminiscent of the medieval guilds. These organizational forms were imposed on the colony without much reference to the question of whether or not they were suitable to the conditions which had to be met. Seigneuries were freely granted, for example, to government officials, members of the clergy, retired officers, merchants, and the like, as a mark of social rank; but it does not appear that the majority of these grantees invested much capital in their estates or exerted themselves to procure settlers. Feudal forms of social organization, it need hardly be said, were necessarily modified to some extent in their application to the North American environment and it is probable that they made the colony stronger in a military sense than it would otherwise have been, but they inevitably inhibited the development of a commercial economy.

In these circumstances it was not surprising that large sectors of the colonial economy remained virtually isolated from commercial transactions of any sort. With the exception of certain necessary items of consumption such as salt, the rural household was almost entirely self-sufficient, and was content to remain so. Acreage under cultivation was extended more as a means of providing subsistence for new families than as a means of providing a surplus for sale.

The relatively low rate of immigration, the scarcity of capital and skilled labour, and the authoritarian form of social organization, combined with the ever-present necessity for defence and the competing attractions of the fur trade, prevented New France from developing into the strong and diversified economic base which was necessary for the consolidation of French empire in North America. The failure of attempts at diversification was reflected in the very slight development of trade with the other French possessions in the New World. As far as the French in Newfoundland, Acadia, the West Indies, or Louisiana were concerned, the colony on the St. Lawrence might almost as well not have existed, for they received from there neither the supplies nor the ships which they needed and found there no markets for the products which they had to sell. New France remained a relatively isolated outpost of the mother country, important in the political and military sense because it held the key to the interior of the continent, but valued commercially solely for its fur trade. And even the fur trade, though it provided the colony with almost the whole of its earned income, was esteemed by French statesmen less for the profits it produced than for the territory which it enabled France to control and—nominally, at least—to occupy.

STRENGTH AND WEAKNESSES OF THE FRENCH COLONIES

As long as we confine our attention to the fur trade alone, the period up to 1713 seems to be marked almost uniformly by French gains and French successes. Despite the appearance of new and more vigorous competition from north and south, the French had built a new trading organization to replace that destroyed by the dispersion of the Hurons. Iroquois aggression, backed by the traders of New York and Albany, had been in general successfully contained. The Hudson's Bay Company, with tremendous geographic advantages on its side, had been practically neutralized as a serious source of competition by successful attacks on its North American bases. And in the interior of the continent, with the exploration of the Great Lakes and the Mississippi, the tentacles of French control had been extended until, reaching the Gulf of Mexico, they formed a vast arc which encircled the English colonies on the Atlantic seaboard and threatened to confine them to the narrow coastal plain. These successes had been won by men whose efforts were based on a small and penurious colony, separated from the mother country by three thousand miles of ocean and the narrow estuary of the St. Lawrence, and organized internally more like an armed camp than like a commercial community. As an instrument of empire, the fur trade had given ample evidence of its potentialities.

Nevertheless, there were shadows as well as highlights in the picture. In terms of territory, the expansion of the French empire had vastly outdistanced the slow westward movement of the English colonies, and for this the St. Lawrence fur trade was largely responsible. But control over territory gave no assurance of ability to survive over time. In some respects the fur trade was a source of weakness to New France, not only because the costs of expansion brought in their train the financial difficulties to which we have already referred, but also because it resulted in a highly unbalanced type of development. Furs were the only commodity which New France could produce which was both light enough and valuable enough to stand the costs of transportation from the interior of the continent to the European market. But concentration on the fur trade diverted resources away from other lines of activity and prevented New France from developing as a source of supply and a market for the rest of the French colonial empire. Rapid expansion into the interior was achieved only at the expense of consolidation and integration. What the French empire needed, if it was to hold its own against the slower but surer expansion of the English colonies, was a cheap source of foodstuffs and of shipping services—a commercial and agricultural centre, in short, which could perform approximately the same functions for the French empire as New England did for the English. This was a role which New France was never able to fill.

Under the terms of the Treaty of Utrecht, signed in 1713, France evacuated the Hudson Bay area, as well as Acadia and the south shore of Newfoundland. These territorial losses were occasioned more by Marlborough's victories on the battlefields of Europe than by any developments in North America, but in their implications for the future of the rival colonial empires of France and Britain in the New World they were of great significance. The next half-century, culminating in the Treaty of Paris in 1763, was to witness the continuation of French expansion into the interior, in the face of rapidly growing competitive pressures from the north and the south.

SUGGESTIONS FOR FURTHER READING

BASIC WORKS:

Innis, Harold A., *The Fur Trade in Canada: an Introduction to Canadian Economic History* (New Haven, 1930), Chapter II, pp. 20-84

Morton, Arthur S., *A History of the Canadian West to 1870-71* (Toronto, 1939), Chapters II-III, pp. 22-124

Newbigin, Marion I., *Canada: the Great River, the Lands and the Men* (London, 1926), Chapters VI-X, pp. 95-206

Rich, E. E., *The Hudson's Bay Company, 1670-1870* (London: The Hudson's Bay Record Society, 1958), Volume I, 1670-1763, pp. 61-426

SUPPLEMENTARY WORKS:

Clapham, Sir John, Introduction to E. E. Rich (ed.), *Minutes of the Hudson's Bay Company, 1671-1674* (Toronto: The Champlain Society, 1942)

Clark, G. N., Introduction to E. E. Rich (ed.), *Minutes of the Hudson's Bay Company, 1679-1683: First Part, 1679-82* (Toronto: The Champlain Society, 1945)

Hunt, George T., *The Wars of the Iroquois: A Study in Intertribal Trade Relations* (Madison, 1940), Chapters I-XI, pp. 3-164

Lawson, Murray E., *Fur: A Study in English Mercantilism, 1700-1775* (University of Toronto Studies, History and Economics, 1943)

Taylor, E. G. R., Introduction to E. E. Rich (ed.), *Copy-Book of Letters Outward &c.* (Toronto: The Champlain Society, 1948)

Tyrrell, J. B., Introduction to J. B. Tyrrell (ed.), *Documents Relating to the Early History of Hudson Bay* (Toronto: The Champlain Society, 1931)

Wrong, George M., *The Rise and Fall of New France* (2 vols.; New York 1928), Chapters XIV-XXIII, pp. 352-621

CHAPTER V

WAR AND TRADE IN THE NORTH ATLANTIC:
1713–1776

THE FRENCH FISHERIES AFTER 1713

THE terms of the Treaty of Utrecht were a serious set-back to French interests in North America and made the task of consolidation even harder than it had been before. In the North Atlantic the French response was to shorten their lines of defence and reinforce their key positions. Of vital importance was the fact that the treaty permitted them to retain Cape Breton Island, where in 1714-15 they constructed Louisbourg, the strongest military and naval base in North America. From the strategic point of view the site was well chosen. Louisbourg commanded the entrance to the Gulf of St. Lawrence, the vital gateway to Quebec, Montreal, and the string of forts which now extended down the Ohio and the Mississippi to New Orleans. As long as Louisbourg was securely held, Quebec could not be attacked from the sea. But the new fortress also had an offensive function, for it dominated the northern sea route from New England to Europe and could in time of war serve as a centre for commerce raiders and as a base for attacks on New England, Newfoundland, and Nova Scotia.

Louisbourg was a formidable fortress to attack, either by sea or by land. Its weakness lay not in its location nor in its fortifications, but in the fact that it was almost completely dependent upon supplies brought in by sea. Consequently, if any hostile power could secure command of the sea and prevent incoming convoys from reaching Louisbourg, it was not likely that the fortress could be held for long against determined attack. In this respect Louisbourg reflected the strategic weakness of the whole French empire in North America. The French hold on Louisbourg, Quebec, Montreal, and the forts in the interior depended upon the maintenance of open communications with France. These lines of communication could not be kept open unless France could achieve and retain naval superiority in the North Atlantic. Logistics and sea-power were the final arbiters in the struggle for North America.

In an attempt to develop a source of supply for Louisbourg, agriculture and settlement were encouraged in Prince Edward Island, but without much success. Provisions were also obtained from the French inhabitants of Nova Scotia, now nominally under British rule, until their expulsion in 1755. In some years supplies were imported from New France, although generally that colony was hard pressed to meet its own requirements, and provisions were also purchased in large quantities from New England. But on the whole the supply position of Louisbourg remained very insecure.

The French fisheries, however, continued to flourish. Deprived of their bases and drying-sites on the south coast of Newfoundland, French fishing-ships concentrated their efforts on the Bank fishery and on the dry fishery off the shores of Cape Breton, the Gaspé, and the north shore of the Gulf of St. Lawrence, besides continuing active on the northern and western coasts of Newfoundland. Many of the ships in the Bank fishery made no contact with the mainland or Newfoundland at all, but sailed, sometimes twice a year, from their home ports to the Banks, salted their catch in their holds, and then sold it in Nantes, Rouen, Bordeaux, La Rochelle, and Paris. The dry fishery in the Gaspé peninsula was carried on along the same general lines as had been developed in Newfoundland, except that no permanent year-round bases were established. Instead, the crews of the fishing-ships built temporary shelters on the shore and fished from small boats, drying their catch on flakes or on the open beaches. On the northern and western shores of Newfoundland, where the French retained fishing rights, a similar technique was used. In Cape Breton itself there developed a resident fishery, carried on in small boats and sloops from permanent bases on land, which produced about 8,000 tons of fish annually. In this region the fishing-ships from French home ports continued to play an important role, but their share of the total catch declined relative to that of the settlers.

The characteristics which should be noted about the French fishery in this period are three in number. First, the French retained important advantages in production and marketing. Their curing methods were better than those practised by the English, and they could market their catch more quickly in Europe. In the dry fishery, particularly in the northern part of Newfoundland, timber was more plentiful, drying-beaches more numerous, and congestion much less of a problem than in the Avalon peninsula, the centre of the English dry fishery. In the green or Bank fishery plentiful supplies of cheap salt available at home ports not only shortened the total length of the voyage but also made possible more thorough curing of the fish on board ship. Grading of the catch by quality and size enabled the fisheries to meet special demands in the home markets and to demand higher prices. In consequence, despite increasingly severe competition from New England and Newfoundland, the French fishermen were able to hold their own in the European market and even demand premium prices for their catch. Between 1739 and 1744, when Britain was at war with Spain, the French fishermen took over the Spanish market completely and succeeded in retaining their foothold after the conclusion of hostilities.

Secondly, as a means of carrying on the fishery, the French continued to rely heavily on the large fishing-ship operating out of a home port on the Channel or Biscay coasts. A resident fishery carried on by small boats developed in Cape Breton under the immediate protection of Louisbourg, but elsewhere, whether in the dry fishery or on the Banks, the relatively large ship of between 100 and 200 tons remained characteristic of the French fisheries in the North Atlantic. This contrasts sharply with developments in the English fishery after 1713; after that date, as we shall see, large ships based on ports in Devon, Cornwall, and Dorset came to play only a minor part in the fisheries, except as supply vessels. In other words, the English fisheries off the coasts of Newfoundland, Nova Scotia, and New England after 1713 were carried on mostly by smaller ships operating from near-by ports in North America, while the French fisheries in the same general area continued to be carried on mostly by the fishing fleets of the mother country. This was partly a consequence of the spread of English settlement, but it also reflected the dominant importance of the domestic market in the case of France and of foreign markets in the case of England.

Thirdly, the French fisheries after 1713 were geographically dispersed. This was typical of the French fisheries throughout their history but became more pronounced after the loss of Nova Scotia and the south shore of Newfoundland. Partly for this reason the French fishing-bases were slow to develop into permanent settlements. This was true even on Cape Breton, where a determined effort was made to establish a central base. The English fishing-ships, in contrast, showed a definite tendency to concentrate in particular areas, even to the point where congestion and overcrowding became a real problem. These points of concentration later developed into permanent settlements and finally into trading and shipping centres. The French fisheries did not show this tendency to concentrate, partly because they were carried on from a large number of dispersed ports in the mother country.

NEWFOUNDLAND: SETTLEMENT AND THE FISHERIES

The British fishery at Newfoundland had been badly disorganized by the war but after 1713 it entered upon a period of rapid development. This development took place, however, along rather different lines from those which had characterized its earlier growth. In particular, the ship-owners of the English West Country ports, who had previously been actively engaged in the fishery, now turned their attention more and more to general trade with Newfoundland, bringing out supplies for the settlers and byeboatkeepers and purchasing fish from them. A few ports, such as Bideford and Barnstaple, continued to send out ships purely for the fishery as before, but most of the West Country ships after 1713 sailed to Newfoundland to trade rather than to fish. The principal reason for this seems to have been the high cost of labour in the west of England and the competition of the resident fishery in New England. The New England fisheries attracted many skilled seamen away from England and the consequent scarcity of labour and high wage rates, despite attempts to hire men in Ireland, forced the West Country ship-owners out of the fisheries and into trade. This was, of course, not an entirely new development, for the share of the West Country in the Newfoundland fisheries had been declining for many years, but it reached its culmination after 1713. One consequence was that the pressure which the West Country merchants had earlier exerted on the British govern-ment whenever they thought their interests in Newfoundland were threatened now dwindled sharply. The old arguments against settlement and byeboatkeeping continued to be heard, and the Board of Trade still echoed the old proposals for forced removal of the settlers, but nobody took them very seriously any longer. In this respect, at least, the road was open for Newfoundland to develop politically along more normal colonial lines.

The settlers and byeboatkeepers in Newfoundland had also suffered severely during the war and they too felt the competition of New England, not only in lower prices and restricted markets for their fish, but also in rising labour costs and the draining away of skilled men. In 1708 wages on Newfoundland had been between £12 and £14 a season; by 1715 they had risen to between £20 and £30. Prosperity did not really return to the industry until after 1722. After that date, however, expansion was rapid. The total catch, which was only 88,469 quintals in 1716 (20 quintals make one long ton), increased to 506,406 quintals in 1749 and 695,866 quintals in 1774.

Besides the relative decline of the West Country fishing fleets, the most important characteristics of the Newfoundland fishery in the period after 1713 were the extension of the in-shore fisheries along the south and east coasts and the development of a Bank fishery carried on by small ships based on Newfoundland harbours. The settlers were at first slow to move into the coastal areas from which the French had been expelled, but by 1730, with steadily increasing congestion in the older harbours and off-shore fishing areas, they had begun to move north and west and by the 1740's English fishermen were operating off the coast of Labrador. The Avalon peninsula, however, remained the most important dry-fishing area. In this area the recovery of the in-shore fisheries after 1713 was delayed by a series of very poor seasons and by the growing problem of overcrowding. In these circumstances the English fishermen, besides ex-

tending their in-shore fisheries into new areas, began to move out onto
the Banks. This was, for them, a new departure, involving larger boats
and different curing techniques, although the French had previously
practised it successfully. Instead of fishing close to the shore from open
boats, the English fishermen now began using decked ships, such as
sloops and schooners. These larger and more seaworthy vessels enabled
them to stay at sea for several weeks at a time, so that they could fish on
the Banks until they were fully loaded and then return to port, unload
their catch for drying, and sail immediately to the Banks again. At the
same time division of labour was introduced, with special gangs of men
remaining on shore to look after the drying, instead of the ships' crews
drying the fish themselves as formerly. These techniques tended to
result in poorer quality and lower prices, since the English did not salt
their catch in the holds of their ships as carefully as did the French and
were not in the habit of grading their fish. Nevertheless, as regards costs
of operation and the total quantity of fish caught, these methods were
certainly more efficient than the older ones.

The byeboatkeepers were very successful in developing the Bank fishery
and after 1713 they increased rapidly in numbers, from 286 in 1716 to
554 in 1751. Their share of the total catch declined, however, relative
to that of the permanent settlers, who were responsible for almost two-
thirds of the total in 1764 as compared with just over one-third in 1716.

At first the settlers laboured under a number of handicaps, not least
among which were extreme poverty, the lack of profitable employment
during the winter months, the scarcity of skilled men, and the absence of
an effective government authority. Now that the West Country ships
were concentrating more and more on trade and on the Bank fishery, the
so-called "admirals" who had formerly exercised jurisdiction of a sort
over the harbours ceased to pay serious attention to their duties, and even
the naval commanders, with certain notable exceptions, seem to have been
content to let matters drift. The result was that for more than a decade
after 1713 the English settlements on Newfoundland were left without
any effective local government. The Newfoundland Act of 1699 was by
now completely inapplicable, but for many years the British government
took no action to remedy the situation, fearing probably that the establishment of a civil government would entail considerable expense and
that it might be difficult to defend the island in the event of renewed
war with France.

Administrative neglect, lawlessness, and social disorganization, combined
with the difficulty of retaining experienced seamen in the face of the
competing attractions of New England, held back the growth of the
permanent settlements and the resident fishery. More than one contemporary observer described the settlers as little better than slaves. Debt
was a serious problem. The settlers relied entirely upon the fisheries for

a living and a succession of bad seasons was sufficient to reduce many of them to a state of dependence upon the merchants who sold them provisions and liquor on credit. Those who worked for hire on the fishing-ships were paid not in money, but in fish, which they then had to hand over to the merchants to whom they were indebted. In the absence of law courts, debts were often collected by force—a practice which was probably not unconnected with the steady emigration from the island to New England.

Conditions seem to have improved considerably after 1729, when the first governor was appointed and magistrates' courts established. At first it was not very clear what jurisdiction the governor and the justices of the peace were entitled to exercise over the English fishermen, particularly with respect to taxation, and the fishing "admirals" were inclined to insist upon their traditional rights. Nevertheless, the setting up of the rudiments of civil government brought greater security to life and property and more settled conditions generally. This was reflected in the growth of population—from 3,295 in 1716 to 10,949 in 1774—and in the gradual expansion of settlement along the south and east coasts.

Newfoundland's importance as a trading centre—a half-way house, as it were, between Europe and the American colonies—increased greatly after 1713. St. John's in particular developed into a busy port of call with a small but prosperous merchant class and a large export-import trade. The principal business of these merchants was the importing of supplies for the settlers and the fisheries and the exporting of dried cod, but in addition a very active re-export or entrepôt trade, much of it illegal, was carried on, particularly in West Indian products and European manufactured goods and wines. Ships from New England, New York, and Pennsylvania typically brought cargoes of such things as livestock, lumber, staves, bricks, bread, flour, and rum, together with West Indian goods like sugar, molasses, tobacco, and dye-woods. Most of these cargoes were not imported for consumption in Newfoundland but for re-export to Europe. In payment merchants from the American colonies took British and European manufactures, dried fish for the West Indies market, and bills of exchange on London. Transporting settlers and indentured servants from Newfoundland to the mainland colonies was also a regular source of profit.

Despite this active trade with the American colonies, the greater part of Newfoundland's exports of fish still went to Europe and commercial ties with Britain remained strong. While the number of trading-ships from the American colonies increased from 31 in 1716 to 66 in 1749, the number of sack ships from Britain increased in the same period from 30 to 125, not to mention the British fishing-ships which by this time were engaging actively in trade. It is true that in the years after 1713 English merchants who had commercial interests in Newfoundland complained bitterly about the competition of American traders, but, in terms of fish exports at least, it does not appear that their dominant position was seriously challenged. Newfoundland remained economically oriented toward Britain, rather than toward the mainland colonies.

NOVA SCOTIA UNDER BRITISH RULE

In Nova Scotia after 1713 events followed a rather different pattern from those in Newfoundland. Despite France's loss of sovereignty over the area, there was at first little change in settlement and French influence remained strong, not only among the Acadians but also among the Indians. A small British garrison was maintained at Annapolis Royal (the former Port Royal) and an important dry fishery developed at Canso, but until the establishment of Halifax in 1749 there was no attempt to encourage immigration (in fact, immigration from New England was actively discouraged) and Nova Scotia was very largely neglected by the British government.

Nevertheless, just as the Acadian settlements around the Bay of Fundy were regularly visited by New England traders, so the fisheries on the east coast of the peninsula were not neglected by New England fishermen. The Gut of Canso, in particular, being near to the Banks and with ample space available for drying, became the centre of a busy dry fishery. This was at first carried on almost entirely by New England schooners and produced mostly an inferior grade of fish suitable for sale in the West Indies. But English sack ships also were active at Canso, bringing in supplies for the fishery and exporting the better grades of fish to Spain and Portugal. For a time it looked as if Canso, like St. John's, might develop into an important commercial centre, for it stood at an apex of two triangular patterns of trade—that carried on by American merchants between Boston, Canso, and Spain, and that carried on by the sack ships between England, Canso, and Spain. But two factors prevented such a development. First, the production of a grade of dried fish suitable for the Spanish and Portuguese markets really called for a boat fishery operated from permanent land bases rather than the schooner fishery carried on by the New Englanders. And secondly, Canso was too close to the powerful French base at Louisbourg, itself an important fishing and trading centre, for secure permanent settlement to be possible. In consequence, after a very promising start, the dry fishery at Canso declined in the 1730's and 1740's, and during the two wars with France (1744-8 and 1755-63) it was badly disrupted.

The importance and at the same time the strategic weakness of the French fortress at Louisbourg were both clearly demonstrated during the first of these two wars, the War of the Austrian Succession. French forces based on Louisbourg captured Canso in 1744 and almost succeeded in taking Annapolis, while New England shipping suffered serious losses at the hands of French privateers. In the following year, however, a large force from New England with British naval support captured Louisbourg, which by this time was almost denuded of ammunition and provisions as a result of the interception of relief convoys from France. Much to the disgust of the New Englanders, however, the Treaty of Aix-la-Chapelle which ended the war returned Louisbourg to France in exchange for Madras, the important British stronghold in India, and certain French conquests in the Low Countries.

As far as North America was concerned, the war left the situation practically unchanged and the Treaty did nothing to remove the sources of conflict. Louisbourg, though temporarily weakened, remained a serious threat both to the British settlements in Newfoundland and Nova Scotia and to the shipping and northern land frontier of New England. Meanwhile in the interior colonial traders, the forerunners of settlement, were already encroaching upon French preserves in the Ohio valley. Both France and England were temporarily exhausted by the war but neither anticipated a long interval of peace before the next outbreak of hostilities.

As a consequence, the British government embarked upon a considerably more active policy in Nova Scotia. Two major steps were taken to counteract and reduce the strength of the French position at Louisbourg. In the first place, the Acadians were ordered to take an unequivocal oath of allegiance to the British Crown. Many of them refused to do this, unless the oath were so qualified as to be meaningless. The Acadians themselves had not taken up arms against the British during the war, but on the other hand they continued to supply a steady stream of foodstuffs, mostly livestock, to Louisbourg. In particular, an active trade which the British were powerless to prevent was carried on across the Isthmus of Chignecto from the rich Acadian farms around the Bay of Minas. In these circumstances the governor and council of the province, who were highly sympathetic to the policies and aspirations of New England, decided in 1755 that the Acadians should be expelled entirely. The British government acquiesced in this decision and it was put into effect immediately; during the next few years over six thousand Acadians were forcibly removed from Nova Scotia.

At the same time the British government began constructing forts and establishing settlements. Most important of all was the founding of Halifax in 1749. With a fine natural harbour, Halifax was intended to counterbalance Louisbourg, to secure the eastern flank of the continental colonies, to serve as a secure base for commerce and naval operations in the North Atlantic, and to protect the fisheries and the settlements which were to be established on the east coast of the peninsula. Immigration from Britain to the new base was encouraged, but within a few years settlers and traders from New England had come to form the majority of its civil population. A German settlement was formed at Lunenburg in 1753 and a small fort (Fort Lawrence) was constructed in 1750 on the Isthmus of Chignecto to oppose the French garrison at Fort Beauséjour. The hostility of the Indians and the threat of French attack prevented further progress. The east coast, with the exception of Halifax and Lunenburg, remained unoccupied until after the conquest of Canada, when New England fishermen and Scottish emigrants began to form settlements.

IMPERIAL CONFLICTS IN NORTH AMERICA: THE ROLE OF NEW ENGLAND

Throughout this period of war and uneasy truce, when the opposing empires of France and Britain were preparing themselves for the final conflict in North America, New England exercised a powerful influence upon the policies of both sides and upon their relative strength. New England merchants traded with the French without restraint, as they would with anyone; but when hostilities broke out it was New England that provided most of the supplies, the men, and the transports for the expeditions against the citadels of French power. Louisbourg depended upon New England for food and for the very sloops with which the French carried on their dry fishery. But it was a New England merchant who commanded the land forces which captured Louisbourg in 1745 and it was New England's interests which led to the expulsion of the Acadians ten years later.

By the middle of the eighteenth century the continued presence of the French in North America was coming to be regarded as an unendurable threat to the security and future growth of the British continental colonies. This threat had two principal aspects: maritime and continental. As regards the former, Louisbourg menaced New England's commerce and fisheries in the North Atlantic. As regards the latter, French expansion down the valleys of the Ohio and Mississippi—an expansion not by means of settlement but by means of the fur trade, alliances with the Indians, and the construction of forts—threatened to confine the Atlantic colonies to the narrow coastal plain and prevent their expansion across the mountains into the rich lands of the interior. In general the southern colonies, particularly Virginia (which claimed title to the Ohio valley), were more concerned with the continental danger, and the northern colonies, particularly Massachusetts, with the maritime. But the New England colonies were also keenly aware of the insecurity of their landward frontiers, as was New York, the centre of the colonial fur trade. As long as the French continued to hold New France, the south shore of the Gulf of St. Lawrence as far as Chignecto, and Cape Breton, New England's

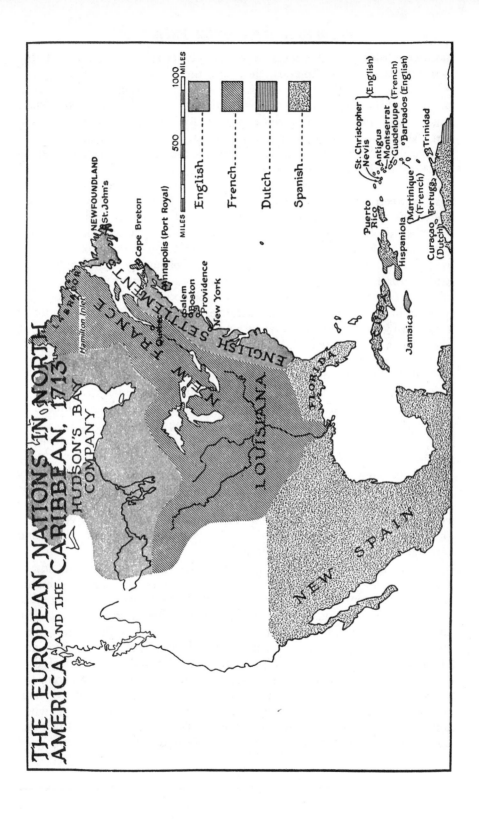

THE EUROPEAN NATIONS IN NORTH AMERICA AND THE CARIBBEAN, 1713

English
French
Dutch
Spanish

MILES
1000
500
MILES

HUDSON'S BAY COMPANY

Hamilton Inlet

LABRADOR

NEWFOUNDLAND
St. John's
Cape Breton
Annapolis (Port Royal)
Quebec
Salem
Boston
Providence
New York

NEW FRANCE

ENGLISH SETTLEMENTS

LOUISIANA

FLORIDA

NEW SPAIN

CUBA

Jamaica

Puerto Rico
Hispaniola
Tortuga
Curaçao (Dutch)

St. Christopher
Nevis
(English)
Antigua
Montserrat
Guadeloupe (French)
Barbados (English)
Martinique (French)
Trinidad

northern frontier was dangerously open to attack. Of all the British possessions in North America, therefore, the New England colonies and New York were the most suspicious of French designs and the most aggressive in demanding the eradication of French power in North America. When the war which was to achieve this goal finally broke out, Massachusetts, Connecticut, and New York provided about 70 per cent of all the colonial troops involved, although they had only about one-third of the white population.

If any war can be called inevitable, that word can be applied to the war between France and England which was formally declared in 1755. In North America, where hostilities began before the formal declaration was issued, the expansion of the two imperial powers had created a situation which was inherently unstable. Into the British colonies there had poured for over a hundred years a stream of immigrants who, together with natural increase, had raised the population to over 1,400,000, that of New England alone numbering over 400,000. The population of New France in the same year was just over 55,000, with perhaps another 6,000 in Cape Breton. Yet France held the continental hinterland beyond the Appalachians and by her highly successful Indian policy aggressively repulsed any attempts on the part of the British seaboard colonies to extend the frontiers of trade and settlement into the interior. The British colonies regarded themselves as encircled and confined by the string of French forts in the interior, from Fort Frontenac on Lake Ontario to New Orleans on the Mississippi, and by the bastions of Quebec and Louisbourg to the north. The French, for their part, saw the steady northward push of trade and settlement from New England gradually narrowing their hold upon the entrances to the Gulf of St. Lawrence and jeopardizing the security of their vital communications with the mother country. In general terms the issue was clear: for how long could the nation which held the St. Lawrence maintain its control of the continental hinterland against the westward thrust of trade and settlement from the Atlantic seaboard?

Despite their much smaller population the French had certain advantages on their side, of which probably the most important was their highly centralized system of colonial government. This enabled them to mobilize a larger proportion of their available resources for military effort and to take quicker action in emergencies. The British colonies, in contrast, were reluctant to co-operate with each other and were inclined to resent any attempt on the part of the British government to induce them to follow uniform policies. Each of them tended to interpret the situation from the point of view of its own local interests, to be zealous and aggressive when its own borders were threatened, but passive and procrastinating when some other colony required assistance. Besides this, in more than one colony political conflict between the governor and the Assembly frustrated attempts to mobilize troops and raise money. Particularism and internal conflicts, in short, prevented the colonies from uniting in their own defence and from exerting against the French the full military effort of which they were potentially capable.

Although the colonies looked to Britain to shoulder the greater part of the burden involved in crushing French power in North America, in their commercial policy they paid scant attention to imperial legislation. This was particularly true of New England; the southern staple-producing colonies, whose trade was mostly direct with Britain and whose merchants depended on British capital and credit facilities, were more easily reconciled to their place in the imperial system. New England, however, had by the middle of the eighteenth century developed into a commercial centre whose interests were in many respects in direct conflict with those of the mother country. The most obvious symptom of this conflict was the prevalence of illegal trade—not only technical infractions of the now highly complex code of legislation embodied in the Acts of Trade, but also direct trade with hostile powers, and in particular with France. Of all the continental colonies New England was probably the most aggressive in seeking the destruction of French power; yet at the same time New England, in times of peace and war alike, profited from trade with the French colonial possessions, providing for them the shipping and supply services which the French empire itself was unable to provide. The explanation of this apparent paradox is to be found in the nature of the economy which had developed in New England. Lacking within its own borders an exportable staple round which its economic life might have been organized, New England had developed and prospered by trading, by selling in the highest market and buying in the lowest. To such an economy national boundaries are significant chiefly because they give rise to price differentials which can be exploited by trade. Because the French in North America threatened the security of New England's commerce and of her landward frontier, New England wished French power crushed. But while the French colonies remained in existence and while a profit could be gained from trading with them, the merchants of New England saw no reason to refrain from participating in that trade.

As in the period before 1713 exports of dried fish, particularly to the West Indies, Spain, and Portugal, remained the mainstay of New England's commerce and provided the basic outward cargo for trading voyages. From 1743 to 1763, however, the size of the fishing fleets and of the total catch declined, largely as a consequence of the diversion of seamen to naval duties and of marketing difficulties in Europe during the wars with Spain and France. Increasing demands for foodstuffs, timber, horses, and the poorer grades of fish in the West Indies partially offset this decline in European markets, and the West Indies trade came to occupy a position of major importance in New England's balance of payments.

It was estimated in 1731 that revenues from sales of fish and other products in the West Indies were sufficient to pay not only for return cargoes of rum and molasses, but also for all the salt, provisions, and equipment used in the New England fisheries. Revenue from sales of fish in Europe, if this estimate is correct, represented clear profit and could be expended entirely on imports of European wines and manufactured goods. Any reduction in the West Indies trade, in consequence, was bound to have serious repercussions upon New England.

Until the end of the seventeenth century the British sugar plantations in the West Indies had supplied not only the domestic market in Britain but also almost all the demand in Europe. After 1713, however, this was no longer the case. French sugar, which was cheaper and of excellent quality, now undersold the British product in Europe and the British planters were forced to confine themselves to the British and North American markets, in which they had a legal monopoly. Compared to the French, the British planters were high-cost producers; the soil of the British islands was becoming exhausted, and many of the plantation owners were heavily in debt. The French producers, who had developed their plantations largely by reinvesting profits, were relatively free from debt, had the advantage of richer soil, and also knew how to get more work out of their slaves. In addition, British sugar exported to England had to pay heavy duties—a 4½ per cent export duty in the West Indies and a 15 per cent import duty in Britain. French duties on sugar were relatively light.

Both the British and the French West Indies had to import most of their provisions, horses, lumber, and livestock. With the development of the plantation system, the demand for slaves had grown rapidly, but for reasons which differed between the two groups of islands. The British planters, with their exhausted soil, had to employ more and more slaves per acre. On the French islands, where the soil was less exhausted, fewer hands per acre were needed, but the total acreage under cultivation was expanding. On both the British and the French islands the slave population increased very rapidly and with it the need for imports of foodstuffs, particularly dried fish. These imports were obtained principally from the British North American colonies.

Trade between the British mainland colonies and the French West Indies increased very greatly after 1713 and aroused vigorous protests from the British plantation owners. The grounds for their complaints were not that the trade was illegal, for the colonies were quite at liberty to export non-enumerated commodities to any part of the world, at least during peace-time. Rather, they claimed that, by exporting provisions to the French islands, New England was raising the price of provisions imported by the British plantations, and thus aggravating the unfavourable cost differential under which the British planters were already labouring. The assistance of

New England, they alleged, was enabling the French to undersell British sugar in the European market. In addition, by purchasing French sugar and molasses, New England was narrowing the market for the British product and evading payment of the duty on British sugar shipped to the mainland colonies. A further ground of complaint arose from the increasing tendency of New England traders to demand payment in specie (usually Spanish pieces of eight) for supplies sold to the British plantations, and then to expend this specie in purchases of molasses and sugar in the French islands. Almost all the metallic coins in circulation in the British West Indies were obtained by trade with the Spanish American colonies, and this drain of specie to the French islands was alleged to be a considerable hardship, since it cut down the amount of money in circulation and made it harder for the planters to pay their debts.

Between 1720 and 1739 the British sugar industry in the West Indies experienced a severe depression, occasioned chiefly by a falling off in exports to Europe. Recovery did not come until the secular increase in sugar consumption in Britain, together with favourable legislation, once more raised prices to remunerative levels. During this period of depression the political power of the West Indies plantation owners was brought into play to check the growing trade between New England and the French West Indies, and in 1733 the British Parliament passed the Molasses Act, which imposed prohibitive duties on sugar, molasses, and rum imported into the British North American colonies from the foreign West Indies. This statute was passed against the strenuous opposition of New England and represented a major political victory for the West Indies interests.

If the Molasses Act had been enforced it would have had disastrous results not only for the French West Indies but also for New England, whose ability to import manufactured goods from Britain was directly dependent upon her earnings from shipping and trade. The members of the British Board of Trade had recognized this fact in 1721 when, commenting on earlier proposals to halt the trade with the French West Indies, they had pointed out that Britain's exports to North America exceeded her imports from there by about £200,000 per annum and that it was the trade and shipping of the northern colonies which covered this deficit. In securing the passing of the Molasses Act, the West Indies plantation owners won an apparent victory not only over New England but also over British manufacturers.

From the start, however, the Act was completely ineffective in achieving its major purpose. Trade with the French West Indies was not halted; the price of provisions sold to the British West Indies was not reduced; and the market for British sugar, molasses, and rum in the American colonies did not increase. The principal effects of the Act were, in fact, to convert legal traders into smugglers, to encourage widespread disregard for British commercial legislation, and to induce many American ships to avoid the British West Indies entirely, thus raising freight rates and the cost of imports. It was not until 1764, in the stormy period between the conquest of Canada and the American Revolution, that serious attempts were made to enforce the Act.

It is clear, indeed, that the economic advantages that the trade offered and its importance for the prosperity of New England and the French West Indies were too great for any but the most repressive and rigorously enforced legislation to be effective. The British islands could absorb only a small proportion of the products which American traders had to sell and could supply only a small proportion of the tropical products which they wished to buy. The French islands could supply sugar and molasses more cheaply and were ready purchasers of New England produce. When French sugar delivered in New England was priced at six or seven shillings a hundredweight less than the English product, what merchant could hope to obey the letter of the law and stay in business? The trade between New England and the French West Indies was, indeed, a reflection of the fact that both the French and the British colonial empires in the New World were out of balance. The British Empire, in terms of purchasing power and productive capacity, was overweighted on the side of the temperate-zone colonies, the French on the side of tropical possessions. New France could not supply the French West Indies; the British West Indies could not absorb the production of New England. Trade between the rival empires reflected the price differentials to which this lack of balance gave rise.

Trade with the French West Indies was the most conspicuous example of how New England refused to be confined within the bounds of British commercial legislation, but it was by no means the only one. Newfoundland, Cape Breton, Nova Scotia, and the Dutch and Danish possessions in the Caribbean were also important smuggling centres. By the 1750's there was hardly a merchant in any of the northern colonies who was not involved in illicit trade. Public opinion in the colonies approved of this trade, holding that it was indispensable to their welfare, and many customs officials connived in it. By the middle of the eighteenth century British control over the economic activities of the American colonies had patently begun to break down.

As long as the French empire in North America continued to jeopardize the security of the British colonies, however, it was not likely that this breakdown in economic control would develop into a general movement toward political independence. Against the disadvantages of restraints on trade there had to be balanced the security provided by British sea-power and British troops. Not until after the conquest of Canada, when the threat to their landward frontiers had been removed, did the continental colonies begin to move rapidly toward revolution. And when the revolution came, resentment at the restraints imposed by British commercial legislation was only one of several factors involved, and probably not the most important. The American Revolution was as much a revolt against privilege within the colonies as it was a revolt against control from England. Illicit trade 'was important more as a symptom of the inability of the first British Empire to adjust to changing economic circumstances than as a cause of revolution.

THE END OF FRENCH DOMINION IN NORTH AMERICA

There is no need for us to follow in detail the campaigns and tactics of the war which destroyed French dominion in North America, but we should note the influence of certain economic factors on the final outcome. France was a continental power, largely self-sufficient in terms of resources. In an economic sense the possession of overseas colonies was a less urgent matter for her than it was for Britain. Those colonies which France did establish in North America, on the St. Lawrence and in the Caribbean, were single-product, staple-producing areas, dependent not upon large-scale emigration from France for their labour force but upon the Indians in the case of New France and upon negro slaves in the case of the West Indies. In comparison with British emigration to the New World, French emigration was very small indeed. France, too, had extensive land frontiers to defend in Europe; the demands of continental security made large armies indispensable and thus lessened the attention and the resources which could be devoted to naval expansion. But overseas colonies could not be held in time of war without winning and holding command of the sea.

Britain, in contrast, was an island power, without land frontiers, and highly dependent on overseas trade. The resources provided by her overseas possessions were indispensable to her standard of living and to her ability to wage war. With a domestic population only about one-quarter that of France, she nevertheless furnished a much larger volume of emigrants to her colonies, while at the same time securing command of the sea through her naval policy. Her possessions in the New World included not only staple-producing areas but also one important group of colonies which had developed their own shipping and commerce and which had become the focus for an increasingly active colonial trade.

British and French colonial expansion in the New World had, in short, followed different patterns. These patterns were determined not only by the resources, climate, and topography of the areas within which the colonies were established, but also by the resources and requirements of the mother countries. In terms of geographical extent, French expansion had been much more rapid, this being partly a result of the fur trade and partly of the highly militarized character of French colonial government. British expansion had been much less impressive in terms of the space occupied, for the frontier of settlement necessarily moved more slowly than the frontier of the fur trade, but it was more closely consolidated and based upon greater resources of population and capital. French influence penetrated far into the interior, but settlement was confined to the St. Lawrence below Lake Ontario. British influence penetrated no farther westward than the Appalachians, but settlement extended up the entire Atlantic seaboard from Florida to northern New Hampshire.

War was formally declared between Britain and France in May, 1756, although hostilities had actually begun in North America two years earlier. French weakness at sea proved the decisive factor. A British expedition against French forts in the Ohio valley was a dismal failure, but this was partially offset by the capture of Fort Beauséjour in 1755, a success which established British control in the Bay of Fundy and disrupted French communications between Louisbourg and Quebec. British strategy now centred round a naval blockade of the French home ports and an attack in force against Louisbourg, to be followed by a two-pronged drive against Quebec, with land forces attacking by way of the Champlain-Richelieu valley and a naval force by way of the St. Lawrence. Amherst, with powerful naval support, laid siege to and took Louisbourg in 1758. The attack by land against Quebec was held up by a skilful French delaying action, but a powerful naval force dispatched from Europe successfully forced its way up the St. Lawrence and landed troops above Quebec. The fortress capitulated in September, 1759, and the remainder of the French forces surrendered at Montreal twelve months later. Apart from a successful French attack on St. John's in 1762, the scene of hostilities in the New World now shifted to the Caribbean where, before the end of the war, British forces captured all the French sugar colonies except Santo Domingo and Cuba.

The conquests in the West Indies figured largely in the negotiations for exchanges of territory which led up to the Treaty of Paris in 1763. The French negotiators asserted that they would rather continue the war than give up both Canada and the sugar islands. The question therefore arose whether Britain should retain the captured French islands, in particular Guadeloupe, and return Canada to France, or retain Canada and return Guadeloupe. There were many good arguments for the first alternative. Guadeloupe was a very rich island producing each year about half a million pounds' worth of sugar and cotton, while Canada, which was commonly thought of as little more than a waste of ice and snow, produced only a few thousand pounds' worth of furs. The retention of Guadeloupe would strengthen Britain's strategic position in the Caribbean and also help to reduce the exorbitant price of sugar in the British market. At the same time it could easily be defended by a naval force, whereas Canada would require a large army and expensive fortifications. On the other hand, to return Canada to France would certainly be a very unpopular step in the American colonies and would recreate the very situation which had caused the war in the first place.

Although considerable controversy was aroused, the issue was never really in doubt. The destruction of French power in Canada had been the principal object of the war, while the conquests in the West Indies had been more or less windfalls, important considerations for bargaining purposes but not major objectives. The influence of the West India planters, to the extent that it influenced the decision, was on the side of giving up Guadeloupe, since the retention of the island would have adversely affected the price of sugar in the British market. But the security of the mainland colonies was probably a more important consideration.

Nevertheless, it is interesting to speculate what the outcome might have been if the decision had been reversed. The retention of Guadeloupe would certainly have done much to improve the balance between northern and tropical possessions within the British Empire and thus have mitigated the problem of illicit trade which was to be the source of so much friction in the following years. Revenue from Guadeloupe's exports, too, would have made it easier for the British government to pay the cost of the war. The most interesting question of all, however, is whether, if Canada had remained French, the American Revolution would have been postponed or even averted entirely. These are hypothetical questions, to which it is impossible to give certain answers, but they help to illustrate the significance of the decision which in fact was made.

THE BRITISH POSITION AFTER 1763: THE AMERICAN REVOLUTION

After 1763 the British Empire in North America included a number of very diverse areas, ranging from the West Indies, with their strong political influence in England, to the Atlantic colonies, with their highly valued tradition of representative government, to Quebec, a conquered territory with a population entirely alien to British rule, and finally to Hudson Bay, still under the control of a chartered company. To govern successfully this highly complex empire was a task which would have tested the abilities of even the wisest administration, and this the British government during this period certainly was not. Before twenty years had passed, thirteen of these colonies had asserted and achieved their political independence from the mother country and had set themselves up as the nucleus of a new national state. For two brief decades there existed the possibility of uniting all the British possessions in North America within a single imperial economy. This possibility was not realized.

To understand why certain of the North American colonies sought independence while others did not, it is necessary to bear in mind at least two considerations: first, that the colonies did not all follow the same pattern in their internal political and economic life; and secondly, that they differed widely in the degree to which they felt membership in Britain's mercantilist empire to be a burden on them. To some of the colonies—for example, the West Indies and Canada—incorporation within Britain's mercantilist system was a great benefit, since it assured an exclusive market for their staples. To others, such as the New England colonies, it appeared to bring no benefits, but only inconveniences and prohibitions. To still others, such as Virginia and Maryland, the balance of advantage and disadvantage was uncertain.

The destruction of French power in North America removed the common danger which had reconciled the Atlantic colonies to the restraints of British mercantilism. At the same time it encouraged the British government to attempt the enforcement of imperial legislation which earlier had been ignored or evaded, particularly the Navigation Acts. The consolidation of the empire was therefore undertaken at a time when the disappearance of an external threat had removed the strongest single factor which had held that empire together. In addition, certain exigencies arising directly out of the war provided new sources of friction. Since the war had been fought at least partly on behalf of the colonies, it seemed reasonable to the British government that they should bear part of the cost. From this there developed the attempt on the part of the British Parliament to levy taxes in the colonies and impose tariffs on colonial commerce, as a means not of directing trade but of raising revenue. This was bitterly resented by the influential merchants of the seaport towns, already incensed by more rigid enforcement of the Acts of Trade. Further, the cession to Britain of Canada and of the continental hinterland as far west as the Mississippi confronted the British government with the necessity of devising a policy for the use and disposal of western lands and for the control of the fur trade. The policy adopted —the setting up of an Indian reserve beyond the Appalachians in 1763 and the annexation to Quebec of the territory north of the Ohio and west of Pennsylvania in 1774—alienated colonial land speculators and fur-traders, particularly in Virginia, and cast Britain in the role previously played by France, that of the chief obstacle in the way of westward expansion.

Serious sources of friction though these might be in the thirteen Atlantic colonies, they were matters of lesser moment in Quebec, Nova Scotia, Newfoundland, and the West Indies. None of these areas had developed economically along lines which brought them into conflict with Britain. Each of them fitted neatly into the mercantilist scheme—Canada with her furs, Newfoundland with her fish, Nova Scotia with her fish, furs, and naval stores, and the West Indies with sugar. The control of western lands was, to be sure, of vital consequence to the fur-trading merchants of the St. Lawrence, but British policy was on their side, and, though many of them had formerly had close ties with New York and Albany, they showed little enthusiasm for the revolutionary cause. The *habitants* of Quebec, too, were apathetic; deserted, as they felt, by France, and by no means harshly treated by their British conquerors, they had little reason to sympathize with the aspirations of New England. The planters of the West Indies, whose wealth and influence had from the beginning been based upon British mercantilism, were unlikely to join in a struggle for its destruction; while Newfoundland, whose history had for so many years been dominated by British fishing fleets and British merchants, was no more than beginning to develop as a settled colony. And even Nova Scotia, though a large part of her population had come from New England and though more than half her trade was with the mainland colonies to the south, remained securely within Britain's orbit, for Britain still maintained a garrison at Halifax, incidentally providing the colony with an important source of sterling exchange, and British export-import firms still financed much of Nova Scotia's foreign and domestic commerce.

To assert that economic factors alone determined which of Britain's colonial possessions in North America remained within the empire would be nonsense. No social movement of such general scope and impact as the American Revolution could possibly have been generated by economic interests alone. But it is important to be aware of the role which economic factors played. Britain's mercantilist empire was held together by a highly complex code of legislation known as the Acts of Trade. The purpose of these laws was to encourage in the colonies those types of economic activity which supplemented the resources of the mother country and to prohibit those types which competed with the mother country. Capital and labour were to be channelled into certain types of investment and diverted from others. In certain of the colonies the resource pattern was such that development along the prescribed lines followed naturally from the pursuit of self-interest. In others, however, the character of the available resources and the adoption of business methods which paralleled those of the mother country led to the diversion of capital and labour into types of activity which competed with the interests of the mother country and finally to the development of rival commercial centres. Within Britain's mercantilist empire there arose competing mercantile systems, centring round the major seaports of the colonies. The resulting strains in the imperial structure encouraged a movement toward independence, in which the northern colonies, the foci of intercolonial trade, took the lead. In the southern or staple-producing colonies, which were intrinsically better adapted to their assigned role in the imperial system, restrictions on westward expansion, the exhaustion of seaboard lands, and the burden of debt owed to British capitalists fostered resistance to a continuation of colonial status. Areas whose westward expansion was not threatened, whose staple exports found ready markets in Britain and Europe, and whose resources fitted them for their assigned place in Britain's mercantilist economy, showed no inclination to withdraw from the imperial system.

The eighteenth century had seen the disintegration of two colonial empires in North America; the nineteenth was to witness the creation of two transcontinental nations. At the turn of the century one of these nations existed only as a scarcely recognized possibility, the other more as a promise and an experiment than as a reality. To the north, British power remained securely established in Newfoundland, Nova Scotia, and Quebec. But these areas were still separate colonies, the only links between them being provided by trade and by their common membership in the imperial system. To the south, on the Atlantic seaboard, the nucleus of a new nation had already come into being, a loose federation of sovereign states, still harassed by internal jealousies and dissensions but unified by their common struggle against Britain and by the common tasks which now faced them. The withdrawal of these states from the imperial system opened up new opportunities for the colonies which had retained their allegiance to Britain, but at the same time it created new problems for them. To Nova Scotia the opportunity was now open to take over the role within the empire which New England had formerly played, as a source of shipping, supplies, and naval stores. In Quebec the way was open for British capital and enterprise to enter the continental fur trade by way of the St. Lawrence and to tap the resources of the interior more effectively than had so far been possible either from Hudson Bay or from the Atlantic seaboard. But, in the future, both in the maritime areas and in the interior, the states of the young American republic were certain to provide aggressive competition. The vigorous expansion of their economic life had already driven them out of one empire and had helped to destroy another. In the years to come the continuation and acceleration of this expansion was to set the pace for the growth and consolidation of the economy to the north and, at times, to threaten its very survival.

SUGGESTIONS FOR FURTHER READING

BASIC WORKS:

Innis, Harold A., *The Cod Fisheries, the History of an International Economy* (Toronto and New Haven, 1940) Chapters VI-VII, pp. 144-213

Lounsbury, Ralph G., *The British Fishery at Newfoundland, 1634-1763* (New Haven, 1934), Chapters VII-X, pp. 245-336

Nettels, Curtis P., *The Roots of American Civilization: A History of American*

Colonial Life (New York and London, 1938), Chapters XXI-XXII, pp. 569-629

Saunders, S. A., *Studies in the Economy of the Maritime Provinces* (Toronto, 1939), pp. 17-102

SUPPLEMENTARY WORKS:

Brebner, J. Bartlet, *New England's Outpost: Acadia before the Conquest of Canada* (New York, 1927), Chapters III-IX, pp. 57-263

Brebner, J. Bartlet, *North Atlantic Triangle: the Interplay of Canada, the United States and Great Britain* (Toronto and New Haven, 1945), Chapter III, pp. 30-45

Graham, Gerald S., *Empire of the North Atlantic: The Maritime Struggle for North America* (Toronto, 1950), Chapters VIII-X, pp. 143-216

Pares, Richard, *War and Trade in the West Indies 1739-1763* (Oxford, 1936), Chapters V, VIII, IX, pp. 179-226, 326-470

Pitman, Frank W., *The Development of the British West Indies, 1700-1763* (New Haven, 1917), Chapters IX-XIV, pp. 189-360

CHAPTER VI

THE CONTINENTAL FUR TRADE: 1713–1776

THE TRADE FROM HUDSON BAY

THROUGHOUT the troubled years from 1686 to 1713, the Hudson's Bay Company had managed to retain its foothold on the Bay and to preserve—indeed, to improve—its organization. The flow of furs across the Atlantic to the London auctions had never been completely interrupted, for though the French controlled most of the posts around the Bay the Company held Fort Nelson until 1694 and Fort Albany and Moose Factory thereafter, and from these bases it was able to carry on a limited but regular trade. French competition even in its most aggressive form had not put the Company out of business.

One result of the inroads made by the French was to encourage the Company to take its first hesitant steps toward establishing more direct relations with the tribes of the interior in order to induce them to send their beaver to the Bay. It was for this purpose that young Henry Kelsey was sent into the Assiniboine country in 1690. Although he brought back much valuable information, Kelsey did not succeed in his principal objective, for the western or Plains Indians whom he met on his journey of exploration were ignorant of the art of canoe-building and reluctant to attempt the long and hazardous expedition to the Bay. This reluctance is not hard to understand, for food supplies were scarce in the immediate vicinity of the Bay. The only tribes who were prepared to make the journey regularly were the Crees and the Assiniboines, who knew how to build canoes and could feed themselves by hunting and fishing while they made their way to the Company's posts. This was, it should be noted, a difficulty which had not handicapped the French on the St. Lawrence to the same extent, for food supplies, particularly of Indian corn, were relatively easy to obtain on the St. Lawrence route. Compared with the French, the English on Hudson Bay may seem to have been remarkably slow to set about exploring the interior and making direct contact with the western tribes. This was in part at least a matter of a deliberately conservative policy, but in part it reflected the difficulty of obtaining food supplies for long journeys to the interior. For many years after Kelsey's journey the Company made no further effort to extend its trade in the interior, but remained dependent upon the Crees and the Assiniboines to act as its middlemen.

By the time the French, under the terms of the Treaty of Utrecht, evacuated the posts which they had captured on Hudson Bay, the English company had built up an effective trading organization and had acquired considerable experience in dealing with the Indians. The next twenty-five years of its history were a period of considerable prosperity. Each year the Company exported goods worth from £5,000 to £6,000, of which about three-quarters were trade goods, and imported furs which, selling at a price of around four shillings a pound, brought in revenue of between £22,000 and £30,000 annually. After costs of administration (estimated at £12,245 in 1739 and £21,702 in 1744), wages and freight charges had been paid, there still remained net revenue sufficient to pay steady dividends and accumulate reserves for future contingencies. In the early years it had been necessary to purchase most of the trade goods from France, for the Indians were already familiar with French commodities and usually demanded them from the Company. But now most of the trade goods were manufactured and purchased in England and, though some of the trading personnel alleged that the French still had the advantage in terms of quality, the Company was able to secure important economies in procurement.

It remained true, however, that the most careful management and the most scrupulous attention to economy were necessary if the trade was to show a profit. The figures we have cited of the value of the Company's annual exports and imports may give an impression of fat profit margins, but actually this was not the case. The posts on the Bay were too far removed from London for any kind of direct supervision to be possible, and all the attention of the Company's able governor, Sir Bibye Lake, and his committee of directors was required to hold down the costs of doing business. Freight costs in particular were heavy, because the cargoes going to and coming from the Bay were not balanced. Ships went out fully loaded with heavy trade goods and returned with light, compact cargoes of furs, together with large quantities of ballast. The total shipping tonnage required by the Company, in other words, was determined by the out-going cargoes and was always larger than what would have been necessary merely to carry the furs to market. In addition the posts on the Bay had to be maintained and fortified, while in England the Company's rights and privileges had to be defended by political action, which tended to be expensive.

The Hudson's Bay Company, in short, like the French on the St. Lawrence, found the costs of carrying on the fur trade a serious problem. To reduce the burden of these costs, two alternative courses of action seemed appropriate: either to increase greatly the quantity of furs traded, so that the overhead costs could be spread over a greater volume of output; or to cut total costs to the minimum by close attention to economy, by efficient administration and accounting, and by avoiding like the plague any expenditures that were not absolutely necessary. The first of these policies was that followed by the French; the second was the one adopted, in this period, by the Hudson's Bay Company. The two policies had very different consequences: the French pushed rapidly westward, always seeking new tribes and new sources of supply; the Company sat quietly in its posts on the Bay, waiting for the Indians to bring down their furs, and highly reluctant to undertake any penetration of the interior, either by building posts or by sending parties of Europeans to trade, until ultimately forced to do so in 1754. The French policy, in a word, was one of aggressive expansion; the Company's, one of passive defence.

While this is so, the Hudson's Bay Company did have the important advantage of being able to bring in its trade goods by sea to bases that were considerably closer to the fur-producing areas of the northwest than Montreal and Quebec. Despite the difficulties of navigation in the Bay, the shortness of the season during which supplies could be brought in and furs taken out, and the inhospitable environment of the trading-posts, this advantage was sufficient to insure that the Company, assuming efficient management, would provide serious competition for the French. Over the long run, indeed, the economies of the Bay route were to prove decisive. The French were, man for man, the better traders; they understood the Indians far better than most of the Company's men; and they gave generous credit. The competitive advantage of the Company lay not in its personnel nor in its trading methods but in the possession of a cheaper route. During the period from 1713 to 1763 the St. Lawrence fur trade was to be extended as far and carried on as vigorously as it possibly could, given the technological conditions of water transportation; but the inherent superiority of the Bay route became more, not less, obvious as the years passed.

Particularly important for the Company's ability to withstand French competition was the fact that from posts on the western shore of the Bay it could tap areas which were beyond the effective reach of French traders. The Nelson and Churchill Rivers were the keys to the rich fur country north and west of Lake Winnipeg, and after 1713, with the re-establishment of Fort York and Fort Prince of Wales (Churchill), these rivers became the mainstay of the Company's trade. The forts on James Bay at the mouths of the Albany and Moose Rivers, on the other hand, drew on the area north of Lake Superior and were, in consequence, directly exposed to French competition. Different trading methods were necessary at these southern posts; lower prices were charged and a greater variety of trade goods provided. At Fort York and Churchill attempts were made to increase trade by dissuading the Indians from making war on each other and by encouraging tribes from the north and west to come to the posts themselves. But these policies had little success and the Company remained dependent on the Crees and the Assiniboines to distribute trade goods in the interior and to bring furs to the Bay. With the exception of a journey to the Slave River area undertaken by William Stewart in 1716, the Company made no effort to promote trade by sending its own employees into the interior until 1754 when, in a belated and ineffective attempt to combat French competition, Anthony Henday was sent to the Saskatchewan.

During most of the period with which we are now dealing, however, the Company can have felt under no particular pressure to adopt a more vigorous trading policy, for the profits which were derived from the posts on the Bay were by no means unsatisfactory. The capitalization of the Company was tripled in 1720; in the following year a dividend of only 5 per cent was paid but thereafter, from 1722 to the end of the 1750's, the annual dividend never fell below 7 per cent, even during war years, and was usually either 8 or 10 per cent. The total number of furs sold by the Company during this period tended to fall off, particularly after 1750, but on the other hand fur prices rose and the earnings of the Company remained relatively steady. French competition was felt in the total quantity of furs reaching the Company, but not immediately in the profits which the Company earned. Thus the need for an active policy of expansion cannot have seemed urgent, at least before 1750. To those who took a longer view of the matter, however, the fact that the Company was successfully maintaining its absolute rate of earnings can hardly have seemed good grounds for complacency, for the fur trade as a whole was expanding. As the French pushed their trading-posts ever farther westward, the Company's relative share of the trade declined. It began to look as if French expansion would pre-empt effective control of the hinterland and confine the Company permanently to its posts on the shore of the Bay.

THE TRADE FROM THE ST. LAWRENCE

The Treaty of Utrecht compelled the French to evacuate the captured posts on Hudson Bay and to search for some new means of limiting the competition of the English company. This was no very difficult problem to solve. Before 1713 English competition had been neutralized by attacks on the Company's posts; after 1713 it was to be met by attacks on the Company's sources of supply. Under the terms of the Treaty the French had recognized British sovereignty over the lands in the immediate vicinity of the Bay, but they had carefully avoided any admission of British rights in the interior. But it was in the interior that the furs were obtained which eventually found their way, through the agency of Indian middlemen, down to the Bay. If the French could intercept and divert these supplies of furs, they could damage the Company's trade quite as effectively as by direct attacks upon its posts.

In the period after 1713, then, the scene of the struggle between the French traders and the Hudson's Bay Company shifted from the shores of the Bay to the interior, and in particular to the territory northwest of Lake Superior, around Lake Winnipeg, and in the Saskatchewan valley. French expansion into this area was undoubtedly stimulated by the depletion of fur resources around Lake Michigan and the upper Mississippi and by the Fox Wars, which made access to the fur areas south of the Great Lakes uncertain and dangerous. The northwest was already known to be a rich source of prime quality furs and had the further advantage of being beyond the range of competition from the Atlantic seaboard. If any further incentive was required for the French to turn their attention to the northwest, it was provided by the knowledge that the Hudson's Bay Company depended on this region for its fur supplies and, as a result of its policy of building no trading-posts of its own except on the Bay, was singularly vulnerable to competition in the interior. Every consideration seemed to point to expansion into the northwest as the next step in French policy. Between 1680 and 1700 the French trading system, following the lead of Jolliet, Marquette, and La Salle, had crossed the height of land south of Lake Michigan and entered the Mississippi drainage basin. Now, between 1730 and 1760, with La Vérendrye and his sons blazing the trail, it was to cross the height of land west of Lake Superior and enter the drainage basin of Hudson Bay.

There were three principal canoe routes leading west from Lake Superior. Following any one of them, a traveller could, by a series of portages, cross the height of land which separated streams flowing into the St. Lawrence from streams flowing into Hudson Bay. The most southerly of these routes was that from Fond du Lac, at the southwest corner of Lake Superior. The northernmost was the route from Kaministiquia, the site of the modern Fort William. Between these two there was the Grand Portage route from the mouth of the Pigeon River—a route which was later to become one of the major transport arteries of the St. Lawrence fur trade.

When, after peace came in 1713, fur markets began to open up once again, the possibility of establishing posts at strategic points on these routes was given serious consideration by the French. It was pointed out that a post at Kaministiquia, together with one at Rainy Lake and one on Lake Winnipeg, would enable French traders to deal directly with the Crees and the Assiniboines in what is now the province of Manitoba. If these tribes could be induced to sell their furs to the French, might not the English be forced to abandon their posts on the Bay entirely, for, deprived of their Indian middlemen, how would they obtain furs? It seemed likely, too, that these Indians would prefer to deal with the French, for by doing so they would be spared the necessity for the long and often hungry journey to the Bay. The Kaministiquia route seemed best for this purpose, for it led northwest from Lake Superior and cut directly across some of the principal rivers which the Indians were accustomed to follow on their way to the Company's posts. A trading-post was therefore established at Kaministiquia in 1717.

The southerly or Fond du Lac route led into the territory of the Sioux Indians, who had previously occupied the advantageous position of middlemen between the western tribes and the fur-trading centre at Green Bay on Lake Michigan. They were, in consequence, inclined to oppose French attempts to by-pass them and trade directly with the western tribes. Partly to placate them and partly as a tactical measure during the second Fox War, a trading-post was maintained among the Sioux between 1727 and 1737.

The Grand Portage route was not used in the years immediately following 1713, despite the fact that, of the three routes, it gave the most convenient access to Rainy Lake, the gateway to Lake of the Woods, Lake Winnipeg, and the whole northwest. It was this route, however, which La Vérendrye selected for his first journey of exploration in 1731. Placed in charge of a trading-post on Lake Nipigon in 1726, La Vérendrye had become obsessed with the idea of finding, west of Lake Superior, a great river flowing to the Pacific, just as the St. Lawrence flowed east to the Atlantic. To find this river was the principal object of his explorations, although to be sure he showed himself well aware of the importance of the fur trade—and with good reason, for much of the capital for his venture was provided by fur-trade merchants. La Vérendrye, of course, never found such a river, for the Rocky Mountains, the existence of which was barely suspected at this time, stood between him and the Pacific. But in the course of their search, he and his sons opened up for French trade vast areas of the northwest and made possible one of the most remarkable spurts of expansion in the history of New France.

La Vérendrye at first hoped to obtain support for his explorations from the French king, but in this he was disappointed. He did receive, however, a monopoly grant of the fur trade in the country which he proposed to explore, and with this asset to his name he managed to secure financial backing from private merchants in Montreal. In the summer of 1731 he set out for the west with a party of about fifty men. He wintered at Kaministiquia but sent his nephew, La Jemeraye, on ahead over the Grand Portage route with a small party of men to build a fort on Rainy Lake. This was, as far as is known, the first time that European traders had used the Grand Portage route. La Jemeraye built Fort St. Pierre and wintered there, carrying on a thriving trade with the Indians in the meantime. In the following year La Vérendrye brought up the rest of the expedition over Grand Portage, paused for a short while at Fort St.

Pierre, and then pushed on to Lake of the Woods, where Fort St. Charles was constructed. He then sent his eldest son ahead to Lake Winnipeg and there, at the mouth of the Red River, Fort Maurepas was built in 1733. La Vérendrye then returned to Montreal for supplies, while his sons, having explored the foot of Lake Winnipeg, pushed up the Red River and the Assiniboine as far as the site of the present city of Portage la Prairie, where in 1736 they established Fort La Reine.

With the construction of Fort La Reine the gap between Lake Superior and Lake Winnipeg was finally closed. Within the space of five short years the French had thrust into the heart of the Hudson's Bay Company's supply area and had established themselves firmly across one of the Company's principal arteries of trade—the Indian canoe route leading from the Assiniboine River across Lake Winnipeg and down the Nelson or the Hayes to York Factory. Not content with this, in the next few years they pushed steadily north. In 1738 Fort Dauphin was built on Lake Winnipegosis, and in 1739, with the construction of Fort Bourbon, French trade reached the Saskatchewan. This was, in a sense, the culmination of La Vérendrye's campaign, at least as far as the fur trade was concerned. The forts later constructed farther up the Saskatchewan—Fort Paskoyac at The Pas and Fort à la Corne near the Forks—served merely to consolidate the French position and block lesser routes to the Bay. By the end of the 1740's the major task had been accomplished: French trading-posts had been established on every important canoe route (save only the Churchill) leading to the Bay; the valleys of the Saskatchewan and the Assiniboine had been incorporated into the St. Lawrence trading system.

The opening up of these new trading areas and, about the same time, the reopening of the Lake Michigan area with the end of the Fox Wars brought considerable prosperity to the French fur trade. The new posts established west of Lake Superior brought an immediate increase in fur supplies, from 146,395 *livres* of furs received at Montreal in 1717 to 221,000 *livres* in 1733, but on the whole the French in this period were not so much troubled by violent fluctuations in the volume of furs coming on the market as they had been previously. The volume of production remained relatively stable from year to year, with the trend rising gradually to a peak between 1740 and 1745. On the average it appears that about half of all the furs came from the area around Lake Michigan and half from the area tributary to Lake Superior, including both the western posts and those north of the Lake. Partly because of the new stability in production and partly because fur prices in Europe tended to increase over the period, marketing problems were much less serious than they had been before 1713 and there was not the same necessity for restricting production.

The business organization of the trade in this period showed few important departures from the earlier lines. The export trade in furs between New France and Europe remained generally under monopoly control, while the trade in the interior was, with the exception of certain posts, controlled by a licensing system. In 1717 monopoly rights in the export trade were sold to the Compagnie d'Occident for a period of twenty-five years. All furs were to be sold to this Company at fixed prices. The merchants of the colony protested strongly against this arrangement, alleging that company control had been tried in the past and had failed miserably, and the monopoly grant was revoked in 1720. For about a year thereafter the trade in furs was open to individual competition, the only restriction being that a tax had to be paid to the Company on all beaver imported into France. This tax was generally evaded, and monopoly control was, in consequence, re-established in 1721. Another experiment in free trade was tried later in that year but it too was a failure and the Company's rights were put into effect once again. The reason for the continuation of monopoly control, of course, was not so much that a single large organization could carry on the export trade in furs more efficiently than the private merchants (though the Company probably did secure certain economies of scale in storage, shipping, and marketing), but that the sale of monopoly privileges was a convenient way of raising government revenue. The vacillating policy pursued by the government of New France between 1717 and 1722 was probably one of the factors which retarded the expansion of the trade in those years.

As regards the trade in the interior, the failure of the various licensing schemes tried in the period before 1713 had led to a policy of restricting trade to posts where it could be carried on under military supervision. This policy had worked very imperfectly, and after 1713 the first opportunity was taken to return to the older system. General amnesties were issued for the benefit of those traders who had violated the earlier regulations and a new licensing system was put into force in 1715. As before, it proved almost unworkable, particularly in competitive conditions. Some of the posts were exposed to English competition and some were not; under a system of licences, traders naturally preferred to go to the sheltered posts, leaving the competitive areas more or less open to English encroachment. In addition, the setting up of a separate French jurisdiction in Louisiana introduced new complications, since it meant that traders who violated the regulations in New France could escape to New Orleans. The licensing system was therefore dropped in 1720. In 1728, however, it was reintroduced, but only for posts in competitive areas. For trading rights in these areas, where it was necessary that prices should be kept as low as possible in order to check English traders, licences were issued, but posts in other districts, where monopoly was feasible, were leased by auction. In other words, traders who went to posts which were free from English competition had to pay for the privilege, while those who bore the brunt of meeting competition had merely to secure a permit. There was also a third category of posts, including Niagara and Frontenac, which could not be run at a profit but which nevertheless had to be kept open to check the activities of the New York traders. These posts were subsidized by the government and were known as the King's posts.

Criticisms of mismanagement in one part of the trade or another were by no means uncommon in this period, but it remains true to say that during the 1740's and 1750's the fur trade of New France reached its highest level of efficiency. In respect to supplies, finance, and marketing, control was highly centralized at Montreal and Quebec, but in the interior great reliance was placed on the initiative and skill of the individual traders, who functioned as more or less independent agents within the larger organization. Thus strength and flexibility were combined to produce a highly effective trading system.

Within little more than a decade the French had extended the limits of their trade into the heart of the Hudson Bay drainage basin, while their explorers had penetrated south into the "bad lands" of the Missouri River system and west to the foothills of the Rockies. This was a remarkable record of expansion in the face of highly adverse conditions. Nevertheless, by the early 1750's it was becoming evident that the St. Lawrence fur trade had been extended as far west as was possible, at least with the capital, organization, and means of transport that were then available. French explorers could, to be sure, push still farther west if they wanted to and if they could secure financial support; the question was whether traders could follow them and still hope to obtain a profit after all the expenses of conducting business over such vast distances had been paid. Transport costs had, of course, been a problem of the trade ever since its inception, but now, with the opening up of the northwest and the construction of trading-posts half-way across the continent from Montreal, they became the major factor limiting further expansion. Ever-increasing transport charges and the capital cost of financing trading ventures over very great distances cut into profit margins which had never been large and set a definite boundary to the geographical area which could profitably be exploited from Montreal.

Signs that this boundary had been reached, if indeed it had not already been passed, became increasingly common after the French moved into the Saskatchewan valley around the middle of the century. For example, French traders in this area would accept from the Indians only the lightest and finest of furs; the heavier and coarser varieties, which were not valuable enough in proportion to their weight to be worth transporting to Montreal, they told the Indians to take to Hudson Bay. And again, French traders tried to obtain the heavier kinds of trade goods, such as kettles, fire-arms, ammunition, and hatchets, from the posts of

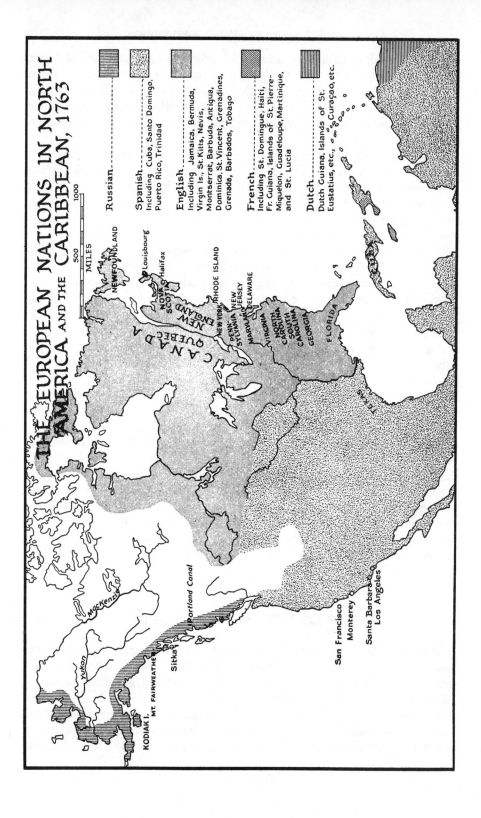

THE EUROPEAN NATIONS IN NORTH AMERICA AND THE CARIBBEAN, 1763

Russian

Spanish
Including Cuba, Santo Domingo,
Puerto Rico, Trinidad

English
Including Jamaica, Bermuda,
Virgin Is, St. Kitts, Nevis,
Montserrat, Barbuda, Antigua,
Dominica, St. Vincent, Grenadines,
Grenada, Barbados, Tobago

French
Including St. Domingue, Haiti,
Fr. Guiana, Islands of St. Pierre-
Miquelon, Guadeloupe, Martinique,
and St. Lucia

Dutch
Dutch Guiana, Islands of St.
Eustatius, etc., Curaçao, etc.

MILES
500   1000

NEWFOUNDLAND
Louisbourg
Halifax
NOVA SCOTIA
NEW ENGLAND
NEW YORK
RHODE ISLAND
PENNSYLVANIA
NEW JERSEY
MARYLAND
DELAWARE
VIRGINIA
NORTH CAROLINA
SOUTH CAROLINA
GEORGIA
FLORIDA
CANADA
QUEBEC
TEXAS

KODIAK I.
MT. FAIRWEATHER
Sitka
Portland Canal
MacKenzie
Yukon

San Francisco
Monterey
Santa Barbara
Los Angeles

the Hudson's Bay Company, instead of bringing them all the way from Montreal. Apparently on at least one occasion they opened direct negotiations with York Factory for this purpose, but more often they seem to have obtained these goods from Indians whom they sent to the Company's posts to trade, with specific instructions as to what goods to bring back.

Evidence of this kind suggests that the French traders operating west of Lake Superior were under considerable pressure to reduce their transport costs and that, to do this, they confined their trade as far as possible to commodities that were high in value and low in weight. And this in turn suggests that they had now pushed as far west as their transport system could take them. The pull of the European market diminished with distance. At Montreal and Quebec furs were the only product which could stand the costs of transport to Europe. On Lake Winnipeg and the lower Saskatchewan, only the lightest and finest of furs could do so. Beyond Fort à la Corne, the westernmost extension of the French trading system, not even the best of furs would repay the costs of securing and selling them.

All this was true, of course, only for the French trading system as it existed in the middle of the eighteenth century. A rise in the price of beaver would have made it commercially feasible to extend the trade still farther west; a reorganization of the transport system—such as, for example, the establishment of supply bases in the interior or the use of large ships on the Great Lakes—would have had the same effect. The limit of expansion which the French traders met on the Saskatchewan was not something final and immutable; it was an organizational and technological limit, a matter of the way business was done and the facilities that were employed. After 1760, when English, Scots, and Yankee merchants took over the Montreal fur trade, means were found to make renewed expansion possible—an expansion which, before the end of the century, was to reach the shores of the Pacific. But the innovations in organization and transport methods which made this possible were not within the reach of the French traders in 1750.

THE TRADE FROM ALBANY AND NEW YORK

With the French from the St. Lawrence operating at or near the maximum range from their bases at Montreal and Quebec, and the English on Hudson Bay content to follow an unaggressive policy of "live and let live", the fur trade north and west of the Great Lakes seemed, in the years around 1750, to have reached a sort of competitive equilibrium. The English had the advantage of being able to bring in supplies by ocean-going vessels to posts close to the best fur areas. The French had the advantage of posts strategically located upstream from the Company's bases, besides their greater skill in trading with the Indians and willingness to extend longer credit. Neither party was, for the time being, in a position to do serious damage to the trade of the other, by peaceful means at least. The French might intercept the Indians on their way to the Company's posts and pre-empt the best of their furs, but the limitations of their transport system prevented them from doing much more than skim the cream off the Company's trade. The Company, in its turn, might have begun building competitive posts in the interior and might conceivably have felt impelled, perhaps for reasons of national ambition or in the interests of its own corporate survival, to challenge the French claim to control of the continental hinterland. But, from a commercial point of view, the need for such a policy can hardly have seemed very great, while the gains to be derived from disrupting what was, after all, a tolerably comfortable situation were highly uncertain.

South of the St. Lawrence-Great Lakes line, in contrast, forces were at work which made the achievement of an equilibrium of this kind impossible. In this area, as in the northwest, the basic French strategy may be described as one of encirclement. But whereas in the northwest French expansion meant the encirclement merely of a few trading-posts on Hudson Bay, south of the Great Lakes the French lines of communication and trade from Lake Ontario to the Gulf of Mexico cut across the rear of the Atlantic colonies, with their rapidly growing populations, high immigration rates, and steadily advancing frontiers of settlement. The conflict in this area, in consequence, was not merely one between two fur-trading systems; the expansive forces of land settlement and land speculation also had to be reckoned with.

In the years immediately after 1713, however, these difficulties were still in the future. Conflict was still confined to the fur trade, the principal contestants being, as before, the Albany merchants and their Iroquois allies on the one hand and the French traders of Montreal on the other. An important advantage on the side of the Albany traders was the greater cheapness of their trade goods, particularly rum, iron kettles, and woollen blankets—an advantage so marked, indeed, that an extensive trade in English manufactures developed between Albany and Montreal, through the agency of certain Iroquois Indians who had transferred their allegiance. The French traders must have paid considerably more for these imported goods than they cost in Albany, but apparently the price differential between French and English manufactures was large enough to make the trade commercially attractive.

The trade with Montreal enabled certain of the Albany merchants to secure furs from the French in exchange for English goods; in 1725 about 15 per cent of all furs reaching Albany were obtained by this method. One influential group of merchants, however, with the support of the governor, strongly opposed trade with Montreal, on the grounds that it would serve only to strengthen French influence over the Indians and reduce the competitive advantage of the Albany traders. Laws were therefore passed by the New York legislature forbidding the sale of English manufactured goods to New France. The result was a marked decrease in the volume of goods imported at New York for the fur trade and an increase in direct importation from Europe to Montreal. New York importers and British merchants therefore protested against the laws and were instrumental in having them disallowed in 1729. The French, for their part, made no effort to suppress the trade, since they benefited greatly from being able to obtain English goods, and trade between Albany and Montreal continued without interruption, except in time of war, from 1729 until the conquest of Canada.

By far the greater part of the furs reaching Albany were obtained, not through the French, but from the Indians, either by direct trade or through the agency of the Iroquois. In these branches of the trade the most significant development in the years after 1713 was the increasing extent to which Albany traders, following the example of the French, began to go to the west themselves and, by-passing the Iroquois, to trade directly with the western tribes. Within a few years of the end of the war trading parties from Albany were active south of Lake Ontario and by the 1720's they were penetrating still farther west. By 1725 68 per cent of the furs reaching Albany were brought in by local traders and only 17 per cent by the Iroquois.

The most important step in this new policy of expansion was the establishment of Fort Oswego on Lake Ontario in 1722. Although at first it was little more than a small and vulnerable trading outpost, the founding of Oswego nevertheless marked the beginning of a new and more bitter phase in the traditional conflict between New York and Montreal. Since Frontenac had ended the Iroquois menace in 1696, French traders had regarded the lower Lakes as their private preserve. Fort Oswego cut the ground from under this conception. Albany traders were now in a position to sever a vitally important French transport route to the west, to divert to New York a large proportion of the Indian trade from the upper Lakes to Montreal, and to undermine the allegiance to the French of the western tribes. With cheaper trade goods, rum, and a position on the flank of one of the principal Indian canoe routes, the traders at Oswego threatened to do immense damage to the French fur trade.

The French were unable to destroy Oswego by force without running the risk of war, a risk which they were then unwilling to take. At the same time they could not hope to compete successfully with the Oswego traders merely on the basis of prices because of the higher cost of their trade goods. Accordingly they fell back on a continuation and extension of their old policy of building military forts at strategic points on the main trade routes. These forts were designed first of all to prevent further English expansion, particularly in areas vital to the security of French communications with the interior, and secondly to serve as trading-posts, where the Indians could be induced to part with their furs before reaching Oswego. Fort Niagara, which had been allowed to fall into disrepair, was reconstructed in 1726; this post, together with Fort Frontenac at the eastern end of Lake Ontario, bore the main brunt of meeting New York competition around the lower Lakes. In 1749 Fort Rouillé was built, near the site of the present city of Toronto, to block the portage route between Lake Ontario and Georgian Bay which was much used by northern Indians on their way to Oswego. As a second line of defence, a post was maintained at Detroit to seal off Lakes Huron and Michigan from New York, and new forts were built at Vincennes on the Wabash in 1727 and at Sault Ste. Marie in 1751.

In addition to building these posts, the function of which was primarily defensive, the French also made preparations to take the offensive, when the time came, against the Atlantic colonies, and in particular against New York, which represented the most immediate danger both commercially and in a military sense. To this end a strong fort was built in 1731 at Crown Point on Lake Champlain. As a site for a trading-post Crown Point had little to recommend it and in fact the pretence that trade was the object was not seriously maintained. The fort was really designed to act as a base for attacks on New York and New England, or in other words to serve a strategic function in the Champlain valley analogous to that served in the North Atlantic by Louisbourg. In particular it was designed to threaten the town of Albany, which was almost defenceless against attack from this quarter.

FUR TRADE AND SETTLEMENT IN THE OHIO VALLEY

From the point of view of the Atlantic colonies, however, Crown Point was merely the most obvious manifestation of the generally menacing alignment of the French empire in North America. If New York was, of all the English colonies, the most directly exposed to French attack, nevertheless the others had good reason to feel insecure, for French control of the territory between the Appalachians and the Mississippi presented a clear threat to their landward frontiers and an obstacle which, unless removed, would forever block their expansion westward over the mountains into the rich plains of the interior. To confine the English colonies to the coastal strip and reserve for France the country beyond the Appalachians was, in fact, one of the major goals of French policy in this period. To hold the trans-Appalachian territory by settlement was not within French power, and this, combined with the failure to secure command of the North Atlantic sea-lanes, was perhaps the fundamental weakness of the French position. But the fortified posts of the fur trade, stretching in a vast arc from Montreal to New Orleans, might well suffice to restrain the westward expansion of the English colonies, for the frontiers of settlement of these colonies, being far removed from the seaports and the centres of government, were typically weak and defenceless. The French forts themselves, compared to the huge area to be controlled, were relatively few in number and widely dispersed, and most of them were little more than stockades; nevertheless, they did much to maintain French influence among the Indians, besides serving as communication centres and bases for raiding parties.

The most important of these French forts were located at strategic points on the two principal canoe routes from Montreal to the west. The older route, still much used, led up the Ottawa River across portages to Georgian Bay and then across Lake Huron. There it divided into two branches, one going west to Lake Superior and one south to Lake Michigan. On the western branch the major forts were at Sault Ste. Marie and Kaministiquia; on the southerly, at Michilimackinac and Green Bay and on the Chicago and St. Joseph Rivers. These forts guarded the vital portages leading to Lake Winnipeg and the northwest in the former case and to the Mississippi basin in the latter. Beyond the portages there were, in the northwest, Forts St. Pierre, St. Charles, Maurepas, La Reine, and the others built by La Vérendrye and his successors, and, in the Mississippi basin, Fort Marin at the junction of the Wisconsin and the Mississippi and Fort de Chartres in the Illinois country, on the border of Louisiana. The second principal canoe route led up the St. Lawrence from Montreal to Lake Ontario. One branch then went across the Toronto portage to Georgian Bay, while another led across the Niagara portage to Lake Erie and thence to Detroit. Forts Frontenac, Rouillé, Niagara, and Detroit covered the vital points on this route. From Detroit a route led up the Maumee River into the Ohio valley and thence to the Mississippi. Fort Miami on the Maumee River and Forts Quiatanon and Vincennes on the Wabash were the centres of French influence in this area.

The routes which led to the Mississippi by way of Lake Erie and the Ohio River had not been much used by the French in the period before 1713, although they had been known at least since La Salle's explorations. The principal reason for this was probably that for many years Lakes Erie and Ontario had been rendered useless as regular transport routes by the presence of the Iroquois. Most of the traffic to and from the west therefore passed over the Ottawa River-Lake Nipissing-Georgian Bay route, which by-passed Lake Erie entirely. The consequence was that when the French sought to establish regular lines of communication with the Mississippi valley they concentrated their attention at first on the portages at the foot of Lake Michigan.

By the middle of the eighteenth century, however, the Iroquois were no longer a serious menace in a military sense, although their competition in the fur trade was still a nuisance. At the same time the rising transport costs which accompanied the westward extension of the trade encouraged attempts to use the Lake Ontario-Lake Erie route to the west in addition to the older Ottawa River route. For these reasons, and also because of the serious competition now provided by the New York traders at Oswego, the French began, around the middle of the eighteenth century, to devote considerably more attention than formerly to the territory around the lower Lakes, and in particular to the various canoe routes which led from Lake Ontario and Lake Erie to the tributaries of the Ohio and thence to the Mississippi. These routes provided shorter and easier means of access to the Mississippi valley than the Lake Michigan portage routes. But they also had considerable strategic importance, for they passed through territory which lay, as it were, just outside the back door of certain of the English colonies, notably Pennsylvania and Virginia. As the tension between France and Britain in North America increased, it became urgent that the Ohio country be brought definitely under French control without further delay.

Traders from Pennsylvania and Virginia had been active in this area at least since the 1720's, for several easy routes led across the mountains from the coastal strip. While New York concentrated on the Oswego and Albany trade, these middle colonies challenged French interests in the valleys of the Ohio and the Allegheny. Access to cheaper English trade goods enabled them to make serious inroads upon the French trade, and by 1740 their competition was being felt at French posts as far west as Detroit.

Even more ominous from the French point of view, however, were the activities of English land speculators and land settlement companies. With the increase of population in Pennsylvania and Virginia, the frontier of settlement was moving steadily westward. Ahead of this frontier and hard on the heels of the fur-traders, the agents of the capitalists of the seaport towns, seeking a more profitable avenue of investment than tobacco or maritime commerce, staked out their claims to lands not yet occupied. This was a much more serious threat to French interests than was English competition in the fur trade, for the French empire in the New World, starved of immigrants from the mother country, had no effective defence against the inexorable westward march of English settlement—none, that is to say, short of war.

The best routes across the mountains into the Ohio country started in Pennsylvania, but the legislature of that colony, being much under Quaker influence, was reluctant to take any steps which might precipitate war with the Indians. In Virginia, on the other hand, the colonial government followed a vigorous expansionist policy and gave full support to the influential capitalists who were interested in opening up the country west of the mountains for settlement. The first important step was taken in 1744 when the Iroquois, claiming to speak for all the tribes involved, ceded to Virginia all their lands within the alleged boundaries of that colony. Certain of the leading members of the colonial aristocracy then organized a company, known as the Ohio Company, which obtained from the King an initial grant of 200,000 acres of land on the banks of the Ohio River, with the promise of a larger grant to follow if a hundred families were settled on the first tract within seven years. The Ohio Company lost no time in sending an agent to the west to survey its land grant, and in 1752 it obtained from the Indians permission to construct a fort at the junction of the Allegheny and Monongahela Rivers.

This move represented a thrust into the heart of the French trading and transport system and provoked an immediate reaction. French forces captured and destroyed the important English fort and trading-post at Pickawillany on the Miami River in 1752 and in the following year took possession of Fort Venango on the Allegheny. The fort which the Ohio Company had begun to build at the forks of the Ohio River was destroyed and Fort Duquesne built in its place. Troops sent from Virginia to enforce the Company's claims were defeated and compelled to withdraw. By the summer of 1754 Virginia and New France were at war.

THE ATLANTIC COLONIES AND WESTWARD EXPANSION

The skirmishes in the Ohio valley marked the beginning of a struggle which, broadening into the Seven Years' War in 1756, was to end with the destruction of the French empire in North America. That the first blood was shed in the capture of an English trading-post and the repelling of an English land settlement company was, in a sense, historically appropriate, for the Seven Years' War, unlike previous wars between France and Britain, was fought primarily over colonial issues. What France sought to gain from the war was not increased power in Europe, but supremacy in North America. Had this not been the case she could never have found herself allied with Austria against Britain and Prussia, for Austria was France's traditional opponent in the European struggle for power. It was only because the stakes had changed that this new alignment of powers was possible.

The increasing tension between the French and the British empires in North America reached the point of open conflict when, to the competition between two fur-trading systems, there was added the competition between the fur trade and settlement. It was the formation of the Ohio Company and the proposal to establish permanent English settlements on the Ohio River that provided the immediate occasion for a resort to arms. The latter conflict, though it may have been aggravated by nationalistic hostility, did not arise to any large extent from the fact that the land settlement interests involved were British and the fur-trade interests predominantly French. It arose fundamentally from the fact that the fur trade and settlement could not coexist in the same area. If the country beyond the Appalachians was to be reserved for the fur trade, the Atlantic colonies would necessarily have to give up all ambitions for a westward extension of settlement. This would be true no matter what authority interposed the barrier. The fact that, in the mid-1750's, it was the French who sought to block settlement beyond the mountains is important for an explanation of the outbreak of war. But the destruction of the French empire did not solve the problem; it merely converted it from a source of conflict between two empires into a source of conflict within the empire which survived.

When, therefore, after the conquest of Canada, the British government issued a proclamation which stated that for the time being colonial settlement should extend no farther westward than a line running through the sources of the rivers which flowed into the Atlantic, colonial land speculators and other advocates of expansion had some reason to wonder whether the destruction of French power had brought all the advantages which had been anticipated. The new boundary line laid down in 1763 was, to be sure, intended merely as a temporary expedient—a means of pacifying the Indians after the bloody uprisings of Pontiac's conspiracy. But it demonstrated, nevertheless, that British policy in regard to western lands would not necessarily be shaped to suit the needs of the American colonies. The fact of the matter was that it was largely for reasons of defence that Britain had, in the period before 1760, encouraged the westward expansion of settlement. But now, with French power in Canada crushed and Spain confined to the territory west of the Mississippi, the urgency of such defence measures had vanished and the opportunity had arisen for considering more carefully how the vast region west of the mountains should be administered. Such consideration involved not only, nor perhaps even principally, the interests of the Atlantic colonies; the welfare of Britain's Indian allies had also to be weighed, together with the profits of the St. Lawrence fur trade, the returns on British capital invested in the seaboard lands of the established colonies, and, in a broader context, the allegiance and dependence on the mother country of all the various members of the imperial family. Several of the Atlantic colonies had already evinced a most improper spirit of independence; to give them unrestricted access to the western lands would hardly weaken that spirit. It was, in a word, a highly complicated question, and one quite without precedent in the history of Britain's maritime empire. The British statesmen who were responsible for finding a viable solution can hardly be blamed for deciding, for the moment, to do nothing—nothing, that is to say, beyond laying it down that the territory between the Appalachians and the Mississippi was to remain for the time being an Indian reserve and that English settlement in that region was not to be permitted.

Since this decision deprived the colonial governors of the power to make further grants of western lands, it was bitterly resented by the land speculators, particularly in the southern group of colonies. These speculators were for the most part drawn from the richest and most influential merchant and planter families and their hostility to the western land policy of the British government in these years was by no means least important among the developments which made the American Revolution possible. But if the terms of the Proclamation of 1763 were bad enough, the details of the permanent policy which began to emerge in the next few years were far worse. The guiding idea behind this policy was that settlement of the western lands ought to proceed slowly and under the direct supervision of the British government. No arrangement which might weaken the ties which bound the colonies to the mother country was to be permitted. To this end a boundary line was to be established, west of which settlement was forbidden. This line would be moved slowly westward from time to time, as the country east of it filled up and as the British government completed arrangements for the purchase of land from the Indians. A policy less to the liking of the colonial expansionists would have been hard to find. And to make matters still worse, the Quebec Act of 1774 annexed to Canada all the territory north of the Ohio and east of the Mississippi, with the object of prohibiting settlement in this area entirely and keeping it as a permanent Indian reserve. The fur trade in this area was to be regulated by the governor of the province of Quebec, and it was clearly intended that it should be carried on by way of the St. Lawrence rather than from New York or Pennsylvania.

What these policies added up to was the virtual exclusion of the Atlantic colonies from the west. The Indian boundary line prevented colonial business men from seeking the rich profits of land speculation and the Quebec Act excluded them from the northern fur trade. To many of them it must have seemed, indeed, as if the result of the Seven Years' War and the changes in imperial policy which had taken place since then had been merely to set up the British government in the place of the French as the principal obstacle to western expansion. The aggressive hostility which had previously been directed against the French was now turned against the mother country, and resentment at restrictions on westward expansion blended with and reinforced resentment at restrictions on sea-borne commerce. Just as many of the colonial merchants whose capital was invested in maritime commerce were coming to believe that continued membership in the imperial system was inconsistent with the prosperity of colonial trade, so many of those who had looked to the fur trade or to land speculation for their profit were gradually realizing that they could not both achieve their ambitions and retain their allegiance to Britain. With the disappearance of the French danger, tendencies toward independence and self-determination which had always been present in the English colonies acquired new strength. It was as if, on the ruins of the French empire, a new imperialism had appeared— a continental imperialism that found its origin in the growing economic strength of the Atlantic colonies, in their hunger for western lands, and in their resistance to the regulations of the mother country.

The conquered territory of New France, however, now known as the province of Quebec, shared neither the hostility of the Atlantic colonies to the western lands policy of the British government nor their resentment against the Acts of Trade. What reason could there be for the merchants of Montreal and Quebec to feel injured by restrictions on settlement in the west when the only west which concerned them was the west of the fur trade—a west which would inevitably be destroyed if settlement was permitted? The western lands policy of the British government was, in fact, precisely what was required to strengthen the St. Lawrence fur trade against competition from New York and Pennsylvania, as several of the larger Albany fur-trading firms recognized when, in the years after 1770, they moved their base of operations to Montreal. Settlement in the west had never been an urgent matter in New France and it would not become a matter of importance for the province of Quebec until many years had passed. At the time of the conquest the settled part of the province was confined to the banks of the St. Lawrence between Quebec and Montreal. There was no question here of a pressure of population upon available land resources. Westward expansion meant expansion of the fur trade, not of settlement. Consequently the imperial regulations which in the Atlantic colonies were regarded as restrictions on expansion appeared in Quebec more like measures to make further expansion possible. And partly for this reason, when the Atlantic colonies took up arms against the mother country, they were not joined by the new British province on the St. Lawrence.

The conquest of Canada had confronted the British government with the problem of how to administer the vast territory in the interior of North America which the French had won and exploited by means of the fur trade. The solution finally arrived at, embodied in the Indian line regulations of 1768 and the Quebec Act of 1774, was essentially a compromise, involving the reservation for the fur trade of large areas north of the Ohio, to be controlled from Quebec, and the gradual settlement of the remainder under the supervision of the British government. This arrangement at least had the merit that it attached to Canada part, though by no means all, of the hinterland south of the Great Lakes which had been tributary to the St. Lawrence during the French regime. The plan failed, primarily because it imposed restrictions on the use and disposal of western lands which the Atlantic colonies would not accept. The War of Independence was fought partly in order to insure the removal of these restrictions. The Treaty of 1783 which ended the War completely erased all traces of the policy which had been so painfully devised; all the territory south of the Great Lakes and east of the Mississippi, save only Spanish Florida, was now annexed to the American confederacy. To Canada there remained only fragments of the great hinterland which, less than twenty-five years before, had paid tribute to Montreal.

SUGGESTIONS FOR FURTHER READING

BASIC WORKS:

Innis, Harold A., *The Fur Trade in Canada: an Introduction to Canadian Economic History* (New Haven, 1930), Chapter II, pp. 84-151

Nettels, Curtis P., *The Roots of American Civilization: A History of American Colonial Life* (New York and London, 1938), Chapters XXI-XXIII, pp. 569-659

Newbigin, Marion I., *Canada, the Great River, the Lands and the Men* (London, 1926), Chapters XI-XIII and Epilogue, pp. 207-300

Rich, E. E., *The Hudson's Bay Company, 1670-1870* (London: The Hudson's Bay Record Society, 1958), Volume I, 1670-1763, pp. 427-661

Rich, E. E., Introduction to *James Isham's Observations on Hudsons Bay, 1743* (Toronto: The Champlain Society, 1949)

SUPPLEMENTARY WORKS:

Alvord, Clarence W., *The Mississippi Valley in British Politics, A Study of the Trade, Land Speculation, and Experiments in Imperialism Culminating in the American Revolution* (2 vols.; Cleveland, 1917), Preface and Vol. I, Chapters I-VII, Vol. II, Chapters II, III, and VIII

Burpee, Lawrence J., *The Search for the Western Sea* (2 vols.; Toronto, 1935), Vol. I, Part II, pp. 193-287

McIlwain, Charles H., Introduction to Peter Wraxall, *An Abridgement of the Indian Affairs contained in Four Folio Volumes, transacted in the Colony of New York, from the Year 1678 to the Year 1751* (Cambridge, Mass., 1915)

Wrong, George M., *The Rise and Fall of New France* (2 vols.; New York, 1928), Vol. II, Chapters XXVI and XXVII, Part 2, pp. 687-734 and 742-61

CHAPTER VII

RECONSTRUCTION IN BRITISH NORTH AMERICA: 1783–1815

BRITISH POLICY TOWARD THE UNITED STATES AFTER 1783

THE British government, in the years between the fall of the French empire and the beginning of the American Revolution, had been faced with a nearly impossible task. The empire in North America for which it was responsible was no balanced structure of mutually complementary parts, such as mercantilist theory assumed, but rather a mixture of diverse and competitive units which together presented almost insurmountable obstacles to consolidation into a single economic system. Merely to hold all the component parts of this sprawling empire in allegiance to the British Crown would have taxed the abilities of the wisest of administrators. To preserve their allegiance and at the same time co-ordinate their economic growth would certainly have necessitated a complete overhaul of the methods and principles which governed the workings of the old colonial system. In the event, the necessary readjustments were not carried through in time and the first British Empire disintegrated. The problems of administering so vast and heterogeneous an empire proved too great for British statesmen.

In some respects the withdrawal from the empire of the thirteen Atlantic colonies simplified the problem of governing those which remained within the fold. The areas which had left the imperial system were the more aggressive and economically advanced; those which remained were the backward members of the family, areas which fitted neatly into a still predominantly mercantilist system and which were too weak as yet to claim independence of the mother country. Most of the latter areas presented no great difficulties for Britain. In Quebec, to be sure, there were special problems of administration to be faced, but elsewhere no acute sources of conflict were evident. In the Hudson Bay territory control by chartered company was still a highly satisfactory form of government since permanent settlement, at least on the shores of the Bay, was obviously out of the question. In Newfoundland issues of settlement, local government, and control of the fisheries were not pressing for the moment. And even in Nova Scotia, the only colony with an Assembly of its own which had chosen to remain within the empire, the situation was in 1783 one of comparative quiet. The economic life of these areas was still firmly tied to British markets and sources of capital. Continued membership in the imperial system not only did them no obvious injury; it also held out the prospect of positive benefits, especially now that they could expect protection against the competition of the more advanced areas which, by asserting their political independence, had cut themselves off from the privileges of the British navigation laws.

But was it so certain that the new American states would be excluded entirely from the privileges of participation in Britain's trading system? Was it in Britain's interests that they should be? The Atlantic colonies had been lost to Britain politically; but did that necessarily mean that they were lost to her commercially as well? There were powerful groups within the British Empire—the West Indies planters, for instance—who considered it by no means in their interests that the American states should be barred from imperial trade. And there was, too, an increasing tendency among the leaders of opinion in Britain to look askance at the morass of detailed regulations which made up the Acts of Trade and to suggest that perhaps they might not be quite the last word on commercial policy. Adam Smith had, to be sure, given them his approval in 1776, but not without qualifications. The ideal of a self-sufficient empire was no longer as sacrosanct as it had once been.

The ending of the War of Independence had, in fact, opened up a possibility which had not existed before: the possibility of modifying the Navigation Acts in such a way as to extend their privileges, on a reciprocal basis, to nations which did not admit allegiance to the British Crown but which could nevertheless advance the prosperity of the British Empire by trade. It was admittedly no more than a possibility, and one which developed not from any fundamental change in belief but rather from the painfully obvious gap in the imperial trading system which had been left by the defection of the Atlantic colonies. But for a time it looked as if it might become reality. The provisional agreement signed with the American peace commissioners in November, 1782, had included a promise that a commercial treaty of mutual advantage would be arranged as soon as possible. And early in 1783 William Pitt introduced a bill in the House of Commons which would have put this promise into effect. For a short time British imperial policy hesitated at the cross-roads. Should a new and more liberal trading policy be adopted, such as would permit the United States to trade freely with British possessions? Or should the attempt be made to build a new empire on the same principles as the old, with the carrying-trade reserved for British ships, and foreign countries—including the United States—barred from the markets of the British colonies?

This issue aroused considerable public controversy in Britain in 1783 and 1784. The West Indies interests were in favour of permitting the free importation of American foodstuffs and lumber in American ships, for they had no confidence that the sugar plantations of the Caribbean could be supplied either from Britain or from British North America. The shipowners and shipbuilders of Britain, on the other hand, argued that the traditional policy of reserving British imperial trade for British shipping should be maintained intact. Any breach in this policy would, they asserted, endanger the strength of the British navy and the security of the nation. Involved in the controversy, too, was the whole question of Britain's economic relations with her remaining colonies, particularly Canada, Nova Scotia, and Newfoundland. The role which these possessions would play in the imperial trading system depended upon the policy adopted toward the United States.

The strongest argument against any relaxation of the Navigation Acts was the assertion that it would imperil Britain's naval strength, and it was this consideration which led the British government to decide in 1784 that the United States should be treated exactly like any other foreign country in all matters relating to maritime trade. This decision was taken not so much as a result of any pressure exerted by vested interests but rather because it was in accord with the most hallowed tradition of British commercial policy—the principle that the empire should depend as little as possible upon foreign supplies and foreign shipping. When balanced against the solid authority of this tradition, the fears of the West Indies planters and the theories of the new generation of *laissez-faire* economists were of little moment. It was true that Britain had lost about one-third of her merchant marine as a consequence of the rebellion of the Atlantic colonies; but British and colonial shipbuilders, with the timber resources of Nova Scotia and Quebec to supplement supplies from the Baltic, could soon make up the deficiency. It was true that the West Indies had in the past relied upon the middle and southern Atlantic colonies for food, lumber, and a host of other necessities; but the remaining British colonies in North America and Britain herself could surely supply what was required and retain the shipping profits besides. It was true that the merchants of Nova Scotia and Quebec had so far given little indication that, handicapped as they were by distance and inexperience, they could take over the functions previously performed by their counterparts in New England; but it did not seem improbable that, encouraged by suitable legislation, they could before long build up their own trading connections and take over the intercolonial trade themselves. In any event no convincing reasons had yet been produced for abandoning the policy which had served in the past.

To decide upon this policy and to give it the formal sanction of law was no very difficult matter; to put it into effect was rather more complicated. The British North American colonies were still in many respects economically dependent upon the United States. Before they could hope to take the place of the American states as sources of supply, new resources had to be developed and new trading connections forged. This necessarily took time. Meanwhile there were urgent problems of relief and settlement to be faced, particularly in Nova Scotia and the old province of Quebec where large numbers of Loyalist refugees had to be fed and succoured. The pressure of these immediate problems, combined with proximity to the United States and the impossibility of preventing smuggling, inevitably led to modifications in the imperial blueprint laid down in 1784 and in the end forced its abandonment. To the story of how these readjustments took place in the various British colonies we shall now turn our attention.

NEWFOUNDLAND

Of all Britain's possessions in the New World Newfoundland was still regarded as second in importance only to the West Indies. From the point of view of the wealth and security of the mother country the island was, in the opinion of the British Board of Trade, worth more than Canada and Louisiana combined. Its value lay not in its inhabitants— these had always been unwanted—but in the employment its fisheries gave to British ships and British seamen. As one contemporary writer expressed it, Newfoundland was like a great ship moored near the Banks during the fishing season for the convenience of English fishermen.

We have already seen how, from the 1630's on, settlement on Newfoundland had been systematically discouraged in the interests of preserving the fisheries for the fishing fleets of the English West Country ports, and how, despite this discouragement, settlement did slowly take hold. But in spite of the appearance of a resident fishery and the increase of population, British policy toward Newfoundland did not change. In 1775, indeed, the traditional policy had been vigorously reaffirmed in an important statute known as Palliser's Act, the stated purpose of which was to restore control of the Newfoundland fisheries to British fishermen. To this end bounties were to be paid to ships sailing from British ports, owned and manned by persons resident in Britain, which went to the Newfoundland Banks to fish. No fishing-ships were to be permitted to carry passengers to Newfoundland without special permission and, to insure that the crews of the fishing-ships did not remain on the island, a portion of their wages was to be held back until their return to England.

To the extent that it was aimed at reviving the declining West Country fishing industry, Palliser's Act was little more than a repetition of earlier legislation. But it had a further purpose. In combination with the Restraining Act, passed in the same year, it was intended to check the expansion of New England. The Restraining Act, passed as a measure of retaliation against the American non-importation agreements, prohibited New England ships from participating in the Newfoundland fisheries and laid it down that New England was to trade only with Great Britain, Ireland, and the British West Indies. In so far as Newfoundland was concerned, the intent of the two Acts taken together was to build up the Bank fishery carried on from England, to weaken the resident fishery, and to cut the commercial ties between New England and Newfoundland. Regarded in this light, the Acts formed a counterpart to the Quebec Act; they were designed to check the expansion of the Atlantic colonies to the northeast, just as the Quebec Act was designed to check their expansion to the west.

Although Palliser's Act did encourage some expansion in the Bank fishery, it had no serious repercussions on settlement in Newfoundland and its effects were in any case overshadowed by the changes which accompanied the American Revolution. After 1776 Newfoundland was completely cut off from the American provisions which had previously been imported to feed her population and supply the fisheries. To some extent the loss of American supplies was made good by shipments from Britain, Nova Scotia, and the West Indies, but these were not sufficient to prevent a serious rise in prices. The population of the island fell slightly during the Revolution and the number of byeboatkeepers was drastically reduced. The Bank fishery on the whole flourished, despite losses to American privateers, for the temporary exclusion of American shipments brought good prices in European markets.

The conclusion of the War of Independence raised two issues of great importance for Newfoundland. The first related to American and French rights in the British North Atlantic fisheries, and the second to trade between Newfoundland and the United States. Regarding the first issue, the Treaty of Versailles stated that Americans were to continue to enjoy unmolested the right to fish in the in-shore waters of British possessions in North America as well as on the Banks and in the Gulf of St. Lawrence, and that they should be permitted to dry and cure fish on any unsettled parts of the coasts of Nova Scotia, the Magdalen Islands, and Labrador (but not Newfoundland). The French, under the terms of the Treaty, retained possession of the islands of St. Pierre and Miquelon, but agreed to give up their fishing rights on the east coast of Newfoundland north of Cape Bonavista in exchange for an extension of their rights on the west coast as far south as Cape Ray. These French rights were to prove the source of continual friction and were not finally extinguished until 1904.

Before the Revolution Newfoundland had obtained about half her supplies of food from Britain and half from the American colonies. Supplies obtained from Canada and Nova Scotia were negligible. There was no agriculture on the island beyond small vegetable gardens, so that the settlers were completely dependent on imports. After the end of the

Revolutionary War the English West Country merchants tried to induce the British government to prohibit entirely trade between Newfoundland and the American states, in the hope that, by reducing food imports, this would check the growth of settlement and the resident fishery. Prices on the island in 1783 and 1784 rose to such heights, however, that the governor on his own initiative permitted American supplies to be landed. When the question came before the British Parliament an act was passed which represented a compromise between free importation and the complete exclusion of American supplies which the West Country merchants demanded. Permission was granted for bread, flour, and livestock from the United States to be imported into Newfoundland, but only in British-built and British-owned ships and only if the importer had a licence from the Commissioner of Customs. This Act was originally for one year only but it was later extended and other commodities, such as tar, lumber, and pitch, were brought under the licensing scheme. In 1788, when the matter came up for reconsideration, a Regulating Act was passed which authorized the governor to continue importation from the United States when circumstances warranted it, but only in British vessels.

These statutes adhered firmly to the principle that, even if American supplies were admitted into Newfoundland, they should not be carried in American ships. The essential object of the Navigation Acts—the monopoly of the carrying-trade—was thereby preserved. But it was by no means easy in practice to prevent the Americans from shipping directly to Newfoundland, for the Treaty of 1783 had granted them access to the in-shore fisheries, and the coastline, with its many small bays and inlets, was admirably suited for smuggling. No matter what laws might be placed on the statute books, cheap American foodstuffs were still essential to the resident fishery. The governor of the island estimated in 1807 that 90 per cent of the molasses consumed in Newfoundland came originally from the French West Indies and was smuggled in by way of the United States. And skilled fishermen continued to leave Newfoundland in American ships to escape debt or in the hope of earning better wages in New England.

The British government's attempt to limit the importation of American supplies and its attempt to check the expansion of the resident fishery were two aspects of the same policy. It was clear that settlement on the island could not flourish without cheap food imports. Any measure, therefore, which restricted imports of American foodstuffs would handicap the resident fishery and benefit the West Country fishing-ships. This traditional policy of discouraging settlement was followed after 1783 just as it had been earlier, despite the increasing urgency with which Newfoundland merchants and their allies in Britain demanded that interests other than those of the West Country ports be given due recognition.

In 1785 these merchants succeeded in having introduced into the

House of Commons a bill which demanded, in effect, that Newfoundland be granted the rights of a British colony. Among other things, they sought to have repealed those clauses of Palliser's Act which made it compulsory for fishermen to return to England at the end of each season, and they requested that persons resident on the island should be permitted to own parts of the shore line as private property. The latter demand was a particularly delicate matter. Residents on the island had been in the habit of selling, leasing, and mortgaging real property as if they owned it. But as the island was not legally a colony, their property rights were at best highly questionable. The demand that private property in land be recognized was, in essence, a demand for colonial status.

The reaction of the British government to this move was to pass in 1786 an act which repeated with only slight modifications the restrictive regulations which had been contained in Palliser's Act. A new system of bounties to fishing-ships sailing from British ports was introduced and a few other minor changes were made. But there was no significant change in policy, and private property rights in land were not admitted. The British government was still determined to do everything in its power to prevent Newfoundland from developing as a colony. The fisheries were to be carried on by British ships sailing from British ports, not by residents on the island.

This policy was completely unworkable in view of the situation which had actually developed in Newfoundland. The falling off in the West Country fishing fleets had gone too far for the trend to be halted by backward-looking legislation. Even in years of high prices and with the added assistance of government bounties, the West Country merchants could hardly cover their costs and many of them were forced into bankruptcy. With the growth of population, the accumulation of capital, and the development of a local trading organization in Newfoundland, the resident fishers and the byeboatkeepers took over the dominant share of the fisheries. The West Country fishing-ships were more and more forced into marginal areas, such as the northern shore of Newfoundland and the Labrador coast, and into the seal and salmon fisheries.

In proposing to suppress settlement and restore the West Country fishing industry the British government was attempting to turn back the clock. Not surprisingly, the results were slight. The passing of the Act of 1786 gave a slight boost to the West Country industry, but the declining trend soon reasserted itself. The total catch of the West Country ships rose from 131,650 quintals in 1784 to 412,550 quintals in 1788, but then fell back once again to 97,815 quintals in 1789 and 160,910 in 1792. The total tonnage of the fishing-ships operating off Newfoundland was 22,535 in 1784; by 1788 the figure had risen to 34,846, but by 1792 it had fallen again to a mere 18,838. Meanwhile the total catch of the resident fishery had increased from 212,616 quintals in 1784 to

457,105 in 1788 and 395,900 in 1792, while the number of boats owned by byeboatkeepers had risen from 344 in 1784 to 583 in 1791. There were, of course, fluctuations from year to year in response to changes in prices and fishing conditions, and the statistics are probably not completely accurate, but the general trends are clear. The Newfoundland fisheries by the last decade of the eighteenth century were carried on predominantly by permanent residents on the island and by byeboatkeepers operating from shore bases by the season. The West Country fishing-ships in this period were never responsible for as much as one-half the total catch, and their share was declining.

The outbreak of war with France in 1793 accentuated these tendencies. The number of fishing-ships from England fell drastically and byeboat-keeping declined, partly because of the impressment of English seamen into the navy. But the resident fishery flourished, despite the high price of food imports and the difficulty of securing European salt. The loss of markets in Spain and Portugal was partly offset by increased exports to the United States and, especially after the passing of the American Embargo Act of 1807, to the West Indies. In general the war years were a period of considerable prosperity for local merchants and many large fortunes were accumulated; the ordinary settlers, squeezed between rising prices for foodstuffs and falling prices for dried cod, did not fare so well. The end of the war was followed by a serious depression, caused partly by the reappearance of French and American competition. By this time, however, the resident fishery in Newfoundland was firmly established and its dominance over the West Country unquestioned. The population in the meantime had increased rapidly, from just over 10,000 in 1785 to more than 35,000 in 1815. These developments were to bring, in the years after 1815, an irresistible pressure for reforms in the island's government and legal institutions. Echoes of the ancient policy of restricting settlement and encouraging the West Country fleets were still heard, but more and more they sounded like wistful imaginings of what might have been rather than serious proposals for action. By 1815 the control of the island's only industry was firmly in the hands of its inhabitants. Finally in 1824 Britain's first possession in the New World was officially recognized as a colony and eight years later it received the grant of representative government.

NOVA SCOTIA, NEW BRUNSWICK, CAPE BRETON, AND PRINCE EDWARD ISLAND

In 1784 Nova Scotia was divided up into the four new provinces of Nova Scotia, New Brunswick, Cape Breton, and Prince Edward Island. The functions which these maritime provinces were expected to perform in the new empire were, in an economic sense, much the same as their neighbour, New England, had performed in the old. They were to serve as a centre for shipping and shipbuilding, as a base for the North Atlantic fisheries, and as a source of provisions and lumber for Newfoundland and the West Indies.

In so far as their natural resources were concerned, the maritime provinces appeared well equipped to perform these functions effectively. In Nova Scotia and New Brunswick there were magnificent timber resources, including the white pine which was essential for masts and spars. The richness of the Bank and in-shore fisheries was well known. Agriculture in Nova Scotia was relatively undeveloped, except around the Bay of Fundy, while in New Brunswick it was almost non-existent. But the Loyalist settlers, almost 32,000 in number, who had sought refuge in the maritime provinces after the American Revolution would before long be in a position to produce foodstuffs for export, and in addition supplies could be obtained from Quebec. The prospects, in short, were by no means discouraging; in the new trading system which was to link together Britain's remaining possessions in the New World and bind them to the mother country, the maritime provinces were to play a vital part.

Of special importance was the expectation that Nova Scotia could take the place of New England as a source of supplies for the British West Indies. The British government was at first inclined to prohibit trade between the United States and the West Indies entirely, even in British ships, but this was soon recognized to be impossible. The West Indies plantations had to be supplied somehow, and in 1783 the American states still provided the only convenient source of foodstuffs and lumber. Regulations were therefore issued which permitted British (but not American) ships to carry lumber, livestock, flour, grain, staves, and all kinds of naval stores from American ports to the West Indies. The long-run intention was to build up two great triangles of trade. The first was to be between Britain, the United States, and the West Indies. Manufactured goods would be exported to the United States in British ships. These ships would then take on cargoes of lumber and foodstuffs in American ports and carry them to the West Indies. Then they would take cargoes of tropical products back to Britain. The second triangle was to be between Britain, Nova Scotia, and the West Indies. Foodstuffs and lumber would be exported from Nova Scotia to the West Indies; rum, sugar, and molasses would then be taken to Britain, and manufactured goods brought back to Nova Scotia. These "long-haul" shipments would give employment to British ships and seamen, keep the carrying-trade out of foreign hands, and insure that the West Indies plantations were fully supplied with the cheap foodstuffs they needed.

Eventually, it was expected, foodstuffs and lumber from the British colonies would take the place of American supplies in the West Indies market. Small quantities of grain had been exported from Acadia during the French regime and there seemed no obvious reason why, now that the province had a much larger population, these exports should not become larger and more regular. To be sure, in the first few years after 1783 imports of foodstuffs from the United States would be indispensable. This was to be expected, for most of the newly arrived Loyalists were city folk and unaccustomed to dirtying their hands with the crude toil of pioneer agriculture. But these were transitional difficulties; there were few who doubted that before long Nova Scotia would be able to feed her own population and produce a surplus for export.

The situation began to be more disturbing when, long after the problems of Loyalist settlement had been disposed of, Nova Scotia continued to be a net importer of foodstuffs from the United States. Prince Edward Island alone among the four maritime colonies attained self-sufficiency in agricultural produce. The other three were from the start dependent on American supplies and became increasingly so as time went on. The principal reasons for this failure to become self-supporting in food were, first, that lumbering and the fisheries attracted men away from farming, and, secondly, that foodstuffs could be imported cheaply and easily from the American states. Most of those who did take up farming as a full-time occupation concentrated on cattle-raising, which required less man-power than wheat-growing. In these circumstances, hopes of excluding American produce from the West Indies grew dim.

Progress in lumbering and shipbuilding also was at first slower than had been anticipated. Between 1783 and 1790 many sawmills were built near the harbours and the larger streams, several shipments were sent to the Caribbean, and for a while the prospects of the lumbering industry seemed bright. But soon the more easily accessible stands of timber had been cut down and operations had to be pushed farther and farther inland, away from natural transportation facilities. Costs immediately began to rise and before long timber merchants in New Brunswick and Nova Scotia found themselves unable to compete with American prices. In addition, neither Nova Scotia nor New Brunswick possessed resources of white oak; consequently they could not meet the demands of the West Indies planters for staves, which were indispensable for the manufacture of casks and barrels. After 1790 occasional cargoes of lumber and staves were still sent to the West Indies but mostly they were American in origin, smuggled into the provinces so that they could be shipped to the Caribbean in British vessels. Exports to Britain, in this period, were negligible. The principal limiting factors in development were the absence of good roads and natural waterways in the interior and the scarcity of capital.

The lumber industry did not again enjoy prosperity until after 1809. In that year the British government imposed high duties on foreign timber imported into Britain. Colonial timber was admitted free so that the colonies enjoyed a large tariff preference. The intention of this legislation was to safeguard the timber supplies of the Royal Navy. New sources of supply were to be developed in North America so that Britain would not be crippled by the loss of Baltic supplies which then seemed imminent as a result of Napoleon's conquests and his alliance with Russia. This tariff preference was doubled in 1810 and increased again in 1811 and 1812 to a level which much more than compensated for the higher costs of transport from North America. The result was an unprecedented boom in the lumber industry, in Upper and Lower Canada as well as in the Maritimes. Many leading British importing firms previously connected with the Baltic trade now turned their attention to North America, received large contracts from the British government, and invested their capital in the cutting and shipping of colonial timber. Shipping tonnage employed in the North American timber trade rose from 21,782 in 1802 to 91,660 in 1807, 110,759 in 1814, and 340,537 in 1819.

Shipbuilding had been an important industry in the colonies before the American Revolution. Not only did it provide the facilities for inter-colonial trade; it also furnished colonial merchants with a means of earning sterling. To send a ship to Britain with a cargo and sell both ship and cargo on arrival had been a very convenient way to pay for American imports, especially since shipbuilding costs were as much as 30 per cent lower in the colonies than they were in Britain. For the same reasons it was to be expected that shipbuilding would be one of the first industries to develop in Nova Scotia and New Brunswick. The need to rebuild the British merchant fleet, seriously weakened by the loss of American shipping, provided an added stimulus. Within a few years after 1783 ship-yards were in operation in every important harbour of the maritime provinces. By 1796 no less than ninety-three square-rigged ships had been built in New Brunswick alone, not to mention seventy-one sloops and schooners. Most of these ships were sold in Britain. For the coasting and West Indies trade the type usually built was the schooner of between 150 and 200 tons, a type which was easier to handle in narrow waters than a square-rigged ship and which required a smaller crew.

In the opinion of some British observers the ships built in the maritime provinces in this period were crudely designed and built of inferior materials. The splendid reputation of the Nova Scotia schooner was not acquired until a later date. Nevertheless, for the first few years after 1783 demand was brisk and the shipyards of the colonies were kept busy. After 1791 development followed a more erratic course. The outbreak of war with France in 1793 was followed by a short but hectic boom and then by a period of slack activity. During the remainder of the period up to 1815 high material and labour costs kept the industry generally depressed, but there were occasional periods of considerable prosperity, as for instance during the short interval of peace after the Treaty of Amiens (1802) and after the passing of the Embargo Act by the American government in 1807.

The fishing industry of the maritime colonies increased rapidly during and immediately after the American Revolution, particularly in Nova Scotia and Cape Breton. The coming of the Loyalists meant both a larger local market and a larger resident labour force. At first the fishery was carried on mostly in small boats and was confined to in-shore waters. The boats would stay at sea for one or two days only, and their catch was intended principally for local consumption. By the first decade of the nineteenth century, however, Nova Scotia fishermen were using larger boats and were taking from half to two-thirds of their catch off the coast of Labrador and in the Gulf of St. Lawrence. Cod was still the mainstay of the industry, but large quantities of mackerel, herring, and salmon were also caught.

The prosperity of the industry hinged on the availability of markets and cheap supplies. Developments in the fisheries were therefore closely linked to changes in Nova Scotia's trading position. The imperial legislation which governed the admission of American produce to the West Indies and to Nova Scotia profoundly influenced the expansion of the Nova Scotia fisheries, as did wars in Europe and the competition of American and Newfoundland fish in the markets of the Mediterranean.

The exclusion of American shipping from the West Indies after 1783 contributed directly to the growth of the fishing industry in Nova Scotia and to the forging of commercial connections between the two areas. Ships took fish to the West Indies and either returned directly to Nova Scotia with salt, molasses, and rum, or else put in at American ports to pick up cargoes of flour, corn, and other foodstuffs. Since the ships were built and the voyages organized "on shares", men with very little capital could engage in this trade, and every settlement along the coast had at least one or two vessels sailing to the West Indies. This combination of maritime trade and the fisheries encouraged in Nova Scotia a type of commercial development very similar to that which had characterized New England. Almost every able-bodied man was engaged in commerce of some kind. The scattering of settlements and harbours along the coast, combined with the relatively low cost of the basic unit of enterprise—the trading- or fishing-ship—meant that no single place or group dominated the economic life of the province. Halifax was, however, the most important commercial centre, because it was the port where most of the imports from England were landed.

Trade with the West Indies would certainly have been larger and more profitable if Nova Scotia had been able to develop a surplus of agricultural products for export. But this was not the only handicap. Nova Scotia merchants, partly through inexperience and partly because certain import- ant items, such as oak for staves, were not available, had difficulty making up suitable cargoes for the Caribbean market. Perishable commodities such as flour, fresh provisions, and livestock tended to spoil on the long voyage; the middle and southern Atlantic states had an important advantage in their ability to ship such cargoes quickly and regularly. The result of these difficulties was that trade relations between Nova Scotia, the United States, and the West Indies developed along lines very different from those which had been planned in the years following the Revolution. A triangular trade did develop, but it was a triangle by which Nova Scotia imported provisions, foodstuffs, and West Indian goods from the United States and paid for these imports by selling fish to American merchants. Direct trade between Nova Scotia and the West Indies tended to decrease, while indirect trade by way of the United States increased.

This was particularly true after 1793. The outbreak of war between Britain and France sent marine insurance rates in Nova Scotia 10 to 12½ per cent above those payable by neutral shippers in the United States. At the same time the governors of the West Indies islands were given authority to admit American produce in American ships when, in their opinion, circumstances warranted it. By this step the Navigation Acts were, in effect, suspended and American merchants were granted free access to the British West Indies. The result was a period of great prosperity for American, particularly New England, shipping. The total tonnage of American ships entering American ports from the British West Indies jumped to 58,989 in the year ending September 30, 1794, as compared with an average of only 4,461 in the three previous years. In these circumstances, Nova Scotia merchants found that it paid better to sell their fish in the United States for export to the West Indies in American ships than to export directly to the West Indies from Nova Scotia in British ships.

By 1804 direct trade between Nova Scotia and the West Indies had practically ceased. If the concessions granted to American shipping had been withdrawn, this trade would certainly have revived speedily. But instead of cancelling or diminishing the privileges which had been granted, the British government seemed on the verge of concluding a commercial treaty with the United States which would have made them permanent. Against this proposal the colonial merchants and their agents in London protested vigorously. They had on their side all the well-worn arguments which had for so many years been used to defend and justify the Navigation Acts; all that they asked for was the commercial preference and protection to which, as they believed, their allegiance to Britain entitled them. But their protests had little effect. To be sure, certain of the regulations were tightened up. The West Indies governors, for example, were instructed to admit American commodities only at times of real and great necessity, and only if Britain or the British North American colonies could not provide the necessary goods. Certain anomalous duties which favoured American as against colonial shippers were removed, and some of the West Indies islands even gave small bounties on imports of colonial fish. But beyond these minor changes nothing was done to offset the disadvantages under which the northern colonies laboured. Britain was fighting for her life against Napoleon and was disinclined to insist that the Navigation Acts be enforced to the letter, especially when American shipping was involved. And the West Indies planters, although their political power in England was already on the wane, were still influential enough to insure that their need for cheap American foodstuffs was not forgotten by imperial policy-makers.

Assistance for the northern colonies came from an unexpected quarter: the United States government. In December, 1807, the American Congress passed the Embargo Act, a measure which, with certain supplementary legislation, prohibited all commerce whatsoever out of American ports. In intention at least this was an act of retaliation against Britain and France. Just over a year before, Napoleon had issued the Berlin Decree, which declared that the British Isles were in a state of blockade and that there should be no commerce between Britain and neutral nations. The British government responded with a series of orders in council which prohibited neutrals from trading directly with ports which excluded British ships. Since the principal neutral carrier by this time was the United States, these measures, if enforced, were certain to do severe damage to American trade. Tension between the United States and Britain was heightened at this critical juncture by an incident in which four alleged deserters were forcibly taken off an American vessel by a ship of the British Navy. Thomas Jefferson, who was then president of the United States, believing that the services of American shipping were indispensable to the belligerents, decided to enforce greater respect for American rights on the high seas by keeping every American ship in harbour. The Embargo Act, a singularly ill-advised piece of legislation, was the result.

No British legislation short of a declaration of war could possibly have done as much harm to American shipping as did the Embargo Act. This was particularly obvious in the case of the West Indies trade. All the protests, petitions, and complaints of the Nova Scotia merchants and British shipbuilders had not been able to keep American shipping from trading with the British colonies in the Caribbean. Now the American Congress had performed that service for them.

This, then, was the opportunity for which the merchants of Nova Scotia and New Brunswick had waited. They were not slow to respond. Within less than a year British North American ports were handling more ships than was the whole of the United States, and most of these ships were carrying cargoes destined for the Caribbean. Imports into the maritime colonies for re-export to the Caribbean increased rapidly. In the summer of 1808 the governors of Nova Scotia and New Brunswick, acting on their own initiative, had authorized the admission of certain enumerated goods in either British or American ships, when these goods were intended for re-export to the West Indies. This action was later ratified by the British government. The Embargo Act was highly unpopular in New England and an active smuggling trade developed, cargoes being exchanged at sea, or carried across the frontier overland, or even brought directly into British ports by American ships, in defiance of their own government. These American imports, combined with British colonial produce, added up to a total volume of trade which made it possible for the West Indies to be supplied without undue difficulty. The merchants of the northern colonies had, it seemed, made good their claim that, if only American shipping were excluded, they could supply the West Indies themselves.

With minor modifications this state of affairs persisted up to and after the outbreak of war between Britain and the United States in 1812. The Embargo Act, which had forbidden American trade with all foreign countries, was repealed in 1809, but, as far as trade with France and Britain was concerned, the Nonintercourse Act which was passed in its place imposed even stricter prohibitions. Napoleon withdrew his restrictions on neutral shipping in August, 1810, and thereafter the Nonintercourse Act was applied against Britain only. The British government in the meantime interposed no serious obstacle to the busy and profitable trade which had grown up between the northern colonies and New England. In the summer of 1809, certainly, a proclamation was issued which confined the import trade of Nova Scotia and New Brunswick to British ships, but this seems to have been no more than a gesture and there is no evidence that any real difficulties were placed in the way of American shippers. Even this nominal restriction was removed in 1811, when permission was given for certain important products—wheat, bread, biscuit, flour, pitch, tar, and turpentine—to be landed at three designated ports in the maritime colonies (Halifax, St. Andrews, and Saint John) in ships of any nationality except French. These arrangements were continued until 1815.

For the maritime colonies as a whole the period from 1808 to 1815 was one of remarkable economic expansion. At the beginning of the period Nova Scotia and New Brunswick were hardly more than names on the map. Their settlements and towns were, for the most part, primitive pioneer communities, where men considered themselves fortunate if they could make enough from farming or the fisheries to support themselves and their families. By the end of the period the harbours and towns of the colonies were among the busiest and most prosperous of the Atlantic seaboard. Fortunes were being made and capital was being accumulated. Nova Scotia and New Brunswick had established themselves as active members of the North Atlantic trading system. Their merchants and ship captains had acquired the skill, experience, and confidence which, before many years had passed, would enable them to challenge the supremacy of New England.

Except in the case of the lumber industry, this burst of development was not stimulated to any large extent by the commercial preferences which the maritime colonies received from Britain, nor did it result from the maturing of any long-term plans for imperial integration. It resulted rather from a highly unique conjuncture of circumstances, involving positive miscalculations in American foreign policy, which dislocated the normal patterns of trade and temporarily cancelled out the advantages of competing supply areas, particularly New England. Over the whole period with which we have been dealing, indeed, the development of New Brunswick and Nova Scotia was affected less by deliberate policies looking toward the consolidation of Britain's remaining empire than it was by measures of temporary expediency adopted to meet the exigencies of war and preparation for war. It was not so much as a consequence of the spread of free-trade theories that the years after 1793 saw one concession after another made to American commercial interests, but rather because of the compromises which Britain, in the interests of national survival, was forced to make in the traditional policies to which, in theory, most of her statesmen still adhered. The old empire which had broken up in 1776 had never in fact been as closely integrated as mercantilist theory had demanded. The new empire which began to coalesce after 1783 was from the start a creation, not of mercantilism, but of compromises with mercantilism.

THE OLD PROVINCE OF QUEBEC

The province of Quebec as it existed in the years immediately before the American Revolution was a very much larger political unit than the province which bears that name today. According to the Quebec Act of 1774 it included the whole of Labrador to the east, while to the north it extended as far as the height of land which marked the limit of Rupert's Land, or the Hudson's Bay Company's territories. Its southern boundary followed the right bank of the St. Lawrence above Montreal and the southern shore of Lake Ontario and Lake Erie; then it skirted the western boundary of Pennsylvania until it reached the Ohio, followed that river as far as its junction with the Mississippi, and then followed the Mississippi northwest to its source. The old province of Quebec included, in short, an immense stretch of territory in the interior, extending far beyond the boundaries of the Canada of today.

The American Revolution had two immediate consequences for the province of Quebec. Firstly, it stripped the province of most of its vast hinterland. The peace settlement of 1783 laid down a boundary in the interior which left the colony on the St. Lawrence no more than a small fraction of the territory to which it had formerly laid claim. The same boundary, only slightly modified by later events, has determined the limits of present-day Canada east of the Rockies. Between Montreal and the Atlantic there was, to be sure, little change. The boundary was to follow the St. Croix River from its estuary to its source and then head due north to the height of land which separated the rivers flowing into the Atlantic from those flowing into the St. Lawrence. Then it was to follow this height of land to the Connecticut River, pass down the river to the forty-fifth parallel, and then head due west to the St. Lawrence. These two sections of the boundary were not laid down as unambiguously as they might have been, as later disputes were to show, but at least they marked no very radical departures from past history. The first section was supposed to follow the ancient boundaries of Nova Scotia, while the second was identical with the corresponding section as defined in the Quebec Act. West of Montreal, however, the situation was very different. In this area the boundary passed through the middle of the St. Lawrence-Great Lakes water system as far as the northwest corner of Lake Superior. Then the line was supposed to head straight west until it met the Mississippi.

Today we are so accustomed to think of a line very close to this as forming the Canadian-American boundary that it is a little difficult to appreciate the immense loss of territory which the peace settlement of 1783 entailed and to grasp how profoundly it affected and constrained the whole future development of Canada. None of the territory between the Ohio, the Great Lakes, and the Mississippi had actually been captured and held by the Americans during the war; when negotiations for peace began, British military control of the area was undisputed. In so far as trade was concerned, even the American negotiators admitted that this region was much more accessible from the St. Lawrence than from the states of the Atlantic seaboard. Why then was this vast area, which in later years was to prove so rich in resources and so strategically located in the continental economy, given up so readily? The reason seems to have been partly ignorance. The British government was not well informed as to the commercial value of the territory which was ceded; even the Montreal fur-traders, who might have been expected to make their opinions heard, were not consulted during the negotiations nor permitted to present their case until the matter was already decided. In addition there was a definite inclination on the part of many members of the British Parliament and ministry to make a generous peace with the Americans in the hope of winning them away from their European allies, and this inclination the American diplomats skilfully exploited. It was anticipated, too, that the treaty of peace would be accompanied by a later commercial treaty which would guarantee, among other things, that British and American citizens would have free access to the territory in the interior on either side of the boundary for purposes of trade. This commercial treaty was never actually signed, partly because British shipping interests opposed the revision of the Navigation Acts which certain of its clauses would have entailed. But it was only on the understanding that the boundary in the interior would be, as it were, non-existent from a commercial point of view that the British government accepted it.

Even in the light of these explanations, however, the question may well be raised whether the cession of the territory south of the Lakes was indispensable to the conclusion of a tolerable peace, and whether perhaps some less open-handed concessions of territory might not, with more determined bargaining, have proved acceptable to the Americans. The full implications of the boundary settlement were not to become evident until many years later, when Canada's railways were searching for a route to the west, but even in 1783 the loss was recognized as severe. To many Canadians the treaty of 1783 has seemed the first if not the only example of the readiness with which British governments, in the hope of gaining American good will, have sacrificed Canadian interests.

The area which had been given up by the treaty was not actually evacuated immediately, for the fur-traders of Montreal clung desperately to the hope that the boundary agreement might be revised, and the British government, belatedly conscious of the implications of the new line, found excuses to retain the western posts. Not until the signing of Jay's Treaty in 1794 were the British garrisons withdrawn. And those whose fortunes were most closely linked to the development of the St. Lawrence economy —the Montreal merchants—did not quite give up hope of regaining the lost territory south of the Great Lakes until after the War of 1812, when the Treaty of Ghent reaffirmed the boundary. Even after that the dream of controlling commercially the lands which had been lost politically continued for more than half a century to influence their plans and projects. Quebec's former greatness was never quite forgotten; the belief that the St. Lawrence River was in some sense the natural and proper avenue for the commerce of the west exercised an enduring influence upon the development of the Canadian economy and has in fact persisted as an important element in the formation of policy until the present day.

The second major consequence of the Revolution was the coming of the Loyalists, which gave to the old province of Quebec, if we except small groups of merchants and officials, its first English-speaking population. There were at least 5,500 of these Loyalists—more if we include demobilized British troops. The precise number is uncertain because no accurate count was taken of those who reached the western part of the province over land and it is not easy to say precisely when the Loyalist arrivals (in the strict sense of the term) ceased and the later American immigration began. For the most part they were a different social type from the Loyalists who had gone to the maritime provinces or to England. Many of them were experienced farmers from the back country of New York, Pennsylvania, and New Jersey, and they brought with them the accumulated "know-how" of generations of frontier agriculture. In this respect they were undoubtedly the most useful type of immigrant the province could possibly have received at this time.

Some of the Loyalists who came to the St. Lawrence settled in the eastern sections of the province of Quebec, on the Bay of Chaleur and at Gaspé, and at various places where there already was a French-speaking population, such as Sorel. Most of them, however, found their new homes in what is now the province of Ontario, particularly on the north shore of the St. Lawrence between Montreal and Kingston, on the Bay of Quinté, and in the Niagara peninsula. In the first few years after their arrival they received assistance in various forms from the British government. Fifty acres of land were given free of charge to each unmarried civilian Loyalist and one hundred to the head of a family, together with fifty for each of his dependants. Former members of Loyalist regiments received larger grants, ranging from one hundred acres for a private to five hundred for a subaltern and one thousand for a former field officer. Rations were provided without charge until the end of 1786, together with essential clothing and a small stock of seed grain and agricultural implements. Grist mills were built at Niagara and Kingston and the settler's grain was ground at government expense. This assistance, together with their previous experience of frontier farming, enabled most of the Loyalists to get their farms into production by the fall of 1786. The fact that most of the settlers had been comrades in arms and were accustomed to military discipline gave the new settlements considerable strength and solidarity.

THE ESTABLISHMENT OF UPPER CANADA

The demands of these Loyalists for the laws and social institutions with which they were familiar, particularly for representative government, led the British government to conclude that it was inadvisable to maintain under the same political jurisdiction both the French in the lower parts of the province and the newly-arrived English-speaking settlers. In 1791, therefore, two new provinces were created, called Upper and Lower Canada, the boundary between them being roughly the same as the boundary between Ontario and Quebec today. The formation of Upper Canada represented something of an innovation in British imperial practice, for it was the first British colony to be without a seaport. It was anticipated, however, that Montreal would serve as the seaport and distributing centre for the upper province, even though it was actually in Lower Canada, and with this end in view the Constitutional Act of 1791 reserved to the imperial government the authority to regulate trade between the two provinces. The fact that Upper Canada had no access to the sea except through Lower Canada, however, was to have profound implications in later years, particularly on government fiscal and transportation policy.

The presence of the Loyalists and their descendants left a distinct imprint on the social and political life of Upper Canada—one which can still be detected today. In terms of numbers, however, it was not many years before members of Loyalist families formed a minority of the total population. The reason lay in the large immigration from the United States which began soon after 1790 and continued until the outbreak of war in 1812. There are no reliable statistics for this American immigration. In 1812, however, a contemporary writer estimated that 80 per cent of the population of Upper Canada were of American birth or descent, only one-quarter of these being Loyalists and their children. The Loyalist element in the population was, in short, considerably outnumbered by 1812.

This differs markedly from the situation in Nova Scotia, where Loyalist families continued to be for many years the dominant element in the population. This contrast, with its profound consequences for the economic, political, and intellectual development of the two provinces, is to be explained mainly by differences in geographic location. Nova Scotia was relatively isolated from large-scale population movements once the original influx of Loyalists had ended; immigration into the province from Britain did not become large until after 1815. Upper Canada, on the other hand, was situated across one of the principal migration routes from the Atlantic seaboard to the rich lands of the Ohio and upper Mississippi valleys. The western part of the province in particular served as a kind of thoroughfare for the thousands of Americans who began moving west around 1800. Many of the Americans who entered Upper Canada at Niagara left the province again at Detroit, but others remained in British territory and the western part of the province soon came to have a distinctively American character.

It must not be imagined that the Americans who settled in Upper Canada were attracted by the virtues of British colonial government. Possibly this was a factor in a few cases, but for most of the American immigrants Upper Canada seemed a good place in which to settle because the land was fertile and freely granted, because the Indians were not hostile (in contrast to the situation on the American side of the line), and because it was conveniently reached from the valleys of the Hudson and the Mohawk, the avenues by which most of those who started out from New England and New York to reach the west crossed the Appalachian barrier. Nationalist sentiment and a preference for this form of government over that was a very minor factor, during these years at least, in determining the direction of population movement. Cheap land was a much more important consideration.

Land was cheap in Upper Canada because the provincial government made very generous grants, not only to Loyalists, but also to other immigrants. Particularly after the arrival of the province's first lieutenant-governor, John Graves Simcoe, an active policy of encouraging American immigration was followed, and land grants, made almost without cost to the recipient, were a prominent feature of that policy. As a rule, two hundred acres were granted to each immigrant who applied, paid the necessary fees, and took the oath of allegiance. It was by no means uncommon, however, for larger grants to be made to persons who had large families or who for one reason or another appeared able to keep a larger area under cultivation. For a time after 1792 Simcoe experimented with what was called the "leader and associates" system; this involved making a large grant to one or two individuals who promised to bring in settlers to occupy the lands granted. Most of these "leaders", however, turned out to be land speculators who were more interested in holding on to their grants in the hope of making a profit by selling them at some future date than in bringing in settlers, and the system was therefore abandoned.

The land-grant policy of the provincial government seems, in general, to have been quite effective in encouraging immigration. But it had other less desirable effects. In particular it led to extensive speculation, because grants were made far more rapidly than the land was actually settled. The original Loyalist grants had been relatively free from this tendency, but free grants were also made to the children of Loyalists as soon as they came of age, to retired officers of the army and navy, and to leading members of the executive government. Many of these later grants were not occupied or settled but held instead as speculations, in the hope that some day, as the surrounding territory filled up and developed, they would be worth large sums of money.

It is undeniable that the land-granting activities of the provincial government were badly mismanaged and that there were many abuses and a certain amount of official corruption. But that the economic development of the province was retarded as a consequence of these shortcomings is by no means so evident. Most historians who have looked into the question in recent years are inclined to believe that land speculation and abuses in land granting, however important they may have been as causes of political discontent and sources of popular resentment, did not significantly retard the process of settlement, at least before 1815. This conclusion probably applies even to the highly controversial Crown and

Clergy Reserves, the sections of land—amounting to two-sevenths of each township—which were held back from settlement to provide funds for the support of the government and the Protestant clergy.

If this is correct, we may safely conclude that the expansion ot the area of agricultural settlement in Upper Canada depended directly on the rate of immigration. It was the steady flow of immigrants from the United States which, more than any other single factor, set the pace for the development of Upper Canada in the period before 1812. Of course there was inevitably an interval between the time when an immigrant secured his land and the time when he first had a surplus of agricultural produce for sale. The length of this time-lag depended upon several factors: his skill as a farmer, the amount of capital he brought with him, the locality in which he chose to settle, and so on. Most important of all, it depended upon whether there was an effective demand for his produce. And this in turn depended upon the existence of markets and transportation facilities.

In these respects the settlers in Upper Canada had several advantages. At a time when roads were almost non-existent, the Great Lakes and the St. Lawrence provided a cheap and convenient means of transportation. Good markets were available, too, in the critical early years. As a matter of deliberate policy, the government had located the original Loyalist settlements near the military posts at Montreal, Kingston, Niagara, and Detroit, so that the garrisons could be provisioned in part at least by local produce. These military markets were especially important because they were one of the few means the settler had of obtaining cash. Furthermore, he could be sure of getting a good price for his flour, for the government paid, at each post in Upper Canada, the price for which flour was selling in Lower Canada plus most of the expense which would have been involved in transporting it upriver from Lachine. The fur trade, too, was a source of demand for foodstuffs, for few of the western posts produced more than a fraction of their own requirements and it was to the advantage of fur-traders to purchase what they needed in Upper Canada rather than carry it upstream from Montreal. And lastly, for a few years after 1796 the American settlements which were slowly growing up south of Lake Ontario and Lake Erie purchased sizable amounts of foodstuffs from Upper Canada, for settlement in this area lagged behind progress in the British province. The early Loyalist immigration, together with the fact that the British did not evacuate the posts south of the Lakes until 1796, meant that Upper Canada had, for once, a lead in development of several years over western New York.

These markets in the interior made possible an unusually rapid transition in Upper Canada from a stage of almost complete self-sufficiency to a stage when relatively large quantities of foodstuffs were available for sale. Within three years of the formation of the province the merchants and farmers of Upper Canada were seeking outside markets. Exports of agricultural produce down the St. Lawrence seem to have begun in 1794, when 12,823 bushels of wheat were consigned to Montreal along with small quantities of flour, and to have increased rapidly in volume after 1800. These shipments marked the beginning of a trade which was to be the mainstay of Upper Canada's economy for the next three-quarters of a century. The markets in the interior were important advantages in the early years, for they saved the farmer the heavy expense of shipping his produce downriver to Montreal, but they were short-lived and limited in capacity. The American settlements south of the Lakes had ceased importing foodstuffs from Upper Canada by 1800; the fur trade and the military garrisons could absorb only a small fraction of the growing quantities of agricultural produce which were seeking a market. It was the export trade in wheat and flour down the St. Lawrence that held the key to Upper Canada's future.

The demand for Upper Canada wheat and flour in Montreal was derived from the demand for food imports in Britain. Ordinarily the British protective tariff embodied in the Corn Laws, together with heavy transport costs on the Atlantic crossing, made it unprofitable to ship foodstuffs from North America to Britain. In the ten years or so after 1800, however, a series of bad harvests in Britain and the occasional interruption of supplies from the Baltic countries during the Napoleonic Wars made the Corn Laws inoperative, and there developed, in consequence, a strong demand for Upper Canada breadstuffs. The return of more normal conditions of supply in 1815 was to mean, for a time, the disappearance of this demand, but for the present it provided a strong stimulus to trade and agriculture in the upper province. The West Indies also provided a market for Upper Canada wheat and flour but, as we have seen, American competition in this area was severe.

To handle this trade in foodstuffs, every established settlement in Upper Canada had at least one resident merchant. Very often he owned a flour mill and usually also a store where he sold the hardware, textiles, and spices which the settlers could not provide for themselves. Several of the more important of these merchants—men like Richard Cartwright at Kingston and Robert Hamilton at Niagara—had originally set themselves up in business by becoming contractors to the army garrisons and suppliers to the fur trade. All of them carried on business with the aid of credit from Montreal firms, for whom they acted, in fact if not in law, as purchasing and distributing agents. Some of them became rich, by the standards of the time, although their wealth was more likely to take the form of land grants, taken in payment of debts, than of money.

The merchants of Upper Canada were, as a group, little liked by the settlers, for they were the only source of credit in the province and inevitably the settlers tended to get into debt to them. There were no banks at this time to supply paper money and the coins in circulation were of many different nationalities and usually in very poor condition. To make up for this lack of a circulating medium and to facilitate their own business transactions, many of the merchants issued their own notes, which were called "bons". Though certainly better than no circulating medium at all, the merchants' notes had serious drawbacks. If the settler for some reason wished to obtain legal tender, the merchant would give him, not the full nominal value of the notes he offered in exchange, but considerably less. And of course, if the merchant happened to go bankrupt, the notes he had issued became worthless.

But despite these characteristic difficulties of a pioneer economy, Upper Canada had by 1812 made very considerable progress. Along the northern shore of Lake Ontario there now stretched an almost unbroken chain of settlements, which in some places, to be sure, extended no farther back than the first concession line, but elsewhere, as in the Niagara peninsula, extended several miles inland from the lake-shore. North of Lake Erie, too, there were flourishing communities in the valleys of the Thames and Grand Rivers, along Dundas Street, and in the Talbot settlement. An export trade in wheat and flour had got under way and the transition to a commercial economy, at least in the older settlements and those most accessible to water transportation, was well advanced. The difficulties which lay ahead, once the immediate danger of American invasion was passed, were serious, but they were difficulties of growth, not of mere survival.

In Lower Canada, meanwhile, the English-speaking commercial group which had moved in at the time of the conquest was growing in size, wealth, and political influence. By 1812 the business men who made up this group were of three principal types: the fur-traders, the export-import merchants, and the timber merchants. The first of them to arrive had been the sutlers and army contractors who, arriving with the victorious British forces, were quick to appreciate the opportunities for profit which the opening up of the St. Lawrence to British capital had created. Some of these army contractors, like Alexander Henry, turned to the fur trade almost immediately. Hard on their heels came some of the most experienced and enterprising of the Albany firms—Phyn, Ellice & Company, who moved their base of operations to Quebec in 1770, Peter Pond, Simon McTavish, and several others. After 1784, when the new Loyalist settlements began to appear on the St. Lawrence above Montreal and north of Lake Ontario, the export-import firms grew in importance. Such firms were usually partnerships and made their profit from exporting the wheat, flour, and potash which came down the St. Lawrence from Upper Canada and importing manufactured goods from England for sale in the new settlements. After 1807 a new group of entrepreneurs appeared on the scene: the timber merchants who financed and organized the export of square timber to England, under the shelter of tariff preferences, for use in the construction industry.

Such were, in these early years, the main components of the Montreal commercial community. The history of the St. Lawrence economy during the next three-quarters of a century is largely the story of the successes and failures, the achievements and disappointments, of this relatively small group of men. In spite of their small numbers, and in spite of the fact that they were, so to speak, isolated in the midst of an unsympathetic French-Canadian culture, they were able to exert a profound influence on government policy, because they were persistent, knew exactly what they wanted, and could make their demands known, both in Canada and, through their business connections, in England. What they wanted in the period before 1812 was, first, political power in Canada, and second, freedom to expand the boundaries of their trading system in the interior. How they achieved the first of these objectives does not directly concern us here. Their struggle to achieve the second is best told in connection with the two staple trades which, in this period, made the commercial empire of the St. Lawrence a reality: the fur trade, and the trade in square timber.

SUGGESTIONS FOR FURTHER READING

BASIC WORKS:

Graham, Gerald S., *Sea Power and British North America, 1783-1820: a Study in British Colonial Policy* (Cambridge, Mass., 1941), Chapters I-XVI, pp. 3-278

Innis, Harold A., *The Cod Fisheries: the History of an International Economy* (Toronto and New Haven, 1940), Chapters VII-X, pp. 183-322

Jones, Robert L., *History of Agriculture in Ontario, 1613-1880* (Toronto, 1948) Chapters I and II, pp. 1-35

SUPPLEMENTARY WORKS:

Benns, F. Lee, *The American Struggle for the British West India Carrying-Trade, 1815-1830* (Bloomington, Indiana, 1923), Chapter I, pp. 7-28

Brebner, J. Bartlet, *North Atlantic Triangle: the Interplay of Canada, the United States, and Great Britain* (Toronto and New Haven, 1945), Chapters IV and V, pp. 46-87

Burt, Alfred L., *The Old Province of Quebec* (Toronto, 1933), Chapter XV, pp. 357-99

Burt, Alfred L., *The United States, Great Britain, and British North America from the Revolution to the Establishment of Peace after the War of 1812* (Toronto, 1940), Chapters I-IV, pp. 1-70

Creighton, D. G., *The Commercial Empire of the St. Lawrence 1760-1850* (Toronto, 1937), Chapters I-IV, pp. 1-115

Hansen, Marcus L., and J. Bartlet Brebner, *The Mingling of the Canadian and American Peoples: Volume I, Historical* (Toronto, 1940), Chapters III and IV, pp. 43-90

PART II

ESCAPE FROM COLONIALISM

CHAPTER VIII

THE CONTINENTAL FUR TRADE AND WESTWARD EXPANSION: 1776–1821

INTRODUCTION

AFTER the conquest of Canada the St. Lawrence fur trade was taken ovei by a group of English, Scottish, and American merchants who, with credit obtained from British exporting firms, quickly rebuilt the trading system in the interior which had originally been created by the French. With the assistance of important innovations in transportation and supply, these merchants within a few years were able to extend their trade into the Athabasca region and as far west as the Rocky Mountains. The larger capital requirements which accompanied the extension of the trade to the west encouraged the formation of the North West Company, a syndicate of the more important Montreal fur-trading firms which finally suppressed all competition from the St. Lawrence. In the interior, however, the Hudson's Bay Company provided serious competition from the north and the American Fur Company from the south and later on the Pacific coast. Explorations financed by the North West Company meanwhile extended the limits of the St. Lawrence fur trade to the Mackenzie River basin in the Arctic and the Fraser and Columbia River basins on the Pacific slope. Increasingly severe competition from the Hudson's Bay Company after 1809, culminating in the attempt to establish an agricultural settlement on the Red River, led to open violence between the two organizations and finally to their amalgamation in 1821. The union of the two companies marked the end of the St. Lawrence fur trade.

RECONSTRUCTION OF THE ST. LAWRENCE FUR TRADE: THE NORTH WEST COMPANY

The fur trade west of Lake Superior as it had been carried on in the later days of the French regime did not revive until several years after the conquest. In 1761 Alexander Henry and others had traded as far west as Michilimackinac, but the danger and uncertainty which accompanied Pontiac's Rebellion, a serious Indian uprising, prevented further advance. By 1766, however, at least one French-Canadian trader had reached the Saskatchewan; within the next few years he was followed by upwards of a score of traders from Montreal, some of whom had previously been active in the fur trade at Albany. Throughout the Seven

Years' War the Indians in the west had been almost entirely deprived of European goods, except for what they could get from Hudson Bay, and the market which these Montreal traders found waiting for them was an eager one.

The Indians were at first inclined to be distrustful of these new arrivals, but the habits of trade which had been built up during the French regime soon reasserted themselves—as indeed they were bound to do, for the Indians had long since forgotten how to live without European goods. The English-speaking traders, too, took over almost without change the trading methods which the French had evolved, and relied upon French Canadians, with their indispensable knowledge of rivers and canoes, to serve as *voyageurs,* interpreters, and guides. This marriage of British capital and enterprise with French experience and ability made possible a very rapid reconstruction of the western fur trade and provided the outstanding example of co-operation between the two nationalities after the conquest.

If there were few changes in the organization of the trade in the interior, the same was not true of the trade between Montreal and Europe. The capture of Canada meant the end of the period of royal monopoly and the opening of the trade, under governmental supervision, to all British subjects. England and not France was now the market for the furs which were shipped from the St. Lawrence and the source of supply for most of the manufactured goods required for trade with the Indians. A whole new set of business connections had to be forged between Montreal and London; new sources of credit had to be found and new arrangements made for the procuring of trade goods and the marketing of furs. These changes made it very difficult for the French-Canadian merchants who had previously been interested in the fur trade to continue in that line of business, for few of them had the necessary commercial connections in England. In their place there appeared at Montreal a new group of English and Scottish firms which made it their business to supply goods on credit to fur-traders in the interior and to organize the shipping of furs to England. These firms, which typically took the form of partnerships, soon came to occupy a commanding posi tion in the St. Lawrence fur trade. Those which survived over the years did so largely because of their ability to secure credit in England when needed and their shrewdness in selecting the traders whom they would finance from year to year in the interior.

These mercantile firms and their English correspondents proved very effective spokesmen and lobbyists for the St. Lawrence fur trade. In England they managed as early as 1764 to secure the reduction of the import duty on beaver to a nominal one penny per skin. After April, 1765, a full-time lobbyist was maintained in London to represent the interests of the Montreal and Quebec traders. In Canada too they successfully resisted close government supervision of the trade and were finally successful in securing relaxation of the regulations to which they objected. After the suppression of Pontiac's Rebellion in 1763 the government had attempted, as the French had earlier, to confine the trade to military posts. Every trader was required to take out a licence and to give security that he would obey the orders of the military commander of the post where he carried on trade. Against these restrictions the merchants protested vigorously, arguing that it was ridiculous to expect the Indians to come to the military posts to trade and that the effect of the regulations would be to ruin the St. Lawrence trade and benefit the trade of New York and Albany. Their protests were at least partly responsible for the passing of the Quebec Act in 1774, which placed the whole of the fur-trading area in the interior, except Rupert's Land, under the jurisdiction of the province of Quebec. During the American Revolution regulations were issued banning all private vessels on the Great Lakes and stipulating that all private shipments should be carried in government vessels. These restrictions, too, the fur-trading firms strongly opposed, especially when they were kept in force after 1783. The government, however, fearful lest by granting permission for private individuals to operate shipping on the Lakes they might encourage illicit trade with the United States, were slow to modify their policy and it was not until 1789 that free construction and navigation of merchant vessels on all the Lakes was permitted. In these and other matters the fur-trading firms of Montreal, by constant pressure on the responsible officials, were able to secure the changes in policy which they desired.

But it was not only in political matters that the Montreal firms learned the advantages of joint action. In their business relations also they showed almost from the start a willingness to unite their separate interests and engage in joint ventures. At first co-operation went no further than a temporary agreement to suspend competition. Thus in 1775 Alexander Henry noted that four competing sets of traders on the Saskatchewan had agreed "to join their stock, and when the season was over, to divide the skins and meat". But these informal and short-lived agreements among traders in the interior were soon followed, if indeed they were not accompanied, by more permanent forms of association among the supply houses at Montreal, and as early as 1776 a loose union of partnerships had come into existence under the name of the North West Company. Probably this association was merely an agreement for a single year. This was true, in any case, of the agreement signed in 1779. By 1780, however, the firms involved were prepared to make more extensive commitments, for the agreement signed in that year was intended to last until 1783. Actually it lasted only two years, but by this time the advantages of carrying on the trade through a single organization had become so clear that a new agreement was signed almost immediately.

The purpose of these agreements was to suppress competition in the St. Lawrence fur trade and thus to enable the participating firms to share in the greater profits likely to accrue from monopoly. In a sense, therefore, they were merely a repetition of the characteristic pattern of organization in the St. Lawrence fur trade: just as English-speaking traders adopted French trading methods in the interior, so they followed the French example of monopoly in finance and forwarding. But the North West Company was a very different type of business from the government monopolies of the French regime. It was not even a true company, as the word is ordinarily used, for it was never incorporated and it had no charter. It was, essentially, an association of partnerships, a joint enterprise in which (as Sir Alexander Mackenzie expressed it) the firms interested in the northwest trade "joined their stock together, and made one common interest". The firms which associated with each other in this way did not at first lose their separate identities; they merely agreed that, for a specified number of years, they would carry on the fur trade as one firm. The profits were divided up at the end of each year, and there was no share capital as we understand the term today. The absence of share capital and the practice of distributing profits annually meant that the North West Company could not accumulate large financial reserves; it was an organization designed for an expanding trade, not for a stable or declining one.

In 1779 the North West Company was made up of eight fur-trading firms, each of which held two shares. The number of shares was increased from time to time—from sixteen in 1779 to twenty in 1787, forty-six in 1795, ninety-six in 1802, and one hundred in 1804—and the participating firms and individuals changed. There is no need for us to trace these changes in detail, but we should note two very important developments to which they gave rise: the appearance of a sharp distinction in function between the "wintering partners" of the Company (those who carried on the trade west of Lake Superior) and the Montreal partners; and the rise to a dominant position in the organization of the firm of McTavish, Frobisher & Company (later McTavish, McGillivrays & Company). These developments were closely related.

Simon McTavish had first entered business in Montreal in 1774 after some previous experience in the fur trade at Albany. With his junior partner he held two shares in the North West Company by the agreement of 1779. By 1783 he had increased this interest to three shares out of sixteen and by 1787 to four out of twenty. In the latter year he entered into partnership with Joseph Frobisher, who himself owned three shares. The junior members of the new partnership owned four shares between them, so that as a firm McTavish, Frobisher & Company owned a total of eleven out of twenty shares—which was, of course, a controlling interest in the organization. This dominant position was consolidated by the agreement of 1790, which laid it down that McTavish, Frobisher & Company should handle all the business of the North West Company in Montreal. This meant that, as agents for the Company, they were to import the necessary goods from England, store them at Montreal, and pack and forward them to the posts in the interior. In addition they had to supply all the cash and credit required to conduct the business of the Company, engage the necessary labour, and act as the Company's attorneys. For these services McTavish, Frobisher & Company received, besides the profit on their shares, a small commission on the value of all the transactions they concluded on behalf of the North West Company.

Nothing could be further from the truth than to think of Simon McTavish and his partners as exercising dictatorial control over the North West Company, in these early years at any rate. The wintering partners, with their intimate knowledge of trading conditions, played a vital role in determining policy and in the last analysis the profits of the Company depended on their initiative and energy. The annual meetings of the Company at Grand Portage and later at Fort William, when the wintering partners met and conferred with the representatives of the Montreal agents, were very far from being merely formal occasions. And the influence of the English firms which supplied credit to Montreal and saw to the marketing of furs in London cannot be overlooked. Nevertheless there were tendencies inherent in the development of the trade which accentuated the importance of the Montreal agents. The capital costs of expansion west of Lake Superior had been the factor initially responsible for the formation of the North West Company; every further expansion of the trade, by increasing the need for working capital and the complexity of the supply system, enhanced the critical role played by the firm which secured credit from England and maintained the Company's basic transportation system. By the first decade of the nineteenth century it was normal for three years to elapse between the time goods were ordered in England and the time when the furs to pay for them were sold in London. In these circumstances the credit-worthiness and reputation of the Montreal agents were clearly of critical importance.

Simon McTavish died in 1804 and his nephew, William McGillivray, took over his position in the North West Company, the name of the Montreal agency being changed in 1806 to McTavish, McGillivrays & Company. During most of this period, when the fur trade and with it the North West Company was expanding rapidly, relations between the wintering partners and the Montreal agents seem in general to have been harmonious; not until about 1800 do the first symptoms of a conflict of interest become evident. In the early years, indeed, the principal problem of the North West Company was not internal unity but external competition. Unlike the Hudson's Bay Company, which possessed under the terms of its royal charter exclusive trading rights in Rupert's Land, the North West Company had no legal right to a monopoly of the fur trade on the St. Lawrence. It could hope to retain a monopoly position only as long as it could by its own efforts prevent competition from arising or crush it after it had arisen. There was an ever-present danger that persons excluded from the North West Company or former partners in the Company who felt themselves badly treated would set up their own trading organization. This actually happened on several occasions. In 1783 the firm of Gregory, McLeod & Company, which had long been interested in the fur trade but which had been excluded from the North West Company agreement of that year, succeeded in securing the services of several experienced western traders who had also been left out of the agreement, and for four years provided the North West Company with very determined competition. Growing hostility between the rival organizations culminated in the murder of John Ross, one of the partners of this firm, by Peter Pond, a North West Company trader, in the Athabasca country in 1786, and in the following year a merger was arranged, the number of shares in the North West Company being increased from sixteen to twenty in order to accommodate the surviving partners of Gregory, McLeod & Company. An even more serious threat appeared in 1797. In 1796, it will be remembered, Great Britain had, under the terms of Jay's Treaty, evacuated the western lake posts, including Detroit and Michilimackinac. This meant that, within a few years, British firms formerly engaged in the fur trade in this area had either to quit the business entirely or else try to force their way into the trade west of Lake Superior in competition with the North West Company. Two Montreal firms accepted the challenge: Parker, Gerrard & Ogilvie, and Forsyth, Richardson & Company. In 1798 the latter firm, which was a subsidiary of the powerful London house of Phyn, Ellice & Company, amalgamated with Leith, Jamieson & Company of Detroit to form an organization which they called the New North West Company. For several years these firms competed independently with the North West Company but in 1800 they joined forces to form what was known as the XY Company. In 1802 they were joined by Sir Alexander Mackenzie, the famous explorer and a former partner in the North West Company, and the firm name was again changed, this time to Sir Alexander Mackenzie & Company.

In terms of the capital it could command and the ability of its management, this rival organization seems to have been at least as strong as the North West Company. In terms of its trading personnel, however, it was definitely weaker, for by this time almost all the experienced traders were firmly tied to the older concern. Nevertheless for several years the XY Company (to use the name by which it is commonly known) furnished very serious opposition indeed to the North West Company. To be sure, relations between the wintering partners of the

rival companies never reached the degree of violence which had characterized the struggle with Gregory, McLeod & Company (perhaps partly
because by this time Simon McTavish and the wintering partners of
the North West Company did not see eye to eye on all matters), but
financially the conflict was very intense and damaging to both parties.
Some indication of its severity is provided by the amount of alcohol
distributed to the Indians, for rum and competition always went hand
in hand in the fur trade. The North West Company alone used 16,299
gallons in trade in the single year 1803, as compared with an annual
average between 1806 and 1810 of only 9,700 gallons. Before long both
organizations were losing money, important fur areas were becoming
exhausted, and relations with the Indians were deteriorating rapidly. The
death of McTavish in 1804 opened the way to amalgamation, and in
November of that year the XY Company was absorbed by the North
West Company. Twenty-five shares out of a total of one hundred in
the combined organization were allotted to the former members of the
XY Company, and its wintering partners were also given shares. But
McTavish, Frobisher & Company retained their position as sole agents
of the North West Company and Sir Alexander Mackenzie was excluded
from any further participation in the fur trade. While the terms of
union were by no means unfair, the North West Company clearly ended
the struggle in better condition than its rival.

TRADING ORGANIZATION AND WESTWARD EXPANSION

The period following the absorption of the XY Company saw the
St. Lawrence fur trade attain its greatest geographical extent and its
greatest commercial success. By this time the North West Company had
a very complete system of posts in the Saskatchewan and Athabasca districts, while Mackenzie's explorations had opened up the Mackenzie River
area in 1789 and had shown the way to the Pacific in 1792-3. The
only remaining area in which expansion was still possible was the Pacific
slope. Ever since the voyages of Captain Cook the commercial potentialities of this region had been recognized; now it seemed as if further delay
in establishing posts beyond the Rockies might have serious consequences,
for Lewis and Clark, the American explorers, had reached the mouth of
the Columbia River by land in November, 1805, and the whole of the
Pacific slope as far north as Russian Alaska might soon be pre-empted by
the United States. Beginning in 1806, therefore, the North West Company
made a determined push into this area. Simon Fraser established Fort
St. James and Fort George on the upper Fraser River in 1806 and 1807
and descended the river as far as its mouth in 1808. Meanwhile David
Thompson, a wintering partner who had formerly been an employee of
the Hudson's Bay Company, crossed the Rockies from the Saskatchewan

in 1807 and built posts in the Kootenay region. In 1811 he travelled down the Columbia River to the ocean, only to find that an American post had already been built at the mouth of the river. With the establishment of these posts west of the Rockies the North West Company added to its territories the district of New Caledonia. The purchase of the American post on the Columbia in 1813 left the Montreal organization in undisputed control of the trade of the Pacific slope, and in 1814 the first shipment of furs was sent direct from the Columbia River to China.

This push to the Pacific brought into being Canada's first transcontinental economic system—a trading empire which extended literally from ocean to ocean. Basic to its survival and functioning were the existence of a demand for furs in Europe, the possession of iron, gunpowder, and / alcohol by European traders, and the use of the canoe on the natural waterways of the Precambrian Shield. In all these respects the traders of the North West Company possessed advantages which their French predecessors had lacked; they were, in consequence, enabled to extend the fur trade far beyond the limits which it had reached in the latter days of the French regime. The marketing of furs in London and the arrangements for their re-export to Europe were more efficient than during the French period; price fluctuations were, of course, still important, but the North West Company was not cursed with periodic crises of over-supply as the French monopolies had been. British manufactured goods, too, the fruits of the Industrial Revolution, were cheap and of good quality. A list of the principal trade goods drawn up in 1811 mentions blankets, woollen and cotton cloth, linen, hardware of all kinds (particularly brass, copper, and tin kettles), painters' colours, fire-arms, powder, ball, shot, and flints. Before the conquest the availability of these goods had enabled Albany to make serious inroads on the French trade, despite the use of an inferior transport route; after the conquest Montreal had the benefit both of English manufactures and of the St. Lawrence route and was quickly able to outdistance Albany. In addition Montreal traders could now supply two very important trade goods—Brazilian tobacco and West India rum—which had not been available to the French. Besides cheaper manufactures, Britain also supplied for the Montreal fur trade longer and more generous credit—a factor whose importance in permitting extension of the trade over longer distances it would be hard to over-estimate. The consolidation of trading interests in Montreal and the close personal and business connections that existed between firms in Montreal and firms in England were instrumental in securing a continuous flow of credit that showed no obvious signs of drying up even when three years elapsed between order and remittance; at no time before 1815 do the operations of the North West Company appear to have been restricted by lack of working capital.

In essentials, trade in the interior was carried on along lines which had been evolved during the French regime. But the growing complexity of transporting men, furs, and trade goods over vast distances made necessary certain innovations in supply methods and much tighter scheduling of consignments. Goods destined for use in the trade were shipped from England to arrive at Quebec not later than November. During the winter they were transported upriver to Montreal, carefully repacked in "pieces" of ninety pounds each, and then freighted to Lachine for transport up the Ottawa in the early spring. From Lachine westward the indispensable means of transportation remained the canoe; the most used route was that by the Ottawa to Lake Nipissing and thence to Georgian Bay by way of French River. Important new developments were the construction of larger canoes and the use of ships on the Great Lakes. There were two principal types of canoes, one used on the trunk line between Lachine and Grand Portage and the other west of Grand Portage. The former type, the *canot du maître*, was manufactured for the North West Company at Three Rivers and at the island of St. Joseph near Michilimackinac; it was about thirty-six feet long and six feet wide in the middle, carried about four tons, and required a crew of eight to ten men. The latter, the *canot du nord*, was about half this size, carried not more than one and a half tons, and required a crew of four or five men. Both types were made from birch bark for the skin, and cedar for the ribs and strakes. During the whole of the period with which we are now concerned the canoe remained the chief means of transport for the Montreal fur trade. Several of the Montreal firms, however, had previously been located at Albany and, operating from this base, they had learned to use the Lake Ontario-Lake Erie route rather than the Ottawa River and to rely on boats and small ships rather than canoes. For heavier and less urgent cargoes, these practices were continued after the conquest. There is no record of a ship being built by the North West Company on Lake Ontario, but a schooner, the *Beaver*, was built on Lake Huron in 1785, and by 1790 the Company had two small ships on Lake Superior. To reduce freight costs, increasing use was made of ships after 1800. A canal was built at Sault Ste. Marie in 1797 or 1798 to enable ships to pass between Lake Huron and Lake Superior, and extensive use was made of the portages at Niagara and between Toronto and Georgian Bay.

Costs were reduced not only by the use of vessels of larger capacity but also by the development of supply bases in the interior. A certain amount of agriculture was carried on at Grand Portage and Fort William and at some of the older-established posts, particularly between Grand Portage and Red River and in the Saskatchewan. Fish was an important product at Michilimackinac and a staple article of diet at the posts in the Athabasca and Great Slave Lake regions. Extensions of trade into the Mackenzie River basin and beyond the Rockies implied increasing reliance upon pemmican as a compact and nourishing foodstuff for transport personnel. In the supply of pemmican the Plains Indians, who were experienced buffalo hunters, came to occupy a strategic position. As these Indians had no access to good fur supplies, they had at first been neglected by the Montreal traders in favour of the Indians of the wooded country to the north. By the first decade of the nineteenth century, however, liberal supplies of rum, as well as their growing familiarity with fire-arms, tobacco, and woollen clothing, had made them dependent upon European traders and thereafter the North West Company counted on them for pemmican supplies. But the warlike proclivities of the Plains Indians made them a very unreliable source of supply and dependence on them for pemmican was a serious weakness in the North West Company's supply system.

These improvements in transport and supply facilities made expansion possible; the characteristics of the North West Company's internal organization, combined with the competitive pressure of the Hudson's Bay Company, made it necessary. There were three main ranks in the organization: partner, clerk, and canoeman (*engagé*). The partners had charge of the more important trading departments and received their remuneration in the form of shares in the profits of the trade. Any money they accumulated in this way was left in the hands of the Montreal agents and the partners were paid interest on it. No one could become a partner who had not served his apprenticeship in the fur trade. A partner who wished to retire was allowed to sell his share, but the purchaser was not permitted to participate actively in the affairs of the Company unless he was approved by the other partners. Most of the partners were Scotsmen, a smaller number English, and a very few French. The clerks of the Company were more or less in the situation of apprentices, except that they were paid wages. They were apprenticed to the trade for five or seven years with the eventual prospect of becoming partners, and their function was principally to look after individual posts. Promotion was usually rapid. The ordinary employees of the Company, the canoemen or *voyageurs*, were divided into two classes: those who wintered west of Grand Portage, and those who merely served on the route between there and Montreal. The latter received less than half as much pay as the former and were referred to, half-contemptuously, as pork-eaters (*mangeurs du lard*). Employees who served as guides, interpreters, or steersmen received higher wages and other privileges.

Morale and efficiency in the North West Company depended very directly on uninterrupted expansion. The pay of the clerks was low (although it tended to rise in periods of competition, to prevent loss of personnel to rival organizations); their incentive to put forward their best efforts in the Company's interests lay in the prospect of promotion, and promotion went to the aggressive trader. As for the partners, their

income and their hopes of being able to retire in comfortable circumstances when their physical strength began to fail depended upon the
profits which the Company earned. There was, therefore, a direct connection between the success of the Company and the aspirations of its
trading personnel. But in addition expansion was made necessary by the
very success with which the Company maintained its monopoly position.
As we have seen, when competition arose which was too determined or
too well financed to be crushed out of hand, the typical solution was for
the senior partners in the competing organization to be given shares in
the North West Company. This was certainly a simple and straightforward method of amalgamation, but it did present the problem of what
was to be done with the new wintering partners. Since they could not
easily be absorbed in the existing departments and posts, the solution
usually adopted was to open up new areas. Thus the amalgamation with
Gregory, McLeod & Company in 1787 was followed by the exploration
of the Mackenzie basin in 1788, while the union with the XY Company
in 1804 preceded the establishment of posts on the Pacific slope. The
amalgamation of competing interests in a single organization not only
made expansion possible, by reducing costs and increasing profits; it
also made it necessary, because of the need to provide for surplus personnel
who could not be summarily discharged.

COMPETITION FROM THE UNITED STATES AND HUDSON BAY

At the risk of some over-simplification, the North West Company can
be described as an enterprise which developed in conditions of rapid
expansion and which, having reached the geographical limits of expansion
and being forced to meet increasingly serious competition, found itself
compelled to adjust to conditions of stability with a totally unsuitable
organization and financial structure. Its chief competitor, on the other
hand, the Hudson's Bay Company, was an enterprise which had developed
under conditions of slow growth and which, forced to compete in order
to survive, successfully readjusted its organization and methods to make
rapid expansion possible. The two companies faced many of the same
problems, but the Hudson's Bay Company was able to learn from the
experience of its rival and in addition had the benefit of a shorter route,
more centralized control over trading personnel, and greater financial
reserves.

The severity of the struggle with the Hudson's Bay Company was due
in large part to the fact that after 1800 the Montreal traders found
themselves pushed out of the territory south of the Great Lakes which
had been ceded to the United States by the Treaty of Versailles. For nearly
twenty years after 1783 British traders had enjoyed almost unimpeded

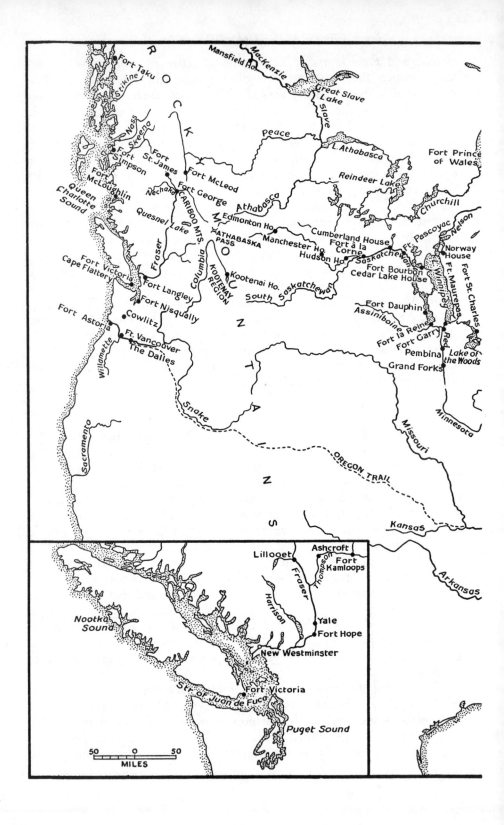

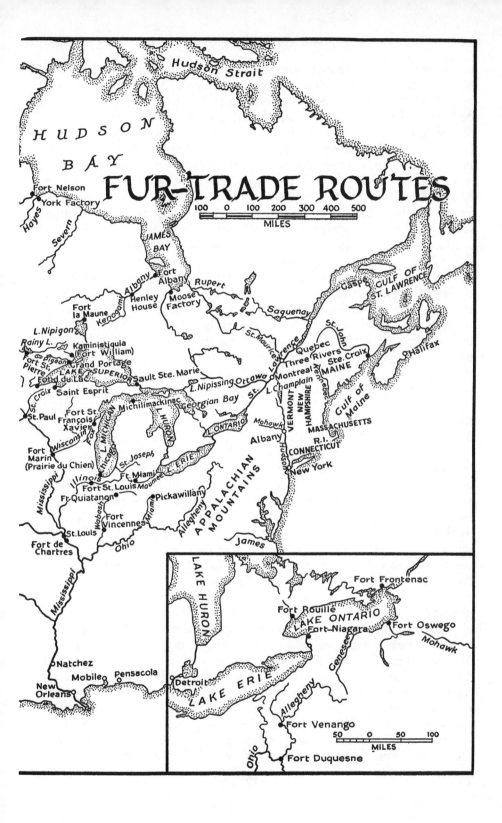

access to this area, although it was in fact American territory; the British garrisons were not withdrawn from the western posts until 1796 and even after that American merchants were slow to challenge the strong position which Montreal firms had built up in this area since the start of the American Revolution. It is not too much to say, indeed, that the fur trade of the territory tributary to Michilimackinac (roughly the present states of Illinois, Michigan, and Wisconsin) was regarded as more lucrative than that of the territory northwest of Lake Superior. Many Montreal firms and individual traders were active in this area, the largest of them being Forsyth, Richardson & Company, and for many years no effective competition was encountered from American traders.

After 1800 the situation changed drastically. Following the withdrawal of the British garrisons from the western posts, the American government began to assert its authority in this area. Government trading-posts were established at Chicago in 1805 and at Michilimackinac in 1809. At the same time serious competition developed in the fur trade. John Jacob Astor, a German immigrant to the United States, had originally established himself as an important figure in the fur trade by shipping furs directly from Montreal to England. After 1794, when direct trade between Canada and the United States became permissible, he changed his base of operations to New York and built up a profitable business importing furs from Montreal and exporting them to London and Europe. Shortly after 1800, recognizing the opportunities opened up by the British evacuation of the western posts, he formed his own trading organization and was soon competing actively in the southwest trade. In 1809 he secured from the New York legislature a charter for the American Fur Company, the initial capitalization being set at one million dollars. Meanwhile in 1806 the Montreal firms interested in the southwest trade had joined together to form the Michilimackinac Company. The senior partners of this Company, John Richardson and William McGillivray, fearing that they would shortly be driven out of the southwest trade entirely, seized the first opportunity to approach Astor and propose a consolidation. At first they were unable to arrive at acceptable terms. In the summer of 1810, however, the wintering partners of the Michilimackinac Company, recognizing the impossibility of resisting both Astor's commercial competition and the hostility of the United States government, sold their interest in the Company to the two Montreal firms, Forsyth, Richardson & Company and McTavish, McGillivrays & Company. These firms then joined with Astor to form the South West Fur Company, equal amounts of capital in the new organization being provided by the Canadian and the American interests. It was agreed that the South West Fur Company should confine its activities to the territorial limits of the United States, on the understanding that the North West Company should restrict itself to British territory; but this did not apply to the Pacific coast, nor to the upper Mississippi. In July, 1811, the North West Company purchased one-third of the interest in the South West Company held by Forsyth, Richardson & Company and McTavish, McGillivrays & Company. The South West Company in its final form therefore represented a union of the most powerful Canadian and American fur-trade interests.

Whatever prospects of survival this international enterprise might have had were destroyed by the outbreak of war in 1812 and by the peace settlement which ended the war. After 1815 British traders were excluded entirely from American territory. This, of course, made it impossible for the South West Company to operate from Montreal and the Canadian interest in the concern was sold to Astor in 1817. This sale completed Montreal's withdrawal from the once important fur trade of the southwest. Astor in the meanwhile had extended his activities to the Pacific coast. He at first offered the North West Company a one-third interest in the trade of this area. When this proposal was rejected he formed the Pacific Fur Company in June, 1810, and built Fort Astoria at the mouth of the Columbia in 1811. As it proved impossible to supply this post by sea during the War of 1812, it was sold to the North West Company in October, 1813.

The withdrawal of Montreal from the trade of the southwest concentrated the forces of expansion toward the northwest and precipitated acute competition with the Hudson's Bay Company. Before the conquest of Canada the Hudson's Bay Company had largely confined its efforts to maintaining posts on the shores of the Bay, relying on Indian middlemen to bring in furs and take back trade goods. A small post, Henley House, had been built a hundred miles inland from Fort Albany in 1743, and a few small-scale expeditions had been sent into the interior, but in general the Company had not departed from a passive policy. The ten years after 1763 saw a marked increase in the number of expeditions into the interior (a total of forty-four being made in the ten-year period) but it was not until 1774 that the Company built its first major trading-post in the hinterland. This was Cumberland House, on Pine Island Lake in the Saskatchewan valley. Its construction marked the beginning of a new and more desperate phase in the competition between Hudson Bay and the St. Lawrence.

Why did the Company adopt this new policy? Its traditional passivity had not been merely the result of conservatism; there were good reasons to support it. Food supplies were very scarce within five hundred miles or so of the shores of the Bay; the barren lands would not support trappers and there was little point in building posts there. Again, the establishment of a series of posts in the interior would mean that the Company would have to build up its own supply system instead of relying on Indian middlemen. Not only would this be a source of considerable expense;

it was also by no means certain that it was technically possible. The Company had no canoes, except a few small ones purchased from the Indians, for two of the indispensable materials for canoe construction—cedar and white birch—did not grow as far north and east as York Factory. Boats of ordinary design drew too much water to pass up the shallow rivers which flowed into the Bay. Lack of a suitable means of transport was by itself sufficient to cast serious doubt on the feasibility of establishing inland posts.

Nevertheless, certain of the Company's officers had always believed that, when and if the French were driven out of North America, it would be necessary to assert the Company's right to exclusive trading privileges in Rupert's Land. To suffer from French competition was one thing; no charter could give protection against that. But to allow British subjects to violate the Company's legal rights was a different matter entirely; to permit this without protest would be, in effect, to give up the Company's most valuable asset—its charter. More than the protection of legal privileges was involved, however. As long as the French held the St. Lawrence, the Hudson's Bay Company at least had a monopoly of the supply of prime northern furs in the London market. But when British firms established themselves in Montreal and sent their traders into the northwest, this advantage disappeared at once.

It was, therefore, no coincidence that the Hudson's Bay Company's decision to abandon its traditional policy and begin building posts in the interior followed within a few months of the time when the competition of British traders based on Montreal began to be felt at the posts on the Bay. It is possible, indeed, to pin-point the precise events that precipitated the decision: the establishment of a trading-post at Cedar Lake on the Saskatchewan by Thomas Corry, a Montreal trader, in 1771, and the desertion to the Hudson's Bay Company of one of Corry's servants, with full information about the methods and plans of the Montreal merchants. Corry's post, situated across the principal route used by the Indians bringing their furs down from Lake Winnipegosis to the Bay, was ideally placed to disrupt the Company's supply system. The information provided by his runaway servant was sufficiently convincing to induce the man in charge at York Factory, hitherto an uncompromising opponent of proposals to build posts in the interior, to write immediately to his superiors in London, urging them to adopt the very policy which he had previously condemned. The gravity of the situation was apparent in the immediate slump in the Company's fur supplies. Fur returns at York Factory were more than one-third below normal in 1772. Thomas Corry, on the other hand, after only two years' trading on the Saskatchewan, was able to return to Montreal and retire permanently from the fur trade, to live in comfort for the rest of his life off the profits of this one venture.

The first inland posts established by the Company—Cumberland House in 1774, Hudson House in 1779, Manchester House in 1786, and Edmonton House in 1795—were supplied by means of small canoes purchased or hired from the Indians and for several years this was the Company's only recourse. But it was never a satisfactory arrangement, for the Indians could not be persuaded to build large canoes of the type used by the Montreal traders. There was only one way to escape from this limitation: to design and build a type of boat which could be used on the shallow rivers draining into the Bay. This step was taken with the introduction of the York boat around 1795 and its rapid improvement in the decade after 1800. The York boat was a keeled boat between thirty and forty feet long, propelled by oars; it required a crew of ten men and could carry 110 "pieces" of ninety pounds each. A modification of this design, with a flat bottom, was used on the Saskatchewan. The shallow draught of the York boat enabled it to be used on most rivers and streams which were passable by canoe, but its weight made it very difficult to portage. Before York boats could be used on the inland routes, roads ten feet wide had to be cut through the bush at every portage and rollers laid down over which the boats could be dragged. The construction of these roads naturally took several years. For heavy freight and for lake transport the York boat was more economical than the canoe, but it was much harder to pull against the current. The consequences could be seen years later in the Company's competitive strength in the Lake Winnipeg area and its relative weakness in Athabasca.

Use of the York boat enabled the Hudson's Bay Company to overcome some of the difficulties which had limited its earlier attempts at expansion. Posts had been built on Reindeer Lake in 1796; Nottingham House and Mansfield House had been established in the Athabasca area in 1802; and by 1804 the Company's servants were active as far to the northwest as Great Slave Lake and the Slave River. Trade was also extended south of Lake Winnipeg; Brandon House was built at the mouth of the Souris River in 1794 and a trading-post established near the site of the former Fort La Reine in 1796. By 1804 the Company was competing actively on the Red and Assiniboine Rivers and among the Indians of the upper Missouri. Transportation and supply problems, however, made it difficult for the Company to maintain these remote trading-posts and to meet competition from Montreal. It was able to dominate the trade in areas close to the Bay, but the disadvantages under which it laboured increased rapidly with distance. The Athabasca area had to be evacuated in 1806 and elsewhere the Company's traders were forced on the defensive. Between 1803 and 1809, indeed, when European markets shrank as a result of Napoleon's conquests, the Company's fortunes declined drastically. Cargoes exported from Hudson Bay to

England, as valued by the British customs, were £38,400 in 1800 and only £15,000 in 1805. In 1808 they fell to a mere £8 and from 1809 to 1814 no dividends were paid.

Recovery from these straits was brought about partly by more extensive use of the York boat and partly by changes in the Company's internal organization. Administrative methods and employment policies which had served adequately when the Company's trade was confined to the posts on the Bay required extensive modification to meet violent competition in the interior. Greater reliance had to be placed on the judgment, initiative, and bargaining ability of the individual trader and less on detailed control from headquarters in London. In making these necessary changes the Company drew heavily on the experience of the North West Company. Colin Robertson, a former partner in the Montreal concern, was employed to advise on employment and wage policies. Largely as a result of his advice the system of paying fixed salaries to employees was abandoned, as far as trading personnel were concerned, and wage payments were substituted which varied in proportion to the profits of each year's trading. Accounts were kept for each post, barter was abolished, and closer control was maintained over the extension of credit to the Indians. Robertson also recommended that the Company should recruit French Canadians for its labour force, but this recommendation was not followed to any large extent. Most of the Company's boatmen, as well as many of its officers and clerks, came from the Orkney Islands in Scotland.

These organizational reforms, combined with improvements in transport methods and the growing experience of its traders enabled the Hudson's Bay Company to return to the attack in 1810. Its competition was now very much more effective than had formerly been the case. York Factory became the principal post on the Bay and the headquarters for the brigades of boats which went to the posts in the interior; attention was concentrated on funnelling supplies through this one depot rather than through several dispersed posts as formerly. Full advantage was taken of the savings in costs which the Hudson Bay route and the use of the York boat made possible, particularly for heavy goods. In 1815 the Company's traders, under the leadership of John Clarke, again entered the Athabasca district and from then until the absorption of the North West Company in 1821 competition became ever more intense.

THE SETTLEMENT AT THE RED RIVER

But the struggle between the companies was not confined to the fur trade. In 1811 Lord Selkirk, a Scottish peer who was a stockholder in the Hudson's Bay Company, received from the Company a grant of land of about 116,000 square miles in extent, lying in what is now Manitoba, Saskatchewan, North Dakota, and Minnesota. His purpose in seeking this grant was to form a colony of Scottish emigrants and thus help to relieve agricultural distress among the Highland crofters. The Company's willingness to make the grant, on the other hand, stemmed from a desire to validate its charter (which had stipulated that it should encourage settlement in Rupert's Land), and the hope that the colony, once established, would serve as a source of foodstuffs and labour for the fur trade. It is probable, however, that in addition to these considerations the directors of the Company were well aware that the founding of Selkirk's colony would be a seriously damaging blow to their Montreal rivals.

Shortly before Selkirk received his grant, the North West Company had proposed a division of territory with the Hudson's Bay Company as a means of averting open conflict. The Montreal firm was willing to give up seventeen posts south of the Saskatchewan but wished to reserve for itself the posts in the northwest. This proposal was unacceptable to the Hudson's Bay Company since it would have meant giving up all claims to a large section of its chartered territory. The counterproposal was made that the North West Company should confine itself to Athabasca and the Pacific slope, but this was rejected out of hand by the Montreal partners on the grounds that by such an arrangement they would give up a great deal while the Hudson's Bay Company would give up nothing. Negotiations therefore broke down. Prospects for a peaceful compromise did not immediately disappear, however, for certain members of the North West Company began buying shares in the Hudson's Bay Company, and for a time it looked as if they might gain control of the board of directors. If this had happened, both fur-trading firms would have been dominated by the same financial interests and some arrangement for peaceful coexistence would certainly have been devised.

The grant to Selkirk and the election to the board of the Hudson's Bay Company of a group friendly to the colonization project destroyed these prospects and made open conflict inevitable. Selkirk's grant covered the network of waterways southwest of Lake Winnipeg and therefore dominated the North West Company's vital communication routes westward from Lake Superior. From this area, too, came the North West Company's indispensable pemmican supplies, more than thirty-five tons of which were required annually for the winter brigades. It was not to be expected that the Montreal traders would permit a colony controlled by the Hudson's Bay Company to be established in this region without resisting it by every means in their power.

Selkirk had already organized two colonization projects—a successful one in Prince Edward Island and a failure in Upper Canada—and his plans for a colony in Assiniboia were by no means as impractical as some people have asserted. If he had received full support from the Hudson's Bay Company and if the North West Company had not found it necessary to oppose his every move, a self-sustaining settlement might well have been established within a few years. But the hostility of the North West Company disrupted his plans from the start. The site chosen for the colony was at the forks of the Red and Assiniboine Rivers, not far from the present city of Winnipeg, and the first settlers, a small party of Scottish and Irish labourers, arrived by way of Hudson Bay in August, 1812. Lack of livestock and of agricultural implements caused serious difficulties during the first two winters and the settlers were compelled to eke out an existence on buffalo meat and potatoes. The expected arrival of a second group of immigrants in 1814, before food supplies were available for them, led the governor of the colony to issue a proclamation forbidding the export of pemmican or any other provisions from the area of Selkirk's grant. This was followed by the seizure of supplies of pemmican which had been intended for the North West Company. Not surprisingly, the partners of the North West Company interpreted these actions as the first steps in the expected campaign to ruin their trade, and at their annual meeting at Fort William in the summer of 1815 they decided that, by fair means or foul, the colony had to be destroyed. Attempts to raise the Cree and Assiniboine Indians against the settlement failed, but the half-breeds who hunted buffalo for the Company (the *Métis*, as they were called) proved more co-operative. The settlers were twice driven from their homes and many of them were induced to depart for Upper Canada. With the killing of the governor of the colony and twenty-one of his followers by a gang of half-breeds at Seven Oaks in June, 1816, relations between the colony and the North West Company approached open warfare. The arrival of Lord Selkirk with a new group of settlers and a regiment of mercenary soldiers saved the colony from complete extinction, but growth and consolidation were clearly impossible as long as the North West Company remained hostile.

THE UNION OF THE COMPANIES

Meanwhile competition between the two organizations in the fur trade was growing more intense and both companies were finding it financially ruinous. The Hudson's Bay Company, however, with its greater financial reserves, proved better able to weather the storm than its rival. In 1811, when negotiations for a division of territory had begun, the attitude of the North West Company partners had been one of easy confidence; by 1820 this complacency had vanished. The change was not due solely to the invasion of Athabasca by Hudson's Bay Company traders in 1815-16; this foray, as a matter of fact, came near to being a major disaster for the Company. Nor did it stem from the happenings at the Red River settlement. It arose, rather, from a reluctant realization that, given moderately efficient management, the Hudson's Bay Company could not only hold its own in the interior but even undercut the Montreal traders. As the Hudson's Bay Company tightened up its internal organization and improved its transport system, the superior advantages of the Bay route over the St. Lawrence became more and more evident. This was especially true for heavy trade goods, which came increasingly into demand as the Indians grew accustomed to European manufactures. According to William McGillivray, who was in a position to know, costs of transport for the Hudson's Bay Company averaged less than half the costs which the North West Company had to pay. By 1820 the Hudson's Bay Company had endured the most violent competition which the North West Company could provide, and it had not only survived but even increased its share of the trade. In these circumstances the opinion of some of the North West Company partners as to what were acceptable terms for a compromise underwent a marked change.

This was true at least of the wintering partners, who had to bear the full brunt of competition and who were not slow to appreciate its destructiveness. The Montreal agents of the Company on the other hand were adamant in their determination to continue the struggle to the end. Relations between the wintering partners and the Montreal agents were already strained, largely as a result of the dictatorial behaviour of the McGillivray brothers, and an open split developed over the question of whether or not a peaceful settlement should be sought with the Hudson's Bay Company. Taking advantage of the fact that the North West Company agreement of 1804 was due to expire in 1822, one of the wintering partners, John McLoughlin, got in touch indirectly with the directors of the Hudson's Bay Company and proposed to them that the wintering partners of the North West Company should give up their association with McTavish, McGillivrays & Company and in future obtain all their supplies of goods from, and deliver all their furs to, the Hudson's Bay Company. Receiving a non-committal reply, McLoughlin went to London late in 1820 in an attempt to get his proposal accepted; there is little doubt that in doing so he was acting as representative of most if not all of the wintering partners. In the meantime the McGillivray brothers, their hands forced by McLoughlin's action, entered into direct negotiations with the Hudson's Bay Company in co-operation with their business associate, Edward Ellice. This made it possible for the directors of the Hudson's Bay Company to play one party off against the other and gravely weakened the bargaining strength of both North West Company groups. Finally, in March, 1821, the directors decided to sign an agreement with the McGillivrays and Ellice, rather than with McLoughlin. An agreement with the wintering partners would have left the Montreal agents free to recruit new trading personnel and to begin the competitive struggle all over again, whereas an agreement with the Montreal supply firms left the wintering partners helpless. Provision was made, however, for the admission of most of the wintering partners into the employment of the Hudson's Bay Company with the rank of chief factors or chief traders.

This agreement between the Hudson's Bay Company on the one hand and the McGillivray brothers and Edward Ellice on the other is one of the most important documents in Canadian economic history. Its importance arises not so much from the fact that it ended a decade of violent competition between two trading companies, but rather from its consequences for the Canadian economy over the next half-century. The agreement stipulated that in future the trade in furs was to be carried on wholly by the Hudson's Bay Company. As far as Montreal was concerned, this meant that the fur trade disappeared entirely, for with trifling exceptions all furs and trade goods handled by the Hudson's Bay Company in the following years went over the cheaper and shorter Bay route. The agreement of 1821 therefore marked the abrupt extinction of the first great staple trade of the St. Lawrence economy.

The victory of the Hudson's Bay Company was certainly due in large measure to the lower transport costs which the Bay route made possible; but this was not the only factor which influenced the final outcome, and taken by itself it would probably not have been sufficient to drive the North West Company out of business. According to an estimate made by the governor of the Hudson's Bay Company in 1814, transportation by way of the St. Lawrence cost the Montreal firm at least £10,000 a year more than the Hudson's Bay Company had to lay out for transportation by the Bay. And besides this the North West Company had to pay an export duty on furs shipped from Quebec which on the average cost it some £30,000 a year; the Hudson's Bay Company did not have to pay this duty. On the other hand, to balance these disadvantages, the North West Company enjoyed the benefit of much more reliable and up-to-date commercial intelligence. The posts on Hudson Bay received news and instructions from England only once a year, because the short navigation season in the Arctic made it impossible for ships to make more than one round trip annually. Reports on trading conditions in North America were out of date before they reached London, while before instructions on policy could be conveyed from London to the posts in the interior, circumstances were likely to have changed so much as to render them inapplicable. All communications, too, between Hudson Bay and London had to be in written form; only occasionally did a chief factor or trader of the Company visit London to talk over the problems of the trade with the directors. The St. Lawrence-Great Lakes route, in contrast, was open for navigation both before and after Hudson Strait, while during the winter messages could be forwarded by way of New York, where the harbour was free from ice all year round. The North West Company, in consequence, was much better informed about changes in market conditions and fur prices than the trading personnel of the Hudson's Bay Company. It was not unknown for a wintering partner of the North West Company to know the results of the Hudson's Bay Company's fur sales before the traders of the Hudson's Bay Company learned them. As a transport system, the Bay route was certainly cheaper than the St. Lawrence; but as a communications system the St. Lawrence route was much more efficient.

The critical weaknesses of the North West Company lay in the looseness of its internal structure. Originally no more than a temporary and informal association of traders, it never entirely rid itself of the defects inherent in this form of organization. The impossibility of building up financial reserves when profits had to be distributed annually meant that the slightest check to expansion was likely to have serious consequences. The fact that all the partners had, at least in principle, an equal voice in the determination of policy certainly contributed to good morale and the exercise of personal initiative, but it also meant that it was very difficult to discipline partners who were guilty of extravagance or violence. The organization suffered from insufficient concentration of authority; when, in the years of acute competition with the Hudson's Bay Company, the McGillivrays attempted to exert centralized control, they succeeded merely in arousing the resentment of the wintering partners. It was in fact impossible to enforce economy measures; the careful accounting and scrupulous frugality which characterized the trading methods of the Hudson's Bay Company were in sharp contrast to the open-handed extravagance and high living of the Montreal traders. For much the same reasons, the Hudson's Bay Company had a better reputation for honesty and justice in dealing with the Indians. The North West Company men were inclined to be over-generous with both liquor and credit, were not above cheating the Indians, and were quick to use violence if they thought it in their interests. Over the long run these practices aroused considerable hostility and undoubtedly made it easier for the Hudson's Bay Company to attract the Indian trade.

To sum up, it would be an over-simplification to ascribe the defeat of the North West Company solely to the lower transport costs of the Bay route. The Montreal company possessed advantages, particularly in regard to commercial communications, which did much to offset its longer lines of supply. The internal organization of the North West Company had, however, evolved in circumstances of steady expansion and was ill adapted for conditions of stable or declining trade. The wide dispersal of authority which had given flexibility and drive to the trading methods of the Company in the earlier period made it impossible to enforce centralized control over policy in the later years when—partly because the geographic limits of the fur trade had been reached and partly because of increasingly effective competition from the north—expansion slowed down. Attempts on the part of the Montreal agents to exercise centralized control alienated the loyalty of the trading personnel and led to conflicts over policy. When expansion was halted, declining profits, rising costs, and deteriorating morale weakened the organization and, in the absence of financial reserves, left it vulnerable to internal disunity. Absorption by the Hudson's Bay Company in 1821 meant the end of Canada's first transcontinental economic system. Competition from the north disrupted the east-west lines of trade which had been extended from Montreal to the Pacific and control over the fur trade came to be concentrated in an organization with headquarters in London. For the next half-century the economic development of the St. Lawrence lowlands on the one hand and of the western prairies and the Pacific slope on the other followed almost completely independent courses.

SUGGESTIONS FOR FURTHER READING

BASIC WORKS:

Davidson, Gordon C., *The North West Company* (Berkeley, 1918), Chapters I-VIII, pp. 1-248

Glover, Richard, Introduction to E. E. Rich (ed.), *Cumberland House Journals and Inland Journal, 1775-82, First Series, 1775-79* (London: The Hudson's Bay Record Society, 1951), pp. xiii-xciii

Innis, Harold A., *The Fur Trade in Canada: an Introduction to Canadian Economic History* (New Haven, 1930), Chapter III, pp. 152-284

Martin, Chester, Introduction to E. E. Rich (ed.), *Journal of Occurrences in the Athabasca Department by George Simpson, 1820 and 1821, and Report* (Toronto: The Champlain Society, 1938), pp. xiii-lix

SUPPLEMENTARY WORKS:

Creighton, Donald G., *The Commercial Empire of the St. Lawrence, 1760-1850* (Toronto, 1937), Part II, Chapter VII, pp. 175-204

Glazebrook, G. P. de T., *A History of Transportation in Canada* (Toronto, 1938), Part I, Chapter II, pp. 25-61

Martin, Chester, *Lord Selkirk's Work in Canada* (Oxford, 1916), Chapters I-XII, pp. 15-195

Morton, Arthur S., *A History of the Canadian West to 1870-71* (Toronto, 1938), Chapters V-VII, pp. 256-622

Pritchett, John P., *The Red River Valley, 1811-1849: A Regional Study* (Toronto, 1942), Chapters I-XX, pp. 1-222

CHAPTER IX

THE TIMBER TRADE

ORIGINS OF THE NORTH AMERICAN TIMBER TRADE

CANADA's first staple trade, the trade in beaver fur, had been founded upon the existence of a demand in Europe for a commodity which was available in large quantities in North America and upon the creation of transport facilities which brought demand and supply together. The Canadian timber trade, which developed during the fur trade's closing decades, similarly depended upon the presence in North America of large and easily accessible supplies of a commodity greatly in demand in Europe, but it differed from the fur trade in its transport requirements, in its relation to immigration and settlement, and in the type of market which it served. Analysis of the role of the timber trade in the economic development of Canada requires that we investigate these differences. But before doing so we must ask why the Canadian timber trade developed when it did, and what were the circumstances which gave to the Canadian economy its second great staple just at the time when its first, the fur trade, was nearing its end.

Ever since the late fifteenth century England had been under the necessity of drawing on foreign sources of supply for the timber with which to build and repair her navy. Naval constructors and designers firmly believed that there was no really satisfactory substitute for English oak, but the shortage of this preferred wood compelled them, from 1500 on, to use foreign timber to an increasing extent. And even during the rare periods when, for the frames and planking of Britain's ships of the line, adequate supplies of English oak were available, for the masts and spars it was necessary to import timber from abroad, since there were in England no pine trees large enough for these purposes.

England's position as a nation state in Europe and in the New World depended upon her strength as a sea power. Unlike the continental nations, she could dispense with a large standing army, but she could not with impunity neglect her navy. Maintenance of naval strength depended, however, upon uninterrupted access in peace and in war to the essential materials from which fighting ships were constructed. Naval timber was, up to 1862, as essential an element in war and diplomacy as oil is today. No European nation could hope to retain the status of a first-class power without an assured supply of oak timber and pine masts.

From the end of the fifteenth century until the beginning of the nineteenth Britain regularly imported the naval and other timber which she required from the countries round the Baltic Sea. Baltic ports such as Stettin, Dantzig, Memel, Riga and St. Petersburg developed and flourished by exporting timber to Britain, and the vast forests of northern Europe and the Scandinavian peninsula were heavily drawn on to supplement Britain's own shrinking woodlands. Dependence on this area for naval timber, however, involved Britain in some very complex diplomatic problems and proved a serious strategic weakness, since during time of war strong naval forces had to be committed to the tasks of keeping open the entrance to the Baltic and convoying the timber ships. As a result, the supply of Baltic timber was at best precarious. During the first Dutch War (1652-4), for example, the Danes closed the Baltic to British ships, producing a major crisis in the royal dockyards. Similar crises recurred in 1715 and again in 1800 and 1806. The danger was not merely that the British navy might be temporarily weakened by a passing scarcity of needed materials. There was also a very serious risk that if Britain once lost command of the sea she might never, as a result of her dependence on Baltic timber, be able to regain it. Baltic timber was essential to Britain's navy, but Britain could be sure of obtaining that timber only as long as she had a fleet powerful enough to keep the entrance to the Baltic open against all adversaries. A single serious naval defeat would both increase the need for naval timber and deprive Britain of the power to obtain it. Adequate reserve supplies at the British dockyards and a consistent policy of encouraging native timber supplies might have diminished these dangers, but corruption and mismanagement in the naval administration prevented these desirable steps from being taken.

The hazards involved in dependence on the Baltic led Britain at an early date to look to her American colonies as an alternative source of supply. The entire Atlantic coast of North America, at the time of the first English settlements, was an almost unbroken forest which contained all the types of wood which the naval dockyards required, as well as several whose value was still not recognized: white and red pine grew in the north, oak in the middle colonies, cypress, cedar, live oak and other as yet unfamiliar woods in the south. The huge white pines of the northern colonies were particularly valuable, for they could provide the great masts and spars needed for Britain's ships of the line. This type of tree was found growing in a wide belt which extended westward from the seaboard between Nova Scotia and New Brunswick, across the upper Hudson and Connecticut River valleys, into the drainage basins of the St. Lawrence and the Ottawa. The first shipments of masts from this region reached the naval dockyards in 1653 and it was not long before a regular trade developed, the centre of which in North America was Portsmouth, New Hampshire, at the mouth of the Piscataqua River.

For the next century and a quarter almost all the great masts used by the Royal Navy came from this area.

Apart from masts colonial timber was regarded as practically worthless for naval purposes. This was partly a reflection of the conservatism of the dockyard officials and partly of the fact that colonial timber was generally not allowed to season properly but was used to build and repair ships while it was still green, so that it was very susceptible to dry rot. Nevertheless, private firms could not be induced to participate in the mast trade unless they were enabled to diversify their operations and spread their risks by cutting and shipping other kinds of timber as well. A sizable investment of capital was involved in cutting the huge trees and transporting them to England; the trade could not be organized efficiently nor carried on profitably on the basis of masts alone. It was in the interests of the British naval authorities, therefore, to encourage the development of a general lumber trade in the colonies, and from the beginning of the eighteenth century bounties were given for this purpose.

Little encouragement was really needed. Throughout the seventeenth and eighteenth centuries and well into the nineteenth, wood was the universal building material. Exports to Britain, even when not used directly for naval construction, relieved the demands on English timber. In the colonies, housing and shipbuilding provided a market for sawn lumber—the sawmill driven by water-power was a commonplace in North America while still a rarity in Britain—and the use of barrels as containers for every commodity that could be poured or packed meant an insatiable demand for staves, an important item in trade with the West Indies. As far as the settler was concerned, the forest was an enemy which had to be destroyed as quickly as possible if settlement and agriculture were to proceed. If there was a market for timber, the settler would sell it for what it would bring; if there was not, he would burn it or let it rot. The important thing was to get the ground cleared.

The combination of a large and increasing demand with seemingly inexhaustible resources meant ruthless exploitation and the rapid disappearance of the best and most accessible timber. As early as 1729 the British government found it necessary to enforce a policy of conservation to preserve the valued mast pines from destruction. The "broad arrow" policy, so called from the mark which was cut with an axe on the trees reserved for the navy, was the result. In the American colonies the regulations provoked wide opposition and were very imperfectly enforced.

THE NOVA SCOTIA AND NEW BRUNSWICK MAST TRADE

One reason for encouraging the North American timber trade had been that the Baltic trade, involving as it did an excess of imports over exports and dependence upon foreigners, was repugnant to mercantilist thinking, whereas the North American trade was within the empire. All the profits of cutting and shipping remained in British or colonial hands, while the source of supply was securely within the control of the British government. These considerations of policy were rudely upset by the outbreak of the American Revolution. Secure in their confidence that colonial supplies could not suddenly be withdrawn by the dictate of a foreign government, the British naval authorities had done little to build up a reserve stock of large pine masts or to develop alternative sources of supply. The result was that, in the sea fighting of the Revolutionary War, particularly after the intervention of France, the effectiveness of the Royal Navy was severely reduced by the shortage of masts. New construction was retarded, repairs delayed, and the ability of the ships of the line to endure punishment during bad weather or in action against the enemy seriously weakened for lack of the great pines which, since the days of Oliver Cromwell, the North American colonies had supplied.

In this crisis the British government turned for masts not only to the Baltic countries but also to the North American colonies which had remained loyal. In Nova Scotia (which then included New Brunswick) trees had been cut for masts as early as 1710, when Port Royal first fell to the British; the "broad arrow" regulations had been enforced in the colony since 1721 and extensive stretches of pine timber had been reserved for naval purposes. By 1772 Nova Scotia was exporting to Britain about half as many masts annually as was Portsmouth, the traditional centre of the mast trade.

The pine forests of Nova Scotia proper provided the Halifax dockyard with an adequate supply of masts throughout the Revolutionary War, but none reached Britain from this area. To take the place of New Hampshire as the principal source of American masts for the British dockyards, the government turned to the virgin forests of what is now New Brunswick, then practically an unsettled wilderness, and the St. John River, stretching deep into the hinterland, became the new centre of the mast trade. The first contracts for masts to be cut in this area were signed in 1779. Several cargoes were sent to Halifax in the next few years but it was 1782 before the first shipment was sent to England.

The opening up of this new supply area came too late to alleviate appreciably the shortage of masts during the Revolutionary War. In the years of peace which followed, however, the navy continued to rely upon New Brunswick for its masts rather than return to its old sources of supply in New England. Britain clearly could no longer count upon being able to obtain masts from the now independent American republic, and New Brunswick contained, in any case, a greater number of the very large pines than did the depleted New Hampshire forests. New England ports continued for some years to send masts to Britain—in 1787 they shipped 297 masts as against 200 from New Brunswick and a mere 16 from Quebec—but their share of the total naval supply declined rapidly. As a matter of policy the Navy Board gave its long-term mast contracts to British timber firms operating on the St. John and after about 1795 practically all the masts used by the navy came from New Brunswick. This remained true until 1804, when the centre of activity shifted to the St. Lawrence.

The large pine masts which were brought down the St. John and shipped to England sold for a price which more than covered the heavy freight costs of the transatlantic voyage. But this was not true of other kinds of lumber which, unlike masts, could be obtained easily and cheaply either in England or from sources of supply like the Baltic much nearer than North America. Freight costs from North America to England were on the average in this period fully three times as high as from the Baltic. In addition the cost of labour in North America was very much higher, sometimes six times as much, than it was in northern Europe, and the timber trade of the Baltic ports had reached a degree of organization and efficiency which far surpassed that of the colonies. In these circumstances a general export trade in lumber from the North American provinces to Britain had no chance to develop. Unlike furs, which were light, compact, and valuable, and could therefore easily bear the costs of shipment to Britain, lumber was a large and bulky product, low in value in proportion to its weight. Freight costs were a large percentage of the final selling price, usually more than half. The only kinds of timber which it paid to export to Britain were large masts, which brought a scarcity price, and the timber used to build colonial ships, which provided its own transportation.

If Europe had remained at peace, this situation might have persisted for many years. As far as the general demand for lumber in Europe was concerned, North America was a high-cost supply area, excluded from the market by distance and heavy freight costs. The Napoleonic Wars, however, completely disrupted normal supply-and-demand relationships. Just as the Dutch Wars of the seventeenth century had led to the development of the colonial mast trade, so the danger of being cut off from foreign supplies during the long war with France which began in 1793 led the British government to encourage, by means of tariff protection, a general export trade in timber from the North American provinces.

THE CRISIS OF 1804 AND THE QUEBEC TRADE

A shortage of English oak, partly the result of an ill-timed economy campaign on the part of the naval authorities, together with the abnormal demand occasioned by a heavy programme of new construction, brought about this sudden change in policy. In 1793, at the beginning of the struggle with France, the British naval dockyards had been adequately stocked with supplies of oak timber accumulated during the years of peace. By 1803, however, when the war at sea entered upon a new and more active phase, these stocks were exhausted and new supplies of English oak were almost unobtainable. An intensive search was made for alternative sources of supply and large quantities of oak were imported from the Baltic. At the same time the first steps were taken to obtain supplies of oak and pine timber other than masts from the British colonies in North America. The important but relatively small-scale naval mast trade which had developed in New Brunswick was now abandoned completely and the entire naval timber trade, including not only masts but also oak for the hulls and planking, was shifted to Quebec. A large contract for naval timber from the St. Lawrence was given to the British firm of Scott, Idles & Company in 1804, and skilled shipwrights and carpenters were sent out from England to supervise the work.

The British timber crisis of 1804 ushered in a period of rapid expansion which soon included much more than naval supplies. Naval contracts gave the initial impetus to development but could not alone support a general lumber trade. Long-term investment and planning demanded some more permanent foundation—specifically, a tariff preference in the British market. In this connection the expansion of French military power in Europe played a crucial role. Until the end of 1806 the Baltic timber ports had found it possible to trade quite freely with Britain and the navy had obtained large and very valuable cargoes of oak and fir timber from that region. In November, 1806, however, Napoleon issued the Berlin Decree, which declared Britain to be in a state of blockade and closed all the ports of the French empire and its dependent states to British ships. By the middle of 1807 Russia, Prussia and Denmark had announced their adherence to the policy. This meant that Britain was, in theory at least, completely cut off from Baltic timber, for, although a British fleet held naval control of the Baltic, Napoleon's troops occupied the key harbours of Dantzig, Memel and Stettin, while his ally, Tsar Alexander of Russia, closed Riga and St. Petersburg to British trade. Timber prices in Britain promptly shot upward as imports shrank, and a critical shortage of all varieties of timber became immediately evident. Memel fir timber, which brought 15s. a load in the fall of 1806, was selling for £9 in the early months of 1808 and £16 in 1809. Imports of oak timber and plank from Prussia fell from 4,230 loads in 1807 to 27 in 1808, recovering slightly to 388 in 1809, while imports from Russia fell from 297 loads in 1806 to 3 in 1807 and 19 in 1808.

Exclusion from the Baltic timber trade threatened serious consequences not only for the Royal Navy but also for the entire British economy, dependent as it was on cheap timber for a multitude of construction purposes. From no source other than the North American colonies could supplies of timber large enough to offset the loss of the Baltic trade be drawn, at least within a reasonable period of time. A beginning had already been made, thanks to the naval contracts given out in 1804 and later years. What was necessary now was to attract other firms into the business and to induce them to invest their capital on a long-term basis in the North American rather than the Baltic trade. No mere temporary spell of high prices would do this. No large timber firm would shift its operations and its organization from the Baltic to the St. Lawrence without some assurance against the risk of being left stranded in a high-cost supply area when Napoleon's armies retreated and prices fell back to more normal levels. Britain could get all the timber it wanted from Quebec; but the price which had to be paid was the imposition of heavy duties on timber imported from the Baltic. If the British consumer was to be supplied with timber from British North America, he had to pay for that timber a price which at least covered the costs of trans-atlantic shipment plus a reasonable profit margin. Such a price could be maintained only by imposing import duties on timber from the Baltic.

These considerations were forcibly brought to the attention of the British government by certain large timber-importing firms who made the imposition of duties on Baltic timber a condition, so to speak, of investing their capital in the development of the Quebec trade. The result was that the duties on foreign timber, which had been in existence at relatively low levels since 1795, were gradually stepped up until firms engaged in the colonial trade enjoyed a very substantial preference indeed. The duty on foreign timber, which was a mere 10s. a load in 1795, stood at 25s. a load in 1805 and 34s. 8d. in 1810. In 1814 it reached its maximum of 65s. a load. Reduced to 55s. in 1821, it remained at that level until 1842. Through this entire period colonial timber entered Britain free, except for a nominal duty between 1821 and 1842.

These differential duties provided the foundation on which the Quebec timber trade was built. At their height, from 1811 on, they were more than sufficient to offset the disadvantages of distance from the British market and to insure that the price paid by the British consumer remained at a level high enough to make shipment from the North American colonies financially profitable. Without such a large measure of tariff preference in the British market the Canadian timber trade would long have remained what it was in 1804—a small-scale trade, dependent on naval contracts and confined largely to masts.

While this is so, the question may well be raised whether the price exacted was not unnecessarily high. Like all protective tariffs, the differential duties proved easier to impose than to remove. In the course of time they created vested interests who stubbornly opposed proposals for reductions. The costs to the British economy of maintaining artificially high prices for an essential construction material during a period of rapid industrialization, while not easy to estimate, must have been very considerable. To offset this is the fact that the development of the Quebec trade undoubtedly relieved Britain from complete dependence on the Baltic.

The most direct and immediate beneficiaries of the differential duties were British timber-importing firms. Scott, Idles & Company had received a naval contract for masts and timber in 1804 on very attractive terms and for several years they had a monopoly of the naval supply. Their strongest rival, Henry Usborne, had first come to Quebec on private business in 1801, while other firms, such as Pollock, Gilmour & Company, had had long experience in the Baltic trade before turning to North America in the years after 1807. Most of these timber firms were not independent Canadian enterprises but branches of British firms. They were usually managed by a relative of one of the partners in the British firm, a son or a cousin, who ran the business in North America partly on his own initiative, partly on orders from England. Some timber firms owned their own fleets of timber ships, but most were content to rely on the large numbers of independently-owned ships which called annually at Quebec and Saint John, the centres of the trade in Lower Canada and the Maritimes respectively, in the hope of picking up a cargo.

In contrast to the characteristic tendency in the fur trade, the timber firms of Quebec and Saint John showed little inclination to amalgamate into a single monopolistic organization. This was partly due to the fact that they were subsidiaries of strong British concerns, partly to the ease with which new enterprises could enter the industry, and partly to the nature of the market. Fur was a luxury article with a narrow market geographically concentrated in London, while timber was a general construction material with a wide variety of uses and areas of consumption. But the persistence of competition in the timber trade also reflected the fact that, initially, no large investments of fixed capital were required. The timber firms of Quebec and Saint John did not themselves undertake logging operations. They were purely middlemen, buying the timber which was brought down the rivers to the seaports and consigning it to their parent firms in England. The actual cutting of the timber, including the search for suitable stands and the hazardous business of floating the rafts downstream to the seaport, was in the hands of small independent operators who worked on contract for the timber buyers. It was not at all unusual, in the early years of the trade, for gangs of no more than five or six men to try their luck at timber-making, often in the hope of earning a little hard cash to extend or improve the farms which were their principal source of livelihood. These small operators were financed from year to year by the timber buyers of the seaports. Their credit requirements were small and little or no capital equipment was needed. In such circumstances monopoly organization had little chance to develop and the industry remained highly competitive. As time went on, of course, the capital and credit requirements of the trade grew larger, particularly after the introduction of privately-built and -owned timber "slides" on the Ottawa, and the size of the typical timber-cutting firm increased. But in the early years it was essentially a small-unit industry.

The protection afforded in the British market by the differential duties guaranteed that the Canadian timber trade as a whole would be able to compete on equal terms with the Baltic, but it did not guarantee stability of prices nor the profitability of particular firms. On the whole the timber trade had the reputation of being very speculative and risky; a few firms, through exceptionally good management, were able to survive for long periods, but the general rate of failures was high. The principal source of uncertainty lay in the year-to-year fluctuations of prices in Britain. The construction industry, which was the chief market for Canadian timber, was then, as it still is, particularly vulnerable to the swings of the business cycle. A falling off in construction contracts had an immediate and accelerated reaction on the demand for Canadian timber. On the supply side there were sharp and largely unpredictable variations in the quantity of timber shipped to Britain from Canada and the Baltic, these variations reflecting partly weather conditions, since a heavy fall of snow during the winter was essential if the timber was to be got out of the forests and floated downriver in the spring. In addition, commercial news was slow to travel from Britain to Canada, for the sailing-ship was still the only transatlantic means of communication; news of changes in market conditions in Britain generally arrived too late for merchants in Canada to make appropriate adjustments in supply. High prices in one year might induce large shipments the year after, even though demand in the meantime had sagged. These time-lags and imperfections in communication created serious uncertainties to which the timber merchant had to adjust as best he could. Trouble usually showed itself first in a tightening of credit, passed along from the parent firm in Britain, which was in close touch with the market, to the subsidiary firm in Quebec and Saint John, and finally to the timber-cutting contractor seeking an advance to cover his next year's operations.

The raw material for the timber industry was drawn from the great forests of red and white pine which in those days covered the entire watershed of the St. Lawrence River. The St. Lawrence and its tributaries, particularly the Ottawa, provided the essential means of transportation and set the boundaries of profitable exploitation. The fur trade, because of its use of the canoe and the light, compact nature of its product, had been quickly and easily extended over the low heights of land which separated one drainage basin from another—from the St.

Lawrence to Hudson Bay, the Mackenzie River, and the Pacific coast. Not so the timber trade; rafts of timber could be floated downstream, but not against the current. The consequence was that each major timber port had a well-defined geographical area to draw upon which could not be significantly extended, at least in the days before the railroad. It did not make much difference, however, whether part of that area was within the territory of a foreign nation. American timber areas south of the St. Lawrence and on the Maine-New Brunswick boundary were tributary to Quebec and Saint John rather than to American seaports.

Until the late 1820's almost all the timber sent from British North America to Britain was in the form of what was called "square timber". As the name suggests, production of square timber involved felling the tree and cutting four flat sides on the trunk with a broad axe. No sawing was done until the timber reached Britain. In some ways this was a very inefficient method of utilizing the available forest resources. In the "squaring" process some of the best wood in the tree, amounting to at least a third of the total cubic capacity, was removed and left lying in the forest, where it constituted a serious fire hazard. If a tree had the slightest trace of rot in its heart (something which could be ascertained only after it had been felled) it was discarded, even though its outer sections contained excellent wood. Only the best and soundest trees were taken and, needless to say, no attention was given to reforestation.

Such extravagant practices in cutting, together with the damage caused by forest fires, meant that the rate of exploitation was rapid, and the centres of activity moved steadily farther and farther up the river valleys and into the hinterland. The timber for the first naval contracts in the Quebec trade appears to have been cut on the Richelieu River, and during its early years the industry drew mainly on the forests around the lower St. Lawrence and Ottawa. By 1820, however, rafts were coming down the St. Lawrence from the eastern end of Lake Ontario. With the opening of the Welland Canal in 1829 the territory around Lake Erie was opened up for timber operations, while the increasing use of steamboats in the 1830's and 1840's made it possible to tow large rafts across the Lakes. By the end of the 1840's timber was arriving at Quebec from as far west as southern Lake Huron. The same inexorable movement in search of new forest resources was apparent on the Ottawa. The first man to exploit the timber resources of the upper Ottawa was Philemon Wright, an immigrant from Massachusetts. In 1800 Wright established a small settlement at Hull, near the foot of the Chaudière rapids, and in 1806 he sent his first raft of timber down the river to Montreal and thence to Quebec. Others soon followed in Wright's footsteps and within a few years there developed on the Ottawa and its tributaries a timber trade which was to surpass and outlive that of the St. Lawrence.

THE IMPACT ON AGRICULTURAL SETTLEMENT AND IMMIGRATION

Timber operations on the St. Lawrence and on the Ottawa had many characteristics in common, but there were also a number of differences. In the first place, the relationship between the timber industry and agriculture was not the same on the two rivers. On the St. Lawrence and around the lower Lakes the cutting of timber was largely incidental to the clearing of land for settlement. The settler had to get the timber off his land before he could start to raise a crop. The valley of the Ottawa, on the other hand, contained relatively little land suitable for permanent agricultural use. In this region, therefore, the cutting of timber had little relation to the clearing of land for agriculture, except in cases where small farms were established to supply the logging camps. In the second place, the organization of the industry was not the same on the St. Lawrence as it was on the Ottawa. On the St. Lawrence, where there was little need for timber firms to organize cutting operations themselves, the rafting of timber to Quebec developed as a specialized business. On the Ottawa, timber-making (as it was called) and rafting were usually in the same hands and specialization did not develop to the same extent. Thirdly, there were certain differences in techniques. On the Ottawa, with its frequently narrow channel and swift current, the unit of which rafts were made up—the "crib", as it was called—was much smaller than the large "drams" which made up the St. Lawrence rafts. Designed to be quickly taken apart and put together again when descending rapids and waterfalls, the Ottawa River raft was easier to build than the St. Lawrence type and called for fewer special skills in construction.

One of the firms engaged in the St. Lawrence trade was D. D. Calvin & Company, and in several ways this concern exemplifies the organization and growth of the industry in this area. Delano Dexter Calvin was an American by birth, and the first rafts of timber he sent down the St. Lawrence to Quebec came from northern New York state. In 1836, however, he set up a branch of his business at Garden Island, near Kingston, and this branch soon grew into the headquarters of his business, largely because of its strategic location. Not only did it have a good harbour; it was also a convenient place to store timber and construct rafts before attempting the hazardous descent of the St. Lawrence. From the start the firm's staple commodity was oak timber, obtained first from northern New York, later from western Upper Canada, and still later from Ohio and Michigan. Pine was also dealt in, but in small quantities and largely for the reason that rafts could not be made from oak alone, since oak was a heavy wood and lacked buoyancy. There seem to have been few periods in which the firm did not cut some of its own timber, but this was always of minor importance. Rafting other people's timber was the mainstay of the business, the activity from which the firm always made money, whether or not the timber in the rafts sold at a profit. Frequently, however, especially when prices were high, Calvin & Company would extend credit to timber producers, either by direct loans or by means of informal partnerships, and from the late 1840's onward the firm always had its agents buying timber for its account in the west. By the 1860's Calvin & Company had branched out into a wide variety of ancillary activities, including the building and operating of wooden ships, towing and salvage work, and a general freight and forwarding business between Quebec, Montreal, and the lake-ports. Rafting to Quebec, however, always remained the heart of the business.

A firm like Calvin & Company, which grew and prospered by rafting other people's timber and was only occasionally involved in timber-making itself, was normal on the St. Lawrence but almost unknown on the Ottawa. Much of the St. Lawrence supply came from farmers who engaged in timber-making only as a necessary preliminary to clearing the soil. Given these supply conditions, a firm could confine its activities to rafting and still be sure of plenty of business. On the Ottawa agricultural settlement was much more dispersed and good farming land less common. A timber firm had to secure its raw material for itself, by cutting timber on Crown lands. There was, accordingly, less opportunity for specialization in rafting to develop.

Timber-making on the St. Lawrence followed settlement and the expansion of agriculture. On the Ottawa and its tributaries, in contrast, agriculture tended to follow the timber industry. Timber-making and agriculture were both seasonal activities, the busiest part of the year for the one being the slack season for the other. The timber camps, too, were excellent markets for agricultural produce; all the food had to be brought in from outside, and high transport costs meant high prices. There was, therefore, a strong temptation to try to combine farming and timber-making. A man would establish a small farm near an active lumbering area and work on it for part of the year, counting on being able to sell his produce to the camps at a good price. Then, when winter began, he would hire himself out as a lumberjack, taking his team of oxen with him if he had one. The results of such attempts to combine the two occupations were not always happy. A man who tried to be both lumberjack and farmer usually had little success in either capacity. Very little of the land in the Ottawa valley—not more than one-eighth of the total area—was suitable for permanent agricultural use, and few of the farms which were established to take advantage of the high prices in the lumber camps were able to provide a decent living for their owner after the camps moved on to new areas.

This problem was by no means as acute on the Ottawa, however, as it was in New Brunswick, where the agricultural labour force was seriously reduced by the high wages which could be earned in the lumber camps and in the associated industry of shipbuilding. In Upper Canada, on the other hand, the two occupations hardly came into conflict at all. Until the late 1830's timber production in this area was almost entirely for the local market, for distance from Quebec and the difficulties of rafting timber across the Lakes meant that the square-timber trade had little chance to develop. In the 1830's and 1840's the completion of the Welland Canal and the use of steam tugs opened up a trade in sawn lumber to the United States and to some extent in square timber to Quebec, but by then settlement was well established, the accessible land was largely in the hands of small farmers, and there were no extensive tracts of Crown lands left for large-scale timber operations. In this area, accordingly, the lumber industry remained subsidiary to agriculture. The farmer found the sale of his unwanted timber a useful supplementary source of income, but there was not the same temptation as there was on the Ottawa or in New Brunswick for him to neglect his regular occupation.

As far as the development of British North America as a whole was concerned, the effects of the timber trade on immigration were of more importance than its harmful consequences for agriculture and settlement in particular areas. Probably in no respect did the fur trade and the timber trade stand in sharper contrast than in their relation to immigration. In the fur trade a compact, valuable product was shipped to England and heavy manufactured goods were shipped back. The cargoes, that is to say, were unbalanced, more shipping space being required on the outward voyage from Britain than on the return journey. Unbalanced cargoes always meant high transport costs, since the freight being shipped in one direction had to bear the expense of the unused capacity moving in the other. There was, therefore, real pressure to decrease the degree of unused capacity by reducing imports and increasing the quantity of furs to be exported. In the timber trade precisely the opposite problem had to be faced. A bulky product, low in value in proportion to the shipping space which it occupied, was exported to Britain, and unused capacity tended to develop on the return leg of the voyage as the timber ships returned empty or lightly loaded from Britain to North America. Once again, unused capacity meant high freight costs, and in the timber trade such costs were a much larger fraction of the final price than in the fur trade. Pressure therefore developed to find a paying cargo which the timber ships could carry when they returned to Quebec or Saint John for a new load of timber. What the cargo might be was of less importance than that it should offset to some extent the costs of the otherwise unremunerative voyage. Various commodities met this requirement, notably salt, large quantities of which were shipped at cheap rates from Britain to

New Brunswick for use in the fishing industry. The most important return cargo for the timber ships was, however, immigrants.

As can well be imagined, conditions aboard the timber ships were far from ideal from the point of view of the immigrants. The timber trade provided the last employment for ships which were too old, too ill-founded, and too ill-manned to be used in any other kind of commercial traffic. A sailing-ship would carry timber when it would carry nothing else. Add to this the fact that effective supervision of immigrant traffic was non-existent, that the immigrants themselves were often weakened by poverty and under-nourishment before ever they left the British Isles, that the ships were owned and captained by men who looked to the timber trade as their main source of profits and regarded the immigrants as a side-line, and the oft-described horrors of the immigrant ship become more easily understandable, if not for that reason more quickly to be condoned. Fundamentally, the importance of the timber trade for immigration lay in the fact that to the push of poverty in the British Isles and the pull of hopes for a better and wider life in the colonies there was now added the crucial factor of cheap transatlantic fares, as owners and operators of timber ships sought to cover the costs of unused capacity on the east-west voyage. The conjuncture of these three factors explains the great upsurge of immigration into British North America in the third and fourth decades of the nineteenth century.

THE END OF THE BRITISH PREFERENCES: NEW PRODUCTS AND NEW MARKETS

The social dislocation caused by the spread of the industrial system in Britain was not least important among the factors which induced these thousands of people to take what was probably the most difficult decision of their lives—the decision to emigrate. But industrialization also brought with it a change in economic thought and policy which in a different way was to have a decisive effect on the Canadian timber trade. As the new doctrines of free trade gained ever wider acceptance, the old tariffs and restrictions on commerce by means of which, in a hazardous and hostile world, Britain had sought protection and security came under increasingly determined attack. The greatest victory of the advocates of free trade was, of course, the repeal of the Corn Laws in 1846. Less conspicuous but no less indicative of Britain's new-found confidence in her own industrial strength and military security was the reduction in the same period of the differential duties on timber.

For more than twenty years after 1821 there had been no change in the duties on foreign timber entering the British market. During this period the Canadian timber trade, passing beyond the stage of a war-stimulated infant industry, had reached maturity in organization and technique, as larger firms established their positions and smaller fly-by-night concerns were squeezed out of existence. The first serious reduction in the tariff preference enjoyed by colonial square timber came in 1842, when the duty on foreign imports was cut from 55 shillings to 30 shillings a load. Further reductions followed quickly in 1845, 1846, 1848 and 1851. Finally in 1860 the duty on foreign timber was abolished entirely.

As might be expected, these tariff changes caused very disturbed conditions in the timber trade, not only because they cut into the profit margins of firms importing from North America, but also because the expectation of reductions in the duties led to periodic gluts on the British market. Importers would throw supplies on the market in the hope of anticipating a further reduction in the preference, thus causing more serious price falls than the tariff changes alone would have occasioned. The survival of the industry as a whole, however, was not threatened. In general, the reduction in the duties on foreign timber does not seem to have caused a serious decline in the absolute amounts of Canadian square timber sold in Britain. What seems to have happened is that the trend of Canadian imports, which had previously been rising, flattened out, increases in total consumption being met by larger imports from the Baltic. In 1859, for the first time since 1816, British imports of square timber from the Baltic exceeded imports from British North America.

Two related developments helped to cushion the shock of the abolition of the differential duties. The first was the growing importance of the export trade in deals, or sawn lumber, and the second was the appearance of a market for Canadian lumber within North America itself. Deals were softwood planks, two or three inches thick. Their manufacture had developed in British North America under the protection of the differential duties, just as the square-timber trade had, and from about 1815 onward increasing quantities had been shipped to Britain. But because they were a more highly manufactured product than square timber, requiring more technical skill, more capital equipment, and—particularly when exported to Britain—much greater uniformity in quality and dimensions, Canadian deals were slow to win a foothold in the British market and until about 1835 imports from Canada to Britain were smaller than imports from the Baltic. After the abolition of the preferential duties, imports from Canada continued to increase but at a slower rate, while imports from the Baltic rapidly took over the larger share of the market. In the meantime, however, new markets had developed for Canadian deals in North America.

The forests north of Lake Ontario and Lake Erie had contributed to some extent to the square-timber trade, but by no means as largely as had the Ottawa valley. With the growth of settlement and the appearance of towns in this area, however, there had developed an active local market for deals and other forms of lumber. If water-power was available, a sawmill was the first piece of fixed capital equipment that a new settlement acquired, once a flour mill had been erected. This local market became more important as population increased and as transportation facilities on the Lakes and on land were improved. The quality and exact dimensions of the lumber were not such critical matters as they were in the export trade to Britain, and the smaller trees could be put to good use.

Much the same process had been taking place on the American side of the Lakes. In the lumber trade, as in the case of fur, the political boundary line at first meant very little. The natural geographic boundaries of the Great Lakes drainage basin were much more important. American timber was sent down the St. Lawrence and exported to Britain, and from the very earliest days lumber as well as foodstuffs and salt was traded across the Lakes.

In the 1840's and 1850's, however, something new began to happen. Great cities were growing up in the United States, not only on the eastern seaboard but also in the midwest, at Chicago, while in New England industrialism had taken firm root. In the United States, as in Great Britain, the growth of cities and the spread of industry meant huge demands for lumber, the universal building material. The forest resources which were available near at hand to these growing metropolitan centres rapidly dwindled and became inadequate. Inexorably they reached northward for Canadian lumber. For the first time there developed, within North America, a large-scale market for a Canadian staple.

THE TARIFF AND THE AMERICAN MARKET

That the American market for lumber came to development in the period when the British market had ceased to expand was, of course, a matter of chance rather than of design. It was during the boom of the mid-1840's that exports of deals and saw logs to the United States first attained sizable dimensions. Further growth of the trade depended largely on improvements in transportation and changes in the American tariff. Chicago could draw directly on the timber of the upper Lakes, but the industrial cities of the American Atlantic seaboard, once the forest resources of their own relatively small drainage basins were exhausted, had to build first canals and then railroads before they could reach over the low heights of land and tap Canadian supplies. The timber trade to Britain had been based on wind and water—sailing-ships on the Atlantic and rafts on the St. Lawrence and the Ottawa. The lumber trade to the United States was based on steam-power—railroads reaching north and northwest from American consumption centres, and steam-driven saw-mills near the centres of production in Canada. Typical of such railroads was the Ogdensburg Railroad, completed in 1850 from Boston to the south bank of the St. Lawrence and extended into the Ottawa valley by means of a Canadian railway, the Bytown and Prescott, in 1854. New York meanwhile was reaching westward toward the timber of the upper Lakes, and in 1853 the New York Central system was completed. During these same years large amounts of American capital were invested in Canadian sawmills, particularly in the Bytown (Ottawa) area.

Inevitably, such a large-scale realignment of trade relations had political repercussions. Within less than a decade the statutes which had given form and meaning to Britain's old colonial system had been swept away: the timber preferences lowered in 1842; the Corn Laws repealed in 1846; the Navigation Acts removed from the statute books in 1849. The leaders of opinion in Britain seemed determined that the colonies should stand on their own feet, economically as well as politically, and pay their own way in the world of international commerce. This new conception of colonial status entailed, for the North American provinces, an abrupt and painful economic readjustment. As the preferences which they had enjoyed in the British market disappeared, the pull of American markets to the south grew stronger. Cast adrift, as they felt, by the mother country, the politicians and merchants of the British North American colonies turned to the United States. Some of them, reluctant to cut the sentimental ties with Britain and too prudent to commit their fortunes unreservedly to the American republic, sought merely closer economic relations; others wished political union as well. Almost all joined in seeking, as a first step, what they called reciprocity. This meant, in practice, free admission of the natural products of each country to the markets of the other.

Among the business groups most anxious to secure reciprocity with the United States were the lumber merchants. They had always been free trade in their sympathies, at least as far as the Canadian market was concerned, and on several occasions had clashed with the Canadian farming interest over the question of free admission of American agricultural products. Imported foodstuffs, particularly salt pork, figured largely in the diet of the lumberjacks and in the costs of the timber producers. With the market for square timber in Britain stagnant and exports of sawn lumber to the United States already swelling rapidly, reciprocity was clearly in their interests.

Selling the idea of reciprocity to the United States entailed a long and tortuous process of diplomatic manoeuvring, and many issues were involved besides those of the lumber industry. The achievement of reciprocity and the precise terms of the agreement which was finally reached will be discussed later in Chapters XI and XVI. At this point we need only observe that, as far as the lumber industry was concerned, the signing of the Reciprocity Treaty in 1854 was the signal for a new and more vigorous burst of expansion. Exports to the United States of planks and boards (which were classed as raw materials and allowed free entry) increased from $1,866,712 in 1854 to $5,043,367 in 1867. And even after reciprocity came to an end in 1866, the growth of the lumber trade with the United States was not seriously retarded. The business cycle, as always in the case of a construction material, caused serious fluctuations, but the growth of population and the expansion of cities, particularly on the eastern seaboard of the United States and in the midwest, meant that the long-term trend continued to rise. The period of the Reciprocity Treaty saw, indeed, a profound reorientation in the external trading relations of the British North American colonies. The American market increased in importance, while the British market suffered a relative decline. This shift was not caused exclusively by reciprocity and it did not reverse itself when reciprocity ended. Britain was never again after 1854 to take as large a proportion of the exports and imports of the North American colonies as she had before. The United States increasingly supplanted Britain as the pace-setter of the Canadian economy and as the principal source of disturbance.

In no area of economic activity was this reorientation more apparent than in the lumber industry. Exports of square timber and deals to Britain continued, to be sure, into the second half of the century, but the advent of the ocean steamship and the increasing use of iron and steel for construction purposes cut into demand. The depression of 1873, for all practical purposes, may be taken as marking the end of the trade. Exports of sawn lumber to the United States continued to grow, however, providing the Canadian provinces with an important source of employment, capital, and dollar earnings. As resources of the best white pine grew scarce, red pine, spruce and other woods previously considered inferior were pressed into service, particularly in the new pulp-and-paper industry. With the construction of railways and, later, the opening of the Canadian west, the lumber industry of eastern Canada expanded beyond the basin of Lake Ontario, the St. Lawrence, and the Ottawa until it covered the entire basin of the Great Lakes and the northern margin of the prairies, wherever forest resources were to be found, as far west as the Rocky Mountains. Meanwhile in British Columbia a lumber industry which had developed initially in response to the demands of the gold-rush in the late 1850's expanded in the closing decades of the nineteenth century to serve markets in the prairie provinces and later in the United States and the Orient.

Throughout this entire period, from the time when the first mast contracts were filled in New Brunswick, the forest resources of the British North American colonies had been exploited primarily to serve the needs of more advanced economies. Canadian wood as masts had served the Royal Navy; as square timber, the factories and houses of industrial Britain; as sawn lumber, the sprawling cities of the United States; and as pulpwood, the printing presses of the world. Whatever the particular form in which it was produced, wood provided the Canadian economy for more than a century with a vitally important staple export—a means whereby the British North American colonies could pay their current expenses in the world of international trade and at the same time attract capital, labour, and enterprise to further their future development. As a staple export, timber bridged the gap between fur and wheat, between the canoe and the railway. Unlike fur, the timber trade called for the destruction of the forests, not for their preservation. In its relation to immigration and settlement it served as a positive accelerating force, whereas the fur trade, on the whole, had delayed and discouraged. Unlike wheat, the timber industry did not involve permanent settlement on the land nor the investment of large amounts of capital in the construction of expensive transportation systems. Its transportation requirements were relatively simple, involving mainly use of the natural waterways of the Precambrian Shield and the Great Lakes. The railroad became a significant factor in the lumber industry only with the opening of the American market and the expansion of north-south trade in the late 1840's. With this shift in the lines of trade, an industry which had developed originally in response to the demands of industrialization in Britain shifted its support to the rapidly industrializing economy of the United States.

SUGGESTIONS FOR FURTHER READING

BASIC WORKS:

Lower, A. R. M., "The Trade in Square Timber", University of Toronto Studies, History and Economics, *Contributions to Canadian Economics*, Vol. VI (1933), pp. 40-61

Lower, A. R. M., *Settlement and the Forest Frontier in Eastern Canada* (Canadian Frontiers of Settlement, Vol. IX, Toronto, 1936), Chapters I-V, pp. 1-57

Lower, A. R. M., *The North American Assault on the Canadian Forest: A History of the Lumber Trade between Canada and the United States* (Toronto, 1938), Chapters I-XIII, pp. 1-159

SUPPLEMENTARY WORKS:

Albion, Robert G., *Forests and Sea Power: The Timber Problem of the Royal Navy, 1652-1862* (Cambridge, Mass., 1926), Chapters I-X, pp. 1-414

Calvin, D. D., *A Saga of the St. Lawrence: Timber and Shipping through Three Generations* (Toronto, 1945), Chapters I-IV, VI-VII, pp. 1-108, 145-74

Innis, Harold A. and A. R. M. Lower, *Select Documents in Canadian Economic History*, 1783-1885 (Toronto, 1933), pp. 266-80, 502-24

Innis, Harold A., "Unused Capacity as a Factor in Canadian Economic History", in *Political Economy in the Modern State* (Toronto, 1946), pp. 201-17

CHAPTER X

THE NORTH PACIFIC: 1783–1821

INTERNATIONAL RIVALRIES ON THE PACIFIC COAST

IN THE emphasis that has been placed on developments in the North Atlantic area and on continental expansion across North America, there is danger of overlooking one of the most strategic regions in our history. Events in the North Pacific helped to shape the destinies of North America in the nineteenth century, and today growing interest in the rich resources of the Pacific coast states of the United States, and in those of British Columbia, Alaska, Eastern Siberia, and Northern China is evidence that this once neglected part of the globe is rapidly becoming one of the most significant areas in world economics and politics. Its early history, like that of the North Atlantic, may be viewed as an extension of European influence in the New World. And again, once beginnings are made, much of its history must be written in terms of a close interplay between Europe and the Americas.

Early rivalries in the North Pacific were part of a world-wide struggle for control of trade routes and strategic resources. Operations began in the late eighteenth century in an inhospitable environment characterized by its remoteness and inaccessibility. For the most part they were based on the exploitation of a staple whose rapid exhaustion forced continual penetration of new areas and made successful conduct of the trade extraordinarily difficult. It was the fortunes of this trade that help to account for the weakness of Spain in this area, the expansion and withdrawal of Russia, the obstacles facing England by sea, and the appearance of the United States and Canada on the Pacific.

Although the economic history of the North Pacific begins with the appearance of the first white trader, claims have been made of the existence of an extensive aboriginal commerce before the appearance of the white man. The Indians of the region once possessed a complex and highly developed social system, and a similarly well-developed economic system makes a plausible and inviting thesis. Numerous references can be found concerning trade and communications established over long distances via the protected coastal waters extending from the Columbia River north to Alaska. Trading commodities are described, e.g., slaves, canoes, oil, dried fish, cedar bark, and dentalium shells, in a network dominated by the Chinooks of the Columbia River region and the Tsimshians far to the north. Great trading marts are said to have existed at the Dalles on the Columbia and in the north near Fort Simpson. Middlemen such as the Makah of Cape Flattery are mentioned, and the trading language of the region, the Chinook Jargon, is described as existing before the white man came.

More recent research, however, provides no support for these claims of an early and extensive aboriginal trade. There is no evidence of exchange on any considerable scale. Raids for slaves and plunder were common, but commercial enterprise as an object in itself was almost unknown. Commerce came with the white trader who carried on an intertribal trade along coastal waters, using native commodities where it paid, and with him developed the Jargon, the universal trade language of the coast. Later, when the sea otter, the great staple of the maritime trade, was mined out in the north, Indian middlemen appeared bartering with the interior tribes for furs desired by the maritime fur trades. Even this offshoot of the white man's trade disappeared when the Hudson's Bay Company established a line of forts to cut such routes to the interior. We must conclude that there is no satisfactory evidence of extensive Indian trade and particularly of a north-south coastal trading network.

SPAIN

As indicated in our first chapter, Spain's claim to a monopoly of the Pacific was a force to be reckoned with in the North Pacific as well as farther south. It was pointed out that her holdings in North America were marginal to her system in South and Central America and that they were in fact more important to her as a defensive position than as an area of potential resource development. As a result, her grip was weaker in North America, too weak to check British expansion in the Carolinas and Georgia. By 1763, Spain had lost the Floridas to England and there seemed little prospect that she could hold in check a power which had gained control of the eastern Mississippi valley, Canada, and important French territories in the Caribbean. Her day in North America, however, was not yet done. When France withdrew from the continent, Spain received Louisiana (New Orleans and the western half of the Mississippi valley). Later, when the American Revolution took England's attention, Spain moved to recover lost ground, and in 1783 we find her back in the Floridas (West Florida, 1779-81, and East Florida, 1783). The Gulf of Mexico became once more a zone of Spanish control.

Over the period from 1787 to 1795, a line of forts was constructed in the Mississippi valley region which gave Spain command of the upper banks of the great river and markedly strengthened her defences against English expansion westward. In addition, new settlements were founded on the Pacific coast in the years 1760-97, and such place names as Los Angeles, San Fernando, Santa Barbara and San Francisco attest to the importance of Spanish influence in this part of the North American continent. Established in Florida, Louisiana and California, Spain could and did provide strong opposition to Anglo-American moves on the continent, and to those of Russians, English, and New Englanders in the North Pacific. In control of the Panama region and well situated to block penetration from the Atlantic round the southern tip of South America, Spain's position in the New World behind the barrier of the two Americas provided a formidable obstacle to foreigners who wished to venture into the North Pacific.

This Spanish recovery in the late eighteenth century provides good support for the adage that empires die slowly. Spain not only extended her territorial control in the New World but also made a strenuous though belated attempt to modify her rigid and outmoded colonial system along more efficient and aggressive lines. Steps were taken to liberalize trade, or in other words to release it from many of the long-established, traditional practices which had prevented a freer expansion of enterprise. The tightly regulated Fleet system was abolished, direct trade was permitted among the colonies and between colonies and mother country, and such chartered organizations as the Caracas Company (1737) and the Royal Philippine Company (1785) were established. These policies had as their objective the bringing of Spain into the main stream of European economic progress. And there appeared for a few brief years the prospect of developing a progressive and expanding trade linking New Spain (Mexico) with the Orient, either by direct trade at Canton, or indirectly through Manila in the Philippines. The valuable sea otter of the northwest coast of North America and the California coast could be picked up from the Indians in exchange for Spanish cloth, copper and other items of trade and used as a means of acquiring Oriental products and particularly the quicksilver of China so badly needed in the mines of New Spain. Spain appeared to have the location and the resources for the development of a thriving trade linking her possessions across the Pacific. Spanish sailors had known of the sea otter, so highly valued in China, a decade or so before published accounts of Captain Cook's voyage to the North Pacific appeared in 1784. Once the news was out, however, ships from England and the United States, some of the former under Portuguese flag, and a few from France appeared in the Pacific in pursuit of a staple which was initially in abundant supply and for which there was a strong market demand.

If Spain had succeeded in dominating this great new staple trade her grip on the whole Pacific region would have been greatly strengthened. Promising beginnings in other lines of commerce had already been made before the sea otter was discovered. The first Spanish galleon crossed the Pacific in 1565, the last in 1815. Her shipping linked Acapulco in

Mexico and Manila in the Philippines in conduct of a trade in which the most valuable spices of the east, silks, brocades and damasks, were exchanged for colonial wares and the silver of Peru. The Philippines were under Spanish control by 1572, and Manila emerged as a great way station between China and Spanish America. There was abundant opportunities here for a commercial nation bent on maximizing its gains from trade. The commerce of Spain, however, was being conducted as a royal monopoly; it was only toward the end of Spanish control that serious attempts were made to liberalize her economic policy and these came too late. Experiments in company conduct of trade came at a time when the chartered company as an instrument of state expansion had seen its best days.

The obstacles which prevented a healthy enterprise expansion in the Pacific in both established and new lines of development may be noted briefly. First, in the seventeenth and eighteenth centuries, Pacific trade was far removed from its weak home base in Europe, a base so weak that only first-rate leadership in the New World made it possible for Spain to hold out as long as she did. Her construction of a Pacific defensive zone from so distant a centre in Europe must be regarded as a remarkable achievement. The area she claimed as her own stretched from the west coast of North America to the eastern periphery of a circle which ran from Kamchatka to south of the equator in Polynesia, with the Philippines as the key point in the whole North Pacific structure of empire. It is little wonder that her policies of exclusion from so vast an area were ineffective in the face of English and French attacks on her shipping, the intervention of New England traders round the Horn and the entry of Russian traders who were to push south from Sitka. Spain's reach was beyond her grasp, but in boldness and imagination her leadership in the New World was unequalled.

Secondly, even in the later eighteenth century and in spite of attempts to liberalize her trading system, Spain's economy never broke loose from medieval controls and the grip of intensive and frequently restrictive regulations laid down in the interest of long-established monopoly positions in the old country. Designs for trade expansion along new lines or into new territories were thwarted by those who saw in them a threat to traditional forms of enterprise. For example, an expanding trade in Oriental silks was held in check by the Andalusian cities who feared the destruction of the domestic silk industry. Similarly, strong monopoly interests in the Philippines in control of the sale of Oriental products in America stood opposed to the plans of trading firms and individuals seeking to open up new avenues of Pacific commerce. The Philippine Company, like the British East India Company in the English system, discouraged a freer and more expansive growth of transpacific enterprise. However, as indicated in our first chapter, England's economy at this time was rapidly freeing itself from traditional restraints on the pursuit of the gains of trade, in contrast to that of Spain which remained strongly medieval in outlook and organization. And it is this continuation of corporate control of Spain's economic life that accounts in good part for her failure to develop a more flexible, innovational trading system in the North Pacific.

Thirdly, Spain's transpacific system suffered from one supremely bad bit of luck. For centuries Spanish ships passed almost within sight of the Hawaiian Islands which are almost directly on the line between Mexico and Manila. The practice of following the northeast trade winds on the way to the Philippines, and on the return the prevailing westerlies, led to her missing the Islands which lay between the zones of prevailing winds. As a great station of supplies and provisions the Islands would have enormously strengthened Spain's position in the Pacific and reduced the misery of the long voyages so graphically described by Professor Morison and others. The New Englanders were to make good use of these Islands in their China trade and even the Russians were to contemplate gaining a foothold in the area.

Summing up at this point: the strength of monopoly elements in Spanish enterprise in the Old World and the New effectively held in check new lines of trade and resource development. These were essential if there was to be successful opposition to the free-ranging enterprisers who were moving into her Pacific preserves. Failure to cope successfully with these intruders hastened her retreat from the northern parts of the Pacific, a retreat which was to end in withdrawal from her holdings in southern North America, in loss of political control of Mexico, and finally, in the destruction of her long-held positions in South America.

RUSSIA

An early threat to Spanish claims in the New World had presented itself with the appearance in the eighteenth century of Russian explorers and traders in northern waters. Professor Kerner has noted the close parallel that may be drawn between the expansion of the fur trade across Siberia to the Pacific and that across North America from the Atlantic to the Pacific coast. In both instances, furs provided the incentive and in both extensive use was made of rivers, lakes, portages and fortified centres or posts. Furs formed the most important item in Russia's domestic and foreign commerce in the sixteenth and seventeenth centuries, they made the greatest contribution to her commercial intercourse with other countries, and the private fur-trader was the most important element in the rise of an independent commercial class. The strong demand for this staple in western Europe in the sixteenth century drew the attention of the state and of private traders to Siberia and led directly to continental expansion across enormous distances.

At first the state gave active support to this exploitation of a resource which represented both an important source of state revenue and a highly liquid emergency reserve. State participation was not effective over great distances, however, and the onward push to the North Pacific was continued in eastern Siberia by individual traders and more actively by private companies. Russia's failure to establish political control over the Amur region in the face of Manchu opposition in the seventeenth century lost to her a potentially rich area of agricultural supplies, a set-back which helped to delay the conquest of Siberia for almost two centuries and proved to be a serious detriment to the successful prosecution of trade in North Pacific waters.

It was on Vitus Bering's second expedition in 1741 (the first was in 1728) that he and his companion, Chirikov, reached the coast of North America. Bering perished on this expedition but Chirikov lived to tell of his exploits. These explorations led to numerous private ventures along the Aleutian chain of islands, although it was not until 1769 that the relation of these islands to the mainland was determined and not until 1783 that Russia established her first permanent base on North America at Kodiak Island. The Russians, aware of Spanish opposition to such intrusion, were in no hurry to publicize their movements, nor had private traders, anxious to escape state taxation (yassack or tribute) by a corrupt officialdom, any incentive for making known these early developments. However, embassy reports from St. Petersburg made known Russian moves and Spain's uneasiness as to Russia's designs led her to move north up the Pacific coast. The beginnings of her occupation of upper California in 1769 was only in part a reaction to Russian expansion, but following 1774 her explorations in northern waters were in direct response to this threat. In 1774 Spain's Perez reached 55 degrees north latitude; other explorers followed in 1775-6 and 1779, although it was not until 1788 that contact was made with the Russians. In the following year Spanish interest in the North Pacific brought her into conflict, not with Russia, however, but with the English traders who followed Cook's steps to Nootka Sound on Vancouver Island. In 1789, Martinez captured four English vessels engaging in the otter trade. Nootka Sound was fortified and missions established. England threatened war and Spain, failing to enlist the support of France, was forced to abandon her exclusive claims to the northwest coast. Following 1790 the whole region was open to the traders who were hardy enough to seek profits in this harsh and inhospitable environment.

Well before this date official Russian explorations had given way to the activities of merchants and adventurers lured by the rich fur resources of eastern Siberia and beyond. The *promyshlenniki*, like the *coureurs de bois* of the French fur trade in North America, hunted the furs over vast distances and in the face of great hardships. Sable and ermine, marten and sea otter found ready markets in Europe and China. The sea otter in particular brought very high prices at Kiakhta on the Russo-Chinese border of Siberia and as early as the 1740's groups of tough enterprisers formed to take advantage of the opportunities present in abundant resources and good returns. Merchants and *promyshlenniki* working on a share basis pushed on to the Aleutian and Kurile Islands in pursuit of the otter. Subject to few regulations and competing fiercely they made their own rules as expansion proceeded. They faced the demands of a harsh and dangerous environment made more difficult by the hatred of the natives whom they treated barbarously and the interference at home of a corrupt officialdom more interested in bribes than in the maintenance of law and order. In the two decades preceding 1790 the mainspring of expansion in the eastern limits of empire was the private merchant who pioneered in a trade which laid the foundations for Russian enterprise in the North Pacific area. Although in the reign of such rulers as Catherine the Great (1762-96) official support was not lacking, it was the private adventurer who bore the risks incurred in this eastern extension of Russian control.

As a result of the great uncertainties of this far-flung commerce, individuals and small groups slowly gave way to larger concerns more capable of coping with the almost overwhelming obstacles facing those who explored, fought and traded in this dangerous environment. The greatest of these was founded by Gregorii Shelekhov and his partner Ivan Golikov in 1781, and under their firm's leadership Kodiak and part of the adjacent mainland was occupied. It was becoming apparent, however, that only a very powerful organization could meet the demands of trade and exploration, and the pressure increased as expansion into the Pacific brought competition with the traders of other powers. The experience of the Russian traders, like that of the North West Company in its early phase, was to underline the fact that intense rivalry among small groups is no way to conduct difficult and dangerous enterprises operating far from their home base. Costs were too high and uncertainties too great for other than the strong unit to survive. Shelekhov and others were realistic enough to see that only by monopoly control of the northwest of America was there any prospect of successful operations in the North Pacific. And further, only government support of such a monopoly could make this great venture sufficiently attractive to encourage the investment of capital and energy necessary if Russian enterprise was to move along the Aleutian chain of islands to North America. Shelekhov showed himself to be equally realistic in his appointment of Alexander Baranov as general manager of his company's operations in the Pacific in 1791, for Baranov was to be one of the great figures of the fur trade in North America, his achievements being matched only by those of Sir George Simpson of the Hudson's Bay Company.

Every argument was used to obtain monopoly rights to North Pacific trade; they included the promotion of imperial interests, the conversion of the natives to Christianity and the benefits of an expanding commerce. Matters came to a head when a rival company applied for incorporation, and finally in 1799 the Russian-American Company emerged to end the long and chaotic rule of competing groups. It was chartered as a monopoly organization and designed to serve as an instrument of Russian expansion in the Pacific area. As its head, Baranov found himself faced with problems which taxed all his managerial ingenuity and skill. Added to those of scarce supplies and difficult market connections were others arising from the intense hostility of the Tlingits of the north and the activities of other traders seeking to establish themselves in the area Russia sought to make her own. Sitka, founded in 1799 to curb the operations of Boston trading ships, was destroyed three years later by natives in a widespread and savage uprising, and it was not until 1805 that peace was restored and steps taken to reorganize the Company's position.

The most crucial problem at this time was that of supplies. Food and provisions were brought in via Yakutsk and Okhotsk, a route too slow and precarious to serve as a satisfactory source of the necessities of life and trade. With the support of Nikolai Rezanov, a favourite of Alexander I, new supply areas were sought to the south in America. Plans for a settlement at the mouth of the Columbia River did not work out, nor did arrangements made with the Spaniards in California. Attempts to establish reciprocal relations with the Hawaiian Islands and Manila also came to nought. A partial solution seemed to have been found when an agreement was made with Astor's American Fur Company by which the Americans were to ship supplies to Sitka and to load Russian furs for Canton. By this arrangement, Baranov expected to reduce his dependence on New England traders and Astor to squeeze out his chief rival, the North West Company. Unfortunately, war between the United States and Great Britain left Astor in a hopeless position, and in 1813 his Pacific centre of operations, Astoria, at the mouth of the Columbia River, was sold to the Canadian company. As a result of his failure in these and similar negotiations Baranov was unable to escape dependence on the New Englanders who supplied as much as one-fifth of his wants.

A more direct attack on the supply problem was made in 1812 when Fort Ross in California (approximately sixty-five miles north of San Francisco) was established as a farming settlement. For more than a quarter of a century this establishment supplied grain and livestock to the Company. But at best supplies from Fort Ross were far from meeting the Company's needs and it was finally sold in 1841 to John Sutter, seven years before gold was discovered at Sutter's Creek and the California gold-rush began. Faced by these limited results, Baranov made the best of a highly uncertain supply situation. Provisions from New England vessels and occasionally limited supplies by sea from St. Petersburg helped to supplement those from the Siberia route and from Fort Ross.

Equally difficult problems were encountered in the marketing of the Company's furs. These had become serious when in the eighteenth century Canton replaced Kiakhta on the Siberian border as the major port of entry, for direct Russian maritime trade with Canton was prohibited as a consequence of strained Russo-Chinese relations. This again led to dependence on the ubiquitous New England trader who was happy to ship Russian furs to Canton for a consideration. Even though this dependence was by no means one-sided, it greatly increased the uncertainties of trade as sea-otter operations extended southward along the Pacific coast of North America, a shift which for a brief period led to co-operation between Yankees and Russians in the taking of the sea otter as well as its carriage to the Chinese market.

Strong Spanish opposition in California waters made bartering for furs with natives a difficult and dangerous operation, and, since the Yankee traders lacked equipment and hunters for catching the sea otter themselves, they looked to the Russians for assistance. The latter were agreeable since arrangements even with competitors brightened the prospect of an eventual Russian move south. In 1803, on the basis of an equal division of the catch, Yankees and Russians worked together in a profitable arrangement to which the Spanish could offer only ineffectual opposition. Baranov regarded this co-operative action as purely temporary, a matter of expedience until the Russian-American Company itself could expand southward. As a step in this direction, an independent hunting expedition was dispatched in 1809 to the otter grounds of San Francisco Bay, but the Spanish authorities stiffened their opposition and this and like ventures failed to yield the profits expected. More success marked the use of Fort Ross as a centre for hunting operations but again stiff Spanish resistance greatly hampered the hunters, and it became increasingly apparent that only by lawful arrangements with the Spanish could the Russians hope to make any substantial progress. However, in spite of overtures designed to permit operations on a share basis with the Spanish, permission for otter-hunting by the Russians was never given. Spanish resistance ceased in 1822 when Mexico achieved her independence, but the change brought little improvement for the Russians. Following a few experimental contacts with them the Mexican government returned to the Spanish policy of excluding all foreigners from adjacent hunting-grounds. Depletion of the fur resources of the area was given as the reason for reserving hunting operations to Mexican residents. Legal restrictions and the depletion of the sea otter in the Fort Ross area led to the abandonment of the Russian centre there.

Baranov's accomplishments in the face of appalling difficulties must be regarded as remarkable, but for all that he was suspended in 1817. He

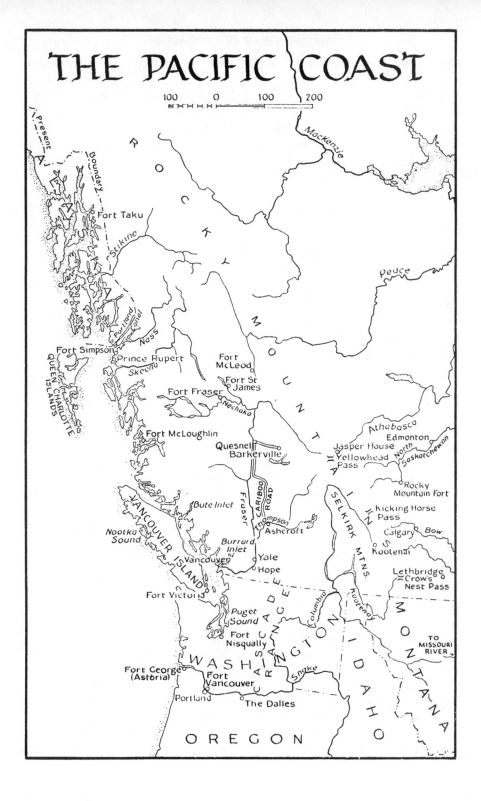

THE PACIFIC COAST

100   0   100   200

died on his homeward voyage in the following year. In spite of the handicaps imposed by the physical environment and unsolvable problems of supplies and markets, this tough and able administrator sought to dominate the whole northwest maritime trade and in the process drive his New England rivals out of the trade altogether. Failure to make the area a Russian fur-trade preserve was the consequence of circumstances beyond his control, but he made the best of the few opportunities presented him in the course of his administration.

At the time of his death, the Russian-American Company's first charter was about to expire. Following a review of the Company's activities, the charter was renewed and in addition Russia, in her famous ukase of 1821, laid claim to exclusive hunting and fishing rights in the waters adjacent to her American and Asiatic holdings. This represented an area extending from Bering Strait south to 51° north latitude on the North American coast, and from Bering Strait to 45° 50' on the Asiatic side. It is important to note that Russian claims included that of sovereignty over the North American mainland south to the 51st parallel. Spain's earlier monopoly demands had evaporated only to be replaced by those of Russia, another power seeking to erect defences against "foreign" intervention and one in no position to enforce its claims against those of England and United States. These nations had common interests arising from the Convention of 1818 in which an agreement had been reached which left the area west of the Rockies open to the citizens of both countries for a period of ten years. The tangled negotiations which followed made clear two closely related facts in the situation at this time: one, that Russia's hold on North America was too weak for effective support of her claims, and two, that the real issue was that of Anglo-American conflict for control in North America, an issue which was decided in this area only in 1846.

In spite of capable and aggressive leadership, there were limitations present in the Russian venture into the Pacific quite as serious as the handicaps imposed by the physical environment and the unsolved problem of supplies. Semi-feudalistic Russia, deeply involved in European affairs, was unable to support her Pacific trade empire to the degree necessary to place it on a firm and lasting basis. Interested officials at times were able to enlist considerable state support, but the Company lacked the political strength of a state agency or of an influential mercantile class. As a result this distant trade was seldom a significant element in state policies and never became part of a comprehensive or well-rounded commercial system. Although attempts were made from time to time to exploit resources other than fur, geography placed too many obstacles in the way of a more diversified development, and as we indicated in discussing the fur trade of the St. Lawrence region, fur has many and serious drawbacks as a support for the empire-builder. As a consequence no strong and aggressive colony emerged which could be effectively integrated with the economy of the mother country.

The Russian-American Company was to continue operations in the northwest until the 1860's, but it had become apparent long before then that its grip on this part of the world was too weak to permit of permanent settlements of any importance on the North American mainland. Only the establishment of a strong position in Siberia and the colonization of this great area would have made possible the expansion of operations in America so forcefully advocated by Baranov. Like the beaver of North America, the sea otter encouraged rapid expansion, but in the process drained man-power and capital from more stable and permanent developments. Exhaustion of the more accessible sea otter along with unsolved problems of supply and markets in the end forced withdrawal from a position whose weakness made a mockery of Russian claims to exclusive control of an area Spain had once claimed as its own.

Control of the Pacific coast region of North America was to be decided by Great Britain and the United States and the issue was to rest finally on the course of continental expansion across North America to the Pacific. The early contestants, Spain and Russia, were to retreat to the margins and finally to leave the Americas altogether. Nevertheless their long participation in North Pacific affairs left its mark on North American economic development. Other powers had to make headway against their pretensions to monopoly and in their attempts to circumvent these were able to capitalize on points of weakness in both systems. It may be concluded that on balance the Yankee traders benefited from the presence of the Russians through their ability to serve as middlemen and as partners in the California hunting-fields. And because of their flexible and aggressive organization of trade they came close to achieving what some Spanish visionaries had sought to achieve, a thriving transpacific trade linking the Orient with the New World. As the maritime flank of a young and expanding continental power, New England in the North Pacific possessed advantages unmatched by the badly handicapped Russian-American Company and the cumbersome slow-moving bureaucracy of Spain. Only England displayed the same commercial drive, and we may note briefly the reasons for her failure to dominate the commerce of the North Pacific in the decades following Captain Cook's explorations in this area.

GREAT BRITAIN

In 1778, when Cook's ships, the *Restoration* and the *Discovery*, had anchored in Nootka Sound, his mariners took aboard sea-otter skins, furs which yielded handsome return when the ships called later at Canton. When the news reached England, other vessels were quickly fitted out to engage in this new line of commerce. They failed, however, to receive any support from the British East India Company whose claims to monopoly of British Pacific trade led some English shipowners to operate under foreign flags. More important to the lack of any sustained interest in this region were the alternative opportunities present elsewhere in world trade. The East India Company, in particular, had much more important interests at stake than the resources of the northwest coast, a region lacking any promise as a market for goods and one whose fur supplies threatened the stability of the Chinese market. A policy of indifference and neglect rather than active monopoly opposition discouraged any development of British trade in this region. And although Captain Vancouver's explorations in 1792 greatly increased England's knowledge of the North Pacific area, early English leadership in this maritime trade quickly gave way before the free-ranging ships of Boston which had all but ousted the handicapped English sea captains by the end of the century. A few ventures were carried out under charter from the East India Company and a number of successful voyages were completed independently, but England's success in linking up her possessions in the North Atlantic had no parallel in the North Pacific. Further, the shadow of Napoleon lay across the continent of Europe and preoccupation with this danger checked interest in the development of a strongly supported transpacific trade.

More definite progress for the British came with the extension of company control across the continent of North America to the Pacific. Although it was a short-cut to the Orient which at first attracted explorers to these shores, it was the fur trade which provided the drive and initiative necessary to transcontinental expansion. As indicated in an earlier chapter, the North West Company, following amalgamation with its rival the XY Company in 1804, led the way in the extension of British enterprise to the Pacific slope, a leadership ended only by its absorption in a greater organization, the Hudson's Bay Company, in 1821. The push to the sea was given new energy with the news in 1807 of the success of the Lewis and Clark expedition across the continent to the south. In that year David Thompson built Kootenai House near Lake Windermere, the first trading-post in the Columbia region. In 1810 he discovered the great Athabasca Pass, an important link in trade connections with the east, and by his explorations laid the groundwork for the Company's trade in the Columbia basin. It was unfortunate that he delayed his journey to the Pacific until 1811 for on his arrival at the mouth of the Columbia he found the Americans had preceded him, with Astoria established as a promising centre of operations of Astor's American Fur Company.

Another representative of the Company, Simon Fraser, in 1805 had built Fort McLeod, the first trading-post west of the Rockies. In 1807, Fort George was built at the confluence of the Nechako and Fraser Rivers, and in the following year the Fraser was explored to its mouth. Through his efforts, New Caledonia, lying between the 49th and 58th parallels, was to become an important district of the Company; as part of the Athabasca Department it embraced the area westward to the coast, bounded on the north by a vaguely defined division between Russian and British interests and on the south by the watershed between the Fraser and Columbia Rivers. The Columbia Department to the south covered the Columbia River watershed including the northern part of what is now Utah. These two administrative divisions were kept in communication through Fort Kamloops at the confluence of the northern and southern branches of the Thompson River, a centre which was also the main link between transcontinental routes and those on the Pacific slope.

The North West Company's Pacific venture raised the familiar problem of supplies and costly communications over great distances. It quickly became apparent that dependence on supplies and markets across the continent must be reduced by maritime arrangements if profits were to be made from the Pacific districts. Further, the market of China, like that of England, called for maritime connections. The purchase of Astoria in 1813 gave the Company the necessary gateway to oceanic commerce. Lack of connections in the Canton market, however, led the North-Westers to rely on American maritime traders for entry into the Orient. From 1813 to 1821 a mutually profitable arrangement enabled the Yankees to take supplies to Astoria, exchange them for furs there, and proceed thence to Canton for Oriental products in demand in Boston and near-by markets. While this aided the North West Company in the operations of its Columbia district, the fact remains that no balanced trading system evolved in the form of a thriving transpacific commerce within the British structure of trade. It was not until after 1821 that more satisfactory maritime connections were established by the Hudson's Bay Company and these were mainly with England.

NEW ENGLAND

By the close of the eighteenth century the advantage in the North Pacific lay with the maritime traders of New England, and for the better part of the next two decades they profitably exploited the long-distance otter trade. For them the beginnings of this trade had occurred at a most opportune time. Looking at the larger picture for a moment, it is well to keep in mind that in his native Massachusetts the merchant was leader in politics and society well into the nineteenth century. Owning or chartering vessels that carried his goods into most ports of the world, he knew the markets of Europe, the West Indies, the Spanish Main, the northwest coast and the Orient. His activities were many and diversified and on his prosperity hinged the welfare of his state. It was an area that lived to a unique degree on its trade, and following the American Revolution the conditions of trade left much to be desired. During the War of Independence privateering had kept much of its shipping employed but peace brought depression, and difficult problems of adjustment emerged to test this commercial state to the utmost. For several decades Great Britain was to aim at the construction of a new and self-sufficient empire free of dependence on the trade and produce of New England and her sister states. The British West Indies, if possible, were to be closed to the new "foreigners" who were to pay heavily for their independence until new lines of enterprise had been discovered. New England's ship-building, like her trade, suffered both from British policies and the strong competition of European nations for the world's carrying-trade and for markets for their products. Agriculture, like her fisheries and commerce, faced post-war dislocation, and civil disorders in 1786-7 attested to the strains present in these difficult years.

Fortunately the situation was not without its bright spots. New England's export staples were badly needed in near-by British possessions and her long experience in smuggling and other forms of evasion stood her in good stead when regulations blocked normal commercial intercourse. But more than the old established trade lines and commodities was necessary to New England's economic recovery, and it was at this crucial point in her history that opportunities in the Pacific drew the more venturesome of her traders to the far northwest coast of America, the Hawaiian Islands and Canton, the fur mart of the Orient. For them, Captain Cook's discovery of the Hawaiian Islands and of the sea otter of Pacific coastal waters and its value in the Canton market was well timed and they quickly turned to advantage this fortunate chain of events.

As early as 1788 Captain Robert Gray's ship *Columbia* had visited the northwest and on his return to Boston two years later there began a new and profitable commerce which linked this New England centre with the northwest coast and Canton. The China trade of the United States had had its beginnings in 1784 with the voyage of the *Empress of China* out of New York and its successful prosecution rested on the discovery of trading commodities which could be exchanged for Oriental wares. Just as the men of Salem found their answer to trade expansion in the spices of the East Indies, those of Boston found theirs in the sea otter of more northerly regions in the Pacific. Other vessels quickly followed in the track of the *Columbia,* and in the early 1790's Boston ships sailing round Cape Horn to the Pacific northwest, the Hawaiian Islands and Canton were moving to dominance of the maritime commerce of this vast area. The Islands occupied a key place in this system of trade, both as a centre of supplies and after 1815 as a source of sandalwood, a staple in abundant supply and good demand in the joss houses of China. The aggressive commercialism of New England, its strength as a centre of shipbuilding and of experienced merchants and seamen constituted elements of strength in enterprise expansion with which other powers had to come to terms.

It was these elements which enabled the Boston traders to cope with the traders and statesmen of Russia and Spain and to exploit profitably the weakness of the monopoly claims of others seeking to exclude them from the sea-otter fields of the Pacific. Operating that small unit of enterprise, the trading vessel, well supplied by a strong and diversified home base, these enterprisers roamed about at will in search of the gains of trade. In a real sense they occupied the key position in the larger network of commerce which linked the Orient with the possessions of Russia, Spain and England on the Pacific shores of North America and with New England in the North Atlantic region. And it was the sea otter which served as an indispensable medium of exchange in a trade which brought teas, nankeens, crepes, and silks to Boston. Free of monopoly controls within their own system of trade, the New Englanders operated in the interstices within and between larger systems which in varying degrees depended on them for supplies and as carriers of pelts to the Canton market. Their central position in North Pacific commerce was unchallenged until the War of 1812 with its unfortunate consequences for long-distance maritime trade.

Two factors were to lead to a rapid decline in the importance of New England's trade in the North Pacific. In the first place, leadership in continental expansion in the United States fell, not to Boston, but to New York, and with this expansion maritime influences in New England as in the nation weakened with growing interest in internal development. The day of the free-ranging Boston trader was not yet past, but it was drawing to a close. Secondly, the rapid depletion of sea otter in northern waters led to a shift of operations to California hunting-grounds and later to the great hides and tallow trade. Increasingly sharp competition in the northwest and the hostility of Indian tribes hastened this shift, although in the end it was the success of the Hudson's Bay Company in the late 1820's in cutting communications with the interior that finally eliminated the maritime trader and established company control over the fur trade of the northwest.

As early as 1796, the activities of New Englanders in California waters had begun with the visit of the Boston ship *Otter* to Monterey. Plans to link voyages to the northwest and to California were soon under way and evidence soon appears of illegal trade with Indians on Spanish territory. The intruders had little to learn about smuggling, but Spanish opposition and the disinterest of California Indians in hunting soon led to co-operation with the Russians under a mutually profitable contract system, an arrangement which continued over the period 1803-12. The outbreak of the Mexican Revolution raised the traders' hopes of a somewhat more stable commerce with the mainland, one based on the exchange of needed supplies there for sea-otter furs. For a brief interval both the California missions and the Russian settlement at Fort Ross utilized the services of the maritimers who roamed the Pacific in search of commodities of trade. However, Spain's continued opposition to dealing with foreign traders and Russia's refusal to resume contract relations with the Yankees led the latter to place an increasingly heavy emphasis on contraband trade. They were helped by weakening Spanish control and the growing needs of the local population which favoured smuggling operations even though Spain continued her obstructive tactics to the end of Spanish power in California in 1822. Mexican independence opened a new era in the California trade and, as the northwest coast lost its appeal, interest increasingly shifted to California as an integral element in the China trade. And in spite of the depletion of the sea otter in California fields a trade in otter- and seal-skins continued to the 1840's when the hides and tallow trade and the whaling industry of the resourceful New Englanders replaced a staple which had for decades provided them with the means of dominating the maritime commerce of the North Pacific.

For a brief interval merchants of Boston and Hawaii carried on a combined trade in furs and hides, but apart from a dwindling flow of furs to Hawaii and thence to the Orient the otter ceased to be of any importance in Pacific commerce. For more than a quarter of a century it had enabled New England to acquire the wares of the Orient, to build a far-ranging transpacific carrying-trade and in so doing to exploit the disabilities of her English, Russian and Spanish rivals. New England's traders, spearheading United States expansion in the North Pacific, roused the nation's interest in the resources of this distant area. Their maritime ventures promoted American settlement in California, drew land-traders to the coast in the 1830's and eventually led to effective demands for military protection of American vessels, merchants and seamen. They had drawn attention to the commercial possibilities of the Pacific coast, and diplomacy and the flag were not slow to follow in their footsteps. Even though this maritime trade was a passing phase in Pacific history, there can be no doubt that United States expansion to the Pacific coast was quickened by the drive and aggressiveness of the merchants and mariners of Boston.

Although New England's trade with Canton was only one aspect of her nation's commercial contacts with the Orient, it has been singled out in these pages because of its strategic role in the history of the North Pacific area. Mention should be made, however, of the maritime ventures of John Jacob Astor in the northwest. As early as 1808 this great enterpriser had decided to tie in the fur trade of the northwest coast with his commercial ventures linking New York with the Canton market. In pursuit of this aim he sent vessels to the Columbia region in the years

1809-11. His ship, the *Enterprise*, in her voyage of 1809-12 made two voyages from Sitka to Canton, but other vessels were less fortunate. The *Tonquin* was blown up on the northwest coast, the *Lark* was wrecked in the Hawaiian Islands and the *Beaver* was blockaded in Canton following the outbreak of the War of 1812. The loss of Astoria was a further blow to his plans. With peace, other vessels were dispatched to the northwest, trading for furs on the California coast and at Norfolk Sound in the north, and for the sandalwood of the Hawaiian Islands. In the 1820's the west coast of South America was to become important as revolutionary movements destroyed Spain's ability to exclude the foreigner, but contacts with the northwest continued over this decade until 1828. Astor's ventures in this region and in California, however, followed the pattern established by the men of Boston, and it is they who must be regarded as the strategic figures in the maritime expansion of the United States in the Pacific area.

THE UNITED STATES: THE LAND TRADE

As the maritime phase of western expansion drew to its close, the continental fur-trader pushed his way westward. Reference has been made to his activities in Canada. Somewhat later, and to the south, individual trappers and trading organizations moved across the continent toward distant Old Oregon and California. The history of the fur trade of the United States in this period cannot be recounted here, but some of its more important features should be noted. In 1809 the St. Louis Missouri Fur Company had been incorporated, and with the inclusion of many of the ablest traders of St. Louis extended operations to the southwest, and in one venture, to the valley of the Columbia. Andrew Henry who built a post on a tributary of the Snake River was the first American trader to operate on the Pacific side of the Mountains. Indian hostilities and a cumbersome and ineffectual organization led to difficulties, and following reorganizations in 1812 and 1819 the Company ceased operations in 1830. The competition of stronger organizations, the Pacific Fur Company (the western branch of the American Fur Company) and the Rocky Mountain Fur Company, hastened its end.

The former, organized by Astor in 1810, was formed mainly of North West Company men. Reference has been made to the outcome of this organization's move to the Pacific coast by sea, the founding of Astoria and the destruction of the *Tonquin*. The Company's overland expedition to the Pacific, following great hardships, reached Astoria in 1812. It is not without interest that the route followed by the expedition on its return journey overland was, with few changes, that of the great Overland Trail of the 1840's, a route running from the Missouri River at the mouth of the Kansas to the mouth of the Columbia River. However, the transfer of Astoria to the North West Company in 1813 ended a venture which, although American in design, had been carried out mainly by British subjects.

To the east, Astor continued his extensive fur-trade activities. In 1816 the American Fur Company superseded the North West and South West Companies in United States territory and in 1822 the American company established its Western Department at St. Louis, its centre of operations in the Missouri and the lower posts on the Mississippi and Illinois. Later the Company extended its operations to participate in the fur trade of the Rocky Mountains, but here strong opposition from the Rocky Mountain Company and other organizations was encountered and this trade was seldom profitable. The activities of the Rocky Mountain Company in its main phase (1822-34) and its relations with the American Fur Company and the Hudson's Bay Company take us beyond the scope of this chapter, but it should be noted that this organization carried the American land trade to California and up the Pacific coast to the Columbia in operations as interesting for their contributions to exploration as for returns to the trader. In the wake of its enterprising hunters, there followed the missionaries and the settlers who were to achieve the permanency of occupation necessary to United States control of present-day Oregon and Washington.

UNITED STATES ADVANCE: SPANISH RETREAT

In the end it was the westward thrust of settlement that determined the ultimate control of the continent. The outcome of the American Revolution had left Spain faced with a more dangerous threat to her possessions than that presented by England and France, European nations with world-wide interests of which North America was only a part. Following 1783, however, the United States emerged to contest a Spanish control which threatened to check westward expansion across the continent from the seaboard. The Atlantic states sought to move across the mountains into the Mississippi valley as the pressure of population and the cupidity of land-speculators led to increased interest in the interior of the continent. In earlier chapters we outlined the opposition of France and later England to the westward movement before the American Revolution. This opposition was broken by the elimination of the French from North America and the thwarting of British attempts to retain control of the interior following the Revolution. To the south, however, Spain's possessions lay across the new and aggressive nation's natural avenues of expansion.

Spain moved to block this westward movement by exclusion of all foreign shipping from the Mississippi, and until Trafalgar her naval power made her a formidable enemy. At the end of the century, her control of Louisiana and the Floridas continued to protect her interests to the west. Unfortunately for her this control was not supported by a strong economic development of the resources of these defence areas. Her settlements, which included Pensacola, Mobile, New Orleans, Natchez and St. Louis, were unprofitable both as markets and as sources of supplies for old Spain. Such products as furs, hides, indigo, lumber and tobacco found a poor market in Spain, and no strong centres emerged to provide effective defence against American penetration. By 1795 navigation of the Mississippi was conceded to this new rival along with control of the east bank of the river. In 1800, Louisiana was returned to France and three years later this enormous area was purchased from France by the United States. The Louisiana Purchase represented a great transfer of territory and the removal of the most serious obstacle to American westward expansion. This transfer has its parallel in Canadian economic history in the purchase of the Hudson's Bay Company territories which permitted uninterrupted expansion west from the St. Lawrence area.

The United States now claimed West Florida as part of Louisiana; in 1810 this territory was annexed (apart from Mobile which was acquired in 1812), and in 1819 the balance of Florida was purchased for $5 million. Recognition was given, however, to Spanish rights in Texas, New Mexico and California. Spain gave up these territories to Mexico in 1822 and it was from Mexico that the United States took them later; Texas was annexed in 1845, California and New Mexico in 1848. By this time Spain had ceased to exist as a political force in the New World. Yet it is important to note that Spanish defensive tactics in Mexico and California had discouraged other European powers from seeking to acquire territories in this region until the population of the New World had increased sufficiently to guarantee freedom of this part of the continent from European intervention.

The early commerce of the North Pacific, based as it was on the rapid exploitation of a highly exhaustible resource, had established no firm footholds on the continent. Like the land fur trade, the maritime trade repelled rather than attracted settlement. Following its decline, there were few prospects of other than a slow and halting rate of progress on the Pacific coast of North America. Great areas to the east of the mountains still awaited the settler, and the isolation of the coastal strip seemed to be a guarantee of a slow rate of change. This outlook changed abruptly when gold was discovered on the Sacramento River in 1848, and later in Oregon, Washington and Idaho, on the Fraser River and in the Cariboo country. Each strike in its turn brought a surge of population, rapid improvements in techniques of transportation and communication, and the beginnings of economic expansion on foundations more solid than the exploitive fur trade could provide. Trade first drew attention to this area, gold gave enormous impetus to its development, and eventually this expansion established the conditions for resumption of Pacific commerce on a more permanent basis.

SUGGESTIONS FOR FURTHER READING

BASIC WORKS:

Caughey, John W., *History of the Pacific Coast of North America* (New York, 1938), Chapters IV-XIII, pp. 47-210

Morison, Samuel Eliot, *The Maritime History of Massachusetts, 1783-1860* (Cambridge, Mass., 1921), Chapters I-VI, pp. 1-78

Ogden, Adele, *The California Sea Otter Trade, 1784-1848* (Berkeley and Los Angeles, 1941), Chapters I-V, pp. 1-94

Tompkins, Stuart Ramsay, *Alaska: Promyshlennik and Sourdough* (Norman, Oklahoma, 1945), Chapters I-X, pp. 1-133

SUPPLEMENTARY WORKS:

Bolton, Herbert Eugene, *History of the Americas: A Syllabus with Maps* (New York, 1935), Lecture XXIX, pp. 158-65, and Lectures XXXIV-XXXIX, pp. 191-228

Chittenden, H. M., *The American Fur Trade of the Far West* (New York, 1935), Vol. I, Part II, Chapters I-XIII, pp. 75-237

Fuller, George W., *A History of the Pacific Northwest* (New York, 1931), Chapters I-VI, pp. 3-109

Kerner, Robert J., *The Urge to the Sea: The Course of Russian History* (Berkeley and Los Angeles, 1942), Chapter I, pp. 1-9, and Chapter IV, pp. 35-88

Porter, Kenneth Wiggins, *John Jacob Astor, Business Man* (Cambridge, Mass., Harvard Studies in Business History, I, 1931), Vol. I, Chapters VI-XI, pp. 129-330, and Vol. II, Chapters XII-XIV, pp. 589-733

CHAPTER XI

THE MARITIME PROVINCES: 1815–1867

INTRODUCTION

AFTER 1815 the fisheries of New England and France quickly recovered from the reverses which they had suffered during the Napoleonic Wars. Nova Scotia, whose fisheries and trade had expanded during this period, sought to meet the revival of competition by demanding that American ships should be excluded from the in-shore fisheries and from trade with the West Indies. The first of these objectives was achieved in 1818, when the in-shore waters of the British North American colonies were closed to American fishers. The United States, however, by imposing retaliatory restrictions on colonial and British shipping, successfully forced entrance into the carrying-trade to the British West Indies and in 1830 won complete freedom of access. Nova Scotia in the meantime, compelled to meet competition from areas which were free from the restrictions of the British colonial system, demanded and won important modifications in imperial trade policy. A considerable expansion of Nova Scotian trade was the result. Friction over the in-shore fisheries continued, however, until a temporary truce was achieved by the signing of the Reciprocity Treaty in 1854. The ending of reciprocity in 1866 and the threat of new and more aggressive moves on the part of the United States hastened the entrance of the province into confederation in 1867. New Brunswick's economy during this period developed around the timber and shipbuilding industries with the fisheries and agriculture playing a minor role. These basic industries reached their peak in the mid-1860's; thereafter, with the advent of the railroad and the iron ship, they began to decline and New Brunswick, like Nova Scotia, turned to federation with the St. Lawrence colonies. Newfoundland, being relatively unaffected by the pull of continental markets in Canada and the United States, remained outside of confederation, preferring to rely upon Britain rather than upon Canada for economic and political support.

CONFLICTS WITH THE UNITED STATES:
(1) THE IN-SHORE FISHERIES

The Treaty of 1783, it will be remembered, had granted to citizens of the United States the privilege of fishing in the in-shore waters of the British North American colonies. In 1814, during the negotiations for peace, Britain took the position that the United States had abrogated the Treaty of 1783 by declaring war in 1812 and that the in-shore fishing privileges had therefore been automatically withdrawn. The American delegation was unwilling to concede the British case but failed to take a firm stand on the issue because of internal disagreements. The matter was therefore left open for future negotiation and the Treaty of Ghent, signed in 1815, contained no reference to the fisheries.

Between 1815 and 1817 the British government, responding to pressure from Nova Scotia, sent naval units into Nova Scotian waters with instructions to warn American ships from fishing within the three-mile limit or using British American ports for any purpose connected with the fisheries. Several small American ships were seized but later released on payment of costs. Finally in 1818 negotiations for a settlement of the issue culminated in the signing of a Convention, the interpretation of which was to prove a source of acute conflict in the future. The United States renounced any liberty which had previously been enjoyed to take, dry, or cure fish "within three marine miles of any of the coasts, bays, creeks or harbours" of the British provinces in North America. American fishers could, however, enter in-shore waters for shelter or to repair damage, purchase wood, or obtain water. To counter-balance American agreement to withdraw from the in-shore fisheries, Britain granted to the United States extensive fishing privileges on the south and west shores of Newfoundland, between the Ramea Islands on the south and Quirpon Island in the north, as well as in the waters around the Magdalen Islands and off the coast of Labrador.

The Convention of 1818 left several questions undecided—such as, for instance, whether the Bay of Fundy should be considered a bay or a part of the open sea, and whether American fishing-ships should be permitted to pass through the Gut of Canso—but in its general intention it was clear enough. The in-shore waters of the British colonies were now closed to American fishing-ships. It remained uncertain whether this advantage could be held permanently or whether, at some time in the future, it might have to be bargained away in return for more eagerly sought concessions from the United States, but for the time being at least the diplomatic victory was sufficient to satisfy the fishing and merchant groups of Nova Scotia. As far as the fishing industry of New England was concerned the effects do not appear to have been very serious. A tariff on imports of cured fish imposed in 1816 and increased bounties granted to fishing-ships in 1819 served to counteract any harmful effects which the Convention might otherwise have produced.

CONFLICTS WITH THE UNITED STATES:
(2) THE WEST INDIES TRADE

The fisheries were, however, by no means the only area in which the maritime colonies and the United States came into conflict. There was also the thorny question of trade with the British West Indies. Nova Scotia's trade with the British islands in the Caribbean had expanded very considerably during the period of the American Embargo and Non-intercourse Acts. The return of peace in 1815, however, raised anew the old question of what part, if any, American shipping should be allowed to play in the trade. By a commercial convention signed in July, 1815, Great Britain and the United States had agreed upon reciprocity of tariffs, but this did not affect the issue of the carrying-trade. American supplies, particularly foodstuffs and lumber, were still indispensable to the sugar islands, for the northern British colonies with the exception of Prince Edward Island still had no agricultural surpluses to dispose of. The question at issue was whether these supplies and the return cargoes of sugar and molasses should be carried in British and colonial shipping only, or whether American ships should be allowed to compete on equal terms. If the latter policy were followed, it seemed highly probable that American shipping, taking full advantage of geographical proximity, would before long monopolize the North American sector of the West Indies trade, leaving for British shipping at most only the transatlantic haul from the West Indies to Britain and back. Fundamentally the question to be decided was whether the profits of the colonial carrying-trade should be reserved for British and colonial shipowners, as traditional colonial policy dictated, or whether they should be shared with Americans in the interests of amicable international relations and cheap imports for the West Indies plantations.

In demanding free access to the markets and carrying-trade of the British West Indies, the United States was in a relatively strong bargaining position. Cheap American supplies were well-nigh indispensable to the prosperity of the British islands, faced as they were with the competition of new and more efficiently organized producing areas, notably in Cuba, while the produce of the British West Indies was of very small importance in the total imports of the United States. American trade with the island of Cuba alone, for instance, exceeded by far the total volume of American trade with all the British islands. Britain, on the other hand, entered the commercial struggle under several handicaps, chief among which were the sharply conflicting interests which had to be reconciled if a consistent position toward the demands of the American government was to be maintained. The traditional policy of colonial monopoly, to which Britain still adhered in principle, indicated that American shipping should be rigorously excluded from the carrying-trade. The interests of the British and colonial shipping industry and of imperial security alike demanded that the task of provisioning the Caribbean islands should not be permitted to fall into the hands of a potential enemy. More was involved than just the intercolonial trade. From the point of view of British shipowners the trade between American and West Indian ports was merely one side of a great triangle, the other two sides of which were the transatlantic hauls from Britain to the United States and from the West Indies to Britain. As long as British vessels had a monopoly of the trade on the two legs of the triangle which met at the West Indies, they could easily underbid American ships in the competitive direct trade between Britain and the United States. If the West Indies trade was lost to the United States, the long haul across the Atlantic might soon follow. On the other hand, the West Indies plantation owners, though their influence in English politics was fast waning, retained sufficient power to make their demands heard in high places. What they demanded —rather, what they insisted they could not do without—was the admission to the British West Indies of the cheapest foodstuffs that could be obtained, no matter where they came from, in ships that offered the lowest freight rates that were available, no matter what their home port and nationality. Any other policy, they argued, would spell ruin to the sugar plantations. In opposition to these claims stood the commercial interests of Nova Scotia and New Brunswick, dominant in the provincial legislatures and not without influence in Whitehall—a group that had tasted the fruits of prosperity during the temporary suspension of American competition after 1807 and that was now in no mood to stand idly by while the mother country extended to the United States privileges which rightly belonged only to loyal colonies. Divided though they might be on smaller matters, on this issue the fishing and the merchant interests of the provinces spoke with one voice, for American dried fish was as serious a source of competition in the West Indies trade as American shipping. Arguing that American vessels, if once they were allowed a share in the West Indies carrying-trade, would soon dominate it completely, they insisted on a policy of complete exclusion.

THE PERIOD OF RETALIATORY LEGISLATION

It is unnecessary to examine in detail the diplomatic strategy involved in the struggle for the West Indies carrying-trade; the objectives sought by each side and the consequences for the regions involved are of more importance than the tactics adopted. The position of the United States government was that there should be no discrimination against American shipping in trade with areas to which American produce was admitted. If the British government chose to prohibit American produce from entering the West Indies, it could certainly do so; but as long as American goods were permitted to enter that market, American ships should be allowed to compete on equal terms with British for the business of carrying them. Expansion of the carrying-trade and the American merchant marine was the principal objective. The British government, on the other hand, held that it was entirely legitimate and proper to give the preference to British shipping in the West Indies trade if the prosperity of any part of the empire would thereby be advanced. Needless to say, settlement of the issue depended less on the rights and wrongs of each side's arguments than it did on the effectiveness of American retaliatory measures.

By 1816 three-quarters of the shipping tonnage employed in trade with the British West Indies was of British registration; less than 20 per cent by value of the merchandise imported into the British islands from the United States was carried in American vessels. It was clear that, unless some remedial action were taken, American shipping would soon be squeezed out of the trade entirely. Faced with increasing restiveness among the mercantile and shipping interests, the American government passed an Act late in 1816 which imposed an additional tonnage duty of $2 on foreign vessels arriving in the United States from ports to which American ships were ordinarily not allowed to go (i.e., from the British West Indies). The weakness of this measure was that it left the British triangular trade intact; the discriminatory duties did not apply to British ships arriving in the United States from Britain and then proceeding to the West Indies with cargoes of American produce. The same was true of the Navigation Act passed by the American Congress in March, 1817. This statute confined the importation into the United States of British West Indies produce to American ships and ships owned by merchants of those colonies; but it did not prohibit British ships from carrying American produce to the British West Indies.

Since the triangular trade, the mainstay of British shipping in the Atlantic, was not affected, these American statutes did not induce the British government to modify its stand in any significant way. To be sure, a conciliatory gesture was made. The British government offered to open the West Indies ports to American ships, provided that certain restrictions on tonnage and type of cargo were agreed to. The ships engaged in the trade were to be single-decked, which meant in effect not more than thirty tons burden, or much smaller than those usually employed in the trade; and the prohibited goods were either those which, like sugar and coffee, the United States was most interested in importing from the British West Indies, or else those, like lumber, fish, salted provisions and livestock, which American merchants most wished to export there.

The concessions offered by the British government were, in fact, almost valueless and the American government quickly rejected them, choosing instead to continue and intensify its policy of commercial retaliation. The next step in this policy was an attempt to destroy the British triangular trade which had been unharmed by the earlier measures. This was effected by the passing of a new Navigation Act in 1818. This Act provided that American ports should be closed to British vessels coming from ports ordinarily closed to American ships; and in addition that British vessels loading in American ports should be required to give bond that they would not land their cargoes in ports to which American ships did not have access.

The Navigation Act of 1818 proved very effective. Since British ships were now prohibited from taking American produce from the United States to the West Indies, the traditional triangular trade was severely damaged. British shipping tonnage entering American ports fell from 174,935 in 1817 to 36,333 in 1819. At this point, however, the northern colonies of Nova Scotia and New Brunswick began to play an important role. American legislation up to 1818 had been directed against the British monopoly of the direct trade between the United States and the West Indies. Was it not possible to circumvent this legislation by routing American produce indirectly through the northern colonies? Such a circuitous trade would avoid the American restrictions and at the same time bring prosperity to the shipping and shipbuilding industries of Nova Scotia and New Brunswick.

This policy was put into effect by the Free Port Act, passed by the British Parliament in 1818. This Act permitted a wide range of American products to be imported into designated North American ports either in British or American ships. These imports could then be re-exported to Britain or to other British possessions, but only in British ships (colonial ships were, of course, considered as British). Saint John in New Brunswick and Halifax in Nova Scotia were declared free ports in May, 1818; St. George and Hamilton in Bermuda had enjoyed a similar status since 1812, and St. Andrews in New Brunswick was added to the list in 1821. The effect of the Free Port Act was to neutralize to a very large extent the American Navigation Act, as American ships were now free to export American produce to the specified harbours in the northern colonies and exchange their cargoes there for West Indian produce. The amount of American produce reaching the British West Indies by this northern route increased from just over $2¼ million in 1818 to more than $3 million in 1819. The carrying-trade between Saint John and Halifax and the West Indies fell almost entirely into the hands of colonial shipowners and the local shipbuilding industries prospered accordingly. Consumers in the West Indies, on the other hand, had to pay the bill for the more roundabout voyage in the form of higher prices for American imports; but some relief was given to the planters by a second statute which permitted them to import foodstuffs from any colony or possession in America which was under the dominion of a European state, provided only that such imports were carried in British ships. The purpose of this Act was mainly to secure American supplies by way of the Danish and Swedish islands in the Caribbean.

The American reaction was to pass a new and stricter Navigation Act which laid it down that after September 30, 1820, all American harbours should be closed to British vessels coming not only from ports ordinarily closed to American shipping but from all British colonial ports in North America without exception. Further, the Act prohibited the importation of goods, even in American vessels, from British colonial ports unless such goods were imported directly from the colony which produced them. Both sections of the new Act were aimed against the trade of Halifax and Saint John, which by this time were in a fair way to establishing their position as entrepôts in the trade between the United States and the British West Indies.

The consequences of this American legislation were highly damaging both to the shipping of the northern colonies and to British trade in general. The British West Indies were now unable to import American provisions either directly from the United States or indirectly by way of the northern colonies. Prices in the islands rose rapidly, there was considerable distress, and vigorous protests were lodged with the British government. On the other hand, the very effectiveness of the legislation provoked opposition within the United States, particularly from the southern states. Southern planters were distrustful of measures which seemed to sacrifice the interests of agriculture for the benefit of the maritime commerce of New York and New England. Loss of domestic support for the policy of retaliation was finally to undermine the bargaining position of the American government.

High prices in the British West Indies and strongly worded protests from the legislatures of the islands compelled the British government to retreat from the position taken in 1819. The need to consider the conflicting interests of the northern colonies, however, still prevented any wholesale concessions. A compromise solution was sought in the West Indian and American Trade Act, passed in 1822. This Act provided that the same list of articles might be imported into the British West Indies directly from the United States in American ships as might be imported indirectly by way of Nova Scotia and New Brunswick. Passed by the British Parliament against the strenuous opposition of British shipowners but with the support of the West Indies planters, the American Trade Act represented a very significant change in policy. In effect it amounted to an abandonment of the northern route; the commercial interests of New Brunswick and Nova Scotia were sacrificed for the benefit of the West Indies. The northern colonies were not entirely forgotten, however. In the first place, fish and salted provisions, two of the principal products exported from these colonies to the West Indies, were specifically excluded from the statute. These two products could be shipped to the West Indies only in British ships. And secondly, the Act imposed additional tariffs of about 10 per cent ad valorem on livestock, lumber, and provisions imported into the British West Indies directly from the United States. Imports from the British North American colonies did not have to pay these duties. In this way an attempt was made to satisfy the demands of the West Indies planters while at the same time conserving the gains which had been made by New Brunswick and Nova Scotia.

The American government, though resentful at the failure to secure complete equality of treatment, decided to take advantage of the British concessions and in August, 1822, opened American ports to British ships coming from the British West Indies and from the North American colonies when carrying the produce of those regions. Certain discriminatory duties on imports were retained, together with the foreign tonnage duties, but a statute passed in March, 1823, provided that these should be removed as soon as the British government removed the discriminatory duties levied on direct imports into the West Indies from the United States. The only remaining barrier to complete freedom of trade in the West Indies was, therefore, the preferential duties levied for the benefit of Nova Scotia and New Brunswick. American negotiators in London in the fall of 1823 demanded that these preferences also be abandoned, but the British government was unwilling to take this final step and for the time being negotiations were deadlocked.

From the British point of view the consequences of the West Indian and American Trade Act and of the American Act of the following year were most unsatisfactory. As the shippers of Nova Scotia and New Brunswick had warned would be the case, the result of opening the West Indies ports to American vessels was that British and colonial ships were rapidly edged out of the trade. By the end of 1824 American shipping had won a substantial monopoly of the carrying-trade to the British islands. At the same time the American and British discriminatory duties were proving a heavy burden on the sugar-planters, already labouring under high production costs, while the merchants of Nova Scotia and New Brunswick were daily threatened with bankruptcy.

Disinclined to provoke the American administration into new restrictions but anxious to assist both the West Indies and the northern colonies, the British government undertook a major revision of its colonial trade policy. This revision was embodied in three important statutes which took effect in January, 1826. The first provided for the admission into the British West Indies and British North America of the produce of all countries of America, Europe, Africa, and western Asia and laid down the duties to be collected. Only dried fish, salted provisions, and a few other articles were specifically excluded. The second confined the direct trade between the colonies and Great Britain to British ships. And the third offered to open the carrying-trade of the colonies to all countries which, if they had colonies, extended similar privileges to Britain, or which, if they had no colonies, extended most-favoured-nation treatment to British vessels. The ports of the colonies were to be closed to all countries which did not comply with these conditions. At the same time customs procedures were greatly simplified and the free-port system was extended.

The design which lay back of this new colonial policy had several objectives. In the first place it represented an attempt to supply the British West Indies from sources other than the United States—particularly Europe, the British North American colonies, and the newly liberated Spanish colonies in Central and South America. In the second place it was part of a broader strategy which aimed at curbing American expansionism. There was at this time no little concern in Britain regarding American pretensions at leadership in the New World. The Monroe Doctrine, announced in 1823, seemed to many observers a clear statement of an intention on the part of the United States to carve out its own sphere of influence in the Caribbean and Latin America. And in the third place the new policy was intended to placate the commercial interests of New Brunswick and Nova Scotia, now more insistent than ever in their demands for protection against American competition. Taken together, these objectives added up to a systematic attempt to reinforce the British colonial system in the New World by effecting a viable reconciliation between the interests of the West Indies, the last stronghold of colonial monopoly, and those of the new commercial colonies to the north. A much less conciliatory attitude toward the United States accompanied the new policy.

The American government was now faced with two alternatives: either to grant Britain the status of "most favoured nation" in all matters affecting foreign commerce (which would have involved the removal of all legislation discriminating against British ships and cargoes), and thus gain admission to the West Indies trade, or to retain the discriminatory duties and thereby accept exclusion of American shipping from the West Indies. No immediate move was made to accept either alternative. The British government thereupon issued an order in council which once again closed British West Indies ports to American ships. Despite the fact that it could now muster very little domestic support for its policies, the American government had no alternative but to reimpose the Navigation Acts of 1818 and 1820. American ports were therefore closed to British ships coming from any British colony in the western hemisphere.

THE FINAL COMPROMISE

As far as restrictions on shipping were concerned, matters now stood very much as they had in 1818—so much so that the bitter economic warfare of the intervening years seemed to have brought no real change in the situation of any of the contestants. This was not exactly true, however. The British West Indies, for example, suffered no real hardship from the reimposition of the American Navigation Laws in 1826; sufficient supplies of American provisions continued to reach the plantations by way of the non-British islands in the Caribbean and also, though illegally, the British North American colonies. True, this meant that much of the carrying-trade was left to American shipping, but even this was becoming less of a bone of contention than had once been the case. The shipowners and merchants of Halifax and Saint John had learned to look elsewhere for markets and were less completely dependent on the West Indies trade than they had formerly been. British legislation in 1823 had permitted the maritime colonies to export their produce directly to certain ports in Europe, and the transatlantic trade had grown increasingly important. In Britain, too, political sentiment was coming to look with favour on the idea of a compromise with the United States; the decline in political influence of the West Indies planters, signalized most dramatically by the emancipation of the slaves in 1834, meant that policies other than doctrinaire mercantilism could be tried. Belatedly, a new philosophy of international trade was making its appearance; there was more room to manoeuvre, more freedom to experiment.

But it was in the United States that sentiment changed most dramatically. The policy of commercial retaliation against Britain had never had the unqualified support of American farmers, particularly in the southern states. The fight for free access to the British West Indies was waged essentially for the benefit of the merchants and shipowners of New England and New York; it was difficult to convince other sections of the electorate, for whom retaliation usually meant loss of export markets, that the interests of the nation as a whole were at stake. A shift in political alignments gave this hostile agrarian sentiment an opportunity to express itself in action. The election of Andrew Jackson as president in 1828 brought into power an administration which was much less friendly to the northern shipping interests than its predecessor had been and which was prepared to adopt a radically different approach to the West Indies question.

Given these changes in attitude on each side, a compromise solution was not difficult to attain. Before the end of 1830 agreement had been reached on mutual concessions. On October 5, a presidential proclamation was issued which repealed the American Acts of 1818, 1820, and 1823, removed the discriminatory duties, and declared the ports of the United States open to British ships from any British colony in the New World. One month later the British government issued an order in council which permitted American ships of all types to carry cargoes of American produce to British colonies and to export goods to any part of the world from those colonies. American ships were to receive exactly the same treatment and pay the same tonnage duties in colonial ports as would British ships coming from the United States. Britain retained the right, however, to impose discriminatory import duties in her colonies to encourage the importation of products from other parts of the empire.

This "reciprocity agreement of 1830", as it is sometimes called, gave to American merchants and shipowners the prize for which they had long struggled: equal treatment with British vessels in the West Indies carrying-trade. For fifteen years Great Britain and the United States had vied with each other in imposing restrictions on one another's shipping. Finally, it seemed, the United States had triumphed. Yet the victory was to some extent an empty one. It is not much of an exaggeration, indeed, to say that, by the time Great Britain permitted the United States to trade freely with the British West Indies, the United States was no longer much interested in doing so. In the first place there had developed in Cuba and Puerto Rico new Caribbean markets and sources of supply which were free from British regulation. Even when their ports were open to American ships, the British islands, it was estimated, took only about one-seventh of all American exports to the Caribbean. Secondly, the West Indies trade, which was essentially a matter of short voyages in small ships, was no longer as important as it had once been in the total foreign commerce of the United States. By 1830 the shipowners of the northern states had learned that there was greater profit to be had in the long hauls to South America and round Cape Horn to the Pacific and the Orient. And thirdly, the growth of industry in the United States and the development of a large domestic market were giving a new cast to American economic policy. Tariff protection, westward expansion, and the improvement of internal transportation, rather than the fostering of the merchant marine, were coming to be regarded as the keys to prosperity.

But what of Nova Scotia and New Brunswick? The merchants of these northern colonies had strenuously opposed the British concessions, for the exclusion of American shipping had brought considerable prosperity to their maritime trade and shipyards. The reciprocity agreement seemed to knock the foundation out from under their colonial economies. Both provinces were injured by the agreement, Nova Scotia more than her sister colony since New Brunswick had the timber industry to fall back on. So far as the carrying-trade was concerned the shipowners of the two provinces now had to meet the chill wind of American competition without the protection of imperial navigation laws and labouring too under the twin handicaps of greater distance from sources of supply and smaller capital resources. To be sure, the British government took prompt action to offset the shock of the reciprocity agreement. In the first place the British North American colonies were given the power to impose their own protective tariffs; and secondly, after 1830, additional duties were levied in the West Indies on certain essential commodities when they were imported directly from foreign countries but not when they were imported from another British colony. The intention of both these steps was clearly to assist the shipping interests of Nova Scotia and New Brunswick, since American produce could be imported into these provinces duty-free and then re-exported to the West Indies as coming from a British colony. The net result was that the trade between the United States and the maritime colonies came to be shared between American and British (including colonial) ships; but American ships were unable to secure much of a foothold in the trade from the Maritimes to England and to the West Indies, which continued to be monopolized by ships of British registry. The old triangular trade, in short, remained in British and colonial hands, as it had been originally, and the profits of this trade continued to be the chief reliance of the merchants of the maritime provinces.

ECONOMIC BACKGROUND OF THE MARITIME PROVINCES BEFORE CONFEDERATION

Despite occasional reverses, developments during the years between 1815 and 1830 were on the whole not unfavourable to the maritime provinces. The struggle over the West Indies trade was, in a sense, merely the final stage in the dissolution of the old British colonial system—a system which, badly shaken by the American Revolution, had been painfully reconstructed between 1783 and 1815. One factor which had precipitated the American Revolution had been the conflict between the commercial colonies of New England and the plantation colonies of the British West Indies. Opposed by the entrenched political power of the West Indian planters and unable to secure the modifications in imperial trade policy which they required, the merchants of the New England colonies had thrown their full weight behind the fight for colonial independence.

Nova Scotia and New Brunswick, in the period after 1815, played very much the same role in the imperial structure as New England had before 1776. Both were commercial colonies, making their living mostly by trade and the fisheries; both found their interests in conflict with the interests of the British West Indies. Unlike New England, however, Nova Scotia and New Brunswick were able to force modifications in colonial policy in their own interests. They could do this because the period after 1815 was far from an exact parallel with the period before 1776. The British West Indies had lost much of their prosperity and much of their political influence in England. British parliaments had become more responsive to the demands of the temperate-zone colonies. Conceptions of the meaning of empire had subtly altered. Perhaps most important, there now was continually before the eyes of the men responsible for policy formation in England the precedent of the American Revolution and the ineluctable fact of the existence of the United States as a power to be reckoned with. It was the ability of the United States to carry through a programme of commercial retaliation on the classic mercantilist pattern which compelled Britain to modify its imperial trade policy.

But if the Navigation Laws of the United States were the hammer that cracked the old colonial system, the insistent demands of Nova Scotia and New Brunswick for fair treatment were the anvil. Loyal colonies could not be expected to remain loyal if the United States were granted all the privileges of membership in Britain's colonial system but expected to bear none of the burdens. Concessions to the United States had to be matched by concessions to the colonies. A progressive liberalization of imperial legislation and an expansion and widening of colonial trade were the result. Free ports, free warehousing facilities, permission to export direct to Europe, the abolition of innumerable sinecures and fees in the customs service, an immense simplification in tariff procedures, and finally control over their own revenues and expenditures—these were among the benefits which the maritime colonies reaped from the struggle for the West Indies trade.

One handicap under which both maritime colonies continued to labour in this period was the slowness of their agricultural development. Failure to make progress in this direction was responsible for dependence on the United States for supplies of foodstuffs for use in the fisheries and for re-export to the West Indies and Newfoundland. Nova Scotian farmers continued to concentrate on livestock and dairy products, where transport costs lessened the effects of American competition, and were reluctant to turn to wheat and flour, partly because of the lack of tariff protection; duties on American agricultural imports imposed in 1820 and increased in 1821 and 1826 were confined to horses, oxen, cows, sheep, and hogs. In New Brunswick commercial farming remained ancillary to the timber industry and only small and occasional surpluses were available for export. Only from Prince Edward Island were agricultural exports relatively large; as early as 1831 the Island had begun to export wheat to England.

Agricultural development in Nova Scotia and New Brunswick was limited by the characteristics of the immigrants from Europe, the scattering of population in small sea-coast settlements, the lack of good roads, the concentration of credit and mercantile ability on overseas trade, the prevalence of farming practices which were poor even by contemporary standards, and the absence of protection against American imports. Immigration into the two provinces, which had fallen off sharply during the American Revolution and the Napoleonic Wars, picked up again after 1815, reached a peak during the 1840's, and declined after 1855. There are no official figures of immigrant arrivals but some conception of the size of the inflow can be derived from population statistics. The population of New Brunswick, which was 74,176 in 1824, reached 119,457 in 1834, 156,162 in 1840, and 193,800 in 1851, an increase of about 161 per cent over the 27-year period. Over approximately the same period (1825-51) the population of Nova Scotia rose from 104,000 to 276,854, an increase of about 166 per cent. These figures underestimate the volume of immigration and the rate of natural increase, since throughout these years there was a steady exodus of population from the maritime provinces, particularly to New England. Nevertheless, it is clear that in absolute numbers immigration into the maritime provinces was smaller than immigration into the St. Lawrence colonies and very much smaller than immigration into the United States. The principal immigrant streams passed either south of Nova Scotia, to the American Atlantic cities, or north, to Quebec and Montreal.

The main elements among the immigrants who came to the maritime provinces were Highland Scots and southern Irish. In Nova Scotia the Scots settled mainly along the eastern seaboard of the peninsula, where they formed a series of small and relatively isolated communities, the nuclei of the small towns scattered along that coast today. The Irish immigrants usually concentrated in the larger towns and showed little interest in purchasing and settling land. Unlike other immigrant groups in Nova Scotia, they did not establish themselves in homogeneous farming communities but preferred to make their living in the fisheries or as lumberjacks or as labourers in the towns and later in the railway construction camps. In New Brunswick the main areas of settlement in the period before 1850 were the upper St. John valley, the shore of the Bay of Fundy, and the south shore of Chaleur Bay.

Many of the Scots immigrants were ill-prepared for the farming conditions which they met on their arrival in the New World and had a hard struggle to establish themselves. Clearing virgin forest in Nova Scotia or New Brunswick was very different from the kind of farming they had been used to in their native Highlands and there was not much opportunity for earlier arrivals to pass on their stock of experience to those who came later. One consequence of this was that throughout both provinces the general standard of farming practice was very low, even by comparison with what was usual in other parts of North America. Improvement in Nova Scotia dates from 1818, when there appeared in the *Acadian Recorder* a series of letters on scientific agriculture signed by "Agricola". These letters aroused wide interest; agricultural societies were formed in various parts of the province, with a government-sponsored central organization in Halifax, and a general raising of standards and widening of agricultural knowledge soon became evident.

The author of the "Agricola" letters was John Young, an immigrant from the Lowlands of Scotland who had established himself as a merchant in Halifax. Probably Young's interest in improving local agriculture stemmed less from his business concerns than from the contrast between the methods practised in Nova Scotia and those which he had seen as a young man in his native Stirlingshire, for on the whole the merchants of the maritime provinces had very little to do with local farming. They dealt in agricultural products, certainly, but usually only those which they imported from the United States and then either sold locally or re-exported to Newfoundland and the West Indies. The lack of good roads, the dispersion of settlement, and the quicker profits to be won in maritime commerce gave the merchants little encouragement to invest their capital in local trade. An efficient internal marketing organization was slow to develop and the money economy penetrated only tardily to the smaller settlements. If the pioneer farmer seemed reluctant to improve his methods and increase his output, part of the reason was simply that, if he did produce a surplus over and above his own requirements, there was no one near by to give him cash or credit for it. For a Halifax merchant interested in the triangular trade to the West Indies, it was probably less trouble to pick up a cargo of foodstuffs in Philadelphia, Baltimore, or some other southern port than to secure one locally.

Despite these disadvantages, in both provinces the growth of population and the gradual extension of land under cultivation brought increases in agricultural output, and by the 1830's the farmers' vote was becoming a factor to be reckoned with in provincial politics. Tariff protection for agriculture was, of course, a long way off. Both provinces were net importers of foodstuffs and the mercantile and fishing interests would not tolerate duties on American imports. The growth of a distinct agricultural interest is shown rather in such things as the blocking of proposals for additional subsidies to the fishery in Nova Scotia in 1833, recommendations by committees of the Assembly for bounties on flour made from local wheat, and demands for expenditures on roads and bridges and control over the public revenue. It was 1850, however, before Nova Scotia had anything like an adequate road system to give the interior settlements access to the seaport markets. By that date there were new problems to be faced, particularly the falling off of immigration. The area under cultivation in Nova Scotia today is not much larger than it was in 1860.

THE LUMBER INDUSTRY IN NEW BRUNSWICK

For most purposes it is possible to treat Nova Scotia and New Brunswick as a single economic unit in this period, for their natural resources were very similar and they were affected in much the same way by external developments. But there was one important difference between them, namely the key role played in the economy of New Brunswick by the lumber industry. In Nova Scotia as in New Brunswick much of the land area had originally been covered with a magnificent pine forest, and in the early years of British occupation an important timber trade had developed in this province also. In Nova Scotia, however, unlike all the other North American colonies, ownership of timber went with ownership of the land on which it stood, and the Crown never attempted to retain title to timber reserves. The result was that the British and colonial governments could exercise no control over forest policy and the available timber resources were quickly and ruthlessly exploited. This fact, combined with the greater total forest area in New Brunswick, explains why Nova Scotia plays only a minor part in the North American lumber trade after 1815. Production was large enough to support a prosperous shipbuilding industry, but exports to Britain and the West Indies were small both absolutely and compared with those of New Brunswick.

We have discussed in Chapter IX the development of the naval mast trade in New Brunswick after the American Revolution. Naval contractors after 1804 shifted their attention to the St. Lawrence colonies, but in 1808 and 1809, in response to increases in the British duties on Baltic timber, the New Brunswick timber trade revived and entered upon a new period of expansion. For the next forty years lumbering was to be the major industry of the province, overshadowing even the fisheries and far surpassing agriculture in the numbers it employed and in its contribution to external trade. The industry had two principal divisions: that producing square timber for the British market, and that specializing in deals, staves, and other forms of sawn lumber for the West Indies. The square-timber trade New Brunswick shared with Upper and Lower Canada; the West Indies trade was shared with Nova Scotia and the United States.

While the lumber industry provided New Brunswick with a means of attracting immigrants and capital and an important source of foreign exchange, it was by no means without its drawbacks. In particular it resulted in a very unbalanced type of development. In New Brunswick there was no clearly marked division between natural forest land and natural farm land. The rivers which gave the lumberman an easy way of floating his rafts down to the sea also gave the settler easy access to the fertile valleys of the interior. This meant that farming and lumbering in New Brunswick were very closely intermingled; they employed partly the same labour force and they were carried on in much the same areas. The consequences for the development of agriculture were, on balance, unfortunate. The high wages and exciting life of the lumber camps attracted many of the younger men away from the farms and induced many settlers to try to combine agriculture and lumbering. Very few succeeded; the man who attempted to combine the two occupations usually failed in both and ended up hopelessly in debt to one of the seaport merchants, if indeed he did not take the easy way out and head for the United States. Few of these small-scale operators had the capital and judgment necessary to survive the fluctuations of what was notoriously a gambler's industry. Profit margins were slim and freight costs inflexible; a drop of a few shillings in the British price often spelled catastrophe for the part-time lumberman in New Brunswick.

Nevertheless, as long as there was a market in Britain and the West Indies there was no shortage of men who were more than willing to forsake the dull routine of farming and try their luck at lumber-making.

During the first great boom between 1815 and 1825 hectic prosperity in the lumbering industry and in the closely-related industry of shipbuilding sucked labour out of agriculture and the province became entirely dependent for its foodstuffs on imports from the United States and, to a lesser extent, from the other British provinces. Local agriculture simply could not compete for labour against the high wages and prospect of quick profits offered by lumbering. A sharp fall in timber prices in 1825, following a stock-market crisis and slump in building activity in Britain, caused great distress and drove many of the weaker producers into bankruptcy, but by 1830 the pattern had reasserted itself. The province was still importing its foodstuffs from the United States and lumber remained the only significant export. An even more severe crisis in 1842 led to new efforts to encourage farming but it was not until the late 1850's that the province began to grow an appreciably larger proportion of its food requirements. The decline of the market for square timber in Britain and the increasing scarcity of good quality pine in New Brunswick were the principal factors responsible for this change. Exports of New Brunswick pine fell from 100,000 tons in 1856 to 27,174 tons in 1865.

In concentrating their energies and capital on the lumber industry the settlers and merchants of New Brunswick were merely taking the course which appeared to be suggested by self-interest. The industry was admittedly risky and speculative and its social repercussions were not above criticism, but timber was after all a cash crop which required neither planting nor ploughing. The interests of the province as a whole, however, would probably have been better served in the long run by a less specialized form of development. Lumber exports, to be sure, paid for most of New Brunswick's imports during this period, but it seems likely that the greater part of the profits went to the shippers rather than to the primary producers and that more of the accumulated earnings were remitted to England than were retained in the province. If this is so, the lumber industry can have done little to promote capital accumulation and provide a sound base for future growth. Furthermore, specialization on the lumber industry meant that New Brunswick was staking its future prosperity on the stability of a very few large markets. The catastrophic repercussions on the whole provincial economy when the British market temporarily failed, as it did in 1825 and 1842, were merely a foretaste of what was bound to happen when that market entered upon a secular decline. New export markets would then have to be found in a hurry and there were only two directions in which New Brunswick could look: the United States, and central Canada.

In both New Brunswick and Nova Scotia the shipbuilding industry entered upon a period of spectacular growth after 1815. In those days of wooden ships even the smallest outport was likely to have a shipyard, for good timber was readily available and the necessary know-how was widely distributed among the men of the coastal settlements. It used to be said, indeed, that a man could build his own ship, grow his own cargo, sail it to the West Indies himself, sell both ship and cargo, and return with a handsome profit to show for his enterprise. This can have been true only in the earliest years of British settlement, however; after 1815 farming, shipbuilding and maritime trade became more specialized and certain towns, such as Pictou, Yarmouth, and Lunenburg in Nova Scotia, acquired a reputation of their own as shipbuilding centres. In numbers Nova Scotia built more ships than New Brunswick, but in terms of tonnage the positions were reversed, for Nova Scotian shipyards built a great number of small craft for the coastal trade. Large vessels for sale in Britain and Europe were built to some extent in Nova Scotia but principally in the north-shore ports of New Brunswick and around Saint John. It was in these years that there was developed the Nova Scotian schooner, a beautiful craft that quickly won well-deserved fame in Atlantic waters. Locally built ships not only enabled the maritime provinces to take over a large share of the colonial carrying-trade but also had a ready sale abroad and contributed very substantially to the balance of payments. Nor were Nova Scotian business men backward in adopting the new technology of steam power; it was a merchant of Halifax, Samuel Cunard, who in 1840 initiated the first regular transatlantic steamship service. By the 1860's several small lines of steamships, partly supported by provincial subsidies, had been organized to ply between the ports of the north shore and those of the Bay of Fundy, while during the summer months there were connections with Quebec also. On the St. John River steamboats ran as far upstream as Woodstock, while on the Atlantic Halifax had regular steamer connections with Liverpool, Boston, Newfoundland, and the Bahamas.

The healthy growth in Nova Scotia and New Brunswick of activities connected with the sea and the forest—the fisheries, shipbuilding, the carrying-trade, and the lumber industry—was in sharp contrast with the sluggish development of agriculture. Like New England in an earlier period, the maritime provinces were developing as commercial, trading economies; but unlike New England they remained dependent on imports of food. Exports of lumber and dried fish to the West Indies and of square timber and ships to Europe enabled them to pay for these food imports and for the manufactured goods which they bought from Britain. New Brunswick's economy, because of the timber industry, was more directly oriented toward the British market; for Nova Scotia the West Indies market, an indirect means of earning sterling exchange, was of greater concern.

THE MARITIMES AND RECIPROCITY

The fact that the prosperity of the maritime provinces depended on access to overseas markets meant that they were very vulnerable to developments in international trade and tariff policy over which they themselves had little or no control. Nova Scotia's economy was badly shaken by the admission of American ships to the West Indies trade in 1830; New Brunswick was faced with a major crisis when, in the early 1840's, the British timber preferences were reduced. As staple-producing regions, both colonies found that reliable and predictable markets for their major exports were indispensable to growth.

In the late 1840's and early 1850's, as Britain took the final steps toward complete free trade, opinion in Nova Scotia and New Brunswick became increasingly in favour of seeking some arrangement whereby markets for the natural products of the Maritimes might be secured in the United States. The origins of this policy were to be found not in the Maritimes but in Upper Canada and Montreal, where for some years past certain leading business men and politicians had been pressing for what they called reciprocity, or the free admission into British North America and the United States of each other's natural products. The reciprocity movement had gained strength steadily as Britain made clear her intention to remove the last vestiges of colonial preference. In 1846, in response to pressure from the colonies, the attainment of reciprocity between British North America and the United States became the official policy of the British government and negotiations were opened in Washington to sound out the attitude of the American administration.

In central Canada reciprocity with the United States seemed to offer only benefits and no drawbacks. In the Maritimes the balance of advantage was not so clear. It is true that in the period between 1846 and 1850 New Brunswick was very anxious to gain access to the American market. The lumber industry, shaken by the reduction in the British timber preferences, saw in reciprocity the key to the American market, while provincial shipbuilders, distrustful of the foreign competition which was expected to follow the abolition of the Navigation Acts in 1849, wanted the right to register colonial-built vessels as American when sold in the United States. In Nova Scotia, too, reciprocity proposals at first met with a very favourable reception, while the legislature of Prince Edward Island as early as March, 1849, passed an act providing for the free admission of American natural products as soon as the American Congress took parallel action. Only in Newfoundland, where the merchants were little concerned with the American market, was there a complete lack of interest.

After 1852, however, there was in each of the maritime colonies a marked change in sentiment. Partly this was due to the return of prosperity after the disturbed business conditions and poor harvests of the previous years. But a more significant factor was the intrusion of the fisheries as a key issue. Almost from the start of the negotiations for reciprocity the American government had demanded access to the coastal fisheries of the maritime colonies in order to balance the greater benefits which, it was alleged, British North America would derive from the treaty. The thorny question which the British government had fondly hoped had been settled for good by the Convention of 1818 now arose once again to complicate the course of diplomacy.

In the first flush of enthusiasm the maritime provinces had been willing to barter the coastal fisheries for reciprocity. With the return of better business conditions, however, reciprocity began to seem less indispensable and there became evident a growing reluctance to sign away rights which had been so stubbornly defended in the past. This was particularly true in Nova Scotia. In 1850 the legislature of that province, in passing resolutions in favour of reciprocity, had rejected amendments which stipulated that under no circumstances should the fisheries be opened to the United States; the general opinion had then been that reciprocity in agricultural produce, lumber, and fish was adequate compensation for the loss of exclusive rights to the in-shore fisheries. But by 1852 public sentiment had changed radically and proposals that the British government should open the coastal fisheries to Americans in return for reciprocity were most vigorously opposed. This opposition continued right up to the signing of the Reciprocity Treaty in 1854.

Under these conditions, if the maritime provinces alone had been involved, it seems highly improbable that reciprocity would ever have been achieved. By 1854 opinion against the opening of the fisheries had hardened to such a degree that no local legislature could possibly have followed a contrary course. But the significance of the reciprocity negotiations lies precisely in the fact that they were conducted on behalf of the British North American provinces as a whole. The British government, in negotiating with the American administration, spoke for all the colonies, not for some only, and its bargaining strength rested largely on its ability to offer concessions in one area in exchange for advantages in another. The only concession which really carried weight in the negotiations was the fisheries. The principal obstacle which the British and Canadian negotiators had to face was simply disinterest: the American Congress, obsessed with the impending crisis over slavery, had little time or patience for foreign trade policy. No politically influential group in the United States thought that it had much to gain, and none (except when reciprocity was tied to the slavery and annexation issues) thought it had very much to lose. Only when the in-shore fisheries of the maritime provinces were thrown into the balance did the ponderous machinery of American politics begin to move.

It is worth noting, however, that it was not the commercial value of the fisheries that won votes for reciprocity but rather the desire to avoid an armed clash with Britain. In 1852, in response to repeated requests from the maritime colonies, the British government had announced its intention of defending the in-shore fisheries against American encroachments by force if necessary, and the naval squadron in Nova Scotian waters had been reinforced with this end in view. The main point at issue was the interpretation of the clause in the Convention of 1818 by which the United States had renounced the right of fishing within three miles of the shore of the British colonies. Was this three-mile limit to follow the coastline exactly, or was it to be drawn from headland to headland? The distinction was a not unimportant one, particularly in the Bay of Fundy, and it had occasioned sporadic friction, at times with explosive possibilities, ever since 1818. The British government, which took the second interpretation as correct, now appeared determined to back up its stand by force. The American government, for its part, evinced little inclination to submit meekly to what public opinion regarded as British aggression. When American naval units were sent to the fishing-grounds to oppose the reinforced British squadron, the situation became very critical indeed and open acts of war seemed by no means improbable. Such were the circumstances in which the American Congress, reluctant to provoke an open breach with Britain at a time when domestic dissension was at its height, turned with a new interest to the subject of reciprocity and found therein attractions, including a settlement of the fisheries question, which had been overlooked in the past.

So it was that Nova Scotia and New Brunswick, having seen the United States admitted to the West Indies carrying-trade in 1830, saw their other long-defended bastion, the coastal fisheries, opened to Americans in 1854. This concession, combined with the rather high-handed manner in which the British government had handled the negotiations in their final stages, meant that the advent of reciprocity was greeted with considerable hostility and resentment in the Maritimes. To be sure, the legislatures of these provinces were not slow to pass the statutes required to put the treaty into effect, but this was only because, having lost the in-shore fisheries, they were understandably anxious not to lose whatever compensating advantages the treaty might bring. These advantages were not inconsiderable. One item which the maritime provinces had initially sought —the admission of colonial shipping to American coastal privileges and to American registration when sold in the United States—was not included in the final agreement. But the treaty did bring free admission into the United States of colonial fish and lumber of all kinds, not to mention coal, gypsum, stone, lard, and various other products of less importance. Whether these benefits were sufficient to compensate, in a purely commercial sense, for the loss of exclusive rights to the coastal fisheries was a question not easy to determine. Opinion in the maritime provinces inclined to the view that they were not. But reciprocity was, after 1854, a fact, not a proposal, and the merchants, lumbermen, and fishers of the maritime provinces set out to make the best of the new opportunities and challenges which the treaty had brought.

The period during which the Reciprocity Treaty was in force (1854-66) was, with the exception of a sharp recession in 1857, one of considerable prosperity and rapid growth for the maritime colonies, as it was also for central Canada. Free access to the American market for the staple exports of these colonies was certainly one factor, though by no means the only one, which made this prosperity possible. In the first five years of the treaty, from 1854 to 1859, the total exports to the United States of all the British North American colonies other than central Canada increased from $2,206,-102 to $5,518,834, or in percentage terms from 100 to 250. Imports from the United States into these provinces increased from $7,266,154 to $9,213,832, or from 100 to 127 per cent. If we take the value of the exports of each province separately to the United States in 1854 as 100, by 1866 New Brunswick's exports had risen to 400, Nova Scotia's to 208, Newfoundland's to 314, and Prince Edward Island's to 131. The corresponding indices of imports, if each province's 1854 values are taken as 100, are 109, 141, 125, and 190. Figures for the terminal years alone obscure the fact that there were quite marked year-to-year fluctuations in both imports and exports (New Brunswick's imports from the United States, for instance, jumped by more than a fifth between 1865 and 1866), and part of the increases noted must be ascribed to the continuation of rising trends which began before the treaty was signed and continued after it was abrogated; but it is clear, nevertheless, that trade between the United States and the maritime colonies expanded very rapidly during the years of reciprocity.

It must be borne in mind, however, that other factors than reciprocity influenced the economic development of the maritime provinces during this period. The secular expansion of world trade meant that the demand for wooden sailing-ships remained strong, since for long voyages, particularly to parts of the world with few coaling stations, these vessels were still unrivalled. Even without reciprocity the lumbering and shipbuilding industries would have flourished by supplying this demand; one estimate places the average value of ships exported annually from New Brunswick, Nova Scotia, and Prince Edward Island in this period at £400,000. Central Canada probably benefited more than did the Maritimes from the Crimean War (1854-6) which, by cutting Britain off from her usual supplies of Black Sea wheat, stimulated grain exports from North America; but the outbreak of the American Civil War in 1861 brought immediate and substantial economic benefits to all the British provinces. Central Canada and the Maritimes profited alike from the appearance of a strong demand in the northern states for horses, meat, wool, and lumber. American shipyards turned to naval construction, thus freeing shipbuilders in Nova Scotia and New Brunswick from their most serious source of competition, while the merchants of Halifax and Saint John reaped handsome profits both from running the blockade and from a greatly increased trade with the West Indies. These developments would certainly have given a very powerful stimulus to the economies of the maritime provinces even in the absence of reciprocity.

RAILWAYS AND CONFEDERATION

One of the most interesting developments of the reciprocity period was the building of the first railways in the maritime provinces. In Chapter XIV we shall discuss in detail the construction and financing of the early railways; here we are more interested in what the coming of the railway meant to the maritime colonies and its relation to confederation in 1867. In New Brunswick during the years from 1853 to 1866 no less than 218 miles of railway were built; Nova Scotia during the same period constructed 147 miles. These figures seem small in comparison with the 1,974 miles which central Canada had completed by 1860; they are small also in comparison with the size of the railway projects which were planned and with the efforts which were put into raising the capital to build them. In the Maritimes even more than in central Canada the gap between plan and achievement in railway construction was uncomfortably large.

The planning of railways which were to link the maritime colonies to the St. Lawrence valley and to the grain-producing areas of the American west was not, of course, unconnected with reciprocity. From the American point of view, the privilege of using Canadian transportation routes, particularly the St. Lawrence waterway system, was not least among the benefits which reciprocity had brought. The lines originally planned in Nova Scotia and New Brunswick—the Saint Andrews and Quebec, the European and North America, and later the Intercolonial—were, as their names suggest, all intended to draw the through trade in agricultural exports from the midwest to the ice-free ports of the Maritimes, particularly during the winter season when the St. Lawrence sea and river route was closed. This grand ambition was, by and large, destined to disappointment. But while it lasted it had two very important and related effects. It linked the Maritimes for the first time with the continental expansionism which then as in the days of the fur trade sparked the ambitions of Montreal. And it brought the governments of the maritime provinces into the London capital market as borrowers.

By the end of 1866 Nova Scotia had invested over $6¼ million in railways and New Brunswick more than $4½ million. The capital for these investments was almost all borrowed from other countries, principally from England, and it was obtained only in return for commitments to pay interest and principal. The ability of the maritime provinces to meet these commitments rested upon their ability to find markets for their exports. The burden of the debts themselves was not serious, given a continuation of prosperity. But the revenue on which the governments of the maritime provinces relied to service the debts was obtained almost entirely from import duties. Consequently a falling off in external trade was bound to have serious repercussions not only on the commercial interests immediately involved but also on the governments' finances. By incurring debts to build the railways which they so earnestly desired, the maritime provinces had, as it were, given hostages to fortune. By increasing the burden of fixed charges on their revenues, they had curtailed their ability to withstand adversity. The tapering off of railway construction itself promised to bring difficulties as a direct result of the curtailment of government expenditures. In addition there were serious problems of structural change: the railways threatened the economic life of the smaller outports, though they benefited the cities at which they terminated and the immediate areas through which they ran. The coastal trade, too, was endangered by the new means of land transportation.

The early 1860's, in short, were a period in which a number of very fundamental changes were taking place in the economic life of the maritime provinces. But their impact was gradual and outwardly things went along very much as they had before. Nova Scotia and New Brunswick were still essentially maritime commercial economies. Despite the discovery and exploitation of coal deposits in Cape Breton, industrialism had hardly yet had any direct effect upon them. They still looked outward to the sea, as they had always done. They continued to rely upon their traditional means of livelihood: the fisheries, agriculture, the forests, shipbuilding, and maritime trade. Nevertheless, the strains of the new industrial age were slowly making themselves felt. The pull of the continent, with its railroads and its great cities, was becoming stronger, and the pull of the sea, with its infinite variety of trade routes and world-wide markets, was becoming weaker. Where before the forces of geography and technology had worked toward division, with each province going more or less its own way within the framework laid down by the mother country, now they were working toward centralization. The Reciprocity Treaty, opening to the exporters of the maritime provinces the continental markets of the United States, had been one evidence of this trend and had reinforced it. The railways of central Canada and the Maritimes, stretching out tentacles toward each other but not yet meeting, marked the next stage. Only Newfoundland, whose principal markets were still in Europe and the West Indies, remained almost wholly unaffected by the new tendencies.

The abrogation of the Reciprocity Treaty by the United States accelerated developments which otherwise would have come about more slowly. Reciprocity came to an end in March, 1866, but its demise had been anticipated for several years previously. The problem which arose was to find some acceptable substitute. The loss of preferences in the British market had been followed by a successful search for preferred markets in the United States. Now these preferences too were gone, while Britain was more determinedly committed to free trade than before. The North American colonies, it seemed, were faced with the unwelcome prospect of having to learn how to survive and grow in a world which was no longer willing to give their products specially favoured treatment.

The clearest way, and the one which held out the most prospect of suc-cess, by which the North American colonies could offset the shock of exclusion from the United States market was by trading more among themselves. If preferences in Britain and the United States were not to be had, the colonies could at least give preferences to each other. Com-mercial union of the British North American provinces would weld them into a single vast trading area within which products might be freely exchanged. If the markets of all the provinces could be opened to the industries of each, an economic system would be created which, by lessen-ing dependence on external markets, would offer greater stability than the economies of the separate provinces could hope for, and which, because of the diversity and complementarity of its resources, would have a greater potential for growth. The colonial policy which Britain had seen fit to adopt, the aggressive tactics of the United States, and the pressures of the new industrial system, with its expensive railways and large public debts—these developments called for the creation of larger and more cen-tralized economic structures than had existed in the era of water-power and wooden ships. In the eyes of many contemporary observers, the only way in which the British colonies in North America could retain some measure of control over their own destinies was by federation.

It would be far from the truth, however, to say that the maritime prov-inces were forced into confederation by economic necessity. On the contrary, the period before 1867 has often been called the golden age of the Mari-times, an age when the present was prosperous and the future bright. The gales of industrialism did not hit their economies with full force until after confederation. Whatever was true of central Canada, in the Maritimes confederation was regarded not as an avenue of escape from political dead-lock and economic stagnation but as a means whereby certain very specific and positive ends could be achieved. By confederation the Maritimes would get their railways, the arteries of the new dominion. By confederation they would strengthen their position against the United States in the coastal fisheries, now thrown open to dispute once again with the end of recipro-city. The chain of events which was finally to lead to confederation started, let us remember, with an interprovincial conference held at Charlottetown, the capital of Prince Edward Island, in 1864—a conference called by the maritime provinces to discuss a maritime federation. Faced with the impending end of reciprocity and the need for renewed defence against the United States in the fisheries, Nova Scotia, New Brunswick, and Prince Edward Island turned first to local federation as a matter of choice and convenience. Only later, on the initiative of central Canada, was this proposal broadened to include a federation of all the British colonies in North America, a scheme which had at first seemed beyond realization. When confederation became a reality the economies of the maritime provinces were still to all appearances sound and healthy. These conditions, however, were not to last.

SUGGESTIONS FOR FURTHER READING

BASIC WORKS:

Benns, F. Lee, *The American Struggle for the British West India Carrying-Trade* (Bloomington, Indiana, 1923), Chapters I-VI, pp. 7-188

Creighton, D. G., *British North America at Confederation: A Study Prepared for the Royal Commission on Dominion-Provincial Relations* (Ottawa, 1939), Sections I, II, IV, and X, pp. 7-12, 22-28, 59-61

Innis, Harold A., *The Cod Fisheries: the History of an International Economy* (Toronto and New Haven, 1946), Chapters IX-XI, pp. 227-374

Lower, A. R. M., *The North American Assault on the Canadian Forest* (Toronto, 1938), Chapters VII, VIII, XI, and XII, pp. 64-88, 123-47

Masters, D. C., *The Reciprocity Treaty of 1854* (Toronto, 1937), Part I, Chapters I-IV, pp. 3-109

SUPPLEMENTARY WORKS:

Lower, A. R. M., *Settlement and the Forest Frontier in Eastern Canada* (Canadian Frontiers of Settlement, Vol. IX, Toronto, 1936), Chapter III, pp. 28-37

Ragatz, Lowell J., *The Fall of the Planter Class in the British Caribbean, 1763-1833* (New York, 1928), Chapters I-XII, pp. 3-457

Saunders, S. A., *The Economic History of the Maritime Provinces: A Study Prepared for the Royal Commission on Dominion-Provincial Relations* (Ottawa, 1939), Section I, pp. 1-13

Setser, Vernon G., *The Commercial Reciprocity Policy of the United States, 1774-1829* (Philadelphia, 1937), Chapter VI and Conclusion, pp. 182-260

Trotter, Reginald G., *Canadian Federation, its Origins and Achievement: A Study in Nation Building* (Toronto, 1924), Part I, Chapters I-X, pp. 3-140, and Chapter XXIII, pp. 309-20

CHAPTER XII

THE ST. LAWRENCE LOWLANDS, 1815–1849
TRANSPORTATION

NEW STAPLES AND NEW PROBLEMS

THE absorption of the North West Company by the Hudson's Bay Company in 1821 reflected and contributed to profound changes in the development of the area tributary to the St. Lawrence River. With the disappearance of the North West Company, the merchants of Montreal lost the first great staple upon which their dreams of continental empire had been built. Thenceforth the fur trade was to be carried on from bases on Hudson Bay and on the Pacific coast. The old commercial link which for so long had tied the St. Lawrence to the economies of Europe had gone.

Meanwhile, and fortunately for the survival of British dominion in North America, new staples were appearing on the St. Lawrence: the timber trade, brought into being and maintained by tariff preferences in the British market; and the trade in the agricultural exports of the settlements in Upper Canada and the American midwestern states. These new staples resembled the fur trade in that they geared the rate of economic growth in the Canadas to developments in overseas markets over which Canadians themselves had little or no control; but in other respects their characteristics were very different. They demanded a new type of transportation system and new methods of securing capital and credit. They required a labour force vastly larger in quantity and possessing different skills. And they had different repercussions upon the societies within which their exploitation was carried out. For the next two decades at least the major problems of the Canadian colonies on the St. Lawrence were to be the problems involved in readjusting their social and economic organization to the requirements of these new staples.

To understand the nature of these problems it is necessary to keep in mind what was taking place in the British economy in the same period, since it was the expansion of the British economy which provided much of the driving force, in terms of markets, capital, and man-power, behind Canadian growth. The British economy in these years was entering upon the last stages in its transition from a predominantly agricultural to a predominantly industrial economy. At the same time, to meet the demands of her workers for cheap food and of her factories for cheap raw materials, Britain was moving rapidly toward a system of free trade.

Both these developments had profound implications for the role of colonies in the imperial system. On the one hand the growth of industrialism in Britain opened up large and potentially profitable markets for colonial exports. But on the other, the movement toward free trade broke down the old mercantilist system of colonial preferences, a system which had been designed to afford to the products of Britain's overseas possessions a favoured position in the markets of the mother country. Industrialism and free trade together, therefore, presented to the North American colonies both an opportunity and a challenge: the opportunity to supply the expanding industrial economy of Britain with food and raw materials, and the challenge of meeting the competition of other sources of supply in the open markets of Britain without the traditional protection of preferential duties. To meet this challenge and to seize this opportunity were the tasks facing the Canadian economy in the first half of the nineteenth century.

A successful outcome was by no means inevitable or predictable. To adjust the economy of the Canadian colonies to the impact of free trade and industrialism in Britain was no easy task. The costs of adjustment were high. Very large investments of capital were required to finance the construction of the transportation system which the new staples demanded. This capital was not available in British North America. Agricultural settlement, too, had to be pushed rapidly forward and immigration encouraged. Banks had to be established, roads built, canals dug, and new forms of business organization developed. The state itself had to accept new responsibilities for development and for the provision of facilities which private enterprise could not itself supply. All this and more had to be done, not in an atmosphere of confident security, but amid doubts and uncertainties, at a time when many in Britain were vigorously arguing that the mother country, in her own interests, should rid herself of her overseas dependencies, when in the Canadas themselves men of property and influence were questioning the wisdom of maintaining the imperial connection, and when in the aggressively expanding American republic to the south hopes for a peaceful assimilation of the Canadian colonies were being more confidently voiced than ever before. Further, in both Upper and Lower Canada political discontents were accumulating which were finally to explode in armed rebellion. Economic readjustments, therefore, had to be carried through in an atmosphere of social disturbance, when in each of the provinces on the St. Lawrence the form and content of colonial government were undergoing drastic change.

THE IMPACT OF THE ERIE CANAL

Attempts to improve the transportation facilities of the St. Lawrence and the Great Lakes were the first and most obvious consequence of the shift to the new staples. For the old staple, fur, a luxury article high in value in relation to its weight, little artificial improvement of the natural water routes had been required. But for the new agricultural staples, low in value in relation to their weight, transport costs were a crucial matter. The final price of these agricultural products was set in the markets of Liverpool and London; how much of this price the settler in Upper Canada or Ohio received as income, and what this income was worth to him in terms of what he could buy with it, depended on how much he had to pay for transportation. The prosperity and indeed the survival of the new commercial system which was being built up on the St. Lawrence to replace the vanished fur trade depended on the improvement, by means of canals, of the route from the growing settlements of the interior to tidewater at Montreal.

The limitations of the St. Lawrence-Great Lakes route to the interior were sharply emphasized by the completion of the Erie Canal in 1825. This canal, linking the port of New York with Buffalo harbour on Lake Erie, provided a new route by which agricultural products could be shipped from the west to the Atlantic seaboard and manufactured goods from the seaboard to the west. This new route was directly competitive with and considerably cheaper than the old St. Lawrence-Great Lakes route. Previously, the American midwestern states had been seriously handicapped in their development by the high costs of exporting their agricultural surpluses and of importing the manufactured goods which they required. They could send their exports either overland, with great expense and difficulty, to New York and other eastern markets, or by river boat down the Ohio and Mississippi, or, lastly, over the Niagara portage, across Lake Ontario, and down the St. Lawrence to Montreal. For their manufactured imports they had relied very heavily on the St. Lawrence route, since Montreal firms shipping by this water route had been able to undersell New York firms, shipping largely overland, by a substantial margin.

The completion of the Erie Canal meant a fundamental change in this pattern of trade. New York shippers to the west now had the benefit of freight charges considerably lower than those paid by their Montreal rivals, while firms shipping agricultural products to the east naturally preferred the cheap and direct Erie Canal route to the slow and expensive transport system of the St. Lawrence, with its numerous rapids, portages, and transshipments. On the one hand, therefore, the Erie Canal, by substantially lowering freight rates to and from the west, boosted the development of the area around Lake Erie; on the other, by establishing a differential in freight rates which favoured New York and handicapped Montreal, it destroyed the earlier advantage of the Canadian route. It is no great exaggeration, indeed, to say that the completion of the Erie Canal reduced Montreal's commercial hinterland by at least half. Before 1825 the territory around Lake Erie, both Canadian and American, had been in a commercial sense tributary to Montreal. After 1825 the American states in this area were dominated by New York, while the western peninsula of Upper Canada, with easy access to New York via the Erie Canal but still cut off from Montreal by the Niagara peninsula and the rapids on the St. Lawrence, was, from an economic point of view, disputed territory.

It took the Canadian provinces on the St. Lawrence almost a quarter of a century to complete their answer to the competitive challenge posed by the Erie Canal in 1825. Not until 1848 could the Canadian colonies announce the completion of a through route from Lake Erie to tidewater by way of the St. Lawrence which was comparable in freight costs and capacity to New York's Erie Canal, and by that date the Erie itself was losing ground in the face of a new source of competition: the American railroads. This delayed reaction had very serious long-term consequences; the ground which had been lost was never quite recovered.

Business men and politicians in Upper Canada and Montreal were quick to recognize the threat which the Erie Canal posed to the St. Lawrence economy, but many obstacles—geographical, political, economic, and technological—had to be surmounted before an adequate response could be made. Geographic factors were partly responsible for the slow completion of the Canadian route. From an engineering point of view, the construction of the Erie Canal had been relatively easy. A depth of only four feet simplified problems of lock construction; advantage had been taken of the rivers and lakes of northern New York state to serve as feeders for the canal; and throughout the whole route no very great heights of land nor sudden changes in level had been encountered. The problem of the Canadian route was fundamentally different. Here there was a long stretch of navigable water—Lake Ontario—which required no artificial improvement at all. But at either end, so to speak, of this stretch there were very serious obstacles indeed. Between Lake Ontario and Montreal there was a series of rapids on the St. Lawrence River, from the Long Sault below Prescott to the Coteau, Cedars, Cascades, and finally the Lachine rapids just above Montreal. These were passable by small boats and rafts on the downward trip, but were not navigable against the current. At the other end of Lake Ontario was the Niagara peninsula, where the great Falls on the Niagara River interposed a complete break in navigation. Here a portage of eleven and a half miles was necessary to overcome an abrupt difference in level between Lake Erie and Lake Ontario of over three hundred feet. Whereas the Erie Canal, therefore, was seen as a single project and was constructed as a unit, the Great Lakes-St. Lawrence route seemed to present a variety of problems and to invite a series of piecemeal, unco-ordinated attempts at local improvements.

These geographic factors took on added significance in combination with the economic and political obstacles to canal construction. Capital was not easily attracted to a new country. Large-scale public works were still highly speculative ventures in those days, and to mobilize large amounts of capital for fixed investments in a relatively little-known colony was a difficult task, especially since within the Canadas themselves there were no large reservoirs of wealth to be tapped. In addition, whether the canals were to be built by private enterprise or by government, they required trained engineers, experienced contractors, and large administrative organizations. In all these respects the Canadian colonies started practically from scratch. The path from commercialism to industrialism was not a smooth one.

The political obstacles were probably the most serious of all. If a co-ordinated and determined effort had been made, the Canadian canal system could have been completed long before 1848. Such an effort was not made, and for this political factors were primarily responsible. In 1791 a natural geographic unit, the St. Lawrence lowlands, had been broken politically into two parts by the formation of Upper and Lower Canada. Lower Canada, predominantly French-speaking and Catholic, with its own cherished culture, fearing submergence in a materialistic Anglo-American population which was increasing rapidly in numbers, was deeply suspicious of the kind of progress likely to be achieved by the construction of expensive canals and the extension of commercial agriculture. The merchants of Montreal, the strongest advocates of canal construction, were a small group isolated in a culture which did not place a high value on their activities and aspirations. Their close alliance with the executive government, in the form of the governor and his Councils, aggravated rather than eased the situation, since it made parliamentary grants for canal construction a political issue which symbolized the conflict between the commercialism of the Anglo-American community and the traditionalism of French Canada. In Upper Canada the emergence of strong commercial interests in timber and agriculture provided a major stimulus to canal construction, since these interests saw themselves cut off from overseas markets unless transportation disabilities were overcome. But in this province, too, government aid for canal construction became embroiled in political conflicts, and the commercial interests, in close alliance with the executive government, found themselves opposed by a vigorous reform movement profoundly suspicious of their aims and methods.

But quite apart from the effects of political disunity within the provinces, the fact that there were two provinces and two legislatures made the task of achieving concerted action in the field of transportation extremely difficult. In the first place, neither one of the provinces separately could command the credit in the international capital market which a single legislature, commanding the revenues of the entire St. Lawrence economy, could reasonably have expected to attain. In the second place, construction of the canals to uniform dimensions and in the most convenient order required agreement upon a single policy and the formation of responsible agencies to insure execution of that policy. This was not done; the canal-building programme envisaged by the government of Upper Canada found little support in the Assembly of Lower Canada, while the occasional appointment of joint committees by the two legislatures proved no effective substitute for the creation of a permanent administrative body with adequate authority and powers of supervision. And in the third place, the existence of two separate legislative bodies presented problems of allocating costs and benefits. The most serious obstacles in the through route, after the opening of the Welland Canal in 1829, were the rapids in the stretch of the St. Lawrence which lay within the jurisdiction of Lower Canada. The greatest benefits, on the other hand, which would result from the construction of canals around these rapids would accrue to Upper Canada and to the small mercantile community of Montreal. Why should one province burden itself with debt to assist the other? Only men who saw the St. Lawrence lowlands as an economic unit could rise above such concern with local interests and prejudices.

THE RIDEAU CANAL

There was one powerful body which might have been expected to con-cern itself with the St. Lawrence economy as a whole and which had authority sufficient to reconcile or override divergent interests: the British government. The improvement of the St. Lawrence-Great Lakes transportation route, after all, involved not only the regional interests of Upper and Lower Canada; it involved also the survival of British dominion in North America both from the point of view of economic prosperity and as a matter of military security. Unfortunately, these points of view were not completely reconcilable. Economic interests, as interpreted by the commercial groups of Upper and Lower Canada, and strategic interests, as interpreted by the British Army and Colonial Office, did not coincide. Unlike the situation in New York state, where the principal through transport route, the Erie Canal, ran back from the frontier to the port, the Canadian through route ran parallel to the frontier, and indeed for a considerable distance formed the boundary line. It was therefore highly vulnerable to American attack, as had been forcibly demonstrated during the War of 1812.

This conflict between commercial and strategic interests seriously limited the participation of the British government in the improvement of the St. Lawrence-Great Lakes route. The difficulties which had been experienced in supplying British forces in Upper Canada and the British fleets on Lakes Ontario and Erie during the War of 1812 had indeed convinced the British colonial authorities that something would have to be done to improve transport facilities between the lower Lakes and the sea. But at the same time the war had strongly impressed upon them the difficulty of defending the St. Lawrence River and the Niagara peninsula against American attack. The British government, therefore, consistently took as its primary and overriding responsibility the maintenance of the military security of the Canadian provinces, even although this might entail as a consequence the perpetuation of barriers to economic prosperity.

The presence of this attitude on the part of the British government did not mean a completely negative policy in the field of transportation. Substantial aid was given to the Lachine Canal in 1821, and to the Welland Canal project in 1828, although in the case of the Welland certain restrictions were imposed upon the choice of the route. More directly, the British government in 1826 undertook the construction of the Rideau Canal as a military work, financed entirely without burden on the Canadian provincial legislatures.

The Rideau Canal was designed to open up a line of communications between Montreal and Kingston which would be independent of the St. Lawrence and which could be defended in the event of American attack. With this end in view, an officer of the Royal Engineers was instructed in 1816 to survey the ground between Kingston on Lake Ontario and the point where the Rideau River joined the Ottawa, at the site of the present city of Ottawa. The officer reported that the project was feasible. Five years later, in 1821, when the legislature of Upper Canada appointed commissioners to consider the improvement of internal navigation, the British government offered to contribute £70,000 toward the cost of a canal constructed along this route. The offer was refused, since the legislature considered that such a canal would have little commercial value in comparison with the St. Lawrence canals which they hoped to see constructed. The British government therefore decided to proceed independently, and construction began in 1826 under the supervision of Colonel By of the Royal Engineers. The canal was finally completed in 1834.

The initial estimate of the probable cost of the Rideau Canal was £169,000. The final cost is generally given as about £1,000,000. Substantial miscalculations of costs were by no means uncommon in canal projects of this period, but in the case of the Rideau the discrepancy between estimated and final costs is so large as to call for some comment. An important factor was the changes which were made in the dimensions. The original plan had called for locks measuring 100 feet by 20 feet, or the same size as the locks on the Lachine Canal which we shall discuss shortly. Before beginning construction, however, Colonel By proposed that these dimensions should be increased to 150 feet by 50 feet in order that the canal might accommodate steamboats. This proposal was opposed by the administrator of Lower Canada on the ground that the smaller dimensions were quite adequate for military purposes. A compromise was finally reached by which the locks were to be 134 feet by 33 feet, with

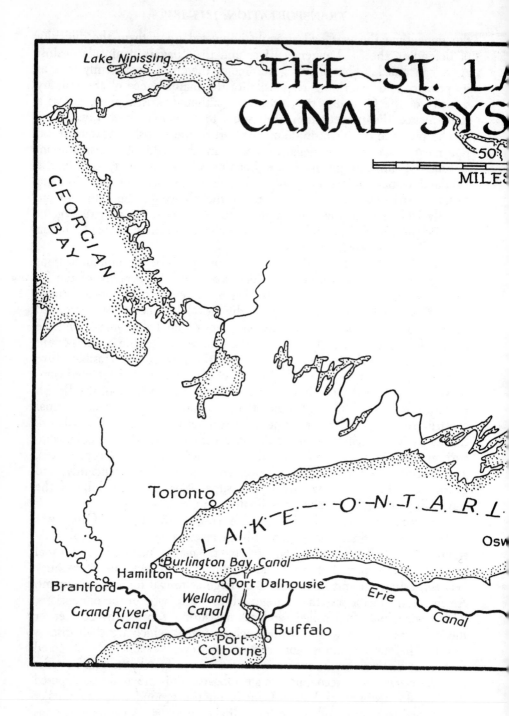

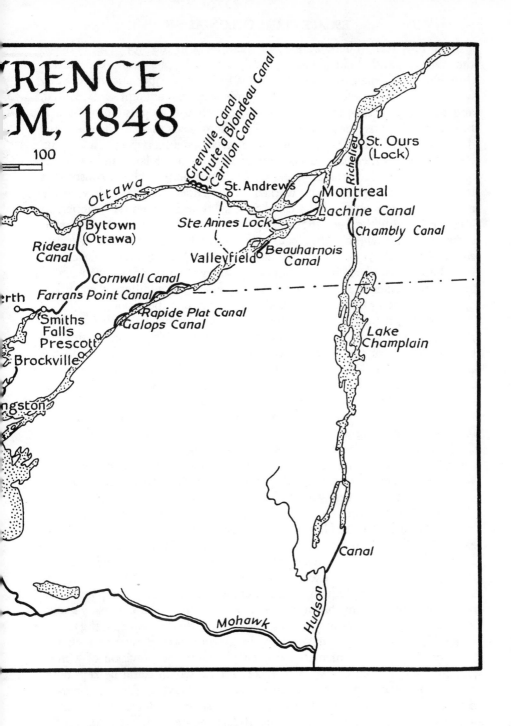

RENCE
M, 1848

100

Grenville Canal
Chute à Blondeau Canal
Carillon Canal

St. Ours
(Lock)

Richelieu

Ottawa   St. Andrews

Montreal

Lachine Canal

Bytown
(Ottawa)   Ste. Annes Lock

Chambly Canal

Rideau
Canal   Valleyfield

Beauharnois
Canal

Cornwall Canal

erth   Farrans Point Canal

Rapide Plat Canal

Lake
Champlain

Smiths
Falls   Galops Canal

Prescott

Brockville

ngston

Canal

Mohawk   Hudson

a depth of 5 feet. There were 47 of these locks in the 133 miles between the Ottawa and Lake Ontario, and the lock pits were constructed throughout of expensive masonry, instead of the cheaper and more easily worked timber. An effort was made to minimize the amount of excavation and rock-cutting required by making as much use as possible of natural lakes and streams, dams being built where necessary to increase the depth of water. This practice may have saved some money in construction costs, but it resulted in the flooding of large areas of land and—a consequence of some importance—meant that it was impossible to construct a tow-path. The engineers who worked on the Rideau appear to have made a serious attempt to build the canal in a solid and substantial manner, in accordance with the best engineering standards of the time; but it seems rather doubtful whether they paid sufficient attention to costs or took into consideration the question whether standards of construction developed for a heavily populated and capital-rich country such as Britain were suited to the requirements of the Canadas. There was, in addition, a good deal of sickness among the labourers and some laxity of supervision.

The cost of the canal was a matter of little importance from the Canadian point of view, except in so far as it deterred the British government from future ventures of the same kind. What was important was that, with the completion of the Rideau and, in the same year, of the three shorter canals on the Ottawa at the Carillon, Chute à Blondeau, and Grenville rapids, there was opened up a new transport route from the interior to Montreal. Unfortunately, this new route left much to be desired. Its capacity was limited. Since there was no tow-path on the Rideau, it was difficult for small sailing craft such as lake schooners and sloops to navigate it without the assistance of steam tow-boats. On the other hand, since the depth was only 5 feet, it was not suitable for large steamboats. Further, the dimensions of the largest vessel which could pass from Montreal to Kingston by this route were determined, not by the dimensions of the Rideau, but by the locks on the Grenville Canal on the Ottawa which, in a classic example of bad planning, had been built with a width of only 19¼ feet. Last but not least, for many years there was no lock at the rapids at St. Anne's, near Montreal, except one built in 1816 by the St. Andrews Forwarding Company which, in an attempt to enforce its monopoly of the forwarding and towing business, restricted its use to the Company's own vessels. No lock for general traffic was built at this point until 1843.

The Ottawa-Rideau canal system, in a word, served well enough the primary purpose for which it had been planned: the provision of a military supply-line from tidewater to Lake Ontario which could be kept open even though the upper St. Lawrence might be closed by American attack. But as a commercial route it was never of great importance. It is possible, indeed, that the construction of the Rideau actually delayed Montreal's counter-attack against the inroads which New York had made on the western trade, for the reason that it diverted attention from the urgency of improving the St. Lawrence route—the only policy which, as we can now see in retrospect, might have enabled Montreal to reassert its commercial dominance over the lower Lakes. It is difficult to believe that an earlier start would not have been made with the canalization of the St. Lawrence if the Rideau had not been built. However this may be, it seems evident that the completion of the Ottawa-Rideau system in 1834 signally failed to recover the ground which had been lost to the Erie Canal in 1825.

THE LACHINE CANAL

An essential link, both in the Ottawa-Rideau system and in the St. Lawrence route, was the canal at the Lachine rapids, on the bend of the St. Lawrence south of the island of Montreal. A small canal at this point had actually been begun in the year 1700, under the French regime, but it had not been completed by the time of the Conquest. Transport difficulties during the the War of 1812 re-emphasized the importance of the project, and in 1815 the legislature of Lower Canada appropriated £25,000 for the purpose and appointed three commissioners to supervise construction. A survey made by an officer of the Royal Engineers, however, resulted in an estimate of costs almost twice this figure, and the project was temporarily shelved. In 1819, in response to a petition from a group of private citizens, mostly Montreal merchants, the legislature chartered a private company to undertake construction, one of the conditions of the charter being that the work should be completed within three years. The Company hired an English engineer and had new surveys made, but soon ran into financial difficulties and in 1821 appealed to the legislature for an extension of time and other changes in the charter. By this date only £89,000 out of a total capital stock of £150,000 had been subscribed, and of this a substantial part had been contributed by the British and provincial governments. The legislature responded to the appeal by revoking the Comany's charter and undertaking the work itself (though the executive responsibility remained in much the same hands). Compensation was paid to the private stockholders for the money which they had actually expended. Under the government's auspices the work was pushed rapidly forward and the canal was opened for traffic in August, 1824. Its construction, at a total cost of £109,601, was financed entirely by the government of Lower Canada, with the exception of £10,000 contributed by the British government on condition that government vessels and stores should be permitted to pass the canal without paying toll.

Approximately 8½ miles in length and with a depth of 5 feet, the Lachine Canal had 6 stone locks measuring 100 feet by 20 feet. Its construction was the only important project in the field of canal transportation undertaken by Lower Canada in the period before 1840. To be sure, in 1830 work was begun on the Chambly Canal, on the Richelieu River, though it was not completed until 1843, and in 1817 three small canals originally built by the Royal Engineers between 1779 and 1783 at the Cascades, the Cedars, and Coteau du Lac were enlarged to accommodate large boats. In 1834 plans were drawn up for enlarging these latter canals still further, but no additional construction was actually undertaken, partly because of political disagreements in the Lower Canada legislature, and partly because of the thinly veiled opposition of the British government to any improvements in the navigation of this highly vulnerable stretch of the river.

THE WELLAND CANAL

In Upper Canada the drive for expanding markets for the province's growing agricultural surpluses led to strong and widespread pressure for canal construction. All groups within the province shared, to a greater or less degree, in the desire for transport improvement, although they came to differ seriously over questions of expense and administration.

The first project to be undertaken was the construction of a canal across the Niagara peninsula. This was particularly important, both for commercial and military reasons. Commercially, the Niagara peninsula represented the greatest single obstacle in the through route. The only means of transport over it was a portage from a point on the Niagara River just above the Falls to the town of Queenston. The necessity for this portage, entailing two trans-shipments and considerable expense, effectively diverted most of the Lake Erie trade to Buffalo harbour and thence down the Erie Canal to New York. The construction of a Niagara canal was therefore a matter of prime importance if Montreal was to secure any significant portion of the western trade. The development of the western districts of Upper Canada, too, was likely to be seriously retarded—or, what was little better, reduced to insecure dependence on American transport routes and tariff policies—if they were left without a means of sending their produce to the Montreal market.

From the strategic point of view, the experience of the British fleets on the lower Lakes during the War of 1812 had made it perfectly clear that the western peninsula of Upper Canada and the line of communication with points farther west could not be defended against American attack in the absence of naval superiority on Lake Erie. The construction of a Niagara canal would make it unnecessary to maintain a separate fleet and naval base on that lake and would greatly facilitate the movement of military supplies and troops westward. The conclusion in 1817 of the Rush-Bagot agreement between Britain and the United States, which limited the naval force which each nation could maintain on the Lakes, does not seem to have significantly lessened the importance which was attached to the Niagara project by military and naval strategists.

So obvious an impediment to commerce was the Niagara barrier that attempts to surmount or circumvent it had been contemplated almost from the earliest days of British settlement in the area. One of the first tasks undertaken by Simcoe, Upper Canada's first lieutenant-governor, had been the construction of two overland roads, Yonge Street and Dundas Street, which were essentially designed as means of freeing British communications with the west from dependence on Niagara and Lake Erie. These roads were laid out to serve the needs of military communications and settlement rather than as trade routes, but the North West Company at least had been quick to see the advantages of Yonge Street as a short cut from Lake Ontario to Georgian Bay. In 1793 Robert Hamilton, a Niagara merchant, had proposed to Simcoe that there should be constructed a paved road at the Niagara portage and a canal with a lock at the rapids below Fort Erie, and six years later he and two other merchants petitioned the legislature for permission to begin the work. Nothing further, however, was done at the time. As in other cases, transport difficulties during the War of 1812 were responsible for a revival of interest in the project, which received a further impetus from the short-lived but hectic burst of agricultural prosperity immediately after the war. Late in 1818 a young man named William Hamilton Merritt, a merchant and mill-owner of the town of St. Catharines in the Niagara peninsula, together with a few other local business men, presented a petition to the legislature in which they claimed that a canal could easily be built from the Welland River, which entered the Niagara River above the Falls, to Twelve Mile Creek, a small stream which emptied into Lake Ontario. They asked that official surveys should be made. A select committee appointed by the legislature to look into the matter reported favourably on the project and recommended that a private company should be chartered to build the canal. At this stage, however, the project was allowed to lapse temporarily, as difficulties which had arisen over the division of customs duties with Lower Canada had sharply curtailed provincial revenues, while the slump in agricultural prices which began in 1819 had plunged Merritt and his associates into private financial embarrassments.

In 1823 Merritt returned to the attack and succeeded in collecting sufficient funds to have a survey made of the route which he had originally proposed and which, incidentally, passed through his property near St. Catharines. A petition was submitted to the legislature, and in January, 1824, a private company was chartered with the title of the Welland Canal Company. Its capital stock was only £40,000. Serious obstacles were encountered in getting even this amount subscribed, partly because the plans which the Company was following at this point called for a canal only four feet deep. It was soon realized that this depth was insufficient, since the canal, if it was to have any commercial utility, would have to be large enough to accommodate lake schooners. Early in 1825, therefore, a new charter was secured which increased the capital stock to £200,000 and which stipulated that the locks should have a depth of at least eight feet.

Construction had actually begun during 1824 and was pushed rapidly ahead after the new charter was secured. As before, however, considerable difficulty was experienced in raising capital. Private investors in Upper and Lower Canada subscribed a little over £17,500, and in 1826 the Company received from the government of Upper Canada the first in a series of loans and stock subscriptions which, before the canal finally passed into government ownership, were to amount to a total of over £275,000. The government of Lower Canada, rather unexpectedly, also invested in the Company to the amount of £25,000, while a loan of £50,000 sterling was secured from the British government by mortgaging the canal and its profits. In addition, a substantial block of shares, totalling almost £70,000, was purchased by a group of investors in New York state, among whom John B. Yates, an Albany lottery manager, was the most conspicuous figure. This influx of American venture capital, which distinguishes the Welland from all other Canadian canals, was of crucial importance in the Company's early years.

With the aid of these sources of capital, the canal was opened for traffic from Lake Ontario to the Welland River, and thence by way of the Niagara to Lake Erie, late in 1829. The dimensions of its locks, which were built of wood, were 100 feet by 22 feet, with a depth of 8 feet. Unexpected construction problems had led to several departures from the original plan, and in particular had necessitated the construction of a long feeder which ran almost the entire length of the Niagara peninsula, from the Grand River estuary, to supply water for the canal. This feeder proved a continual source of trouble, and in addition the passage of ships up the Niagara River was hazardous and slow. In 1830, therefore, conscious of these drawbacks, the directors decided to extend the canal directly to Lake Erie and at the same time to convert the feeder into a navigable branch of the canal. These tasks fully occupied their attention and finances until 1833, when the direct cut to Lake Erie was opened.

If traffic through the canal had developed as rapidly as had been anticipated, the Company might at this point have begun to emerge from its financial straits. Unfortunately, the initial flow of traffic was small. Several factors were responsible for this. In the first place, a series of mishaps and accidents damaged confidence in the canal. Lower freight costs were not in themselves sufficient to induce shippers to patronize the Welland rather than the Erie; they also had to be able to count on sending their goods through without delay. Secondly, shipping on Lake Erie was at this time dominated by American vessels. American forwarders not only had a natural preference for the familiar American route; they also were in many cases dependent on credit extended by commercial houses in Buffalo and New York. Thirdly, the Welland Canal was not in all respects suitable for the class of vessel then navigating the Lakes. The development of traffic through the Welland had to wait upon the construction of a class of vessel especially designed for the canal—ships with flat bottoms, straight stems, centre-boards, and short bowsprits, the forerunners of the present-day "canallers".

In addition, the advantages which the Welland might otherwise have possessed over the Erie were seriously diminished by the fact that the St. Lawrence canals had not yet been completed. No single section of the St. Lawrence-Great Lakes route could develop its full potentialities until the entire route had been completed. For this reason, the Welland Canal in its early years relied heavily on American traffic, particularly traffic between ports on Lake Erie, such as Cleveland, and the port of Oswego on Lake Ontario, which had recently been connected to the Erie Canal by the completion of the Oswego Canal in 1828. The expectation that this subsidiary route could be developed had, of course, been much in the minds of the American investors in the Company. It was perhaps paradoxical but not unnatural that for the first few years after the Welland Canal was opened it was more important as a link in an American, rather than a Canadian, transport system.

Because of the slow development of traffic, revenue from tolls on the Welland Canal, amounting to only £5,754 in 1836, was insufficient to pay for routine upkeep and maintenance, and the physical condition of the canal deteriorated steadily, the wooden lock pits in particular falling rapidly into disrepair. In 1836, therefore, a petition was submitted by the private stockholders requesting that the provincial government should purchase the canal. No immediate action was taken on the request, but in March, 1837, the government assumed effective control by stipulating as a condition of making a large loan to the Company that it should have the right to appoint a majority of the board of directors. Full government ownership of the canal was secured by an act passed in 1841 (amended in 1843) which bought out the private stockholders by giving them government bonds in exchange for their shares in the Company.

THE CORNWALL CANAL

With the exception of such minor works as the Burlington Bay, Desjardins, and Grand River canals, the only other canal project undertaken in Upper Canada before the union of the provinces was the Cornwall Canal on the St. Lawrence. This was designed to avoid the Long Sault rapids at the head of Lake St. Francis, the only section of the St. Lawrence which Upper Canada could undertake to improve without the co-operation of

Lower Canada. Proposals to construct such a canal had been presented to the legislature of Upper Canada as early as 1816, and in 1818 a joint commission appointed by the legislatures of both provinces had recommended that an early start be made with the construction of canals on this stretch of the river. No action was taken on this recommendation, although in 1826 plans were drawn up and submitted to the legislature. In 1830, however, the town of Brockville, fearing that it would suffer commercially from the completion of the Ottawa-Rideau system, had a survey made of one possible route for a canal around the Long Sault rapids and urged the legislature to take action in the matter. In response to considerable pressure from the citizens of Brockville, the legislature in 1832 passed a resolution approving the construction of the canal and in the following year commissioners were appointed to supervise the work. Construction was begun in 1834.

Perhaps partly because of the difficulties which were being experienced by the Welland Canal Company, it was taken for granted from the outset that the Cornwall Canal should be strictly a governmental work. To finance the project, the province floated a series of loans in London and for a time work went ahead briskly. Unfortunately, the severe depression which began in 1837, combined with the Canadian rebellions of the same year, made it impossible for the provincial government to sell its bonds. Work on the Cornwall Canal was therefore suspended in 1837; it was not resumed until 1842. Completed in 1843, the canal is said to have cost over one and a half million dollars. It had a length of eleven and a half miles and six locks measuring 200 by 55 feet, with a depth of 9 feet.

THE COMPLETION OF THE ST. LAWRENCE CANAL SYSTEM

For the Canadian colonies on the St. Lawrence the years between 1836 and 1841 were a period of considerable unrest. Falling agricultural prices and acute shortage of credit caused severe hardship for farmer and merchant alike, while political deadlock and the interruption in the flow of capital imports brought plans for transport improvement to a standstill. Both commercially and constitutionally, the colonies appeared to have reached an impasse.

The appointment of Lord Durham as Governor-General of the British North American colonies marked the beginning of a new period of development. Conscious of the extent to which political unrest had been aggravated by commercial and agricultural depression, particularly in Upper Canada, Durham lost no time in calling to the attention of the British government the urgent necessity for completing the St. Lawrence canal system. On Durham's instructions, an officer of the Royal Engineers, Lt.-Col. Phillpotts, prepared two very able reports on the subject, in which he argued strongly that the future prosperity of the St. Lawrence colonies depended upon the completion of the chain of canals between Lake Erie and tidewater. "Unless," he asserted, "we open an uninterrupted navigation for *large freight steamers,* capable of carrying a cargo of at least 300 tons, *without trans-shipment* before they arrive at Montreal or Quebec, we have no chance whatever of securing any great portion of that vast and important trade which must ere long be carried on between the Western States and the Atlantic Ocean." He urged that the canals which had already been built (the Welland and Lachine) should be enlarged to a depth of nine feet, that the Cornwall Canal should be pushed rapidly to completion, and that canals of the same dimensions as the Cornwall Canal should be constructed around the remaining rapids on the St. Lawrence as quickly as possible.

Financing the construction of these canals remained the major problem. Upper Canada was at this time practically bankrupt, while Lower Canada, though financially in better condition because of her much smaller public debt, could hardly be expected to shoulder the burden alone. Union of the two provinces promised not only to ease political difficulties and facilitate the constitutional changes then in contemplation but also to provide a more solid foundation for new attempts to raise capital in London. The British government therefore offered, as an inducement to Upper Canada to enter the union and as a means of re-establishing the credit of Canadian securities in the London money market, to guarantee the payment of interest on a new Canadian loan of one and a half million pounds sterling. This guarantee would in effect convert the bonds of the Canadian government into first-class gilt-edged securities, the equivalent of the bonds of the British government.

This imperial loan was initially supposed to be applied to the redemption of the outstanding debts of the two provinces, the intention being that, if new capital was required to finance public works, new Canadian securities, without the guarantee of the British government, would be issued. Mainly because of the continuing depression, this plan was abandoned, as it appeared improbable that a new issue of Canadian government securities would sell at anything like their nominal value. In 1842, therefore, the legislature of the now united provinces of Canada decided to use the proceeds of the imperial loan to complete the St. Lawrence and Welland Canals, leaving the existing provincial debt unredeemed. The British government made no objection to this arrangement and, in consequence, the construction of the Canadian canal system was resumed in 1842, after five years of inactivity.

Under the capable supervision of the Board of Works, the programme of construction and enlargement was pushed ahead vigorously. The Cornwall Canal, as we have already noted, was opened for navigation in 1843. In the previous year a start had been made on the Beauharnois

Canal, constructed on the north shore of the St. Lawrence around the Cascades, Cedars, and Coteau rapids; this canal was completed at the end of 1845. In 1844 work was begun on the Farran's Point, Rapide Plat, and Galops Canals (known collectively as the Williamsburg Canals) between the Cornwall Canal and Lake Ontario. These were opened for navigation in 1847. Lastly, between 1843 and 1848 the Lachine Canal was enlarged to a depth of nine feet. Between 1842 and 1845 the Welland Canal also had been rebuilt and enlarged.

CANADA'S STAKE IN THE ST. LAWRENCE CANALS

By 1848, therefore, a chain of first-class canals, built to uniform dimensions, had been constructed to provide a complete system of navigable waterways from Lake Erie to the sea. Thus was the task completed which had occupied the St. Lawrence colonies for over a quarter of a century. Its accomplishment had not been easy; the outstanding debt of the province, amounting in 1850 to over two and a half million pounds, bore witness both to the magnitude of the undertaking and to the seriousness of the commitment which had been made.

For the St. Lawrence canals represented not only a magnificent system of inland waterways; they represented also a massive investment in the future. Their value as an investment depended not at all on how much had been spent on them in the past, but entirely on how well in the future they would serve the interests of the nation which had built them. The grand design which had inspired this canal system rested upon the confident assumption that, once the canals were completed, the St. Lawrence route, by its greater cheapness and capacity, would attract a substantial —perhaps the greatest—part of the agricultural exports of Upper Canada and the American midwest. The debt to which the canals had given rise represented, in effect, the overhead costs which the St. Lawrence economy had incurred in the effort to establish itself as the great through route from the Atlantic to the interior. But the world in which the St. Lawrence colonies found themselves at mid-century was not the world in which their canal system had been planned. A new source of competition had appeared: the railroad, cheaper than waterways as a means of transportation for many classes of commodities and, unlike waterways, able to operate effectively during the winter months. The American states were now expanding rapidly in economic strength and appeared to be outdistancing by far the development of those areas in North America which still acknowledged allegiance to the British Crown. And in Britain the disintegration of the old colonial system, symbolized in the repeal of the Corn Laws and the Navigation Acts, appeared to remove the very foundations upon which the St. Lawrence economy had been built. The completion of the St.

Lawrence canals indeed marked the accomplishment of a great task; but the horizons which opened up when the task was finished seemed to promise only greater problems and new difficulties in the future.

SUGGESTIONS FOR FURTHER READING

BASIC WORKS:

Glazebrook, G. P. de T., *A History of Transportation in Canada* (Toronto, 1938), pp. 75-97

Patton, M. J., "Shipping and Canals", in A. Shortt and A. G. Doughty, eds., *Canada and its Provinces* (22 vols.; Toronto, 1914-17), Vol. 10, Part II, pp. 475-535

SUPPLEMENTARY WORKS:

Aitken, Hugh G. J., *The Welland Canal Company: A Study in Canadian Enterprise* (Cambridge, Mass., 1954)

Cuthbertson, George A., *Freshwater: A History and Narrative of the Great Lakes* (New York, 1931), pp. 203-51

Keefer, Thomas C., *The Canals of Canada* (Montreal, 1894)

Kingsford, William, *The Canadian Canals* (Toronto, 1865)

Whitford, Noble E., *History of the Canal System of the State of New York* (2 vols.; Albany, 1906)

CHAPTER XIII

THE ST. LAWRENCE LOWLANDS, 1815–1849: IMMIGRATION, LAND SETTLEMENT, AGRICULTURE, AND TRADE POLICY

IMMIGRATION

In 1815, on the conclusion of the war with the United States, the political authorities of Upper and Lower Canada instituted a policy of excluding American settlers. Such a policy was, of course, difficult to enforce, for it was not easy to distinguish an American from a resident of Upper Canada once he had crossed the frontier, and certainly it did not completely shut off the influx of American immigrants. It appears probable, however, that it did divert toward Ohio many of the westward-moving American migrants who would otherwise have taken the easy route into Upper Canada by way of the Niagara peninsula. The opening of the Erie Canal in 1825, the growth of shipping on Lake Erie, and the construction of land routes south of the lake, were factors which reinforced this tendency.

It was expected that immigrants from Britain would fill the gap left by the exclusion of Americans. This expectation was in harmony not only with Upper Canada's need for settlers but also with a growing sentiment in Britain which favoured emigration as a cure for unemployment, poverty, social unrest, and rising taxes on real estate. Various schemes for large-scale emigration which were proposed and put into action during the 1820's and 1830's reflected the belief that the social costs of industrialism and cyclical unemployment in Britain could be minimized by sending the "surplus" population to the thinly settled colonies overseas.

Statistics for the number of immigrants who came from the British Isles to the St. Lawrence colonies and remained there as residents are rather unreliable. It appears, however, that the number of immigrants arriving at Quebec rose from about 12,600 in 1827 to 28,000 in 1830 and over 66,000 in 1832. A large proportion of these immigrants, however, estimated in some years to be as much as a half, did not remain in the Canadas but moved on into the United States. On the other hand, many immigrants who finally settled in Upper Canada, particularly those with more than average reserves of cash, preferred to land in New York and take the Erie Canal route to the interior. Statistics of arrivals at Quebec, therefore, do not accurately reflect the true volume of immigration.

It is possible to be somewhat more definite about the trend and the periods of greatest inflow. Immigration was small immediately after the end of the war in 1815. Only some 700 are said to have arrived in that year. A few groups of unemployed workers and demobilized soldiers came out with the assistance of the British government before 1818, notably those who formed the Rideau settlements in Upper Canada, but these experiments in state-assisted emigration were costly and were soon abandoned. The great increase in the rate of immigration began in the 1820's, when the expansion of the timber trade, bringing with it the problem of securing return cargoes for the ships which carried timber to England, reduced the cost of the transatlantic voyage. In the same period several of the American Atlantic states, concerned over the number of poor immigrants who were arriving, began to impose taxes on immigration and thus deflected part of the flow to British North American ports. Large numbers of immigrants arrived in each year between 1826 and 1832. Epidemics of cholera in 1832 and 1834 and the Canadian rebellions of 1837 resulted in a substantial decrease in arrivals—and indeed in some emigration from the Canadas to the United States—but the movement picked up again in the 1840's. Famine in Ireland in 1845 was followed by the arrival of very large numbers of Irish immigrants in 1846 and 1847. In the latter year as many as 90,000 arrived, bringing with them a serious outbreak of cholera. The flow slackened somewhat in the following years, partly because of the growing scarcity of good land in Upper Canada, partly because of restrictions imposed because of the poverty and low resistance to disease of these Irish immigrants.

Various schemes for government or parish assistance to people wishing to emigrate from the British Isles were in operation during these years but they were in the aggregate relatively unimportant. Most of the immigrants made the crossing entirely on their own initiative, without financial assistance from any outside body or institution. Although agents of shipping companies and other interested persons gave currency to a host of fables regarding the ease of emigrating and the delights of life in North America, the principal force behind the migration was not the pull of independence or prosperity in the Canadas but the push of poverty and unemployment in Britain.

Nevertheless, it would be a mistake to think of these immigrants as being uniformly penniless and without resources. Many of them came over to join kinfolk or friends who were already established in the Canadas and who were in a position to provide assistance during the early years. Many of them, too, particularly those who arrived in the early 1830's, brought over not inconsiderable sums of money—the life savings of families who migrated, not because their situation was already desperate, but because they feared it might shortly become so. Estimates of the amount of capital brought to the Canadas by immigrants are, however, highly unreliable. A

Liverpool newspaper set the figure at an average of £15 per head, but this was probably no more than a guess. Official immigration reports give figures of £250,000 and £600,000 as estimates of the funds brought in by immigrants arriving at Quebec in 1831 and 1832 respectively, and these figures are at least suggestive of the sums involved.

The overwhelming majority of these immigrants came to the Canadas in the expectation of buying land and becoming farmers. A small proportion of them settled in Lower Canada, but the persistence of feudal tenures in this province and the hostility of French Canadians to mass Anglo-Saxon immigration were serious deterrents. By far the greater number went to Upper Canada. One result of this was a shift in the balance of population between the two provinces. The population of Upper Canada, estimated at 157,923 in 1825, increased to 432,159 in 1840 and 791,000 in 1850. That of Lower Canada, estimated at 479,288 in 1825, had increased to 716,670 by 1840 and to 840,000 by 1850. That is to say, while the population of Upper Canada increased by over 400 per cent in the quarter century, the population of Lower Canada increased by only a little over 75 per cent. By 1852 Upper Canada's population exceeded that of Lower Canada. Lower Canada in this period appears to have had a higher death-rate than Upper Canada, but also a higher birth-rate. The shift in the balance of population was due almost entirely to immigration.

LAND SETTLEMENT

The long-run effect of this large-scale immigration upon the economic development of Upper Canada depended upon the rate at which the arrivals could be integrated into the productive organization of the colony. This in turn depended upon the rate at which they could be settled on the land and, by the provision of the necessary capital facilities, particularly for transportation, turned into effective producers of commodities which had market value—in this case, primarily wheat.

For several years after 1815 the government of Upper Canada continued to make free grants of lands to settlers and others, as had been the practice before 1812. In 1827, however, in an attempt to increase provincial revenues and also reduce the corruption and favouritism which had characterized land-granting in the province, a system of selling public land on credit, known as the New South Wales system, was introduced. After 1827, therefore, no further free grants were made, except to militiamen, veterans of the War of 1812, children of Loyalists and (after 1841) settlers on certain specified colonization roads. The immigrant arriving in the province after this date had to purchase his land, either from the Department of Crown Lands or from private owners. The inefficiency of the Crown Lands officials made purchase from the government a slow process and it was not easy to obtain a clear title. Most of the desirable locations had in any case already been alienated. The general practice for immigrants was therefore to purchase land, in the form of an established farm, a cleared lot, or merely a "location", from private land agents or small-scale land speculators.

In terms of the time it took them to become effective agricultural producers, immigrants into Upper Canada are sometimes divided into three classes. Those who arrived without cash resources ordinarily hired themselves out as labourers, either in the lumber industry, or in the canal construction camps, or on farms. After a period of years, when they had accumulated a little money, they could purchase an uncleared lot in the back areas, or lease a farm, perhaps in the Clergy Reserves, or arrange a share-cropping agreement with someone who owned a location which he wanted to see improved. For the first few years after he occupied his land, a settler of this type could hardly hope to have a salable crop, but would rely on outside earnings during the harvest season to maintain himself and his family through the winter. The second class of settlers, those who brought with them a little capital, would usually purchase a location at once, as near to an established community as they could afford. After two or three years, during which they would live on their savings, they could count on having a marketable crop and could look forward to improving and extending their holdings steadily thereafter. A settler of the third class, one who had considerable capital, would either purchase an improved farm at once or else buy a location and pay for having it cleared, so that a cash crop would be obtained within a relatively short time.

The rate at which immigrants became farmers depended, therefore, primarily on the amount of capital which they could command. The process of assimilating immigrants into the productive organization of the colony was essentially, from the economic point of view, a process of investment. The capital required for each individual settler (or, more correctly, for each family) varied, of course, from year to year and from one part of the province to another, but, during the period with which we are concerned, it can never have been much less than £200, and this only on the assumption that the settler was prepared to take up a location of uncleared land in the back areas, away from the lake-shore and the main transport routes. Near a village or one of the older settlements, land cost from £4 to £8 an acre in the early 1820's, whereas in the back areas it could be purchased for from two to three shillings an acre. In the Talbot settlement north of Lake Erie a partially cleared farm of 200 acres, with a log house and a barn already built, could be bought for £250 in the 1820's. Near the lake-shore, and in relatively thickly settled areas such as the Niagara district, such a farm would cost between £800 and £900. By the mid-1830's a tract of a hundred acres of good land anywhere in

Upper Canada cost at least £100. In addition to the purchase price of his land, a new settler required £100 as a bare minimum to buy the necessary livestock and implements and to pay for help in getting his land cleared. In brief, it required a considerable sum of money, invested over a period of several years, for an immigrant to establish himself as a settler.

The system of selling both public and private lands on credit, as well as such forms of community co-operation as logging- and harvesting-bees, served to minimize the settler's need for cash. Important also were the activities of the colonization companies, of which the Canada Company in Upper Canada and the British-American Land Company in Lower Canada were the most conspicuous. Formed in 1823 with a capital of one million pounds sterling, most of which was subscribed by British merchants, the Canada Company originally proposed to purchase from the British government all the unassigned lands in the province and resell them at a profit to settlers. This proposal proving unacceptable, the Company then offered to take over the Clergy and Crown Reserves. The Clergy Reserves were later excluded from the transaction and a tract of one million acres of land in the London and Western districts, known as the Huron Tract, substituted. The Company was formally chartered in June, 1825; it purchased from the British government all the Crown Reserves and the Huron Tract and agreed to pay in return the sum of £348,860 in instalments over a period of sixteen years. Two-thirds of this sum was to be paid directly to the provincial government, while the remainder was to be expended on local improvements and public works on the Company's lands.

The organization of the British-American Land Company in Lower Canada followed a similar pattern. In 1825 the promoters, several of whom were interested also in the Canada Company, proposed to the Governor-General that they should purchase all the ungranted lands belonging to the Crown in the surveyed townships of Lower Canada, together with one-half or the whole of the Clergy Reserves. This proposal was not accepted, but six years later another and more successful attempt was made. Chartered in 1834, the Company secured control of 847,661 acres of land at a cost of £120,000, payable in ten years. Half of this purchase price was to be laid out in improvements and public works; the remainder was to be paid directly to the provincial government. The greater part of the acreage involved was in the area known as the Eastern Townships, on the border of Maine, New Hampshire, and Vermont, a region which had already been partially settled by immigrants from the United States.

Both of these land companies aroused considerable hostility among the reform elements in Upper and Lower Canada, who resented the transfer of such a large portion of the natural resources of the provinces to the control of private commercial interests based on London. Much of this resentment, however, seems to have had a political rather than an economic origin. The annual instalments which the companies had contracted to pay to the provincial governments were used to finance the civil list, or in other words the salaries of the permanent executive officers of government. This, of course, rendered the executive branch of the provincial government to that extent independent of the legislative branch; and since the main strength of the reform parties was in the elected Assemblies and the main strength of their opponents in the appointed Executive and Legislative Councils, the land companies were inevitably drawn into the arena of political conflict.

From the economic point of view these political complications were of secondary importance. Both companies appear to have made substantial contributions to accelerating the rate of immigration and settlement, principally because of the capital facilities which they provided. The Canada Company, for example, built sawmills and grist mills, brick kilns, schoolhouses, roads, and a steamboat. Equally important were its efforts to spread information about the Canadas in Europe and the British Isles and to insure that immigrants arriving at Quebec proceeded to Upper Canada and did not drift south to the United States. Immigrants who undertook to purchase land from the Company were provided with transportation from Quebec to the head of Lake Ontario. The British-American Company, too, greatly improved the condition of the roads in its section of Lower Canada and was instrumental in encouraging numbers of English speaking settlers to take up land in the Eastern Townships, in spite of a general reluctance on the part of immigrants to settle in what was regarded as a purely French-speaking province. The British-American Company encountered more serious financial difficulties than did its counterpart in Upper Canada and was forced to suspend its payments to the provincial government after only three instalments had been paid. The Canada Company, despite early difficulties, was more successful, partly because, as a general rule, it dealt only with immigrants who had some capital when they arrived, partly because the stream of immigration was more easily directed toward Upper Canada than it was to the Eastern Townships.

The importance of these companies for the development of the St. Lawrence colonies lay in the fact that they provided capital facilities and a measure of guidance which helped to tide the immigrant over the first few difficult years. Not only did they contribute to increasing the rate of immigration and the proportion of immigrants who remained in the Canadas; they also cut down the interval between the time when an immigrant arrived and the time when he became an effective producer. Whether or not some other type of organization could have performed the same functions more efficiently must remain an open question.

CROPS AND FARMING METHODS

Agricultural techniques remained rather primitive throughout the whole of this period. A few areas in Upper Canada and a few groups of immigrants formed exceptions to this statement. The Pennsylvania Germans and the Lowland Scots, for example, acquired reputations as first-class farmers wherever they settled. Native Upper Canadians, however, and the general run of American immigrants practised the unsystematic type of extensive agriculture typical of the North American frontier, and these set the general tone of farming practice in the province.

Visitors to Upper Canada from Britain were inclined to be highly critical of the agricultural practices which they encountered, and contrasted them unfavourably with the careful ploughing and planned rotations which were becoming common in England. Extensive agriculture of the type generally practised in Upper Canada was, however, by no means irrational in terms of the economic situation of the province. Capital was very scarce and land relatively cheap; in many areas transport facilities were quite inadequate and the absence of cash markets encouraged self-sufficiency and provided little incentive to intensify production. Many of those who owned and occupied land, too, were farmers only in a special sense of the word, since they made their living not by farming one area continuously, but rather by clearing a location, selling it at a profit, moving on to another location, and repeating the process so long as purchasers of cleared farms were available. These "professional settlers", as they are sometimes called, had little reason to adopt improved techniques of husbandry.

Scarcity of capital and the lack of cash markets explain the prevalence of many agricultural practices which seem wasteful and inefficient. The initial clearing of the ground, for example, was usually accomplished either by "girdling" the trees—cutting a ring out of the trunk—and leaving them to die, or by felling them, cutting them into logs, and burning them. Whichever method was used, very large quantities of timber were destroyed without any useful product resulting except, when the logs were burned, the potash which was exported to Europe for use in the chemical and textile industries. The first crops taken off newly cleared land, too, were obtained merely by sowing wheat round the stumps and scratching it in with a harrow, since the ground was, at this stage, rich enough to require no deep ploughing or manure. Each year the backwoods farmer would clear four or five acres of new land and sow it with wheat in this way, raising potatoes, Indian corn, rye, or buckwheat on the land from which a wheat crop had been taken the year before. After a few years the stumps could be removed or burned, and the land was then ready for the plough.

In the older parts of Upper Canada, where the land had been cleared for several decades and where transport facilities and local markets were available, agricultural techniques were in general rather less primitive. The staple product was, of course, wheat, which was a cash crop and required less capital investment than other branches of farming, but other crops, such as peas, barley, rye, and buckwheat, were grown for domestic consumption. Farming methods varied considerably from one locality to another. In some areas wheat was sown year after year on the same piece of land, until the soil became exhausted. Then it would be allowed to lie fallow for a few years, and again sown with wheat for several years in a row. This "wheat mining", as it was called, was not in line with the best English and European practice but, where land was cheap and labour and capital expensive, it was by no means unreasonable, especially since wheat was a crop which in most years could be sold for cash. Other farmers, however, and particularly those on old cleared farms in the Niagara peninsula and along the north shore of Lake Ontario, practised something like a regular rotation of crops and ordinarily did not sow the same land with wheat for two years in succession. Some merely allowed the land to lie fallow each alternate year; others interspersed crops of spring or fall wheat with peas, oats, or barley, and allowed the land to recuperate as meadow or pasture for four or five years after two wheat crops had been taken from it.

Agricultural implements were few and simple until the late 1830's. The backwoods farmer, in addition to his usual assortment of axes, spades, hoes, and so on, had only one labour-saving implement of any importance. This was a heavy harrow, made of three large timbers fastened in the form of a triangle, fitted with iron teeth and drawn by oxen. On the older cleared farms this would be supplemented by a grain cradle, a wagon, and a plough. During the 1840's these implements were improved and new ones added. The old "Loyalist plough", constructed almost entirely of wood, was partially displaced by the American cast-iron plough and the Scotch swing or wheelless plough, but designs and preferences varied widely. Lighter types of harrow made their appearance in the late 1840's, together with cultivators, grain drills, and wooden rollers. The revolving hayrake, introduced from the United States about 1840, quickly became popular. Early Hussey and McCormick reapers, however, which made their appearance in Upper Canada in 1843 and 1847 respectively, were slow to win acceptance, the Hussey machine because it required a team of eleven men to operate it, the McCormick because of its originally flimsy construction. Threshing-machines had come into general use by 1843.

AGRICULTURAL CREDIT AND MARKETING

The adoption of improved agricultural implements and the diffusion of more systematic farming practices reflected the spread of a money economy, the growth of an export demand for wheat and flour, and the improvement of transport facilities. The construction of canals, the expansion of lake shipping, the extension of roads into the interior, and the appearance of banks widened the area of commercialized agriculture and trading and broke down the self-sufficiency of the frontier farm. One important figure in the spread of the commercial economy was the country merchant, the man who set up a general store, supplied the settlers with the few necessities which they could not provide themselves, such as tea, spices, ironware, and the finer textiles, and received in return such agricultural products as were available. These merchants, although they themselves operated with very slender resources, ordinarily gave their customers generous credit and encouraged them to take goods in trade rather than demand cash. In the more remote localities, indeed, and in times of depression, cash sales and purchases were rare. Potash and wheat were the only crops which, in most years at least, the settler could count on being able to sell for cash.

Performing functions similar to those of the country merchants but on a larger scale were two other types of business men: millers and grain dealers. These were to be found principally in the larger settlements, in the lake ports, and, in the case of millers, near reliable sources of waterpower. Millers sometimes worked on a "custom" basis: that is, they ground wheat for the settlers and retained a share of the flour as a fee for their services. Very often, however, the miller would also act as a grain dealer, buying wheat from the settlers, milling it, and shipping it on his own account to Montreal. Flour, being more valuable and less bulky than wheat, was cheaper to ship, so that there was a strong incentive for anyone interested in the grain business in Upper Canada either to build a mill himself or enter into partnership with a miller. Integration of milling with storekeeping in a single enterprise was very common and had several advantages, since it assured a quicker turnover of merchandise and a steady flow of customers to the store. Grain dealers acted as agents of Upper Canada millers or of Montreal commercial houses and ordinarily paid cash for the wheat they purchased. Both millers and dealers usually offered better rates of exchange than did the country storekeepers, partly because they carried on a more extensive business, partly because, being near to water transportation, their costs were lower. Wherever transport facilities made it possible, therefore, settlers preferred to take their wheat to a miller or a dealer at one of the many small harbours along the north shore of Lake Ontario and Lake Erie, or in the Niagara peninsula. If we could chart on a map of Upper Canada the prices offered for wheat at any point of time, the prices would be highest at lake ports and near navigable rivers, and would become progressively lower at places farther away from water transportation, finally reaching zero in the back areas where, because of high transport costs, wheat had literally no commercial value. The geographical extension of commercial agriculture was dependent upon the extension of transport facilities, the arteries of the St. Lawrence commercial system.

Large-scale milling enterprises developed in Upper Canada, particularly at Gananoque and in the Niagara peninsula, in the 1830's and 1840's under the encouragement of favourable tariff legislation. Credit for their operations, as for those of the grain dealers, was provided either by the banks of Upper and Lower Canada or by exporting firms in Montreal. These Montreal firms, in turn, were financed by British grain importers. From the markets of Liverpool and London to the millers and merchants of Upper Canada there stretched a chain of debts and credits, paralleling in the sphere of finance the physical transport system of the St. Lawrence and the North Atlantic. The strength of this chain depended basically upon the price of wheat in the British markets and upon the British tariffs which governed access to those markets.

BRITISH AND CANADIAN AGRICULTURAL TARIFFS

The commercial interests of the Canadas during the period from 1815 until the repeal of the Corn Laws in 1846 pursued two main objectives: to secure entry into Britain for Canadian grain, preferably free of duty but failing that at a lower rate than was applied to other overseas sources of supply; and to establish the Great Lakes-St. Lawrence route as the principal corridor for the export of grain from the American midwest. The attempt to achieve both these objectives led them into policies which were not entirely consistent with each other and which came to conflict sharply with the interests of other groups in the provinces, particularly the agricultural interests of Upper Canada, who demanded protection from American agricultural imports. Both objectives, of course, conflicted with the British agricultural interests, who relied upon the Corn Laws to limit the importation of overseas grain; on the other hand they were at least in some respects in harmony with the growing acceptance of free-trade doctrines in Britain, particularly among manufacturers and industrial workers, who sought cheap food imports as a means of lowering costs of production and increasing real wages.

The British Corn Law of 1815 allowed Canadian wheat to enter Britain when the British price rose above 67s. a quarter (one shilling at this time was worth about 25 cents; a quarter of wheat is eight bushels); foreign wheat was excluded until the British price rose to 80s. This arrangement appeared to afford a substantial preference to Canadian exporters and in fact, in 1815 and 1816, when the British price rose above 67s., large quantities of Canadian grain were shipped to England. In the following years, however, good harvests in Britain brought lower prices, and imports of Canadian grain ceased, so that the preference was rendered of no value. The disappearance of the export market for grain considerably aggravated the depression of 1819-21 in Upper Canada, and in 1822 the law was modified. The price which would exclude Canadian grain was lowered to 59s.; when prices rose above this level, colonial wheat was to be admitted, not free as before, but on payment of a duty.

The level of the "import point" was, however, only one source of objections. From the point of view of Canadian exporters an equally serious defect in the arrangement was its unpredictability. Forecasts of future price movements and harvest conditions in Britain were highly unreliable and slow to reach Montreal, while prices could change drastically during the transatlantic voyage. The Canadian exporter, in consequence, had no means of knowing, when he shipped grain from Montreal, whether or not it would be admitted to Britain for sale. This caused very serious commercial difficulties since, if the cargo exported had to be kept in bond in a British port until prices rose, the exporter was in grave danger of bankruptcy, unless he could get his credit extended.

Various changes in the law were made during the 1820's in an attempt to remedy these difficulties. In 1825 a temporary regulation permitted Canadian wheat to enter Britain at all times on payment of a duty of 5s. a quarter, no matter what the British price might be, and in 1827 a similar regulation provided that this duty should be cut to 6d. a quarter when the British price exceeded 67s. Canadian flour was granted similar treatment. In 1828 the regulation of the previous year was made permanent. From 1825 on, therefore, Canadian exporters were at least assured that they would be able to sell their shipments at some price. Although they were still denied the free entry which they sought, they enjoyed a considerable preference over foreign sources of supply, for foreign wheat had to pay much higher rates of duty, rising to 20s. 8d. when the British price fell to 67s.

One of the reasons why the British government was reluctant to grant free entry was the fear that the British market might be flooded by American flour which, shipped to Canada, milled there, and exported by way of the St. Lawrence, would seek entrance to Britain as Canadian produce. And to bring this about was, of course, one of the principal objectives of the Canadian commercial interests. Millers and forwarders of Upper Canada no less than the Montreal merchants regarded it as a matter of prime importance that as large a volume as possible of the wheat and flour of the American midwestern states should reach the Atlantic by the St. Lawrence route. With this end in view the Upper Canada legislature in 1818 passed an act which removed almost all prohibitions on trade with the United States and in the following years proceeded, independently of Lower Canada, to impose a schedule of tariffs which, while it levied duties on a wide range of American manufactures, admitted American wheat, flour, and timber free of duty when destined for export.

Agricultural depression in the Canadas and the closing of the British ports brought attempts to modify this policy. In 1822 the Canada Trade Act, passed by the imperial Parliament in an attempt to establish a uniform and comprehensive system of tariffs for both provinces, levied duties on American agricultural products entering both Canadas. The duties were relatively heavy, amounting to 1s. a bushel on wheat and 5s. a barrel on flour. In 1831, however, when the Colonial Trade Act was passed by the British Parliament, all duties on agricultural products entering the British North American colonies were repealed. The passing of this Act represented an important victory for the commercial interests.

Tariff legislation in this period, in short, generally favoured the attainment of the second objective sought by the Canadian commercial interests: the free admission of American wheat and flour for export by the St. Lawrence. At the same time the virtual impossibility of enforcing the Navigation Acts on the Great Lakes, formally recognized in 1830, encouraged the expansion of lake shipping and the consignment of American produce in American ships to Canadian ports. Up to 1831 the pursuance of this policy aroused little resentment among Canadian farmers, principally because the resumption of grain exports after 1822 and the expansion of immigration brought considerable agricultural prosperity. Both Upper and Lower Canada in these years exported wheat and flour, but whereas in the case of Upper Canada the exports represented a net surplus, Lower Canada was dependent upon imports from Upper Canada and from the United States to meet local requirements. After 1831, however, the situation changed abruptly for the worse in both provinces, when partial crop failures in the Canadas, combined with excellent harvests and low prices in Britain, sharply reduced exports. Amid widespread agrarian and commercial distress, acute conflict developed between the agricultural interests of the Canadas, anxious to limit the importation of American grain, and the merchants of Montreal and Upper Canada, who sought to continue the policy of free importation. The onset of an acute commercial crisis in 1837, followed by a period of commercial depression in Europe and North America, brought the conflict to a head and accentuated political discontent.

THE TARIFF AND AGRARIAN DISCONTENT

The British Corn Law of 1828 did assure Canadian exporters of admission to the British market and granted them a substantial preference over foreign sources of supply. But it by no means guaranteed remunerative prices, and when grain prices in England were low, as in years of good harvests, high transport costs on the St. Lawrence route and on the Atlantic, together with the 5s. import duty in Britain, closed the export market to

Canadian producers as decisively as any legislative prohibition. A series of excellent British harvests between 1831 and 1835 lowered prices in Britain to an average well below 67s. a quarter and reduced Canadian exports to a sporadic trickle. In 1834-5 wheat prices in the Toronto area had fallen to 32 to 38 cents a bushel. Even for settlers with easy access to lake transportation, such prices did not cover costs, while for those in the back areas they meant, if not starvation, at least acute hardship. The prosperity of the commercial sector of the economy depended, in effect, upon the price of wheat, and when the British market failed there were few alternatives. The maritime provinces and the British West Indies were, it is true, open to Canadian grain, but they could absorb only limited quantities and were more cheaply supplied from the American Atlantic ports than from Montreal.

Difficulties with the British market encouraged Canadian producers to test the possibilities of exportation to the United States, where, partly in consequence of the larger internal market, better transport facilities, and the growth of industry in the eastern states, grain prices during the 1830's were generally higher than in Upper Canada. Normally a duty of 25 cents a bushel, imposed in 1824, excluded Canadian grain, but between 1835 and 1838, when the wheat crop failed in parts of the United States, prices rose high enough to compensate for this duty and wheat was imported from time to time from Upper Canada, 236,000 bushels being imported in 1835 alone. Crop conditions were not good in Upper Canada, but what surplus there was found its way to New York, Michigan, and Illinois, rather than to Montreal. These were, however, exceptional conditions and did little to relieve the difficulties of Upper Canada farmers. Lower Canada also in this period suffered severely from crop failures, largely because of the ravages of wheat rust and the wheat midge. The amount of wheat grown in this province was, even in good years, not much greater than that required for local consumption, large exports from the Richelieu region being almost exactly offset by imports from Upper Canada, New York, and Ohio. Crop failures in the 1830's, particularly in 1835, caused great distress and necessitated the importation of flour from New York and even from Europe to meet local requirements. By the early 1840's Lower Canada farmers had largely abandoned wheat-growing and were forced to turn instead to coarse grains, such as oats and barley. For these crops, unfortunately, there was no export demand.

Agrarian depression in Upper Canada precipitated attacks upon imperial trade policy. The operation of the Colonial Trade Act of 1831 which, it will be recalled, repealed all duties on the importation of American agricultural produce, was blamed for the disastrously low prices which Upper Canada farmers faced when the British market failed them. If they were to be excluded by protective tariffs from the American and British markets, why should American farmers be permitted free entrance to the markets of the Canadas? Faced in their home markets with American competition in the only things they produced which had cash value, the agricultural interests raised the cry for tariff protection and provincial control over trade policy. Agitation for an agricultural tariff reached a peak in 1835 when a bill "to afford a proper protection and encouragement to those engaged in agricultural pursuits and other operations" was introduced into the Upper Canada legislature. Passed by the Assembly but rejected by the Legislative Council, the measure would have levied high rates of duty on a wide range of American agricultural products.

Partly because the demand for agricultural protection was at an early stage taken up by the Reform party which, whatever its influence in the Assembly, could do little against the veto power of the Lieutenant-Governor and the Tory-dominated Legislative Council, no tariff on imports of American agricultural products was authorized by the government of Upper Canada up to the union of the provinces in 1840. Political unrest was, however, considerably aggravated by the failure to provide agricultural protection, and the cleavage of interests between the farming population and the merchants, accentuated to be sure by serious crop failures in both provinces and by the severe credit stringency which accompanied the onset of depression throughout Europe and North America, is believed to have been one of the principal economic causes of the rebellions of 1837. Fundamentally, the agrarian and the commercial interests found themselves in opposition to one another because they had different conceptions of the function which the Canadas were to play in the world economy. As far as the merchants were concerned, the prime objective was to reassert the dominance of the St. Lawrence as the principal trade route by which the grain-producing areas of the hinterland, whether Canadian or American, would export their produce and import their manufactures. The canalization of the St. Lawrence, the free importation of American produce, and the fight for preferential entry to the British market were the cornerstones of their ambition. The future growth and prosperity of the Canadian economy, in their eyes, revolved around the success of the St. Lawrence trade route. The farmers, on the other hand, were interested primarily in the prices which they received for the goods they produced. They did not share the merchants' enthusiasm for the establishment of the St. Lawrence as a truly international trade route since, as they saw it, the importation of American produce necessarily reduced the share of the market open to Canadian producers. The prosperity and growth of the Canadas, they believed, depended not upon the profits of the carrying-trade, but upon guaranteeing Canadian farmers freedom from American competition in the markets which were available.

Economic issues were inevitably confused by political struggles. Not content with denouncing the lack of agricultural protection, the farmers also condemned other parts of the merchants' programme, such as the construction of canals, while those who accepted the leadership of the more radical reformers found the source of their troubles, not in particular legislative acts, but in the functioning of the colonial system as a whole. In many respects, indeed, the interests of the merchants and those of the farmers did not conflict, but coincided. Both groups had much to gain from the construction of the St. Lawrence and Welland Canals. Both believed that a partial solution to their problems was to be found in free access to the British market. But the times were not conducive to clear thinking on economic matters. It is doubtful, indeed, whether free importation of American produce was as damaging to the interests of Canadian farmers as was believed. To be sure, in some years, as in 1839, a general crop failure in Upper Canada resulted in heavy imports of American wheat and flour. And it seems very probable that the importation of American livestock did to some extent discourage Canadian farmers from turning to dairying and stock-breeding when the wheat market failed them. But in most years between 1835 and 1840 Upper Canada was exporting grain to the United States, rather than importing it, and one cannot confidently assert that it would have proved an over-all benefit to Upper Canada to have shut out American wheat and flour in years of general crop failure in the province. There was little in the merchants' programme, regarded as a complete whole, which was in conflict with agrarian interests; trouble arose because one section of this programme—the free importation of American foodstuffs—became effective before the other two objectives —the canalization of the St. Lawrence and free entry to the British market —were realized. If the prices of agricultural products were lower in the Canadas than they were in the United States, the explanation was to be found less in the free admission of American produce than in the high transport costs which excluded Canadian exporters from the markets of Liverpool and London. Persistent crop failures, acute credit stringency, and the ravages of wheat rust and the wheat midge were probably more to be blamed for the difficulties of Canadian farmers in the late 1830's than was the lack of tariff protection.

THE TARIFF AS A SOURCE OF REVENUE

Tariff policy in the Canadas was, of course, only partially a matter of protection. It was also a matter of government revenues. Direct taxation was of very minor importance in both provinces. Upper Canada levied small land and general property taxes, but in Lower Canada direct taxes were practically non-existent, if we ignore ecclesiastical tithes. Both legislatures therefore depended for the bulk of their disposable revenue upon receipts from customs duties. Since smuggling in Upper Canada was so easy and common, this meant in effect that both Upper and Lower Canada had to draw by far the larger part of their government revenues from duties collected at Quebec, the only port of entry where trade was sufficiently regular and concentrated to be taxed.

The proportion in which this revenue should be divided between the two provinces was a constant source of disagreement. Free trade between the provinces had been established by the Constitutional Act, so that it was not open to Upper Canada to tax goods passing the interprovincial boundary. An agreement was therefore arrived at in 1795 whereby one-eighth of all customs revenues collected at Quebec was to be paid to Upper Canada. This arrangement broke down in 1797, and from that year until 1816 Upper Canada maintained a customs inspector at Coteau du Lac on the St. Lawrence to keep track of the goods entering the province by that route. Customs revenues were divided between the provinces according to the proportion of total imports at Quebec which was recorded as entering Upper Canada. In 1817 Lower Canada made a lump sum grant to Upper Canada and in 1818 agreed to transfer one-fifth of the customs revenues. In 1819, however, the arrangement broke down completely, as the legislature of Lower Canada failed to pass the usual bill appointing commissioners to negotiate with Upper Canada. For three years thereafter, until the passing of the Canada Trade Act in 1822, the upper province received no share of the Quebec customs revenues whatsoever. The Canada Trade Act set Upper Canada's share at one-fifth and laid it down that, after 1824, the proportion was to be adjusted every three years in accordance with the percentage of imports consumed in each province. Although these percentages could be calculated only very approximately, the arrangement lasted until 1840.

The inconvenience and friction caused by the necessity for dividing the customs revenue was considerable, but the repercussions upon Upper Canada went far beyond mere administrative difficulties. Since the customs duties were levied in Lower Canada, the legislature of that province had, in effect, sole jurisdiction over the rates of duty to be imposed, at least as far as imports by the St. Lawrence route were concerned. Upper Canada could indeed pass legislation taxing imports from the United States, but when every creek entering Lake Ontario or Lake Erie invited the attention of smugglers, the possibilities of enforcing such legislation were very limited. The revenue which the government of Upper Canada could command, therefore, depended almost entirely upon the tariffs which Lower Canada saw fit to impose. If both provinces had had the same need for revenue, this might not have proved a serious drawback. But as a matter of fact Upper Canada, with a rapidly expanding population and growing agricultural surpluses, stood in much greater need of government expenditures, particularly for the construction of canals, roads, and bridges, than did Lower Canada with its slower rate of population growth and very different attitude toward commercialism. And this difficulty was quite apart from the cyclical fluctuations in revenues which dependence on customs duties necessarily implied: the provincial governments, perpetually in need of money, found it far from easy to cut back their expenditures when, in a depression, revenues from the customs declined.

The schedule of import duties levied at Quebec in this period was very complicated and there is no need for us to examine it in detail. The backbone of the schedule was a general *ad valorem* tariff of 2½ per cent. This tariff was first imposed by the colonial legislatures in 1813 and remained in force until 1839; it provided both provinces with most of their government revenue throughout this period. In practice it was levied principally on imports of manufactured goods from Britain. Besides this general tariff there were specific revenue duties on such things as wines, spirits, and tobacco, and also a free list which included salt meat, fish, wheat, peas, furs, and skins. From 1819 on, specific duties were levied on certain imports from the United States. Most imports from that country, however, were either admitted free or were excluded entirely by statute.

The Canada Trade Act, passed by the British Parliament in 1822, made few important changes in the rates, but levied duties on certain commodities which had previously entered Lower Canada free, such as wheat, flour, and lumber. Of wider scope was a statute passed by the imperial Parliament in 1825. This act, in the first place, considerably enlarged the list of goods which could legally be imported into the Canadas from countries other than Great Britain; but, secondly, it imposed new *ad valorem* rates on a long list of commodities and raised the general rate (which applied to all dutiable imports for which no specific rate was laid down) to 15 per cent, as compared to the former 2½ per cent.

This large increase in the general rate aroused protests from Canadian merchants, as it applied not only to goods imported for local consumption but also to goods imported for processing and re-export. Various concessions were therefore granted in the following years, culminating in the repeal of all duties on agricultural imports from the United States in the Colonial Trade Act of 1831. Two years later the free list was extended by imperial legislation to include wood and lumber, salt, drugs, cotton, fruits, and various other commodities. Finally, in 1839, the legislature of Lower Canada increased the level of the general duties by making the 2½ per cent colonial tariff which had been in force since 1813 additional to, instead of part of, the 15 per cent imperial tariff imposed in 1825.

TARIFF POLICY AFTER 1840; THE REPEAL OF THE CORN LAWS

The union of the provinces in 1840 removed the source of the long-continued conflict over the division of the customs revenues, permitted the floating of new provincial loans in Britain for the completion of the canal system, and made necessary the consolidation of the provincial tariff schedules. The general provincial tariff was raised to 5 per cent in an attempt to secure additional revenue, and various minor changes were made in the specific duties.

The demand for protective, as distinct from revenue, tariffs, however, continued strong among the agricultural interests. In 1842 the farmers of Canada West (the former Upper Canada) petitioned the British government for free admission of Canadian wheat to England, together with the imposition of a duty on American grain entering Canada. The merchants of Montreal and their allies, the millers and shippers of Canada West, had, of course, no objection to the first part of this petition, but strenuously opposed the second. Agricultural interests in Britain, on the other hand, offered strong opposition to the first part of the proposal. The consequence was that the petition was rejected and a bill which had been drawn up to admit Canadian wheat at a nominal duty and tax American produce entering Canada was dropped. In its place there was passed a compromise measure which imposed a sliding scale of duties on colonial wheat, ranging from 1s. a quarter when the British price was 58s. or over to 5s. when it was less than 55s. This represented a considerable improvement in the position of Canadian farmers and exporters, but was much less than had been hoped for.

The failure of this petition so aggravated tension between the conflicting interests in Canada that the first opportunity was seized to attempt a reconciliation. This opportunity was provided by a dispatch received from the Colonial Secretary which seemed to imply that, if Canada imposed a tariff on American wheat, Britain would remove or reduce the duties on Canadian wheat and flour entering Britain. In consequence the Canadian legislature late in 1842 passed its first truly protectionist agricultural tariff, imposing a duty of 3s. a quarter on American wheat; in the following year similar duties were levied on other American produce. These statutes represented a signal victory for the protectionist group and a set-back for the commercial interests. The blow to the merchants and shippers was offset, however, by the passing of the Canada Corn Act by the imperial Parliament in 1843. This statute levied a nominal duty of 1s. a quarter on imports of Canadian wheat, no matter what the British price might be. This was a very substantial concession indeed; its effects were obvious in an increase in the quantities of American wheat imported into Canada for milling and re-export and in the expansion of milling and forwarding facilities in Upper Canada.

The imposition of a protective tariff on American agricultural products and the passing of the Canada Corn Act in the year following accomplished the seemingly impossible task of giving both the agricultural and the commercial interests what they wanted. The provincial duty was not and was not intended to be so high as to prevent American wheat from being imported into Canada, milled there, and shipped to Britain as colonial flour. The Canada Corn Act gave Canadian farmers an assured market for their grain and at the same time made it profitable for American exporters to use the St. Lawrence route, in spite of the tariff and higher freight costs. For a time, then, it looked as if a viable compromise had been reached between the demands of the conflicting groups.

The solution, however, was not one which could endure. The tariff concessions granted to Canadian wheat-growers and exporters by the British government were politically possible only because of the growing strength of the free-trade movement in Britain. But free-trade doctrine did not envisage the retention of preferential duties on colonial exports as a permanent feature of British trade policy. Such preferences were merely a temporary compromise and were, in fact, inconsistent with the final objective, which was the free admission to British markets of the products of *all* nations, with no particular favour granted to colonies as against other sources of supply. Canadian farmers and merchants, on the other hand, although they had long sought free entry to the British market, had no desire to see the same treatment extended to foreign countries. The passing of the Canada Corn Act was for them the culmination of their efforts, whereas to the free-traders of Britain it was merely a minor victory in a continuing struggle.

That the preference granted by the Canada Corn Act might be short-lived was a possibility which few Canadian farmers and merchants seriously considered. The great expansion in wheat acreage and of the milling industry in Canada West bore witness to their confidence that the concession would prove to be permanent. This confidence was rudely shattered in 1846 when it was learned that the British government had repealed the Corn Laws and that within three years all protective duties on imports of overseas grain into Britain would be abolished. This, of course, meant that after that date Canadian grain would enjoy no preference over other sources of supply.

Meanwhile the United States had been taking steps to regain the export traffic which had been lost to the St. Lawrence route by the passing of the Canada Corn Act. In 1845 and in 1846 the American Congress passed drawback acts which permitted Canadian grain to be exported in bond to New York by way of the Erie Canal without paying the American import duty, thus enabling Canadian exporters to take advantage of the lower ocean-shipping rates from New York to England. The loss of the British preference would in any event have greatly reduced the advantages of the St. Lawrence route. The American bonding legislation nullified them completely. In an attempt to prevent the loss of the through trade the Canadian legislature in 1846 repealed the 3s. duty on imports of American grain, except that which was intended for consumption in Canada, but this proved of little effect. Not only was the through trade of the American midwestern states lost to the St. Lawrence; the export trade of Canada West also began to move to the Atlantic over American transport routes. In 1850 the volume of Upper Canada wheat exported through the United States was more than fifteen times greater than that exported by way of the St. Lawrence.

The groups in Canada most seriously injured by the repeal of the Corn Laws were not the farmers, but the merchants of Montreal. The American bonding legislation, excellent harvests in 1847, 1848, and 1849, and the beginning of an export trade in grain to the United States, not for re-export to Britain but for American consumption, brought continuing prosperity to the farmers of Canada West, while the farmers of Canada East, driven out of wheat production by the ravages of wheat rust and the wheat midge, reaped substantial benefits from the appearance of an American demand for oats, barley, poultry, eggs, and butter in the summer of 1849. For the Montreal merchants and the St. Lawrence shipping interests, on the other hand, the loss of the British preference was a major disaster. Their fortunes were committed to the St. Lawrence route, and their commercial organization had been built around it. The repeal of the Corn Laws and the passing of bonding legislation in the United States, threatening as it did the loss of their commercial hinterland not only in the American midwest but also in Canada West, seemed to destroy the economic rationale of the whole St. Lawrence commercial system, to undercut the basis of the costly canal-building programme which was at last nearing completion, and to remove the last economic benefits which might be derived from membership in the British imperial system.

Meanwhile the forces leading to a closer integration of the Canadian economy with that of the United States were growing in strength. From the days of the fur trade the Canadian economy had developed around an east-west axis, with the St. Lawrence as the major artery of commerce and Montreal as the major entrepôt and point of trans-shipment. Now this orientation was changing, as Canadian products moved in increasing volume, not eastward down the St. Lawrence, but south to the markets and trade routes of the United States, and as American railroads, backed by the capital of New York, Boston, and Philadelphia, crept out to tap the whole frontier of Canada West and the townships along the St. Lawrence. The strains of this reorientation were felt most severely in Montreal, the hinge-point of the St. Lawrence economy. Its political implications were evident in the Annexation Manifesto of 1849. Industrialism in Britain had brought the repeal of the Corn Laws and the breakdown of the system of colonial preferences upon which the economy of the St. Lawrence had been based; but industrialism in the United States, though still in its infancy, was already opening new markets for Canadian staples.

SUGGESTIONS FOR FURTHER READING

BASIC WORKS:

Creighton, Donald G., *The Commercial Empire of the St. Lawrence, 1760-1850* (Toronto, 1937), Chapters VIII-XIII

Jones, Robert L., *History of Agriculture in Ontario, 1613-1880* (Toronto, 1948), Chapters III-VI, VIII-X

McDiarmid, Orville J., *Commercial Policy in the Canadian Economy* (Cambridge, Mass., 1946), Chapters III-IV

MacDonald, Norman, *Canada, 1763-1841: Immigration and Settlement* (London, New York, and Toronto, 1939)

SUPPLEMENTARY WORKS:

Cowan, Helen I., *British Emigration to British North America, 1783-1837* (University of Toronto Studies, History and Economics, Vol. IV, No. 2, 1928)

Patterson, Gilbert, *Land Settlement in Upper Canada, 1783-1840* (16th Report of the Department of Archives for the Province of Ontario, 1920. Toronto, 1921)

Tucker, Gilbert N., *The Canadian Commercial Revolution, 1845-1851* (New Haven, 1936)

CHAPTER XIV

THE COMING OF THE RAILWAY

CANADIAN ECONOMIC POLICY AFTER 1850

By the middle of the nineteenth century the Canadian colonies on the St. Lawrence, united politically in 1840, had laid the foundations of a unified commercial economy, based upon the exploitation of timber resources, the production of wheat, the construction of a uniform system of inland waterways, and the development of an elaborate network of commercial credit centring on Montreal, the point where the commerce of the interior and the commerce of the North Atlantic met. The repeal of the Corn Laws, symbolizing dramatically the end of an era in which the political bonds of empire had been maintained and reinforced by ties of mutual economic dependence, dealt this painfully evolved commercial economy a serious blow. The loss of the British preferences on wheat in 1846, the reduction in the preferences on timber in 1845 and 1846, and the onset of severe depression throughout Europe and North America in 1847 were followed by political disturbance and commercial distress in Canada, which found their outlet in renewed agitation for political amalgamation with the United States, particularly among those commercial groups who had previously been most dependent upon the trade with Britain. "I would willingly remain a subject of Her Majesty," wrote Jacob Keefer, an Upper Canada business man, in 1849, "if I could afford it; but having built my hopes upon the continued prosperity of Canada and that foundation having failed, the reflection that I am a British subject does not afford substantial relief."

The movement for annexation to the United States, however, failed to gain momentum, and the political and economic leaders of Canada turned to the task of adjusting the Canadian economy to the new challenges and dangers which faced it. This process of adjustment involved two principal lines of policy: first, the attempt to develop further the export trade in foodstuffs and raw materials to the United States, culminating in the Reciprocity Treaty of 1854; and secondly, the attempt to regain for the St. Lawrence route and for Montreal some part of the through trade in grain exports from the American midwest to Europe. This latter aspiration involved the construction of trunk-line railways, culminating in the completion of the Grand Trunk Railway from Sarnia, Ontario, to Portland, Maine, in 1860. These two broad lines of policy were in an important sense complementary. The divisive effects of dependence upon American markets and transport routes, implied by the expansion of the export trade to the south, were to be offset by the strengthening of the east-west transportation axis, with railways supplementing the older system of natural and artificial waterways.

EARLY RAILWAY PROJECTS

The construction of railways in Canada lagged considerably behind parallel developments in the United States. In part this was due to the fact that domestic sources of capital were very much smaller than in the United States, but the advent of the railway was also delayed by the slow progress made in completing the Canadian canal system. The crisis of 1837 had, to all intents and purposes, marked the end of the canal-building era in the United States, with over 3,000 miles of canals completed. Canada's canal-building programme was barely begun in that year. During the 1840's, when the states of the American Atlantic seaboard were building their first railroad network, Canada was still absorbed in the completion of the St. Lawrence waterway. The government, with its borrowing powers stretched to the limit to finance the canals, had no funds to spare for experiments with railways, and it was in any case by no means obvious to most Canadians that railways would ever compete successfully with the magnificent system of inland waterways which they were then constructing.

Just as the completion of the Erie Canal in 1825 had hastened the construction of the St. Lawrence canal system, so the expansion of the American railroad net and its encroachments upon the commercial hinterland of Montreal provided the stimulus for Canadian railway construction. The St. Lawrence and Welland Canals had been built to draw the export and import trade of the midwest to Montreal. Not only had this objective not been achieved by 1850 but, what was even more ominous, the trade of Canada itself was being attracted to New York and Boston by the new American railroads rather than to Montreal by the St. Lawrence canals. No sooner, therefore, had the Canadian canal system been completed than it became apparent that even more strenuous efforts would be required, not only to challenge the spreading influence of the American Atlantic ports but even to retain the limited traffic which the Canadian route had thus far managed to secure.

Several railway companies were chartered in Canada in the 1830's and early 1840's, but the difficulty of raising capital during a period of depression and political unrest, combined with a concentration of interest in canals, prevented any important construction being undertaken. A few small railways were actually built, however, most of them being of the "portage" type; that is to say, they were built around rapids on the rivers and were intended to supplement water transportation. A line was constructed around the rapids on the Richelieu River in 1836 to facilitate trade and travel between Montreal and New York, and in 1847 a short line was built between Montreal and Lachine. In Upper Canada a railway was built around Niagara Falls in 1839, but the gradients proved to be too steep for the steam locomotives of the day and the carriages had to be drawn by horses.

These minor railways were of trivial importance but they were all that Canada could claim in the way of actual railway construction in the period before 1847. By 1850 over 9,000 miles of railroad track had been laid in the United States; in all the British North American colonies only 66 miles had been laid by that year.

The event which precipitated the beginning of major railway construction in Canada was the passing of bonding or "drawback" legislation by the American Congress in 1845 and 1846 (see Chapter XIII). By threatening to divert through American transport routes all the export trade of western Canada and the American midwestern states, this legislation compelled the commercial interests of Montreal to reconsider the adequacy of the canal programme to which they had pinned their hopes. Two serious defects were immediately apparent. In the first place, Montreal was not a winter port. For almost half the year it was closed to commercial shipping by ice and other dangers of winter navigation. In the second place, it was still seriously handicapped by the fact that ocean freight rates between Montreal and Liverpool were considerably higher than those between the American Atlantic ports and Liverpool. In 1850 the freight on a barrel of flour from New York to Liverpool was 1s. 3½d.; from Montreal it was 3s. 0½d. The cause of this differential was to be found primarily in the fact that New York, with excellent westward connections, was a major importing centre and could offer balanced cargoes for Atlantic shipping, whereas most of the vessels arriving at Montreal came in ballast. The restrictions imposed on foreign shipping, until 1849, by the Navigation Acts and the high insurance and pilotage charges in the Gulf of St. Lawrence were also serious handicaps for Montreal.

The completion of the St. Lawrence canals, while it promised to improve the position of Montreal in regard to internal transport costs, could do nothing to lessen the seriousness of these handicaps in respect to ocean shipping. The only course of action which promised an escape from the difficulty was for Montreal to secure access, by means of a railway, to an Atlantic port which would be open throughout the year and which would enjoy the same or greater advantages in ocean freights as New York. Such a railway, it was argued, would not compete with the St. Lawrence canals nor prejudice the heavy investments which had been made in them. On the contrary, it would add to their value. During the open season exports would be funnelled down through the canals to Montreal and there be trans-shipped into ocean-going vessels; during the winter they would be trans-shipped onto the railway, also at Montreal. The canals would continue to serve their intended function and Montreal would remain the major point of trans-shipment and the traffic gateway of the St. Lawrence economy.

THE ST. LAWRENCE AND ATLANTIC RAILWAY

Some such project as this had for long attracted the attention of politicians and promoters in the maritime colonies. As early as 1829 a proposal had been put forward for a railway from St. Andrews, New Brunswick, to Quebec, and in 1836 a company had been chartered to build it. Unfortunately, the route along which this railway was intended to run passed through certain territory which was claimed both by the state of Maine and by New Brunswick, and when, by the Webster-Ashburton Treaty of 1842, the larger part of this territory was ceded to Maine, the project lost popularity, as the only alternative routes from St. Andrews were considerably longer. Hopes for a railway connection with Quebec did not die, however, and in 1844 backers of the Halifax and Quebec Railway project proposed to build a line from Halifax to Truro, from there to Shediac, and thence to Rivière du Loup and Quebec. But in this project too the question of the route proved a serious stumbling-block, for the co-operation of the legislature of New Brunswick could be secured only on condition that the railway should pass through Saint John. An engineer appointed jointly by the three colonies concerned, a certain Major Robinson, carried out a survey to decide the matter, but in the end recommended neither of the two routes which had been proposed, but rather one which hugged the north coast of New Brunswick, keeping as far as possible from the American frontier. Even if this route had been acceptable to the three provinces, it did not recommend itself at that time to the British government, without whose financial aid the project could not be undertaken.

While the maritime colonies were meeting with these disappointments, Montreal was engaged in negotiations with two American cities, both of which sought the privilege of serving as the terminus of the proposed railway from Montreal to the Atlantic. The two candidates were Portland, in the state of Maine, and Boston. Portland, still a minor city, saw in the prospect of winning the Canadian trade a chance to establish itself as a major seaport, while Boston, long jealous of the Erie Canal, was determined that in this new age of the railway she would not fall behind New York in the struggle for the trade of the interior. Both cities had excellent harbours; Portland was slightly nearer to Liverpool and also to Montreal. The Montrealers were at first inclined to favour Boston but, largely as a result of the energetic salesmanship of John A. Poor, a young lawyer from Bangor, Maine, they finally selected Portland. In 1845 two companies were chartered to construct the railway: one, the Atlantic and St. Lawrence, to build from Portland to the Quebec-Vermont border, and the other, the St. Lawrence and Atlantic, to build the Canadian section.

While the initiative in the early stages of this project came largely from the American promoters, the board of directors of the St. Lawrence and Atlantic included men who were among the leading figures in the Montreal commercial community. Conspicuous in its management was Alexander T. Galt, at this time commissioner of the British-American Land Company which, since the railway would pass through its land in the Eastern Townships, had an obvious interest in its success. Despite this influential backing, however, serious financial problems were encountered from the start. After an appeal to the provincial government for aid had been refused, capital was solicited from the Canadian public, but only £100,000 could be raised in this way. Galt then went to England in an attempt to sell the Company's shares and at first had some success. In 1846, however, the British railway boom ended, bringing with it the collapse of the stock market. The subscriptions which had been promised to the St. Lawrence and Atlantic were wiped out and further efforts to raise capital in England rendered hopeless for the time being. An attempt to market an issue of bonds in the following year also failed. On the strength of the Canadian subscriptions—some of which were paid in the form of pork and eggs for the sustenance of construction gangs—surveys were carried out and some track laid, but progress was painfully slow. In 1849, with only some forty miles of line actually completed, the St. Lawrence and Atlantic again appealed to the legislature for assistance.

THE NORTHERN AND GREAT WESTERN RAILWAYS

Meanwhile in Canada West a number of ambitious railway schemes had been put forward, the two most important of which were the Northern Railway and the Great Western Railway. The Northern developed out of two charters which had been granted by the legislature of Upper Canada before 1837: the Toronto and Lake Simcoe, and the Toronto and Lake Huron. As the titles suggest, both these roads had been planned to strike north from Toronto, roughly along the line of Simcoe's Yonge Street and the old fur-trading portage route. The Northern Railway, following the same general route, had two principal objectives: first, to open up the fertile territory north of Toronto, the development of which had been considerably retarded up to this point by poor transport facilities; and secondly, to form part of a combined rail and water route by which wheat and flour exports from Chicago and the upper Lakes would be funnelled down through Toronto to Lake Ontario, avoiding the circuitous route through the Detroit River and Lake Erie. Despite an ingenious attempt to raise money by means of a lottery, financial difficulties prevented any start being made with construction before 1849.

The Great Western Railway grew out of a charter granted to the London and Gore Railway Company in 1834. Although its promoters, like those of the Northern Railway, hoped to develop substantial local traffic, the principal objective of the Great Western was to form a connecting link between the New York railroads which terminated at Buffalo and the Michigan Central Railroad which terminated at Detroit. Planned to run from the Niagara River to Hamilton and thence to Windsor, the Great Western was designed to provide the New York roads with a through route to the west considerably shorter than any which might be built south of Lake Erie. The Company received its new charter in 1845. Energetic attempts were made to raise capital in Canada, Britain, and the United States in 1847 and 1848, but these were years of severe depression and it proved impossible to raise sufficient funds. A start was made with construction in 1847 but progress was very slow.

GOVERNMENT ASSISTANCE: THE GUARANTEE ACT

By 1849 all three of the major railways then under construction in Canada were in serious difficulties, primarily because they had found it impossible to raise capital in England during a period of commercial depression. The completion of the St. Lawrence canals opened up the possibility of government assistance, and strong pressure was applied in the legislature for some form of subsidy, loan, or guarantee to the railways. In consequence, in April, 1849, Francis Hincks, then inspector-general in the second Baldwin-Lafontaine ministry, proposed to the legislature a scheme for government assistance to railways which had initially been suggested to him by the directors of the St. Lawrence and Atlantic. The proposal was that the government, under certain conditions, should guarantee the interest, at a rate not over 6 per cent, on half the bonds of any railway over seventy-five miles in length, provided that half the railway had already been built. Hincks' resolution was seconded by Sir Allan MacNab, leader of the opposition and president of the Great Western, and the legislature passed it unanimously.

The Guarantee Act, as it was called, did not solve all the problems of the railways, as they still had to build half their line before they became eligible. But the assurance of the guarantee of interest on half their bonded debt, combined with an improvement in general business conditions, made it considerably easier for them to secure capital, and construction was pushed ahead steadily during the next four years. On the St. Lawrence and

Atlantic, Galt took over the presidency and reorganized the management. The line reached Richmond in 1851, Sherbrooke in the following year, and the Vermont border in 1853. Meanwhile the American company, the Atlantic and St. Lawrence, had also been meeting difficulty in raising money, particularly since the state of Maine was prohibited by its constitution from giving aid to railroads or other private businesses, and in 1851 had been obliged to admit its inability to complete the line from Portland to the Canadian border. The St. Lawrence and Atlantic thereupon agreed to build sixteen additional miles of track from the border to Island Pond, Vermont, and floated a special issue of bonds in London to finance the extension. The whole line from the south shore of the St. Lawrence opposite Montreal to Portland was opened for traffic late in 1853.

Meanwhile the Northern and the Great Western Railways, also eligible for assistance under the Guarantee Act, had both been making progress. On the Northern, after much argument over the northern terminus, construction got under way in 1851 and was completed to Collingwood on Georgian Bay by the end of 1854. In later years this line contributed largely to the expansion of Toronto as a distributing point. The Great Western, for its part, once the government guarantee was assured, managed to secure the participation of a group of New York and Boston capitalists, led by Erastus Corning, John Murray Forbes, and John W. Brooks, who had taken over the bankrupt Michigan Central and who were shortly to finance the formation of the New York Central. With this influx of American capital the line was completed from the Niagara River to Windsor in 1855, construction being carried out by a contracting firm headed by Samuel Zimmerman, an American immigrant who won the unenviable title of political boss of Canada West. For the first few years after its completion the Great Western proved highly profitable, partly because of the large volume of local traffic it attracted, partly because for a time it formed part of the only through route from Chicago to Boston and New York.

IMPACT ON CANADA OF RAILWAY CONSTRUCTION IN THE UNITED STATES

By the early 1850's, with the Great Western and the St. Lawrence and Atlantic making steady progress, it looked as if the St. Lawrence economy would shortly be provided with two major railways, each of which formed, as it were, extensions of the canal system which had been completed in 1849. The St. Lawrence and Atlantic provided an extension eastward, from Montreal to Portland, while the Great Western, from Hamilton to Windsor, formed an extension to the west. Between these two railways, from the western end of Lake Ontario to Montreal, no railway was yet under construction.

The expansion of the American railroad system was, however, already making it clear that Montreal could not continue to rely upon the canals to fill this gap in the through route from the west. Each of the major ports of the American Atlantic seaboard by this time had either completed, or was well on the way to completing, a line of railways across the Appalachians; each was striving, by means of the new technology of the railway, to win a share of the western trade. By 1850 New York was linked to Buffalo by a chain of sixteen railways, amalgamated by 1853 to form the New York Central. In 1851 the New York and Erie was completed, providing New York with a second route to the west. By 1852 the Pennsylvania Railroad, planned to connect Philadelphia with Cleveland, had reached Pittsburgh; and in 1853 the Baltimore and Ohio reached Wheeling.

The threat which the merchants and capitalists of Montreal felt most keenly, however, came not from these lines but from the Ogdensburg Railroad, which was completed in 1850. This line ran from Ogdensburg on the south shore of the St. Lawrence to Lake Champlain, where it linked up with roads leading to Boston. As we have already seen, Boston had failed in its bid for selection as the Atlantic terminus of the St. Lawrence and Atlantic; it had, in fact, been prevented even from tapping the Montreal-Portland traffic by a statute passed by the Maine legislature which prohibited the building of branch lines to the south, and by the fact that the St. Lawrence and Atlantic had been constructed with a gauge of 5′ 6″, whereas the standard gauge of the Boston roads was 4′ 8½″. The Ogdensburg Railroad, however, promised to benefit Boston more than any connection with the St. Lawrence and Atlantic could have done, for the reason that it tapped the St. Lawrence trade before that trade reached Montreal, not after. It challenged Montreal's position, in fact, more directly than any of the other American railroads, because it cut into Montreal's hinterland, not at its extremities, but close to its heart, threatening to divert to Boston every ton of cargo which would otherwise pass down the St. Lawrence canals. The New York roads which terminated at Buffalo could divert only the Lake Erie trade; the Ogdensburg road threatened Montreal's hold on Lake Ontario and the Ottawa valley also.

While the completion of these Boston and New York railroads brought higher prices to farmers along the St. Lawrence and throughout Canada West and opened up new markets for coarse grains, livestock, and dairy products, it presented a serious challenge to the commerce of Montreal and indeed to the entire St. Lawrence transport system. Nor were the interests of Montreal likely to be furthered by the appearance of widespread local enthusiasm for railways running, not parallel with the St. Lawrence, but to make connection with American roads which terminated at the frontier.

Typical of such projects were the Bytown and Prescott, proposed in 1851 to connect the Ottawa valley with the Ogdensburg Railroad; the Brockville and Ottawa, proposed in 1852 to make contact with a branch of the New York Central; and the Buffalo and Lake Huron, which eventually linked Buffalo and the town of Goderich. Each of these "feeder" railroads represented an attempt to extend the tentacles of the American transport system into Montreal's commercial hinterland.

It was the threat presented by these American railroads and their proposed Canadian feeders which precipitated the construction of the first Canadian trunk railway. Both political and economic considerations were involved. Annexationist sentiment, though temporarily dormant in Canada, was still very much alive in the United States, and it required little imagination to discern the spectre of "manifest destiny" behind the commercial imperialism of the New York and New England railroads. Economically, it was becoming clear that the canals alone were inadequate to hold together the commercial system of the St. Lawrence in the face of the divisive pulls of American markets and transport routes. Montreal's continued existence as the major entrepôt of the Canadian economy depended upon the construction of a new transport system which, though inevitably paralleling and competing with the newly completed St. Lawrence canals, would weld together the scattered towns and settlements as the canals had failed to do.

But it was not only the urgent need to counter the encroachments of American railroads upon Montreal's Canadian hinterland which impelled the construction of a new transport system for the St. Lawrence economy. Indeed, if Canadian staple exports had been the only prize at stake, it is doubtful whether even the most sanguine would have found much prospect for commercial success in the building of a Canadian trunk-line railway. The real prize, the objective which, if once it were secured, would justify completely the large capital investments involved in the project, was, as it had always been, the trade of the American west. Cut off from their own west by the barrier of Precambrian granite north of Lakes Huron and Superior, Canadians looked south to the vast grain-producing areas of the United States and, by an easy stretch of the imagination, transferred to the age of the railway the dream which had inspired the builders of the St. Lawrence economy since its tenuous beginnings. It was the prospect of tapping the through trade from the American midwest to the Atlantic which alone made the project feasible.

THE EUROPEAN AND NORTH AMERICAN: AN ABORTIVE PROJECT

The most direct policy for the Canadian government to have followed, once the desirability of a trunk-line railway was recognized, would probably have been to charter, and subsidize if necessary, a corporation to build a railway from Montreal to Hamilton, linking up with the St. Lawrence and Atlantic on the east and the Great Western on the west. The principal argument against such a policy—that it depended upon an American port for its Atlantic terminus—did not at this time carry much weight in Montreal. Nova Scotia and New Brunswick, however, were not prepared to give up without a struggle all hopes of participating in the St. Lawrence trade.

The failure of the first two attempts to link the maritime colonies with Montreal and Quebec by railway has already been described. The St. Andrews and Quebec project was abandoned by all except the determined citizens of St. Andrews after the Ashburton Treaty of 1842. The Halifax and Quebec project became seemingly hopeless after the British government refused to grant financial assistance in 1849. Attention then shifted in the maritime colonies to the possibility of obtaining a railway connection with Montreal by constructing, not a direct line from Halifax to Quebec and thence to Montreal, but a line running from Halifax to Saint John and thence to Portland, so as to connect with the St. Lawrence and Atlantic. If Portland was nearer to Liverpool than New York, then Halifax, it was argued, was even nearer than Portland. A line running south to Portland would not only provide a route to Montreal but also, connecting with the New England railroads, would become the principal channel of communication between Europe and the United States. Appropriately christened the European and North American, this project won tremendous popularity throughout the maritime colonies and the New England states, with John A. Poor playing a leading role, as he had done for the St. Lawrence and Atlantic.

The European and North American Railroad was never actually constructed. Despite the high hopes which accompanied its original conception, the project turned out in the end to be a dismal failure. Nevertheless, the planning of the railway and the negotiations which were undertaken on its behalf had very important repercussions on the general strategy of railway building in Canada and on the policies adopted by the governments involved. The promotion and construction of the Grand Trunk Railway, which stemmed directly from the collapse of the European and North American project, cannot be understood without an analysis of the factors responsible for the failure of its ill-fated predecessor. For these reasons the European and North American Railroad deserves more attention than most historical failures require.

As originally planned, the European and North American was to be built jointly by Maine and the two maritime colonies. A single corporation was formed, chartered by each of the three legislatures, so that construction would be carried out under unified management. The total cost was estimated at $12 million. Half of this sum was to be raised by private subscriptions, and half on the guarantee of the governments concerned.

The state of Maine quickly passed the necessary legislation and undertook a survey of the route as far as the New Brunswick boundary. The New Brunswick legislature also passed the charter and authorized a stock subscription. In Nova Scotia, however, events took a dramatic turn which was to alter the character of the whole project. Joseph Howe, a leading figure in provincial politics, gave the scheme his strong support, but argued that the province itself should build that part of the railway which lay within its own borders, since otherwise, he feared, the whole railway would soon come under the control of American capitalists. Recognizing that, even if the railway were built as a public work, finance was certain to be a most serious problem, Howe proposed that the British government should be requested to guarantee the necessary provincial loan. "If it passes into the hands of American capitalists," he argued, "they will possess an interest and an influence in the very bosom of the Province, which sooner or later will cost the Mother Country much more than will be required to construct the Railway." With the guarantee of the British government, Nova Scotia would be sure of finding purchasers for its bonds and in addition would have to pay very much lower interest rates. An obvious precedent was to be found in the guarantee extended to the bonds of the province of Canada in 1841 to insure the completion of the St. Lawrence canal system.

When the Colonial Office at first declined to give this proposal serious consideration or even to make a cash contribution toward the cost of the railway, Howe sailed to England in November, 1850, determined to convince the British government of the merit of his scheme. Once in England he energetically publicized his proposals and finally succeeded in inducing the Colonial Office to reconsider its stand. Howe was informed that, although no assistance would be given to a project which was purely provincial in character, assistance might be given to a project which involved the interests of the Empire as a whole. Specifically, financial aid would be given to the railway project if New Brunswick and Canada would join with Nova Scotia in building the whole road from Halifax to Quebec. It was further stipulated, to safeguard the British tax-payer from loss, that the British North American colonies were to bear the entire cost of the railway and were to impose taxes sufficient to pay the annual interest and set up a sinking-fund for the redemption of the principal. No specific route was laid down; the provinces were not required to follow Major Robinson's northern route if a shorter or better route could be found, but the route finally selected had to be approved by the British government. Nor was there any objection to a connection with American railroads. "The British Government," stated the official dispatch, "would by no means object to its forming part of the plan that it should include provision for establishing a communication between the projected railway and the railways of the United States."

Howe returned from London convinced that he had secured, not only what he had gone to seek, but a great deal more. The British government, he believed, had assured him that, when the stipulated conditions had been met, Parliament would be asked to authorize a guarantee of interest on a provincial loan of £7 million—sufficient to build not only the Portland line, but also a railway from Halifax to Quebec and perhaps even farther west.

The first prerequisite, the co-operation of New Brunswick and Canada, was quickly secured. New Brunswick gladly accepted the proposal and sent its representative, E. B. Chandler, with Howe to Toronto, then the seat of the Canadian government, in June, 1851. The Canadian legislature, dazzled by the prospect of cheap capital, was not slow to accept. The three provinces thereupon formally agreed that they would build the Halifax and Quebec road jointly, while Canada alone would build an extension to Montreal, and New Brunswick alone an extension to the Maine border, to connect with the American section of the European and North American.

These ambitious schemes were based on Howe's assurance that the guarantee of interest on the £7 million loan had been definitely promised, subject only to the approval of the British Parliament. It came, therefore, as a considerable surprise to all concerned when, late in 1851, the Colonial Office stated categorically that the guarantee would not and was never intended to be extended to cover the European and North American project—that is, the road from Halifax to Portland. The British government would have not the slightest objection if this road were built. But the guarantee of interest was to apply only to the railway from Halifax to Quebec.

How this misunderstanding arose is not clear. On his return from England Howe had certainly been convinced that the guarantee would cover the European and North American project, as well as the railway from Halifax to Quebec; his version of the agreement had been widely publicized and had gone uncontradicted for several months. On the other hand, it had certainly been stipulated in the agreement that the route should be subject to the approval of the British government. It seems probable that the Colonial Office, on scrutinizing Howe's proposals more closely, came to the conclusion that the interests of the Empire as a whole provided little justification for subsidizing a railway to the American city of Portland out of the pocket of the British tax-payer, especially if Canada and the maritime provinces were in any case to be linked by a direct line.

Whatever its origin, the misunderstanding wrecked the project. New Brunswick, whose co-operation was essential, declined to support the Halifax and Quebec railway unless it passed through the city of Saint John and the St. John valley, the richest and most densely populated sector

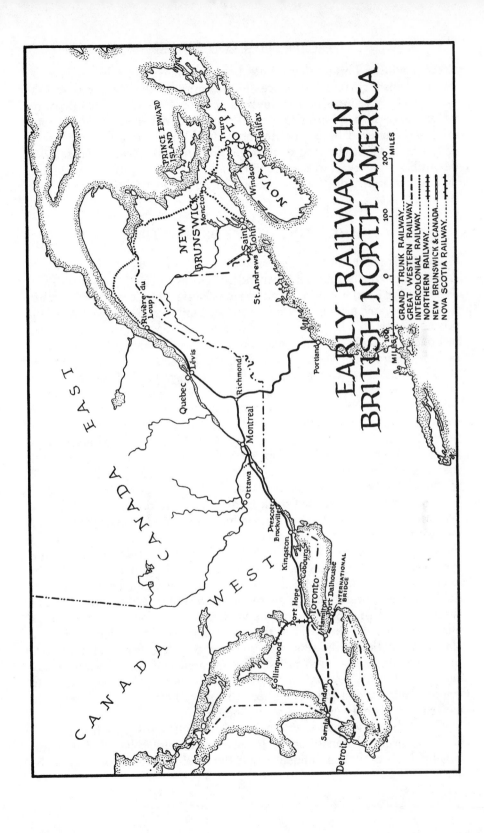

EARLY RAILWAYS IN
BRITISH NORTH AMERICA

MILES
200 100 0 100 200
MILES

GRAND TRUNK RAILWAY........
GREAT WESTERN RAILWAY........
NORTHERN RAILWAY........
NEW BRUNSWICK & CANADA........
NOVA SCOTIA RAILWAY........

PRINCE EDWARD
ISLAND

NOVA SCOTIA

Truro
Halifax
Windsor

NEW
BRUNSWICK

Moncton
Saint John
St. Andrews

Portland

Rivière du
Loup

Lévis
Quebec
Richmond

CANADA EAST

Montreal
Ottawa

CANADA WEST

Prescott
Brockville
Kingston
Cobourg
Port Hope
Port Dalhousie
Toronto
Hamilton
INTERNATIONAL
BRIDGE
Collingwood
Sarnia
London
Detroit

CANADA

of the province. This southern route, however, was completely unacceptable to the British government, since its proximity to the American frontier would sharply reduce its usefulness in the event of war. The only route which the British government would now accept was the northern route originally surveyed by Major Robinson, which ran along the south shore of the Gulf of St. Lawrence, through very unproductive but more easily defensible territory. No compromise could be found between these conflicting demands, and the negotiations ended in deadlock in 1852.

THE ENTRY OF THE BRASSEY FIRM

From this point until Confederation fifteen years later the British North American provinces pursued independent railway policies. New Brunswick decided to proceed with the European and North American project. When it rapidly became evident that the necessary capital could not be raised from private sources, E. B. Chandler, who was then representing the province in London, entered into an agreement with a well-known group of English railway contractors, Messrs. Peto, Brassey, Jackson, and Betts, who had already built more than a quarter of the railways in England, as well as others in France, Spain, and Italy, and who were at this time looking for contracts to employ their idle labour and equipment. These contractors stated that they were willing to build the railway either as a private enterprise or as a government project. The New Brunswick legislature chose the first alternative and in 1852 ratified a contract according to which the Brassey firm was to construct the whole railway from Nova Scotia to the Maine border, on condition that the province provided a subsidy of $32,500 per mile, purchased stock in the railway to the amount of $6,000 per mile, and also lent them $9,400 per mile on the security of a first mortgage. If any additional capital was needed, it was to be raised by the contractors. Construction was begun in 1853. The Brassey firm, however, soon ran into financial difficulties as a result of the collapse of the stock market in England and in 1856 demanded additional assistance from the provincial government. This the legislature declined to provide. The contract was then cancelled and the work taken over by the government, a total of $450,000 being paid to the contractors for the portion which had already been built. By 1860 the line was complete from Saint John to Shediac, a distance of 108 miles. The remainder of the railway was not begun until 1867. During this period, too, some progress was made with the St. Andrews and Quebec project. By 1867, however, this railway was bankrupt, with only one-third of its line completed.

Nova Scotia also entered into negotiations with the Brassey firm in spite of the determined opposition of Joseph Howe, who believed that it was largely because of their influence that the British government had, as he alleged, retracted its offer to guarantee the provincial loan. In 1853, however, when there seemed to be no other way of raising capital for the railway, he agreed to accept their proposals, the contractors offering to raise all the money required if they were given the construction contracts on their own terms. As in the case of New Brunswick, Brassey and his associates failed to carry out their promises and in 1854 they gave up the contract before any construction had been begun. The provincial government then took over the project and in 1858 a line was completed from Halifax to Truro with a branch to Windsor. By 1867 this line was extended to Pictou, giving Halifax railway connections both with the Bay of Fundy and with the Gulf of St. Lawrence. Both these lines, however, were highly vulnerable to competition from coastal shipping, as was the Saint John to Shediac line in New Brunswick.

THE GRAND TRUNK RAILWAY

Each of the maritime provinces, after the collapse of the guarantee negotiations in 1852, turned to the Brassey firm for assistance and, when this policy failed, each was compelled to adopt a policy of government construction. In the province of Canada events followed a rather different course. According to the proposals which Howe and Chandler had brought to Toronto in 1851, Canada was to be allotted £4 million out of the contemplated £7 million guaranteed loan. This sum was believed to be considerably larger than would be necessary to construct merely the Canadian section of the Halifax and Quebec railway. Estimating that construction costs would average between £5,000 and £6,000 per mile, Hincks calculated that, out of the proceeds of the loan, Canada would be able to construct, in addition to its section of the Halifax line, a complete trunk railway from Quebec along the St. Lawrence and the north shore of Lake Ontario to Hamilton, where it would join the Great Western. Accordingly, in the bill which was presented to the Canadian legislature in 1851 to authorize the guaranteed loan, provision was made for the construction of this trunk railway as well as for the Quebec and Halifax. When negotiations for the imperial guarantee broke down, the Quebec and Halifax part of the project was abandoned, but not the trunk-line scheme. Hincks signed a contract with Brassey and his associates according to which they agreed to build the trunk-line railway and to raise all the necessary capital, provided that the Canadian government guaranteed their bonds to the extent of one-half the total cost (later modified to a flat rate guarantee of £3,000 per mile). Arrangements were also made for the Grand Trunk to lease the Montreal to Portland line of the St. Lawrence and Atlantic.

The charter of the Grand Trunk Railway Company of Canada was passed by the Canadian legislature in April, 1853, and the prospectus was issued in London shortly thereafter. The latter was a most impressive document, not only because of the distinguished names associated with the Company, but also because of its confident predictions and the extensive programme of construction which it envisaged. No less than six out of the twelve Canadian directors were members of the Canadian Cabinet: John Ross, solicitor-general for Canada West, who became president; Francis Hincks, inspector-general; Etienne Taché, receiver-general; James Morris, postmaster-general; Malcolm Cameron, president of the Executive Council; and René Caron, speaker of the Legislative Council. To these were added, as directors on behalf of the Canadian government, Thomas Baring and George Carr Glyn, the eminent London bankers who handled Canada's borrowings in England. Peter McGill, president of the Bank of Montreal, Galt, and Holton were also named as directors, but the latter two soon resigned.

As regards the future profitability of the railway, the prospectus was not pessimistic. The various initial advantages were enumerated: its freedom from competition, since it would form the only complete railway system in Canada; the extensive financial guarantees provided by the Canadian government; the fact that 250 miles of the system were already open for traffic; the assurance that construction would be quickly and efficiently carried out, since Messrs. Peto, Brassey, Betts, and Jackson had already contracted for six-sevenths of the work; and lastly the fact that the total cost was already known, since it was "actually defined by the contracts already made, whereby any apprehension of the capital being found insufficient is removed". Reducing these advantages to cash terms, the prospectus estimated average revenue at £25 per mile and average operating costs at 40 per cent of revenue. A rate of profit of 11½ per cent on the share capital was confidently predicted.

The total capital of the Company was set at £9,500,000. By no means all of this, however, was available for immediate distribution to the investing public. In the first place, a total of £2,254,000 had to be set aside for the owners and bondholders of the three roads which the Grand Trunk absorbed: the St. Lawrence and Atlantic, the Quebec and Richmond, and the Ontario, Simcoe, and Huron. Of the remaining £7,246,000, one-half was to be issued in the form of shares, one-quarter (£1,811,500) as bonds guaranteed by the Canadian government (in effect, provincial debentures), and one-quarter as company bonds. Most of the bonds, however, including those which carried the government's guarantee, were reserved for the contractors, to be sold for their account as money was required to pay for construction. The shares were to be sold, mostly in London, by Baring Brothers and Company and Glyn, Mills, and Company, the province's financial agents.

In terms of the amount of capital involved, the building of the Grand Trunk Railway was the largest single investment project undertaken up to that date in Canada. Its success or failure depended primarily on finance, and this in turn depended upon the ability of the Brassey firm, through Barings and Glyn, Mills, to find buyers in England for the Company's bonds. When Hincks had gone to England in 1852, he and his associates had considered it indispensable that the British government should guarantee the necessary loan. The entire project had been conceived and drawn up on the assumption that this guarantee would be obtained. When the guarantee of the British government was refused, the guarantee of the Canadian government was substituted, but no reduction in the dimensions of the project was made to take account of the different capital-raising ability of the new guarantor. The basic problem was, therefore, whether the credit of the Canadian government, supplemented by the financial abilities of the Brassey firm, Barings, and Glyn, Mills, could compensate for the initial failure to secure the guarantee of the British government.

Serious financial difficulties were not slow to appear. By 1855 the Company was unable to pay interest on the bonds which had already been sold, while new issues were almost unmarketable. The directors then turned to the Canadian government for further assistance. A committee of the English stockholders, headed by the governor of the Bank of England, proposed that the Canadian government should give a guarantee of interest at 5 per cent on the entire capital stock. This proposal was rejected by the Canadian cabinet then in office. The very extensive political influence of the Company and the contractors was then brought to bear and a new ministry, acting on the advice of the Governor-General, Lord Elgin, agreed to a compromise. The government guarantee was extended to cover an additional £900,000 of bonds; the Brassey firm was released from its obligation to take up the unsold stock and bonds, on condition that they accepted half their future payments in the Company's much depreciated securities; and the province agreed to relinquish its first mortgage in order to permit an issue of £2 million in preference bonds. Further concessions followed. In the decade after 1855 hardly a year passed without some relaxation of the terms of the agreement between the Company and the Canadian government. By 1867 the total indebtedness of the Grand Trunk Railway to the government of Canada was estimated at over $26 million. This was, however, a debt in name only; in effect it was an outright gift.

While to some extent these difficulties arose from miscalculations and bad timing in the approach to the British investor, to a large degree they reflected unanticipated costs of construction. In the first place, the track taken over from the St. Lawrence and Atlantic was found to be in very poor condition; extensive reconstruction was necessary before the road was fit for regular traffic. Secondly, the Grand Trunk undertook to construct its own line from Toronto to Sarnia. This had not been part of the original plan. In their prospectus, the promoters of the Grand Trunk had referred to the Great Western as "a continuation of the Trunk line, although under a different company", and had cited the advantages to be gained from a connection, through the Great Western, with the railroads of New York and Michigan. Certainly there was little economic justification for constructing another through line west of Toronto. Negotiations for the amalgamation of the two companies failed, however, perhaps partly because of the influence of New York capital in the management of the Great Western (although most of the shares were held in England), partly because the Grand Trunk directors had convinced themselves that they required their own independent connection with Detroit. The influence of Canadian contractors also may have been important. In 1851 Gzowski and Company, a contracting firm in which A. T. Galt and other former directors of the St. Lawrence and Atlantic were partners, had received the contracts for the construction of the Toronto and Guelph Railway. In 1852 this road requested permission from the legislature to extend its line to Sarnia. The railway committee of the legislature decided that to grant this request would be both "unjust and impolitic", since such a road would be an invasion of the territory of the Great Western, of which the government had already paid half the cost, and since there was not enough business for two lines west of Toronto. Hincks, however, thought otherwise. Permission for the Sarnia extension was granted, and the Toronto and Guelph was absorbed into the Grand Trunk system, with Gzowski and Company receiving the contract to build the Toronto to Sarnia line at a fee of £8,000 per mile. No provision had been made for this extension in the original estimates.

For the Toronto to Montreal section, the Brassey firm received £9,000 per mile, but had to accept half their pay in the form of depreciated bonds and shares. They later claimed that they had lost one million pounds by their contracts. Gzowski and Company, on the other hand, received their pay in the form of cash, and the individual members of the firm realized sizable fortunes. Besides the unfavourable financial arrangements, the Brassey firm worked under the handicap of being unfamiliar with North American railway-building techniques. Their previous experience had been in countries where labour was relatively cheap, and they did not use as many or as effective labour-saving devices as American and Canadian contractors. It is not easy, however, to estimate the importance of this factor; the Toronto to Sarnia section, built by Canadian contractors at a lower rate per mile, was later described by an English engineer engaged by the Grand Trunk to report on the whole line as having been constructed "with an excellence of workmanship far beyond the requirements of the contract". The difficulties which the British contractors experienced were due not so much to any attempt on their part to adhere to higher standards of construction than were usual in North America, but rather to their close involvement in the financial difficulties of the railway.

One factor which affected both groups of contractors adversely was the sharp rise in prices which took place during the period of construction. Partly this was due to the effects of the rapid rate of investment itself; the decade of the 1850's, with construction going ahead on several major railways, was a period of heavy capital imports and was characterized by serious inflationary tendencies. While the fact that a large part of the physical capital required by the railways, such as rails and rolling-stock, was imported rather than drawn from domestic sources no doubt made the inflationary impact less than it would otherwise have been, the pressure of the railways' demands upon limited supplies of labour and materials in Canada certainly contributed to the price rise. Wage rates for unskilled railway labour rose 40 per cent between 1853 and 1854. Accentuating this tendency were the effects of the Crimean War upon British demands for Canadian wheat and of the Reciprocity Treaty with the United States upon American demand for a wide range of Canadian raw materials. With wheat at two dollars a bushel and land fetching double its pre-1850 price, contractors' profit margins shrank to vanishing-point, while the cost calculations which had been used to estimate capital requirements became completely unrealistic. The coincidence in time of a massive programme of investment and a period of general prosperity created severe difficulties for the contractors and contributed to the pressure for government aid.

The construction of the road was retarded, but never completely halted, by these financial embarrassments. The section taken over from the St. Lawrence and Atlantic was completed in June, 1853, although maintenance expenses continued high thereafter because of the poor standard of construction. In the following year track was laid from Richmond to Levis, giving Quebec a rail connection, though rather a circuitous one, with Montreal; this line was extended to Rivière du Loup in 1860. On the important central section the line was completed from Montreal to Brockville in 1855, and from Brockville to Toronto in 1856. The Toronto to Sarnia section, in the hands of Gzowski and Company, was completed as far as Stratford in 1856, but construction west of this point was delayed by lack of money and by the protracted negotiations for amalgamation with the Great Western. Not until 1858 did the line reach London, while the final section from London to Sarnia, together with a short line in Michigan from Port Huron, opposite Sarnia, to Detroit, was not completed until 1859. In the same year the Victoria Bridge across the St. Lawrence at Montreal was opened for traffic.

THE GRAND TRUNK IN OPERATION

By 1860, after seven years of construction, the whole line from Sarnia to Portland was ready for use. This did not mean, however, that the problems of the Grand Trunk Railway were over. At the end of 1860 the

Company had a floating debt of over $12 million; its total indebtedness. including the provincial debentures, was almost $60 million. On many sections of the line the track and rolling-stock were already in such poor condition that replacement was urgently necessary. On other sections, such as that from Quebec to Rivière du Loup, the volume of traffic was so small that revenues barely covered operating expenses. Over the line as a whole operating expenses during the next ten years varied between 58 and 85 per cent of gross receipts, instead of the 40 per cent which the prospectus, basing its estimate on English experience, had forecast. Other predictions which had accompanied the planning of the road proved equally fallacious. Construction costs ($63,800 per mile, on the average) had proved much higher than estimates. Certain sections, such as the St. Lawrence and Atlantic and the Detroit and Port Huron, had been purchased at inflated prices. Standards of construction, instead of being up to the best English practice, had been lax, particularly in the sections east of Toronto where the Brassey firm, squeezed between rising costs and limited cash resources, had tried to save money by heavy grades, cheap iron rails, and inadequate ballast.

These defects were reflected in high maintenance costs throughout the next twenty years. But revenues also proved disappointing. For this there were several reasons. In contrast to the assertions of the prospectus, the Grand Trunk proved highly vulnerable to competition. Throughout its length it faced the competition of the St. Lawrence canals, which retained their advantages for bulk staples such as wheat, even though mail, fast freight, and passengers went by rail. In 1859 transport costs between Toronto and Montreal were $3.50 per ton by rail, but only $2 to $3 per ton by water. In competition with other railways, too, both in Canada and in the United States, the Grand Trunk laboured under disadvantages. The Great Western had better connections with Detroit and Chicago. The American roads, pushing westward often in advance of settlement, left only the crumbs of the western trade for the Grand Trunk. Handicapped by its heavy burden of fixed debts, by its high operating costs, by its poor physical equipment, and by the fact that its central management was located in England, the Grand Trunk during the first two decades of its existence failed to attract any significant portion of the export trade of the American west. This failure was reflected in its inability, at any time, to pay a dividend on its ordinary shares.

In view of the fact that the Grand Trunk had been expressly designed for through traffic and that the importance of the western trade for its success had been explicitly recognized from the start, it is surprising to find that in one respect at least the management of the railway followed a policy which could hardly have been expected to do anything but increase its handicaps in competition with its American rivals. This was in connection with the gauge. The St. Lawrence and Atlantic, as we have already noticed, had been built with a gauge of 5′ 6″. There were, it is true, good engineering arguments for preferring this broad gauge to the more usual 4′ 8½″, but the principal reason for selecting it for the Montreal-Portland line was to prevent Boston from tapping the through traffic. In July, 1851, the government of Canada decided that the 5′ 6″ gauge should be the national railway gauge of Canada; as a consequence, the entire Grand Trunk line was constructed with this broad gauge. Now if the reason for choosing this gauge in the first place had been to prevent American lines from tapping through traffic on a Canadian route, it was hardly to be expected that it would be of much assistance to a Canadian line attempting to tap through traffic on American routes. The Grand Trunk system ended at Detroit; its only hope of attracting through traffic from the American west lay in good connections with American roads in Michigan. But these roads used the 4′ 8½″ gauge. The difference in gauge meant that all through traffic had to be trans-shipped, if it was to go over the Grand Trunk line. The necessity for this trans-shipment, combined with the absence of a tunnel or bridge at the Detroit River, did much to neutralize any competitive advantages which the Grand Trunk might otherwise have possessed.

The Great Western had originally been planned to use the 4′ 8½″ gauge, as was natural for a line intended primarily to serve as a connecting link between the Michigan Central and the New York Central. It was, indeed, in the confident expectation that this gauge would be used that Erastus Corning, president of the Utica and Schenectady and later of the New York Central, had induced the New York legislature to pass a law permitting any railroad in that state to subscribe to stock in the Great Western, provided only that the consent of two-thirds of the stockholders in the subscribing road was obtained. About one-fifth ($493,500) of the original capital stock of the Great Western had been provided by New York railroads under this statute, the Utica and Schenectady alone subscribing $200,000. Investments by stockholders of the Michigan Central and in Detroit brought the total American capital invested in the Great Western to approximately $800,000. It is quite clear that very little if any of this capital would have been provided had it not been understood that the Great Western was to use the 4′ 8½″ gauge. In 1851, however, when the Canadian government decided that the standard Canadian gauge should be 5′ 6″, the Great Western, despite vigorous protests from the American stockholders and Corning's personal intervention, was compelled to adopt the new standard. This, of course, largely destroyed the usefulness of the Great Western, at least in terms of its original conception. The change of gauge was especially unfortunate for the Great Western because it would otherwise have enjoyed excellent physical connections with the New York Central by means of a suspension bridge over the Niagara River which was completed in 1854.

There was, of course, no single standard railway gauge even within the United States at this time. The Erie Railroad, for instance, had a 6′ gauge. The adoption of the 5′ 6″ gauge by Canada was, however, a serious and costly error, because it isolated the Canadian trunk roads from the American lines on which they inevitably had to depend for any American freight they hoped to obtain. The Great Western had no connection with the east except via the New York Central or the Erie Railroad, nor with the west except via the Michigan Central or the Michigan Southern, until it built its own line, the Detroit and Milwaukee, in the 1860's. The Grand Trunk, until it acquired its own line to Chicago in 1881, had no connection with the American west except through the Michigan Central or Michigan Southern, both of which were controlled by New York capital. Neither of these Canadian roads could hope to achieve financial success, or even solvency, without good American connections. Recognition of the error did not come until 1870, when both lines, at considerable expense, began relaying their track and converting their rolling-stock to the 4′ 8½″ gauge. Three years earlier the Great Western had attempted a compromise by laying a third rail, so that its tracks could be used by rolling-stock built for either gauge, but this expedient caused several serious accidents and was very unsatisfactory.

GOVERNMENT AID: THE MUNICIPAL LOAN FUND

In principal and interest, the total financial aid extended to railways by the Canadian government under the Guarantee Act and the Grand Trunk charter amounted to approximately $33 million. Whatever the legal form of the assistance, whether guarantee or loan, it amounted in effect to an outright subsidy, since very little of the money was ever repaid. The funds committed under the Guarantee Act and the Grand Trunk legislation, however, by no means exhausted the total of government aid to railways. Considerable sums were also disbursed by the municipalities. In Canada West the Municipal Act of 1849 empowered municipalities to lend money to or invest in road or bridge companies, while most of the railway charters included clauses providing for municipal contributions. The Great Western, for example, under an amendment to its charter authorized in 1850, sold shares to the amount of £25,000 each to the counties of Oxford and Middlesex and the towns of Galt and London, while the town of Hamilton subscribed £100,000. The railway legislation of 1851, inspired by Francis Hincks, made provision for the construction of the trunk-line jointly by the province and by the municipalities if the guaranteed loan proved insufficient.

The legislation which opened the flood-gates of municipal aid to railways was the Municipal Loan Fund Act, devised by Hincks and passed by the legislature in 1852. Its basic idea was very simple. There were, it was argued, numerous opportunities for the construction of useful and profitable railways in Canada, apart from the main trunk-line, if only the capital could be obtained to build them. The difficulty in obtaining capital arose from the fact that the potentialities of these railways, and the credit standing of the municipalities which wished to build them, were not properly appreciated outside Canada. In particular, they were not appreciated in London, where most of the capital would have to be raised. If, however, the credit of all these municipalities could be pooled, and the feasibility of all the local projects examined and sanctioned by the Canadian government, then there was no good reason why the province of Canada, with its superior credit standing, should not float the necessary loans and then lend the money to the municipalities, who would invest it in the railways they desired. This is what the Municipal Loan Fund was designed to do. Each municipality was authorized to issue debentures for aid to railways, canals, harbours, or roads. The debentures of the various municipalities, if approved by the Executive Council, were to be pooled in the Municipal Loan Fund. In proportion to the size of the fund, the receiver-general was authorized to issue provincial debentures. The proceeds of the sale of these provincial debentures were then to be transferred to the municipalities for investment in railways and other useful projects. Each municipality was required to contribute to a central sinking-fund to redeem its debentures at maturity. If it fell behind in its payments, it was to be charged interest; if it continued to default, the provincial government would levy a charge upon the property-holders in the municipality. The receiver-general was authorized to make advances to the fund if, for any reason, payments by the municipalities did not meet charges upon it.

This ingenious scheme was linked to another experiment which was being carried out at the same time, namely the experiment in free banking. Hincks apparently expected that there would be a steady demand for Loan Fund debentures, since they could be used as a basis for note circulation. The free-banking experiment, however, was not a success. The principal defect of the fund, however, lay not in the lack of demand for the debentures, but in the extravagance and over-optimism of the municipalities, particularly in Canada West. If bad planning and bad management were characteristic of the Grand Trunk, they were even more typical of the railways in which the municipalities—each of them convinced that a railway, no matter how poorly constructed or expensive, was the key to prosperity—invested. By 1859 the municipalities in Canada West had raised $7,300,000 by means of the fund and spent $5,800,000 of this sum on railways; arrears of interest totalled $2,300,000. In Canada East, where a more cautious policy was the rule, $2,400,000 had been raised and only $900,000 spent on railways, but even in this part of the province arrears of interest amounted to $300,000.

The provincial government, in setting up the fund, had attempted to make it clear that it was not guaranteeing the bonds of the municipalities nor assuming responsibility for them. But whether or not the province wished to be held responsible for the fund, from the point of view of the investor it was in fact responsible. Provincial debentures had been sold to match the municipal debentures in the fund, and it was not possible for the province to assume responsibility for certain of its debentures and not for others. The safeguards included in the organization of the fund to insure the provincial government against liability proved quite inadequate. As one municipality after another defaulted, pressure built up in the legislature to cancel or postpone payment of arrears. Members of Parliament, after all, had to be elected; the levying of a tax on property-holders in a defaulting municipality was politically impossible. Finally in 1859 the government was forced to close the fund and assume responsibility for its obligations. A total of £3 million was added to the provincial debt in the process.

THE FIRST PERIOD OF RAILWAY-BUILDING: A SUMMARY VIEW

In 1850 there had been 66 miles of railway in all the British North American colonies; in 1860 there were 2,065. Between 1860 and Confederation seven years later only 213 miles were added to this total. The rising prices and hectic prosperity which accompanied this remarkable burst of expansion during the 1850's were typical of a period of rapid capital formation. The total cost of the railways up to 1867 has been estimated at $154,694,853: for 2,188¼ miles in Canada, $145,794,853; for 145 miles in Nova Scotia, approximately $6,380,000; and for 126 miles in New Brunswick, approximately $2,520,000. Total capital imports into Canada during the decade of the 1850's have been estimated at $100 million (including military expenditures), as compared with $35 million between 1841 and 1849 and $25 million between 1827 and 1838. These figures indicate only the primary investments; total capital formation must have been several times higher. They serve, however, to give some idea of the sharp acceleration in the rate of growth which took place during the 1850's.

In Britain industrialism preceded the advent of the railway; in the United States the germs of an industrial economy were already in existence on the Atlantic seaboard before the railroads crossed the Appalachians. Canada, on the other hand, was an almost exclusively agricultural and commercial economy when the first major spurt of railway construction took place. The relative backwardness of Canada meant that, when the railway was introduced, a special set of problems had to be solved which had not been encountered, or had been encountered with less severity, in the United States and Britain. Most of these problems revolved around capital supply. With the exception of a few minor "portage" railways, domestic sources of capital in Canada were insufficient even to make a start with construction. The borrowing ability of the Canadian government was therefore called into play to secure capital from Britain.

While by far the greater part of the capital was obtained from other countries, Canadians participated largely in the work of promotion and construction. In these fields the government as such played a passive or enabling role. The St. Lawrence canals, after disappointing experiments with private construction on the first Welland and Lachine Canals, had been built and financed by the government. The railways, on the other hand, were built by private corporations, operating with very extensive government financial assistance. This change in policy represented in part the growing strength of the Canadian business class and an extension of the activities of this class away from its formerly almost exclusive concern with commerce. It represented also, however, a growing appreciation on the part of Canadian politicians and business men of the greater profit opportunities inherent in private construction. Tutored by the Brassey firm and by American examples, Canadian promoters and contractors proved by no means slow to acquire the skills, both political and financial, necessary for railway construction in North America. The role of the government as such, as distinct from the activities of individual members of the government, was confined to financial assistance and to a largely nominal supervision over policy.

How successful did this partnership between government and private business prove? Our answer must depend largely on the criteria of success we adopt. On the one hand, 2,000 miles of railway were built within a single decade, which was no mean achievement. On the other, the level of government debt was greatly increased: some $33 million was added to the Canadian provincial debt as a result of aid to the Grand Trunk, the Great Western, and the Northern Railways—leaving aside the many smaller ones—before 1867. Was this money prudently and economically expended? The verdict of the private investor—with Grand Trunk ordinary shares selling in London in 1865 at 22 and Great Western at 65—is clear enough. But the private rate of return is not an entirely adequate criterion: we are more concerned here with the economy as a whole. The primary objective of Canadian railway policy in the 1850's, the construction of a trunk-line railway from the Detroit River to the sea, was certainly achieved. A good case can be made, however, for the view that this objective was achieved only at the cost of excessive waste, with excessive drains on the public treasury, and with excessive damage to Canada's credit on the world capital market. It is possible that a policy of direct government construction would have proved more effective.

The long-run importance of these early railways for the economic development of Canada depended less upon whether or not they had been economically and efficiently constructed than upon whether or not they provided a viable solution to the problems which had inspired their inception. These problems, as we have already seen, were basically two in number: first, the problem of maintaining the unity of the St. Lawrence economy in the face of the divisive pulls of American markets and transport routes; and secondly, the problem of re-establishing the position of Montreal as a major entrepôt in the movement of foodstuffs from the American west to Europe.

As regards the first problem, it is clear that the railways acted as a strong centralizing force in the Canadian economy. The numerous feeder railways, many of them built with the assistance of the Municipal Loan Fund, channelled traffic onto the main through routes and stimulated the development of areas which had previously been largely isolated and self-sufficient. The relative failure of the main trunk-lines to attract the western trade was followed by attempts to build up local traffic, particularly after the abrogation of the Reciprocity Treaty in 1866. For the first time Canadian commerce was freed from dependence upon water transportation and, as a consequence, from the seasonal closing of transportation during the winter.

To the second problem, however, the Canadian railways of the 1850's provided no effective answer. The total volume of freight moving eastward on these lines in 1859 amounted to less than 200,000 tons. Over the five-year period, 1855-60, arrivals of grain at Buffalo and Oswego averaged over 27½ million bushels annually; the total exports from Canadian Atlantic ports (i.e., principally from Montreal) over the same period averaged only 672,625 bushels annually. The competition of water transportation and of American railroads, the handicap of the broad gauge and of poor connections in Michigan and farther west, and the continued failure of Montreal to attract the highly remunerative inbound trade in manufactured products from England effectively prevented the Canadian trunk railways from winning the traffic of the American west.

Most important of all, perhaps, when the decade of the 1850's closed there was still no railway in existence between the colony on the St. Lawrence and the maritime colonies of New Brunswick and Nova Scotia. Nor was there any railway in existence or even seriously considered, except as a topic for rhetoric, between Canada and the struggling British colony on the Pacific coast. In the east the failure to secure assistance from Britain, combined with interprovincial disagreements over the route and the competing attractions of Portland, had frustrated attempts to build from Halifax to Quebec. In the west the vast stretch of unproductive territory north of Lakes Superior and Huron, the territorial sovereignty of the Hudson's Bay Company over the prairies, and the long-persisting dream of capturing the American western trade seemed to place prospects for a Canadian transcontinental railway far in the future. And yet the same forces which had impelled Canada into her first major railway programme were soon to lead her to embark on both the eastern line to the Maritimes and the transcontinental line to the Pacific coast. These forces were the desire for national economic unity and the fear of American encroachment upon Canada's hinterland. From the experiments and mistakes of the 1850's Canadian business men and politicians learned the lessons which equipped them to undertake this larger task.

SUGGESTIONS FOR FURTHER READING

BASIC WORKS:

Glazebrook, G. P. de T., *A History of Transportation in Canada* (Toronto, 1938), Chapter V

Innis, Harold A., "Transportation as a Factor in Canadian Economic History", in *Problems of Staple Production in Canada* (Toronto, 1933), pp. 1-16

Innis, Harold A. and A. R. M. Lower, eds., *Select Documents in Canadian Economic History, 1783-1885* (Toronto, 1933), pp. 198-207, 486-98

McLean, S. J., "National Highways Overland", in A. Shortt and A. G. Doughty, eds., *Canada and Its Provinces* (Toronto, 1914), Vol. X, pp. 359-416

Skelton, Oscar D., *The Railway Builders* (Toronto, 1916), Chapters I-V

SUPPLEMENTARY WORKS:

Brown, Thomas S., *A History of the Grand Trunk Railway* (Quebec, 1864)

Jenks, Leland H., *The Migration of British Capital to 1875* (London and New York, 1927), Chapters V and VII

Myers, Gustavus, *History of Canadian Wealth* (Chicago, 1914), Vol. 1, Chapters X-XI

Skelton, Oscar D., *The Life and Times of Sir Alexander Tilloch Galt* (Toronto, 1920), Chapters III-IV

CHAPTER XV

THE CONTINENTAL HINTERLAND AND
THE PACIFIC COAST: 1821–1870

REORGANIZATION OF THE FUR TRADE AFTER 1821

THE long and bitter struggle between the Hudson's Bay Company and the North West Company ended with the amalgamation of the two organizations in 1821. Important advantages on the side of the Hudson's Bay Company in this struggle had been greater financial resources, centralized control over policy, and the lower transport costs of the Bay route. The formation of the new organization, which operated under the name and charter of the Hudson's Bay Company, was followed by attempts to combine these advantages with the trained personnel and efficient operating techniques of the North West Company. The first five years after the merger were occupied with this task: duplication of posts and personnel had to be eliminated; the wastes and extravagances which had developed in the era of competition had to be reduced; the different trading practices had to be blended into a single system; and an effective method of managerial control had to be evolved.

The terms of the amalgamation were complicated, reflecting the several different interests which had to be taken into account. According to the agreement signed on 26 March, 1821, equal amounts of capital in the new concern were to be provided by each of the former organizations. The net profits for the next twenty-one years were to be divided into 100 shares; 20 of these shares were to go to the Hudson's Bay Company shareholders, 20 to the North West Company, 5 to the heirs of Lord Selkirk, 5 to the London agents of the North West Company (William and Simon McGillivray and Edward Ellice), and 40 to the chief factors and chief traders of the Company. The remaining 10 were reserved for contingencies. Three years later the 5 shares allotted to the London agents of the North West Company were converted into Hudson's Bay stock. The dominant influence in the central management of the new Company remained in the hands of the old Hudson's Bay shareholders, although Edward Ellice came to play a very important role; most of the chief factors and chief traders, on the other hand, were former North West Company men.

In terms of organization, the agreement laid it down that the Company was to be managed by a board consisting of two representatives from each party to the agreement, together with the governor and deputy governor of the Hudson's Bay Company. Three years later this arrangement was dropped in favour of the older system of a committee of directors, on which Edward Ellice was the only member previously associated with the North West Company. In North America, responsibility for the immediate supervision of the trade was in the hands of two governors, one for the Northern Department and one for the Southern, who, in consultation with Councils made up from the chief factors in each Department, were to determine the details of each year's operations, the "outfits" to be made up, the wintering residence of the factors and traders, and so on. Within a few years, however, under the authoritarian rule of George Simpson, as governor first of the Northern and later of both Departments, the power of the Councils became largely nominal. Policy was laid down and enforced by Simpson in North America and the governor of the Company in London.

One immediate and very important result of the coalition was that the British government confirmed the Company's charter and also its exclusive rights to trade in areas not included in the charter. During the final stages of the struggle with the North West Company, the rights which the Company claimed under its charter had been seriously called into question. Shortly after the amalgamation, however, an Act of Parliament was passed which not only implied that the Company's charter was valid as far as it applied to Rupert's Land (roughly the Hudson Bay drainage basin), but also granted to the Company for an initial period of twenty-one years the exclusive privilege of trading with the Indians over the whole of the rest of British North America, excepting only the established colonies. This Act, therefore, granted to the Company monopoly rights which were vastly more extensive, in a geographical sense, than any it had enjoyed before.

To supply the fur trade over this large area the new Company relied upon the use of bases on Hudson Bay, combined with the improvement of transport methods in the interior. The St. Lawrence-Great Lakes route used by the North West Company was abandoned so far as freight was concerned, and Fort William, the important junction on that route, was broken up. Boats were substituted for canoes on all the major supply routes and an elaborate system of "brigades" was worked out. The shortness of the season made it essential that the arrivals and departures of these brigades should be very carefully scheduled. Vessels from England arrived at York Factory late in July or early in August and were unloaded there. A year's supply of stores was always maintained at this base, so that supplies for posts in the interior could be dispatched without waiting for the arrival of consignments from England. From York Factory supplies were taken by boat in early summer to Norway House, at the northern end of Lake Winnipeg, which was the major distributing point in the interior and served as the base for the important Athabasca and Mackenzie River posts and later for the Yukon also. Other direct routes ran from York Factory to the Red River and the Saskatchewan.

Improvements in transportation were accompanied by extensive reorganization of the Company's trading system in the interests of economy and efficiency of operation. A more detailed and systematic cost-accounting system was introduced. Where two posts, established during the period of competition, drew on the same fur-supply area, one was eliminated and the Indians encouraged to take their furs to the remaining post. The expensive presents to the Indians were sharply reduced, as were the distribution of liquor and the extension of long credits, though it proved impossible to eliminate these features of the trade entirely. At posts in the interior, in an attempt to reduce incoming cargoes, every effort was made to encourage self-sufficiency in food supplies by the use of potatoes and other vegetables, fish, and pemmican, and in equipment by the collection of dressed leather, buffalo robes, sinews, and so on. The provision without charge of certain items of equipment to the Company's employees was abolished and wages were reduced. Attempts were made to solve the problem of surplus personnel by encouraging early retirement.

Immediately following coalition the territory controlled by the Company was divided for administrative purposes into four districts, laid out primarily according to the principal water transport routes. The watershed of the Columbia River on the Pacific coast and New Caledonia formed one district; the territory bounded by Hudson Bay on the east, the Arctic Ocean on the north, the Rocky Mountains on the west, and the American border on the south formed another. These two districts together formed the Northern Department. The Montreal district, including the two Canadas, the Ottawa valley, and later Labrador, together with the districts east of Hudson Bay and south of James Bay, made up the Southern Department. Each Department had its own Council and, in the beginning, its own governor.

The two governors appointed in 1821 were both Hudson's Bay Company men. George Simpson, who was assigned to the Northern Department, although his previous experience in the fur trade had not been very extensive, had demonstrated his abilities by directing the critical Athabasca campaign of the Hudson's Bay Company in 1820-1. By his energy and tact, as well as by his penetrating appraisals of men and of the requirements of the situation, he quickly reorganized the Northern Department and brought its work up to a high standard of efficiency. William Williams, on the other hand, who took over the Southern Department after having been governor of Rupert's Land since 1818, proved unequal to his task, partly because his territory was exposed to competition from Canada and to some extent from the United States, partly because he was unable to avoid friction with his Council, many of whom were former North West

Company men. Difficulties were also encountered with the former agents of the North West Company in Montreal, now operating under the firm name of McGillivrays, Thain, & Company, who, as party to the amalgamation agreement, retained jurisdiction over the posts on the Ottawa and were anxious to promote use of the St. Lawrence route, whereas the policy of the Company now was to channel all trade through the bases on Hudson Bay. In 1826, therefore, in an attempt to solve these difficulties, Williams was recalled and the Montreal agency abolished; Simpson was given authority over both the Northern and the Southern Departments, as well as the posts on the Ottawa.

Control over the entire fur trade throughout British North America now centred in Simpson's hands, subject only to the superior authority of the London committee. Following the model of the North West Company, some flexibility was permitted in the operations of traders in the interior, particularly in competitive areas such as the Columbia, while the supervision of operating procedures remained the responsibility of the Council; but it was Simpson who formulated policy and who provided the positive leadership necessary for morale and efficiency. A very able and tough administrator who placed the interests of the Company above any personal considerations, Simpson dominated the vast trading empire under his control. His authority was never seriously challenged, except after 1841 by John McLoughlin on the Pacific coast.

The measures promoting greater economy and efficiency which Simpson had introduced in the Northern Department were now generalized throughout the whole organization. Centralized control made possible a policy of conserving fur resources in areas which had been over-trapped during the period of competition, paralleled by a policy of systematically exhausting fur resources in areas which might attract competition. This latter policy was applied with great thoroughness in such competitive areas as the Red River valley, where fur-traders from Minnesota were moving in, and on the Pacific coast, where independent groups of American trappers were active. These cleaned-out areas served, so to speak, as defensive barriers to prevent encroachments upon the Company's preserves. Systematic exhaustion of these areas made it possible to conserve resources in areas which were free from competition, by closing down posts and by encouraging the trapping of furs other than beaver, as for example in the Peace River district and in the area immediately tributary to York Factory. A quota system was instituted for the most exhausted districts and attempts were made to discourage the Indians from hunting beaver in summer. At some posts prices were adjusted so as to favour the production of small furs such as martens, muskrats, and lynx, and discourage the trapping of beaver. These conservation measures were only partly successful. The Indians could not in fact be prevented from hunting beaver in summer, but the closing of posts in exhausted districts and the encouragement given to the trapping of fur-bearing animals other than beaver proved more effective.

The execution of such long-range policies was possible only under monopoly control of the trade. Competition had led to rapid penetration of the continental hinterland but also to rising costs, falling profits, and exhaustion of fur supplies. Monopoly provided the opportunity for consolidation and conservation in the interests of lower costs, higher profits, and long-term survival. In this context, however, the term "monopoly" must be used with care. The Company had no monopoly of the sale of furs in England. Only to a very limited extent could it influence the prices at which its furs should sell, since Russian and American sources of supply provided effective competition in the London and European markets. Attempts to raise prices by withholding supplies were never permanently successful. In North America, on the other hand, the Company had a monopoly in the supply of European goods to the Indians. It provided, except in certain areas, the only market for furs and the only source of supply of manufactured commodities.

Despite the establishment of monopoly and centralized control, however, in certain areas the position of the Company was far from secure. On the Pacific coast the inroads of American fur-traders and later of American settlers accentuated the problems which arose from uncertain political sovereignty over the area, and the Company was forced to withdraw northward. In the Red River valley the Company proved unable to exclude private traders, prevent the strengthening of economic ties with the United States, or maintain political control over the growing settlement. In both these areas the maintenance of monopoly control over the fur trade proved incompatible with the expansion of settlement.

THE HUDSON'S BAY COMPANY ON THE PACIFIC COAST

The territory between the Rocky Mountains and the Pacific coast was divided into two principal fur-trading districts: New Caledonia in the north, an ill-defined area which included the watershed of the Fraser River and its tributaries; and the Columbia in the south, which included the watershed of the Columbia River, or in other words the greater part of the present states of Washington, Oregon, and Idaho, together with parts of Montana, Utah, and southern British Columbia. Although the North West Company had maintained posts in these districts since 1806, the Hudson's Bay Company had paid little attention to the region, and even after amalgamation in 1821 it remained uncertain for several years whether or not it was in the Company's interests to carry on the trade west of the Rocky Mountains. Costs of transport to and from the region were very high; such information as there was about its fur-trading possibilities was not encouraging; and its political future was in doubt. Russia,

Great Britain, and the United States each claimed sovereignty over part or the whole of the region. Britain and the United States had signed a convention in 1818 which provided for joint occupancy for a period of ten years, but this was clearly a temporary compromise. In 1821, too, the Russian government had issued an edict claiming the whole coastal region from Bering Strait to Queen Charlotte Sound, and it was no secret that for a considerable time the Russian-American Company had been planning to establish posts as far south as northern California. In this area, in short, the Hudson's Bay Company could not with any confidence count upon a prolonged period of occupancy, nor could it expect to enjoy the monopoly of trade which it had secured throughout the rest of its dominions. The policies and tactics which it employed east of the Rocky Mountains were not applicable to the situation on the Pacific coast.

Accentuating these political uncertainties was the fact that the region as a whole, and particularly the Columbia basin, was not believed to offer many opportunities for profitable trade. "We understand," wrote the governor and committee to Simpson in 1822, "that hitherto the trade of the Columbia has not been profitable, and from all that we have learnt on the subject we are not sanguine in our expectations of being able to make it so in future." Nevertheless, Simpson was encouraged to look into the matter. This he had already begun to do. In August, 1821, two chief factors and two chief traders—three of them former North West Company men—had been assigned to the Columbia and preliminary reports were already reaching Simpson. These reports made it clear that the reasons for the unprofitability of the Columbia trade lay not in poor fur resources but in low morale and inefficient operating methods. Simpson therefore recommended to the London committee that the Columbia should not be evacuated, arguing that, even if the district did not produce great profits, at least it was not likely to lose money, while continued activity by the Company in this area would serve to check opposition from American traders.

The Company's decision to continue operations in the Columbia and New Caledonia was taken not in the expectation that these operations would prove directly profitable but rather in the hope that they would enable the Company to maintain, as it were, a defence in depth against American and Russian competition, control the Columbia River gateway to the interior, and prevent either Russia or America from dominating the entire Pacific coastal strip. Throughout these years the Company maintained close communication with the British government, largely through the agency of Edward Ellice, and played an active role as an instrument of imperial policy. Little could be done, however, to build up a permanent trading organization in the area until its political status was clarified. A significant step in this direction was taken in 1825, when Britain and Russia agreed that the southern boundary of Russian Alaska should be at 54° 40′ north latitude. There remained the problem of securing agreement between the United States and Britain on the northern limit of American claims. Britain was prepared to accept the Columbia River as the boundary, but this was rejected by the United States. Discussions between Britain and the United States on this issue reached deadlock in July, 1824.

When it became clear that the boundary between British and American jurisdiction on the coast would certainly not be farther south than the Columbia River, the Hudson's Bay Company took prompt steps to exploit to the full the fur resources of the area which they would eventually have to evacuate. In July, 1824, chief factors Alexander Kennedy and John McLoughlin were appointed to the Columbia and in the winter of 1824-5 Simpson visited the area. Fort George (the former Astoria) on the south bank of the Columbia was abandoned and a new post, Fort Vancouver, was constructed on the north bank of the Columbia opposite the mouth of the Willamette River. Particular attention was directed to the Snake River region, south of the Columbia. "If properly managed," wrote Simpson with reference to this region, "no question exists that it would yield handsome profits as we have convincing proof that the country is a rich preserve of Beaver and which for political reasons we should endeavour to destroy as fast as possible." At the same time plans were put into effect to extend trading operations in New Caledonia with a view to cutting off supplies of furs which otherwise would find their way to the Russian posts on the coast.

On Simpson's departure in March, 1825, McLoughlin assumed sole charge of the Columbia district. Systematic planning for the exploitation of his territory was still frustrated by continuing political uncertainties. The joint-occupancy agreement was due to expire in 1828 and for a time it seemed probable that after that date the Company would find itself excluded from the territory south of the Columbia—an eventuality which, in McLoughlin's opinion, would destroy any prospects of carrying on a profitable trade on the Pacific coast. In these circumstances he could do little beyond transfer the more important posts to new sites north of the Columbia, explore the potentialities of the country to the north, particularly in the region of the Fraser and Thompson Rivers, and exploit as best he could, by means of annual expeditions, the fur resources of the disputed territory to the south.

Trading and trapping expeditions to the rich Snake River region south of the Columbia brought the Company into direct competition with American traders but nevertheless, under the capable leadership of Peter Skene Ogden, proved highly productive. Serious difficulties at first arose from large-scale desertions to American traders of the personnel employed on these expeditions, who were mostly not permanent employees but halfbreeds and Indians engaged by the season who were usually heavily in debt to the Company. Increases in the prices allowed for furs and decreases in the prices charged for supplies did much to check this tendency, but nevertheless it was symptomatic of the difficulties involved in transferring practices worked out in monopolistic territory east of the Rockies to the competitive conditions of the Pacific coast. McLoughlin also found it advisable to allow his subordinates considerably wider latitude in arranging the timing of their expeditions than was permitted east of the Rockies. In this period, however, American competition on land, though a source of considerable annoyance, did not prove a serious threat. Although American traders generally offered higher prices for furs, the Company could afford to undersell them in the prices charged for supplies. This competitive advantage was a result of the Company's lower transport costs, since it imported supplies for the Columbia by sea whereas American traders had to bring in their supplies over land. American maritime competition, as we shall see, was a more serious matter.

In August, 1827, the joint-occupancy agreement between the United States and Great Britain was renewed for an indefinite period. This permitted McLoughlin to organize the Snake River expeditions on a more regular basis. Large quantities of high-quality furs were obtained annually from this region, and trapping parties were in the field almost the whole year round. Trading and exploring parties were also sent farther south and penetrated to the Sacramento valley, but returns from this area were never very large. Sporadic attempts were also made to develop the coastal trade to the north, where American trading ships were active. For this purpose it was necessary to build up an inventory of supplies and to increase the number of ships. The schooner *Cadboro* went to the Fraser River in 1827 and established Fort Langley. In 1830 the brig *Eagle* went to the Nass River and in 1834 an unsuccessful attempt was made to establish a post on the Stikine River, which was within Russian territorial limits. A steamboat, the *Beaver,* arrived on the Pacific coast in 1836; by this date the Company had no less than seven vessels regularly engaged in the coastal trade.

These additions to the Company's fleet made it possible to extend trading operations to the north and offer competition to American trading vessels. Compared to the Americans, however, the Company worked under serious disadvantages. It proved difficult to secure experienced sailors and even more difficult to find competent sea captains. The wrecking of the Company's supply ships at the mouth of the Columbia in 1829 and again in 1830 cut down the scale of operations which could be undertaken in these and the immediately following years. Not until 1830 did McLoughlin have the year's inventory of supplies necessary for the equipping of coastal expeditions. McLoughlin, too, had little faith in the profitability of the coastal trade, preferring wherever possible to establish permanent posts on land.

One very important difference between the operations of the American maritime traders and those of the Company's ships lay in the characteristics of the different trading systems in which they were involved. The American ships had no permanent bases on the Pacific coast; their fur-trading operations in this area were merely one component in a far-flung system of exchange which took them from American ports on the Atlantic coast (principally Boston), round Cape Horn to the Hawaiian Islands and the Pacific northwest, thence to China, and thence, after a voyage which usually lasted three years, back to their home ports. This flexible and highly competitive trading system depended for its profitability upon the securing of intermediate cargoes. Furs obtained on the Pacific coast (largely in exchange for supplies sold to the Russians) were sold in China and the proceeds used to purchase silk, tea, and other products which could be sold in the United States. The acute problem of securing balanced cargoes on each link of this multilateral trade explains the eagerness of American maritime traders to fill their ships with furs before making for Canton.

The operations of the Hudson's Bay Company's ships on the Pacific coast, in contrast, were ancillary to the operations of permanent establishments on land. The policies of the Company had been evolved with reference to the needs of an organization which was continental rather than maritime in its outlook. Whereas the American ships arrived at the start and departed at the end of the season, the Company's personnel remained in the area the whole year round. One consequence of this was a marked difference in trading methods and in policy toward the Indians. For obvious reasons of security, it was the policy of the Company to restrict the sale of fire-arms and liquor to the Indians. The American coastal traders had no such scruples and did not hesitate to sell arms and alcohol if by so doing they could get furs which otherwise would have gone to the Company. Faced with competition of this type the Company was forced to raise the prices offered for furs and finally to follow the example of the Americans. In this as in other respects, competition led to a reversion to old North West Company tactics.

The problem of unbalanced cargoes, of course, plagued the Company as well as the American traders. One attempt to solve this problem took the form of encouraging the development of local sources of supply, particularly of agricultural products, in order to reduce incoming cargoes. A determined effort was also made, however, to expand the Company's maritime trading activities, and in particular to break into the Canton market. The major difficulty here lay in the fact that the East India Company enjoyed, under the terms of its charter, exclusive rights to British trade in this area. It was not possible for the Hudson's Bay Company to ship furs directly to Canton and sell them there for its own account. For the first few years after 1821, therefore, the Company followed the practice of consigning beaver to Perkins and Company, a Boston mercantile firm with an agency in Canton, and thus evaded the East India Company's monopoly. Perkins and Company then shipped return cargoes to Boston and credited the Company with the proceeds. This arrangement proved satisfactory as a temporary expedient and provided the Company with an alternative market when fur prices in London were low. But an attempt was also made to come to terms with the East India Company. Simpson in particular believed that some arrangement between the two companies which would permit the Hudson's Bay Company to market its furs directly in Canton was essential if American maritime competition was to be checked. For a time he was hopeful of success, since the competition of these American traders was as much of a nuisance to the East India Company in Canton as it was to the Hudson's Bay Company on the Pacific coast. Negotiations between the two chartered companies ended in failure, however, and after 1828 even the limited trade which had been carried on through the Boston firm appears to have ceased. This failure to secure access to the Canton market seriously weakened the Company's position on the Pacific coast.

While the policy of the London committee of the Company toward American traders was one of uncompromising opposition, toward the Russian-American Fur Company a more conciliatory line was followed. This was partly because both companies had a long-term interest in the area and therefore would benefit by coming to terms with each other, but also, as far as the Hudson's Bay Company was concerned, it was part of the attempt to check American competition. The Russian-American Company was badly handicapped by supply difficulties and had adopted a policy of purchasing supplies from American trading vessels in exchange for furs. Many American ships, indeed, relied upon this trade in supplies to provide them with the furs which they later sold in China. An agreement between the two companies by which the Hudson's Bay Company would undertake to provide the Russian organization with supplies, in return for trading concessions, promised to check American maritime competition more effectively than any direct measures of retaliation.

In 1829 Simpson wrote to Wrangel, the Russian governor at Sitka, informing him that the Hudson's Bay Company intended to extend its trading operations northward along the coast and offering to supply the Russian company with English manufactured goods, cereals, and meat. Wrangel replied that he had no authority to accept such a proposal and suggested that a direct approach should be made to the headquarters of the Russian-American Company in St. Petersburg. The London committee then opened direct negotiations with St. Petersburg, offering to supply the Russians at cost price with whatever quantity of English products they might require for their operations in the North Pacific area, but the Russian reaction was unenthusiastic. A favourable opportunity to raise the matter again did not occur until 1834. In that year the brig *Dryad* attempted to establish a post on the Stikine River but was turned back by the Russians. McLoughlin alleged that the Company suffered a loss of over £22,000 in consequence. This incident and the Company's claim for damages (since British ships had been guaranteed free navigation of the Stikine by the convention of 1825) provided the excuse for appealing to the Foreign Office to apply diplomatic pressure on the Russians. After lengthy negotiations agreement was finally reached in 1839. Under its terms the Russians agreed to cease all trading activities in the mainland portion of the Alaska "panhandle" (the strip of coast about 350 miles in length between the Portland Canal and Mount Fairweather) and to lease this area to the Hudson's Bay Company for a period of ten years. In return, the Hudson's Bay Company agreed to pay an annual rent of 2,000 land-otter skins and to supply the Russians with stated quantities of wheat, flour, butter, pork, and other foodstuffs. This agreement was renewed periodically until Alaska was purchased by the United States in 1867.

The most important immediate result of this agreement was to free the Hudson's Bay Company from competition in the north, both from the Russians and from the Americans. Since the Russians had evacuated their posts and now obtained their supplies from the Hudson's Bay Company, the trade in supplies which had made it profitable for American vessels to visit the coast came to an end. American maritime competition had in any case been decreasing in vigour since about 1834, partly because of the activities of the Company's ships; after 1839 it was of negligible importance.

The agreement with the Russians also provided an opportunity for a reorganization of the Company's trading system. McLoughlin's plan was to construct a chain of trading-posts from Puget Sound to the far north; Forts Langley, Simpson, and McLoughlin had already been established with this end in view. Simpson, however, who visited the area in 1841, was decidedly of the opinion that all the posts except Fort Simpson should be abandoned and the trade carried on by means of the Company's steamship, the *Beaver*, which he proposed should make trips six times a year along the coast and collect furs from the Indians. This policy would, he believed, permit a reduction in personnel, increase the quantity of furs obtained (since many of the more remote tribes would find it difficult to visit the permanent posts) and save the Company upwards of £4,000 a year. McLoughlin vigorously opposed Simpson's proposals but was overruled by the governor and committee of the Company in London. In 1842 he received orders to abandon Forts Taku and McLoughlin and to construct a new depot on the southern end of Vancouver Island (later named Fort Victoria). These instructions were, of course, carried out, but conflict between Simpson and McLoughlin continued and was exacerbated by Simpson's seemingly callous reaction to the murder of McLoughlin's son, an employee of the Company, by his men in April, 1842. Relations between the two men grew increasingly bitter from this time until McLoughlin's removal from office as superintendent of the Columbia Department in 1845.

The rift between McLoughlin and Simpson developed partly because the two men had very different conceptions of the economic future of the Pacific coast and of the role which the Company was to play in that future. Simpson appears to have felt that the progress of settlement would before very long render the Company's position in the area untenable; he was concerned, therefore, not to expand the Company's fixed investment more than was strictly necessary. The whole fur trade of the Pacific coast was for him a limited commitment—a sphere of action by no means to be neglected, but at the same time one in which it would be imprudent of the Company to involve itself too deeply or too irrevocably. McLoughlin on the other hand tended to attach more importance to the long-term interests of the region for which he was responsible. His continued hostility to the idea of carrying on the fur trade by means of coastal shipping was not unconnected with an awareness that such a policy would inevitably limit exploration, settlement, and permanent occupation.

To a certain extent diversification of the Company's economic activities on the Pacific coast was called for by both policies. Simpson, as we have noticed, attached considerable importance to the development of agriculture in the immediate vicinity of the posts as a means of reducing imports. Several small farms were in fact established in the Columbia valley before 1839, that at Fort Vancouver producing in 1832 no less than 3,500 bushels of wheat, 3,000 of barley, 3,000 of peas, 15,000 of potatoes, and 2,000 of oats. The signing of the agreement with the Russians greatly increased the demand for agricultural products and led to the formation of the Puget's Sound Agricultural Company in 1839. This corporation was legally independent of the Hudson's Bay Company but in effect it was a subsidiary. McLoughlin, who had proposed as early as 1832 that such a company should be formed, was put in charge of its local management. As a commercial venture the Puget's Sound Company was not very successful, and McLoughlin frequently had serious difficulty in meeting the deliveries called for in the Russian agreement.

Encouragement to agriculture was accompanied by attempts to build up a more diversified export trade. In 1827 McLoughlin had suggested that a trade in salmon and timber should be developed between the Columbia, the Sandwich Islands, and California. He pointed out that, since the coastal fur trade was a seasonal affair so far as shipping was concerned, the Company's ships and their crews could easily be employed in this wider trade when they would otherwise be unemployed, and that it was essential to exploit all the available resources of the Columbia area if the Company was to compete successfully with American traders. Simpson supported this proposal, and various experiments in the production and marketing of products other than fur were tried in the following years. Small shipments of dried salmon had been sent to England for some years, but they had invariably deteriorated during the long voyage. Trial shipments sent to California and the Sandwich Islands seem to have been more profitable. Proceeds from the sale of salmon and timber in the Sandwich Islands were used to buy an American ship there in 1832. On the whole, however, these attempts at diversification proved disappointing, not because the resources were unavailable, but because the Company had neither the personnel nor the organization necessary to handle a complex trade covering a variety of commodities destined for a number of different markets. Success in the fur trade, as the French had discovered long before, demanded concentration on a single product.

The Company's lack of success in developing a diversified economic base on the Pacific coast reduced its ability to delay or resist American immigration. Individual American fur-traders in the Columbia and Snake River areas had presented little threat, since the Company could usually undersell them and drive them out of business. But the situation was different with regard to American immigrants who came not to trade but to settle. Against these immigrants the weapons of commercial competition were ineffective. In the Columbia district as elsewhere settlement and the fur trade were irreconcilable; with American settlers pouring in across the Oregon Trail by the early 1840's, the Company had no alternative but to beat an orderly but reluctant retreat northward.

The issue of the Company's policy toward settlement in the Columbia district had been raised as early as 1828, when McLoughlin had been faced with the problem of how to deal with freemen and discharged servants of the Company who wished to settle in the fertile Willamette valley. Attempts to prevent or discourage the formation of a small farming colony in this area were unsuccessful, and by the early 1830's it was taken for granted by both Simpson and McLoughlin that the most they could hope to do was to discourage large-scale immigration into the Willamette settlement and try to keep the settlers friendly toward the Company. In neither of these aims were they long successful. Intense American interest in the area—which, in the eyes of many Americans, was already part of the United States—combined with the activities of American Methodist missionaries, led to a steady influx of settlers in the late 1830's and early 1840's. The population of the Willamette settlement grew from 51 adult males in 1838 to 126 adult males in 1841, the total population in the latter year being about 500. In 1842 about 140 persons arrived, and in 1843 the arrival of several large parties of immigrants increased the population by more than 850 persons in a single year. Even larger parties arrived in the years following. In spite of McLoughlin's opposition and the passive resistance of those members of the settlement who had formerly been servants of the Company, a provisional government was organized in May, 1843. At first this government claimed jurisdiction only over the country south of the Columbia; in December, 1844, however, it decided to extend its jurisdiction north of the river. This raised the question of its jurisdiction over the Company. Recognition of the authority of the provisional government in some respects was, McLoughlin felt, unavoidable, since otherwise there would be no peaceful way of protecting the Company's property, recovering debts owed to the Company by American settlers, or preventing desertions on the part of the Company's servants. An agreement was therefore worked out according to which the Company agreed to pay taxes on business done with the local settlers.

The expansion of American settlement made it obvious that agreement between Britain and the United States on the boundary question could not long be delayed. The perpetuation of the joint-occupancy agreement was no longer in the Company's interests, even had it been possible in the light of contemporary expansionist sentiment in the United States. The Snake River area had been thoroughly cleaned out; fur resources in the area south and immediately north of the Columbia River were dwindling rapidly. As early as 1841 Simpson warned the governor and committee in London that it was no longer realistic to hope that the boundary would be drawn along the line of the Columbia River; it was far more likely, he felt, that the United States would insist upon a line through the Straits of Juan de Fuca and thence east roughly along the 48th parallel. Actually Simpson was optimistic in hoping even for this latter line. A strong body of opinion in the United States sought to have the Oregon boundary set not at the Columbia, nor at the line Simpson envisaged, nor at the 49th parallel which formed the boundary across the rest of the western half of the continent, but at 54° 40′ north latitude, the southern boundary of Russian sovereignty. Such a boundary, of course, would have denied British North America any access to the Pacific coast whatsoever. For a time it looked as if this demand would be strongly pressed. James K. Polk, an enthusiastic expansionist, won the Democratic nomination for President in 1844 and proceeded to campaign under the aggressive slogan "Fifty-four forty or fight". When elected, however, he proved less intransigent, partly because a war with Mexico over the annexation of Texas was then pending. A British offer to accept the 49th parallel as the Oregon boundary opened the way for a compromise and, after a certain amount of political manoeuvring, was accepted by Polk. A treaty based on the British offer was signed on 15 June, 1846.

After the signing of the treaty the Company's principal base on the Pacific coast was moved from Fort Vancouver on the Columbia to Fort Victoria on Vancouver Island, and the whole area was put under the charge of chief factor James Douglas, a very capable administrator who had formerly been McLoughlin's chief assistant. The Company retained certain trading interests in the new state of Oregon and in the Territory of Washington, but it was deprived by the treaty of its important agricultural bases at Cowlitz and Nisqually. Attention was therefore directed to developing Vancouver Island as an agricultural and administrative centre, while the focus of fur-trading activity shifted northward to the Fraser and Thompson Rivers. As the Company could no longer use the Columbia River as its main transport route to the interior, the Fraser acquired a new importance.

Meanwhile considerable pressure was being exerted on the British government to encourage the formation of a British colony on the Pacific coast. The directors of the Hudson's Bay Company were naturally anxious that any colony established in this area should be under their control, and with this end in view informed the government that the Company stood ready to receive a grant of all the territories north and west of Rupert's Land which belonged to the Crown. Critics of the Company, on the other hand, pointed out that its record for promoting settlement was hardly an encouraging one, and argued that only by the formation of a vigorous independent colony could British title to the Pacific coast region be made secure. Finally, in the face of considerable parliamentary opposition, a royal grant ceded Vancouver Island to the Company in January, 1849, for an annual rent of seven shillings, on condition that a colony of emigrants from Britain or British possessions should be formed there within five years. No grant of territory on the mainland was made to the Company at this time.

The first governor appointed to the new colony, Richard Blanshard, was not connected with the Company and largely for this reason found himself practically without authority. His resignation in April, 1851, was followed by the appointment of Douglas, who thus became the official representative both of the Company and of the Crown. Progress in forming the colony was very slow. Despite the Company's official undertaking to promote settlement, little in the way of positive encouragement was given. In the absence of such encouragement, the inaccessibility of the colony, the lack of markets, the high price charged for land, and, after 1849, the competing attractions of the California gold-field resulted in a painfully slow rate of growth. A few Scots miners were brought over by the Company to work the Nanaimo coal deposits and some of them remained as settlers. Employees of the Company and a very few independent settlers formed the remainder of the colony.

GOLD AND COLONIZATION

The discovery of gold on the Fraser River in 1856-7 completely transformed the situation. As a staple product, gold had certain characteristics in common with furs—its high value, for example, in relation to its weight, the ready market which it commanded in Europe and elsewhere, and its ability to bear the costs of long-distance transportation—but it required a much larger labour force, it did not involve dependence upon the Indians, and it demanded a very different transport and supply organization. Against settlement based on subsistence agriculture, the Hudson's Bay Company had been able to fight a relatively successful delaying action; settlement based on gold, however, was a development with which a fur-trading organization was not equipped to deal.

A minor gold-rush to the Queen Charlotte Islands in 1852 enabled Douglas to consult with the Colonial Office as to the policy to be pursued in such circumstances. Fearing that the arrival of large numbers of American miners from California would threaten British sovereignty over the area, Douglas sought permission to exclude foreigners from trade. This was refused, but Douglas was appointed lieutenant-governor of the Islands and was instructed to require prospectors and miners to take out licences and pay suitable fees. By the time these instructions arrived the gold-rush to the Islands had ended, but when news of the discovery of gold on the Fraser reached Victoria in 1856 the policy which the Colonial Office had indicated was promptly put into force. In view of the excitement to which the news gave rise in California, Oregon, and Washington Territory, any attempt to exclude or restrict American prospectors would certainly have caused serious trouble. The problem which Douglas faced was not so much whether or not to restrict the influx of Americans miners, but how to preserve a minimum framework of law and order in territory over which he had no political authority. Douglas was governor only of Vancouver Island; on the mainland, although he exercised considerable influence through his position in the Hudson's Bay Company, he had at first no political jurisdiction whatsoever.

A large-scale influx of American miners got under way in April, 1858. By this time placer-mining in California had given way to hydraulic sluicing and quartz-mining, which did not require such a large labour force, and large numbers of prospectors and miners, as well as others with no previous experience in the gold-fields, were available to exploit the new discoveries on the Fraser. The fact that these discoveries were in British territory was no deterrent. By the middle of August, 1858, between twenty-five and thirty thousand persons had arrived at the mouth of the Fraser, most of them having set out from San Francisco. Victoria itself rapidly acquired all the characteristics of a boom town; land values soared and many new mercantile businesses were established.

James Douglas made no attempt to limit this sudden immigration beyond trying to enforce a system of mining licences. Mindful, however, of the interests of the Company he served, he attempted to establish a monopoly of the trade in supplies on the Fraser River, the only means of access to the diggings. In May, 1858, he issued a proclamation which stated that any person attempting to ship supplies up the Fraser for trade without the permission of the Hudson's Bay Company was violating the Company's exclusive trading privileges and would be prosecuted. At the same time he entered into negotiations with the Pacific Mail Steamship Company, an American concern which wished to operate freight and passenger steamers on the lower reaches of the river. According to the agreement which was proposed, these steamers were to carry only Hudson's Bay Company freight and were to pay to the Company two dollars for every passenger carried up the Fraser. In return, the Steamship Company was to be granted exclusive rights to the river transport business.

This arrangement, if carried out, would certainly have proved highly profitable to the Company. Douglas had, however, overstepped his authority and the Colonial Secretary promptly disallowed both his proclamation and the proposed agreement with the Steamship Company. Douglas was reminded that the Hudson's Bay Company was entitled to the exclusive trade with the Indians but possessed no other rights or privileges whatsoever. No obstacle was to be placed in the way of foreign vessels unloading passengers or freight at the mouth of the Fraser, so long as the goods landed were not prohibited under the customs laws. Since it was necessary to maintain the principle that the navigation of the Fraser was open in law to British vessels only, Douglas was to require American and other foreign vessels to obtain a licence from him as the local representative of the Crown. But he was explicitly warned that he was under no circumstances to use his political office to promote the interests of the Company.

The anomalous situation caused by Douglas' lack of authority on the mainland was rectified by his appointment as governor of the new colony of British Columbia, created by an Act of August 2, 1858. In accepting this appointment, Douglas severed all connection with the Hudson's Bay Company, but continued as governor of the separate colony of Vancouver Island. At the same time the Hudson's Bay Company's exclusive rights to trade were revoked in so far as they applied to the territory of British Columbia.

Douglas' principal concerns were the maintenance of law and order among the miners, the prevention of violence between the miners and the Indians, and the improvement of transport facilities from the coast to the upper reaches of the Fraser. The miners themselves proved remarkably peaceable and law-abiding; lynch law and vigilante justice, which had been common in the California gold-fields, were almost non-existent on the Fraser. Part of the reason for this was undoubtedly Douglas's firm but tactful handling of the situation, but it should also be remembered that, since the Fraser provided the only means of escape from the diggings, opportunities for a wanted criminal to evade capture were limited. Many of the miners, too, had had considerable experience in California and were able to draw up and enforce informal codes of mining regulations for their own governance. As regards relations with the Indians, Douglas feared that, in the event of a general Indian uprising, the American miners would appeal to their own government for protection, thus affording a convenient pretext for American annexation of the whole of British Columbia. A few potentially explosive situations of this kind did in fact develop, particularly in the early days of the gold-rush, but, with the assistance of a detachment of Royal Engineers sent out from England, Douglas was able to deal with them successfully.

The first gold discoveries had been on the Thompson River, the Fraser's major tributary, but the sand-bars on the lower reaches of the Fraser were the scene of most of the early prospecting. As these were gradually occupied or worked out, the miners moved farther and farther up the river until by 1859 the focus of activity had reached Quesnel Lake. In 1861 the major rush to the Cariboo got under way. As the miners moved farther inland, the difficulty of bringing in supplies increased. There were no roads; a few Indian trails and the Fraser, where it was navigable, provided the only means of access. Steamboats could travel upriver as far as Yale, but beyond that supplies had to be transported overland. Prices at the miners' camps, in consequence, were extremely high. At Fort Hope on the Fraser a barrel of flour sold for $60 in the summer of 1858, while at Barkerville in the Cariboo, in the spring of 1862, the price is said to have reached $300 per barrel. To reduce these costs, and at the same time to maintain political control over the scattered camps, improvement of transport facilities was indispensable.

To avoid the almost impassable canyons on the Fraser above Yale, a new route was opened up in 1858, largely by volunteer labour, which followed the line of the Harrison and Lillooet Rivers from a point about thirty-five miles above New Westminster to the town of Lillooet on the upper Fraser. This route was very extensively used until 1864, when the Cariboo road was opened for traffic. This road led from Yale to the junction of the Fraser and Thompson Rivers, thence up the Thompson to the town of Ashcroft, and thence north to Quesnel and Barkerville in the Cariboo. Constructed through very difficult country at a cost of $1¼ million, the Cariboo road opened up a through route for freight wagons and fast coaches from the head of steamboat navigation at Yale to the heart of the gold-fields. Transport costs were sharply reduced. The cost of freight from Yale to Camerontown fell from 60 cents a pound in 1863 to 30 cents in 1864 and 15 cents in 1865.

It is estimated that by 1859 the population of British Columbia had increased to 17,000, excluding Indians, but the total varied considerably from year to year and from season to season. By 1861 it had fallen to about 5,000. The quantity of gold produced is very difficult to estimate, since no complete record was kept, but a figure of $25 million has been suggested as the total for the period 1859-71. After 1865, with the decline of placer-mining, the total yield fell off rapidly. For a time, therefore, the economy of the province was highly productive. This did not mean, however, that a firm base had been laid for sustaining a high rate of growth in the future. Of the immigrants attracted by the gold discoveries, only a minority remained as settlers. Of the stores, banks, and other ancillary businesses set up to facilitate the exploitation of the gold-fields, only a few remained after the yield of gold declined. Of the wealth produced on the Fraser and in the Cariboo, only a small fraction was channelled off and invested in other types of economic activity within the province. As gold yields declined, the enduring problem of diversifying the economic life of the province and integrating it into the economy of North America and the Pacific reappeared. This problem, which the hectic prosperity of the gold discoveries had obscured but not solved, was now aggravated by the difficulty of adjusting the colony to a slower rate of growth and to the secular decline of the two staples—fur and gold—upon which it had been built.

These difficulties were reflected in the public finances of the colony. Even during the height of the gold-rushes it had not been easy to meet the expenses of government. The only important sources of revenue were land sales, a customs tariff of 10 per cent, and the liquor and mining licences. An export duty on gold proved impossible to collect and was repealed in 1865. These sources of revenue produced sums which increased from $291,980 in 1861 to $442,985 in 1862, $554,390 in 1863, $520,495 in 1864 and $580,530 in 1865. During each of these years there was a substantial budget deficit. A debt of about $1¼ million had been incurred, mostly to contractors, for the construction of the Cariboo road. To pay off this debt as rapidly as possible, Douglas authorized a system of tolls on the traffic which used the road. But there were limits beyond which a policy of making public improvements pay their own way was not practicable and the funded debt of the province rose steadily, from a mere $26,000 in 1860 to $610,000 in 1863, $820,800 in 1864, and $1,189,830 in 1865.

Such an increase in debt would have been no cause for concern if the prosperity of the colony had not been based so exclusively on gold. But by 1866 the great days of placer-mining were over, immigration ceased, and the revenue from import duties, the mainstay of the public finances, fell off sharply. In these circumstances, with agriculture and industry practically non-existent and the only available markets shut off by the American tariff or the long voyage round Cape Horn, the burden of the debt became a heavy one. Partly as an economy measure, the colonies of Vancouver Island and British Columbia were united in 1866, but this could bring no permanent relief. The need of the colony on the Pacific coast was for immigrants, capital, and markets. Only by union with some larger and richer economic system could these be obtained. To British Columbia, a province on the verge of bankruptcy, only two choices were open: annexation by the United States, or confederation with the other British colonies in North America.

THE COLONY AT THE RED RIVER

Meanwhile at the Red River, half-way across the continent, Lord Selkirk's colony was struggling to establish itself. With the union of the Hudson's Bay Company and the North West Company, the earlier dangers of forcible expulsion were removed, and efforts were made to develop the colony as a source of agricultural and labour supplies for the fur trade. Trading personnel rendered superfluous by the amalgamation were encouraged to settle at Fort Garry, as it was expected that they would form a stable element in the colony and remain well disposed to the Company. Partly as a result of this policy, partly through the arrival of a large party of Swiss immigrants, the population of the settlement doubled between 1820 and 1822. By 1826 it had passed 2,000.

In 1818, 1819, and to a lesser extent in 1820, locust plagues devastated the crops of the colony and seed grain had to be brought in from Prairie du Chien on the Mississippi. A severe flood in 1826 caused extensive damage and resulted in a loss of population. Many of the Swiss settlers made their way to the United States, while a number of the French departed for Lower Canada. Despite these setbacks, by the early 1830's the colony had achieved a certain degree of economic stability and permanence. Governor Simpson of the Hudson's Bay Company, who had referred to the flood of 1826 as "an extinguisher to the hope of Red River ever retaining the name of Settlement", was able to report within a few years that the colony was "in the most perfect state of tranquillity" and enjoying considerable prosperity. Under these circumstances the officers of the Company, who in the years immediately following 1821 had been decidedly unfriendly to the colony, began to take a more positive interest in its welfare, and in 1835 the sixth Earl of Selkirk agreed to sell the Assiniboia grant back to the Company for the sum of £84,111 sterling.

By this date the Company's fur-trading operations were significantly dependent upon the settlement as a source of labour and agricultural supplies. Pemmican, biscuit, cheese, butter, and many other products were regularly purchased by the Company from the settlers and distributed throughout the trading area east of the Rockies, thus enabling the Company to reduce its imports from England. Purchases of flour from the Red River settlement increased from 200 cwt. in 1825 to 1,200 cwt. in 1833. As regards labour supply, the brigades of York boats which operated between York Factory, Norway House, and the Red River were manned by settlers hired at the Red River settlement, as were the brigades which carried supplies for the Athabasca, Peace, and Mackenzie River districts. By hiring these settlers for the season and paying them by the "piece" (the unit in which trade goods were packed), the Company was spared the expense of maintaining a permanent labour force and was enabled to effect sharp reductions in transport costs. The freight per "piece" between York Factory and the Red River, for example, fell from 25s. in 1825 to 16s. in 1840.

But it was not only because of its growing importance as a source of labour and supplies that the Company desired to exercise direct control over the settlement. It was also because the settlers had shown a persistent tendency to ignore the Company's claims to exclusive trading rights. It was very difficult to prevent the settlers from trading with the Indians; many of them were experienced fur-traders and had little taste for the drudgery and disappointments of pioneer agriculture. The Company controlled the trade routes leading north from the settlement, but not those leading south to the Mississippi and Minnesota Rivers. The result was that after 1821 an active trade in furs and liquor developed between the Red River colony and American posts in what later became upper Minnesota.

The Company's attempt to prevent this trade at first proved unavailing. In 1821 and 1822 John Clarke, chief factor at Fort Garry, declared that all trade between the settlers and the Indians was illegal, and was supported in his stand by Governor Simpson. Any goods which the settlers might require were to be obtained from the Company's store; any furs which the Indians wished to dispose of were to be sold only to the Company. Bulger, governor of the colony, immediately protested to the executors of the Selkirk estate and to the governor of the Company in London, claiming that the settlers had the right to trade as they pleased. The governor of the Company supported Bulger, pointing out in a letter to Simpson that the Company had no right to prevent the Indians from trading in provisions or to prevent the settlers from obtaining furs for their own use.

From this time until 1835 the settlers at the Red River enjoyed practically complete freedom of trade. In practice, of course, so far as agricultural produce was concerned, the only available market was the Hudson's Bay Company, which purchased all that the settlers had to sell. The Company's store, too, was the cheapest source of supply for imported goods, which were sold to the settlers at the same prices as were charged the Company's personnel. This monopoly situation was the result not of any chartered rights, but of the colony's isolation. High transport costs prevented the settlers from seeking other markets for their produce and effectively excluded independent competition in the sale of imported goods. Had it not been for the market and the supply facilities provided by the fur trade, the colony could not have maintained itself.

The private trade in furs which was carried on by the settlers at Red River provided the only exception to the otherwise close economic control which the Company exercised over the colony. This private trade was never very extensive; it was no immediate threat to the profits of the Company. The reason why the Company attempted so strenuously to suppress it was that it represented the advance guard, so to speak, of American economic penetration north of the international boundary. Settlers at the Red River, particularly the *Métis* or half-breeds, secured furs from the Indians, usually in exchange for liquor, carried them by familiar routes across the frontier, and sold them to American traders at posts on the upper Mississippi and on the upper reaches of the Red River. One reason for the initial establishment of the Red River settlement had been to interpose a barrier to American penetration northwards. The development of close economic ties between the settlement and American traders threatened to convert what had been intended as a line of defence into a hostile salient. It was only a matter of a few years before the American agricultural frontier would extend to the upper Mississippi; when that happened, the tide of settlement, diverted northward by the high, dry lands to the west, would inevitably tend to flow down the fertile Red River valley and invade Assiniboia. This was the long-term danger which the private trade of the settlers at Red River ominously foreshadowed.

When the Company assumed direct control of the colony in 1835, one of its first acts was to impose a tariff of 7½ per cent on all imports and exports. Ostensibly intended to provide revenue for the civil government, this measure was actually designed to check the activities of the private traders. Reduced to 5 per cent in 1836 and to 4 per cent in 1837, the tariff aroused considerable resentment among the settlers. It proved largely ineffective as a means of checking the smuggling trade and was later supplemented by more direct repressive action. Consignments of goods sent out of the colony were carefully examined and frequently confiscated; a system of mail censorship was introduced; the houses of persons suspected of smuggling were searched, force being used if necessary; and a new form of land deed was devised, which compelled anyone receiving land from the Company to undertake that he would not engage in trade in furs, skins, or dressed leather. Persons known to be engaged in the illegal fur trade were denied the privilege of importing goods from England in the Company's ships.

Despite these repressive measures, private trade grew in volume. Furs and skins sold at American posts brought much higher prices than they did at the posts of the Hudson's Bay Company, so that the trade was profitable enough to offset the serious risks involved. Pembina, on the American side of the international boundary, developed into an important trading centre where merchandise destined for Red River was stored until it could be smuggled across the border. In 1843 the American Fur

Company, with posts at Pembina and Grand Forks, established a line of carts between Pembina and St. Paul on the Mississippi to handle the Red River trade; by the end of the 1840's this transport system was carrying furs valued at about $20,000 annually. Other American trading companies established themselves at Pembina and carried on a regular trade with Red River. After 1844, according to a contemporary account, almost every person in the Red River settlement who had any means traded in furs.

Faced by overt defiance of its trading regulations and by a growing reluctance on the part of the police and magistrates to take action against offenders, the Company was driven to seek more direct means of enforcing its policies. An opportunity was provided by the Oregon crisis of 1846, when fear of American attack induced the British government to send a detachment of troops to Fort Garry. Military government was proclaimed in the colony in the fall of 1846, and for the next two years the private trade in furs was effectively halted. The withdrawal of the garrison in 1848, however, was followed by renewed activity on the part of private traders and by considerable popular agitation against Company control. The conflict came to a head in 1849 with the arrest of four settlers on charges of private trading. Amid intense excitement, several hundred armed settlers threatened to take the law into their own hands and succeeded in inducing the presiding magistrate, a salaried employee of the Company, to dismiss the cases. This was interpreted by the settlers to mean that trade would thenceforth be free and that the Company had given up its claim to exclusive trading rights. It was in fact clear that nothing short of the presence of troops could put a stop to private trading. The Company therefore abandoned its attempts to enforce its monopoly in the Red River area and permitted the settlers to trade as they chose.

By this time (1849) the settlement had a population of 5,291, with over 6,000 acres of land under cultivation. In spite of the conflict generated over the issue of private trade, the development of the colony was probably limited less by the repressive policies of the Company than by inadequate transport facilities and the lack of an exportable staple. The stubborn resistance of the settlers to restrictions on private trading in furs was in large part a reflection of the fact that there was no other product available which could stand the cost of transportation to outside markets.

During the early years of the settlement a series of determined efforts had been made to find a staple product around which an economically self-sustaining colony would be built. For a time considerable attention was given to wool. A buffalo wool company was established to dress skins and weave coarse cloth for the local market and to export the finer wool to England. The product failed to win acceptance in England, however, and the company went into bankruptcy in 1825. An experimental farm was established on the Assiniboine River above Fort Garry and stocked at considerable expense with cattle, horses, and sheep, only to collapse through mismanagement in 1822. Attempts were also made to bring in sheep from Missouri and Kentucky, a tallow company was founded, and flax-growing was encouraged. Each of these experiments represented an effort to find a product for which there was a demand in England, Canada, or the United States, which could be produced by the settlers, and which was sufficiently high in value in relation to weight to stand the costs of transport from the settlement to the outside market; each of them ended in failure. Any margin of profit which remained after all transport costs had been paid was swallowed up by inefficient management.

Transport costs also ruled out wheat as a staple export. A transport system which was adequate for the fur trade was not adequate for a bulky and low-valued commodity like wheat. Climatic difficulties, too, limited the development of wheat cultivation. It is estimated that on the average the wheat used at Red River took 137 days to mature. Only in exceptional years could the harvest begin before the middle of September. The risk of damage by frost or high winds was therefore great.

The experience with wheat cultivation in the Red River area coloured the attitude of the Hudson's Bay Company officers and of other informed observers to the eventual prospect of large-scale settlement in the prairie territories. In 1857 a select committee of the British House of Commons conducted a careful inquiry into the affairs of the Company and incidentally devoted considerable attention to the possibility of colonizing the areas which the Company controlled. It was notable that those witnesses who had the most intimate acquaintance with the Red River colony were most sceptical about the feasibility of agricultural settlement in the prairies. This was not to be ascribed solely to the fur-traders' traditional hostility to settlement; it reflected also the disappointments and difficulties of agriculture at the Red River colony over more than a quarter of a century. No doubt it was true, as some critics urged, that the Company had not done all in its power to encourage agriculture in the settlement. No doubt the market provided by the fur trade was neither very large nor very lucrative. No doubt information about the climate and soil of the prairies was sadly inadequate. But it remained true, then as now, that extensive cereal cultivation on the prairies was not possible without both cheap transportation to the sea and an early-ripening wheat. Neither of these prerequisites was available to the Red River farmers in 1857. Red Fife wheat, developed in the early 1840's, was still sown only in parts of Upper Canada and New York. Canada's railway system still terminated at the Detroit River.

THE WEST ENTERS CONFEDERATION

In 1867, when the British North America Act was passing the British Parliament, and the colonies of Canada, New Brunswick, and Nova Scotia were preparing to unite in a single confederation, the governor of British Columbia sent a cablegram to the Colonial Office which read: "Can provision be made in the bill before parliament for the admission of British Columbia to Canadian confederation?" The answer which he received can hardly have been unexpected. The Colonial Office informed him that "the question must . . . await the time when the intervening territory now under the control of the Hudson's Bay Company shall have been incorporated with the confederation."

In Canada, particularly in Upper Canada, interest in the possibility of opening up the western prairies for settlement had been growing for more than a decade. Inseparably connected with this were proposals for a confederation of the British North American colonies and for the establishment of a single nation with dominion from sea to sea. Of the many factors which contributed to this grand design, not least important was a growing awareness that, if the prairies and the colony on the Pacific coast were not soon incorporated into a Canadian confederation, it was highly probable that they would be absorbed by the United States.

Both British Columbia and the Red River settlement were cut off from the other British colonies in North America by distance; both had developed close economic ties with the United States. Almost the entire external trade of British Columbia was with San Francisco, the focus of the trade routes of the Pacific and the terminus (in 1869) of the first transcontinental railway. Only a few ships each year arrived from England, while transportation eastward over land was confined to the fur trade. Immigration from Britain was almost non-existent; mail to Britain had to bear American postage stamps if it was to be taken out of the colony. When, in 1867, the United States purchased Alaska, British Columbia found herself sandwiched between American territory to the north and to the south; the nearest British possessions were Hong Kong to the west and the Red River settlement to the east. There was no future for the colony so long as it remained an isolated British outpost; every economic consideration seemed to point to annexation by the United States as the only practicable solution.

At the Red River settlement the same prospect appeared imminent. By the end of the 1850's even the Hudson's Bay Company had begun to bring in its supplies and mail from the south, using the routes which formerly had served the smuggling trade. When Governor Simpson wished to visit the colony, he took the train to Chicago. Trade between Fort Garry and St. Paul provided employment for fifteen hundred wagons, and steamboats had begun to ply on the river in 1859. By 1869 the governor of the colony had come to regard annexation by the United States as inevitable, and even stated his opinion that "it is for the interest of the settlers here that annexation should take place at once."

But annexation was not to come so easily. Both in British Columbia and at the Red River there were substantial sections of the population which found it impossible to regard with enthusiasm the prospect of absorption by the United States. And in Canada and Great Britain there were men in positions of influence who saw in confederation and westward expansion a possible solution to many seemingly insoluble difficulties. In the field of politics, confederation and transcontinental expansion promised an escape from the chronic situation of deadlock in the Canadian Parliament, where the development of the double-majority system had made it necessary for a government to obtain support from majorities of both the English- and the French-speaking members. And in the field of business, expansion to the west appeared to offer to the bankrupt Grand Trunk Railway almost the only prospect of eventual financial solvency. Political and economic necessities mutually reinforced each other; while the politicians of Canada and the maritime provinces, supported and encouraged by the British government, were moving cautiously in the direction of agreement, a small group of financiers were quietly consummating the sales of real estate which were to make the formation of a transcontinental dominion possible.

Edward W. Watkin, who became president of the Grand Trunk Railway in 1861, was convinced that the only solution to the road's continuing difficulties lay in expansion. His final goal was to make the Grand Trunk a transcontinental railroad, by constructing or leasing extensions eastward to Halifax and westward through Chicago and St. Paul to Red River and thence to the Pacific coast. To achieve this goal it was necessary to come to terms with the Hudson's Bay Company, through whose territory the line to the Pacific would have to run. As a first step in this direction Watkin proposed the construction of a transcontinental telegraph line, to be financed in part by the governments of Canada and British Columbia, and requested the Hudson's Bay Company to give a grant of land, consisting of a strip ten miles wide, along which the telegraph could run. This scheme was, of course, designed to prepare the way for the railway. The Company declined to consider the request.

As the Company seemed determined to block his plans, Watkin concluded that there was no alternative but to buy the Company. This was arranged without much difficulty. Thomas Baring and George Carr Glyn, London bankers to the Grand Trunk and the Canadian government, had in 1863 been associated with the establishment of the International Financial Society, an institution modelled on the famous French investment banking firm, the Crédit Mobilier, and this newly established Society was seeking attractive opportunities for investing its funds. The shares of the Hudson's Bay Company were held in relatively few hands and the Duke of Newcastle, the Colonial Minister, had already unofficially ascertained that they could be purchased for £1½ million, which was cheap to anyone thinking in terms of railways and settlement. Watkin, Baring and Glyn therefore agreed that the International Financial Society should purchase the property and charter of the Hudson's Bay Company for this amount. The sale was carried out in June, 1863.

This transaction put an entirely new complexion upon the problem of creating a transcontinental economy. The old Hudson's Bay Company, an organization which looked to the trade in furs for its profits, had been at best lukewarm, at worst hostile to settlement upon its domains. To the new Hudson's Bay Company, in contrast, the fur trade was almost a side-line; profits were to be made from sales of land incidental to the opening up of the west for large-scale settlement. Control over Rupert's Land was now vested in a group of men who had a direct interest in facilitating confederation and accelerating the process of westward expansion.

The British North America Act, uniting the provinces of Canada, New Brunswick, and Nova Scotia into a single confederation, passed the British Parliament in March, 1867, and went into effect on July 1st of that year. In June, 1869, the Canadian Parliament passed an act which provided for the temporary government of Rupert's Land and the northwest territory when united with Canada. Meanwhile negotiations had been proceeding between the Hudson's Bay Company, the imperial government, and the government of Canada to reach agreement upon the terms and date on which the Company's territories should be transferred from the Company to the Dominion of Canada. The terms finally agreed to were that the Company should surrender its charter to the Crown; as compensation for this surrender it was to receive from the government of Canada a cash payment of £300,000; in addition it was to retain one-twentieth part of the land in each township established in Rupert's Land, together with blocks of land surrounding each of its trading-posts. All titles to land already alienated by the Company were to be confirmed by Canada, and the Company was to be free to carry on its trade, as a private corporation, without hindrance.

The date originally set for the transfer was December 1, 1869, but unforeseen difficulties with the settlers at Red River forced delay. The sale of the Hudson's Bay Company to the International Financial Society had done much to lower the prestige of the Company among the settlers, while the fact that no consideration had been given to their interests had resulted in low morale among the Company's fur-trading personnel. The settlers regarded with suspicion the arrangements made for the government of the colony after its transfer to Canada; in particular they were concerned over the validity of their claims to the land which they occupied, since many of them, particularly the half-breeds, could produce no documentary evidence of ownership. The arrogance of a number of recent immigrants from Canada and the tactlessness of the Canadian government in sending surveying parties to the colony before the date of the transfer precipitated the appearance of organized resistance among the settlers. The future governor of the colony, William McDougall, was prevented from entering the settlement in October, 1869, and in November a party of half-breeds under the leadership of Louis Riel occupied Fort Garry and set up a provisional government. When December 1 arrived, therefore, the Canadian government refused to accept the transfer of the colony, as it was reluctant to shoulder the financial burden of suppressing the insurrection by force.

The task of finding a solution to this potentially explosive situation fell to the lot of Donald Smith (later Lord Strathcona), an officer of the Hudson's Bay Company, who was sent to Red River by the Canadian government as special commissioner in December, 1869. By February, 1870, Smith had succeeded in inducing the settlers to draw up a list of demands and to agree to send a delegation to Ottawa to discuss terms for the admission of the settlement to the Dominion. The most important of these demands, in the form in which they were finally presented to the Canadian government, were that the settlement should become a province enjoying equal rights with the other provinces, that it should be represented in both houses of the federal Parliament, that the arrangement of all local customs and usages (that is, matters of language, religion, and education) should be left to the control of the local legislature, that the property rights of the inhabitants should be respected, and that the lands and other natural resources should be under the control of the province and not of the Dominion. All these demands were accepted by the Canadian government in May, with the important exception that control of natural resources was reserved for the Dominion. The final agreement was ratified by the Canadian Parliament in the form of the Manitoba Act of 1870.

In June, 1870, the Hudson's Bay Company surrendered its charter to the Crown, the stipulated £300,000 was paid to the Company by the Canadian government, and Rupert's Land, together with the North West Territory, was transferred to the Dominion. The way was now clear for the admission of British Columbia also into the confederation. "It is quite clear," wrote Sir John A. Macdonald in 1869, "that no time should be lost . . . in putting the screws on Vancouver Island." The death in 1869 of Frederick Seymour, governor of the colony, who had been noticeably unenthusiastic toward confederation, was followed by the appointment of Anthony Musgrave with instructions from the British government to give his full support to the federation movement. Delegates from the province opened negotiations with the Canadian government in June, 1870, and reached agreement early in July. The Dominion government agreed to take over the debt of British Columbia and in addition to make a yearly grant of $35,000 plus 80 cents per head of the population (estimated in 1870 at 60,000) until the total population should reach

400,000, after which the grant would remain constant. In addition, since the per capita debt of British Columbia was less than those of the other provinces, the Dominion government was to pay to the province 5 per cent annually on the difference between the actual debt of British Columbia and a debt computed at the rate of $27.77 per capita (the rate already agreed upon for Nova Scotia and New Brunswick). The Dominion government also agreed to begin the construction of a transcontinental railroad to the Pacific coast within two years and to complete it in ten.

TRANSCONTINENTAL DOMINION: A NEW OPPORTUNITY

Throughout this period, from 1821 to 1870, the Hudson's Bay Company had played the role of a great conservative force, preserving under British influence isolated outposts of trade and settlement which formed the nuclei of territories eventually admitted to the Canadian confederation as provinces. If the Company had not been established on the Pacific coast when the tide of American immigration began to flow over the Oregon trail, it is more than doubtful whether the northern limit of American expansion could have been held at the 49th parallel. If a base of administration and supply had not been in existence on Vancouver Island when gold was discovered on the Fraser, the entire Pacific coast would now almost certainly be American territory. If throughout Rupert's Land and the northwest the Company had not maintained its trading monopoly, and if at the Red River, the point where the river systems of Hudson Bay and the Mississippi met, a permanent settlement controlled by the Company had not been established, the northward infiltration of American traders and settlers might well have pre-empted the Canadian west for the American republic. In each of these areas the Hudson's Bay Company over half a century carried out a prolonged and dogged holding operation, conserving the seed-beds of future provinces in the course of furthering its own corporate interests. The boundaries of the Canadian nation of today are set, not by the territory which the fur trade could win, but by the territory which it could hold against the advance of the American frontier.

By the end of the 1860's, however, this task was becoming too great for the resources of a trading company. Both British Columbia and Red River were rapidly being drawn into the economic orbit of American commercial and financial centres. British Columbia was part of the commercial hinterland of San Francisco, the Red River colony of Pembina and St. Paul. In each area geography and commerce combined to strengthen economic ties with the south. To offset these tendencies two things were necessary: the opening of the Canadian west for settlement, and the construction of a Canadian transcontinental railway. The purchase of the Hudson's Bay Company in 1863 and the confederation of Canada and the maritime provinces in 1867 together made these objectives possible of attainment. In 1821, with the bankruptcy of the North West Company, Canada's first transcontinental economic system, based on fur and the canoe, had been destroyed. Now, half a century later, a new transcontinental system was to be created, based on settlement, wheat, and the railway.

SUGGESTIONS FOR FURTHER READING

BASIC WORKS:

Innis, Harold A., *The Fur Trade in Canada: an Introduction to Canadian Economic History* (New Haven, 1930), Chapter IV, pp. 285-344

Innis, Harold A., Introduction to R. H. Fleming (ed.), *Minutes of Council, Northern Department of Rupert Land, 1821-31* (Toronto: The Champlain Society, 1940; E. E. Rich, general editor), pp. xi-lxxvii

Lamb, W. Kaye, Introductions to E. E. Rich (ed.), *The Letters of John McLoughlin, First Series, 1825-38* (Toronto: The Champlain Society, 1941), pp. ix-cxxviii; *Second Series, 1839-44* (1943), pp. xi-xlix; *Third Series, 1844-46* (1944), pp. xi-lxiii

Morton, Arthur S. and Chester Martin, *History of Prairie Settlement and "Dominion Lands" Policy* (Toronto, 1938), pp. 30-44, 195-223

SUPPLEMENTARY WORKS:

Brebner, J. Bartlet, *North Atlantic Triangle: the Interplay of Canada, the United States, and Great Britain* (Toronto and New Haven, 1945), Chapter X, pp. 165-81

Howay, F. W., W. N. Sage, and H. F. Angus, *British Columbia and the United States* (Toronto, 1942), Chapters IV-VIII, pp. 41-217

Morton, Arthur S., *A History of the Canadian West to 1870-71* (London, Toronto, and New York, 1939), Chapters VIII-XIII, pp. 623-932

Pritchett, John P., *The Red River Valley, 1811-1849, A Regional Study* (Toronto, 1942), Chapters XX-XXIV, pp. 215-71

CHAPTER XVI

THE STRATEGY OF CANADIAN DEVELOPMENT: PART I, 1849 TO CONFEDERATION

INTRODUCTION

THE years between 1849 and 1867 form an important watershed in Canadian history. During this period changes in the technology of communications, particularly the railway and the iron steamship, and changes in the organization of economic life, particularly the expansion of industrialism in Britain and the United States, drastically altered the environment in which the colonies which were later to form the Canadian nation sought to live and grow. Old staple products such as square timber, for many years the chief reliance of the St. Lawrence colonies and New Brunswick, began to decline, and newer staples, notably wheat, grew in importance. Markets in Britain in which the colonies had traditionally enjoyed preferential treatment were now thrown open to all comers in the interests of cheap raw materials and foodstuffs for British industry, and new markets had to be sought in the United States. The St. Lawrence canals, in which great sums of money had been invested, were found inadequate as means of defence against the competition of the steam locomotive in the United States, and new capital had to be raised and new debts incurred to finance the building of railways in Canada. Meanwhile, in the field of politics, the winning of responsible government gave Canadians control over their own tariff policy and made it possible for the colonial governments to assume the overhead costs of development. Weakening military and economic support from the British government, together with the urgent need for railway construction to meet the threat presented by the pace of American expansion into the western prairies, encouraged the North American colonies to draw closer together and explore the possibilities of co-operative action. The achievement of confederation in 1867 signalized the formation of a political unit strong enough to support the construction of a transcontinental railway to the Pacific coast and thus to keep open the road to nationhood.

Some of the developments of this period have been dealt with in earlier chapters. What we must do now is stand back a little from the details and try to understand the general tendency of events—to make out the broad ground-swell of change beneath the individual waves of circumstance. These were the years in which the political and economic framework of Canada as we know it today was being brought into existence. Our task in the present chapter is to understand how this was accomplished, and in particular how forces impinging upon the British North American colonies .from the outside world influenced their growth and gave a distinctive impetus and direction to their endeavours.

TACTICS FOR DEVELOPMENT: TRANSPORTATION AND THE TARIFF

In 1841 the two St. Lawrence colonies of Upper and Lower Canada had been united to form a single political unit. Besides the considerations of political expediency which led to this step, it seemed to make good economic sense. From a commercial point of view the St. Lawrence basin was a single region. The river imposed its unity on the territory through which it ran. It was Upper Canada's indispensable link with the sea. It was Montreal's vital avenue to the Great Lakes. It was the transport system on which depended all hopes of capturing from New York the through trade between the midwestern states and Europe. To unite under one legislature and one executive the two British provinces through which the river ran seemed merely a belated recognition of a geographical imperative.

Perhaps the most important economic consequence of the division of the two provinces before 1841 had been the delay in starting and completing the St. Lawrence canal system. This delay enabled New York, with its Erie and Oswego Canals, to get a head start over Montreal and to take over the lion's share of the trade to and from the middle west. Union of the provinces in 1841, with the aid of a low-interest loan guaranteed by the British government, meant that a single government could assume the entire responsibility for constructing all the waterway improvements which were necessary. This governmental authority, too, commanded sufficient revenues and offered sufficient prospects of permanence for it to be able to sell its bonds to investors in England. The St. Lawrence canal system was, in consequence, completed at the end of 1848.

The Erie Canal, which gave New York its low-cost water route to the Great Lakes, had been completed almost a quarter of a century before, in 1825. The delay in itself was a serious matter, but more serious still was the fact that developments in the world economy had not stood still while Canadians settled their internal difficulties, sold their bonds, and built their canals. The St. Lawrence canal system, taken as a whole, constituted a very costly investment for a young and relatively undeveloped country. The traffic generated within Canada itself—the wheat, flour, lumber and potash sent down the canals to Montreal and the textiles, hardware, machinery, and other manufactured goods sent back up the canals to the interior settlements—could not within the foreseeable future be large enough to make this investment worth while. Only if the St. Lawrence became a through route between Europe and the American midwest, so that the transit trade as well as the local trade passed through the canals, would the project pay its way.

This was the reasoning which lay behind the whole Canadian canal-building programme, from the turning of the first spadeful of earth on the Welland Canal in 1824 to the completion of the last stone lock on the St. Lawrence in 1848. Unless the western trade could be captured, the St. Lawrence canals would inevitably prove a waste of money, no matter what incidental benefits they might bring. The hopes and fortunes of the St. Lawrence commercial system were staked on the feasibility of diverting American traffic away from American transport routes.

To succeed in this aim involved more than just the improvement of navigation facilities on the river. This was one way to reduce freight costs and an essential one; but the St. Lawrence route had other drawbacks besides the rapids between Prescott and Lachine. There was the factor of climate: for five or six months of the year Montreal and Quebec were closed to navigation by ice. And there were the characteristic difficulties of a late start: ships calling at New York could be sure of picking up a cargo because of the volume and variety of traffic which poured through that port, whereas at Montreal they might be held up for weeks, waiting to fill their holds. Again, many of the ships calling at Montreal arrived in ballast, so that the cost of both voyages was thrown on the out-going cargo; New York, on the other hand, was the importing centre for an extensive hinterland, so that shipowners could count on a paying cargo on both legs of the voyage. To the lower ocean freight rates which this made possible, New York could add lower insurance and pilotage charges, safer access to the open sea, and the services of a multitude of specialized brokerage and credit agencies. Geography and the external economies which accompanied an early start and rapid growth gave to New York advantages which were difficult to match.

To offset the competitive disadvantages of the northern route, Canadian merchants exerted themselves to secure favourable tariff legislation from the British and provincial governments. Canadian wheat and flour were granted preferences in the British market by the Corn Laws of 1815, 1822 and 1828. The Colonial Trade Act of 1831 permitted American grain to enter the Canadas free of all import duties and to pass down the St. Lawrence on precisely the same terms as Canadian produce. Finally in 1843 the Canada Corn Act allowed Canadian flour and American wheat ground in Canadian mills to enter Britain free—a decisive step the effects of which on the prosperity of Montreal and the lake ports of Upper

Canada were immediately evident. In the same year, as a gesture to placate the farming interest, the Canadian legislature imposed a small duty on imports of American wheat, but this duty in itself was by no means large enough to prevent American wheat from passing down the St. Lawrence. With this minor exception, by 1843 the steady political pressure of Canadian merchants had effected the removal of every legislative obstacle which might otherwise have impeded American shippers from using the northern route.

The assumption which underlay the merchants' programme was that the construction of canals on the river, together with tariff advantages in the British market, would suffice to make the St. Lawrence route cheaper than its American rivals. In Britain and the United States, however, the march of events rapidly falsified the assumptions on which this belief was based. The repeal of the Corn Laws in 1846 meant that in future Canadian grain imported into Britain would be treated no more favourably than grain from foreign countries. This erased all possibility of offsetting higher freight costs on the St. Lawrence and the Atlantic by lower tariff liability on entering Britain. In the same year the United States government passed a Drawback Act which permitted grain from Upper Canada to be shipped to New York in bond, so that Canadian up-country shippers could use the cheaper American route without paying American import duties.

This double blow effectively neutralized the commercial strategy on which the Canadian business community had pinned its hopes. There was no adequate means of retaliation. The action taken by the British government was no more likely to be reversed by anything Canadians could do than were the tactics of the Americans. The St. Lawrence colonies had organized their economic life around the export of staples to Britain. Farmers had developed their lands and merchants had invested their capital in the expectation that Britain would continue to be their primary market; the whole structure of tariff policy and government debt had been erected on this foundation. Now the British market for Canadian staples appeared to be vanishing as one after another the tariff preferences which had furnished the economic framework of empire were whittled away and discarded. In the race for industrial supremacy in which she already had a head start Britain could not afford to preserve the vestiges of an earlier mercantilist age. Cheap food and cheap raw materials were indispensable to Britain's industrial machine, and to obtain them she was willing to cancel the trading privileges which her overseas colonies had previously enjoyed. The ever-increasing volume of goods which flowed from Britain's factories required world-wide markets for their sale, not markets confined to the colonies of settlement; foreign countries could secure the sterling to buy these goods only if they were permitted to sell their natural products in Britain. Abandonment of the old ideal of a self-contained. self-sufficient empire was the price which Britain paid, not unwillingly, for industrial supremacy.

The full shock of the repeal of the Corn Laws and, simultaneously, the reduction of the timber preferences was felt in Canada in the years between 1847 and 1849. Symptomatic of the resulting confusion, aggravated as it was by depression and political disturbance, was the appearance of the Annexation Manifesto, a vigorous appeal for immediate union with the United States. Annexationist sentiment has never been entirely absent from the Canadian scene: what was remarkable about the Manifesto of 1849 was that among those who signed it were to be found some of the leading business men of Montreal. These men and the community of which they were members had up to this time been the staunchest and most uncompromising advocates of the imperial connection. It was they who, in company with their compatriots in Upper Canada, had built the St. Lawrence commercial system and who, in Lower Canada, had set themselves up as the proponents of progress and development. Why then in 1849 did they suddenly change their views?

To some extent the factors responsible were temporary and ephemeral, just as this outburst of overt annexationism was ephemeral. Tight credit, falling prices and sudden bankruptcies undermined the confidence of more than one merchant. Political discontent and fear that the coming of responsible government would mean submergence by the French-Canadian majority also had their influence. But the causes went deeper than this. It was no coincidence that among the strongest advocates of annexation in 1849 were some who, not many years before, had had the largest stakes in the old British trading system. Fundamental was a sense of abandonment and disorientation—a feeling akin to that of a man who has played the game hard and fair, only to find, with victory almost within his grasp, that the rules have been changed, so that friends become enemies and enemies friends. In the eyes of the merchants who put down their names for annexation, Britain had knocked out the keystone of the imperial trading system, and by so doing had destroyed all that gave meaning and purpose to the St. Lawrence economy.

To the more far-sighted of the Montreal merchants—or perhaps only to those who were lucky enough to have adequate cash balances—this reaction seemed exaggerated and emotional. Grain prices in the United States were at this time several cents a bushel higher than in Canada, partly because of the recent discovery of gold in California, partly because American producers were less dependent on overseas markets. And the pace of economic expansion south of the border, now that recovery from the depression of the early 1840's was well under way, was impressive enough to justify unfavourable comment on the progress of the British colonies. But, on a sober calculation, the future of the St. Lawrence colonies seemed by no means entirely gloomy. The question was whether

Canada, having lost her privileged position in the British market, could hold her own in equal competition with other sources of supply. Could she find other markets, in the United States, in the Maritimes, and in the west, to replace or supplement those on which she had previously relied? The answers to these questions depended less upon political affiliation than upon costs of shipment between the Great Lakes and Liverpool, upon the movement of grain prices in Britain, and upon tariff and transportation policy. Too much had been invested in the St. Lawrence transportation system for it to be abandoned at the first chill blast of international competition. The pattern of growth which it represented had left too deep an impress on Canadian business and public finance for it to be erased in a moment's discouragement. The older strategy of development had indeed been made obsolete by the changes of the mid-century, and a new strategy had to be devised—a strategy which was to involve, as a matter of economic necessity, the building of a transcontinental economy. The key elements in this new strategy were the railway and the tariff.

THE UNITED STATES: ECONOMIC PACE-MAKER

To the Canadian observer the rate of economic expansion in the United States in the middle decades of the nineteenth century could not but seem impressive. Comparisons with the experience of the British colonies were inevitable and provided the framework for many contemporary discussions of government policy. There was a tendency for these comparisons to be made largely in terms of the advantages and disadvantages accruing to colonies which remained politically subordinate to Britain, as against former colonies which had successfully asserted their independence; and, despite the strong element of loyalism in Canada's business community, there were those who did not hesitate to assert that the lagging progress of the northern colonies was to be ascribed largely to the fact that they had chosen to remain dependencies of manufacturing Britain. There was more than a grain of truth in these arguments. The role which the northern colonies played in the imperial trading system was that of primary producers. This was their reason for being, the economic justification for the considerable sums which the British tax-payer contributed to their maintenance and defence. In terms of the natural resources which, with the technology of that time, were available for exploitation, it was a role which they were well fitted to play. But it had certain definite disadvantages for their stability and rate of growth. Concentration on the production of a few primary staples—fur, timber, fish and wheat—meant weakness in other lines of activity, failure to diversify, and serious vulnerability to changes in marketing conditions over which colonial politicians and business men could exercise little or no control. The simplicity of economic structure which characterized the Canadian colonies in this period reflected the unbalanced, highly specialized type of development which empire-building on the mercantilist model had tried to implant in all colonies and which in some, where the resource pattern was suitable, it had actually succeeded in generating.

The economic system which had developed in the United States by the middle of the nineteenth century was based upon a much greater variety of resources and a much more complex pattern of internal and external trade than was the case in the British colonies. This very diversity of resources had been in large measure responsible for the original withdrawal of the thirteen colonies from the British mercantile system in 1776. Since that date to the rich and varied resource base there had been added other sources of strength: a form of government which imposed minimal restrictions on individual initiative; a set of social values which accorded high prestige to wealth without demanding close scrutiny of how wealth was obtained; a disposition on the part of mechanics and business men to borrow and experiment, so that already there had developed a distinctive "American system" of manufacture; and, last but by no means least, two great inflows of wealth from Europe—the one an inflow of immigrants, most of them persons in the prime of life, already trained in some craft or skill, and the other an inflow of capital, as European investors eagerly snapped up the bonds of American state governments. By combining all these sources of strength the business and political leaders of the American republic had put together an economic system geared to expansion. It was a system which carried within itself serious sources of instability, as the crisis of 1837 had shown; but, partly because of the very looseness and flexibility of its organization, it was capable of a very high rate of growth and quick recovery from setbacks. In the early 1850's, despite ominous signs of internal stress, this economy was expanding very rapidly.

This, then, was the nation which served as pace-setter for the British colonies to the north. Not all those who watched its progress from across the border were prepared to admit that Americans, individually or collectively, were entitled to much credit for their productive achievements. R. B. Sullivan of Toronto, for example, pointed out in 1838 that ". . . the British people express their wonder at American enterprize and industry, when in fact the greatest part of the money which paid for these improvements (Rail Roads, Canals, and other public works) came from London, and the labourers who made them from Ireland, leaving to America the very easy task of employing other people with other peoples' money." Sullivan's remarks, and his implied comparison with the situation in Upper and Lower Canada, were highly pertinent. The best estimate of the British capital invested in these two Canadian provinces between 1827 and 1849 places the total at no more than $25 million (excluding military expenditures), a figure far surpassed by exports of British capital to the United States in the same period. Immigration into the British colonies was, as we have had occasion to note, very much smaller than immigration into the United States, where a total of just over two million persons are recorded as having arrived from Europe between 1820 and 1850. The whole population of the province of Canada in the latter year barely exceeded 1.6 million. The Canadian colonies in the first half of the nineteenth century, in short, received considerably smaller infusions of capital and labour from Europe than did the American states. And this was not all. Many of the American states repudiated their debts to Britain in the disturbed financial conditions of the early 1840's, and thus freed themselves from the burden of interest payments. To the Canadian colonies, on the other hand, simply because they were colonies, repudiation of debts to Britain was unthinkable.

But the reasons why European capital and labour were attracted more readily to the United States than to Canada had little to do with colonial status as such. Geography had been kind to the American republic. Both to east and west of the thirteen original states of the Atlantic seaboard there lay vast areas rich in natural resources, offering almost unlimited fields of exploitation for an aggressive and ambitious people. To the east there was the ocean, a source of wealth both directly because of its fisheries and indirectly because of the markets to which it gave access. To the west there were, beyond the Appalachians, the great plains of the interior, stretching wide and fertile to the Mississippi and beyond that to the Rockies and the Pacific. The ocean to the east and the continental hinterland to the west provided the citizens of the American nation with room for expansion and sources of wealth ready for the taking. Each of them opened up a frontier, in the one case a frontier of maritime trade, in the other a frontier of settlement. It was the existence of these two frontiers which enabled the American states to grow, within half a century, from a string of colonial outposts on the periphery of the civilized world to a strong and independent nation, eagerly reaching out for the continental empire which she believed to be her manifest destiny.

The North American colonies which had remained within the imperial system had no such easy fields of expansion open to them. On both the maritime and the continental frontiers they were confronted by much more serious obstacles than those facing the United States. On the sea Britain's Navigation Laws, until their abolition in 1849, restricted the ports to which their ships could sail and the markets in which they could sell their produce. On land, geography interposed barriers between the open prairies of the west and the colonies which had access to the ocean. The northern spearhead of the Appalachians split the maritime provinces off from the St. Lawrence lowlands. The interminable miles of Precambrian granite north of Lakes Huron and Superior separated the St. Lawrence colonies from the western plains. From the close of the St. Lawrence fur trade in 1821 until the construction of the first Canadian transcontinental railway in 1885 the St. Lawrence colonies had, for all practical purposes, no continental hinterland of their own. Hence the attraction of the much more accessible American hinterland and Montreal's obsession with the through trade of the American west. Not until the railway had rebuilt, in vastly different form, the transcontinental economy originally created by the fur-trader's canoe did an expanding western frontier under Canadian control become possible.

The maritime frontier had provided the American colonies with their first opportunities for economic expansion. Up to the end of the eighteenth century settlement and agriculture were confined to the coastal strip east of the Appalachians. Such manufacturing as existed was small in scale; the use of power-driven machinery was confined to flour- and saw-milling. Markets on land were very limited, and the sea and coastal rivers provided literally the only means of cheap transportation. In these circumstances maritime trade was the means whereby most of the early American fortunes were made and the source from which much of the capital used to finance later development was originally derived.

By the second quarter of the nineteenth century, however, this phase of development was drawing to a close. American shipping was still very active on the sea-lanes of the world, but the relative importance of maritime trade in the American economy as a whole was declining. The better lands east of the Appalachians had by this time all been occupied, and settlement had burst over the mountains onto the fertile plains east of the Mississippi. More and more the attention of men and governments was turning to westward expansion and the problems which accompanied it—particularly the building and financing of roads and canals. After 1815, when, as one contemporary observer put it, all America seemed to be on the move, the focus of American economic life moved away from the sea and toward the hinterland. The continental, not the maritime, frontier now furnished the major avenue of expansion and field for investment.

As foreign commerce declined in importance and agriculture in the eastern states began to feel the competition of the new grain-producing areas in the middle west, the capital which had accumulated in the hands of eastern business men found its way increasingly into manufacturing, particularly into textiles. The waterfalls of the eastern rivers provided convenient sources of power, the swelling stream of immigrants provided a labour supply, and, once the initial technical secrets had been learned from England, native engineering skills and ingenuity were more than adequate to develop a workable technology. The New England states, which formerly had led the way in the development of maritime trade, now became pioneers in the development of industrialism. Where once

Boston capital had gone into shipping ventures to the West Indies, South America, California, or the Orient, now it went into textile mills in Lawrence, Lowell, Chicopee, or Fall River.

As a consequence of these two parallel lines of development there came into being a kind of regional specialization which was to be characteristic of the American economy for the remainder of the century and which provides much of the explanation for its rapid growth. To the west there was the advancing frontier of agricultural settlement, moving forward not steadily but irregularly and unevenly as climate or resources retarded advance in one area and hastened it in another. In the east there were the great industrial towns with their factories and slums. Linking these two areas of the economy there was a physical network—the lines of transport, first roads, then canals, and then railways—and a financial network—the seepage of capital into new areas and new enterprises as opportunities opened up and old fields of investment declined. These geographic shifts in investment caused by the moving frontier, together with population growth and innovations in methods of production, kept the economy expanding and enabled it to recover rapidly from its periodic recessions.

The development of the region west of the Appalachians had initially been limited by poor transportation facilities. Here, as in Canada, settlement and trade at first followed the navigable rivers. The Mississippi, navigable for more than 2,000 miles upstream from New Orleans, and its great tributaries, the Ohio and the Missouri, were the major arteries of trade and enabled the pioneer settlers in the interior to get their products to market. Upstream traffic on these rivers was, however, very slow and difficult. The introduction of the steamboat after 1807 helped considerably, but it was still easier and cheaper for the settlers to bring in such manufactured goods as they could not do without over the mountains from the eastern seaports rather than up the rivers from New Orleans. A kind of triangular trade developed by which the staple exports of the trans-Appalachian region moved south to the Gulf of Mexico while essential imports were brought in by road and river from the Atlantic seaboard. After about 1825, however, this pattern, which had bound the northeast, the west, and the south into a single interdependent economic system, began to break down. The completion of the Erie Canal and the other transportation improvements financed by the states of the eastern seaboard made it possible for the settlers of the old northwest (roughly the present states of Ohio, Indiana, Michigan and Illinois) to send their staple exports directly to the Atlantic seaports more cheaply than they could be sent to New Orleans. The pattern of internal trade began to change. By the mid-1840's New York and Pennsylvania had made serious inroads into the trade of the Ohio valley, while New Orleans was well on the way to becoming almost exclusively a cotton port.

The pace of these changes was accelerated by the introduction of the railroad. A demonstrated success in England by 1830 and in the United States by 1840, the combination of iron rails and steam locomotive made available a means of transportation which did not freeze up in winter and which could penetrate into areas which lacked the water resources and natural channels necessary for the construction of canals. The great canal-building era in the United States came to a close with the depression of 1837; by 1840, 2,818 miles of railroad had been laid and by 1850, 9,022 miles. Almost all of this mileage was confined to the Atlantic seaboard. In the decade of the 1850's the railroad crossed the Appalachians, traversed the old northwest, and reached the Mississippi. By 1860, 31,246 miles of track had been laid, nearly half of which were west of the Appalachians. The railroad had caught up with the frontier and, barring minor interruptions where bridges or inter-system connections were lacking, through routes were available all the way from the Atlantic seaports to the edge of settlement.

If canals had weakened the links between the western frontier and the South, railroads threatened to cut them completely. Already the invention of the cotton gin, the availability of Negro labour, and the insatiable demands of Europe's textile factories had made of the South an economic region almost wholly dependent on a single crop—cotton—and had encouraged in that region the development of a society committed to the preservation of the institution of slavery. The railroad disrupted the old trade patterns which had tied this region to the agricultural frontier of the middle west, linking that frontier instead directly to the seaports of New England and the middle Atlantic states. This inevitably meant a major realignment of power in the national government. The economic alliance between west and east which the railroad had cemented found its immediate and direct reflection in politics. The major issue around which this alliance was formed and tested was the extension of slavery from the South to the new western states, particularly Kansas and Nebraska. This was the issue which, successive attempts at compromise having failed, brought the nation to civil war.

So it was that the westward march of the continental frontier, often thought of as a process by which social tensions were eased and diffused, served in this instance as a source of conflict and disunity. Few but fanatics wished originally to extirpate slavery in the states where it was already an established institution; it was its extension into new states brought into being by the movement of the frontier that was the sticking-point. In this sense the Civil War was an incident in the spread of commerce across the continent from the eastern seaboard where it had first taken root as an offshoot of European civilization. Conflict on the maritime frontier between Britain and her colonies had precipitated the American Revolution; conflict on the continental frontier between the industrial states of the northeast and the staple-producing states of the South precipitated the Civil War.

THE RECIPROCITY TREATY

The American Civil War and the tensions which led up to it influenced the economic development of the British North American provinces in several ways. Before the outbreak of hostilities the uneasy political balance between North and South made possible the passing of the Reciprocity Treaty. During the war new markets were opened up in the United States for Canadian exports, thus cushioning to some extent the loss of preferences in Britain. The final victory of the North, bringing into power a party committed to high tariffs and industrial expansion, destroyed the precarious political balance which had made reciprocity possible and presented the British provinces with a serious military and economic threat to their southern borders. At the same time, by removing restraints on the expansion of American settlement west of the Mississippi, the end of the war jeopardized the security of the Canadian west and hastened the movement toward confederation and the transfer of the Hudson's Bay Company's territories to the new dominion.

As far as the province of Canada was concerned, it was to be expected that, when the first shock of free trade in Britain made itself felt, business men and politicians alike should promptly turn to the building of closer economic relationships with the United States. It was not a matter of finding completely new markets or forming completely new commercial ties, but rather of strengthening and supplementing ones that already existed. To map-makers and diplomats, rivers and lakes might seem admirably suited to serve as boundaries between political units, but to the merchant and the forwarder, in an age when bulky low-value staples moved afloat if they moved at all, waterways tended to unite rather than divide. Before the coming of the railway the basins of Lakes Erie and Ontario formed a single economic area, the unity of which was only to a very minor degree marred by the tariffs and other restrictions on commerce which governments imposed. The abandonment as early as 1825 of all attempts to enforce the Navigation Acts on the Lakes illustrates the impossibility of applying mercantilist policies in this area. The shores of the Lakes offered innumerable small harbours suitable for use by sloops and schooners. To keep watch over all of them so that trade might be taxed, prohibited, or measured would have entailed an intolerably large financial burden. Most of the shipments across the Lakes consequently went unrecorded in official statistics, for import and export figures are characteristically by-products of customs administration. The size and importance of this international trade on the Lakes therefore tends to be underestimated in comparison with the trade on the St. Lawrence which, since it was concentrated in a single channel, was more easily measured and taxed. But our interpretation of developments during the period of reciprocity would be very seriously distorted if we lost sight of the fact that in the area of the lower Lakes commercial relations between Canada and the United States—particularly between Upper Canada and western New York state—had always been close.

Partly because of this background, Upper Canada business men were among the first to seize upon the idea of reciprocity, publicize it, and convert it into an objective of government policy. The arguments they used were simple. The British colonies in North America, if they were to find markets for their exports, had to devise some substitute for the system of imperial preferences which was now disappearing. To follow the mother country in its unilateral adoption of free trade was neither economically desirable nor, considering the strength of the farming interest in Canada, politically possible. To run to the other extreme and seek immediate economic and political union with the United States would entail the sacrifice of a host of valued institutions and traditions, not least among them the incipient sense of national identity and the tradition of loyalty to Britain. But was there not a middle way? Was it not possible to attain some of the economic advantages of union with the United States without loss of political independence or cultural integrity? Could this not be brought about by a process of reciprocal reductions or abolitions of tariffs, as for instance by the removal by each participating country of all customs duties on imports of natural products from the others?

Reciprocity meant, in short, the attempt to create in North America a single market area, covering several distinct political jurisdictions, in which certain specified types of products could be freely exchanged. Seen in this light, partial and limited economic union between the British North American colonies and the United States was presented as an alternative to annexation—indeed as the only feasible alternative. This was the context in which reciprocity won the support not only of increasing numbers in Canada and the Maritimes, but also of the British government. With a few notable exceptions, political leaders in Britain had long since resigned themselves to the inevitable loss of the North American colonies—or rather, more positively, had convinced themselves that the sooner the mother country could rid herself of her overseas dependencies the better. But a willingness to cast off expensive colonies did not necessarily imply an equal willingness to see those colonies snapped up by the United States, a nation whose appetite for territory had already been demonstrated in Texas and Oregon. Reciprocity seemed, therefore, to offer the possibility of a very satisfactory compromise. It was inconsistent with the doctrines of unqualified free trade to which Britain was now committed; its immediate effect, indeed, would be to establish in the colonies differential duties against Britain. But, perhaps because of a half-felt suspicion that economic policies suited to an industrial economy selling in world markets were not necessarily equally well adapted to the needs of a relatively undeveloped colony, this issue was not publicly pressed. Britain had undermined her own ability to control colonial tariff policy by abandoning the system of imperial preferences; self-governing colonies could not be denied the right which Britain herself had exercised to shape her commercial policy in her own interests rather than the interests of the Empire as a whole.

To sell the idea of reciprocity to the American Congress and administration was a much more difficult matter. On tariff questions North and South traditionally stood in opposition. The South, a plantation economy, desired low tariffs in order to lower the price of imported goods and reduce costs of production for exports of raw materials. The North, an economy of small farms and factories, was strongly protectionist. On broad economic grounds southern sentiment might have been expected to be for reciprocity, northern against it. This alignment, however, was radically distorted by the slavery issue. The balance of political power between slave and non-slave states was so delicate that any large accession of territory was certain to upset it. Many believed that reciprocity with the British colonies would soon be followed by political union. Even the possibility that this might happen was enough to provoke the South into violent opposition. The prospect of the admission to the American federation of new non-slave states was not one which the representatives of the South in Congress could contemplate with equanimity.

While the negotiations for reciprocity were immeasurably complicated by the sectional dispute over slavery, no less serious an obstacle to success was simply indifference. American politicians, as the Canadian representatives in Washington soon discovered, knew little about the British American colonies and cared less. The only private interest groups which felt immediately stirred to action were groups which felt their welfare threatened: the wheat-growers of Virginia and Maryland, for example, and the coal-owners of Pennsylvania. The exclusion of manufactured goods from the proposed agreement, though no doubt essential if it was to stand any chance of acceptance, meant that business interests on the whole remained apathetic. In addition there was a good deal of anti-British prejudice, recently inflamed by the dispute over British claims to control of the Nicaragua canal route in Central America.

In combination, these difficulties were sufficient to make quick and easy attainment of reciprocity out of the question. Even to get the matter considered was far from easy. Attempts to secure the abolition of duties on natural products by parallel legislation were abandoned in 1852; thereafter efforts were concentrated on obtaining the desired result by means of a treaty, a mode of procedure calculated to give the American administration a freer hand and reduce the possibility of action being blocked in the House of Representatives. But there were still serious obstacles. Two things above all were essential to success: southern political leaders had to be convinced that reciprocity would forestall, not precipitate, annexation; and the administration had to be given some impelling reason to seek an early and decisive solution. Both of these prerequisites were met between 1852 and 1854, the one by Lord Elgin's brilliant personal diplomacy in Washington at the end of May, 1854, and the other by the British government's announcement in 1852 that it intended to back up by force its interpretation of the fisheries convention of 1818.

Whether Britain, involved already in the Crimean crisis, and the United States, harassed by internal dissension, would have gone to war over the fisheries is very much open to question. The mere possibility of war at that juncture, however, was sufficient to place the reciprocity issue in a very different light. In itself reciprocity was still regarded with little enthusiasm in the United States; the desire for a settlement of the fisheries dispute, on the other hand, was immediate and urgent. The American administration, in consequence, found itself for the first time assured of congressional support for an agreement which would include both the fisheries and reciprocity. There was, indeed, some danger that the fisheries issue might edge reciprocity out of the area of negotiation entirely. Certainly by the time agreement was finally reached settlement of the fisheries dispute had become the principal objective in the eyes of the British and American negotiators and reciprocity little more than a concession included at the insistence of the colonies.

The Reciprocity Treaty was signed on June 5, 1854, and approved by the American Senate on August 4. Approval by the legislatures of Great Britain, Canada, Nova Scotia, New Brunswick and Newfoundland followed within the next twelve months, though by administrative arrangement the terms of the Treaty were put into effect before the end of 1854. Its principal provisions may be summarized as follows: American fishermen were permitted free access to the coastal fisheries of the British colonies and were allowed to land on the shores of the colonies for the purpose of drying their nets and curing their fish. Fishermen from the British colonies received similar privileges in the American coastal fisheries north of the 36th parallel. Import duties were abolished on a wide range of natural products when imported into the British North American colonies from the United States and vice versa. These included grain, flour and other breadstuffs, fish, livestock, fresh or cured meat, coal, timber, lumber, and several other natural products of less importance. American vessels were admitted to the use of the St. Lawrence and other Canadian canals on the same terms as British and colonial vessels, while the United States government granted corresponding privileges on Lake Michigan and undertook to recommend that the individual states take similar action on the canals under their jurisdiction. The Treaty was to remain in force for ten years, after which it could be terminated by either side at twelve months' notice.

For New Brunswick, Nova Scotia and Newfoundland the most important privilege secured by the Treaty was the free admission of their fish into the American market. This was the concession which compensated to some extent for the bitterly resented admission of the Americans to the in-shore fisheries. New Brunswick also stood to benefit considerably from the removal of the duties on lumber, for the reductions in the British timber preferences had been a severe blow. Abolition of the lumber duties was an important factor for the province of Canada also, though overshadowed by what was for the St. Lawrence colony by far the major concession: free trade in wheat and flour.

THE NATIONAL POLICY: ITS ORIGIN AND MEANING

Not least among the elements which had made the signing of the Treaty possible was the fact that, by the time the American government had succeeded in convincing itself that reciprocity was desirable, the British colonies were by no means as anxious to obtain it as they had been earlier. In 1849 and 1850 either annexation or reciprocity had been regarded as indispensable. By 1853 it had become possible to believe that the British colonies could get along without either. Reciprocity was still regarded as excellent in principle and certain to bring considerable material benefits, but it was no longer thought of as a prerequisite to the survival of the North American provinces as self-governing communities within the British Empire. A third alternative had opened up. Could not the British provinces, by strengthening the commercial ties among themselves and by exploiting the new possibilities created by the railway, maintain their position in the international economy without relying exclusively upon preferential treatment either in Britain or the United States? They had already secured self-government, within certain imprecise but flexible limits; soon they would successfully assert their right to control their own tariff policy. Could they not, by using these closely related devices, the railway and the tariff, so develop their resources and organize their trade as to create something approaching a national economy of their own?

Recognition that such a policy was possible did much to ease the task of the British and colonial diplomats negotiating for reciprocity in Washington. And, when reciprocity was lost in 1866, this was the policy which pointed the way toward confederation and transcontinental expansion. Its origins are not hard to find. All the provinces (with the exception of Newfoundland and, far away on the Pacific coast, British

Columbia) had been shaken by the removal of the preferences on wheat and timber and felt the need to draw closer together for mutual support and defence. The railway for the first time made it possible to overcome the barriers of distance and climate which had kept the maritime provinces apart from their sister colony on the St. Lawrence. If railways were to be built, and if a common commercial policy toward the United States was to be developed and maintained, the separate colonies had to learn how to act in concert. Failure to do so would inevitably result, if not in annexation by the United States, at least in economic domination—a development already foreshadowed by the shipment of Upper Canada wheat over New York routes for sale in New York markets, and in the uncomfortably conspicuous role which the citizens of Portland, Maine, were playing in the railway projects of Montreal and Saint John.

At first the outlines of the new policy were far from clear. Protection, free trade, annexation, reciprocity—all had their advocates in the British provinces in the early 1850's. Basic to the slow formulation of an economic strategy on which all or most could agree was the realization that the abolition of the preferences on wheat and flour and the reductions in the preferences on timber, though they had certainly caused great commercial distress, had not destroyed all prospects of growth—and this despite the fact that, in the case of wheat, the transition had been sharper and more sudden than originally intended. When Peel had proposed the repeal of the Corn Laws in 1846, he had suggested that, to ease the difficulties of adjustment in the British possessions overseas, a small preference on colonial grain should be maintained for three more years. In fact the appearance of famine in Ireland led to the absolute suspension of all but nominal registration duties in January, 1847, so that the colonial preference was swept away before its appointed time. But this did not mean the disappearance of the British market for Canadian grain—quite the contrary. Exports of wheat and flour from the St. Lawrence, which had been 2,507,392 bushels in 1845 and 3,312,757 bushels in 1846, rose to 3,883,156 bushels in 1847. The annual average for the five years 1842-6 was 2,208,436 bushels; for the five years after 1846 it was 3,719,885.

The repeal of the Corn Laws, in fact, did not cause serious injury to the Canadian farmer. Some had feared that Canadian grain, deprived of its tariff advantages, would be edged out of the British market by foreign grain from the Baltic, the Russian Black Sea ports, and the United States. But this did not happen. Part of the explanation lay in the fact that British wheat prices fell neither as fast nor as far as had been expected. The annual average prices in 1846, 1847, and 1848 were 54s. 8d., 69s. 9d., and 50s. respectively; in the three previous years they had been 50s. 1d., 51s. 3d., and 50s. 10d. It was not until 1851 that the annual average price fell temporarily to the very low figure of 38s. 6d. By the end of 1848, too, the St. Lawrence canals were ready for use, bringing very substantial reductions in forwarding costs. The rate for shipping a barrel of flour from Toronto to Montreal, which earlier had ranged between 2s. and 3s., fell immediately after 1848 to between 1s. and 1s. 6d. With British prices still at remunerative levels and transport costs on the inland waterways cut in half, the Upper Canada farmer had little immediate cause to regret the loss of the British wheat preference.

It was not the farmers but the merchants and millers who were seriously penalized by the loss of the British preferences. The flour-milling industry had expanded considerably since 1843, partly to accommodate existing business but more in anticipation of future increases in volume. This speculative development came to an abrupt end in 1846. The Montreal wholesalers and grain dealers were also badly hurt. Most of these merchant houses operated on a slim profit margin and with small reserves of capital. During 1846 and the early part of 1847 they had shipped unusually large quantities of grain to Britain to meet the temporary scarcity occasioned by the Irish famine, and the break in prices which began in June, 1847, found many of them financially over-extended. Nor was the timber industry spared. The reduction in the timber preferences in itself would have necessitated a painful readjustment; to this was added in 1847 a drastic slump in demand as the railway construction boom in Britain came to an end. From the middle of 1847 until the end of 1849 the commercial life of Montreal and Quebec was practically stagnant.

The crisis which the St. Lawrence economy experienced between 1847 and 1849 was a very painful one. Its impact, however, was largely confined to the commercial life of the towns, and it was not of long duration. To contemporary minds it was not easy to distinguish between short- and long-run difficulties, and the effects on business confidence were all of a piece. The end of a major investment boom in Britain coincided with the end of the old British tariff system and, incidentally, with a period of great tension in Canadian politics. Deep depression in Britain and political violence in Canada were alike temporary factors; the long-run problem was whether or not the St. Lawrence economy could survive the revolution in British trade policy.

The purpose of the reciprocity movement was to offset the loss of the British preferences by building up alternative and supplementary markets in the United States. But this policy, aimed as it was at the development of north-south lines of trade, did not and was not intended to involve an abandonment of the east-west trade routes around which the St. Lawrence economy had been built. The development of trade with the United States went on simultaneously with efforts to maintain and extend trade with Britain. The old channels of commerce which led down the St. Lawrence to Montreal and the Atlantic were to be deepened at the same time as new channels were dug leading south to the United States. The two lines of policy were complementary, not alternatives.

It had long been clear that only a very substantial difference in costs would induce American shippers in the western states to send their produce eastward down the St. Lawrence rather than over the competing American routes. Mere equality in costs on the inland waterways, or even a small differential in favour of Canada, was not sufficient, for the American routes passed through an extensive home market and terminated at ports which could offer lower freight costs on the Atlantic crossing. Before 1846 supporters of the Canadian route had counted on their tariff advantages in the British market to provide the necessary cost differential; after 1846 this was no longer possible. The St. Lawrence route now had to be evaluated on its merits.

The completion of the St. Lawrence canal system at the end of 1848, cutting in half costs of shipment from Lake Ontario to Montreal, freed the Canadian route from the worst of its handicaps. Attention immediately turned to Montreal's other major disadvantage: the higher ocean freight charges which shippers from Montreal had to pay as compared with shippers from New York. Primary responsibility for this unfavourable differential was placed on the Navigation Acts which, it was alleged, prevented foreign vessels from entering the Canadian grain trade and thus, by restricting the supply of shipping, drove up the price. Between 1847 and 1849, therefore, business interests in Canada and to a lesser extent in the other colonies pressed vigorously for the repeal of the Navigation Acts, arguing that, if Britain abolished part of her old commercial policy, she should abolish it completely. The old colonial system had been a matter of reciprocal restrictions and privileges: if the privileges were withdrawn, the restrictions should be also. It was unjust to repeal merely those statutes which had benefited the colonies and leave untouched those which had penalized them in the interests of preserving Britain's monopoly of the carrying-trade. The British government, which had taken a firm stand against restrictions on commerce of any kind, found these arguments difficult to refute, and the Navigation Acts were accordingly repealed in May, 1849.

The repeal of the Navigation Acts coincided with the end of the depression which had hung over Canadian business since 1847, and also with the conclusion of an agreement between Canada and the other North American colonies for reciprocal free trade in natural products. It is, accordingly, very difficult to assess what effect, if any, the abolition of the Acts had on Canadian trade. British ocean freight rates had in any case been falling since 1847 and continued to do so until 1852. Extensive new construction in excess of current demand during the previous boom, together with the advent of faster and larger iron sailing-ships and steamers, meant a secular tendency toward lower rates. Some ships of foreign registration called at Montreal after 1849 which would not have been seen in that port in earlier years, but the number was never large. It seems improbable, in short, that repeal caused any immediate substantial reduction in ocean freight rates in the Canadian grain trade. Above all, the relative position of Montreal as compared with New York showed no significant improvement. Various estimates have been made of ocean freight rates at the two ports in the early 1850's, and some show a greatei differential in favour of New York than others; most agree, however, that rates at New York averaged at least 50 per cent lower than at Montreal. Later in the 1850's the persistence of this large unfavourable differential was to lead the government to experiment with subsidies to ocean steamship lines.

The net result of all these changes during the late 1840's was that Canada succeeded in maintaining her position in the British grain market, despite the loss of tariff preferences. Experience had shown that Canadian wheat could be produced and shipped to England at costs low enough to allow farmers and merchants, in most years, a reasonable return on their investments of labour and capital. As regards the through trade from the American middle west, however, Montreal was unable, despite the completion of the St. Lawrence canals, to improve her position relative to New York. The bulk of the through trade from the continental hinterland to the Atlantic seaboard still passed over American transport routes. To the extent that the diverting of this trade down the St. Lawrence had been an objective of the Canadian canal-building programme, that programme had proved a failure. To the extent, however, that the canals enabled Canadian producers to compete in world markets, they were a success.

While the maintenance of trade with Britain and the development of trade with the United States were the major themes of Canadian commercial policy in these years, they were not the only ones. Trade with the maritime provinces also attracted increasing attention. We have already mentioned the interprovincial reciprocity agreement of 1849, providing for free trade in natural products among the British colonies. This agreement seems to have stimulated an immediate and substantial increase in shipment of breadstuffs from Montreal to the Maritimes. Exports of flour from the province of Canada to the maritime provinces, for example, increased from 19,500 barrels in 1844 to 79,000 barrels in 1849, and then jumped sharply to 141,000 barrels in 1850. In the short run these new markets had much to do with Montreal's recovery from depression in 1849. A more important long-run consequence was to emphasize the possibilities of interprovincial economic co-operation. Free trade in natural products among the British North American colonies in 1849 and their joint adoption of reciprocity toward the United States in 1854 clearly reflected a growing recognition that their economic interests were interdependent.

RAILWAYS AND THE TARIFF

Interest in the maritime provinces as markets for Canadian produce coincided with the drawing up of plans for trunk-line railways. Up to this time the freeze-up of the St. Lawrence in winter had meant that for almost six months of every year Canada's business life came to a standstill. To Canada's business and political leaders the railway was first and foremost a means of abolishing this perennial stagnation. To their counterparts in the maritime provinces, the railway was a means of converting small struggling seaports into major centres of international commerce. For too many years the principal arteries of trade between the New World and Europe had by-passed the Maritimes, passing either north to the St. Lawrence or south to New York and Boston. Railways would channel these trade routes through the maritime provinces instead of past them and enable their seaports to assume the role for which geography had, it was believed, intended them—that of great international emporia upon which the transport systems of ocean and continent would converge.

Promoters and politicians alike, whether in Canada or in the Maritimes, realized that the railway was certain to cause profound changes in the directions of trade and the location of production. With few exceptions, however, they described the changes which they hoped to bring about in terms taken over almost without modification from the age of canals and water-borne transport which was then coming to a close. The themes which had consistently run through all of Canadian history up to this point were still there, restated more firmly and clearly than ever. The cardinal objective was still the capture of the American western trade. The great aim was still to make the St. Lawrence the principal corridor of commerce between Britain and the continental hinterland, and the hinterland was still conceived of as the American states of the Mississippi basin. From this point of view the great advantage of the railways over the canals was that they made long-distance transportation possible in winter and thus could give Canada access to an ice-free Atlantic port. Few if any had the vision to see that the coming of the railway did more than make the traditional goals of the Canadian economy easier to attain; few realized that the whole framework of possibilities within which the Canadian economy was to develop had been profoundly altered. Specifically, the railway made it possible for the British provinces, for the first time, to lay claim to their own hinterland and to look to their own west as a field of development. The barrier of the Precambrian Shield which, since the end of the fur trade, had cut the St. Lawrence colonies off from all economic contact with the prairies west of Lake Superior could now be surmounted. The formation of a single national economic system, including not only the Maritimes and the St. Lawrence colonies but also the prairies and the isolated colony on the Pacific coast, was now for the first time a feasible objective.

Awareness of these new horizons was slow in dawning. The North American colonies were not ill suited to the age of wind and water which was passing away, and the problems and opportunities which the new age of steam and iron would present were still matters for speculation. The immediate consequences of the coming of the railway, however, were direct and unmistakable. The influx of construction capital from Britain, with its effects multiplied throughout the whole economy, provided the solid foundation for a remarkable period of prosperity in the early and middle fifties. Speculation in land, building, and general construction, encouraged by the world-wide tendency toward rising prices and falling interest rates which followed the gold discoveries in California and Australia, rode on top of the investment boom and created an atmosphere of heady optimism. Montreal's import trade expanded rapidly, from £1.7 million in 1847 to £4.1 million in 1854, with iron, coal, textiles, and hardware of all kinds making up the bulk of the increase. Rising prices and a brisk home market for foodstuffs brought prosperity to the farming population, already reaping the benefits of the Crimean War, which had interrupted the export of Russian wheat, and of a series of bad harvests in Britain. The establishment of railway depots, maintenance sheds, foundries and engineering shops introduced Canada for the first time to the technology of heavy industry. All these were the outward and visible signs of the revolution which the railway had brought.

But the construction of railways had other effects which, though perhaps less predictable, were to prove more important in the long run. Canada's late start in railway construction, together with the very considerable uncertainties facing the private investor, had made necessary a policy of extensive government assistance, mostly in the form of government guarantees of interest on the bonds of railway companies. In the early 1850's these guarantees had played an essential part in attracting British capital and in inducing British railway construction firms to accept contracts in Canada. While prosperity lasted in Britain and Canada the government was not called upon to make good these guarantees, for the railway companies had little difficulty in marketing their securities and raising money to meet their obligations. In 1857, however, a recession brought the boom to a close, leaving the Canadian railways, particularly the Grand Trunk, in a very difficult position. The main line of the Grand Trunk from Sarnia to Montreal was not yet completed, and neither was the Victoria Bridge across the St. Lawrence. The Great Western and Northern Railways were little better off. There had not been time for traffic to develop and the collapse of the stock market in Britain, making it impossible to raise new capital, confronted the companies with the imminent danger of bankruptcy. This was a prospect which neither the directors of the companies nor the ministers of the government—who were in many cases the same people—were prepared to face. At the same time a number of the municipalities which had incurred debts under the Municipal Loan Fund found it impossible to meet their obligations. The provincial government had not formally guaranteed the Fund, but failure to pay interest when due would certainly have ruined Canada's credit in London. Consequently the province found it necessary to make large advances to enable the Fund to meet its obligations.

The railway guarantees alone added in effect more than £7½ million, on which 6 per cent interest was due annually, to the public debt of the province of Canada. Prior to 1857 this sum had been a charge on the revenues of the railway companies; after that date almost the whole of the interest had to be paid from the revenues of the province. The sources of revenue available to the provincial government at this time consisted almost exclusively of customs duties. There were other minor sources of income, but the tariff on imports was by far the largest. Revenue from import duties fluctuated in a very characteristic pattern, increasing in times of prosperity when imports were large and decreasing in depression. The onset of depression in 1857 meant that Canadian public revenues were subjected to an unusually large and unanticipated drain precisely at the time when, under the existing tariff, revenues had been sharply reduced.

Alexander T. Galt, who was minister of finance at this time and had been intimately associated with the Grand Trunk management, realized that this state of affairs was likely to continue for several years, since the railway companies could hardly hope to get on their feet financially until business conditions improved, if then. If the Canadian government was not to follow the railways into bankruptcy, it was imperative that new sources of revenue be found immediately. Direct taxation being impossible for political and administrative reasons, there was no alternative but to increase the tariff.

The Canadian government had been under pressure to revise the tariff for some time. Within a year of the signing of the Reciprocity Treaty a movement had got under way, originating primarily in the Toronto-Hamilton area, the objective of which was to secure tariff protection for Canadian manufacturers. Supporters of this movement argued that, under the Canadian tariff as it then existed, manufactured goods were imported at very low rates of duty while raw materials (except when imported under the Reciprocity Treaty) had to pay high rates. Many of these imported manufactured goods, they alleged, could easily be produced in Canada with the available labour force, if the rates of duty were increased. They accordingly proposed that the duty on manufactured goods which could be made in Canada should be increased to 25 or 30 per cent, while the duties on imports of raw materials, tea, coffee, sugar and molasses, should be substantially reduced.

This was far from being the first proposal for a protective tariff in Canada. It was, however, the first serious move in the direction of industrial, as contrasted with agricultural, protection, and in this sense reflected the profound changes which, within a relatively few years, the Canadian economy had experienced. The rates of duty proposed were very moderate compared with the American tariff. The significant factor was that protection was demanded in order to encourage the production of manufactures, which with few and trifling exceptions Canada, as an agricultural and raw-material-producing economy, had so far been content to import.

The financial crisis of 1858 enabled Galt to satisfy this protectionist pressure group and simultaneously broaden the sources of revenue on which the government could draw. In 1859 he raised the duties on a wide range of manufactured goods (including hardware, machinery, clothing, cotton and woollen textiles and tobacco) to 20 per cent *ad valorem* (25 per cent in the case of clothing) as compared with 15 per cent in 1856. Duties on sugar were scheduled to be reduced from 40 per cent in 1859 to 15 per cent in 1862, and those on tea and coffee from 15 per cent to 5 per cent in the same period. In general outline, therefore, Galt's new schedule of duties followed the change which the advocates of protection for industry had suggested.

Quite apart from their domestic repercussions, these tariff changes provoked vigorous protests in the United States and Britain, the sources of most of Canada's imported manufactures, and set in motion processes which were finally to lead to the cancellation of the Reciprocity Treaty and to the winning of colonial fiscal autonomy. During its first three years reciprocity had proved very popular both in Canada and the United States. By 1858, however, considerable criticism of the effects of the Treaty had begun to make itself heard, particularly from business groups in Buffalo, New York, and Philadelphia who felt themselves injured, or expected to be injured, by the diversion of through traffic down the St. Lawrence and the Grand Trunk. The imposition in Canada of increased duties on manufactures provided these groups with the opportunity they needed to launch a full-scale attack on reciprocity. Canada had, they alleged, violated the spirit if not the letter of the Treaty. The prospect of increased exports of manufactures to Canada had been, in their view, the consideration which had induced the United States to accept the Treaty in the first place. If this advantage was to be withdrawn, then reciprocity had turned out a very bad bargain and the Treaty should be abrogated at the first opportunity.

Galt's tariff certainly furnished opponents of reciprocity with excellent polemical material, but it seems probable that, had this pretext not been available, some other would have been found and the Treaty abrogated anyway. The victory of the protectionist North in the Civil War had destroyed the delicate regional balance in American politics which had made acceptance of the Treaty possible. Fear of the Canadian railway-building programme, resentment at alleged pro-Southern sentiments and policies in Britain during the Civil War, together with the dissatisfaction of a number of forwarders and manufacturers in Buffalo and New York, created a situation in which few could find good arguments to support reciprocity while many found good reason to oppose. The new Canadian tariff on manufactures may have caused some loss of business to American exporters but of more importance was the fact that it served as an emotional focus for anti-reciprocity sentiment and provided an excuse for ending the Treaty. Formal cancellation had to wait until March, 1866, but the end was in no doubt many years before that.

Exporters in Britain, too, found Galt's tariff by no means to their taste and protested to their government against what they considered improper behaviour in a British colony. This provided Galt with the opportunity to assert publicly Canada's right as a self-governing colony to determine her own commercial and fiscal policy. In reply to a protest emanating from manufacturing interests in Sheffield, England, he pointed out, first, that the new duties were absolutely necessary as revenue measures and secondly, that the people of Canada were entitled to decide for themselves how and to what extent they should be taxed. This uncompromising assertion of fiscal autonomy was allowed to pass unchallenged by the British government. To have questioned Galt's position would, indeed, have been to make nonsense of the theory of colonial self-government. If self-government meant anything, it meant control over the raising and spending of public revenue. It was not as revenue measures, however, that the Sheffield manufacturers had objected to the new duties but rather to their protectionist character. The effect and intent of Galt's tariff, as they saw it, was not so much to tax imports but rather to keep them out. Galt in reply argued that the protectionist function of the duties was quite incidental, and there is no reason to doubt that, as regards the specific changes he had made, he meant what he said. Nevertheless, the new duties on manufactures did serve as the thin edge of the wedge for later tariffs which were admittedly protectionist in their aim. This is what the Sheffield manufacturers foresaw and feared, and in this sense Galt's rebuttal missed the point.

The fact that a colony could with impunity assert its right to decide upon its own commercial and fiscal policies, even when those policies conflicted with the interests of the mother country, high-lighted the profound changes which had taken place in the British Empire since the coming of industrialism. The imperial government had in effect abrogated its authority to control the external economic relations of the North

American colonies, except by treaty. The deliberate destruction of the system of imperial preferences and the repeal of the Navigation Laws had obliterated the formal statutory framework of economic privileges and restrictions which had held the old empire together. The grant of responsible government in the colonies necessarily entailed the cession to colonial legislatures of the power of taxation and consequently the right to impose tariffs as they saw fit. More concretely, the British Possessions Act of 1846 had explicitly empowered the colonial legislatures to repeal any or all tariffs imposed on them by the imperial Parliament, including duties by which a preference had been granted to British ships and products. The intention behind this Act had been to make it easier for the colonies to follow Britain's example and adopt free trade. But, whether intended or not, the statute implied a complete surrender by Britain of control over the fiscal systems of the self-governing colonies, except in respect to the treaty-making power. The limited right which the colonies had enjoyed up to this point of imposing duties for local revenue purposes was now enlarged to include the right which Britain in the past had jealously guarded as the inalienable prerogative of the mother country: the right to impose duties for the control of imperial trade.

Three years after the new duties went into effect, in a report on the Reciprocity Treaty, Galt found occasion to present a more elaborate defence of his policy. Sales of British manufactures in Canada, he argued, were limited by high costs of transport, particularly the cost of moving imported goods from the seaport where they were first landed to the place of final consumption. These costs raised the prices of imports and consequently lowered the real income which Canadians earned by their exports. The same costs, of course, had to be borne by produce which was exported, with the same final result: smaller sales of British manufactures and a lower standard of living for Canadian consumers. The duties on imported manufactures were levied in order to raise money to pay for cost-reducing improvements in transportation, such as railways. If, by raising import duties 5 per cent, sufficient revenue was obtained to reduce costs of transport 10 per cent, then the net result was a *reduction*, not an increase, in the total cost of importing goods into Canada. Consequently, as a result of the duties, the Canadian producer in reality was less protected from overseas competition than before, not more. The British manufacturer would gain from increased sales and the Canadian consumer from lower prices. The cost of imports would fall and the income earned from exports would increase.

In this as in his earlier statement Galt stressed that the primary aim of the tariff was to raise revenue, not to protect Canadian manufacturers. So far from the new duties being protectionist in nature, they left the Canadian manufacturer more exposed to competition than ever before. The new emphasis in Galt's argument was the direct connection which he made between tariff policy and transportation. The tariff was necessary, he argued, in order that Canada might have railways. This close relation between the tariff and the railways was to become even more intimate in later years. Canadian railways were predominantly east-west lines; the tariff became a device whereby traffic could be encouraged to move along these lines and discouraged from moving on north-south lines to and from the United States. Important as it was in the years before confederation, this use of the tariff was to become vital with the construction of the transcontinental railways and the opening of the Canadian west. In Galt's day the function of the tariff was to raise money to build railways; after confederation its function was to create traffic for them. The tariff, by interposing a cost barrier to the flow of goods across the national frontier and particularly from the south, channelled traffic between eastern and western Canada along the transcontinental railways. This made possible the development of industry in eastern Canada, behind the protection of the tariff, to support the agricultural development of the west. The tariff and the transcontinental railways tied together the various specialized regions into a single interdependent system and made the creation of a Canadian national economy possible.

All this was far in the distance when Galt imposed and defended his very moderate import duties. Yet it is interesting to note that even then the level of profits (or deficits) on the Canadian trunk-line railways depended on the level of the tariff, as is fundamentally still the case, despite the intervention of a multitude of complicating factors, at the present day. The railways and the hesitant beginnings of Canadian industry were already setting their mark upon national policy.

The movement of the North American provinces toward confederation was also in large part a reflection of the problems and prerequisites of railway construction. The insistent demand in the Maritimes for an intercolonial railway to connect them with the St. Lawrence was perhaps the most important single factor impelling them, whatever their doubts and reservations, toward confederation. The need in central Canada, after the loss of reciprocity, for new markets in the east and in the west which could be reached only by railways was largely responsible for the support which the confederation movement received in that province from business interests. For the Red River colony and even more for British Columbia, railway connections with the east were indispensable if they were to avoid absorption by the United States. Despite the variety of their circumstances, one problem which all the provinces had when they approached confederation was the problem of railway debt. The assumption of these debts by the central government was a prerequisite for the formation of the dominion.

AN OVER-ALL VIEW

To sum up, in the first half of the nineteenth century the economic development of the British colonies in North America had been based upon the production of raw materials for export to Britain. A system of preferential tariffs in the mother country enabled these colonies to surmount the barriers of distance and climate and to attract labour and capital for development. In 1846, however, a cumulative series of political and economic changes in Britain precipitated the abandonment of the system of colonial preferences. Relations between the colonies and the mother country entered upon a new phase in which the colonies were expected to survive without special tariff privileges. This revolutionary change undermined the economic strategy upon which the colonies had so far based their plans and investments, and compelled them to evolve a new strategy which would enable them to market their produce and so obtain the resources which were necessary for survival and growth. Fundamental to this new strategy was the manipulation of the tariff and the construction of railways. Railway construction was designed to lower still further the costs of the St. Lawrence route and to convert the seaports of the maritime provinces into outlets for the western trade. The tariff was used as a bargaining weapon to secure access to foreign markets, particularly the United States, as a means of securing government revenue, and incidentally as a means of protecting local industry. Difficulties experienced in financing railway construction and in maintaining access to the American market after the Civil War encouraged consultation between the colonies with a view to securing complete intercolonial free trade and the completion of the intercolonial railway system. This in turn, combined with political difficulties in central Canada and the fear of American encroachments in the maritime fisheries and in the Red River area, led to confederation. Confederation represented the formation of a political unit equipped under the British North America Act with authority and resources adequate for the implementation of the new strategy. The adoption of a national policy of industrial protection and the construction of a transcontinental railway marked the beginning of the next phase in development.

SUGGESTIONS FOR FURTHER READING

BASIC WORKS:

Creighton, Donald G., *British North America at Confederation: A Study Prepared for the Royal Commission on Dominion-Provincial Relations* (Ottawa, 1939), Part I, Sections I-X, pp. 7-61

Innis, Harold A., *Problems of Staple Production in Canada* (Toronto, 1933), Part I, Chapters I and II, pp. 1-23

Innis, Harold A., *Political Economy in the Modern State* (Toronto, 1946), Chapters VIII and IX, pp. 145-200

SUPPLEMENTARY WORKS:

McDiarmid, Orville J., *Commercial Policy in the Canadian Economy* (Cambridge, Mass., 1946), Chapter IV, pp. 61-92

Masters, Donald C., *The Reciprocity Treaty of 1854* (Toronto, 1937), Part II, Chapters I-IV, pp. 113-226, and "Epilogue", pp. 227-42

Tucker, Gilbert N., *The Canadian Commercial Revolution, 1845-1851* (New Haven, 1936), Chapters III-X, pp. 48-223

PART III

TRANSCONTINENTAL ECONOMY

CHAPTER XVII

THE STRATEGY OF CANADIAN DEVELOPMENT: PART II, CONFEDERATION AND THE NATIONAL POLICY

CANADA AFTER CONFEDERATION

THE uniting of the four provinces of Ontario, Quebec, New Brunswick and Nova Scotia in 1867 stands out as one of the great episodes of Canadian political history. On the one hand, it established the political framework necessary to the building of a nation in the northern half of the North American continent; on the other, it provided a more explicit formulation of the new strategy of Canadian development which had made its appearance in the 1850's. Yet in the implementation of this strategy Confederation was less a fulfilment of nationalistic aspirations than a bare beginning on the task of creating a strong and unified state in transcontinental British North America. The economic underpinnings of the new edifice were still far from complete, and the weak structure of 1867 was soon to be tested by serious internal tensions, by the western expansion of the United States, and by world depression. The broadening of political union by the inclusion of new provinces and the declaration of independence in the National Policy of 1879 brought greater strength and a greater unity of purpose, but the three decades following Confederation, the most critical phase in Canadian economic history, seemed to many a prolonged period of marking time, of frustration and hopes long deferred. Not until the turn of the century did the programme of nation-building begin to pay off in the spectacular expansion of the years preceding the First World War.

The decision to establish and consolidate a new transcontinental nation in North America had been made in the decades preceding 1867. From the vantage-point of the present, it is apparent that there was no realistic alternative to acceptance of the challenge of nationhood. The construction of canals and early railways underlined the decision to avoid continental integration with the United States. The general strategy is clear in expansionist policies designed to integrate British North American possessions and to strengthen the British connection. Loss of British preferences forced the provinces of Canada and the Maritimes to rely more directly on their own efforts and resources but produced no marked realignment in attitudes or policies, which continued to stress the necessity of measures to offset the growing power of the United States. Nor does

Galt's tariff statement with its affirmation of independence in fiscal matters suggest any departure from the policy of strengthening Canada's east-west axis. The end of the Reciprocity Treaty further emphasized the need to create a stronger national unity under Canadian leadership.

Confederation in a real sense represented a response to conditions in which the range of choice was limited by past decisions and by changing relations with the mother country and the United States. The obvious and perhaps only line of action was the integration of the St. Lawrence and maritime regions, economically and politically, with the objective of establishing a strong base for expansion to western regions threatened by encroachments from the south. Much of the drive to this expansion was provided by the necessity of coping with the problem of public debts incurred in transportation improvements and by the threat of unused capacity in canal and railway facilities which, if not met, could undermine the financial structure of the young country. Inability to capture the trade of the interior of the continent for the St. Lawrence system had the unfortunate consequence that, in terms of her market and resource developments, Canada had over-built and over-extended her transportation system, a situation which could be met only by the development of the new and more abundant resources of the western plains. The Fathers of Confederation had not created this problem but it was their lot to find a solution.

Not only was the drive to expansion great and the range of choice limited, but the obstacles and uncertainties faced were many and varied. Geographically, little was known of the physical environment of the west even though exploratory surveys had been carried out in the late 1850's. In particular, the problem of adapting prevailing agricultural techniques to the difficult prairie setting was not satisfactorily solved for decades. Economically, uncertainties associated with world market conditions and capital and man-power supplies persisted until almost the end of the century; over this period real capital formation proceeded at a much slower pace than in the 1850's and the first decade of the twentieth century. Politically, Rupert's Land and the North West Territories remained under the control of the Hudson's Bay Company, and Prince Edward Island and British Columbia had still to be brought into the federation of provinces. Internal tensions took many forms over these difficult decades. Maritime unrest centring on tariffs, the Red River uprising of 1869 and the North West Rebellion of 1885 with its unhappy repercussions in Quebec, Manitoba's attacks on railway monopoly, and more generally, sharp disagreement in the area of federal-provincial relations—such questions as these taxed the ingenuity of the Dominion's statesmen to the utmost. In Canada's external relations, failure to renew reciprocal trade agreements with the United States hastened the turn to the protective tariffs of 1879.

Yet in spite of serious and persisting issues faced on many fronts, the framework of the new Dominion was brought to completion in the years between Confederation and the turn of the century, and the foundations of a transcontinental economy were laid sufficiently well to withstand the strains and dislocations of two world wars. The closing decades of the nineteenth century may be viewed as a period of consolidation and extension of gains achieved in the 1850's. The rate of economic advance was moderate in comparison to that of other periods but it was nevertheless an era of sustained growth in the face of great obstacles. It is true that external stimuli so important in the decade preceding the First World War were largely lacking and that technological advance was slow to the end of the century, but in view of the range of problems encountered the period from 1867 to 1900 must be regarded as one of solid and substantial achievement in nation-building.

It is not difficult to discern the essential and formative elements in the evolution of the political and economic structure that was emerging over these decades. The larger design was present from the beginning; the creation of a federal system dominated by a central government whose primary and overriding responsibility was the creation of a strong continental unity embracing the scattered and diverse regions of British North America. The detailed programme back of this design appeared slowly and in piecemeal fashion, but by 1879, the year in which the National Policy was formulated, the parts of a comprehensive and more or less complete pattern had fallen into place: a transcontinental railway, protective tariffs, land settlement policy, the promotion of immigration. Agricultural development of the west was basic to the whole programme, and wheat was to become the new staple to which the transcontinental economy was geared, the means of attracting capital and immigrants and of creating a mass market for the materials and manufactured products of the other regions of the Dominion. The unity lost in 1821 was to be restored by a programme of national planning in which private enterprise, strongly backed by the state, was to create the strong though vulnerable structure of the twentieth-century Canadian economy.

THE FEDERATION ARRANGEMENTS

From the vantage-point of the present, it is easy to see the obstacles which faced the Fathers of Confederation in their attempt to build a new nation in North America. It is apparent that these were greater than they realized at the time and it is fortunate that there were present elements of strength which enabled them to push ahead with the task of unifying the scattered and diverse regions which were to constitute, with the addition of Newfoundland, the Canada of today. Geographically, the odds appeared to be heavily against the nation-builders. The vast area to be defended and developed, the natural north-south divisions of the North American continent, the barriers of the Canadian Shield and the western Cordillera—these alone seemed to be sufficient to rule out effective integration of the different regions of the country. Yet in this geographic background there were assets as well as liabilities. The St. Lawrence River system with all its drawbacks continued to play its historic role of unifying the St. Lawrence Lowlands, the heart of the economy then as now. The possibility of working out from this central area to the far west on the basis of a single resource in demand in external markets had already been demonstrated by the fur trade, and in wheat the physical environment was once more to provide a strategic staple for this purpose. An east-west alignment linking Canada with Europe via the shortest of Atlantic crossings had appeared as a response to geographic conditions, and over the nineteenth century the natural lines of development showed no deviation from this pattern. To the south, the proximity of the United States resulted in strong pressures for a unity which would have come more slowly if fears of intervention or absorption had not been so great.

Economic factors also presented obstacles to national integration. Differences in resource development in the major regions led to pronounced differences in outlook, and emphasis on the needs and aspirations of local communities reduced interest in the building of a national economy. Of a population of 3,690,000 more than 80 per cent were engaged in agriculture and extractive activities and most of the remainder were in manufacturing and industry carried on in small, relatively isolated establishments. It would be difficult to find a contrast more striking than that between this essentially rural economy of the Confederation provinces and the prosperous industrial nation of today. On the other hand, there were important economic assets to be taken into account. The boom of the 1850's with its large influx of capital and migrants, and the general stimulus of railway construction representing an investment exceeding $100,000,000, had provided both a strong base for expansion across the continent and the confidence that this expansion could be achieved without dependence on outside intervention. This change in attitude is clearly apparent before Confederation; without it there could have been no vision of a great area of internal free trade, of a strong and diversified economy, and a domestic market large enough to absorb much of the country's agricultural and manufacturing production. A sound banking and currency system had emerged by Confederation, while in long-term finance Galt's fiscal policies had effectively linked tariff revenues and investment in transportation improvements. The framework of a nation had been erected, much valuable experience had been gained, and, as indicated, the necessity of continued efforts to round out the structure and to meet obligations incurred in the past by further development of transportation facilities provided a drive strong enough to overcome obstacles to national unity.

It was in the area of politics, however, that strategic decisions were made and implemented. Political union was a first step and it was not taken easily. The union of Upper and Lower Canada had shown the way, but cultural and religious differences continued to divide these provinces which were inseparably linked, in spite of their differences, by the centralizing tendencies of the St. Lawrence system. Yet this uneasy union had demonstrated the importance of constructing a wider and stronger political base for expansion, and without it it is very doubtful that outside capital would have been attracted in the volume it reached in the decade following 1840. And it was the province of Canada which played the leading part in bringing about the general federation of the St. Lawrence and maritime provinces as an alternative to regional federations which would undoubtedly have delayed the larger unity which emerged in 1867. The passing of the British North America Act in the spring of 1867, in its linking of four provinces, appears now as a natural and logical consequence of the weaker and more limited union of 1840.

By this enactment, the Dominion Parliament was given all powers essential to defence of this new nation, to the development of its resources, and to extension of jurisdiction to territories still to be integrated in a larger national system. In section 91 of the Act, among the twenty-nine specific powers listed were control of the armed forces, the raising of money by any mode of taxation, the regulation of trade and commerce, banking, credit, currency and bankruptcy, criminal law, postal services, the fisheries, patents and copyrights, and in the area of communication such matters as navigation and shipping, railways, canals and telegraphs. In all matters not specifically assigned to provincial governments the central government had general authority to enact laws for "the peace, order and good government of Canada". These were very extensive powers, but they were matched by heavy responsibilities, for the Dominion government was to provide the drive and direction necessary for the creation of an independent transcontinental nation.

The provinces, on the other hand, were granted very modest powers. These were set out in sixteen headings under section 92 of the British North America Act and related mainly to such matters of local concern as property and civil rights, civil law, provincial company charters, municipal government, hospitals and asylums, licences, and (what seemed of very minor importance at that time) the right to raise money by direct taxation to meet government expenses. Education was regarded as a provincial matter subject to Dominion intervention in questions involving legal rights in denominational schools. Legislation concerning immigration and agriculture could be enacted both by the provinces and the Dominion, but the latter had the last word in cases of dispute. In sum, the Dominion government was given wide and general powers, any residual or unspecified powers were assigned to it, and the provinces were left with jurisdiction over matters considered to be of local or particular interest. A major task of construction lay ahead, and concentration of control in the hands of the central government was regarded as a matter of necessity. Other provisions of the Act, such as the improvement of the St. Lawrence canal system, the opening of communications with the west, and completion of the Intercolonial Railway within six months, implied burdens which no decentralized structure could have borne.

The financial arrangements set out under the Act reflect this distribution of powers and responsibilities. Assumption by the Dominion of the costs of defence, of the major part of heavy expenditures on transportation, of administration of the complex apparatus of central government, and of almost the entire burden of provincial indebtedness underlined the importance of federal revenues. Control of customs and excise taxes, from which the provinces as a whole had derived more than 80 per cent of their revenues, was turned over to the Dominion. These taxes, along with stamp duties and bank imposts, formed the major source of revenue for the federal government at this time. The unlimited right to impose taxation in any form provided a guarantee that the Dominion's income would match future demands on its resources. The provinces, although relieved of much of their indebtedness, required income for such services as civil government and the maintenance of justice, for education, charitable services and the promotion of agriculture. It was not expected that there would be call for large expenditures since neither education nor social welfare were the costly items they have since become. To provide for these relatively minor functions, the provinces had the right to raise revenues by licences, permits and fees, they were in receipt of income derived from their control of their natural resources, and they had the right (along with the Dominion) to raise money by direct taxation. This last was of limited importance since direct taxes on land, property, or income were very minor items in the government accounts of this period. In effect, minor provincial responsibilities were matched by slender sources of income.

It was recognized, however, that the provinces in giving up their major sources of revenue had not been relieved to the same extent of financial burdens, and to enable them to balance their budgets provision was made for various forms of Dominion assistance. In general this took the form of annual grants, including per capita subsidies, special grants-in-aid, and in some instances special annual subsidies usually for limited periods. Adjustments were made from time to time, including concessions to Nova Scotia in 1869, special arrangements made when Manitoba, British Columbia and Prince Edward Island became provinces, and a general revision in 1873 to meet the complaints of Ontario and Quebec. In these adjustments there was no significant deviation from the policies and procedures set out in 1867, and no shift from the balance of federal-provincial powers set out in the British North America Act. The intention of the Fathers of Confederation was clear: no province was to have the power to question the federal government's control of the future course of the nation's economic development. If Canada had remained a relatively simple staple-producing economy, this control might have remained strong and unchallenged over a long period. Yet an almost inevitable consequence of success in this venture in nation-building was the appearance of strains in this centralized structure, strains serious enough to bring the powers of the central government increasingly in question as the nation moved into the era of modern industrialism.

Judicial interpretations of the constitution unfavourable to Dominion leadership and a steady enlargement of the functions of provincial governments have combined to produce a federation quite different from that intended by the framers of Confederation. The division of powers as visualized by them could not be explicitly stated in terms fully applicable to twentieth-century Canada; interpretation of the residual powers vested in the Dominion government and redefinition of provincial powers appearing under the heading of "property and civil rights" have, for example, led to a shrinking of the federal power not contemplated at Confederation. A wide range of legislative control has been granted to, or assumed by, the provinces in such vitally important fields as social legislation, industrial regulations and other activities which were of minor importance in 1867. Two world wars and the depression of the 1930's were to result in profound changes in Dominion-provincial relations. New and unforeseen responsibilities of provincial governments have brought with them heavy financial burdens, and the search for additional sources of revenue has brought the provinces into conflict with the Dominion. Resort to income and sales taxes and succession duties, sources of revenue which have become of the greatest importance in public finance, has led to controversy over the proper distribution of the proceeds of these taxes and the best machinery for collecting them. No permanent basis has been found for settlement of this issue of federal-provincial jurisdictions and it remains a crucial problem for the administrations of our time. It is true that the Confederation arrangements provided effective and realistic solutions to the problems of a nation scarcely on the threshold of industrialism, but a combination of changes—economic, political and legislative—has given new strength to the force of regionalism which a centralized structure had been designed to overcome. The challenge of the present is to strengthen and buttress a national unity threatened by forces as strong as any faced by the nation-builders of almost a century ago.

THE DEVELOPMENT OF A NATIONAL ECONOMY

As a major event in Canadian political history, Confederation has received its due measure of attention. The British North America Act spelled out in a general way the aims and objectives of the legislators of the time and the means whereby these were to be implemented. Viewed in terms of the evolution of the Canadian economy, however, it appears as but a step and a halting one in the pursuance of a strategy clearly in evidence in the decades immediately preceding Confederation. In its essential elements, this strategy remained unchanged over the nineteenth century. In some important respects, however, changes in detail occurred with changing economic and political conditions. As the vision of a commercial empire of the St. Lawrence faded, a larger vision took its place. This has come to bear the label "National Policy", a term which has been applied both to the programme of creating a Canadian nation and, in a much more restricted meaning, to the system of protective tariffs which was adopted in 1878. The broader use of the term is now widely accepted and for our purposes is preferable to its narrower application. This makes the problem of its exact definition more difficult, since it embraces a range of elements which by Confederation had not been woven into any clear-cut pattern. On the other hand, the main ingredients are easily discerned: the central place of the St. Lawrence area as the basis for continental expansion, the reliance on transportation improvements to provide the backbone of this expansion, the emphasis on a few staple products for export to European markets, the encouragement of developments in finance and secondary industries to support this structure, and finally the slow shift to tariffs to round out this broadly conceived policy of economic growth. It is important at this point to note the forces which modified this policy and led finally to its more explicit formulation in 1878.

Of the internal changes which left their mark on policy none was more important than the shift from commercialism, with its reliance on short-term capital investment in trade, to industrialism, with its emphasis on long-term fixed investments and large capital outlays. This shift began with the construction of canals and brought with it a heavy and continued pressure for full utilization of the new transportation system. Without the reduction of unused capacity to a minimum there was little prospect of meeting fixed financial obligations or of achieving the prosperity necessary to continued expansion. This became a matter of overriding importance with the approaching end of reciprocal tariff relations with the United States and, equally important, the recognition that expansion across the Canadian Shield to the northwest had become a matter of survival as an independent national entity. This meant no abandonment of established policies, but rather their co-ordination and amplification to meet a new and greater challenge. The basic ingredients were present; it remained to produce a unified plan in which each would make an effective contribution. To link transportation, tariffs, land policy, banking and public finance in a more closely-knit pattern, to foster agriculture and industry in the St. Lawrence provinces and the lumbering and fisheries of the Maritimes, and to create in the process a larger and more unified economic structure—these were preliminary steps in the development of a national economy. A great area of internal free trade and a stronger bargaining position with other nations could be expected to result from the attainment of this objective. The Confederation arrangements laid down the main lines of policy, but it was more than a decade before the various pieces could be said to have fallen in place.

The years immediately following Confederation were prosperous and the young nation got off to a good start. This prosperity, short-lived as it was, provided a happy contrast with the gloom of the years preceding Confederation, a period when fears of stagnation seemed to be well founded. At that time, the limits of expansion appeared to have been reached and a heavy debt burden oppressed the spirits of the most optimistic. Worse still, a substantial net emigration was under way, much of it to a neighbour expanding at a rate which made the Canadian scene appear dismal by contrast, a neighbour, moreover, no longer interested in reciprocal trade. The Washington negotiations of 1871, it is true, ended a period of bickering over in-shore fishing rights, but in the settlement which provided for monetary compensation for United States activities in Canadian fishing areas, Canada's suggestions of reciprocity in trade were rejected. Federal union seemed to be the only way out of a situation in which each province faced difficulties which only a larger unity could hope to overcome. And for a brief spell better times seemed to indicate that a new and more promising start had been made. World market conditions were extremely favourable, and the stimulus of expanding exports was felt throughout the economy. Canadian exports increased from $58 million in 1868 to a total of $89 million in 1874, and imports over the same period rose from $73 million to $128 million. Exports to Great Britain doubled in this period, and even without reciprocity United States imports of Canadian produce increased by almost one-third. Dominion revenues reflected this prosperity; these doubled over this period, customs revenues alone increasing from $9 million to $14 million, and tax returns showing an increase of 60 per cent. Paid-up banking capital increased by a similar percentage, and nineteen new banks came into existence. The total debt of the Dominion climbed from $93 million to $141 million, but buoyant revenues relieved qualms for the time being. Increased activity in manufacturing, transportation and exchange was accompanied by heavy immigration into the country, and despite the presence of strong speculative elements in this boom, Canada seemed to be safely on the road to a strong and prosperous nationhood.

In this period of world prosperity the new transcontinental economy came into being. The canals of the St. Lawrence were deepened and completion of the Intercolonial Railway strengthened ties with the maritime provinces. Prince Edward Island, cold to Confederation proposals in the sixties but now saddled with a debt of $4 million, much of it incurred in railway construction, became part of the Dominion in 1873. To the west, negotiations were concluded in 1867 for transfer of title to Rupert's Land from the Hudson's Bay Company to the Crown and thence to the Canadian government. By the Rupert's Land Act of 1868, two centuries of the Company's rule came to an end. Manitoba became a province in 1870, and with the Manitoba Act of this year Dominion lands policy began to take shape. In contrast to the four original provinces which retained their natural resources without question, the ungranted and waste lands of Manitoba and the entire northwest passed under the control of the federal government to be administered for "purposes of the Dominion". Under homestead regulations as set out in Dominion Orders in Council in 1871 and incorporated in the Dominion Lands Act of 1872, settlers, on paying a registration fee of $10, could file a claim on 160 acres of land. Title to this land could be secured at the end of a three-year period if homestead requirements of cultivation had been met. In addition, pre-emption rights on adjoining quarter sections could be secured at a price to be set by the government. This huge area of the west was to be used as a magnet to attract the immigrants necessary to produce wheat, the key staple of the economy for the next four decades.

There is a close parallel between this acquisition of territory by the Dominion and the Louisiana Purchase in the United States; both removed a major obstacle to western expansion and both gave new momentum to transcontinental expansion. In Canada, this transfer ". . . transformed the Dominion from a federation of equal provinces into an empire with a quarter of a continent of 'Dominion Lands' under direct federal administration. For sixty years this vast domain was 'administered by the Government of Canada' until the historic 'purposes of the Dominion' were fairly achieved, so far as public lands could help to achieve them." (Chester Martin, "Dominion Lands Policy", p. 196, in *Canadian Frontiers of Settlement*, Vol. II, Macmillan, 1938.)

Before settlement could spread in large volume into the Canadian west, adequate transportation was essential, and here also the public domain was put to good use. When British Columbia, its gold-rushes a thing of the past and its debt burden too much a thing of the present, entered the Dominion in 1871, the federal government was committed to constructing within a period of ten years a Pacific railway linking this province with the St. Lawrence region. This was considerably better than the Pacific wagon road the British Columbia delegates had bargained for, but it greatly increased the pressure on the Dominion to push to the Pacific. Construction of a railway over this vast distance entailed expenditures enormous for so weak an economy and by 1873 the Dominion had committed itself to expenditures of $30 million for construction of the Canadian Pacific Railway. The most important form of assistance, however, was to consist of grants of public lands to the Pacific Railway syndicate; in 1873, 50 million acres of western lands were set aside for this purpose. Although this amount was eventually scaled down, railway land grants were to dominate Dominion land policies for the next two decades. Assistance in this form declined after 1894, but by 1908 31,800,000 acres of public land had been granted to railway contractors. This aspect of land policy is discussed more fully in Chapter XVIII, but the central place of prairie lands in national policies should be noted at this point, for in a real sense they provided the basic element in what was essentially a system of national planning. In addition to railway land grants, almost 60 million acres (59,777,000) had been granted under homestead regulations by 1930; the Hudson's Bay Company received 6,630,000 acres in the fertile belt as part of its compensation for relinquishing control in 1870; and one-eighteenth of all western lands were set aside as school grants with approximately 4,900,000 acres sold to raise revenues for educational purposes (gross proceeds of these sales were $73,700,000). When Saskatchewan and Alberta became provinces in 1905, the Dominion retained its control of Crown lands in these provinces, although British Columbia had been granted the same control over its natural resources as that possessed by the original Confederation provinces. Dominion lands policy, as an aspect of nation-building, came to an end when the public lands of the prairie provinces were transferred to provincial control in 1930. The railways had been built and the land settled by this date, and although there has been much controversy about the justice of this policy and the distribution of the burdens entailed in national development it is clear that there was no alternative to the use of land grants on a lavish scale if the purposes of the Dominion were to be achieved.

THE PROTECTIVE TARIFF

Transportation, public finance, and land policy had become closely linked in the prosperous six-year period following Confederation, while territorial acquisitions had produced a transcontinental unity of a sort. But the element which was to become most closely identified with the term "National Policy", the protective tariff, did not take on importance until 1879. Good times help to account for this late resort to high protection. Further, hopes for reciprocity with the United States were not yet dead. The strenuous opposition of the maritime provinces also checked any pronounced move in the direction of high tariffs, and domestic industries were not yet sufficiently strong or vocal to make their demands effective. And for a time Dominion concern with revenues to meet the heavy debt burdens assumed at Confederation led to stress on the revenue aspect of tariffs. As a result there was little change in the tariff structure before 1879; raw materials and most semi-finished goods entered the country free of duty; a duty of 15 per cent *ad valorem* was levied on most manufactured goods and this was increased to 17½ per cent in 1874; higher rates were levied on luxury goods. A policy of "incidental protection" appeared to be most generally acceptable for the time being, and even the slight increase of 1874 was a result of revenue needs. The average duty on all imports stood at about 20½ per cent, a slight increase since Confederation but scarcely a significant move to protection. The events of the next five years were to bring the issue of protective tariffs to the fore and, more broadly, to lead to the formulation of a policy best described as economic nationalism.

In 1873, slump replaced prosperity in world markets and for the remainder of the seventies the rate of expansion declined sharply. The stimulus of a strong external demand for Canadian produce disappeared as economic conditions in Great Britain and the United States deteriorated. Contraction of credit and declining investment and trade in these countries struck at the foundations of Canada's short-lived prosperity and gloom quickly replaced the optimism of the preceding years. There was a painful contrast between the apparent stagnation of these years and the boom of the 1850's and the period immediately following Confederation. The economy of the new country was extremely vulnerable to external changes, and the combination of a heavy burden of indebtedness and a declining level of national income placed a serious strain on a weak economic structure. To make matters worse, the whole period to 1896 was one of periodic and prolonged slumps interrupted by brief periods of recovery. Although recent studies show that the widespread pessimism of the period as a whole was scarcely justified in view of the fact that the growth of the economy, although moderate, was continuous over the last quarter of the nineteenth century, the events of the later seventies did indicate that the objectives of the Fathers of Confederation were not to be attained without a prolonged struggle. Depression hit with full force in 1876 and continued until 1879. Exports declined to a low level of $71 million in the latter year and imports to $82 million. The price level had fallen by 20 per cent from the level of 1873. Trade in Canadian forest products was hard hit and exports of lumber products fell to one-half the volume of 1873. Beginning in 1875, commercial failures displayed a sharp increase, paid-up capital of the banks fell by more than $6.5 million between this year and 1879, and bank loans and circulation contracted sharply over this four-year period. Bank failures brought heavy losses to creditors and shareholders. It was not until the fall of 1879 that market conditions improved, and for a brief period increased immigration and resumption of large-scale investment in railway construction seemed to indicate that the worst was over.

Nevertheless, this period of depression and gloom with its threat of failure left a deep and lasting mark on national policies. Of the greatest significance was a strong move to high protection as a solution for the nation's economic ills. The reasons for this change in policy and its implications for later developments may be noted briefly. In the first place, declining public revenues and fears of national bankruptcy led to a search for more adequate sources of revenue, and higher tariffs seemed to offer one way out of financial difficulties. Secondly, and more important, domestic industry had suffered the full impact of depression; price declines in manufactured goods had been much more serious than were those in raw materials. Although the competitive power of the United States was still not great, the failure to achieve reciprocal trade relations led Canadian manufacturers to emphasize more strongly a domestic market which they felt should be reserved for them. Falling transportation costs had made Canadian industry more vulnerable to external competition, and falling prices of manufactured goods in Great Britain and the United States further threatened Canadian manufacturing interests. Thirdly, it was becoming apparent that a more rapid rate of industrialization was essential if progress was to be made with plans for a better balanced, more diversified and more tightly integrated economic development. Without a strong industrial base there could be little hope of lessening Canada's dependence on external conditions for her prosperity. And finally, and less tangible, there is apparent in the increasing appeals to national feeling the growing conviction that the nation must work out its own destiny, free of outside intervention and the necessity of appealing for better terms to powers interested in their own national designs. The sense of "manifest destiny" so apparent in the United States of the 1840's was much less in evidence in the Canada of the 1870's, but in the national policy formulations of 1879 this feeling was by no means absent. In sum, a policy of protection had its appeal to national sentiment, it offered a way out of depression, and it promised a stronger and less vulnerable economy. It should be noted, too, that it had its uses as a political issue and was not without its appeal to an increasing anti-United States sentiment in the country.

The result was a more complex tariff structure in which particular attention was given to protection of goods which were manufactured or which could be manufactured in Canada. On items not otherwise specified, the general level was raised from 17½ per cent to 20 per cent. Textiles were given special consideration and the iron and steel industry received substantial new protection. Duties on semi-finished goods and industrial materials ranged from 10 to 20 per cent, those on fully manufactured industrial equipment and machinery were in the neighbourhood of 25 per cent, and on finished consumer goods in common use up to 30 pei cent. Protection on such products as glass and chinaware, boots and shoes, and furniture varied from 25 to 30 per cent. Agricultural duties, although of little actual assistance, improved the farmers' morale, and a specific duty on coal of 50 cents per ton improved Nova Scotia's competitive position in this product in the central provinces. The trend to higher protection of domestic industries continued to 1887. Higher duties on iron and steel, farm machinery and textiles, and administrative changes which reinforced the protective features of tariff legislation completed the shift from revenue tariffs and incidental protection to a policy of high tariffs which has continued with few basic changes until very recently.

At the time of this transition to protectionism the bulk of federal revenues was derived from tariffs, and with renewed plans for transcontinental railway construction with its heavy financial demands, tariffs and railways became inseparably linked in a programme of western expansion. High protection to Canadian industry appeared to have two beneficial effects: where goods were kept out of the country by high tariffs and domestic production thereby encouraged, improved prospects for an east-west traffic provided a guarantee of earnings on the transportation system; where goods entered over tariff barriers, the resulting revenues could be applied to meeting railway deficits resulting from loss of traffic. This feature of national policy, the protective tariff, thus rounded out a broad, consistent and comprehensive programme of national planning from which there were few deviations before 1930. It was a programme of economic nationalism, one in which railways and steamships, tariffs and industrial development, and the wheat of the prairies formed the essential elements of a structure which had been evolving since at least as early as the mid-nineteenth century. For the next fifty years a combination of private enterprise and strong state support served the nation through the difficult years of the eighties and nineties, the boom decade preceding the First World War, the war itself, and the hectic and uneven prosperity of the 1920's. Only with the great depression of the 1930's, the end of Canada's western frontier, and a changed political and social climate did this general programme undergo substantial modification. Whether we label it as "the national policy", economic nationalism, or simply "the old industrialism" of wheat, railways and tariffs, the objectives were clear for all to see. Equally clear were the consequences of this policy: a strong economic and political unity to 1930, a better balanced and diversified though vulnerable transcontinental economy, and a rise to a "middle nation" role in world affairs. Colony had given way to nation, and for the time being the pull of the United States economy was held firmly in check.

THE RATE OF DEVELOPMENT: RETARDING FACTORS

Although there has been a tendency to underestimate the rate of progress of the Canadian economy over the period from 1874 to 1886, it is true that economic growth was much slower over these decades than had been anticipated. Population changes, in particular, were highly discouraging. In spite of federal land policies, railway construction and immigration propaganda, a population of some 3,600,000 in 1871 had increased to barely 5,370,000 at the turn of the century. This was scarcely the growth that had been expected and certainly one well below a rate sufficient to people the empty spaces of the west. An average annual rate of increase of 1.61 per cent in the 1870's dropped to 1.13 per cent in the 1880's and in the last decade of the century to as low as 1.06 per cent. Immigration was not absent; more than 1,500,000 immigrants entered the country in this period. But heavy emigration, approaching two million, much of it Canadian-born, indicated that Canada had unwillingly become a temporary residence and a vestibule for settlers whose final destination was the United States. Nor was Canada's trade position any more encouraging. Although both imports and exports more than doubled in these decades, this was a very modest increase from small beginnings and far overshadowed by the expansion of the early twentieth century. The effects of a persistent decline in prices were offset to some degree by improving terms of trade, since the prices of manufactured goods fell more rapidly than those of lumber and agricultural products exported from the country, but higher tariffs weakened any stimulus this might have had for the economy. British investment funds found outlets at home, in United States railway bonds in the seventies, and in South American ventures in the eighties, but it was not until as late as 1903 that they began to move in volume to finance Canadian development. A respectable rate of progress in the 1870's had come close to a standstill by the nineties, and regional and provincial dissatisfaction with Dominion policies steadily increased as the century drew to a close. Without strong external stimuli, the most aggressive of national policies could make little headway, and these were lacking at this time.

This disappointingly slow rate of progress has been attributed to a number of factors. Unfavourable world conditions have been held to explain Canada's inability to attract and hold population and capital in the volume anticipated. Yet other new countries, rich in resources and lacking in labour and capital, fared better than Canada. Bouts of depression in Europe made for a strong push of migration from that area and the New World stood to gain in population from the difficulties of the Old. Canada's pulling power, however, was more than matched by that of Australia, Argentina, and the American west, and in spite of the zeal displayed in the federal government's developmental policies Canadian wheat exports, the basis of Canadian expansion, displayed little change at a time when the exports of other new countries were climbing rapidly. Again, the difficulty of adapting the agricultural techniques of the day to the production of wheat in the difficult prairie environment appears to have disillusioned many of the newcomers to the Canadian west, and this drawback, combined with relatively high railway and ocean freight rates, retarded the extension of wheat-growing in this part of the continent. But the most decisive factor in relegating Canada to a very minor role in the world migration and capital movements of this period must be sought in the weight and momentum of United States expansion westward. The northern nation had to wait its turn until the twentieth century when the westward-moving frontier swung north to the Canadian prairies. In contrast to the inter-war years of this century and the present, a period whose tempo of economic growth is greatly increased by United States capital and enterprise, the later nineteenth century, so far as Canada was concerned, is best summed up as a period of consolidation and waiting until world interest, its capital and its labour, were attracted in volume to the hitherto neglected northern half of North America. Meanwhile, men and money turned to other wests than Canada's.

It was only when the best lands in the United States had been alienated, her agricultural surplus reduced by her growing domestic market, and her forest resources nearly exhausted that Canada's national policy began to pay long-awaited dividends. A brief survey of developments in the United States in the late nineteenth century underlines the minor place occupied by Canada in this phase of North American economic history. In the United States, the moving frontier of the west was the dominant influence in national expansion over the eight decades preceding 1896. In contrast to Canada, where the frontiers of settlement were curbed and controlled in the interests of a unity threatened by United States penetration, the frontiers of the United States, with its security against outside intervention, constituted an expansive, energizing force which greatly accelerated the rate of economic advance. Similarly, Canada's emphasis on a centralized political structure necessary to hold and develop a transcontinental area contrasts sharply with the freedom of frontier regions in the United States. The preoccupation of United States historians (and novelists) with the open frontier as a dynamic force in the country's development has no counterpart in Canadian studies.

This aspect of United States history was of the greatest significance to the rate and character of Canada's growth and its salient features should be noted. In 1860, the population of Canada's neighbour was approximately 31.5 million. The westward movement had reached the area bordering the west bank of the Mississippi, and jumping to the far west had led to economic beginnings in Old Oregon and California. Among the western states which had been admitted to the Union were Louisiana (1812), Missouri (1821), Arkansas (1836), Texas (1845), Iowa (1846), Minnesota (1858), and on the Pacific coast California (1850) and Oregon (1859). Between 1860 and 1890, the period of the "last frontier" in the United States, other regions were admitted to statehood: Kansas (1861), Nevada (1864), Nebraska (1867), Colorado (1876), North Dakota, South Dakota, Montana and Washington (1889), Wyoming (1890). In 1860, the 97th meridian had roughly marked out the limits of western advance (apart from the Pacific coast); by 1890, population had been attracted in volume to settle and develop the region between this line of advance and the scattered settlements of the coast. Miners, ranchers, and farmers pushed into this huge area and before the end of the century frontier expansion had ceased to be the dynamic element it had been since almost the beginning of the century. For Canada, the greater attractions of this area to the south and the momentum of this push westward from a strong and diversified eastern base of operations provided a challenge which could not be effectively met, and it was only when the best lands were alienated in the United States that Canada's great age of western expansion could begin.

The magnitude of United States development in these years of Canada's slow advance is apparent from a brief glance at the principal features of that country's expansion over the thirty years following the Civil War. Over this period population increased in each decade by approximately one-quarter; in 1880 it had risen to 50 million, in 1890 to 63 million, and by 1900 had exceeded 75 million. Annual immigration closely reflected the ups and downs of the business cycle but reached impressive peaks in the good years; in 1867, the figure exceeded 300,000, in 1870 it approached 400,000 and in 1874 close to 460,000 arrivals were recorded. The greatest influx occurred in 1882 with almost 789,000 immigrants; in 1892, 580,000 entered the country. Unlike Canadian experience, emigration does not appear to have been a significant factor at any time over these decades. Agricultural development paralleled this high rate of population increase, and over the half-century following 1860 more than 500 million acres of new land came into cultivation. It is true that agricultural development suffered severely from periods of depression, that lack of experience in semi-arid areas led to difficulties, and that by 1890 the value of agricultural production was exceeded by the net value of manufactured products; but to the end of the century farming remained the backbone of western expansion. Railway construction, the vast area of free or cheap fertile land, and revolutionary advances in farm practices and equipment enabled agriculture to keep pace until the close of the frontier phase of United States history.

Back of western expansion over this period were spectacular developments in railroad transportation and an industrial revolution of great magnitude. Land policies and high tariffs were other strategic elements in the nation's economic growth. By 1870, 53,000 miles of railway had been built and four-fifths of this construction was east of the Mississippi; in 1887, 82,000 miles of railroad were in operation, and by 1890 railroad mileage had increased fivefold since 1860 to 167,000. By 1900 the total was almost 200,000, roughly the mileage of all European nations combined. The introduction of the Bessemer process had provided cheap steel in the 1860's and technological improvements kept pace with railway construction. The Union and Central Pacific Railroads joined at Ogden, Utah, in 1869, the Northern Pacific was completed in 1883 and the Great Northern a decade later. Settlement in the west spread with the growing railway network and land policies supported both. In many areas, the trapper, the miner, and the rancher preceded the farmer, but it was agriculture which provided the base for large-scale population expansion in the west. Adoption of the homestead principle in 1862, a measure opposed earlier by the southern states, made available large areas of free land in exchange for settlement; 160 acres of surveyed public domain could be acquired after five years' continuous occupation and payment of a registration fee. Public lands were thus to be used to promote settlement in the national interest, and they served this purpose as the primary means of hastening western expansion. An evaluation of this legislation cannot be attempted here, but we may note that it was frequently modified and not always wisely, that widespread abuses quickly crept in, and that owing in part to the rush of settlement no national policy of planned development was pursued. Less than half the land acquired by settlers was free land; the larger part was obtained by purchase from speculators, railroads, or states. On the other hand, the Homestead Act had the effect of greatly increasing the pulling power of land in western expansion, for the prospect of free land was a bait difficult to resist, even though selling agencies frequently managed to intervene between the settler and the land he sought.

Land was also used to speed the construction of railroads, the pacemaker of western settlement. Approximately 135 million acres were granted by the federal government for this purpose and state assistance in this form exceeded 50 million acres. One-fourth of Minnesota and Washington was turned over for railroad grants along with substantial areas in other western states. Not only did this "land" bonus greatly stimulate railroad construction, it gave new momentum to western development in the form of the colonization activities of railroad companies. Rapid disposal of much of these lands on credit at $4 to $5 per acre both yielded revenues from their sale and increased traffic resulting from the growth of settlement. Free or cheap land drew man-power and capital on a scale unequalled in the history of "open frontiers".

Closely allied with this westward-moving wave of settlement was a rate of industrial growth sufficient to make the United States the leading industrial power of the twentieth century. In every respect conditions were highly favourable to industrial progress, and the industrial revolution of the post-Civil War period appears as one of the most dramatic events in economic history. An enormous area of free trade, of unrestricted enterprise, of freedom from external attack or the threat of serious social or political unrest, an area moreover of rich, varied and increasingly accessible resources, the United States of this period was blessed with an almost fantastically endowed environment for rapid and unrestrained economic growth. The Civil War had provided a strong stimulus for factory-made products, and one of its major consequences was the rise to dominance of the industrial north with its economic philosophy of laissez-faire—a philosophy or outlook which stressed freedom of enterprise and in particular freedom from government intervention in economic affairs. This was qualified in one important respect, the continuation and even extension of the high tariffs which had appeared as a result of the financial needs of government in the Civil War period. The general level of tariffs had increased from roughly 20 per cent in 1860 to 47 per cent by the end of the war, and in spite of expectations of a lowering of tariffs after the war high tariffs had come to stay. There has been little deviation since from this strongly protectionist policy.

More significant to industrial progress, however, were the country's rich natural resources, the large-scale migration of cheap and skilled labour from Europe, and the large and growing domestic market which offered inducements to enterprise unequalled in the economic history of any other power. The rise of the corporation as the characteristic form of enterprise and the later emergence of strong trade unions were to raise issues of freedom and control which remain major problems today. Big business and colourful personalities dominated the development of such basic resources as petroleum, iron ore, copper, coal and coke. This was an age of iron and steel, and impressive progress was made in this sector of economic growth. In 1869 capital invested in the iron and steel industry amounted to $122 million and value of production approached $207 million; by the close of the century capital had increased to $414 million and value of production to $804 million. Light manufactures, including the processing of food and kindred products, the production of textiles, boots and shoes, kept pace with the more spectacular heavy industries. Mass production and mass consumption quickly became the distinctive marks of the United States economy.

This was the giant to which Canadian enterprise and statesmanship had to accommodate itself. Two dynamic frontiers to the south, the agricultural and the industrial, drew men and capital on a scale which dwarfed Canada's efforts, and Canadian economic history bears witness to the consequences of the proximity of her huge and boisterous neighbour.

It was only as the western land frontier ceased to be a major force in United States expansion that interest could be attracted to the opportunities present in Canadian development. This change along with the return of better conditions in Europe was to provide the conditions necessary to the fulfilment of the objectives of the Fathers of Confederation, and, for a brief interval, the first decade of the present century, the rate if not the magnitude of growth in the Canadian economy was to compare favourably with that of the United States.

THE DAWN OF PROSPERITY

Indications of better times to come made their appearance as early as 1896. The prolonged downward movement of world prices gave way in that year to a moderate movement upward. Substantial additions to the world's gold stocks in a period in which the gold standard was operating effectively helped to bring about this change. This was only one of a number of highly favourable circumstances which appeared at this time to bring prosperity to the Canadian economy. Not only was the selling-price of Canadian exports moving upward, but the cost of transporting wheat, Canada's key staple, was dropping sharply. Further, cheap land and a high level of technical efficiency greatly strengthened Canada's competitive position in world markets. In the period to 1913, the average price of Canada's exports increased by 32 per cent, and of particular importance, the price of wheat at Liverpool rose from 84 cents per bushel in 1896 to $1.13 in 1913, an increase of almost one-third. The spread of industrialization in Europe and the expanding urban populations of that continent supported a strong and increasing demand for foodstuffs from abroad. The same factors in the United States led to a greater domestic absorption of agricultural production there. This declining export surplus in the United States along with the shrinking of the "open frontier" led to an increasing pressure of overseas demand on Canadian resources. On the other hand, the average price of Canada's imports rose only 24 per cent over the period 1896-1913, and the cost of transporting wheat from Regina to Liverpool declined from 26.7 cents in 1896 to 20.8 cents in 1903, increasing again only in 1912 to approximately the level of 1896. Favourable prices of manufactured goods and cheaper transportation coincided with rising prices to bring prosperity to the Canadian west. "In this *conjuncture* lay the economic stimulus which caused the occupation of 73 million acres of land between 1901 and 1916." (Mackintosh, *Economic Problems of the Prairie Provinces*, Vol. IV, p. 10.)

There is ample statistical evidence of Canada's progress in these boom years. Population increased by over 1,800,000 in the decade 1901-11, an increase greater than over the whole period 1871-1901. A prairie population of little more than one-quarter million in 1891 and less than 420,000 in 1901 exceeded 1,300,000 by 1911. Immigrant arrivals, which numbered 82,000 in 1891 and less than 50,000 ten years later, climbed to almost 190,000 in 1906 and exceeded 400,000 in 1913. The country's ability to absorb population increased dramatically over these years, and emigration ceased to be the serious problem it had been. Canada's export trade also reflected the remarkable prosperity of the period. Total merchandise exports of approximately $65 million in 1870 reached a level of $183 million by 1900; in 1910 they exceeded $298 million and by 1913 were close to $380 million. Imports of merchandise for home consumption, which had amounted to $67 million in 1870, were in excess of $172 million by 1900; by 1910 these had increased to $370 million and in 1913 the value of imports was greater than $670 million. This excess of imports over exports over most of the first decade of this century was made possible by the very large volume of long-term investment attracted to the country in these years. For reasons indicated above, terms of trade were substantially in Canada's favour, or in other words the ratio between prices received from exports and those paid for imports was decidedly to her advantage. Banking statistics tell a similar story of good times; the total liabilities of chartered banks, which amounted to approximately $72 million in 1870, had increased to $320 million at the end of the century; by 1913 they were in excess of $1 billion. Strong external stimuli were clearly giving the young economy a lift which had been lacking in the preceding decades. The demand for Canadian foodstuffs was one of these; another and closely related stimulus was the huge capital inflow which began early in the century and continued to the outbreak of the First World War.

The influx of capital was a basic element in an upward movement which, following the years of recovery, 1896-1901, achieved momentum in 1902-3 and took on the proportions of a boom in the years 1909-13. Funds reached the country through various channels; immigrants brought capital with them, investors in search of quick returns from land and other speculations were attracted, and, much the most important, Canadian securities were sold in very large volume in the London money market by governments and railway companies for developmental purposes. British and continental funds began to move on a scale sufficient to dominate this phase of the country's growth. The vast area of Canada and the bulky character of its products necessitated large supplies of capital for transportation and related improvements, and for agricultural, manufacturing and mining development. By 1913, more than $2 billion had been invested in railways alone, the larger part of this sum since 1900. Domestic supplies of capital were much too limited to provide the huge sums needed and it fell mainly to the British investor to meet the capital requirements of the Canadian economy of this period.

The British investor was encouraged to do so for a number of reasons. For two decades most of his investments had been made at home, and a growing scarcity of good domestic investment outlets led him to look elsewhere. Further, the rate of capital accumulation in the United States was so great as to reduce substantially the need for borrowing from London; this country's increasing independence of capital imports and indications of her emergence as the world's leading creditor nation produced reactions in Great Britain. The tendency to increase investment in the home market was counteracted by a declining rate of interest there; this had fallen from 3.20 per cent in 1875 to 2.76 per cent in 1900 and as a consequence the British investor sought other fields of investment in the early years of the twentieth century. Over the period 1903-12, British capital exports as a percentage of total British investment increased from 8 to 48 per cent. Most of this went to countries other than the United States, and Canada became one of the most important beneficiaries of this change in the volume and distribution of British capital investment.

In every respect conditions were favourable to a high level of prosperity in the Canadian economy of the early twentieth century. The spread of industrialism in Europe created a demand for Canada's export staples, a source of cheap manufactured goods for Canadian consumption, and a growing volume of capital for investment in Canadian expansion. In North America, the northward shift of the frontier to the Canadian prairies, the shrinking export surplus of the United States, and that country's declining demand for foreign capital helped to heighten European interest in Canada. Further, technological progress in agriculture, mining and manufacturing in the United States undoubtedly accelerated the rate of Canada's growth since there were few barriers to the entry of technical innovations, most of which could be readily applied to Canadian resource development. In Canada itself, the economic and political bases of expansion had been laid before the end of the century. A national policy based on the closely interrelated elements of railway construction, tariff policies and wheat production for the world markets had been formulated. It remained to implement more effectively the national design visualized by Confederation.

By the close of the century, a growing volume of man-power and capital was being attracted to exploit the country's rich and varied resources. Net capital imports increased from $30 million in 1900 to $60 million in 1904, jumped to $110 million in 1905, and, following a setback in 1907, increased astronomically over the period 1908 to 1913 from $218 million to more than $540 million. In the peak years 1900 to 1913, capital imports averaged almost $400 million a year, and payments abroad on interest and dividends approximately $115 million. Like the boom of the 1850's, this period of capital influx and large-scale immigration produced a stronger and more diversified economy. Although prairie agriculture was the key activity in early twentieth-century expansion, the hydro-electric power and pulp-and-paper industries of Ontario and Quebec made substantial headway; important progress was made in sawmill and logging operations in British Columbia; and the coal-mines of Nova Scotia and Alberta, the gold of the Yukon, the lead-zinc-copper of southern British Columbia and the silver of Ontario drew men and capital for their exploitation. Capital invested in manufacturing operations amounted to \$1¼ billion by 1910, and an increasing proportion of the population was being attracted to the industrial, financial and distributing centres of the economy. A new Canada was emerging, a stronger and better balanced economy able to absorb a population increase exceeding 183,000 annually in the decade 1901-11. Sixty per cent of this increase was accounted for by the western provinces, 38 per cent by Ontario and Quebec, and only 2 per cent by the Maritimes. An expanding domestic market stimulated manufacturing and industrial development in central Canada, while the wheat economy of the west provided the income from exports on which the progress of the economy largely depended in this period.

Geography and economics combined to make Canada primarily a trading nation. A small population on the one hand and a vast output of wheat and later newsprint and base metals on the other ensured a very large export surplus and a very heavy dependence on returns from foreign trade. In this period, the lack or scarcity of certain strategic resources also ensured a heavy dependence on imports, including coal for the industries of Ontario and Quebec, and petroleum, iron ore and various tropical and semi-tropical products in demand in the Canadian market. The sale of surplus products in world markets provided the means of payment for these commodities and the income necessary for repayment of the borrowings necessary to growth in this stage of Canadian development. The size of the country and the dispersion of its resources resulted in heavy initial capital investment, and only a very large export trade could support the huge expenditures incurred in this process of nation-building.

As important as the size of Canada's external trade was its distribution. In the period of 1867-96, trade with Great Britain had been of primary importance; British goods supplied a large part of Canada's import requirements, and a slowly increasing volume of Canadian lumber, wheat, fish, fur, cattle and cheese found its way to the British market. As early as 1883, however, imports from the United States exceeded those from Great Britain and by 1896 more than half Canada's imports originated in the former country; by 1913 the United States was supplying Canada with more than two-thirds of her imports, and the mother country's share had fallen to barely one-fifth. Canadian exports to Great Britain, on the other hand, remained at a high level; these doubled in the decade following 1896 and exceeded \$215 million in 1914. The British market absorbed in the neighbourhood of 50 per cent of Canada's exports over the period to 1914, while the United States' share was little more than one-third. It was in these years that the much-studied triangular system of trade between Canada, Great Britain and the United States took form. Although British investments in the period 1900-13 exceeded $1.75 billion, Canada's merchandise exports to Great Britain exceeded this sum by $670 million. Conversely, a United States capital investment in Canada of $630 million was exceeded by a Canadian import surplus from that country of $1,700 million. Canada was borrowing on a vast scale from the mother country, but she was buying in an equally great volume from the United States.

It is not difficult to account for the scale of Canada's imports from her neighbour. The proximity of the United States, Canadians' familiarity with its products and capital equipment, and the economies of mass production gave that country a preferred position among Canadian consumers. The Canadian environment was not unlike that of the United States and it was relatively easy for the business men of the latter to supply Canadians with the volume and variety of products desired. The location of branch plants in Canada and the smaller country's reliance on the technological and managerial skills of the larger further channelled Canadian purchasing power to the United States. Cheap transportation for bulky products was another factor of importance. In short, United States enterprise was in a better position to meet Canada's import needs than that of any other country. The resulting excess of imports over Canadian exports to the United States was paid for in large part in pounds sterling derived from a favourable or active balance of trade with Great Britain and from the large sums borrowed from British investors. These payments in sterling by Canada to the United States could be used by the latter to pay for the commodities and services of Great Britain and of other countries which in turn could trade in large volume with the British. In this way, increased supplies of pounds sterling, the great international medium of exchange at this time, originated in British loans to Canada. The result was a strong stimulus to world trade. The process by which this large capital inflow was absorbed by Canada and the part played by monetary and trade factors in the mechanism of adjustment of international balances has been analysed in detail by Jacob Viner and others.

This pattern of trade and foreign investment so basic to Canada's growth was to be radically changed in the inter-war years of this century, but it provided one of the mainsprings of progress in this great boom period. British capital and the advanced technology of the United States combined to telescope a process of development which reached a fever pitch in the years 1909-13. There were signs, however, of difficulties ahead. In the first place, although Canada's export trade remained fairly well diversified to 1907, in the following years wheat and to some extent other grains increased in relative importance to a point where the country's specialization in a single export staple could be described as extreme. In other words, Canada's prosperity had become too closely geared to the income derived from wheat. The dangers of excessive reliance on the ups and downs in prices and output of a single staple had already been demonstrated in the days of the fur and lumber trades. In 1913, one-third of her total exports was in the form of grain and grain products. Later events were to underline the disadvantages of this pre-eminence of the "wheat economy" in Canadian trade. Dependence on this staple to support a transcontinental system of railways, to provide buying power for the lumber and related activities of the Pacific and the manufacturing and industrial complex of central Canada helps to explain the speculative, uneven character of Canada's economic growth at this stage.

Secondly, heavy dependence on the United States as a centre of strategic imports assumed either the continuation of large-scale borrowings from the mother country over a prolonged period or, failing this, easier access to the United States market for Canadian produce if Canadian purchases in the United States were to continue at a high level. Canada's bargaining position in her relations with her neighbour was, unfortunately, extremely weak. Canadian products constituted a very minor item in United States trade and in spite of a growing interest in Canadian forest products and non-ferrous metals there was no possibility of coping effectively with tariff policies damaging to Canada's external trade.

Thirdly, the growing interest of United States enterprise in Canadian resources and the beginnings of a volume of capital investment which was later to assume very large proportions were to threaten the economic and even the political unity which seemed to be so solidly established by the progress of the early twentieth century. As indicated early in this chapter, this unity was based on a transcontinental system of railways and the exploitation of staples destined mainly for the British market. The costs of railway construction necessitated a large and balanced traffic of wheat to the eastern seaboard and of manufactured products of central Canada westward to the wheat areas. Any marked decline in this traffic constituted a threat to Canadian unity. This threat was to take the form of movements in United States investment and market demands which in effect pulled traffic south from adjacent regions in Canada. Any weakening of European markets would greatly increase this threat; this was to occur with the unfortunate developments of later decades in this century. In short, inherent in the process which gave the Canadian economy its great lift in the decade preceding the First World War were elements of uncertainty which were to create complex problems for the statesmen of a later day. The events of this period led to the emergence of a strong and progressive nation in the north of this continent, but these same events were to increase the strength of external influences in Canadian affairs.

THE STRATEGY OF DEVELOPMENT: A SUMMARY

The principal features of what might well be termed the "European phase" of Canadian national policy have been outlined in the preceding pages. The Canadian economy was to be geared to the expanding industrialism of Europe. It was a policy shaped by Canada's unique geographic environment, by the strength of British ties, and by the almost overwhelming competitive power of the United States. In its general design it presented few deviations from the pattern of development which had emerged with the fur and timber trades of earlier times. The scale was greater and the picture more complex, but the "old industrialism", which first appeared in Canada with canal and early railway construction and persisted into the inter-war period of the twentieth century, laid the foundations for the Canadian economy of today. It may be summed up as a national programme expressed in terms of staples and transportation, tariffs and railways, land and immigration policies, and the buttressing of enterprise by government ownership and support. It was unfortunate that efforts to fit Canada more effectively into a pattern of world trade increased the vulnerability of the economy to external changes beyond her control and to unpredictable shifts in commercial policy on the part of those with whom she traded. This phase of increasing dependence is not an uncommon one in the history of new countries, and for most it appears as an inevitable step on the road to greater economic maturity.

It was only in the culminating years of this programme that capital, man-power and enterprise could be attracted in sufficient volume to complete the process of building the strong and unified economy which had been visualized at Confederation. In spite of the halting rate of advance and the numerous set-backs and disappointments encountered, it raised the economy to a new plateau of economic development. Viewed in perspective, it marks the close of one era and the beginnings of another. Just as the country's growth in the period of fur and timber had set the stage for the industrialism of canals and railways and the components added following Confederation, the second phase outlined in this chapter was to take Canada into the third and present phase, that of the new industrialism of the mid-twentieth century. Signs of changes which were to take Canada into this modern phase may be discerned in the late nineteenth and early twentieth century. Gold and base-metal mining, the production of pulp and paper, and the development of the country's power resources were to spearhead Canada's progress to the advanced state of development she occupies today, but over the period dealt with in this chapter these and related advances in the mining of new metals and in new forms of transportation were not the pace-setters they are now.

In the half-century following Confederation, the federal government had become committed to the achievement and maintenance of a national unity based on wheat, railways, tariffs, on iron and coal, and on the continuance of close relations with Europe. The speed of United States expansion over this period forced the Canadian government's hand in the push westward from a weak base in eastern Canada. European connections in terms of markets, capital and labour enabled Canadian enterprise and government to consolidate their hold on the northern half of the North American continent. More recent developments threaten this transcontinental structure by strengthening regional influences in the economy. In opposition to an east-west alignment of the economy, lines of trade run increasingly north and south, tying in the various regions of the country with metropolitan centres in the adjacent areas of the United States. The growing demand of the United States for Canada's natural resources, the huge volume of that country's investment in Canadian development, and the increasing intervention of United States enterprise in Canadian economic affairs now strengthen the divisive influences of geography. The resources of developing areas of the country are now largely controlled by the provinces rather than by the federal government, and a consistent national policy has become increasingly difficult to pursue as the better-endowed provinces challenge the latter's control of Canada's resource development. New lines of strategy are now called for. The causes and consequences of these changes in economic policy will be examined more fully in Chapter XXI.

SUGGESTIONS FOR FURTHER READING

BASIC WORKS:

Brown, George W., (ed.), *Canada* (Berkeley, 1950), Part II, pp. 155-277

Creighton, D. G., *British North America at Confederation: A Study prepared for the Royal Commission on Dominion-Provincial Relations* (Ottawa, 1939)

Fowke, V. C., "The National Policy—Old and New", *Canadian Journal of Economics and Political Science* (August, 1952), pp. 271-86

McDiarmid, Orville J., *Commercial Policy in the Canadian Economy* (Cambridge, Mass., 1946), Chapters VII-X

Mackintosh, W. A., *Economic Problems of the Prairie Provinces* (Canadian Frontiers of Settlement, Vol. IV, Toronto, 1935), Chapters I and II, Appendix A

Morton, Arthur S., and Chester Martin, *History of Prairie Settlement and "Dominion Lands" Policy* (Canadian Frontiers of Settlement, Vol. II, Toronto, 1938), Part II, Chapters II, VII-X, XII-XIII

Report of the Royal Commission on Dominion-Provincial Relations, Book 1. *Canada: 1867-1939* (Ottawa, 1940), Chapters I-III

Williamson, Harold F., *The Growth of the American Economy* (New York, 1953), Chapters XVIII-XXVII

SUPPLEMENTARY WORKS:

Brebner, J. Bartlet, *North Atlantic Triangle: the Interplay of Canada, the United States, and Great Britain* (Toronto and New Haven, 1945), Chapters XXIII and XXIV

Faulkner, H. U., *American Economic History* (New York, 1949), Chapters XVIII, XX, and XXIII

Hartland, Penelope, "Factors in the Economic Growth in Canada", *Journal of Economic History* (Vol. XV, No. 1, 1955), pp. 13-22

Heaton, Herbert, "Other Wests Than Ours", *The Tasks of Economic History* (Supplement VI, 1946), pp. 50-62

Knox, F. A., *Dominion Monetary Policy, 1929-34: A Study prepared for the Royal Commission on Dominion-Provincial Relations* (Ottawa, 1939)

Viner, J., *Canada's Balance of International Indebtedness, 1900-1930* (Cambridge, Mass., 1924)

Wright, Chester W., *Economic History of the United States* (New York, 1941), Chapters XXIX-XXX, XXXIII-XXXIV

CHAPTER XVIII

THE TRANSCONTINENTAL RAILWAYS

RAILWAYS AND CONFEDERATION: THE INTERCOLONIAL

THE confederation of the maritime provinces and central Canada in 1867, the purchase of Rupert's Land in 1869, and the admission of British Columbia to the federation in 1870 brought into being a new nation in North America. Political union, however, stood little chance of survival unless it was complemented by economic union. This was necessarily a slow and difficult process. It was not enough merely to abolish tariffs between the provinces and interpose tariffs between them and the outside world. The tariff as an instrument of economic development could not be effective unless the various regions of Canada, with their diverse resources, could specialize in those types of production for which they had differential advantages. Such regional specialization depended upon the creation of transportation facilities which would permit products and labour to move cheaply and easily from one part of the country to another. Economic unification, in a word, depended upon the improvement of communications, and specifically upon the construction of railways.

Two railway projects in particular were indispensable. One was the construction of a line between central Canada and the Maritimes, the other the construction of a line from central Canada across the western prairies to the Pacific coast. The first of these lines had been insisted upon by the maritime provinces, the second chiefly by central Canada, though it also had strong support in British Columbia. It was considered essential that both lines should pass wholly through Canadian territory, partly for strategic reasons, partly through fear that traffic would be diverted over American routes.

Since 1852, when negotiations for joint construction of an intercolonial railway had ended in deadlock, the maritime provinces and central Canada had followed independent policies of railway construction. By Confederation Nova Scotia had constructed a line linking Halifax with the Bay of Fundy at Truro, while in New Brunswick Saint John had rail connection with the Gulf of St. Lawrence by a line running northeast through Moncton to Shediac. In central Canada the Grand Trunk line extended as far as Rivière du Loup, 125 miles east of Quebec. Between Rivière du Loup and Truro there was only wilderness; no private company had plans for bridging this five-hundred-mile gap, nor could the provinces

separately command sufficient resources for the task. The maritime provinces therefore made the early construction of a railway between these
points by the new federal government an explicit condition of their entry
into Confederation.

The issue upon which negotiations had broken down in the 1850's
and which still bedevilled the project was that of the route. Military
security and commercial convenience were in conflict. Any railway from
Montreal or Quebec to the Maritimes which sought the cheapest and most
convenient route would necessarily have to cut through northern Maine.
Any line which passed wholly through British (that is, Canadian) territory would necessarily have to parallel very closely the south shore of
the Gulf of St. Lawrence, avoiding the great northward bulge of the
American boundary. The latter route, since it would inevitably be much
longer and more exposed to water competition than the international
route, could offer few attractions for the promoter and investor. And since
it would by-pass the settled and productive southern and western sections
of New Brunswick, in the St. John valley, it could expect only half-
hearted support from the legislature of that province.

The British government, whose financial support for the project was
indispensable, declined to sanction any route which passed through
American territory. This was the position which it had taken in 1851,
when it had refused to support the European and North American project;
the threat of American attack during and immediately after the Civil
War confirmed its judgment. From the military point of view the value
of the proposed railway was that it would make it possible for troops to
be moved in winter from the British naval base at Halifax to Quebec
and Montreal to repel or discourage American invasion. Clearly this
advantage would be completely lost if the line passed through or near
American territory. The British government therefore remained firm in
its insistence that aid would be given only if the proposed intercolonial
railway followed the northern or coastal route.

Despite determined efforts, these conflicting interests could not be
reconciled. The demand for a rail connection between the Maritimes and
central Canada was so great, however, that throughout the 1850's and
1860's attempts continued to find some compromise solution, but without
success. Finally in 1863 the province of Canada proposed that a survey
of the alternative routes and their probable costs should be made by a
commission of three engineers, one appointed by Canada, one by the
maritime provinces, and one by the British government. This suggestion
was at first accepted with alacrity by the other parties to the negotiations,
but so many difficulties arose that in the end Canada decided to go ahead
independently. An experienced Canadian engineer, Sandford Fleming,
was selected to take charge of the work and a start was made with the
surveys in the spring of 1864.

Fleming submitted his report in February, 1865. At the time of Con-federation, however, the question of the route was still undecided, and the British North America Act, though it included an explicit agreement that the road would be built, said nothing about the route to be followed. But a decision could not be long delayed and in 1868, in response to a request from the government, Fleming gave it as his considered opinion that the northern route was preferable, on the grounds that it was safer from American attack and would be better suited for through traffic, provided that a port for Atlantic shipping were constructed on the Bay of Chaleur. The circuitous all-Canadian route was accordingly selected and construction was begun under government supervision in December, 1868. Completed from Rivière du Loup to Truro in July, 1876, the road cost a total of $34,363,896 and was financed entirely by the federal gov-ernment with the assistance of an imperial guarantee.

Too much influence on these decisions should not be ascribed to Fleming, for the British government had made it quite clear that only the northern route was acceptable. Fleming's influence is seen more clearly in the way in which the road was built. Very high standards of construction were adhered to throughout. Steel rails were used instead of iron, and iron bridges instead of wood. No expense was spared to make the road as durable as possible. These high standards reflected Fleming's belief that local traffic would be relatively unimportant in the road's earnings, since it passed through sparsely settled and for the most part infertile territory. He was convinced, on the other hand, that the Intercolonial could attract through traffic if freight rates were kept low enough, and consequently believed that high initial costs were perfectly justifiable as the price which had to be paid for lower expenses for maintenance and repair later. It is possible to argue, however, with the advantage of hind-sight, that Fleming's belief in the future of the Inter-colonial as a trunk-line carrier had little foundation in reality. Since the road's only connections with the west were by way of the Grand Trunk and the St. Lawrence canals, it could hope for no greater success in attracting through freight than could these routes. The selection of the northern route in New Brunswick meant that the road was permanently handicapped by additional and, from an economic point of view, useless mileage, as well as being exposed to serious competition from coastal shipping. By insisting on high initial standards of construction, Fleming saddled the road with high capital costs per mile of track; by agreeing to the northern route the government made it very improbable that the road could ever attract a volume of traffic sufficient to pay interest on those costs.

These difficulties were later aggravated by the competition of more direct lines from Montreal and Quebec to the seaboard. From the start the Grand Trunk line to Portland, formerly the St. Lawrence and Atlantic, was a competitor for western freight. Eastern extensions of the transcontinental lines constructed after 1885 presented a more serious threat. In July, 1890, the Canadian Pacific Railway, by construction and leasing, completed a "short line" through Maine which gave a direct connection between Montreal and Saint John. Later in the same year it negotiated an agreement with the Intercolonial for exchange of traffic at Saint John for Halifax. These arrangements gave the Canadian Pacific an outlet to the seaboard which was, between Montreal and Halifax, 101 miles shorter than the Intercolonial and, between Montreal and Saint John, 279 miles shorter. In 1914 the completion of the eastern section of the National Transcontinental from Quebec to Moncton added a second short route from central Canada to the Maritimes. Against these competing roads, built without reference to military strategy, the Intercolonial could do little. Handicapped as it was by a circuitous route, heavy capital costs, freight rates kept low for political reasons, and mediocre management, it was hard pressed to cover its operating costs even in years of prosperity and never paid interest on the capital expended on its construction. By ordinary business standards it was an undoubted failure.

In the light of the circumstances in which the Intercolonial was planned, however, and the purposes which it was intended to serve, ordinary business standards are clearly inappropriate for gauging its success. Since the objectives aimed at were political and strategic in nature, the value of the road should be appraised in terms of whether it achieved these objectives, whether some other less costly method would have served equally well, and whether the objectives themselves were soundly conceived. From this point of view it must be admitted that the strategic value of the road was very questionable. The danger of overt military aggression by the United States was not of long duration; and it may be doubted whether there was much point in insisting that the route of the Intercolonial should be as far distant from the American boundary as possible when the Intercolonial's only western outlet, the Grand Trunk, enjoyed no such geographical margin of safety. As an instrument of national unity the Intercolonial was probably more effective: the economic logic which lay behind the insistence of the maritime provinces that the road be built was not wholly erroneous, though the degree to which railway connection with central Canada would adversely affect industrial development in the Maritimes was underestimated and the degree to which it would open up markets for Nova Scotian coal and New Brunswick lumber exaggerated. Since the road was under government control, however, freight rates on the Intercolonial were probably more susceptible to manipulation in the interests of forwarders and producers than on the private lines; consequently the Intercolonial did serve the Maritimes as a measure of insurance against flagrantly unfavourable discrimination by competing carriers. Both this function and the strategic objective, however, could have been served equally well by a railway built more cheaply and with less emphasis on heavy, durable construction. On balance the evidence suggests that the purposes which the Intercolonial was intended to serve could have been achieved with a less massive investment of capital.

THE PACIFIC RAILWAY: ABORTIVE PROPOSALS

With the completion of the Intercolonial the federal government was free to concentrate its attention and finances on the second of the two major railway projects for which it had accepted responsibility: the line from central Canada to the Pacific coast. An undertaking had been given to British Columbia in 1871 that such a road would be begun within two years of the admission of that province to the Dominion and completed within ten. It soon became clear, however, that this promise could not be fulfilled. Much of the territory through which the railway would have to be built was as yet unexplored and unsurveyed. It was by no means certain that a pass could be found through the Rockies with grades gradual enough to make a railway feasible. The suitability of the prairies for agricultural settlement was still a matter of dispute. The premier, Sir John A. Macdonald, had stated his conviction that the road should be built by private capitalists, with the assistance of government subsidies of cash and land, but the uncertainties involved were so great that for several years no one, could be found who was willing to undertake the task.

There was, however, one group of capitalists who had been involved in the transcontinental project from the beginning and who still had a large stake in seeing it carried through to completion under their management. The leading members of this group were the directors and executive officers of the Grand Trunk Railway. The president of the Grand Trunk, Edward Watkin, had played a significant though largely behind-the-scenes part in bringing the Confederation negotiations to a successful conclusion and had been knighted for his pains. Earlier, as we have seen, he had taken the lead in buying out the old fur-trading management of the Hudson's Bay Company and thus had paved the way for the transfer of Rupert's Land to the Dominion. Throughout these long and complicated negotiations Watkin had steadily pursued one unchanging objective: the conversion of the Grand Trunk into a transcontinental railway. This was, in his view, the only strategy which offered any hope of long-term profitability for the Grand Trunk system.

The interests of the Grand Trunk Railway and of the new Dominion of Canada were therefore in principle identical, at least in so far as the need for transcontinental expansion was concerned. The eastern extension to the Maritimes and the western extension to the Pacific were no less indispensable to the one than to the other. This community of interest was clearly recognized by Watkin and his associates, as was the policy which it implied: both extensions, when completed, had to be under Grand Trunk control. The government might build the railways if it chose, but the Grand Trunk, unless it wished to stand quietly by and watch a formidable new competitor appear on the scene, had to be responsible for their operation.

It had been taken for granted both by Watkin and by Sir John A. Macdonald that the Intercolonial upon completion should be operated by the Grand Trunk. Watkin, however, was edged out of office in 1869 and Macdonald's Conservative government was defeated in the elections of 1873. The Liberal government under Alexander Mackenzie which took office in 1874 was by no means as well disposed toward the Grand Trunk as its predecessor had been and, when the Intercolonial was completed, decided in favour of government operation. This was a serious setback to the policy which Watkin had laid down. The eastern extension had slipped through the Grand Trunk's grasp. Would the Pacific project also escape capture?

Although the Grand Trunk and the government saw eye to eye on the need for a Pacific railway, their views as to precisely how it should be built did not coincide. From the government's point of view it was essential that the line should run entirely through British territory. This implied construction through northern Ontario, round the north shore of Lake Superior to Fort William, thence to Fort Garry (Winnipeg) and thence across the prairies to the Rockies and the Pacific coast. Such a line would undoubtedly prove very difficult and expensive to construct; it would pass through terrain which (as was then believed) was unlikely ever to generate traffic, particularly the section across the Precambrian Shield north of Lake Superior; and it would be entirely separate from and to some extent competitive with the Grand Trunk's existing system in southern Ontario. For these reasons the government's plan was totally unacceptable to the Grand Trunk management. "I am quite clear," the managing director wrote in 1872, "that railways from Fort Garry around the north shore of Lake Superior and Lake Nipissing could not be built except at a frightful cost, when built could not be worked successfully in winter, and if it could be worked would have no traffic to carry upon it."

The scheme which the Grand Trunk proposed as an alternative to the government plan was one which reduced to the minimum the need for new construction and new capital expenditure. As in the government plan, a new railway was to be constructed in the west, from Fort William to Winnipeg and thence to the Pacific. In the east the Grand Trunk's existing line from Quebec to Sarnia was to be used. But—and this was the basic difference from the government plan—between Sarnia and the west reliance was to be placed on American railroads across Michigan, Illinois, and Minnesota (supplemented by shipping on the upper Lakes during the open season). In this way the need to build a Canadian line north of Lake Superior would be avoided completely. All that would be necessary to complete a through rail connection between western and central Canada was the construction of a relatively short branch line from Winnipeg to Pembina, to link up with the American railways.

If in the case of the Intercolonial the government had found sufficient reason to veto the economically preferable route simply because of the fact that it passed through American territory, it was hardly likely that they would look with favour on this plan for the western transcontinental. The railway, after all, was not intended to be merely a method of transporting goods from one place to another; it was also an instrument of national unification. How could it serve this purpose if the vital link between east and west remained under the control of a foreign power? One of the major objectives of Confederation had been to preserve the western prairies north of the 49th parallel for Canada. Was this objective likely to be achieved by a plan which deliberately fed traffic to and from the west onto American railroads? However attractive the Grand Trunk's proposal might be in terms of time and money to be saved in the short run, it did not conform to the long-term strategy of Canadian national policy.

By refusing to discard these proposals, the Grand Trunk interests excluded themselves for the time being from participation in the plan for western expansion. It is conceivable that if no other group had come forward the government might in the end have come round to their way of thinking and accepted the Grand Trunk plan as a temporary expedient, hoping that in this way a start at least might be made with railway building and settlement in the prairies and that at some later date the all-Canadian route across the Precambrian Shield north of Lake Superior might be added when traffic volume justified the investment. The consequences which such a choice would have had for Canadian development must of course remain a matter for speculation, but it is worth noting that the Grand Trunk management, in emphasizing the very large investment required to construct a railway across the Canadian Shield and the improbability that this region would, within the foreseeable future, generate traffic for the system, were singling out a factor which has underlain the financial problems of the Canadian transcontinental railways up to the present day. The costs of constructing such a railway, as reflected, for example, in the deficits of the Canadian National Railways, are an index of the obstacles which geography placed in the way of national unity.

The Grand Trunk interests, however, were not the only entrepreneurs with whom the government was in communication. During 1871 an offer to build the railway had been received from a group of American promoters headed by Jay Cooke, president of the Northern Pacific Railway. Chartered by the American Congress in 1864, the Northern Pacific had been empowered to build a railway from some point on Lake Superior to Portland, Oregon. In 1871 its line had reached the Red River. Its promoters were interested in the possibility of obtaining a Canadian charter for two reasons: first, because it would enable them to expand northward into the Canadian prairies and thus develop settlement and traffic in an area which the other American railroads could not touch; and secondly because it would permit them to build a railway in eastern Canada to link up with their subsidiary, the Vermont Central, and thus give them access to Boston by way of Montreal.

Jay Cooke and his associates first approached Sir Francis Hincks, minister of finance in the Macdonald government. Hincks foresaw that the syndicate's offer would stand little chance of acceptance if presented as a purely American proposition and therefore urged them, unofficially, to secure Canadian participation. At the same time he approached Sir Hugh Allan, a prominent Canadian business man, and suggested that he get in touch with the Northern Pacific group. Allan took his advice, came to an understanding with Cooke, secured additional backing in Canada, and in December, 1871, formally submitted to Macdonald's government a proposal to build the Canadian transcontinental.

Sir Hugh Allan had made his reputation in Canadian business as head of the Allan steamship line, one of the earliest transatlantic lines to offer regular mail and passenger service between Quebec and Liverpool. More recently, however, he had entered railroading with his promotion of the North Shore Railway, a line running from Quebec westward, the purpose of which was, from Allan's point of view, to provide traffic for his ships and free him from dependence on the Grand Trunk. The alliance between Allan and Cooke meant that the American group had acquired as their Canadian representative a man who, far from being a mere figurehead, had considerable experience in transportation and who was in addition well versed in the intricacies of Canadian politics. This did not mean, however, that all opposition in Canada disappeared. Business interests in Ontario, particularly in Toronto and Hamilton, alleged that if Allan were permitted to dominate the project the terminus of the transcontinental line would inevitably be at Quebec (the implication being that Allan was still primarily working for the interests of his shipping line). These critics also asserted that the American capitalists associated with Allan were not really interested in building a Canadian transcontinental at all, but merely wished to get control of the project in order to delay construction and suppress a potential source of competition with the Northern Pacific. The Grand Trunk interests too, already hostile to Allan because of his North Shore venture, opposed his association with this larger project.

This opposition crystallized in the formation of a rival syndicate known as the Interoceanic Railway Company. This syndicate, led by D. L. MacPherson, represented a coalition of Toronto and Grand Trunk interests, whereas Allan's organization, the Canada Pacific, was backed by Montreal and Quebec and by the Northern Pacific. Both groups sought and received charters and promises of financial assistance. Efforts by the government to bring about an amalgamation of the two concerns at first proved abortive, but after the elections of August, 1872, in which Macdonald's government was returned to office, a new company was formed under the name of the Canadian Pacific Railway. Ontario and Quebec were both represented on the board of this new organization, but the fact that Allan was president left little doubt as to which of the rival syndicates had won the advantage. To the new concern the government granted a charter and promised assistance in the form of a cash subsidy of $30 million and a land grant of 50 million acres. It was stipulated, however, that the American interests which had previously backed Allan should be excluded from participation. Allan acquiesced in this demand and severed his connection with the Northern Pacific group.

What followed made it clear that Allan had badly over-played his hand. The American interests, resentful at being excluded from the new agreement, made public some of Allan's personal letters which disclosed that the expenses of certain leading members of the Conservative party in the previous election had been heavily subsidized by Allan with funds provided by the Northern Pacific. A major political scandal developed and Macdonald's Conservative government was forced to resign in November, 1873. Shortly thereafter the Canadian Pacific company, which had in any event been experiencing very great difficulty in raising capital in England, gave up its charter.

SURVEYS AND GOVERNMENT CONSTRUCTION

With the advent to power of the Liberal party under Alexander Mackenzie at the end of 1873 the Pacific project entered upon a new phase. Unable to find a group of capitalists able and willing to undertake the task without dependence on American backing, the government decided to begin construction itself, but to proceed cautiously and slowly, using the existing water communications wherever possible between the Rocky Mountains and the eastern terminus and not laying track much ahead of the expansion of settlement. This new policy made necessary a revision of the terms of union with British Columbia, a step which evoked strong protests in that province. The dispute was submitted to arbitration, and in November, 1874, the Earl of Carnarvon, secretary of state for the colonies, proposed a compromise which was accepted by both parties; the most important modification was that the railway was to be completed before December 31, 1890, at least as far as to link up with the American railway system at the western end of Lake Superior.

In accordance with this new policy, the Liberal government in the next few years pushed ahead gradually with the improvement of parts of the old land-and-water route to the west and with the construction of railways in certain vital sections. The so-called "Dawson route" from Lake Superior to the Red River settlement was improved; a survey for possible routes in British Columbia and through the mountains was put in hand; and some sections of railway track were actually laid west of the Red River. A line was completed between Fort Garry and the United States boundary, providing a link with the St. Paul and Pacific, an American road, while in eastern Canada provision was made for the extension of the Canada Central Railway to Georgian Bay in order to provide a better connection for shipping on the upper Lakes. These relatively small-scale projects proved in the aggregate a useful if unspectacular achievement, but progress was retarded not only by the difficulty of raising capital in a period of depression but also by the limited executive capacity of the recently organized federal government and by the scarcity of engineering ability. Popular demands for more rapid progress and the difficulty experienced in exercising administrative control from central Canada over construction in the prairies led the government to offer once again to contract out parts or the whole of the work to private organizations. The offer at first evoked no response.

On the surface Canada's progress with the building of the transcontinental railway in these years may appear largely a story of graft and intrigue on the one hand and penny-pinching over-cautiousness on the other. Nevertheless, independent of the manoeuvrings of politicians and promoters, there was slowly emerging a more realistic sense of the dimensions of the undertaking and a more rational appreciation of the problems involved. Very little was known of the agricultural possibilities of the western prairies when the transcontinental railway project was first accepted as government policy, and the possibility of finding a suitable route was open to question. The dissipation of these and other uncertainties was the work of a number of engineers and surveyors whose names made little impression on the general public but whose role nevertheless was of vital importance.

The fur-traders who had originally been responsible for the exploration of the prairies, the passes through the mountains, and the interior of the Pacific coastal strip had not been interested in agricultural settlement; their eyes had been trained to search for water transport routes with easy portages, rather than the straight lines and low grades which the railway engineer hoped to find. The first official reports on the feasibility of large-scale agricultural settlement in the west were prepared by three expeditions sent out by the government of the province of Canada in

1857 and 1858. The first of these expeditions, under the leadership of George Gladman, explored the route from Lake Superior to the Red River and the valley of the Assiniboine as far west as Portage la Prairie. The second and third, under H. Y. Hind and S. J. Dawson, covered the territory between Red River and the South Saskatchewan and that lying north and west of Red River.

In general the reports submitted by the leaders of these expeditions were optimistic—more so, as later experience proved, than the situation justified. Hind, for example, although he considered the drainage basin of the South Saskatchewan "unfit for the permanent habitation of man" because of low rainfall, was convinced that, from a few miles west of Lake of the Woods to the Rocky Mountains, there stretched a continuous belt of fertile territory, curving northward around the edge of the so-called American desert, which was highly suitable for settlement and cultivation. Any railway, wrote Hind, which passed through this fertile belt would eventually enjoy the great advantage of "being fed by an agricultural population from one extremity to the other". This served to offset to some extent the pessimistic reports circulated by the officers of the Hudson's Bay Company.

Somewhat less encouraging, however, was a report submitted in 1863 by a certain Captain Palliser, an explorer and engineer appointed by the British government to report on the country west of Lake Superior. Palliser gave it as his considered opinion that, as a consequence of the choice of the 49th parallel as the international boundary, it would prove impossible to construct a transcontinental railway exclusively through British territory. He believed that settlers would be brought in by ship to the head of Lake Superior, and he was prepared to recommend the construction of a railway across the prairies. But he did not consider that a direct rail link between western and central Canada would be feasible. As for the topography and agricultural possibilities of the prairies, he in general corroborated Hind's conclusions. Part of the American desert—that great tract of semi-arid land which had, in the United States, blocked the continuous expansion of settlement from the Mississippi to the Pacific coast— projected northward into western Canada. This intruding wedge of arid land later came to be known as "Palliser's triangle". Its base lay along the international boundary between 100 degrees west longitude and the foot of the Rocky Mountains, while its apex (or rather its northern boundary, for Palliser's detailed account made it clear that it was not strictly a triangle but more nearly a pentagon) extended north as far as the 52nd parallel of latitude. Within this semi-arid area, in Palliser's opinion, settlement was impossible. Farther to the north, however, there stretched the fertile belt which Hind also had described, a great "rainbow" of territory eminently suitable for agriculture which included the valleys of the Red, the Assiniboine, and the North Saskatchewan Rivers. Within this belt settlement was, according to Palliser's report, entirely feasible, although he believed that cattle-raising was likely to be more successful than wheat-growing because of frost hazards.

These surveys and reports provided the factual basis for the transcontinental projects of the 1870's. They were not significantly altered until 1880 when—if we may anticipate the sequence of events a little—John Macoun, a botanist attached to the engineering staff of the Canadian Pacific Railway, prepared a highly optimistic report, based partly on information supplied by railway surveying parties, which in important respects contradicted the testimony of Hind and Palliser. Specifically, Macoun reported that much of the territory which Palliser had classed as arid was in fact perfectly suitable for agriculture and pasture. Palliser had been deceived, it was alleged, in concluding that the treeless prairie which made up much of "Palliser's triangle" had too little rainfall to be of any use for agriculture. The apparent aridity of this area, according to Macoun, was due to the clayey nature of the soil, which would not hold the moisture unless and until it was broken up by the plough. By this process of reasoning Macoun was able to increase substantially the total area in the west which could be classed as fit for agricultural settlement. Between Manitoba and the Rockies there were, he estimated, not less than 150 million acres of land which could support an agricultural population.

RAILWAY LAND GRANTS

The extent and location of the land fit for agricultural settlement in the west were not matters for mere abstract curiosity. They were directly relevant to the amount and kind of government assistance which a transcontinental railway company could count on receiving and for the route which would be chosen. Information as to rainfall, temperatures, and soil types, incomplete and unreliable as it was, provided the factual basis for both public and private planning.

It had been assumed almost without question from the first discussion of the project that part of the assistance which the government would provide to a transcontinental railway company would take the form of a land grant. In the United States, in spite of constitutional difficulties which did not exist in the case of Canada, the use of unoccupied land to assist projects of public benefit and accelerate the process of settlement had become an accepted practice, and approximately 150 million acres of land had been granted to western railways between 1850 and 1870. The policy was discontinued in the United States in 1871; the same year saw its inception in Canada. In approving the resolution in favour of the railway to British Columbia the Canadian House of Commons stipulated that the public aid to be given "should consist of such liberal grants of land, and such subsidy in money, or other aid, not increasing the present rate of taxation, as the Parliament of Canada shall hereafter determine." Assistance to railways in the form of guarantees of bonded debt had been tried in Canada in the 1850's and 1860's, and the memory was still painful. Assistance to the transcontinental project was to take the form of outright grants of land and money, a method which had the semblance at least of limiting the government's obligations to fixed and predictable amounts.

In accordance with this policy the federal government offered in 1872 to any private company which would undertake to build the transcontinental railway a land grant of not more than 50 million acres, the lands to be located on either side of the railway in blocks not more than 20 miles deep and between 6 and 12 miles in frontage on the railway. The blocks were to be laid out in such a way that each one granted to the company on one side of the railway should be opposite a block of the same width reserved for the government on the other side. This was, it should be noted, a departure from the American method of locating railway lands by alternate sections, the idea being that the method proposed by the Canadian government would encourage compactness of settlement. The offer made to Sir Hugh Allan's company in 1872 included a land grant of this size and type, supplemented by $30 million in cash; but in a further departure from American practice which was to prove important later, a clause was inconspicuously inserted in the contract stating that the lands granted to the company were to be "of the fair average quality of the land in the sections of the country best adapted for settlement". According to the American method the railway company had had to take "pot luck", as it were, with the quality of the alternate sections which it received. The "fair average quality" clause in the Canadian contract marked the introduction of an entirely novel principle which entitled the company to reject inferior sections. Cancellation of the Allan contract nullified the effect of the clause in this case, but it was to reappear in modified form in later agreements.

After the "Pacific scandal" Mackenzie's Liberal government offered as an inducement to private capitalists $10,000 in cash and 20,000 acres of land per mile of track, the land to be in alternate blocks of 20 square miles, each block having a frontage of between 3 and 6 miles on the line of the railway. On this basis the total amount granted would have been approximately 54 million acres. This offer, as we have already observed, evoked no response. Sir John A. Macdonald, whose party returned to office in 1878, stepped up the land grant offer to 100 million acres, a very substantial increase which, if put into effect, would have involved handing over to the railway company all ungranted land within twenty miles on either side of the track. In June, 1879, the system of large blocks was abandoned and the American system of alternate sections, each of 640 acres, adopted. The principal reason for this change was the need to compete with the very liberal conditions of land sale offered by American railways, particularly the Northern Pacific and the St. Paul, Minneapolis and Manitoba.

This was the situation as of the year 1880. With certain significant exceptions the Canadian government had adopted the American system of land grants to western railways. Despite successive increases in the total quantity of land offered, no acceptable proposition had been received from private railway interests since the failure of Allan's scheme in 1873. On the other hand, surveys of the western prairies had made it clear that by no means all of the total land area was suitable for cultivation. If we accept John Macoun's calculation as a rough indication of contemporary thinking on the subject, then Macdonald's offer of 100 million acres represented two-thirds of the total area believed to be fit for agriculture and pasture. More recent estimates suggest that Macoun erred on the side of over-optimism.

THE SEARCH FOR A ROUTE

Choice of the route to be followed by the railway across the prairies depended on reports as to the location of the fertile areas and on the discovery of suitable passes through the mountains. The job of finding the best route was given by the government to Sandford Fleming, who was appointed chief engineer in 1871. Though somewhat distracted by his work for the Intercolonial, Fleming conducted over the next nine years a very exhaustive series of surveys which made it clear that a feasible route was available, though it would undoubtedly be very expensive.

To avoid the unpleasant necessity of choosing between Montreal and Toronto as the eastern terminus, the government decided that the proposed railway should start at some point on Lake Nipissing in northern Ontario, leaving it up to private groups to build connections from this point to the major cities. Westward from this terminus the route had to pass through three distinct areas. First there was the thousand miles of wood and muskeg across the Canadian Shield north of Lakes Huron and Superior, from Lake Nipissing to the Red River—very difficult territory which had never been thoroughly explored. Construction over this terrain would certainly involve problems unlike any which railway engineers had previously encountered in North America. Westward from the Red River there stretched the prairie region, in which no serious engineering problems were anticipated. Beyond the prairies there was the mountain section, the most difficult of all. This section had three principal topographic features, running roughly parallel to each other from north to south: first the Rocky Mountain chain, then an intervening high plateau, and finally the coastal range, rising almost directly from the ocean.

In each of these sections the engineering and surveying parties had to meet different problems and work within different limitations. In the section north of Lake Superior the engineer's freedom of choice was limited to deciding how far inland from the shore of the Lake the line should run, and from the point of view of construction costs or probable traffic the exact location was a matter of marginal importance. Nor was there much room for choice in the section between the head of Lake Superior (the present Fort William) and the Red River: the line could head either for Selkirk or for the rapidly growing city of Winnipeg, but if it was to remain within Canadian territory it had to pass north of Lake of the Woods. As for the prairie section, the work of Hind and Palliser made it highly desirable that the line should run through the fertile belt, or in other words that it should take a northerly route (that is, in the general direction of the present city of Edmonton) rather than a southerly one close to the Canadian-American border. The feasibility of this northerly route, however, depended on the discovery of a suitable pass through the Rockies and the Cascades and thence to the coast. This was, at the time when Fleming began his surveys, the biggest single uncertainty involved in the choice of a route.

The selection of a pass through the mountains involved not only consideration of distances and gradients but also of the location of the Pacific terminus. By 1873 Fleming had made up his mind that the Yellowhead Pass offered the most suitable route through the Rockies. A vigorous dispute arose, however, over whether the line west of the mountains should head for Burrard Inlet (that is, the present city of Vancouver) or alternatively should seek a more northerly terminus at Bute Inlet. If the latter were chosen it would be possible to build a bridge across to Vancouver Island, so that Victoria could retain its position as the major seaport of the area. Fleming, however, gave his final judgment in favour of a line from Yellowhead Pass to Burrard Inlet by way of the Thompson and Fraser Rivers. Though far from popular in British Columbia, this selection was accepted by the government.

Adoption of Yellowhead Pass made it possible for Fleming to run his route across the prairies through the "fertile belt". Beginning at Fort William, he proposed that the line should head for Selkirk, as it would be rather easier to bridge the Red River here than at Winnipeg. Crossing Lake Manitoba at the Narrows, the line was to run almost in a straight line from Selkirk to Edmonton and thence to Yellowhead Pass, through relatively easy territory with low gradients. After the original surveys had been completed the expansion of settlement around Winnipeg made it desirable to discard the line running through Selkirk and a new route was laid out passing through Winnipeg and thence running south of Lake Manitoba to join the line originally proposed. For the section north of Lake Superior between Fort William and Lake Nipissing three possible routes had been found by the end of 1873. The decision of the Liberal government to use water transportation for this section, however, meant that no final selection of the route was made before 1880.

Selection of a route by Fleming and its approval by the government did not, of course, imply that any transcontinental railway which received government aid would necessarily have to follow that route. It meant only that at least one feasible route was available. As we shall see, the first Canadian transcontinental railway did not follow Fleming's route. Nevertheless, the work of the government engineers and surveying parties in the years before 1880 did much to clear away the fog of uncertainty which had earlier obscured the transcontinental project. Planners of the second and third transcontinentals—the Canadian Northern and the Grand Trunk Pacific—relied heavily on their findings.

CHARTERING OF THE CANADIAN PACIFIC RAILWAY COMPANY

The policy of the Liberal government which took office in 1873 had been to proceed gradually with the work of construction, making maximum use of water communications where such existed. The positive results of this policy were to allow time for careful surveys to be completed and to postpone a full-scale attack upon the building of the railway until business conditions improved. As to the prudence of the policy there was little question. The meagreness of the results, however, led to increasingly sharp criticism. Protests against the slowness with which progress was being made reflected partly recovery from the depression of 1873-9 and partly an awareness of Canada's increasing ability to tackle the job of building a transcontinental railway system. The decade of the 1870's was not a period of rapid economic growth in Canada, as measured by any of the usual indices, but it was a period when the gains of previous years of prosperity were being consolidated. In an economic sense Canada was better able to support the construction of a transcontinental railway in 1880 than in 1870. The disparity between political union and the level of economic development necessary to fulfil the terms of the union was smaller at the end of the decade than it had been at the beginning. Nevertheless, the task was still a formidable one. The population of the United States at the time when the first Pacific railway was built in that country was approximately 30 million; the population of Canada in 1880 was just over 4 million.

By 1880, almost ten years after the pledge to build the transcontinental railway had been given, surveys had been completed for the whole route, Manitoba had been linked indirectly with central Canada both over American railways and by a Canadian line to the head of Lake Superior, and a start had been made with construction in British Columbia. The

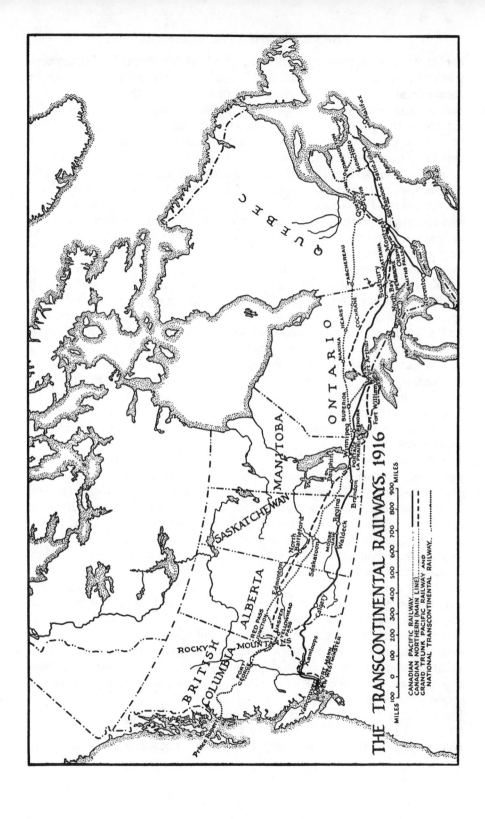

THE TRANSCONTINENTAL RAILWAYS, 1916

MILES 100 0 100 200 300 400 500 600 700 800 900 MILES

CANADIAN PACIFIC RAILWAY. _____
CANADIAN NORTHERN (MAIN LINE) ....
GRAND TRUNK PACIFIC RAILWAY AND
    NATIONAL TRANSCONTINENTAL RAILWAY. ....

QUEBEC

ONTARIO

MANITOBA

SASKATCHEWAN

ALBERTA

BRITISH COLUMBIA

ROCKY MOUNTAINS

Halifax
St.John
Sherbrooke
MONTREAL
OTTAWA
Smiths Falls
PEMBROKE
MATTAWA
Toronto
North Bay
Sudbury
Quebec
TASCHEREAU
COCHRANE
HEARST
MAKINA
Fort Armour
Fort William
SUPERIOR
Winnipeg
PORTAGE LA PRAIRIE
Dauphin
Brandon
Regina
MOOSE JAW
Waldeck
North Battleford
Saskatoon
Edmonton
RED PASS JUNCTION
JASPER
YELLOWHEAD
FORT GEORGE
Kamloops
Calgary
PORT MANN
NEW WESTMINSTER
Vancouver
Victoria
Prince Rupert

return of relative prosperity in 1879 provided Macdonald's Conservative government, which had ousted the Liberals in 1878, with an opportunity to accelerate the rate of progress by contracting for the construction of the transcontinental with a group of private capitalists. This implied a return to the policy of 1870-3. The stipulation which had marked the earlier negotiations—that the contracting parties should be free from American control—was still in force.

The failure of English investors to come forward with an acceptable proposal, the deep-seated suspicion of American capital, and the refusal of the Grand Trunk to consider any project involving construction north of Lake Superior left the Canadian government in a very difficult situation. It was all very well to decide, as a matter of policy, that the work would go forward more quickly if a private company took it over; but what if no private company wanted the job? This was the impasse which Macdonald's government faced and to which for more than two years it could find no solution. A possible way out did not appear until the late spring of 1880, when negotiations were opened between the government and a group of business men associated with an American midwestern railway, the St. Paul, Minneapolis and Manitoba. Thereafter events moved quickly. By August, 1880, an understanding had been reached on the amount and terms of government aid. A contract was signed in October and submitted to Parliament for ratification in December. In February of the following year the act ratifying the contract and chartering the Canadian Pacific Railway Company received the royal assent and became law.

The men who formed the nucleus of the Canadian Pacific syndicate had originally made their fortunes by a highly successful reorganization of a twice-bankrupt Minnesota railway, the St. Paul and Pacific. Chartered in 1857 as the Minnesota and Pacific, this railway had been planned to run from St. Paul on the Mississippi to Breckenridge on the Red River. In spite of receiving a large land grant and a cash subsidy from the state legislature, it had gone into bankruptcy before any track was laid. After reorganization as the St. Paul and Pacific a large bond issue was floated in Holland and the line was completed from St. Paul to Breckenridge. The company again became bankrupt, however, and, at the instigation of the Dutch bondholders, was placed in receivership in 1873.

The misfortunes of the St. Paul and Pacific up to this point had been due almost entirely to inefficient and unscrupulous management; fundamentally the road was a sound project, if it could cut loose from past indebtedness. This was particularly clear to two business men of Canadian origin who were living in St. Paul at this time: Norman W. Kittson, a former factor of the Hudson's Bay Company, and James J. Hill, owner of a coal and lumber yard. Kittson and Hill were shareholders in a company which operated steamboats on the Red River. They saw in the St. Paul and Pacific a railway which, if properly developed and managed, would provide them with a direct route from the Red River across Minnesota to the Mississippi and thence over connecting roads to Chicago and the east. Also interested in their project was Donald A. Smith, chief commissioner of the Hudson's Bay Company, who regularly passed through St. Paul on his visits to the east and was well aware what a connection by rail to Chicago would mean for the Red River colony. Smith, Kittson and Hill, acting together, decided to secure control of the St. Paul and Pacific and to develop it, in conjunction initially with steamboats on the Red River, as part of a through route to the Canadian and American west.

The essential first step in this scheme was to raise enough capital to buy out the Dutch bondholders who held the mortgage on the road. Here Smith, who had good business connections in Montreal, played the crucial role. At his urging George Stephen, president of the Bank of Montreal, and Richard B. Angus, general manager of that bank, took the opportunity of a visit to Chicago in 1876 to inspect the St. Paul and Pacific and consult with Kittson and Hill. Like Smith, they were immediately impressed with the line's possibilities and agreed to join the group. An option to purchase was obtained from the Dutch bondholders, most of whom had considered their investment as good as lost, and sufficient cash was raised, partly by a loan from the Bank of Montreal, to free the company from its immediate liabilities, meet current expenses, and complete the laying of track as far as the Canadian border, where it met the government road being built south from Winnipeg. Stephen and his associates then formed a new company, the St. Paul, Minneapolis and Manitoba, which purchased the Dutch bonds and foreclosed the mortgage, thus securing control of the railway and with it the Minnesota land grant of two and a half million acres. The entire property was now in the hands of the original syndicate, which had been joined in the meantime by John S. Kennedy, a New York banker who had formerly acted as the representative of the Dutch investors.

The possibility of inducing the St. Paul syndicate to undertake the construction of the Canadian transcontinental was first mentioned to Macdonald's government by J. H. Pope, a political associate of the premier, in 1880, and, as we have seen, negotiations were promptly begun and moved rapidly to a successful conclusion. The characteristics which made the syndicate highly suitable candidates for the project are obvious enough: they had demonstrated their ability to raise capital and lay track quickly; they could work smoothly as a team; they had experience in constructing and operating a western railroad; and, with the unimportant exception of Kennedy, they were Canadians. It was, if anything, a point in their favour that the St. Paul was an upstart road independent as yet of any of the major American systems, and that its reorganization had been carried through without the assistance of the great New York investment banking-houses. There could be no grounds for alleging American domination in this case.

The presence of Stephen and Angus in the original syndicate meant that Montreal was certain to be strongly represented in the inner councils of the new organization. This representation was strengthened still further by the addition to the group during 1880 of Duncan McIntyre, a Montreal business man. McIntyre owned a controlling interest in the Canada Central Railway which, with a line already built from Brockville to Pembroke via Ottawa and an extension under construction to Callander on Lake Nipissing, was admirably suited to serve as the eastern outlet for the transcontinental. Selection of McIntyre as one of the original directors and later as first vice-president made it beyond question that Montreal, rather than Toronto, would be the future eastern terminus of the Canadian Pacific Railway. Other additions to the organizing group represented alliances with overseas sources of capital: the French banking firm of Cohen, Reinach & Company, the Société Générale, and the London firm of Morton, Rose & Company (on behalf of their New York affiliate, Morton, Bliss & Company) joined the syndicate during 1880. With these accessions of strength, the membership of the group was complete. The contract signed on October 21, 1880, bore the names of Charles Tupper on behalf of the Canadian government, and, on behalf of the syndicate, George Stephen, Duncan McIntyre, James J. Hill, John S. Kennedy, Morton, Rose & Company, and Cohen, Reinach & Company. Donald A. Smith's name did not appear, largely because of the personal antipathy between him and the premier, but he continued to play a very important part in the company. Hill withdrew from the company in 1883 in protest against the decision to build north of Lake Superior and devoted himself entirely to the St. Paul, Minneapolis and Manitoba, which he later developed into the Great Northern system. Shortly thereafter Kennedy also left the organization.

THE C.P.R. CONTRACT

The contract, when submitted to Parliament for ratification, met with considerable criticism from the opposition, on the grounds that its provisions for government aid were unduly generous. The offer of a rival syndicate, representing principally Ontario business interests, to build the road on terms more advantageous to the government was, however, refused, and the contract was finally approved in the House of Commons by a vote of 128 to 49. Its principal clauses were as follows:

(1) The Canadian Pacific Railway was to receive, as a direct subsidy from the government, $25 million in cash and 25 million acres of land.

The land grant was to be in alternate sections of 640 acres, 24 miles deep on each side of the railway from Winnipeg to Jasper House; sections unfit for settlement in this stretch of territory were to be replaced by grants elsewhere in the west or by a similar grant along the company's branch lines. Land needed for workshops, stations, roadbed, and so on was also granted free of charge.

(2) Those sections of the railway already completed by the government were to be handed over to the company without charge, while other sections already under contract—specifically those between Selkirk and Lake Superior and, on the Pacific coast, between Kamloops and Port Moody—were to be completed at the government's expense. The cost of these sections, amounting to some 710 miles of track, was estimated at $37,785,320, including the cost of surveys.

(3) All material required for the construction and operation of the railway, and the entire capital stock, were to be exempt from taxation for ever. The land granted was to be exempt from taxation for twenty years, unless sold or occupied in the meantime. Material required for construction was to be admitted free of import duty.

(4) The freight rates charged by the company were to be free from parliamentary regulation until 10 per cent profit had been earned on the capital expended on construction.

(5) The construction of any competing railway between the main line of the C.P.R. and the American boundary was prohibited for twenty years, the only exceptions being lines which (i) ran southwest or west of southwest, and (ii) did not approach within fifteen miles of the boundary.

(6) The capital stock was set at $25 million (later increased to $100 million), and the company was empowered to issue bonds up to $25 million on the security of the land grant, these bonds to be held by the government and sold (all but one-fifth) for the benefit of the company.

(7) The whole line was to be completed by 1 May, 1891, to standards of construction at least as good as those of the Union Pacific Railway in the United States when first constructed. The gauge was to be 4 feet 8½ inches.

An appraisal of whether or not these terms were unduly favourable to the company must take into account the efforts which governments of both major political parties had previously made to find a group of private business men able and willing to build the transcontinental, but without success. The offer of the rival Ontario syndicate to accept less favourable terms was, it would seem, largely a political manoeuvre; certainly there had been ample time for such an offer to be made before the C.P.R. contract was submitted to Parliament. As regards the land grant, it should be noted that very much larger quantities of land had been offered earlier: in 1872 the Conservative government had been prepared to appropriate 50 million acres, and in 1878 100 million. The grant actually made to the C.P.R. was small relative to what had previously been regarded as necessary. The so-called "monopoly clause", prohibiting the construction of competing railways between the line of the C.P.R. and the Canadian-American boundary was designed in the first instance to prevent American railroads from thrusting branches into C.P.R. territory; it later proved the source of much dissension between provincial and federal governments and was cancelled before the twenty-year term expired.

An important feature of the contract was the absence of any provision for a government guarantee of interest on the company's bonds. This mode of assistance had been characteristic of Canadian railroad construction in the 1850's, reaching its peak in the legislation in aid of the Grand Trunk and in the operations of the Municipal Loan Fund. By 1880, largely because of the disastrous consequences of the policy as applied to the Grand Trunk, a definite revulsion had set in. Government guarantees of interest had the advantage that, at the time when they were granted, they entailed no immediate financial burden on the government. This removed a very salutary check on the extension of assistance, however, and made the eventual burden on the public revenues difficult if not impossible to predict. Direct subsidies in cash and land avoided these difficulties: the credit of the government and the credit of the railway company remained separate; the total burden on the public revenues could be accurately estimated and measures taken to counterbalance it.

BUILDING THE C.P.R.

The contract stated that the route to be followed by the railway was to be the one already selected by the government surveyors: that is to say, it would run from Lake Nipissing to Selkirk, across the prairies to Edmonton, and then through the Yellowhead Pass and the valleys of the Fraser and the Thompson to Burrard Inlet. Shortly after the organization of the company, however, very substantial changes were made in this route. The most important of these changes was the decision to follow a more southerly route across the prairies, running the line much closer to the American boundary than had originally been planned, heading from Winnipeg toward Calgary rather than Edmonton and making use of the Kicking Horse Pass through the Rockies rather than the Yellowhead. This decision meant that the western section of the C.P.R. would run, not through the "fertile belt" as earlier surveyors had indicated, but through "Palliser's triangle", the tract of semi-arid land which, it had been assumed, would prove unfit for settlement. Macoun's report of 1880, however, strongly suggested that the difficulties of agricultural settlement in this area had been greatly exaggerated, and the southern route promised to be considerably shorter. The principal factor inducing the company to select the southern route was probably the wish to tap American traffic and to prevent American railroads, particularly the Northern Pacific, from tapping Canadian traffic after the twenty-year statutory monopoly had expired; but the expectation of quicker construction, economies in operating costs, and the greater competitive strength which would result from a shorter line were also relevant.

In construction as in the surveys the engineer played a crucial role. Initially two American-trained men were put in charge: A. B. Stickney as general superintendent and General Rosser as chief engineer. The rate of progress under these men proved unsatisfactory, however, and at the end of 1881 they were replaced by William C. Van Horne as general manager and T. G. Shaughnessy as purchasing agent. Van Horne and Shaughnessy had both had considerable experience with American western railroads, their last posts before joining the C.P.R. having been as general superintendent and general storekeeper respectively of the Chicago, Milwaukee and St. Paul. They were given very wide powers by the directors of the C.P.R. and proved highly competent. It is generally agreed that, aside from questions of finance, the rapid completion of the C.P.R. was largely due to their good management.

The appointment of Van Horne and Shaughnessy was followed by a very substantial acceleration in the rate of construction. On the section north of Lake Superior, for which government surveys had been less thorough than elsewhere, a start was made with the location of the line in 1882. A route near to the shore of the Lake was chosen, the expectation being that proximity to water transportation would ease the problem of bringing in supplies. Very great engineering difficulties were encountered in this section, however, the cost of construction rising to as much as half a million dollars per mile of track, and progress was painfully slow. By the end of 1883 track had been laid for 100 miles west from Callander and for about 35 miles east from Port Arthur, leaving approximately 520 miles still to be covered. Within the next twelve months, which saw the major effort in this section, the gap was reduced to just over 250 miles and trains were running between Callander and Sudbury. The whole section between Callander and Port Arthur was completed in May, 1885, and passenger trains were running by November of that year.

The prairie section, though not without its problems, was the least difficult of the three and rapid progress was made after Van Horne took charge. By October 3, 1882, track had been laid from Brandon to Regina, and by June of the following year the line had reached the summit of the Rockies. Meanwhile work was being pushed ahead on the government sections: the section between Port Arthur and the Red River was ready for use by the end of 1883, while that from Port Moody to Kamloops was completed late in July, 1885. Construction of the very difficult section through the Rockies and the Selkirks was the final stage. On November

7, 1885, the last gap in the line was closed and in May of the following year the first passenger train was taken through from Montreal to Vancouver.

FINANCE

Completion of the transcontinental line five years ahead of the time stipulated in the contract was undoubtedly a remarkable achievement. Credit must go not only to Van Horne and Shaughnessy, who were primarily responsible for operations in the field, but also to those who were responsible for raising capital and handling relations with the government. Donald A. Smith and George Stephen played the major roles in this sphere. The difficulty of their task was much accentuated by the depressed business conditions which characterized the years 1883 to 1886.

The financing of the C.P.R. was carried out according to a well-defined and, with a single exception, consistently maintained policy. So far as possible the directors avoided issuing bonds (except on the security of the land grant), preferring instead to raise capital by the sale of stock. The intent of this policy was to avoid burdening the road with a heavy fixed debt. Many American railroads had been financed almost entirely by bond issues, and in consequence had experienced great difficulty in avoiding bankruptcy and receivership during the periods of low earnings. By minimizing the proportion of fixed interest debt in the company's capital structure the directors of the C.P.R. hoped to avert these dangers. Fluctuations in earnings could then be absorbed by reducing or passing dividends, without risk that the stockholders might lose control of their property. This element of flexibility, however, was not secured without cost, for bonds would have been much easier to sell than stock. In the long run avoidance of fixed interest obligations gave the C.P.R. greater freedom of action and greater ability to weather depression; in the short run it made it much more difficult to secure funds for construction.

The attempt to build the railway without any bonded debt left the C.P.R. with three principal sources of funds: the land grant, the government subsidy, and the sale of shares to the public. The land grant and the cash subsidy were distributed to the company in instalments as construction progressed. If offered for sale immediately, the company's land would have brought in relatively little money; efforts were therefore directed at encouraging immigration and settlement. In the meantime, to gain some immediate advantage from the grant, bonds were issued on the security of the company's land to the amount of $25 million. During 1881 $10 million of these were sold; the remaining $15 million were used as security for government loans and as a pledge for the fulfilment of the contract. These bonds were later redeemed and cancelled as the lands were sold, so that they were not a permanent addition to the company's capital structure.

The authorized share capital of the company was raised from $25 to $100 million in December, 1882. During 1881 the promoters of the company had subscribed to $5 million at par; in May, 1882, they had allotted themselves $10 million at 25. In December, 1882, a further $30 million was issued at a price of 52½ to a group of New York bankers and eventually sold by them, mostly in Europe. A further $10 million was pledged in New York and Montreal as security for a loan of $5 million and later sold for approximately the amount of the loan. In all, shares to the par value of $65 million were sold up to the winter of 1883, bringing in approximately $31 million in cash to the company's treasury.

The serious discount at which C.P.R. shares found purchasers is to be explained only in part by the speed of construction and the consequent necessity under which the company found itself of throwing shares on the market for what they would bring. There was, in addition, considerable distrust of Canadian railway securities on the part of investors in London and New York and much doubt about the future of the Canadian west as a field for immigration and settlement. These doubts were encouraged by the representatives of the Grand Trunk and of the American trans-continentals. Lack of confidence in the potential earning power of the C.P.R. made the task of raising capital very difficult and, as we shall see, finally forced a partial abandonment of the policy of avoiding bonded debt.

Late in 1883 a determined attempt was made to create a market for the $35 million of stock which remained unsold. On the advice of its financial advisers in New York and London, the company offered to guarantee payment of dividends on the stock at a rate of 3 per cent for a specified term of years. As security for this pledge a total of $16 million was deposited with the Canadian government. This device might well have enabled the remainder of the shares to be sold at reasonable prices, had not the stock market become almost completely demoralized at the end of 1883 by the bankruptcy of the Northern Pacific Railroad in the United States. As matters turned out the new policy of guaranteeing dividends proved quite ineffective, while the deposit of $16 million with the government deprived the company of cash resources which could ill be spared.

The early months of 1884 found the company in a very critical financial position. Stephen, Smith, and McIntyre raised what money they could by pledging personal property to the Bank of Montreal, but the total was quite insufficient. Turning to the government for aid, they asked for a loan of $22½ million for four years at 4 per cent, to be secured by a first mortgage on the C.P.R.'s main line. The government was at first very reluctant but finally consented. The proceeds of this loan provided the immediate relief which was necessary but the progress of construction (at costs substantially higher than had been estimated) soon made a new search for funds unavoidable. The mortgage which had been given to the government, however, made it impossible for the company to borrow elsewhere, while the shares were now almost unsalable. Renewed appeals to the government resulted in an important modification in policy. The $35 million of unsold stock was cancelled and an equal amount of first mortgage bonds issued. These bonds—the first to be issued apart from land grant bonds—were secured by the company's main line, which had earlier been pledged to the government. In lieu of the former security, the company mortgaged to the government all its unsold lands and $20 million of the new bonds. The remaining $15 million were sold in New York and London during 1885. This was the first large influx of British capital which the company had received.

By these expedients sufficient capital was obtained to complete the transcontinental line. While due credit must be paid to the ingenuity and perseverance of Smith and Stephen, it is quite clear that without the financial assistance provided by the government construction would have been seriously delayed and possibly halted completely. In this respect the building of the C.P.R. followed the pattern of previous transportation developments in Canada (the canals built between 1841 and 1848 being the conspicuous exception), with the government playing an indispensable part in securing capital but private enterprise carrying the primary responsibility for organization and management. Unlike such earlier examples as the Welland Canal and the Grand Trunk, however, the success of the C.P.R. in terms of cash profits was almost immediate, and the company was able to pay off its debts to the government very quickly. By the summer of 1886 all obligations to the government had been settled, partly in cash, partly in land.

As we have seen, during the period of construction the C.P.R.'s land grant was more important as security for bond issues and government loans than as a direct source of revenue from sales. Nevertheless, certain features of the grant deserve brief comment. In theory, all lands granted were supposed to be alternate sections directly tributary to the main line and branches, as had been the standard practice in the United States. In negotiating its contract, however, the C.P.R. had stipulated that, if any sections were not "fairly fit for settlement", the company should be entitled to select an equal area elsewhere. As the main line was completed, it became clear that the total acreage which the company was prepared to accept as fit for settlement within the "main-line belt" amounted to only a small fraction of the total grant. (Actually only 5,255,870 acres were finally accepted by the C.P.R. in sections directly adjoining the main line.) To fill out the total acreage promised—reduced to 18,206,986 acres by an agreement between the company and the government in 1891—additional reserves were laid out in areas far removed from the main line. The two largest of these reserves were, first, the Northern Reserve, comprising about 6½ million acres of land accepted by the C.P.R. as "fit for settlement", lying between 52 and 54 degrees north latitude and 104 and 106 degrees west longitude (east of Saskatoon, Saskatchewan); and, secondly, the Southern Reserve, of about 2¼ million acres of acceptable land, lying between the western boundary of Manitoba and the Coteau Hills, and between the southern limit of the main-line belt and the international boundary. These reserves were to prove very valuable in the long run, but they were too remote to contribute to the expansion of traffic on the C.P.R.'s original main line. Added later were the Lake Dauphin Reserve, a smaller area of about 400,000 acres lying on each side of the Lake Dauphin branch line; the Second Northern Reserve, of about 386,000 acres, situated to the east and northeast of Edmonton; and finally, in 1903, the so-called Irrigation Block, an area of about 2.9 million acres of semi-arid land in southern Alberta. The land-grant policy as a whole, both in conception and execution, showed elements of flexibility and adaptability to local conditions which had not been present in the case of the American transcontinentals.

THE CANADIAN NORTHERN

The construction of the first Canadian transcontinental railway was carried through to completion in the face of very considerable uncertainties, particularly those involved in ignorance of the prairie environment and of costs of construction. The success of the project dissipated many of these uncertainties: clearly the risks and difficulties had been overestimated. At the same time the profitability of the C.P.R. called attention to the gains to be won from participation in the development of the Canadian west and encouraged attempts to duplicate the success achieved by the pioneer road. The closing years of the nineteenth century accordingly saw the inception of two additional transcontinental projects, each of them conceived in an atmosphere of confident optimism which contrasted sharply with the fears and hesitations which had preceded the chartering of the Canadian Pacific.

The first of these projects, which later became the Canadian Northern, was the product of the enterprise of two Canadians, William Mackenzie and Donald Mann, who had participated as contractors in the building of the C.P.R. In 1886 these two men entered into partnership and undertook construction contracts on several minor railways in the west as well as on the C.P.R. "short line" through Maine. Their first venture into railway promotion, as distinct from contracting, came in 1896, when they purchased the Lake Manitoba Railway and Canal Company. The charter of this corporation had been granted by the Manitoba legislature in 1889 and carried with it a federal land grant of 6,000 acres per mile for 125 miles; no track had yet been laid, however. Mackenzie and Mann induced the provincial government to guarantee the bonds of the company up to $8,000 per mile for the same distance and also to grant exemption from taxes. With these assets and their knowledge of the contracting business they completed the railway from Gladstone to Dauphin and thence to Lake Winnipegosis. Trains were run over this line for the first time in 1897, running rights over the track of another minor railway giving access to Portage La Prairie and thus to the main line of the C.P.R.

This pioneer railway, operated with the barest minimum of capital equipment, was extended westward in the next few years until in 1900 it entered Saskatchewan. Meanwhile Mackenzie and Mann, under charters from the federal, Ontario, and Manitoba legislatures, had begun constructing a line from Winnipeg to Lake Superior. In 1899, after amalgamation with the Winnipeg Great Northern, the name of the system was changed to the Canadian Northern and three years later the through line from Winnipeg to Port Arthur was completed.

What was probably the decisive event in the development of the Canadian Northern took place in 1901. In 1888 the federal government, yielding to very strong pressure from Manitoba, had cancelled the "monopoly clause" in the C.P.R. contract, prohibiting construction south of the main line. Taking immediate advantage of this, the Manitoba legislature had given the Northern Pacific, the American transcontinental, permission to build north of the border, and in subsequent years the American road had developed a system of about 350 miles of track in the area between Brandon, Winnipeg, and Emerson. When the parent line went into bankruptcy the Manitoba government, reluctant to see its main hope of competition with the C.P.R. disappear, leased from the Northern Pacific its subsidiary lines in Canada. Being unwilling to operate these lines itself, it offered to sub-lease them to private interests. Despite strenuous opposition on the part of the C.P.R., Mackenzie and Mann secured the lease, paying to the provincial government a rental equal to that due to the Northern Pacific and agreeing to reduce rates on certain categories of freight.

This coup converted the Canadian Northern at one stroke into the third largest railway system in Canada and enabled Mackenzie and Mann to link their line between Winnipeg and Lake Superior with their original lines in western Manitoba. In the same year, by acquiring a short line in eastern Canada, they served notice that their interests were not confined to the west. The decision to aim at the development of a transcontinental system seems to have been taken in 1903 or shortly thereafter. By 1905 the Canadian Northern owned almost 350 miles of track in eastern

Canada, including the skeleton of an Ottawa-Montreal-Quebec line and a line across Nova Scotia, while in the prairies its track extended as far west as Edmonton. There remained to be built the sections between Ottawa and Port Arthur and between Edmonton and the Pacific coast—the sections which would inevitably prove the most expensive to construct and generate the least traffic. Following very closely the route through Yellowhead Pass originally mapped by Sandford Fleming, the western section was pushed through to Vancouver in 1915. In the same year the last miles of track were laid on the section east of Port Arthur, the route being located so as to curve north of the C.P.R. line as far as North Bay and then head directly for Ottawa, with extensions going to Toronto, Kingston, Montreal, and Quebec. The whole line was opened for traffic in September, 1915.

The financing of the Canadian Northern was remarkable for a number of reasons. While the C.P.R. had avoided bonded debt as far as possible, relying on stock issues to raise capital, the Canadian Northern was financed mainly by bonds and subsidies. Until 1914, when the federal government became a stockholder, the shares of the company were issued exclusively to the original promoters, ostensibly in return for their services of organization and management. This enabled Mackenzie and Mann to retain control over their various enterprises without investing any of their own money. As a method of financing, however, it had serious disadvantages since, by burdening the railway with heavy fixed charges for interest, it weakened its ability to survive depression or temporary declines in earnings.

With the common stock reserved for the original promoters, the railway's chief sources of capital were three in number: cash subsidies, land grants, and guarantees of bonded debt. The federal government had abandoned its land-grant policy in 1894, but several of the charters under which the Canadian Northern was built had been passed before that date and carried grants with them. In all the Canadian Northern received about 6½ million acres, of which 4 million came from the federal government and the remainder from the governments of Ontario and Quebec. Cash subsidies from the federal government and the governments of Ontario, Quebec, and Manitoba totalled just under $29 million.

The principal method by which government aid was extended to the Canadian Northern was by a revival and extension of the guarantee system. This system had been rejected as unreliable and open to abuse at the time of the chartering of the C.P.R.; in the atmosphere of heady optimism which characterized the opening of the twentieth century it regained its lost popularity. Between 1903 and 1914 the federal government guaranteed the Canadian Northern's bonds to the extent of $105 million, both major political parties approving of and participating in the policy. The provincial governments went even further, extending guarantees which amounted to a total of $130 million; in addition, Nova Scotia made a loan of $5 million. With the help of these guarantees the Canadian Northern had little difficulty in marketing its bonds until the outbreak of the First World War.

THE GRAND TRUNK PACIFIC AND THE NATIONAL TRANSCONTINENTAL

The secular improvement in world economic conditions after about 1890 and, with the disappearance of free land in the United States, the diversion of immigration toward Canada, were probably the main economic features of the environment in which the Canadian Northern had been conceived and created. The rapid development of grain production in the west and the desire to weaken the monopoly position of the C.P.R. made the circumstances even more favourable. The objective economic facts of the situation, however, are not in themselves sufficient to explain the amount of government aid to the Canadian Northern and the open-handed generosity with which it was given. Neither do they account for the promotion, approval by government, and final completion of yet a third transcontinental railway system: the Grand Trunk Pacific. Superimposed on a highly favourable set of economic circumstances was a mood of new confidence and a feeling of new strength. If hazards and dangers had been exaggerated before, now they were all but forgotten. Optimistic expectations and an assertive sense of Canadian nationalism—summed up in the claim that the new century was "Canada's century"—were key features of the climate of opinion in which the new transcontinentals were built.

The Grand Trunk Railway, by refusing to build north of Lake Superior, had disqualified itself from participation in the building of the first Canadian transcontinental in the 1880's. Since then it had seen the C.P.R. not only establish a seemingly impregnable position in traffic between western and central Canada, but also invade territory which the Grand Trunk had previously regarded almost as its private preserve, particularly Quebec and southern Ontario. In this latter area the threat of serious competition from the C.P.R. and the completion in 1873 of the Canada Southern, an American-financed railway running from Windsor to the Niagara River, led to the amalgamation of the Grand Trunk and the Great Western in 1882, a move which, along with the construction of a tunnel under Lake St. Clair in 1890, greatly improved the road's Michigan connections and its ability to secure through freight from Chicago. The improvement in earning capacity proved only temporary, however, and by 1895 the Grand Trunk seemed as far as it had ever been from achieving the status of a profitable railway.

From its earliest days the Grand Trunk had been handicapped by the fact that its stockholders and top management were in England. The attempt to operate a Canadian railway from offices on the other side of the Atlantic had, not surprisingly, met with little success, and in 1895 a new general manager was appointed and given wide powers to effect the reforms which he thought necessary. This man was Charles M. Hays, formerly general manager of the Wabash Railroad in the United States. Hays' influence was immediately felt in a tightening up of administration, the purchase of new equipment, and the rebuilding of certain sections of the line. These changes, however, though highly salutary, were over-shadowed by Hays' announcement in 1902 that the Grand Trunk intended to build westward to the Pacific. Edward Watkin in the 1860's had believed that the only solution to the Grand Trunk's difficulties lay in transcontinental expansion; Hays in 1902 had come to the same conclusion.

Before the federal government gave its approval to the project, important changes were made in the original plan. Hays had proposed to build from North Bay westward, using the Grand Trunk's existing lines to Montreal and Portland for the eastern outlet. Political considerations, however, made it highly desirable that the railway should pass through Quebec city and that its eastern terminus should be in the maritime provinces rather than in Maine. It was believed, too, that it would be greatly in the interests of Ontario and Quebec if the line from Quebec city westward were to run far to the north of the line of the C.P.R., so as to open up for settlement the so-called "clay belt", between the Laurentians and Hudson Bay. To satisfy these various regional demands, Sir Wilfrid Laurier, then prime minister, proposed that the government should build the eastern section of the new transcontinental from Winnipeg to the Maritimes, while the Grand Trunk, through an affiliated company, should build the western section from Winnipeg to the Pacific. On completion, the eastern section was to be leased for fifty years to the Grand Trunk, free of rental for the first three years and at 3 per cent on the cost of construction thereafter.

In accordance with this plan the Grand Trunk Pacific Railway Company was chartered in 1903 with an authorized capital of $45 million (of which only $25 million was actually issued). This company was charged with the construction within five years of a railway from Winnipeg to the Pacific, built to the standards of the Grand Trunk line in central Canada. The government undertook to provide assistance by guaranteeing interest for seven years on the company's bonds to the amount of $13,000 per mile on the prairie section and to an amount equal to three-quarters of the total cost on the mountain section. The remainder of the company's bonds were to be guaranteed by the Grand Trunk Railway Company, which was authorized to hold not less than $24.9 million of the common stock of the Grand Trunk Pacific. In effect this meant that the entire cost of the western section was to be met by the sale of bonds; these bonds would be guaranteed either by the government or by the parent company, the Grand Trunk; and the parent company, by holding all but a negligible portion of the common stock in its affiliate, would be sure of retaining control.

The route chosen for the western section passed through Edmonton and the Yellowhead Pass, as did that of the Canadian Northern. Attempts to work out an arrangement whereby both railways could use the same track through the mountains ended in failure in 1908, as had earlier attempts at amalgamation, and the two lines were built through the Pass side by side. Instead of turning south toward Vancouver, however, like the Canadian Northern, the Grand Trunk Pacific headed northwest down the Fraser and Skeena valleys toward Prince Rupert, 550 miles farther up the coast, where a new city and harbour were to be constructed. Selection of Prince Rupert as the terminus meant that the line west of the Rockies passed through very fertile territory with easy grades; on the other hand, terminal and harbour facilities were non-existent. The whole western section was completed and opened for traffic in September, 1914. The total cost was approximately $140 million.

The eastern section of the railway (known as the National Transcontinental) began at Moncton, New Brunswick, a terminus selected so that the government would not have to choose between Saint John and Halifax. Skirting the Maine boundary, the line headed for Quebec and then struck north and west across the height of land into the drainage basin of Hudson Bay. Passing through the "clay belt", it traversed a great arc north of Lake Abitibi to Cochrane and thence north of Lake Nipigon to Winnipeg, where it met the Grand Trunk Pacific. Branches had originally been planned to link the main line with Fort William, Toronto, and Montreal. Only the first of these was actually built before 1914, but running rights over the Temiskaming and Northern Ontario, a colonization railway built by the Ontario government, gave access to Toronto. The total cost of the whole section from Moncton to Winnipeg, completed late in 1913, was approximately $160 million, as compared with prior estimates of $60 million.

According to the original contract, the Grand Trunk Pacific had undertaken to lease and operate the National Transcontinental when completed. This, however, the Grand Trunk Pacific refused to do, alleging that the railway was not really finished and that the required standards of construction had not been maintained. The government therefore undertook to operate the section from Winnipeg to Moncton itself. At the same time, to enable it to share in the profitable grain traffic from Winnipeg to Lake Superior, it took over from the Grand Trunk Pacific a branch which that company had built from Superior (Sioux Lookout) to Fort William.

BANKRUPTCY AND GOVERNMENT OPERATION:
THE FORMATION OF THE CANADIAN NATIONAL RAILWAYS SYSTEM

In the year which saw the outbreak of the First World War, the Canadian Pacific Railway had an operating surplus of some $30 million. The two newer transcontinentals, in contrast, were financially in a highly insecure position. Far from being able to earn profits on current account, they were still in need of additional capital to complete and round out their systems. In August, 1914, neither the Grand Trunk Pacific nor the Canadian Northern had finished laying track. Barely a start had been made with the construction of terminal facilities and feeders, though the Canadian Northern had a fairly adequate system of branch lines in the west. Traffic had not had time to develop. The rise in wages and prices since 1900, quite apart from underestimation of engineering problems and (as was alleged in the case of the Grand Trunk Pacific and the National Transcontinental) irresponsible mismanagement, had made both systems much more costly than had been anticipated. Exclusive reliance on bonded debt as a means of financing had left them burdened with excessively heavy fixed charges. Both transcontinentals urgently required additional capital investments before they could hope to earn profits; both, in consequence, were hard hit by the outbreak of war, accompanied as it was by a drastic decline in immigration and the cessation of capital imports.

Desperately in need of funds, the two companies turned for aid to the government. Loans were made in 1914, but in 1916, when it became apparent that assistance was still required, a major reconsideration of government policy became necessary. Three alternatives were open: to permit the Grand Trunk Pacific and the Canadian Northern to go into liquidation, so that some or all of their debts would be wiped out; to foreclose the mortgage held by the government, so that both roads would come under government control but without any liquidation of indebtedness; or finally, to give further financial assistance on a temporary basis while the whole matter was thoroughly examined. If the first alternative were chosen the Grand Trunk Railway also would probably be forced into receivership and serious damage would be done to Canada's credit standing in London and New York. Under the second alternative the government would not only have to provide the money which was then needed but also would have to take responsibility for meeting all past debts and for providing capital in future. The third alternative at least avoided the necessity for immediate decision and was finally adopted.

The terms of reference of the royal commission appointed in July, 1916 (known as the Drayton-Acworth commission), were to consider the general problem of transportation in Canada, with particular reference to the desirability of the government's acquiring or reorganizing any or all of the three transcontinental railways. After lengthy hearings, the commissioners submitted a report which recommended that the Grand Trunk, the Grand Trunk Pacific, and the Canadian Northern should be brought under government control. They strongly advised against direct government ownership, however, proposing instead (in the majority report) that ownership of these three railways, together with the Intercolonial and the National Transcontinental, should be vested in an independent and self-perpetuating board of five trustees appointed by Parliament and incorporated as the Dominion Railway Company. The government was to assume responsibility for the existing debts of the component railways. A minority report submitted by A. H. Smith, chairman of the commission and president of the New York Central Railroad, objected to this plan as being unworkable and recommended instead that the Grand Trunk should operate the eastern lines of the Grand Trunk Pacific and the Canadian Northern, while the Canadian Northern should operate the western lines and the government the connecting links. Neither majority nor minority reports recommended that any action should be taken with respect to the Canadian Pacific, except to protect it against unfair competition from railways controlled by the government.

The general principle stated in the majority report of the commission —that the transcontinental railways, apart from the C.P.R., should be operated by a board appointed by Parliament but insulated as far as possible from political pressures—was upheld by the government and put into effect with the formation of the Canadian National Railways in 1920. The transfer of ownership, however, proved somewhat complicated. The government already owned $40 million of stock in the Canadian Northern, which had come into its possession in return for cash subsidies and bond guarantees. The remaining $60 million was owned by Mackenzie and Mann. All that was necessary for the government to secure ownership of the road was for it to purchase Mackenzie's and Mann's holdings. The difficult question was the price to be paid. The Drayton-Acworth commission had concluded that the common stock of the Canadian Northern was worthless, since in their opinion no purchaser would pay for the property a price sufficient to cover its liabilities, and a significant body of opinion in Parliament held that no compensation whatsoever should be paid. Most of the stock owned by Mackenzie and Mann, however, had been pledged to the Canadian Bank of Commerce as security for loans, so that there were important financial interests to be considered. The government therefore agreed to submit the matter to arbitration, with the proviso that not more than $10 million should be paid. The board of arbitration, however, after prolonged hearings, arrived at a figure of $10.8 million, and this was the sum finally agreed upon. In the meantime the government had taken over the management of the railway.

Purchase of the Grand Trunk Pacific proved even more complicated, since the fortunes of the parent company were inextricably involved in the negotiations. The proposition put forward by the Grand Trunk in 1915 was that the government should take over the Grand Trunk Pacific and agree to assume all the liabilities of the Grand Trunk to its affiliate. The government rejected this offer, believing that purchase of the parent company as well as its Pacific subsidiary was necessary for any permanent settlement. Offer and counter-offer for the purchase of both corporations failed to produce agreement and in March, 1919, the government permitted the Grand Trunk Pacific to go into receivership, with the minister of railways and canals acting as official receiver. The Grand Trunk, which the government declined to release from its financial obligations to the Grand Trunk Pacific, finally agreed to sell out to the government in October, 1919. A board of arbitration, with one member submitting a dissenting opinion, concluded that the preference and common stock of the company was without value and on this basis ownership passed to the government. Consolidation of the Grand Trunk into the Canadian National system began immediately and was completed by January, 1923.

At the time when the Canadian National Railways system was formed, the principle of government ownership had few supporters in Canada. Nationalization was undertaken not on grounds of principle but as a pragmatic necessity, to prevent the bankruptcy of enterprises in which many private individuals had invested their savings, the dissolution of transportation systems of great national importance, and the possibility of serious damage to Canada's credit in foreign capital markets. The major argument in its favour was not its intrinsic desirability but the impracticability of all possible alternatives. The apparent inevitability of the step stemmed from the fact that the determining decisions had been taken many years before, when, with one transcontinental railway system barely completed, and that with great difficulty and expense, the Canadian people through their elected representatives had sanctioned the creation of two additional transcontinental systems. We have already referred to the atmosphere of optimism and nationalistic self-confidence in which these later transcontinentals were born; it was not an atmosphere which encouraged precise calculations of costs and returns, nor perhaps, with the knowledge and experience then available, would attempts at calculations of this kind have yielded unambiguous counsel. It may be suggested, however, that even if there were no feasible alternatives to government ownership between 1916 and 1920, the alternatives that were in fact open between 1900 and 1905 received very inadequate consideration. Granted that the national interest required one transcontinental railway north of Lake Superior, did it require three? Granted that the C.P.R.'s monopoly in the west presented certain dangers, were the possibilities of government regulation fully explored? Granted even the desirability of competition in through traffic, would not one strong competitor, adequately equipped with feeders and branch lines in the east and in the west, have proved at least as effective as two weak ones? With the advantages of hind-sight, of course, it is easy to pick out what seem to have been errors and miscalculations, and the tendency to condemn on economic grounds decisions which involved much more than economic issues must be resisted. Nevertheless, the impression that remains is one of haste and over-confidence, of large commitments assumed with little deliberation, of alternatives and compromise solutions too quickly rejected. The repercussions of these errors, if they were errors, are still felt at the present day. National economic unity was the goal and purpose of the transcontinental railways; but the problem of distributing the costs of those railways, particularly in the form of freight rates, has caused and continues to cause acute political conflict.

SUGGESTIONS FOR FURTHER READING

BASIC WORKS:

Glazebrook, G. P. de T., *A History of Transportation in Canada* (Toronto, 1938), Chapters VI-XI, pp. 191-376

Innis, Harold A., *A History of the Canadian Pacific Railway* (Toronto, 1923), Chapters I-III, pp. 1-128

Skelton, Oscar D., *The Railway Builders* (Toronto, 1916), Chapters VI-XI, pp. 92-219

SUPPLEMENTARY WORKS:

Hedges, James B., *The Federal Railway Land Subsidy Policy of Canada* (Cambridge, Mass., 1934), Chapters I and II, pp. 3-67

Innis, Harold A., *Problems of Staple Production in Canada* (Toronto, 1933), Part I, Chapters I and II, pp. 1-23; Part II, Chapters I and II, pp. 24-81

Innis, Harold A., "Memorandum on Transportation" in *Report of the Royal Commission on Transportation* [the "Turgeon Commission"] (Ottawa, 1951), pp. 294-307

Irwin, Leonard B., *Pacific Railways and Nationalism in the Canadian-American Northwest, 1845-1873* (Philadelphia, 1939)

Mackintosh, W. A., *Prairie Settlement: The Geographical Setting* (Toronto, 1934), Chapters I and II, pp. 1-43

CHAPTER XIX

MONEY AND BANKING IN CANADIAN DEVELOPMENT

INTRODUCTION

BASIC to Canada's growth over the centuries has been the evolution of her financial system. From primitive beginnings in the French regime, it has developed to form the complex and efficient network of institutions of today. On this development each of the staples in Canadian economic history has left its mark. The financing of an export trade in fur and timber called for institutions and techniques essential to the exploitation, carriage and marketing of these export commodities. Reference was made in earlier chapters to the provision of credit for the operations of the great fur-trade organizations and the dominant firms in the timber trade, institutions which channelled funds from English sources to finance activities closely tied to the British market. This close alliance of finance and commerce which appears so early in our history was to be a factor of the greatest importance to the banking structure which began to take form in the early nineteenth century.

Concentration on export staples diverted capital, always in short supply in newly developing countries, away from domestic industry and agriculture, and as a consequence institutions for the mobilization and investment of funds in these latter pursuits were slow to appear. In New France, following the failure of company organizations as colonizers, it was the state that undertook to promote internal development. Free improved land, free transportation and money grants were provided to encourage settlement. And it was not long before our first bankers, the merchants of New France, appeared, extending credit, mortgaging lands, helping to alleviate somewhat the chronic scarcity of currency. They also financed small dealers who acted as agents for them in buying provisions for military authorities. Although early agriculture was largely self-sufficient, evidence that farmers were becoming indebted to merchants appears at an early date. We find the latter complaining that because of the scarcity of money they could not collect their debts, and farmers in turn protesting against seizure of grain in payment of overdue claims. This was a far cry from commercial farming with its large capital requirements, but mercantile or store credit was always in demand, for in spite of the adoption of French currency money continued to be very scarce and

445

credit, like barter, was necessary to help overcome this deficiency. However, the weak position of agriculture throughout the period of French rule, frequent resort to inflationary issues of unbacked currency, and the disruption of the colony's economic life as the long struggle with England reached its climax, prevented any healthy development. State finance was not adequate for the task of empire-building and mercantile credit was too limited to play the important role it was to assume at a later date.

Nevertheless, the experience of the French administration was not without its lessons for those who followed, for they also had to cope with problems of capital scarcity and chaotic currency conditions in which a mixture of the coinage of many nations made for great uncertainties in trade. The volume of gold and silver coinage, much of it Spanish, fluctuated with the colony's balance of payments, and serious difficulties resulted from its shrinkage in bad times. The efforts of the French to bring order out of confusion and to meet the pressing need for small coinage failed, but their failure was a consequence of factors largely beyond their control. In the first place, there were strongly speculative elements in the finances of a colony tied to beaver and forced to draw its major public revenues from export taxes on this staple and from import taxes on goods brought into the country in exchange for it. Secondly, the French government had to bear the cost of expensive wars in Europe and North America, and national bankruptcy was at times very close; these difficulties inevitably had repercussions on the finances of the colony on the St. Lawrence. And thirdly, New France suffered from a chronically unfavourable balance of trade with the mother country, so that any supplies of specie which appeared in the colony from whatever source tended to be drained away to Europe.

Experiments with card money illustrate the problems faced by the authorities during their stay in North America. The necessity of making payments to the militia in the face of slow and occasionally interrupted remittances from the mother country led to issues of this primitive paper, which represented simply the intendant's written promise to redeem the cards on the arrival of funds for the year. The first issues appeared in 1685 and for nearly thirty years these were an important part of the money of Canada. In spite of the difficult position of the colony, this medium sufficed for a time to meet the most urgent needs of local circulation even though financial expediency had been the governing factor in its issue. Unfortunately, as a result of financial difficulties in France card money fell to a discount and its holders suffered accordingly. In 1719 all outstanding issues were redeemed at approximately 50 per cent of their face value, and for ten years thereafter the colony was free from this type of currency. In 1729 it was again issued and along with treasury bonds (governmental promissory notes) met the colony's needs until 1745 when the fall of Louisbourg marked the beginnings of decline. There follows a sad history of payments deferred on government paper and card money, increasing inflation, growing corruption and fraud in the colony's finances—events made worse by bad harvests and the not infrequent loss of supply vessels to the English. The Seven Years' War led to large inflationary issues of paper money, a symptom of the fatal weakness of the colony. The later issues of card money were ultimately redeemed at approximately one-quarter of their face value, and this only at the insistence of the British government. Basically, the colony depended for its survival on the mother country and its currency difficulties reflected the inability of Old France to work out a more stable and enduring colonial system in the New World. Later, Canada and the United States were also to experiment with paper issues as aids in the financing of hard-pressed governments, but fortunately in a much more favourable environment than that of the administration of New France.

Conditions were not greatly improved in the first decades of British rule. In spite of attempts to end the chaos of mixed currencies, much confusion remained. In Halifax, Spanish dollars were rated as equivalent to five shillings, and in Montreal to eight shillings, the New York valuation; this difference between "Halifax" and "New York" currencies was only one of many complications faced by the governments and business men of this time. These difficulties and the shortage of satisfactory coinage led merchants to issue bills due or "bons", good at their face value in merchandise. Following the American Revolution, the influx of United Empire Loyalists and the American immigrants who followed on their heels led to rapid expansion of settlement, particularly in Upper Canada, and in spite of unsatisfactory land-grant policies, poor roads and the difficulties facing pioneer agriculture, substantial progress was made in the western province. In the better-settled sections of Upper Canada, the lack of a standard and generally available currency led to increasing difficulties and there are numerous references to the necessity of small traders advancing sums to hard-pressed settlers. These traders were financed largely by Montreal and Quebec merchants who in their turn were financed by "long credits" supplied by English firms to the importers and retailers of those cities. Local merchants or traders bought the surplus commodities of farms, and disposed of salt, rum and dry goods, and within the area served by them these dealers occupied a strategic position in the life of the community. Since capital was lacking and specie scarce they were in an exceptionally favourable position to control the currency through the issue of their own notes which formed the principal circulating medium. But since these issues were limited in quantity, they were entirely inadequate for the trading needs of the colony. Although settlers with surplus products could find outlets in governmental purchases for the needs of military garrisons, in civil establishments, and to a lesser degree in fur-trade posts, these soon became too limited a market. It was a situation which left the settlers very much at the mercy of the merchants they relied on to supply them with goods and dispose of their produce.

The experience of John McGill, whom Governor Simcoe appointed in 1792 as chief commissary officer and special agent for the purchase of supplies for Upper Canada, is enlightening since he served for a time as the official arbiter between the scattered settlers and the merchants with whom they had to deal. The need to protect settlers against exploitation and to aid in the marketing of surplus products led him to make recommendations which included payments in transferable certificates to those providing supplies to the government. These certificates are described by Adam Shortt as the first reliable currency in Upper Canada. They were limited, however, to the actual purchase of supplies and were insufficient in quantity to meet the needs of trade. The local paper currency of the merchants continued to be the primary circulating medium of the early settlers but the certificates served to underline the growing need for a more reliable and generally acceptable paper than existed at the time.

Unsatisfactory currency and credit conditions led in 1792 to the first attempt to establish a bank of issue, discount and deposit. A private organization, the Canadian Banking Company, was formed by an English commercial house in Montreal, but the venture was soon abandoned; the outbreak of war in Europe discouraged the undertaking and it is probable that confidence in paper money issues and familiarity with their use was too limited at this time to permit successful operations. As a result, some of the essential functions of banking continued to be performed by leading Canadian merchants, one of the most important of them being the firm of Forsyth, Richardson and Company of Montreal. Their key position in a system which channelled credit from British houses to the local traders with whom the settlers dealt permitted them to render valuable services, but it was a system which had many drawbacks. Bankruptcy laws were unsatisfactory at this time and heavy losses were occasionally taken by British firms. The issue of private notes by merchants and traders had its risks for those who accepted them in payment and whose lack of confidence was sometimes well founded. Nevertheless, in this and later periods private banks performed important functions and were in many cases very competently managed.

Although attempts to found a bank of issue in Lower Canada in 1806 and the following year failed, the pressure continued. Experiments in the official rating of all coins in circulation led to some improvements in the currency (although it should be noted that such experiments had been going on periodically for more than a century and had been unsuccessful in achieving the primary objective of retaining specie within the colony) and the informal paper currency of merchants helped pave the way for later issues of bank-notes. But it was the problem of war finance which brought the first important changes. To meet the expenses of the War of 1812, the government issued Army Bills, legal-tender notes, all but the smallest of which bore interest and which were in convenient denominations. They were convertible into bills of exchange in the United Kingdom and their use by the colonists as currency over the war years made for confidence in paper money and undoubtedly encouraged acceptance of later note issues by the early banks. The war had provided a strong demand for settlers' products, merchants became affluent, and farmers received higher prices and spare-time employment, enabling them to meet their debts to merchants for the purchase of new goods. Cash payments and short terms of credit tended to replace the former long-credit system, but redemption of the war-time currency was accompanied by serious difficulties which were aggravated by the overextension of credit in the war years.

However, the good faith shown in the redemption of the Army Bills weakened the old prejudice against paper money. They had served as a stable and effective medium of exchange and it became apparent that recovery and continued progress rested upon the establishment of adequate banking facilities. Although store credit was to remain the most important source of carry-over funds for the settlers, bank credit was essential if traders and merchants were to finance their purchases from farmers. The older system of long credit was now becoming quite inadequate for this purpose.

THE FIRST CHARTERED BANKS: EXTERNAL INFLUENCES

Canadian banking history has its beginning with the appearance of the Bank of Montreal in 1817, Canada's first bank of discount, deposit and issue. In the following year, the Quebec Bank and the Bank of Canada, the latter another Montreal bank, were established. These three banks began operations as private partnerships but were granted charters in 1822. The articles of association of the Bank of Montreal, it should be noted, were to become the basis for all later bank charters granted in Lower and Upper Canada, and, with modifications which came with adjustment to the conditions of an expanding economy, they embodied features of banking legislation still important in our day. Of these none was more significant than the absence of restrictions on branch banking.

The charters of these early banks authorized them to receive deposits and to deal in bills of exchange, to issue bank-notes payable on demand in legal coin, to discount notes, and to deal in gold and silver bullion. No provision was made for mortgage-lending by the banks and although loans on the security of land were not always avoided, subsequent events demonstrated the dangers of this practice in the commercial-banking field. Security of banking was sought in the requirement that total debts were not to exceed three times the amount of capital stock paid in plus a sum equal to funds deposited with the bank for safekeeping. Directors were jointly and individually liable for certain actions of their banks and an annual return to shareholders was required. The charters were open to criticism on several counts, including their inadequate provision for tests of solvency and lack of safeguards against excessive issues of bank-notes, but experience was necessary before serious weaknesses became apparent.

From the beginning, external influences played an important part in the evolution of our banking structure. On the one hand, British policies with their emphasis on banking stability exerted at times a strong pressure on our early banking legislation. It is true that the mother country failed in her attempts to extend her currency system throughout the Empire, to make the pound sterling symbol of her rule, and that in spite of British intentions Canada eventually adopted the decimal system and the dollar as her monetary standard; nevertheless, the salutary effects of British influence are clearly apparent throughout Canadian banking history. Until responsible government was achieved in Canada, the Colonial Office maintained close control over Canadian banking practice, and there is no doubt that this control had much to do with the absence of the experimentation so common in the banking history of the United States. On the other hand, the close relations between early Canadian and American mercantile communities meant that Canadian business men were more familiar with United States than with English banking methods, and the common description of the Canadian banking system as a direct descendant of the First Bank of the United States is sufficiently accurate to call for a brief glance at early banking developments in that country.

In the planning of the First Bank of the United States, Alexander Hamilton, first secretary of the treasury, had taken as his model the Bank of England, a private institution but one which was charged with important public responsibilities. The First Bank received a twenty-year charter in 1791 and for the two decades of its existence made important contributions to the nation's financial stability. Its notes had general acceptance throughout the country, and conservative issue-and-loan policies provided restraining influences on state and other banks. Certain features of its operations were important in the evolution of banking in Canada and these may be noted briefly. In the first place, the First Bank represented a great centralization of financial power in one institution, a power which extended over currency, credit, and, to a considerable degree, fiscal policy. Its position as depository of the principal specie reserves of the country and as a creditor of the state banks enabled it to keep these banks in line with its policies since it could demand payment in specie for balances owing to it whenever tendencies to over-expansion became apparent. In effect, it performed many of the functions of a central bank. With its control over currency and its ability to act as a lender of last resort, it could enforce conservative policies in the face of strong speculative pressure. Its success as a great stabilizing influence in banking left a deep impression on Canada's first bankers and, in spite of periodic protests against concentration of power in finance, there have been few deviations in Canada from this preoccupation with strength and stability as the first principles of sound banking.

Secondly, and closely linked with the above, was the establishment of branches by the First Bank in the larger commercial and financial centres. The branch-banking system permitted the Bank to extend its facilities and increase its control throughout the whole banking structure. Its branches served as clearing agencies in their districts and promoted uniform currency and credit conditions throughout the country. They gave both strength and flexibility to the banking system and in these respects compare very favourably with the unit system of banking which was to succeed them in the United States. The guiding principles of United States banking practice at this time—the provision of a widely acceptable and uniform currency, centralization of financial power, emphasis on short-term lending, and the use of branch banking as a means of extending facilities and exercising control—appealed greatly to the leaders of the early commercial and financial community of Canada.

The First Bank of the United States, however, failed to secure renewal of its charter. The concentration of financial power which it represented aroused both the hostility of those who feared monopoly and the envy of the state banks. Political controversy stirred up further opposition. Nevertheless, during the War of 1812, the absence of a national bank was keenly felt, and in 1816 the Second Bank of the United States was granted a charter for a twenty-year period. Although it made highly important contributions to the stability and expansion of the nation's economy, it too failed to outlive its first charter. Dislike of the Second Bank's conservative policies, fear of its great powers, and the agrarian west's dislike of eastern banking control were elements which brought its operations to an end. Later developments, the establishment of an independent Treasury system in 1837 and of unit banking with the organization of the National Banking system in 1863, were to appear to Canadian financial circles as retrogressive steps best avoided in the interests of sound banking.

This early phase of the banking history of the United States underlines fundamental differences between Canadian and United States attitudes towards banking in these formative years. In Canada, the strength of

conservative elements in finance and politics, and the distrust of governmental ventures in the banking field, far outweighed the opposition of
agrarian interests and fears of financial monopoly. The latter sentiment
at times exerted a strong influence, it is true, and Canadian banking
legislation reflects such pressures, but experiments in free banking were
few and governmental intervention kept them within narrow limits.
Alexander Hamilton's policies were congenial to the most powerful elements in Canadian commerce and finance and they never lost their appeal.
It is well to remember, too, that strong centralizing influences were
present in an economy faced in the critical decades preceding Confederation
with the task of nation-building in the face of great geographic obstacles,
loss of a preferred position in the British market and the vastly greater
competitive power of the United States. The difficulties of raising capital
to finance necessary large-scale undertakings were so great as to make
centralized organizations essential in many parts of the Canadian economy.

It should also be noted that the close and long-established connection
between commerce and banking, a connection important in politics as
well as economics, provided for strong resistance to agrarian demands for
free banking and easy-money policies. Later, when western expansion
on the prairies produced new and stronger attacks on eastern financial
control, the Canadian banking system was too strongly established in the
older provinces to be upset. Rather, its strength and the flexibility of
branch-banking operations permitted a more or less natural extension of
its control into new areas. In other words, the timing of expansion into
western Canada, unlike that of the United States, was such that agrarian
discontent made little impression on the Canadian banking structure,
even though strong political movements in the western provinces were
by no means absent.

In addition to the strength of centralizing influences in the Canadian
economy and the timing of western expansion on the prairies, there was
also the fact that no major break or catastrophe occurred in the nineteenth
century to destroy or radically change the financial system that was gradually emerging. In the United States, on the other hand, the Civil War
was to lead to the creation of a new banking system and to the beginnings
of bitter controversy between those who sought retirement of the enormous
issues of irredeemable paper issues in the 1860's and those who opposed
such contraction of the money supply. As a consequence, Canada escaped
the excitement of the Greenback movement and the struggle over
bimetallism, developments which left their mark on the financial structure
of the United States. Canadian banking history is not devoid of keenly
fought controversial issues, but when comparison is made with banking
developments to the south, the absence of any sharp break in this history
or radical departure from principles early established appears as the
most noticeable feature of Canadian banking experience.

FIFTY YEARS OF BANKING EXPERIENCE

The early period of banking in Lower Canada was one of slow progress. Conditions in the 1820's were not conducive to rapid advance and prejudice against commercial banking was strong. Only one additional bank, the City Bank of Montreal, was chartered before 1841 and this in the face of opposition from many members of the Assembly. In Upper Canada the environment was somewhat more favourable, although far from ideal. Merchants and other business men in Kingston established a bank but failed to obtain a charter, and in 1822 the bank closed its doors. This was Canada's first bank failure and a significant one in that it hastened essential reforms. Another institution, the Bank of Kingston, was formed but failed to begin operations within the period of its charter. Finally, in 1821, the Bank of Upper Canada was chartered. This institution opened for business in the following year and quickly attained a practical monopoly of the note issue. From the beginning its associations with the new government of Upper Canada were close, an association not without its dangers as later experience was to demonstrate. It has been described as a child of the Family Compact, and backed by this aristocracy of wealth and political power it sought to establish a monopoly in the banking field. It was in the face of this bank's strong opposition that Kingston's first active chartered bank, the Commercial Bank of the Midland District, was established in 1832.

In the Maritimes the first bank to be established was the Bank of New Brunswick which received its charter in 1820. In Nova Scotia, although attempts were made shortly after the turn of the century to establish banks, the first regular bank charter was granted to the Bank of Nova Scotia in 1832. It is probable that government issues of notes, which first appeared in 1812 and continued to Confederation, delayed the establishment of chartered banking in the province. Although these notes were not always redeemable their history compares very favourably with other and later experiments in the issue of government currency.

As the area of most rapid change, Upper Canada before union in 1840 was the scene of the most important developments in finance. In spite of poor communications, lack of easy access to coast ports, and an unwieldy and inefficient land-grant system, settlement increased substantially and expenditures on public works provided a strong stimulus to commerce and agriculture. Political problems, however, were emerging and banking policy became one of the most controversial issues of the day. The high profits of the Bank of Upper Canada attracted newcomers, but those who sought entry encountered strong opposition and marked difference of opinion quickly became apparent. Basically, controversy took the form of conflict between those who advocated close control over new entries into the banking field in the interests of stability, and others who saw in free banking the answer to the need for more banking capital in the province.

This controversy centred on proposed regulations designed to protect the public interest. The imperial authorities sought to strengthen and improve the banking structure but their suggestions concerning the conditions of extending credit, the question of shareholders' liability, and loans to directors and other aspects of banking practice unfortunately had little effect before the Act of Union. Events quickly proved the need for reform. The early 1830's were years of rapid expansion backed by boom conditions in the United Kingdom. British investments in the United States gave stimulus to developments there and in both these countries, as well as in Canada, strongly speculative elements were present. In the United States, the end of the rule of the Second Bank of the United States was followed by greater freedom in the establishment of banks and by resort to various monetary experiments featured by large and frequently excessive issue of paper money. Thus two opposing influences were acting upon Canadian finance at this time: British pressure for sound commercial-banking practice on the one hand, and on the other, the temptation to experiment along the lines followed in the United States.

The provincial government opposed experimentation in finance while the Reformers as strongly opposed restrictions on the entry of new banks and the necessity for legislative approval of incorporation of banks or additions to their capital. In spite of the government's attitude and the mother country's conservative influence signs of speculative activity made their appearance in trade, finance and real estate. In 1835, a private bank, the Bank of the People, was begun by the Reformers and other private banks soon opened their doors. Some of these were sound institutions, but many were fraudulent undertakings posing as reputable banks. Unauthorized issues of promissory notes for circulation as money were difficult to hold in check and speculators even more difficult to control. Scarcity of good collateral led to an emphasis on loans on personal security and at times these were indistinguishable from loans on land, the only asset many borrowers had at their command. The situation was not improved by strong indications of political influence in the lending policies of some institutions.

Crisis conditions which appeared in Britain in 1836 and, partly as a consequence, in the United States soon had repercussions in Canada. Although speculation had been less violent in Canada and the reaction less severe, Canadian banks were forced to reduce discounts and frequently to suspend specie payments. The Commercial Bank and the Gore Bank at Hamilton suspended in 1837, a year of widespread commercial distress and serious political unrest. The Bank of Upper Canada soon followed suit, although the necessity of its doing so was disputed. Suspension of all three banks was authorized by the government of Upper Canada. All chartered banks in Lower Canada had earlier suspended payment, without legal notice, in the spring of 1837. In the period of suspension, bank-notes were freely accepted in domestic exchange but a shortage of small currency led many merchants to return to the old practice of issuing "bons". A swarm of private banks appeared in this interval to add to the difficulties of the regular banks. The crisis was less severe than in the United States, however, the contraction of lending less sudden, and the Canadian chartered banks weathered the storm without any failures among their ranks.

By 1839 the worst was over. The experience was of value in its chastening effect on those who had failed to see the need for adequate safeguards of the public interest. It was apparent that the banking system was still in a rudimentary state and that there were important lessons still to be learned. The regular banks by severely restricting credit had maintained sufficient strength and stability to continue operations through crisis and depression. Adherence to this policy may be attributed to the strength of conservative influence in Canadian banking and the comparative weakness of democratic pressures on Canadian finance. In any event, no chartered bank failed in Upper Canada over a period of forty years, a more laudable even though less exciting history than that of its neighbour to the south.

One important change which took place in this period was the greater emphasis on liquidity, i.e., shorter terms of repayment for loans. This amounted to a shift from a system of long credit extending usually for about fifteen months to one in which a substantial part of a loan was paid within a period of three months. With improvements in transportation and communication, the financing of both export and domestic trade required less extended accommodation and reduced the need for the locking up of capital for periods which were lengthy from a commercial-banking standpoint. It is true that this increasing emphasis on liquidity was to raise problems for the agriculturist, but there were compensations such as greater currency stability and more adequate financing of those with whom he did business. Cash payments by merchants, millers and grain dealers were facilitated, and along with store credit these met the more pressing short-term financial needs of the farmer. Lack of capital for development was overcome in part by the assistance of land companies, the adoption of a homestead system, and better prospects for capital accumulation as a result of improved transportation to markets. Government assistance in periods of crop failure was common and on occasion assumed substantial proportions. The financial system still had serious limitations from the farmers' standpoint but with supplementary agencies it sufficed to meet his more urgent monetary needs.

The Act of Union in uniting the Canadas removed a major political disability; but the expansion that followed was to create new problems and to enhance the need for more adequate financing of the country's economic development. A major and highly controversial issue which appeared soon after union concerned the relations of the government and the chartered banks. This emerged with Lord Sydenham's proposal that the latter relinquish their right to issue paper money, a privilege which was becoming exclusively theirs. In similar vein, Francis Hincks, chairman of the Joint Committee on Currency and Banking, strongly advocated a provincial bank of issue. These proposals were supported by many who were much less impressed by the virtues of an elastic currency than were the bankers. The notes of the commercial banks were sufficiently secure to warrant confidence in them, but the tendency of note issues to contract sharply in times of depression (with the decline in the banks' assets of short-term commercial paper), led many to believe—and not without some justification—that falling prices were the result of the lack of sufficient money in circulation. To them the provision of note issues which would not shrink in bad times seemed to be the obvious solution. A currency based on government bonds rather than commercial paper was proposed on the grounds that greater stability in the supply of currency would be achieved, and in the process a ready market would be created for the bonds of the hard-pressed provincial government. It was recommended that a bank be established for the issue of notes, and that the commercial banks give up their right of note issue. The new bank would be empowered to issue notes up to a maximum of £1 million backed by 25 per cent in gold and 75 per cent in government securities; more than this amount would be backed in full by gold. The government would also benefit by the saving of interest on the bonds held as backing for this currency. No incentive was given the banks to make this radical change. Further, at this time deposit banking was so limited that loss of the right of note issues was tantamount to loss of ability to conduct banking operations on other than a very restricted scale.

The chartered banks opposed this legislation as detrimental to their interests and certain to reduce their ability to render essential services to their customers. Bankers could argue with good reason that their bank currency had been satisfactory in meeting the changing needs of business, and that bank issues were preferable to a much less elastic government currency. And the strength of the chartered banks in the recent period of crisis had impressed many. Others opposed the principle on the grounds that a provincial bank would increase the power of the Executive against the Assembly. The move was defeated but later proposals were to embody the same principle and later bore fruit in Dominion note issues. However, other proposals of Sydenham and Hincks proved more acceptable. Limitation of the amount of the note circulation of a bank to its paid-up capital was an important step at a time when note issues amounted to approximately half of demand liabilities, and this and like measures did much to strengthen the banking system that was emerging. The source of many of these proposals was the British Treasury, its influence being exercised through the Colonial Office which had the constitutional right to revise or disallow colonial legislation. One writer concludes that credit for the more important of the safeguards in colonial bank charters was the result less of the action of local authorities than of the intervention of the imperial authorities in Canadian banking legislation.

In the general economic expansion which followed until 1847, the banks played a central role, keeping pace with the extension of commerce and agriculture to new districts. Loans and bank circulation increased rapidly, increases in banking capital were authorized, and a period of controversy and strain seemed to have come to an end. To round out the country's credit system, building societies emerged to help meet the demand for more adequate long-term loan facilities. The Upper Canada Trust and Loan Company was incorporated in 1843, the Lambton Loan and Investment Company in 1844, and the Montreal Building Society in the following year. These early companies loaned money on real estate, but restrictions on their borrowing powers and types of investment somewhat limited their operations. Authority to receive deposits and to issue debentures was not given until 1874. Building Society acts in Canada and the maritime provinces in 1846 and later years led to the formation of other societies and by Confederation there were nineteen of these in operation and making returns to the government.

Unfortunately, although substantial progress was apparent in transportation developments, the integration of agricultural settlement, and the opening of new areas for settlement, Canada's sensitivity to conditions external to the economy was very great and new strains soon appeared to test her financial institutions. The appearance of financial crisis in England in 1847 made it clear that Canada's prosperity was bound up with that of the mother country and that speculative elements were by no means absent in her short-lived boom. Depression in 1848 led to numerous commercial failures with heavy losses taken by creditors. British free-trade policies did not help matters; the timber trade in particular was hard hit, but no region or industry escaped. The moves of the United States to checkmate the St. Lawrence system were only too successful, and the realization that Canada's canal system was quite inadequate in the face of her neighbour's railway expansion added to the gloom of these years. Yet it is noteworthy that although Canadian banks were forced to take substantial losses, to reduce dividends, and to draw on reserves, no chartered bank failed and no suspension of specie payments was found to be necessary.

The banking system, however, was not free of criticism. There were general complaints of lack of banking facilities, particularly in the smaller towns, and on its part the provincial government renewed its pressure on the banks in the attempt to widen the market for government securities. The success of a government issue of provincial debentures payable on demand which was introduced into the country's currency at this time led to the revival of proposals for a provincial bank of issue, and the "Act to establish Freedom of Banking" of 1850 reflected the strength of the support given to this project. This took the form of a proposal to establish free banking in the provinces; provision was made for the setting up of small banks and for proper safeguards of their circulation. American influence is apparent in that each bank formed under this Act was to conduct its business at one place only. Banks formed under the Act were to issue notes obtained from the receiver-general of the province in exchange for an equal amount of specified government securities bearing interest. Each bank was required to redeem its notes in specie on demand and the notes were to be receivable at par in payment of public dues. The existing chartered banks were encouraged to give up their rights of circulation and to secure registered notes in return for the deposit of securities. The object of this legislation was clear, i.e., to modify a banking structure in which comparatively few large banks conducted diversified operations through their head offices and branches, by the creation, under general legislation, of numerous small banks whose circulation would be based on the securities of the province and which would operate in a system of unit as opposed to branch banking. In short, the development of the Canadian banking system was to conform more closely to that which was taking shape in the United States as the move to the National Banking system gained impetus there.

The imperial authorities, like the chartered banks, opposed this legislation. It was pointed out that adequate protection against over-issue of notes was lacking, that there was no guarantee of immediate convertibility of notes on demand, and that depreciation of government securities would result from their close connection with paper currency. Only a few "free banks", five in all, appeared under the Act and of these only Molson's Bank attained any importance. The Bank of British North America, operating under royal charter, took advantage of the Act but whether it derived much benefit from it is open to question. Various inducements were offered to the chartered banks to adopt "free banking" principles, but they failed to respond. In the face of their opposition the Act had little effect and was repealed in part in 1866 and completely in the Bank Act of 1880. It is not without interest, however, since it introduced the first general legislation applicable to all banks in the province, it established the principle that bank-notes were a first charge on the issuing banks, and it provided the first illustration in the province of Canada of close connection between paper currency issues and government securities.

The influence of the home government was exerted less successfully in another direction. Over a long period it had attempted to secure adoption of the pounds, shillings, and pence system in the colonies. Commercial and financial connections with the United States were too close, however, to permit implementation of this policy and finally in 1851 the decimal system of dollars and cents was adopted by the province of Canada. This was accepted by the British government in 1853. The province also adopted the gold standard at this time, its standard being defined as the British sovereign of $4.86 ⅔.

By 1854 the chartered banks had clearly won out against the free banks even though later attempts were to be made to establish free banking. In the banking legislation of this year further steps were taken in the direction of a general Bank Act and the firm establishment of the chartered-banking system. Additions to capital stock were authorized, and in the prosperous years which followed the achievement of the Reciprocity Treaty of 1854 the number of chartered banks was increased. Of these, the Bank of Toronto was established in 1855, the Bank of Canada in 1858 (to become the Canadian Bank of Commerce in 1866) and the Royal Bank of Canada in 1859. In all twelve banks were incorporated between 1855 and 1857 inclusive and by the latter year paid-up capital of banks had doubled since 1851, an increase which later events demonstrated to amount to over-expansion of banking operations at this time.

The banks were not only increasing in size and number but in range of activities as well. In 1859 an Act was passed which, in providing additional banking facilities for commercial transactions, was to become of great importance to the financing of the grain, lumber and other trades. Loans could now be made on the security of bills of lading or warehouse receipts for grain and other commodities. Although limited in application at this time, this legislation was gradually extended to empower the banks to lend to farmers, lumbermen and fabricators of raw materials on what was, in effect, chattel mortgage security, a practice which enabled farmers and others to operate more fully on a cash basis. The Act of 1859 was the first step towards the "pledge sections" of our present Bank Act and under its provisions and subsequent amendments much of the grain, lumbering and manufacturing business of today is financed.

The growing strength and prestige of the banking system with its diversified operations augured well for the future but there were still important lessons to be learned. The prosperous conditions of the 1850's were to lead to land speculation, to excessive imports of commodities, and to heavy pressure on the banks for accommodation. A period of feverish expansion reached its peak in 1857 and was brought to an end by commercial crisis in the United States and abroad. This downswing in business along with the crop failures in the same year placed a heavy strain on the economy. The Canadian banks were forced to restrict credit and to take measures to check the drain of gold from the country. Primary producers suffered from delay in getting crops to market, and all the symptoms of a severe depression quickly appeared—declining demand, a drastic fall in values, a sharp increase in business failures and the collapse of the speculative boom in real estate. Although the banks survived the crisis, they were subject to severe criticism centring on the lack of safeguards against excessive note issues and creation of capital beyond the country's requirements. In 1860, Alexander Galt revived the earlier proposal of a government issue but nothing was done at this time. Nor was he any more successful when in 1865 he offered inducements to the banks to surrender their note-issue privileges.

Criticism increased as a result of developments in the next decade. Recovery from depression was slow, and this along with other adverse factors was to spell disaster for the Bank of Upper Canada, a leading banking institution at that time. In the first place, railway construction had led, in its effects on population patterns, to the decline of many centres even as it promoted others. With its operations mainly in the less advantageously situated towns, the Bank of Upper Canada suffered a serious decline in its business. Secondly, the tendency for land to constitute the real security for many loans made it difficult to avoid involvement in land speculation, and the collapse of real-estate values contributed to the failure of the Bank which, because of its political connections, was more deeply involved than most. Advances for political reasons led to losses which were revealed too late for corrective action to be taken. In 1863, it was replaced by the Bank of Montreal as the government's banker and its general banking business contracted steadily until 1866 when it was forced to stop payments. Its failure brought disaster to many of its creditors; its depositors and those who held its notes, stockholders and the government suffered losses which in total were calamitous for the colony at this time. Confidence in the banking structure was further shaken by the failure of the Commercial Bank in 1867, the result in good part of a single large and unfortunate loan rather than of generally unsound banking practice. On the credit side, these bank failures led to a more realistic approach to banking principles and practice, both on the part of the public and the bankers themselves, and to a better understanding of the importance of internal administration and of liquidity in commercial-banking operations.

A closely related development on the eve of Confederation was in the field of government finance. At this time the government of the province was heavily in debt as a result of its support to railway construction, its credit position was weak, and it looked once more to the banking system for assistance. To avoid paying high interest rates on further government borrowings, legislation was passed to permit an issue of provincial notes to the amount of $8,000,000 payable on demand in specie; 20 per cent of the first $5 million and 25 per cent of the remaining $3 million was to be backed by gold, and the rest by government securities.

Inducements were once more offered to the banks to give up their circulation and to take up the issue and redemption of government issues of money. This legislation, the Provincial Note Act of 1866, found little response among the banks. Only the Bank of Montreal, the principal fiscal agent of the government and a bank to which the government was heavily in debt, accepted the government's offer and proceeded to replace a substantial part of its notes with those of the province. The close connection between government needs and currency issues was now established, but there remained difficult questions to be settled in the years following Confederation.

The pioneer in the issue of government notes had been Nova Scotia. Ever since 1812, government paper money had circulated in the form of Treasury notes of the province. Although the issue was not immediately convertible into specie in any great volume and was less elastic than bank-note issues, it served to economize specie when this was scarce and the metal coinage in a chaotic state. This lessened the pressure for banking facilities for a time, but the growing needs of commerce and industry finally led to the chartering of the Bank of Nova Scotia in 1832, the first bank in British North America to have provision for double liability of shareholders in its charter. In the main, the provisions of its charter, as with the charters of other maritime banks, were similar to those granted in Canada. Although private banks with note-issue privileges competed with the chartered banks that emerged, there was confidence in the banking structure and no failure resulted until 1873. The turbulence which marked the early days of banking in Canada was much less in evidence in the maritime provinces before Confederation. Periods of crisis were not escaped, but on the whole the pre-Confederation decade was one of prosperity and the banks of Saint John and Halifax and a few smaller centres reflected the good times of these years. (In Nova Scotia at Confederation, five banks had local charters—the Bank of Nova Scotia, the People's Bank of Halifax, the Union-Bank of Halifax, the Merchants' Bank of Halifax, and the Bank of Yarmouth—while one additional charter was available but unused. In New Brunswick there were four such banks —the Bank of New Brunswick, the Commercial Bank of New Brunswick, the St. Stephen's Bank, and the People's Bank—while one bank was in liquidation and there were five charters not in use.)

On the Pacific coast, chartered banking had its beginning when the Bank of British North America began operations in British Columbia in 1859. In the same year MacDonald's Bank began operations in Victoria; this was a private bank, and well managed, but a robbery brought it to an untimely end in 1864. The Bank of British Columbia received its charter in 1862. The latter bank was established in response to the gold discoveries in this area and continued in operation until 1901 when it was absorbed by the Canadian Bank of Commerce. Its head offices were in

London and its capital was provided from English sources. Provision was made for a considerable expansion of capital and the bank was empowered to establish branches in British Columbia, Vancouver Island and later in North America west of the province of Canada. With the collapse of the mining boom, however, British Columbia marked time until the appearance of the transcontinental railway and no great demand for expansion of banking facilities was felt in these years.

At Confederation eighteen banks were functioning under charters granted by the province of Canada, and nine banks under Nova Scotia and New Brunswick charters; there were ten charters available but not in use at this time. Under the British North America Act, the federal government assumed control of coinage and currency, banking, incorporation of banks, savings banks, bills of exchange and promissory notes, interest and legal tender, and the issue of paper currency, an arrangement which precluded provincial or local experiments with currency and banking. In 1868 the Dominion Notes Act re-enacted the Provincial Notes Act of 1866. Although frequent amendments were made to this legislation, no change in principle appeared until 1918, and the note issues of banks and of the government continued to circulate side by side until very recently. The policy of encouraging the chartered banks to replace their own notes with Dominion notes was not abandoned, but the extension of the legislation of 1866 served mainly to continue arrangements with the Bank of Montreal which at this time had charge of the government issues amounting to $5 million. A bill proposing a bond-secured currency was introduced by Sir John Rose, the first minister of finance, in the session of 1868-9 but it was withdrawn because of lack of support.

AN AUTOMATIC SYSTEM

The period between Confederation and the Bank Act of 1871, the first thorough revision of the new Dominion's banking legislation, was one of keen controversy, the outcome of which was to set the pattern of Canadian banking development until well into the twentieth century. The controversial issues were not new issues, but monetary experiments in the United States in the Civil War period and the immediate post-war years attracted sufficient notice to sharpen prevailing differences of opinion as to the role of the banks and the relations of government finance and commercial banking. There were also questions concerning the stability and efficiency of the banking system to be settled in these critical years of debate and decision.

The immediate problem to be faced following Confederation was the creation of a uniform banking system out of the varied currency and banking arrangements of the different provinces. A temporary measure gave the banks incorporated in the various provinces power to conduct operations over the entire area of the new Dominion and extended over the same territories the prevailing general legislation of the province of Canada. As regards banking reform, greater security for depositors and holders of notes was clearly necessary, as the banking community in the main recognized. The failure of two important banks in the preceding period and the heavy losses taken by others confirmed the need for reform. This question, however, was inextricably bound up with more general banking developments. In some circles, the National Banking system of the United States, with its numerous local banks operating with local capital and managed by local interests, its creation of a wide market for United States bonds, and its apparently secure National Bank note issues backed by government guarantees, seemed to have much to offer. The Bank of Montreal, as the government's banker and sole issuer of provincial notes, and much the strongest bank in the country at this time, advocated a system of local banks and exclusive government note issues extended through the banks on the receipt of Dominion Government bonds as security for circulation. To government leaders, faced with difficult financial problems, a bond-secured circulation had great appeal, and renewed endeavours were made to expand issues of Dominion notes and to encourage the investment of banking capital in government securities. The majority of the banking institutions, on the other hand, raised their long-held objections to such measures; credit contraction would follow conversion of substantial amounts of banking capital into public debt, government issues would be relatively inelastic, flexibility in the adjustment of the supply of money to currency needs would be lacking, and there was no certainty as to the convertibility of government notes. Although there was little that was novel about the pros and cons of this controversy, the strength of opposing elements and the larger area affected led to a more comprehensive review of the functions of the banking system of the time.

In 1870, "An Act respecting Banks and Banking" was passed which, with slight amendments in 1871, established the pattern of Canadian banking for decades to follow. Traces of controversy were apparent in the requirement that banks keep at least one-third of their reserves in the form of Dominion notes. The bank-note issue was limited to the amount of paid-up capital, with no notes of denominations smaller than $4 in circulation; this last measure gave the Dominion government a monopoly of $1 and $2 notes. Dominion notes now circulated along with bank-note issues and under specified conditions might be increased in amount to $9 million, a figure which was increased in later enactments; a gold reserve of 20 per cent was held against this amount and beyond this the gold backing was 100 per cent. In the interests of banking stability, the sections of the Act dealing with capital stock now required that an initial capital to the amount of $500,000 be subscribed, $100,000 of this to be paid in in each of the first two years of operation. Bank shares now carried the double-liability clause, and suspension of payments by a bank for ninety days meant the loss of its charter. Bank charters were to run until 1881 and were subject to revision at that time. Legislation relating to loans on the security of bills of lading and warehouse receipts was extended with respect to the conditions in which loans were made and was to apply to a wider range of Canadian industries; banks could lend against the security of commodities which were stored awaiting marketing, or which were in transit or being converted from raw materials into consumption goods.

In the same year the "Uniform Currency Act" placed all Canada on a dollar basis, the gold content of the Canadian dollar to be the same as that of the United States. Although the Canadian standard coin continued to be defined as the British sovereign of $4.86 ⅔, this was changed in 1910 when the Currency Act of that year defined our standard as a certain weight of fine gold. Since little gold was in circulation, most of it being in the reserves of the Dominion government and the banks, this was in effect a gold bullion standard in contrast with the gold specie standard which had been adopted by the province of Canada in 1851 and had been in effect since 1853. Provision was made for the issue of Canadian gold coinage but this had little result; the Canadian branch of the Royal Mint was not established until 1908, the first Canadian $5 and $10 gold pieces were not struck until 1912, and none have been issued since 1919. Gold coins have never been a popular medium of exchange and when gold is needed for export bullion serves the purpose. Finally, decimal currency, the keeping of accounts in dollars and cents, was extended throughout the Dominion.

These legislative measures were passed in an atmosphere of prosperity and expansion. The entry of the new province of Manitoba in 1870 augured well for western development with its stimulus to new transportation construction and large-scale immigration. Expansion of banking facilities reflected the general optimism of the time; by mid-1873, thirty-three banks were in operation, a net increase of five banks since Confederation. The biggest of these, the Bank of Montreal, the Merchants' Bank of Canada and the Canadian Bank of Commerce, were substantial institutions, and confidence in these and the banking system in general was strengthened by their stability during the United States financial crisis of 1873. The Canadian economy, however, was too sensitive to external influences to escape the shock of crisis and depression elsewhere, speculative excesses appeared once more, and the now familiar pattern of hectic prosperity followed by depression manifested itself. In 1875, a great increase in commercial failures was reported and depression hit with full force in 1876. The carrying and timber trades suffered a severe set-back, but the whole economy felt the pinch. Excess imports on long credit from England had left a heavy burden of mercantile debt, and fixed charges arising out of government assistance to transportation improvements also raised serious problems. The low point of depression was reached in 1879. Although no bank panic resulted, there were bank failures, and creditors and shareholders of defunct banks took heavy losses. Bad investments made in speculative times were written off and once more the young country felt the chastening effect of hard times with their lessons for those unaware of its vulnerability to external influences. By the close of the decade, the worst was over; good crops, improved market conditions, and plans for a transcontinental railway and the opening of the "far west" indicated that the economy had survived one more period of testing.

The stronger banks had demonstrated the importance of a stable financial system, and in spite of the difficult five-year period just endured, no structural changes in Canadian banking were made in the Bank Act of 1881. Bank-notes were made a first lien on banking assets and banks were required to keep 40 per cent of their reserves in the form of Dominion notes. Bank-notes of less than $5 were no longer to be issued or reissued, and notes not multiples of $5 were prohibited. Sections dealing with loans on the security of commodities were further extended. In the same year, the issue of Dominion notes, which in the 1870's had been limited to $12 million, was increased to $20 million; these notes were backed by a reserve of 15 per cent in gold, 10 per cent in gold and securities of the Dominion guaranteed by the British government, and 75 per cent in Dominion of Canada debentures. In 1903, provision was made for a gold reserve of 25 per cent against the first $30 million of Dominion notes issued, the remainder to be backed by government bonds. Beyond this, the gold reserve was 100 per cent. Dominion issues increased so markedly over the early years of the twentieth century that by 1914 the gold reserve against Dominion notes exceeded 85 per cent.

Although commercial banking was now solidly established in its essential elements, signs of dissatisfaction with the functioning of the banking system as a whole were not absent. In the first place, proposals for the establishment of farmers' banks reflected the agriculturists' discontent with bankers' views on "sound banking practice" as well as the influence of the Greenback and Populist movements in the United States with their emphasis on the virtues of easy-money policies. These proposals included the formation of farmers' banks with capital consisting of gold, government bonds and farm mortgages, the issue of Dominion notes secured by first mortgages on farms, and frequently the end of the banks' powers of note issue. Although these proposals were rejected, it was clear that the chartered banks, with their emphasis on liquidity and on commercial loans, were far from being as closely attuned to the needs of the farmer as to those of the merchants, implement companies and others with whom the farmer had business dealings. On the other hand, it was exceedingly doubtful that the banks were in a position to serve without danger to the whole structure both the business community and the farmers whose complex pattern of short-term, intermediate and mortgage credit raised difficult problems for borrowers. The financial system was inadequate from this standpoint, but remedies were to be sought largely outside the field of commercial banking.

In the second place, the depression of the 1870's and developments in the following decade revealed deficiencies in the banking system which called for remedial action. The Bank Act revision of 1890, the first of importance since 1871, bears witness to the lessons learned in these years. The importance of large capital had become increasingly apparent, and the amount of paid-up capital required of a new bank was increased to $250,000. More difficult to remedy were certain defects related to bank-note issues. The fact that the notes of some banks were not always accepted at par by other banks was a source of irritation even though this concerned mainly the notes of smaller banks presented at some distance from head office. Circulation of notes at par in every part of the country was becoming increasingly important with the growth of interprovincial trade and it was obvious that there was room for improvement in this respect. Delays in the redemption of bank-notes between the date of suspension and the date when bank assets were realized had also been a cause of some inconvenience and loss.

Among the proposals made to correct these defects were first, recourse to the so-called "American Plan", and second, the requirement of a fixed reserve against bank-note issues. Against the first proposal, that of a national currency based on public securities, Canadian bankers could argue that while the National Banking system of the United States had provided a sound currency for that country, it was one unresponsive to seasonal and other changes in the need for currency. Since the volume of currency there depended on the amount of eligible government securities held by the banks, it bore little relation to the actual demand for money, and only the growth of deposit banking had prevented this system from exerting a crippling deflationary effect on the economy. Similarly, a fixed reserve against notes would greatly hinder the banking system in meeting the fluctuating demands of the business community for accommodation.

These were effective arguments, and reforms in Canada proceeded along other lines. Circulation of notes at par in all parts of the country was achieved by the establishment of a redemption agency in each province. The security of Canadian currency was gained, without sacrifice of elasticity, by the formation of a Circulation Redemption Fund to which each bank contributed 5 per cent of its circulation, a measure which in effect made the banks mutually responsible for each other's note circulation. In addition, notes were made a first lien on the assets of failed banks.

These remedial measures were taken in preference to the major surgery advocated by some proponents of banking reform. This emphasis on a gradual or evolutionary change in the banking system was in line with the course pursued throughout the nineteenth century. Attempts in 1841, in the late 1860's and in 1890 to introduce measures at variance with the banking community's ideals of sound banking practice failed to alter a pattern marked by adherence to principles laid down at the beginning, by comparative absence of experiment, and by gradual modification of banking practice in the light of experience.

Developments up to 1914 indicate no important changes from this pattern. The Canadian Bankers' Association, formed as a voluntary organization in 1892, was given the status of a public corporation in 1900 and granted the power to establish and regulate clearing-houses for the banks in any part of the country. It was also given certain responsibilities in cases of suspension of failed banks and in respect of the handling of bank-notes. In 1908, the Bank Act was amended to enable banks to issue beyond the statutory limit, i.e., the amount of their paid-up capital. This permitted a temporary increase in note issues when crops were moving to market and money turnover was large. Each bank was enabled to issue notes in excess of the former limit to the amount of 15 per cent of its capital and reserve fund. The excess issues were subject to a tax of 5 per cent to encourage retirement when the pressure had slackened. This privilege, originally restricted to the months of October to January inclusive, was extended in 1912 to include September and February. A more significant change permitting banks to issue notes in excess of their paid-up capital was made in the Bank Act of 1913. Banks could now, at any time of the year, issue such notes by depositing gold or Dominion notes in a Central Gold Reserve, obtaining thereby the right to issue notes equal to the amount deposited. This gave the banks an alternative to excess issues under the legislation of 1908 and these ceased to be of any importance. This special reserve provision, by making the currency dependent on bank holdings of gold and Dominion notes, ended the more or less automatic responsiveness of bank-note issues to the needs of business. Beyond specified limits, the further issue of such notes now depended upon the banks' ability to provide 100 per cent reserves in the form of gold and/or Dominion notes. A measure designed to raise the upper limits to the currency issue had removed one of the most desirable features of earlier bank-note issues. Like the provision for seasonal excess issues, establishment of the Central Gold Reserve appears as an expedient which left considerable room for improvement. In effect, a central bank was becoming a necessity with the growing complexity and range of the country's financial structure, and moves in this direction were not slow in appearing.

A POLICY OF DRIFT

A significant step in the direction of central banking was made in the passing of the Finance Act of 1914, although it appears that the full implications of this enactment were not apparent when it was passed. A war measure at the beginning, it ceased to be emergency legislation in 1923 and remained in force until its repeal in 1934. The outbreak of war had occasioned heavy withdrawals of gold; financial crisis threatened, and to ease the pressure on the banks the minister of finance was empowered, on receipt of specified securities, to advance Dominion notes to the banks so that these could be used as additions to their cash reserves. The volume of such advances to the banks was, however, at all times determined "automatically" on the initiative of the banks; the government apparently did not contemplate instituting any form of deliberate or discretionary control over their credit operations. The gold standard was also temporarily abandoned at this time. Formerly, the banks had increased their cash reserves largely from outside the country by converting call loans in New York into gold and importing this metal for reserve purposes. This arrangement had the virtue of simplicity; when credit expansion was called for, cash reserves could be quickly supplemented by this mechanism of drawing loans on call outside the country. When such short-term loans were reduced to a low level, however, ability to extend credit further was virtually absent. The Finance Act was designed in part to overcome this drawback, but in achieving this end, the Act in effect gave control of the ultimate source of credit, the cash reserves of the banks, into the hand of an agency of government and in so doing may have helped to prepare the way for central banking in the Dominion.

In 1923 the Treasury Board was given administration of the Act which became a permanent feature of the Canadian financial system. The operations of the Board, however, left much to be desired from a central-banking standpoint. Basic problems of credit policy were left untouched, nor was there any adequate provision for management of a note issue no longer convertible into gold. What was in effect a managed system lacked a qualified and responsible agency of management. The gold standard, as re-established in 1926, could not be maintained unless one of two alternatives was adopted. These alternatives were, first, the restoration of the monetary system operating before the war, or second, provision for the establishment of a central bank responsible for Canadian monetary policy.

Advocates of the first alternative were not lacking. The gold standard of pre-war times had many attractive features. In the first place it was an international system, one which linked the price level in each country with prices in all other countries which adhered to the same system. In the second place it was, in a sense, an automatic system: as long as the expansion and contraction of credit in each country was based on the free flow of gold into and out of its monetary stocks, the responsibility of monetary authorities for controlling the supply of money was clearly defined and strictly limited. Perhaps most important of all, it was a well-tried and tested system, and had all the attractions of familiarity. It is true that the operations of this international monetary system had been in actuality much less automatic than is sometimes supposed; whether reference be to the operations of the Bank of England or to the Canadian banking structure, the workability of the system depended on the participants adhering to "the rules of the game". As far as Canada was concerned, gold had long ceased to circulate as money to any extent, but the rule that Dominion notes were payable in gold on demand, that this gold could be freely exported, and that increases in note issues were possible only in response to increases in gold reserves had made this metal the basis of the national credit system. Proponents of a world order in which gold moved freely across national frontiers, in which exchange rates were permitted to fluctuate only within narrow limits, and in which credit expansion and thus the internal price level was tied directly to world economic conditions could point to the progress achieved in terms of expanding international trade and rising living standards. But the highly uncertain world of the 1920's raised new and difficult problems for the monetary authorities of every nation and the feasibility of a return to the pre-war standard was by no means self-evident.

When Canada returned to the gold standard in 1926 it quickly became apparent that a simple return to the procedures of the pre-war era was out of the question. The position of London as the centre of world finance had been seriously weakened by the events of the World War. The pound sterling was no longer the universally accepted medium of exchange which it had once been. Nations were now much more concerned than formerly with the maintenance of national prosperity and self-sufficiency and, in pursuing these goals, were unwilling to let their internal price levels (and indirectly, the level of employment) be determined mainly by the international movement of gold reserves. The gold standard no longer worked as effectively and automatically as had formerly been the case, if only for the simple reason that the monetary authorities of the various trading nations did not permit it to work. In these unfamiliar and threatening conditions Canada found herself, on the one hand, unable to rely on the automatic processes of adjustment to external disturbances which had once proved adequate, and, on the other, lacking any central organization which could accept responsibility for the management of currency and credit in the interest of the nation as a whole. Without such an agency there was little possibility of adhering to an international standard of any kind. Under these conditions the return to the gold standard was clearly ill-advised, and in 1931 the attempt was legally abandoned. In fact the gold standard had ceased to operate effectively, so far as Canada was concerned, in 1929. The uncertainties resulting from the lack of clearly defined monetary policies together with the depression which began in 1929, the failure of export demand for Canada's staples, and the cessation of capital imports led to proposals for remedial action, and in 1933 the Royal Commission on Banking and Currency was appointed to explore the problem. Government acceptance of the commission's proposals led to the establishment of the Bank of Canada and the beginning of central banking operations in 1935.

THE CENTRAL BANK AND RECENT DEVELOPMENTS

The establishment of Canada's central bank rounded out in its essentials a structure which had been slowly evolving for over a century. Somewhat late in the day, the Dominion followed in the path of British and European banking development. The necessity of a central authority responsible for the management of the country's monetary system was now recognized in the creation of an agency responsible for maintaining the external value of the currency, for regulating credit and currency in the national interest, for co-operating with other countries in monetary affairs and for advising the government on monetary policy. More generally, the central bank, according to the preamble of the Act, was ". . . to mitigate by its influence fluctuations in the general level of trade, prices and employment as far as may be possible within the scope of monetary management." It was required to keep a reserve in gold equal to 25 per cent of its liabilities and in the course of its operations assumed control of the Dominion note issue and associated gold reserves. Although under private ownership at the beginning, the Bank became a public institution when provision was made in 1938 for government acquisition of its shares from private stockholders. As fiscal agent of the Dominion government, responsible for management of the public debt, the Bank of Canada made important contributions in the war years, a period in which the banking system, strengthened by the central bank, played a crucial part in the sale of enormous issues of government bonds.

The commission's recommendation that the central bank be given sole rights of note issue led to the provision for the gradual extinction of the issues of the chartered banks. These were not to exceed 25 per cent of paid-up capital of the banks by 1945. Following this date the banks no longer had the right to issue their own notes and arrangements were made for the redemption and retirement of notes coming into the banks' possession. In 1950, the Bank of Canada assumed responsibility for redemption, and an old and highly controversial question was at last settled. The fact that this and other points of controversy awaited settlement until recently is due in good part to the circumstances that the Canadian branch-banking system was highly centralized at an early date, so that its strength and stability lessened the need for central banking as long as conditions favourable to the maintenance of the gold standard prevailed. The experience of the two decades following 1914 demonstrated that these conditions were no longer present and that there was little likelihood that they would ever return.

Although central-banking techniques of monetary leadership are still evolving, no radical departures from present-day practice are in prospect. The Bank of Canada exerts control mainly by operating on the cash reserves of the chartered banks. At times these may wish to increase their borrowings from the central bank and such borrowings are influenced by high or low rates of interest or by limitations on loans. Like other central banks, the Bank of Canada may engage in open-market operations by which it influences the reserves of the commercial banks. Although this technique has not been developed to the same extent in Canada as it has in Great Britain or the United States it is probably the most important of the techniques of control employed by the Bank of Canada. It is based on the central bank's practice of buying and selling securities in the open market; if credit expansion is desired, securities are purchased with cheques on the central bank and these, deposited by the sellers of the securities in their chartered banks, are forwarded to the central bank to form a net addition to the commercial banks' cash reserves; conversely, by selling securities, the central bank reduces cash reserves of the banks and hence their power to extend credit so long as they do not vary to any considerable extent their ratio of cash to demand liabilities. Another important factor, however, is the prestige of the Bank of Canada and its ability to persuade the banks to fall in line with the policies it advocates.

The limited scope of Canada's money market lessens the possibility of effective monetary management by the central bank. Open-market operations have been largely in short-term government securities which have been held almost entirely by the commercial banks; these institutions may resell them to the central bank when they require cash, a practice which leads to an increase in money supply whether or not this is in line with the central bank's general monetary policies. To broaden the money market, attempts are being made to encourage the buying of treasury bills by large corporations, provincial governments and others. In order to invite the co-operation of securities dealers, provision was made in 1953 for day-to-day loans by the banks to authorized security dealers to enable them to carry inventories of treasury bills without loss. In addition, under purchase and resale agreements, the central bank will buy treasury bills and short-term securities from authorized security dealers with a promise to resell at a stipulated price. Since on occasion dealers may be forced to borrow from the central bank and commercial banks at times may find it advisable to do so, the Bank of Canada's rediscount rate is likely to be more effective as an instrument of monetary control than it has been in the past. Although no more than a beginning has been made, the objectives of policy are clear: first, a short-term market with wider scope for participation by corporations, dealers in securities and possibly provincial and municipal governments; second, the creation of a new liquid asset in the form of day-to-day loans, a factor in encouraging the banks to reduce their cash-reserve ratio in the direction of new legal minimum requirements which can be varied by the central bank; and third, and possibly most important, a more sensitive response in the money market to the rediscount policies of the central bank. These changes amount to a closer approach to the Bank of England's techniques of control, and, although the Canadian money market is far from being as complex and well-articulated as that of London, the basic elements are similar.

In recent years, two important developments have increased substantially the scope of banking operations. The Farm Improvements Loan Act of 1944 provides for bank loans to farmers for a wide variety of purposes, and in view of the large volume of loans made under this legislation, it must be regarded as a highly significant advance in the provision of shorter-term credit for agricultural needs. Equally important were the arrangements made in 1954 for bank loans on the security of residential mortgages on new properties. The National Housing Act was amended in that year to permit bank participation in housing finance, a mortgage-insurance system was introduced, and under the Bank Act as changed to permit lending against insured mortgage, the banks had loaned close to $100 million by February, 1955. This entry into the long-term lending field, although it represents no marked deviation from the bankers' long-held adherence to keeping risks to a minimum (since these loans are insured by the federal government), may be viewed as an important step to wider participation by the banks in Canadian economic growth.

While the commercial banks along with trust and loan companies have been the principal depositories of the people's savings, other institutions also perform this function. Savings banks and co-operative credit unions have a long history, and the latter in particular have been expanding very rapidly in the past few years. With respect to savings banks, federal government and provincial institutions and a few private savings banks are now in operation. The Post Office Savings Banks, established in 1867, gradually absorbed various branches of the Government of Canada savings banks until the process of amalgamation was completed in 1929. Deposits in these institutions amounted to approximately $40 million in 1953. The provincial governments of Newfoundland, Ontario and Alberta also operate savings institutions. The Newfoundland Savings Bank deposits exceeded $24 million in 1953, those of the Province of Ontario Savings Office, with its 21 branches, $62 million, while $19 million was on deposit in the 45 Provincial Treasury Branches of Alberta in that year. In Quebec, the Montreal Country and District Savings Bank which was founded in 1846 and La Banque d'Economie de Québec founded two years later have large sums in savings accounts. Credit unions were first established in Quebec in 1900 and one-third of Canada's total are still in that province. The unions are also important in Ontario, British Columbia and Alberta and are increasing rapidly among industrial workers in these provinces. Deposits of these unions in Canada exceeded $290 million in 1952 and loans to members in this year $159 million. Although dwarfed by the commercial banks which had more than $4.5 billion of notice deposits in 1952, these institutions play an important part in the accumulation of small savings and the encouragement of thrift. As such they are valuable elements in Canada's financial system.

Also outside the sphere of commercial-bank operations, the Industrial Development Bank represents an attempt to round out the banking structure by the provision of loans for industrial purposes. Established in 1945, it was designed to ensure the availability of credit to prospectively sound industrial enterprises not able to secure credit elsewhere on reasonable terms and in so doing to supplement the activities of other lending agencies. Its president is the governor of the Bank of Canada, its capital stock of $25 million was subscribed and paid in by the central Bank, and it may raise additional funds by the issue of bonds and debentures. At the end of March, 1953, a sum exceeding $37 million had been loaned to a wide range of small industries and a total of $53,660,000 had been authorized. There are strong indications that the Bank's field of operations will steadily increase as its activities become better known.

Apart from the tardy development of the Canadian money market, the Canadian banking structure has come of age. The evolution of central banking has been slow, but the main steps are clear enough: the legislation of 1868 which permanently established the issue of Dominion notes, the power given the Canadian Bankers' Association in 1900 for better co-ordination of banking activities, the Central Gold Reserve provisions of 1913, the Finance Act of 1914 and 1923, and finally the beginning of formal central-banking operations in 1935. Two features of the Canadian banking system as it has developed help to account for the comparative absence of experimentation and the strong resistance to pressure for adoption of United States banking principles and practice. In the first place, the emphasis on relatively large and powerful institutions which has been characteristic of Canadian banking from the beginning, and the close relations of one or very few of these with government, gave the banks a prestige which was rarely shaken. Economically, their stability and strength in periods of testing appeared in happy contrast to the unsettled conditions of United States banking. Politically, their close relations with the tight-knit commercial community of the cities and larger towns and with government officialdom made successful attacks on their positions extremely difficult. Adherence to the liquidity theory of banking and to the belief in the efficacy of a more or less automatic mechanism of monetary adjustment was strong, and critics, even in high circles, made little headway over the nineteenth century.

In the second place, the efficiency and range of a branch-banking system permitted a degree of centralized control and a concentration of reserves that was absent in the unique unit-banking system of the United States. Ease of expansion into new areas and diversification of loans to enterprises scattered over the country were other virtues which lessened the need for central-banking control. In a world of an effectively functioning gold standard and in an expanding capital-importing economy, the Canadian banking system performed its main functions without benefit of any central agency of monetary management. However, the growing complexity of Canada's twentieth-century economy and the upheavals of two world wars hastened the appearance of central banking even though the measures taken reflect a continued preference for gradual, as opposed to radical, or abrupt, change. It is doubtful that the future will see any departure from this pattern. A high degree of concentration of power in the banking field continues (of our ten banks three control roughly two-thirds of the country's banking assets), and competition has assumed the form characteristic of situations in which a limited number of competitors place heavier emphasis on service than on price differentials. As such the banks continue to form the backbone of the country's financial system, and, along with the Bank of Canada, represent the culmination of a long process of adaptation to the requirements of an economy whose history is best described as one of painful adjustment to external pressures.

SUGGESTIONS FOR FURTHER READING

BASIC WORKS:

Bladen, V. W., *An Introduction to Political Economy* (Toronto, 1951), Chapter IV

Breckenridge, R. M., *The Canadian Banking System, 1817-90* (Toronto, 1894)

Curtis, C. A., "Evolution of Canadian Banking", *Annals of the American Academy of Political and Social Science* (Vol. 253), pp. 115-24

Curtis, C. A., "Banking", *Encyclopedia of Canada*, Vol. I (Toronto, 1935), pp. 151-64

Curtis, C. A., "Currency", *Encyclopedia of Canada*, Vol. II (Toronto, 1935), pp. 159-67

Knox, F. A., *Dominion Monetary Policy: 1929-34* (Prepared for the Royal Commission on Dominion-Provincial Relations; mimeographed)

Plumptre, A. F. W., *Central Banking in the British Dominions* (Toronto, 1940), Chapter IV

Canada Year Book, 1934-5, "Banking in Canada", pp. 967-92

Canada Year Book, 1937, "The Bank of Canada and Its Relations to the Canadian Financial System", pp. 881-5

King's Printer, Ottawa, 1933, *Report of Royal Commission on Banking and Currency in Canada*

SUPPLEMENTARY WORKS:

Bank of Canada, *The Story of Canada's Currency* (Ottawa, 1955)

Beckhart, B. H., "The Banking System of Canada" (in *Foreign Banking Systems* (New York, 1929), Chapter V

Eckhardt, E. M. P., *Manual of Canadian Banking* (Toronto, 1909)

Elliott, G. A., "Canadian Monetary Policy—Drift, Domestic Management and Debts". *Papers and Proceedings of the Canadian Political Science Association* (Vol. VI, 1934)

Jamieson, A. B., *Chartered Banking in Canada* (Toronto, 1952), Part I

McIntosh, R. M. "Broadening the Money Market", *Journal of the Canadian Bankers' Association* (Autumn, 1954). See also *Commerce Journal* (University of Toronto, 1955)

Neufeld, E. P., *Bank of Canada Operations, 1935-54* (Toronto, 1955)

Shortt, Adam, Chapters on Canadian currency, banking and the banking system in Vols. 4, 5, 10 of *Canada and its Provinces* (Toronto, 1914). Also numerous articles on the history of Canadian banking, currency and exchange in *Journal of the Canadian Bankers' Association* (Toronto)

Stokes, Milton L., *The Bank of Canada: The Development and Present Position of Central Banking in Canada* (Toronto, 1939)

CHAPTER XX

THE WHEAT ECONOMY

INTRODUCTION

THE emergence of wheat as Canada's great export staple of the early twentieth century has been a major theme in the literature of Canadian development. This is not surprising, for in the process whereby Canada became a strong trading and industrial nation this staple occupies a central place. It is not too much to say that wheat was the keystone in the arch of Canada's National Policy. Its production and sale made possible the construction of transcontinental railway systems and the extension of political control across the continent to the Pacific.

As with any major undertaking, the cultivation of the wheat-lands of Canada's new west presented a mixture of familiar or established procedures with much that was experimental or novel in aspect. Wheat was scarcely a new product in Canadian history; the beginnings of wheat production and more particularly its importance in the economy of central Canada in the period from 1850 to 1885 have been noted in earlier chapters. To a considerable degree, western expansion based on this staple may be viewed as an extension of cultivation into a new field of operations, or more largely, as a transfer of economic and political institutions, of financial, marketing and transportation systems, from eastern to western Canada. Prairie lands presented a new frontier, a great hinterland to be developed in the national interest, and for decades they remained a frontier dominated from the centre, a hinterland controlled along lines laid down well before large-scale expansion began. The strength and persistence of this control largely account for the importance of protest movements in the politics of the western provinces.

If we take the longer view of Canada's development as a sequence of shifts in emphasis from one export staple to another, no sharp departure from past policies is revealed in the heavy reliance on wheat as a factor in the nation's growth. This is apparent if we note the parallel that may be drawn between wheat and fur as significant elements in continental expansion. Both were staples produced very largely for export markets and both required elaborate and highly expensive systems of transportation. Like the fur trade, wheat production implied close ties with Europe and a strengthening of Old World connections, cultural as well as economic and political. The emergence of the wheat economy consolidated and gave new strength to influences established in the days of the pioneer trade. In marked contrast to developments to the south, there was no turning back on Europe, no break with European traditions, and few indications of any desire to build a new and better world in North America.

Concentration on wheat, as earlier on fur, however, led to serious and persisting difficulties resulting from frequent and unpredictable changes in prices and supplies available for export. This instability was the more serious in each instance because of the economy's dependence on a single export commodity for much of its income, and equally significant, because of the importance of fixed costs incurred largely for necessary investments in transportation improvements. In short, a combination of wide swings in income and a high proportion of costs which did not vary closely with changes in income made a stable or even rate of growth out of the question in both fur and wheat economies. Promotion of the earlier fur trade had made for strongly speculative elements in the country's development and in most respects the shift to wheat did little to lessen uncertainties present in earlier times.

It is true that the change had somewhat different implications for the long run, since wheat had saving graces which fur lacked. The later staple, in contrast to fur, possessed the quality of permanence and in addition provided a strong base for large-scale settlement. This is the case even when soil-mining practices, once an unhappy feature of pioneer agriculture, are taken into account, and more so as better knowledge of soils and closer attention to conservation measures have resulted in a more effective utilization of the nation's soil resources. Nevertheless, these advances have not removed nor greatly curbed wide variations in income resulting from fluctuations in price, quality, and supplies of wheat for the market, and this remains a problem for present-day administrations.

The importance of speculative elements in western expansion based on wheat is not difficult to explain for there was much in this expansion that suggested a venture into the unknown. Although general surveys had been undertaken and nuclei of later settlement had come into being, much remained to be learned of the resource potential of the prairie provinces. The physical environment was much more complex than had been assumed and the agricultural techniques of the British Isles and eastern Canada were not suited for cultivation of prairie soils. Numerous hazards faced wheat-growers in what might accurately be described as a struggle of man against nature. Fortunately for the wheat-farmer, at the turn of the century conditions were sufficiently favourable to enable him to cope fairly effectively with a wide range of uncertainties.

World wheat prices moved sharply upward over the period from 1896 to 1920, the total cost of transporting wheat to Liverpool declined until 1911, and farm productivity increased rapidly as experience was acquired

477

and agricultural techniques were borrowed from adjacent and geographically similar areas in the western United States. A combination of free or cheap land in Canada and the end of cheaper land in the United States helped to ensure that advantage would be taken of these favourable circumstances. Yet in spite of rising wheat prices and falling costs of transportation, the challenge of the Canadian west was met with great difficulty, for the obstacles were great.

These obstacles appeared in many forms. The unexpected complexity of the physical environment of the prairie provinces, the numerous and discouraging hazards which faced wheat-growers over the growing season, and the abrupt and occasionally extreme changes in economic conditions —these in many years made farming very much a gambling operation. Extreme variations in farmers' net income attested to the experimental character of western development. The ups and downs of good years and bad which are characteristic features of a new and pioneer economy, one lacking in diversity and vulnerable to external changes, may perhaps be regarded as an inevitable phase on the road to greater economic maturity, but for the prairie farmer it was far from being an easy road.

The area of this great experiment may be described as the northern extension of the great central plain which stretches south to the Gulf of Mexico. In Canada, its western limit is the Rocky Mountains, its eastern the Canadian Shield, while on the south the international boundary cuts across one of the major geographic regions of the continent. In extent it narrows from a front of 800 miles along the 49th parallel to one of roughly 400 miles on its northern limit, the Arctic Ocean. Relief maps of the Canadian section depict three quite distinct levels of a great plateau, the altitude of which increases gently, although somewhat irregularly, from eastern Manitoba to the Alberta foothills. The easternmost level is generally less than 1,000 feet in altitude; its eastern limit is the Shield and its western limit is defined by the Manitoba Escarpment which runs from the Pembina hills on the border, through Riding and Duck Mountains, and continues roughly northward from this point. Its heart is the fertile Red River valley, a flat plain whose rich soils are evidence of glacial Lake Agassiz which once covered the first prairie level. The second of the three levels appears as a broken plateau of 1,500 feet in altitude, rising at some points to 3,000 feet; its western boundary starts at the Missouri Coteau and follows a line west of Weyburn and Moose Jaw which extends in a northwesterly direction to Battleford and beyond. The third level has the foothills of the Rockies as its western limit and rises generally from a 3,000-foot altitude in the east to roughly 5,000 feet on its western flank.

This great central plain thus displays considerable variety in its topography, and the same is true of such geographic factors as climate, soils and rainfall. Nevertheless there is sufficient uniformity to permit us to generalize about the physical setting in this part of the continent. The settled area of the prairies, an area which lies for the most part southwest of a line drawn from Winnipeg through Prince Albert to Edmonton, may be described as being mainly treeless grass land; its annual average rainfall nowhere exceeds twenty inches, a rate of precipitation which explains a condition ranging from semi-arid to arid. Fortunately, most of the rainfall occurs in the growing season, but in some regions, notably those of southwestern Saskatchewan and southeastern Alberta, the margin between adequate rainfall and drought conditions is exceedingly narrow. Temperature changes reflect the extreme variations of continental interiors, and to the north frost replaces drought as a major hazard for the farmers. Only the development of early maturing varieties of wheat has permitted the extension of agriculture into northern districts.

In general, three broad climatic and soil zones may be defined. The dark-soil, sub-humid northern zone is best suited to dairying and mixed farming; wheat is important, but concentration on this staple is out of the question because of the shortness of the growing season and the poorer quality of the product. To the south, on the other hand, the chestnut or dark brown plains soils of the semi-arid second zone are excellent for wheat-growing and the larger part of the field-crop area is given over to wheat production. Limited precipitation, long cold winters and short hot summers encourage the growth of early-maturing varieties of cereals of high quality and the bulk of Canada's best wheat has been grown in this soil zone. In the southwestern parts of the plain, bitter experience has shown that the light brown soils of the region along with its extreme variations in rainfall are more suited to cattle and sheep than to wheat, although in some districts of southern Alberta irrigation has helped to overcome the more serious handicaps which geography has imposed on this "next-year country".

The essential features of a "wheat economy" appear most clearly in Saskatchewan and at least one writer of importance has restricted the application of the term of this province, whose continued dependence on wheat makes it an ideal area for study of the possibilities and limitations of a one-crop economy. The uneven and eventful history of Saskatchewan reflects in microcosm the problems of the Canada of the early twentieth century. It was fortunate for Canada as a whole that the experience of Saskatchewan in the depression years of the 1930's had no parallel in the national economy of 1900-13. In this province as in its sister provinces, a combination of poor yields and highly adverse world market conditions following 1929 threatened economic collapse; the hazards of wheat production and the uncertainties of supply and demand made it all too apparent that the dominance of wheat had its dangers for sound and progressive economic development.

For some of the hazards facing the wheat-grower of the prairies fairly effective solutions were found. The short growing season led to a search for early-ripening varieties of wheat. Red Fife was introduced at the turn of the century and represented a substantial improvement over earlier varieties used; in 1911, Marquis shortened the period of maturing by roughly a week and produced a higher yield; and in the 1920's Garnet and Reward permitted production in districts formerly too far north for production. These were highly significant advances even though the danger of unseasonable frosts remains to the present day a serious hazard. Rainfall deficiency has been more difficult to cope with and dry-farming techniques have provided only a partial solution. Wheat-stem rust, the cause of heavy losses in particular years, has led to an intensive search for rust-resistant strains, and such varieties as Thatcher, Apex and Renown have helped to check this plant parasite, but the contest between science and this and other plant diseases continues. The depredations of grass-hoppers and other insect pests have been reduced by control measures and the risk of hail loss has been partly met by hail insurance, yet for these too no easy solution is in prospect.

The significance of these numerous hazards is reflected in wide variations in the volume and quality of wheat produced in this far from ideal environment. The average yield per acre in Saskatchewan, for example, has varied from 8.8 bushels in 1900 to a figure in excess of 25 bushels in 1925, with a low point of 2.7 in 1937. For the prairie provinces as a whole, the range of variation is almost as extreme. It is important to note that differences in yield are not offset by price changes; a poor prairie crop cannot by itself induce higher prices in the world market. Quality as well as quantity has displayed considerable variation from one year to the next; the percentage of wheat grown in the prairie provinces which graded No. 3 Northern or better was less than 40 in 1911, but more than 90 in the first two years of this century and again in 1922. These marked fluctuations in volume and grade of product are sufficient by themselves to cause extreme variations in the wheat-farmer's net income, but life for him is made even more uncertain by economic factors over which he has had no control until recently and a very limited control now.

Although both wheat prices and the costs of producing and transporting this commodity to European markets moved in the farmer's favour in the years before World War I, the difficulty of financing operations under conditions of uncertain and fluctuating prices was apparent from the beginning. Institutional credit was highly inflexible in its terms and arrangements for meeting the farmer's financial needs, and the total costs of producing wheat contained a high proportion of fixed charges. Under favourable conditions this incompatibility of variable income and fixed costs need not spell disaster for the farmer, but the experience of the First World War period and later of the depression years of the 1930's underlined the danger of such a price-cost relationship. Inflated prices in the war and immediate post-war periods and a less than proportionate rise in costs led to a marked increase in farm income and to a rate of expansion which necessitated painful adjustments at a later date. When in the early 1930's the price of Canada's best wheat dropped to roughly one-quarter that of the years 1917-20, no corresponding decline in costs occurred to offset the catastrophic decline in returns. Although such extreme variability in farm income was not encountered in the first decade of the twentieth century, the margin between success and failure was frequently a thin one. Conditions were highly precarious for carrying out this great experiment in settling the heart of a continent; success rested on a highly favourable set of circumstances both internal and external to the economy. Reference has been made in earlier chapters to the changing structure of the economies of Great Britain and the United States which made possible the results achieved in this strategic phase of nation-building. In Canada itself, a consistent national policy directed to the exploitation of rich natural resources made the best of the opportunities presented by external changes and in the process prepared the way for the more diversified and better-balanced, though still economically vulnerable, structure of the present.

SECULAR GROWTH AND CYCLICAL PHASES

The "wheat phase" of Canada's National Policy ended only in 1930 with the transfer of natural resources from the Dominion to the prairie provinces. In spite of unsolved problems and discouraging set-backs, the first three decades of the present century represent an era of quite remarkable achievement. It was in these years that wheat played a dominant role in the Canadian economy, even though its contributions were to hasten the rise of other great export staples and an expansion of industrialism which lessened agriculture's relative importance in the economy. Fertile prairie lands were the magnet that drew men and capital to the interior of the continent. At the close of this period more than 88 per cent of the surveyed land area of the prairie provinces had been disposed of "for the purposes of the Dominion". A prairie population of less than 420,000 in 1901 had increased fivefold to 2,350,000 by 1931; that of Manitoba had increased from 255,211 to 700,139, Saskatchewan from 91,379 to 921,795, and Alberta from 73,022 to 731,605. By the close of the period almost one-quarter of Canada's population lived in the western provinces, in contrast with less than 10 per cent in 1901.

Other indices of change are equally impressive. Over these three decades the area of occupied land increased from 15.5 million acres to almost 110 million, or sevenfold, and improved acreage increased elevenfold from 5.6 million acres to roughly 60 million. More than 60 per cent of the gainfully employed in the prairie provinces were engaged in agricultural operations dominated by wheat production. The area of wheat plantings alone increased from 4.3 million acres in 1901 to 26.4 million in 1931. Turning to trade, wheat exports in 1901 yielded less than $7 million, in 1921 almost $311 million, and even in the poor year of 1931 they exceeded $118 million. Of Canada's total export trade, wheat exports increased from less than 4 per cent in 1901 to more than 16 per cent in 1911; by 1921 they were in excess of 25 per cent and had become the nation's most valuable export. In the rush of settlement mistakes were made, and too often discrimination was lacking in the selection of lands for cultivation. Over-optimism is characteristic of new and developing areas and, even when allowance is made for ignorance of growing conditions and quality of soils, indications of irrationality are seldom absent in boom periods. A particularly unfortunate illustration was the opening of the arid regions of southwestern Saskatchewan and eastern Alberta to settlement in 1908; newcomers poured in to break land which, as later experience showed, was more fit for grazing than for cereal crops. Hind-sight is easy and such mistakes were perhaps inevitable at the time, but the costs of later adjustment of farming practices to geographic conditions were to be exceedingly high.

A number of distinct phases may be discerned in this thirty-year period of economic growth. The boom years to 1913 provided an impulse to the economy which raised it to a new plateau of economic achievement; the First World War brought new and striking changes, accelerated a rate of growth already great, and raised difficult problems of readjustment to peace-time conditions; the third and final phase of rapid expansion, that of the 1920's, witnessed recovery and a renewed growth which ended with the Great Depression of the 1930's. The close of Canada's "Dominion Lands" cycle, one which extends back to Confederation, marks the beginning of a less spectacular and expansive period in Canadian agricultural history. Changing world conditions called for closer adaptation of agriculture to its geographic and physical environment rather than further expansion, and a series of bad crop years brought home the dangers of over-specialization. The policies pursued in the Second World War years and the period 1946-55 are evidence that the lesson has been well learned.

THE FIRST PERIOD OF EXPANSION

There is good reason for the close attention historians and economists have given to Canada's boom decade of the early twentieth century, for it marks one of the major turning-points in the evolution of the Canadian economy. As pointed out in Chapter XVIII, statistics of rates of change, whether reference be to increase in population, occupied farm acreage, labour force, national product, manufacturing output or influx of foreign capital, indicate in this period a pace of development matched only in the 1850's and possibly in the decade after 1945. And just as the progress of the economy in the 1850's laid the foundations for subsequent expansion, that of the decade from 1901 to 1911 provided the base for the advances of the war and inter-war years of this century. The boom of the post-World War II period marks this as the culminating phase in a nation's century-long progress from a simple, largely underdeveloped pioneer economy to the complex industrial nation Canada has become today. Hitherto the primary stimulus to growth must be sought in factors external to the economy; it is only very recently that the Canadian economy has begun to display a momentum of its own.

The salient features of the great decade 1901-11 are easily distinguished. After thirty years of waiting and frustrated hopes, it was at last Canada's turn to be drawn into the world network of trade and investment. Not only was there the stimulus provided by such developments as the rapidly growing demand of industrial countries for primary products, the zeal of British investors for capital exports to other areas than the United States, and the end of the land frontier of the American west; in addition, and as important as any of these, was the spectacular rate of technological advance in the United States economy of the late nineteenth and early twentieth centuries, a consequence in part of the huge inflow of cheap labour from southeastern Europe and a remarkably high level of domestic investment in new technologies of production and distribution. Canada's ability to borrow her neighbour's innovations easily and freely contributed greatly to her rate of progress in both agriculture and industry. It is important to note that Canada's agricultural revolution of this period was accompanied and supported by a parallel revolution in Canadian industry. This is apparent if account is taken of the fact that over the first decade of the twentieth century the proportion of gainfully employed engaged in manufacturing remained almost constant in spite of the great increase in agricultural production, that the value of manufactured goods provided for the home market increased at an even faster rate than the value of agricultural production, and that the ratio of urban to total population increased substantially. It is true that wheat production sparked this industrial development, and that prairie settlement created a strong demand for Canadian manufactures, but without the ability to use the technological advances of the United States in industry, mining and related activities, Canadian economic development as a whole must have experienced a substantially slower rate of change.

In agricultural technology too, Canadian borrowings were heavy. The spread of prairie settlement after 1900 depended to a very considerable extent on techniques perfected by her neighbour for cultivation of similar

483

areas in the United States. These borrowings included the use of the chilled-steel plough, the self-binding reaper, the steel-roller mill for the grinding of hard prairie grain, the endless-belt elevator and the box car for hauling grain in bulk. Other borrowings of high value included the use of summer-fallowing for conservation of moisture and the system of rectangular survey which has left its distinctive mark on the prairie landscape. Without these advances, it is very doubtful that world demand could have had the impact it had on the Canadian economy even when resource factors are taken into account. It was the combination of favourable demand-and-supply conditions, supported by technological and capital borrowings, that explains the phenomenal rate of progress that was achieved.

At the close of the first decade, the prairie population exceeded 1.3 million and Saskatchewan had taken her place as the nation's great wheat province; 57.5 million acres had been occupied and about 23 million or 40 per cent of this occupied land had been improved. Homestead entries, which had numbered 8,167 in 1901, reached their peak in 1911 when 44,479 entries were recorded. Canada's wheat production increased from 56 million bushels in 1901 to 231 million bushels a decade later. Before the First World War broke out, 7,500 miles of rail in the prairie provinces had been added to the 4,100 miles which had existed in 1901. Settlement followed the railway over this decade and spread out north and west from the valleys of the Red, the Assiniboine, the Souris and the Qu'Appelle; apart from these valleys, settlers in 1901 had pushed into the inter-lake district of Manitoba, had followed within a narrow range the line of the Canadian Pacific Railway westward, and in a belt stretching from the international boundary of Alberta northward to Edmonton had turned to the development of ranching. Five years later, settlement had blocked out much of the Park Belt and the dark brown prairie soils zone and moved farther north between the lakes in Manitoba. By 1911, the whole of the prairie area had been covered, although over much of the territory population density was low. The arid zone of southwestern Saskatchewan and southeastern Alberta had, unfortunately, been occupied by farmers rather than by ranchers. Settlement in the Peace River valley had begun, settlers were moving steadily into the more settled districts and a slow push north was in evidence. In the following five-year period, a slower rate of progress of the same general character was recorded as the density of population throughout the whole area increased; the movement northward continued, and the Peace River country felt the stimulus of railway construction north from Edmonton. As noted earlier, dry-farming techniques helped the farmer to fight drought in the southern areas, and the appearance of new varieties of wheat permitted a slow though steady march of settlement to northern districts.

Canada's whole economic development hinged on this wave of prairie settlement—a wave which has been described as one of history's greatest population movements. Although the details of the impact on other regions of the country cannot be recorded here, special notice should be taken of the closely related progress in industry and manufacturing in this period, not only because of its rate and magnitude but also because of the significance of its location for later developments. Fostered by high tariffs, stimulated by declining freight rates and the growth of towns and cities, by large-scale expenditures for railway construction and by the buying power of the prairie farmer, Canadian manufacturing registered substantial gains in almost every category. In the first decade of the century, the net value of manufacturing production increased more than two and one-half times, textile production more than doubled, the production of iron and steel and their products increased more than threefold, and flour and grist-mill products almost fivefold. The production of consumer goods and capital equipment and the processing of natural products kept pace with the country's expanding farm output. Significant beginnings were made in the production and export of pulp and paper and non-ferrous metals, items which were later to rival and in some instances surpass wheat as the country's leading export commodity. The lumber mills of British Columbia and the iron and steel industry and the coal mines of Nova Scotia also felt the stimulus of prairie demands, but heavy concentration of manufacturing operations in Ontario and Quebec established these provinces as the industrial heart of the nation. This concentration was to give rise to regional frictions and discontent, but it must be regarded as the logical consequence of National Policy decisions, in that the east-west economic and political alignment of the country, the linking together of its various regions, was greatly strengthened by the growth of industry in the central provinces. Transportation of manufactured products westward to the prairie provinces and of wheat moving eastward to world markets permitted maximum utilization of the nation's transcontinental railway system and made for diffusion of the western farmers' buying power throughout the economy. Whatever the incidence of benefits and burdens of this aspect of National Policy may be, it served the purposes of the nation-builders for the time being.

This critical phase in Canadian economic history appears now as the high point of achievement in the attainment of aims first explicitly formulated in the difficult years following Confederation. The foundations of a stronger and better-integrated economy had been laid, errors in resource utilization had not yet come to light, and the pains of adjustment to less dynamic conditions were matters for the future. The disadvantages of a "staples policy" were not yet clearly apparent, and in any event it is difficult to see that any practicable alternative existed at the time. It is true, of course, that prairie wheat was only one of many agricultural commodities produced in the economy, and a more exhaustive discussion of Canadian agricultural history would have reference to other cereals, to dairying, ranching, and a wide range of specialty crops; but wheat alone could attract the man-power and the capital necessary at this stage of the nation's growth. Similarly, the industries of central Canada, like the fisheries and lumber of British Columbia and the coal and iron of the Maritimes, had their part to play in national development, but the emergence of an adequate home market awaited the exploitation of a resource in heavy demand in other parts of the world. Greater diversity in resource utilization and production and great complexity in economic organization depended on the interest of foreign buyers and foreign investors in the Canadian economy, and wheat aroused this interest.

Even in this early decade, however, there were indications of changes which were to lessen dependence on this export staple. The most significant was the beginning of a slow shift in the centre of the nation's economic gravity back to the Canadian Shield. This great plateau of barren rock had been the dominant geographic feature in the days of the fur trade, and the strong stimulus which wheat gave to other lines of resource utilization was to hasten a structural change of the greatest significance to the economy of today. The extent, consequences and implications of this return to the Shield are the subject of Chapter XXI.

THE WAR PHASE

Before the First World War broke out, there were signs that a period of great prosperity and almost feverish expansion was drawing to a close. As early as 1912 the storm signal of tightening credit in the London money market gave warning of difficulties ahead. By 1913 it had become apparent that British investors were turning from external to domestic investment. British capital exports, which had amounted to almost one-half of total British investment in 1912, turned sharply downward and Canada experienced a marked reduction in capital imports. Boom gave way to depression as the price level of Canadian export staples fell in world markets and the effects of a growing volume of unemployment were felt throughout the economy. There was little to cushion the shock of adverse changes in commodity and capital markets and it became all too clear that the boom-or-bust tendencies of the fur trade were still very strong in twentieth-century Canada. The economy had been geared to a rapid and sustained rate of growth; as this slowed down to a halt, symptoms appeared of over-expansion in railway construction, agricultural production and manufacturing capacity. The poor prairie crop of 1914 further emphasized the dangers inherent in a staples policy. The outbreak of war and the consequent disruption of trade and capital movements for a time threatened disaster to an economy already deep in depression.

Conditions changed abruptly for the better in the following year as a result of the almost insatiable demands of the Allied powers for food supplies and the materials of war. The necessity of making painful adjustments to a more stable or even declining level of world demand disappeared, and the country's development in the war and immediate post-war years exhibits a pattern closely similar to that of the first decade of the century. This is illustrated by the continued importance of external influences in the country's growth, a resumption of expansion of settlement and production in the prairie provinces, a marked increase in the concentration of industry in the central provinces, and a strengthening of the east-west axis of the economy. It is true that British imports had ceased to play a major part in financing the country's growth and that economic ties with the United States were growing steadily stronger, but for the time being no major change occurred in the general character of Canadian expansion or in policies formulated half a century earlier. It was sufficient that the peace-time demands of world markets had been replaced by the more urgent demands of war and that in the process an even greater external stimulus had been imparted to the Canadian economy.

Beginning in 1915, the price of wheat and related products climbed sharply. The result was an unparalleled rate of increase in the area devoted to the production of wheat and other field crops. Rising prices and the bumper crop of 1915 ended the threat of depression, and, perhaps more significant, the need for closer and more effective adaptation of wheat-growing regions to their geographic environment and to a slower rate of growth. The price of No. 1 Northern wheat (Fort William), which had averaged $1.07 per bushel over the period 1910-16, rose to a war-inflated average of $2.31 per bushel in the period 1917-20. From September, 1919, to July, 1920, inclusive, the price of wheat (basis No. 1 Northern, Fort William) held steady at a monthly average of $2.63 per bushel, then rose to $2.67 ⅜ for August, 1920, and in September of that year reached the astronomical level of $2.73 ½. In spite of the poor crops of 1917-19, these prices ensured satisfactory returns for the wheat-farmer. Although wheat remained the dominant export staple, substantial increases were also recorded in exports of other agricultural commodities and prosperous conditions were general over the prairies. By 1919, writes Professor Mackintosh, the acreage under wheat was close to 80 per cent greater than it had been in 1913, the total increase in the area devoted to field crops between 1913 and 1919 approximated the increase which had taken place in the twenty years preceding this hectic period, and the average value of wheat and flour exports in the 1917-19 period was more than double that of 1913. In the war-boom years of 1915-20 more than four million acres were added to the prairie area in wheat production. Over the decade 1911-21 prairie population increased by more than 600,000 to reach a total of almost two million. Population density rose in the better settled areas of the prairies and further expansion occurred in northwestern Saskatchewan and the Peace River area.

Although the impact of war on the manufacturing and mining sectors of the economy was less sharp than in the years of World War II, high prices stimulated production and the adoption of the most advanced techniques of modern industrialism. Base metal output rose sharply, aided by a successful search for improved techniques for the handling of complex ores. By 1921, export returns from nickel, copper, lead and zinc yielded $23.6 million, an increase of $14 million above the figure for 1911. More spectacular was the increase over this decade in the value of exports of wood-pulp and newsprint which rose from $19 million in 1913 to $150 million in 1921. Experience was to show that investment in these products of the forest were quite as speculative in character as investment in the production of wheat.

Manufacturing more than kept pace with the general growth of the economy in these years. To the stimulus of British orders for munitions and war equipment were added the incentives of a booming domestic market, the protection afforded by high ocean freight rates and a steep decline in imports from Europe and the United Kingdom, and tariff policies highly favourable to manufacturing interests. War orders for shells and planes led to a sharp increase in the capacity and diversity of operations of the iron and steel industry. The shift from the comparatively simple staples economy of the early twentieth century to the complex industrial economy of the present was greatly accelerated by these developments. War demands are short-term demands but it is difficult to exaggerate their consequences for the long run.

Although the consequences of the First World War for Canada were many and complex, its more general effects may be noted briefly. Of the greatest importance was the fact that the nation was spared the necessity of devising policies suitable to a slower rate of growth and of attempting corrective measures aimed at closer adaptation of farming practices to the prairie environment. War removed the need for any marked change in the national policies which had proved so successful in the period of the wheat boom, and wheat continued for a brief period longer to hold its dominant position in the economy. Industry and manufacturing might respond to the stimulus of war orders, but basically and with few exceptions they remained largely dependent on the prosperity of the prairie region and the continuance of marketing, financial and transportation arrangements which emphasized the east-west alignment of the economy. The old industrialism of wheat, railways and tariffs, in other words, received a new lease of life in the war years even though in the process the groundwork was being laid for its displacement. The old structure gained new supports for a time but they were temporary supports. Further, there were few signs of weakening of the speculative element so apparent in the days of the wheat boom. Greater diversity in the nation's economic life was encouraged, it is true, but continued and heavy reliance on a very limited number of export products for much of the nation's income was a guarantee that the economy would remain as sensitive to external influences as it had been from its early beginnings in the French regime.

This was true in spite of war-accelerated changes in Canada's pattern of trade and investment. The impetus given to the production and export of non-ferrous metals, pulp and paper greatly strengthened economic ties with the United States. Over the period 1914-18, exports to that country increased from $177 million to $440 million, and imports rose by almost $400 million to a total of $792 million. By 1921 the United States' share of Canada's total external trade was in the neighbourhood of 60 per cent. Imports from the United Kingdom, of course, dropped sharply, and although exports exceeded $860 million in 1918 much of this war-swollen amount was directly financed by Canada herself. The change in the structure of trade was accompanied by a similar change in the direction of capital flows. Over the period 1913-21, the investments of the United States in Canada increased by more than $1.5 billion. By 1920 a major shift in Canada's source of capital imports was well under way. A debtor nation at the beginning of the war, the United States emerged from it as a leading creditor nation, and Canada's proximity and wealth of resources drew American investment funds in increasing volume. On the debit side was the strengthening of regional tensions in the Canadian economy as the capital exports and market demands of her neighbour created pronounced disparities in the rate of progress of different regions. The central provinces and British Columbia as the centre of the new expansion found themselves in increasing conflict with national policies which had evolved in relation to wheat, and this conflict deepened with their growing strength in the economy and their lessening dependence on the prairie market. Although this threat to Canadian unity was still mainly a matter for the future and the wheat era had not yet come to a close, war-time developments undoubtedly hastened structural changes which are at the heart of regional differences today.

THE NINETEEN-TWENTIES

The war-stimulated boom came to an end in 1920 and once more serious depression threatened the economy. Prairie agriculture, in particular, was in a highly precarious condition. To meet war-time demands for foodstuffs, the prairie farmer had expanded production by heavy purchases of land and equipment at inflated prices. In the process he had gone deeply into debt. The prairie economy had become a high-cost economy, and only a continued high level of income would permit the wheat-farmer to carry his heavy burden of indebtedness and to continue in operation on the scale achieved in the war and immediate post-war period. Disaster threatened as the price of wheat dropped steadily from the 1920 peak to as low as $1.07 per bushel (basis No. 1 Northern, Fort William) in 1924, a return less than half that obtained annually over the period 1917-20. Other parts of the economy also faced depression as industry and manufacturing faced shrinking domestic and external markets. The dangers of increased dependence on the United States as an export outlet were demonstrated by that country's turn to higher tariffs in its emergency legislation of 1921 and the Fordney-McCumber tariff of the following year. Imports of farm products were drastically reduced by agricultural duties higher than any previously recorded in United States tariff legislation. As with the depression of 1913-15 there seemed to be no escape from prolonged depression caused by an unfortunate combination of falling export prices and a high level of fixed indebtedness.

Fortunately, at least from a short-run point of view, world conditions improved sufficiently to solve once more the most pressing of the country's economic problems. Post-war reconstruction, the return of monetary stability, and a high and sustained volume of United States foreign lending brought about a fair semblance of economic recovery. It is true that its foundations were unsound, but for a time the threat of depression was lifted from North America and Europe. The price of Canada's main exports moved up once more, and once more Canada's income from her export trade showed a sharp increase. Europe's need for new world foodstuffs, reduced European tariffs against wheat, and falling ocean freight rates strengthened the demand for Canadian grain, and the remunerative price of $1.68 per bushel (basis No. 1 Northern, Fort William) in 1925 encouraged resumption of another, though short-lived, period of expansion. By 1926 the area of improved prairie land had increased to almost 50 million acres and the return from wheat exports amounted to $250 million. Population density increased in the better-settled regions of the prairies, there was further expansion in northern Alberta and Saskatchewan and some extension of cultivation in the Peace River valley. Of particular importance was the progress made in adapting farm practices more closely to soil and climatic conditions; this objective was attained principally in the thirties and later, but in the twenties the beginnings of withdrawal of farming operations from the inter-lake district of Manitoba and the arid zone of the southwest pointed the way to more effective use of prairie land resources.

Once more a wheat boom seemed to be in prospect and the period 1926-9 appeared to mark the resumption of expansion along now familiar lines. Although wheat prices declined from the level of 1925, crop conditions were good until 1928. In that year a record wheat crop of 567 million bushels was produced and Canada's share of world wheat exports increased to approximately 50 per cent. The effects of improved world conditions were strengthened by favourable internal developments. These included reductions in railway freight rates, tariff changes which lowered the level of duties on farm equipment and the benefits to some parts of the prairies resulting from the opening of the Panama Canal. Improved varieties of wheat encouraged further expansion of settlement in the northern districts of Alberta and Saskatchewan. Prairie population increased by some 300,000 in the period 1926-31; the level of 2.3 million which was reached in 1931 was not exceeded until 1936. Wheat continued to dominate the economies of Saskatchewan and Alberta. In Manitoba, on the other hand, the growing importance of mining, power, and pulp-and-paper production brought that province more closely into line with developments in central Canada.

It is now clear that this last spurt of prairie wheat expansion was even more precariously based than the preceding wheat boom had been. The foundations of world prosperity in the period 1925-9 were extremely shaky. Much of Europe's buying power and its hopes of continued recovery rested on the continuance of United States foreign lending. The bulk of United States loans were short-term, however, and when depression struck in that country in 1929-30 and this great stream of capital dried up, the collapse of the European market was inevitable. This change was not unrelated to another unfortunate development, namely the growing strength of economic nationalism on a world-wide scale, with its emphasis on self-sufficiency and its search for means of insulating national economies against external influences. The old internationalism based on regional specialization and a world division of labour had given way to a twentieth-century variant of nationalism hostile to the nineteenth century's dream of a world economy. Support of domestic agriculture in European countries by means of tariffs, subsidies and other aid resulted in a shrinking of external demand for wheat and other grains, and as economic warfare replaced peaceful economic relations, depression in Canada steadily deepened.

These events helped to accelerate the decline of wheat in the Canadian economy; economic trends within the economy reinforced this decline. In Manitoba, a shift back to the Shield got under way—a small-scale version of a much larger shift in the economy as a whole. The wheat boom of 1926-9 in Saskatchewan and Alberta in retrospect appears as the final phase in a long cycle of nation-building. For these provinces, the culmination of this phase led to a period of readjustment long overdue. Even though wheat was to remain a staple of major importance to the economy's prosperity, the new frontier of modern industrialism was rapidly coming into its own. New metals, new forms of transportation, new means of utilizing the country's power resources—these were constituent elements in a technological revolution which is still under way. A combination of rich and varied resources, of advanced techniques, and of the large and increasing demands of the industrial giant to the south was to make Canada increasingly a North American nation. Central Canada, British Columbia, and to some extent Manitoba received the lion's share of the benefits of this structural change, while the maritime provinces occupied a marginal position in these new developments as they had in the old; the wheat provinces of Saskatchewan and Alberta found themselves faced with the task of seeking equilibrium, at a reasonable level of prosperity, in an area which had ceased to dominate the economy's growth.

Let us now sum up the larger features of this great wave of expansion extending over three decades of the twentieth century. Three boom periods may be distinguished: the wheat boom of the first decade, the war-induced boom of 1915-20, and the final upsurge of 1925-9. For two brief spells, roughly from 1913 to 1915 and from 1921 to 1924, economic expansion came to an abrupt halt and in each of these periods there appeared the prospect of a lengthy and painful process of adjustment on two fronts: first, a search for a broader and more diversified base of operations in agriculture and more generally in the economy itself; and second, a move toward a reduction of the economy's extreme dependence on external conditions even if this implied a slower rate of progress. The war period and the recovery of the late twenties averted the necessity for the first adjustment, although important advances were made in this direction in both phases. Little or no progress was made with the second, however, and the economy of 1929-30 was quite as vulnerable as it had been when wheat was king. Shifts in economic conditions and policy in the United States, seldom predictable from the Canadian point of view, steadily increased in importance in Canada's economic and political life as European influences weakened. New resource developments and new market connections increased rather than reduced the elements of uncertainty in Canadian enterprise.

By 1930, wheat had made its major contribution to Canada's growth. By the drive and momentum it had given the economy, it had drawn the man-power, capital and technology necessary to the beginnings of development on a massive scale of the rich resources of the Canadian Shield. It was only as this shift took on large-scale proportions that the fortunes of wheat-producers ceased to exert a decisive influence on the evolution of the economy as a whole.

DEPRESSION AND ADJUSTMENT

A wide range of circumstances seemed to ensure that the end of this third phase of wheat expansion would not be followed, as in the past, by a brief pause, a new surge of settlement, and further growth along the old lines. There were clear indications that for the most part the geographic limits of wheat production had been reached and that in some areas a retreat from wheat-growing was inevitable. Technological improvements in the production of wheat and other field crops were steadily increasing the optimum size of the farm unit and in the process of creating fewer and larger farms were strengthening the movement of population from farm to urban centres. The new industrialism was hastening the relative decline of wheat in the economy as new frontiers of opportunity beckoned the enterpriser and the investor. Externally, the collapse of the European economy and the increasing pull of an expanding United States reinforced structural changes unfavourable to continued emphasis on wheat production. The market demands of the United States centred on Canadian mineral and forest resources, and American investors concentrated largely on Canadian manufacturing, mining and industrial development. United States agricultural protectionism, on the other hand, left little room for Canadian wheat in the United States market. Manitoba had already moved away from its wheat phase and Alberta was to follow later. But it was the Great Depression of the nineteen-thirties which definitely brought the era of wheat to a close.

From 1929 to 1933, the economy experienced a sharp downswing in every sector. World-wide depression struck with great severity an area intrinsically very sensitive to external shocks. The prairie provinces suffered the most from the collapse of world markets and over the decade 1931-41 experienced a net emigration of almost a quarter of a million of their population. The dangers of extreme specialization are best illustrated by the plight of Saskatchewan in the depression years. A combination of drought and low prices brought ruin to a large proportion of the province's population. Over the period of 1930-8 wheat production fell below an average of ten bushels per acre, and in 1937 dropped to less than three bushels per acre. In 1932, Professor Fowke informs us, the best Canadian wheat brought a net return of barely 25 cents per bushel. The estimated net income from wheat sold off the farms in the province dropped from a peak of $218 million in 1928 to $42.3 million in 1933, and in 1937 declined further to $17.8 million. For the wheat economy as a whole the picture was almost as dark. The average annual production of wheat for the period 1920-8 was 220.5 million bushels; for 1928-38, 138 million bushels. The export price of wheat dropped more than 50 per cent over the period 1929-33 and in 1932 the price per bushel was little more than 40 per cent of that of 1929. A fall in volume or price of this order would have brought serious depression; together they spelled ruin.

Although the whole economy faced the rigours of depression, events seemed to conspire against the wheat farmer. In 1930, the United States, Germany, Italy and France sharply increased the degree of protection given to their agriculturists, huge supplies of Russian and United States wheat flooded the world market, and currency depreciation by such competitors as the Argentine and Australia further weakened Canada's position in the world's wheat trade. The fall in per capita income in Saskatchewan far exceeded that in other parts of the country. According to Professor Mackintosh, while Canada's per capita income declined somewhat less than 50 per cent from 1928-9 to 1933, that of Alberta fell more than 60 per cent and Saskatchewan's dropped an almost unbelievable 72 per cent. Nature and man seemed to conspire against the agriculturist with the wheat-farmer as the special target of adversity. National policies, once so favourable, now seemed to turn against him. Adherence to sound money doctrines left him exposed to adverse changes in export markets; on the other hand, measures taken to reduce his debt burden and his level of fixed costs were largely ineffective. Higher tariffs for Canadian manufactures left him with the prospect of buying in a strongly protected home market while at the same time selling in a world market in the face of fierce and unequal competition; as a consequence he had no alternative but to absorb the full shock of world depression. The outcome of this conjuncture of unfavourable conditions was a prolonged history of provincial and federal relief measures on the vast scale necessary to save a large proportion of the farm population from destitution. From 1931 to 1938 the farm relief programme was financed mainly by the federal government, and in Saskatchewan alone some $140 million was expended for relief purposes. The magnitude of the disaster which had afflicted prairie agriculture is reflected in the wide range of governmental measures undertaken to relieve farm distress; these included direct subsidies, minimum-price arrangements, stabilization policies and debt adjustment. Rehabilitation assistance included efforts to promote improvements in cultural practices, land utilization and water conservation. More permanent provision for emergencies arising from widespread crop failure was provided for in the Prairie Farm Assistance Act of 1939. Greater attention was also paid to international negotiations to improve export markets for wheat and other agricultural products, a move necessitated by the increasing intervention of governments in world trade.

When World War II broke out in September, 1939, a repetition of past periods of boom based on rising world demand seemed to be on the way. The bitter lessons of the 1930's, however, had been well learned. Agricultural policy was now directed to curtailing wheat production, and on the other hand to substantially increasing the output of dairy and livestock products. There was good reason for restrictions on wheat production. Higher prices and improved export sales provided incentives to expand wheat acreage and in the spring of 1940 an increase of two million acres in the area of wheat seeded was recorded. A larger crop in 1940-1 in the the face of Germany's military successes in Europe and her dangerous blockade of British ports promised difficulties ahead for farmers and governments alike. In 1941, deliveries to the Canadian Wheat Board were restricted to 230 million bushels annually and each farmer was assigned a quota of 65 per cent of his 1940 wheat acreage. Subsidies were paid to encourage an increase in dairy and livestock production, and compensation was given farmers for land taken out of wheat and diverted to summer-fallow or the production of coarse grains.

As a result of these measures, wheat acreage dropped almost 24 per cent. Prosperity had returned to prairie agriculture but wheat no longer set the pace. In 1939, two-thirds of prairie cash income had been derived from wheat; in 1942 this had dropped to somewhat less than one-third. Livestock production in particular showed a marked increase, and in 1942-3 Alberta's cash income from hogs exceeded that from wheat. It is true that before the end of the war farmers were turning back to wheat, but production of this commodity was now much more effectively adapted to conditions in the various regions of the prairies and it was clear that in the process of adjustment the dependence of the economy on this staple had been permanently reduced. Governmental policies directed to the marketing of wheat through international negotiations now have stability as their primary objective. Export sales of wheat no longer determine the state of the economy even though their contribution to the national income is still a matter of national concern.

Population changes of the 1940's and early 1950's underline the great structural changes taking place in the economy. Although there was a secular or long-run movement of population from the farm to urban centres, the depression years, war-time developments and the industrial boom greatly accelerated the movement from the farm. Saskatchewan bore the brunt of changes adverse to agriculture and her population had declined in the decade following 1931. For the prairie provinces as a whole, population statistics for the period 1941-6 (according to the quinquennial census) showed an absolute decrease for the first time, a loss equivalent to some 85,-000 in excess of the natural increase of the region in this period. Over the decade 1941-51, the country's strictly farm population decreased by 10 per cent, that for Saskatchewan falling by 23 per cent, Manitoba by 31 per cent, Alberta by 11 per cent. More striking was the increase in the urban population of these provinces. In this period, Alberta's urban population increased by 75 per cent, while in Saskatchewan it rose by 32 per cent (the same percentage increase as that of Canada as a whole), and in Manitoba by 26 per cent.

Differential rates of population change in the various provinces throw into clear relief the economic significance of these developments in the economy; over the period 1941-53, years in which Canada's population increased by 25 per cent, the favoured provinces of British Columbia, Ontario, Quebec and Alberta registered increases ranging from 26 per cent (Alberta) to 50 per cent (British Columbia), in sharp contrast with a 4 per cent decline in the population of the wheat province of Saskatchewan. It is true that mechanization of agriculture has strengthened the trend to larger farms and reduced the population necessary for production of the nation's field crops, but quite as important in prairie population change and not unrelated to the rate of mechanization in western agriculture has been the impact of western oil discoveries. These have brought about striking changes not only in Alberta but throughout the prairie economy. Refinery expansion, pipe-line construction and an intensive search for oil throughout western Canada have led to a radical change in the economic outlook of the whole region. This advance of the new industrialism into the heart of the wheat economy has brightened prospects for greater diversity in this formerly highly specialized area of production.

This is not to underrate the contribution which wheat still makes to the economy. The events of the early 1950's demonstrated the strength of Canada's position in the export market; the high quality of the product, the widespread use of advanced techniques of production, and close adaptation of farming practices to soil and climatic conditions are guarantees of a strong competitive position in world trade. It is apparent that in spite of the relative decline of wheat, an extensive area in the prairies is highly suitable for wheat production and that any pronounced shift to other lines of agricultural production would result, in anything like normal times, in a less economic utilization of prairie resources. The great natural advantages of a substantial portion of the prairie provinces for the production of wheat ensure that this staple will remain one of Canada's great export commodities. The excellent crops of the early 1950's helped to bring agricultural income to new levels and the stimulus was felt throughout the entire economy. The production of 688 million bushels in 1952 and 614 million bushels in 1953 mark these as the two biggest crop years in Canadian history. In the great year of 1952 the value of exports of wheat exceeded $620 million or more than 14 per cent of the value of Canada's exports in that year. In the years since World War II, prices showed little deviation from a satisfactory return of $1.80 per bushel (basis No. 1 Northern, Fort William). A series of excellent crops at such prices helped to stimulate boom conditions in the Canadian economy of the mid-twentieth century.

There are indications, however, that the wheat producer still faces serious uncertainties beyond his control. Increasing competition in export markets, a downward secular trend of prices, and a piling up of surplus stocks of wheat in the United States and Canada point to an increasingly serious wheat problem. The success of the major exporting nations in achieving market stability rests on their ability to find a common basis for agreement among themselves in a situation complicated by the surplus-disposal policies of the United States and by the strong position of importing areas in this era of abundance. Canada's high-quality wheat and her low costs of production make her competitive position a strong one, but the likelihood of large and even mounting surpluses of world supplies of wheat raises perplexing problems for the future. Nor are market uncertainties absent in Canada's trade in forest, mineral and factory products. It is obvious, even when increases in the United States demand for Canadian resources are taken into account, that avoidance of extreme fluctuations in the level of activity in Canadian industry and manufacturing must rest largely on the outcome of stabilization measures in the United States. In all sectors of the Canadian economy the influence of that power has become paramount. Its ability to solve its farm surplus problems without hardship to other wheat-producing nations will go far to shape Canada's wheat policy in the future; and similarly, its success in keeping the American economy on an even keel must be regarded as a key factor in the evolution of Canada's new "National Policy".

SOME PROBLEMS OF THE WHEAT ECONOMY

The complex history of western agriculture over the past half-century has been enlivened by numerous controversial issues. Conflicts between the prairie farming community and those who viewed the wheat economy as an instrument of national policy, or as a hinterland to be exploited, were perhaps inevitable. Fears of monopoly in transportation, marketing and finance gave rise to protest movements and the use of political weapons designed to strengthen a weak bargaining position. Basically, there are few novel features in this opposition of western farmers to the domination of non-agrarian interests; reference has been made in earlier chapters to the deep-rooted differences existing between rural and urban sectors of the country's population. The opening of the Canadian west, however, greatly increased the area of potential conflict and in the final years of the old National Policy differences deepened as a long period of expansion drew to a close. Their political and constitutional aspects take us beyond the scope of these pages, but note should be taken of some of the basic economic problems at the heart of the controversies.

RAILWAY RATES

Indications of the western farmers' distrust of monopoly appeared well before the wheat boom began, when strenuous action was taken by the province of Manitoba to break monopoly powers granted in the charter of the Canadian Pacific Railway. These in effect prevented the construction of a competing system of transportation in the Canadian west; Manitoba responded by vigorous attempts to encourage construction of lines to connect with United States railways to the south. These attempts culminated in the passing of the Red River Valley Railway Act, a provincial statute designed to end the Canadian railway's transportation monopoly. This and similar legislation was opposed both by the railway, which feared this threat to its revenue position, and by the federal government, which looked on the transcontinental line as the backbone of its National Policy. Continued pressure and the financial exigencies of the Canadian Pacific Railway led to abandonment of the monopoly clause in 1888 in return for which the railway received substantial financial compensation. Manitoba may be said to have won a political victory, although effective competition awaited the construction of other transcontinental lines. Aid given to the Canadian Northern Railway under the Manitoba Agreement of 1901 hastened the building of a competitive line from Port Arthur to Winnipeg. Boom conditions and support to further railway construction resulted in rapid progress and the early appearance of two additional transcontinental systems.

Pressure to reduce railway rates appeared as another and effective line of attack. In 1897, the Crow's Nest Pass Agreement with the Canadian Pacific Railway provided for lower rates on wheat and flour moving eastward to the head of navigation on Lake Superior; in return for a subsidy of $11,000 per mile, the railway in addition to this reduction in freight rates agreed to build a branch line from Lethbridge, through Crow's Nest Pass, to Nelson, British Columbia; this construction along with lower rates brightened prospects for a larger volume of traffic over Canada's east-west transportation system. Additional reductions were made under the Manitoba Agreement of 1901 when, in return for assistance in the form of bond guarantees and the lease of a section of railway line, the Canadian Northern agreed to lower rates between Manitoba and Lake Superior. This led to a cut in the C.P.R.'s rates in 1903, and in 1914 the lower rates prevailing in Manitoba were extended to the other prairie provinces. As a result of these changes, farmers were given a relatively low rate on grain for export, and complaints about the level of rates gave way to demands for more railways and equipment. Subsequent attempts to effect further reductions met with strong opposition, and in 1948 a royal commission was appointed to deal with this highly complex question. Although the rate structure is still a subject of keen controversy, Professor Currie, in an exhaustive study of the economics of Canadian transportation, concludes that low rates on export grain, although not decisive, were a powerful factor in western expansion.

The construction of the Panama Canal and successful efforts to reduce the level of rates on grain moving to Pacific ports to equality with those on grain moving eastward has encouraged a westward flow from Alberta and some parts of Saskatchewan. Completion of the Hudson Bay Railway, although of less consequence than its promoters had expected, provides one more alternative to the long haul to eastern ports. Since 1930, controversy has centred less on the position of specific industries and more largely on the question of benefits and burdens of railway rates to various regions, but over the early decades of the century strong pressure for lower rates on wheat and other grains undoubtedly improved the farmers' position in world markets. This was in line with National Policy objectives, a fact which greatly improved farmers' prospects for obtaining the reductions they sought.

MARKETING

Other efforts to improve the competitive position of agriculture took the form of attacks on interests in control of marketing arrangements for farm products. These attacks evolved slowly from political pressure applied for limited objectives to support of large-scale organizations which sought first to participate in the marketing of wheat and other grains and later to control, directly or through governmental agencies, the entire marketing process from producer to overseas importer. General regulation of the western grain trade by the federal government had begun as early as 1885, and a system of inspection and grading had been established in 1889, but further improvements were soon sought. An early and important objective was the improvement of conditions for the local storage of grain and its transportation to terminal markets. This brought the farmers into conflict with the line elevator companies operating chains of grain elevators and selling through common agents. These had expanded rapidly with the support of the C.P.R. Dissatisfaction with their operations rested on the absence of competition between elevators at many points, while the position of the elevator companies was further strengthened by the railway's refusal to permit direct loading into railway cars at any point at which there was a standard elevator. This left the farmer with no alternative but to accept the elevator's terms for price, weight, grade and dockage. In response to farmers' protests, a royal commission was appointed in 1899 and in the following year the Manitoba Grain Act was passed by the federal government. By this legislation, a warehouse commissioner was appointed to investigate complaints and provision was made for more adequate inspection; the railway was required to make an impartial distribution of cars and to build loading platforms free of charge where the demand was sufficient. Further complaints led to extensive amendments to this Act in 1908, and in 1912 it was incorporated in the Canada Grain Act —a statute which one authority has referred to as the "Magna Charta of the grain-grower".

Laxity in the enforcement of the Manitoba Grain Act of 1900 led to the beginnings of effective organization by prairie farmers, and we may note the principal phases in the struggle for farmer-control of the western wheat trade. To secure better enforcement of the Manitoba Grain Act, the Territorial Grain Growers' Association was organized in 1901. The Manitoba Grain Growers' Association followed in 1903. Success in securing important amendments to the Act in this year stimulated greater interest in the possibilities of organized effort by farmers, and in 1906 the United

Farmers of Alberta and the Saskatchewan Grain Growers' Association replaced the earlier Territorial Association. Following this initial phase, attention shifted to co-operative action in the marketing of prairie wheat and the Grain Growers' Grain Company began operations as a co-operative commission agent. The activities of this organization quickly brought it into conflict with the private grain trade. The Winnipeg Grain Exchange became the principal target of attack and the issue of farmers versus Exchange emerged as a leading political question of the day.

Difficulties arising from the strong competitive position of the line elevators led to the next phase, that of construction of elevators to compete with established interests in the trade. The government of Manitoba made a beginning in this direction in 1909 but the attempt failed and its elevators were leased to the Grain Growers' Grain Company in 1912. The failure of a government-owned system resulted in greater interest in co-operative action, and in 1911 the Saskatchewan Co-operative Elevator Company was formed. A similar organization established in Alberta in 1913 amalgamated three years later with the Grain Growers' Grain Company to form the United Grain Growers Limited. These two organizations, the Saskatchewan Co-operative Elevator Company and the United Grain Growers Limited, were highly successful in their operations, competing strongly with the private trade and handling up to one-third of the grain sold in the prairie provinces. The farmers were now well represented by their own organizations in both handling and selling activities and for the time being these appeared as an effective response to demands for a better deal for prairie agriculture.

The next phase was hastened by the events of the First World War period. Disturbance of the normal channels of trade led the Dominion government to appoint the Board of Grain Supervisors to regulate and control the marketing of grain. Although this shift to government marketing was aimed mainly at curbing speculative abuses and was regarded as a purely temporary arrangement, attempts to move out of the grain trade at the end of the war were strongly opposed by those who sought increased governmental action to stabilize agricultural returns at a satisfactory level. Post-war conditions forced the government's hand, and although war-time arrangements had been discontinued, it was found necessary in 1919 to create the Canadian Wheat Board to protect Canada's position in the export trade. For this purpose the board was made exclusive marketing agency for Canadian wheat in home and export markets. Although producers were not given the minimum guaranteed price which many sought, they received an initial advance payment for wheat at the time of delivery and participation certificates which enabled them to share in the final distribution of the receipts of the crop. The Board ceased to function in 1920, but conditions in the depression years of 1921-3 led to strong demands for its revival. When these were not successful, the formation of provincial pools appeared as the next significant step in participation by farmers in the marketing of prairie grain.

In 1923 the Alberta Co-operative Wheat Producers Limited was established. In the following year Saskatchewan and Manitoba followed suit, and the Canadian Co-operative Wheat Producers Limited was formed to serve as the Pools' central selling agency. These organizations acted as sales agent for the grower; they gave him an initial payment on delivery and returned to him the price of his wheat minus specified charges. Members were bound by a five-year contract to turn over all their wheat to the Pools under arrangements which left little room for the private trader. The provincial Pools were highly successful up to 1929 and during the twenties expanded their activities to include the operation of grain elevators. Emphasis on direct selling and greater stability in payment helped to hold the support of the producers and more than one-half of prairie wheat acreage was under pool contract when depression struck.

Collapse of prices of 1930 brought an end to this period of successful operations. Initial payments to farmers proved to be too large and the governments of the three prairie provinces were called on to guarantee bank loans to their respective Pools. When conditions worsened, the Dominion government was forced to step in and in effect take over the functions formerly performed by the Pools' central selling agency. The Pools in turn went their own way, serving as co-operative elevator companies but for a time operating on a greatly reduced scale. Each developed its own marketing department; since 1943 these have acted as agents for the purchase and delivery of wheat to a central governmental agency, the Canadian Wheat Board. With the return of better conditions, the Pools have made a strong recovery, adding greatly to their elevator capacity and handling a substantial part of grain marketed, a proportion ranging from one-third in Alberta to more than one-half in Saskatchewan. Although separate organizations, they work closely together to promote agricultural co-operation and to exert political pressure in the farmers' interests. Professor MacGibbon in his study of the grain trade views the situation as one of strong but stabilized competition between producer-owned organizations and the independent interests in the trade.

The retreat of the Pools in 1929-30, however, was to be followed by fundamental changes in marketing arrangements for the sale of Canadian wheat. The federal government was faced at this time with the problem of disposing of the Pools' wheat surplus in a world of depressed and shrinking markets. As depression deepened, the pressure for government participation steadily increased. Farmers' demands ranged from the formation of compulsory pools in control of all wheat-marketing to the setting of a minimum fixed price for wheat. Attacks on the private trade grew in intensity and agitation against the Winnipeg Grain Exchange led to the appointment of a royal commission in 1931. The findings of the commission, however, gave little comfort to the critics of the Exchange. Various measures taken to improve the farmers' conditions included bonus payments, negotiation of an agreement which purported to give Canadian wheat a preferred position in the British market, and support of the International Wheat Agreement of 1933. Designed to achieve greater price stability by adjustment of exports to effective world demand, this Agreement was to be more important for the experience gained than for any benefits it brought to the farmer.

More direct action seemed to be called for, and in 1935 the Canadian Wheat Board was formed as an emergency measure to liquidate surplus wheat stocks. Farmers sold to the Board on a voluntary no-contract basis, a fixed minimum initial price being paid on delivery and certificates being issued to enable farmers to participate in any surplus accruing above the minimum price. Although intended as an emergency institution only, conditions gave the Board a permanency which many farmers sought and which both the private grain trade and the government opposed. The Board served principally as an agency to which the farmers could deliver their grain at a minimum price if the open-market price was not satisfactory. For better or worse the government seemed to be in the business of selling wheat to stay, and the Board appeared as a political compromise between open-market trading and compulsory wheat-marketing through pool or government agencies. In 1941, limitation of the amount of wheat to be accepted by the Board and compensation to growers for reduction of wheat acreage indicated that production was at last recognized to be as important as marketing in the attainment of greater stability of returns.

War once again intervened to strengthen government intervention and in 1943 the Board became sole marketing agent with complete control over Canadian wheat supplies. The primary objectives were, first, to assure the government of adequate supplies to meet its commitments for foodstuffs under Mutual Aid pacts, and secondly, to control prices and avoid the inflationary increases which had led to serious over-expansion of acreage in the First World War period. In return for increased state control of marketing and production, the farmer was protected against excessive fluctuations in export prices. The shift from government support to direct intervention was in part a result of radical changes in the conduct of world trade. During the 1930's private trading through open markets had rapidly declined in the face of governmental policies of bulk purchase and sale and the employment of such devices as import tariffs, quotas and embargoes. Over the period 1935-43, the Canadian government sought to leave room for the private trader but the abnormal conditions of war-time left no alternative to increased governmental control. Prospects for return of private interests in the grain trade depend upon the return of at least an approximation to open-market or free-trade conditions in world commerce.

As a result of tendencies which strengthen the role of the state in international trade, increasing attention has been given to international agreements designed to stabilize prices and production. The British Wheat Agreement of 1946 gave the wheat-farmer security against post-war slump, although over the four-year period of the agreement his returns were substantially lower than would have resulted from freer market operations. A more comprehensive programme of marketing through international arrangements was embarked on in 1949 when forty-two countries signed an agreement to run for four years; this agreement between the major exporters, with the exception of Argentina and Russia, and thirty-seven importing countries concerned the allocation of exports and a maximum and minimum range of prices. Canadian sales were negotiated through the Wheat Board, and in fact sales under international agreement ensure the continuance of governmental monopoly over the marketing of Canadian wheat. A new international agreement was ratified in 1953, but the withdrawal of the United Kingdom and the attitude of importing countries in times of surplus production have weakened the possibility of attaining stability through controlled marketing. Uncertainty as to United States surplus-disposal policies also threatens the success of this agreement.

It is by no means certain that the benefits of centralized governmental control over marketing arrangements outweigh the drawbacks, but until economic nationalism shows signs of weakening no return to multilateral trade and open-market operations can be expected. Canada's expanding population now ensures an improving domestic demand, but dependence on export market conditions must remain heavy so long as she remains a major centre of wheat production. The farmer is no longer without defences against the free play of market forces, and through organized effort and political pressure he has greatly strengthened his bargaining position; whether the shift to governmental monopoly is the best means of ensuring him a fair deal remains a controversial issue which is writ large in national policy debates on the role of state and private enterprise in the economy.

TARIFFS

Western farmers succeeded in hastening revolutionary changes in the organization of the grain trade. They were much less successful in shaping tariff policies to their liking. In spite of repeated attacks on protective tariffs, Canada is today a high-tariff nation. It is not difficult to account for this failure to make progress in the direction of free trade. Although farmers displayed a united front in their attacks on trade barriers, the attacks were seldom as strong and never as sustained as those on the private sectors of the grain trade. More pressing and immediate issues frequently diverted their attention from tariff reforms. Further, over the period of western expansion, a moderate level of tariffs cannot be said to have imposed a serious burden on the wheat economy. Conditions changed for the worse in 1930-2, but in these years there was no possibility of escaping the world trend to high protection.

Not only was the drive to reform the tariff structure weaker than attacks on the grain trade, but the obstacles to successful action were much stronger than had been encountered in marketing reforms. This is true whether reference be to the policies and tactics of the federal government or of private enterprise. In marketing, the government at Ottawa, in recognition of the contributions of the wheat economy to national progress, might reluctantly condone the retreat of private interests in the trade, and, indeed, accept their submergence when world events left little alternative. Farmer opposition to the tariff policies set out in 1879, however, could expect no support, for it threatened the National Policy to which the federal government was so deeply committed. In the first place, the costs of continental expansion were heavy and the sources of governmental revenue limited. As late as the period preceding the First World War, over 70 per cent of federal revenue was raised by customs duties and another 14 per cent by excise taxes. And although personal income and corporation taxes were imposed in 1917, in the inter-war period some two-thirds of federal revenue was derived from tariffs, general sales taxes and specific taxes on liquor and tobacco. Where fiscal needs were so great and dependence on customs revenues so heavy, strong opposition to measures directed toward any substantial lowering of duties was to be expected. Secondly, successful operation of the transcontinental railway rested on a large and increasing east-west traffic, and for this support of domestic industry and manufacturing was essential if wheat shipments to eastern ports were to be more or less balanced by a flow of manufactured goods to the prairies. In other words, railways, wheat and tariffs were inseparably linked; it was the farmer's misfortune that his demands for freer trade brought him so directly into conflict with National Policy objectives. Thirdly, the growing power of United States competition in the twentieth century left no alternative to continued protection of domestic manufacturing and industry. And finally, the reappearance of economic nationalism in the inter-war period called for further measures in defence of domestic industry as economic warfare replaced peaceful exchange. External developments had forced the central government to establish a monopoly of wheat-marketing which many farmers had advocated; conversely, changing world conditions strengthened protectionist sentiments which the western farmer had so consistently opposed. In the one instance, he went with the tide, in the other against it.

If the Canadian government could permit no extensive downward revision of tariff schedules, private enterprise centred in transportation, merchandising and industry was solidly opposed to any moves in this direction. These elements shared a common interest in the expanding prairie market and together they provided much stronger opposition to the farmers' demands than the private grain trade was able to muster. Transportation interests opposed reciprocal trade with the United States as a threat to its east-west traffic, and merchants wished no competition from their American counterparts. But it was that traditional protectionist, the industrialist, who acted as the principal advocate of high tariffs. The Canadian Manufacturers Association, successor in 1887 to the Manufacturers Association of Ontario, reorganized for more effective action in 1900. In view of the rapid growth of the prairie population in the next few decades, the consequent increase in the western farmers' political influence and their turn to large-scale organization to express and implement their demands, the tendency of the industrialist and other protectionist interests to close ranks is not surprising. The tariff issue was clear-cut, the opposing lines sharply drawn, and the federal government was faced with the problem of maintaining a balance which would preserve political peace and at the same time leave its National Policy intact. The western farmer saw no good in a situation in which he sold his products in the face of world competition and bought his necessities in a domestic market rendered less competitive by protective tariffs. His opponents stressed the virtues of a protected home market in which infant industry might grow to maturity and give the economy the diversity it lacked.

Until world depression struck in the 1930's, the federal government sought by concessions and compromise to provide a moderate level of protection to manufacturing and industry. In 1897, on the eve of rapid western expansion, minor changes were made in tariff legislation in response to demands for lower duties; in the following year a British Preferential Tariff was arranged and in 1900 the British preference was increased. In the Tariff Act of 1907, an Intermediate Tariff was introduced which provided for lower duties where satisfactory commercial treaties were negotiated; this innovation, along with the British preference, offered somewhat lower duties on imports from Great Britain and Europe without reducing the level of protection against United States imports. The effect of these conciliatory changes was slight, and the farmers' dissatisfaction was reflected in the aggressive tactics of the period from 1907 to 1911.

Economically and politically the farmers were in a strong position to exert pressure on the government, and the Liberal party undertook to meet their demands for a new reciprocity treaty with the United States. Concurrent legislation was enacted by the United States Congress after a stormy session, but, faced with strong opposition in the Canadian Parliament, the Liberals took the issue to the polls and were defeated. Although the projected treaty had been limited mainly to free trade in natural products, its opponents viewed this legislation as a dangerous step in the wrong direction; their victory in this trial of strength left no doubts as to where the balance of power lay.

The farmers returned to the attack in the early twenties, but apart from reductions in duties on farm implements they made little impression on the tariff structure. Rather, the trend turned sharply against them when world depression led to a marked upward revision in the tariffs of all countries with whom Canada traded. In Canada, moderate tariff protection gave way to high tariffs when the general level of duties on the bulk of imports was increased by nearly 50 per cent. The Empire Trade Agreement of 1932 provided for minor reductions but gave little assistance to the wheat-farmer. High duties and the introduction of a wide range of administrative restrictions on trade imposed heavy burdens on farmers faced with a catastrophic fall in the export price of their products and a level of costs which reflected the strongly protected position of those from whom they bought commodities and services. Exposed to the full force of world competition, their competitive power weakened by an artificially high level of costs, they faced a situation not unlike that which had so severely retarded the development of the maritime provinces' export industries. Only large-scale governmental assistance along other lines saved the wheat economy from total collapse. Later developments in tariff policies, the Canada-United States Agreements of 1935 and 1938, the Canada-United Kingdom Agreement of 1937, and growing interest in the extension of most-favoured-nation agreements under the General Agreement on Tariffs and Trade (GATT) represent a mild retreat from high protection, but the obstacles to any marked reduction in the general level of duties are many and varied. It is reasonable to expect further progress in the extension of reciprocal trading arrangements, but this appears to be a question of long-run policy. In the meantime, the negotiation of international agreements, support of better adjustment of wheat production to world demand, and the encouragement of increased efficiency in the production and transportation of agricultural products must be relied on to strengthen the wheat economy in a high-tariff world.

FARM CREDIT

Quite as important to the western farmer as marketing arrangements for his products and the tariff policies of the federal government is the financial system on which he must depend to meet his complex credit needs. These are complex because of the mixed pattern of short-term, intermediate and mortgage lending which appears under the heading of farm credit, and they have been met with difficulty. A financial structure which had evolved in eastern Canada and which, with western expansion, extended its field of operations to the prairies had somehow to be adapted to the requirements of a community exhibiting extreme variations in income. This process of adaptation was slow and incomplete, and the farmers' dissatisfaction with the lending practices of the commercial banks and long-term lending institutions was heightened by the fact that these organizations were located in the urban centres of the east. Distrust of money power and fears of exploitation by large and impersonal lending institutions gave strength to the demands of a "soft-money" frontier for cheap and abundant credit. The chartered banks, like the Canadian Pacific Railway, the Grain Exchange, and the Canadian Manufacturers Association, were suspect in the farmer's eyes, and governments, federal and provincial, were called on to improve his bargaining position in finance as in other fields. Emphasis on political solutions for farm-credit problems brought these into the broader area of regional conflict; the emergence of Social Credit in Alberta represents the latest step in a long series of attacks on a financial structure solidly established well before twentieth-century expansion began.

The farm-credit problems of the wheat economy were not new problems in Canadian agricultural history. Over the second half of the nineteenth century frequent attempts were made to modify the emerging financial system in the interests of the farmer and some progress was made in providing him with adequate credit facilities. The expansion of commercial agriculture in the central provinces following the completion of the canals and early railways led to heavy demands on the chartered banks which had developed primarily in response to the needs of trade. Those institutions were not well suited to meeting agricultural needs, and widely different views on banking policy quickly led to conflict between farmers and the banking community. The outcome helped to set the stage for later developments in western Canada and some reference to the credit problems of this earlier phase will provide perspective on those of the wheat economy.

The transition to a predominantly commercial agriculture was not made easily. Although capital was attracted to investment in Canadian manufacturing, to transportation and communication and to the wholesale and retail trades, funds for agricultural improvement were slow in appearing even though the need was great. The gradual introduction of farm machinery, new methods of cultivation, and rising land values gave new urgency to the problem of capital scarcity in agriculture. As early as the 1840's, farm finance had become less a matter of obtaining assistance in land settlement, of getting a start, than of attracting funds necessary for the purchase of land whose value was no longer nominal and for the acquisition of equipment no longer primitive and cheap. In the absence of personal security, the farmer had little to offer save his land. The gradual accumulation of the savings of private individuals led to the beginnings of mortgage-lending, but the funds of individual investors fell far short of the demand and interest rates were as high as 25 per cent per annum. Banks assisted to some extent, but land was regarded by them as an unsuitable form of security for commercial-bank loans, an attitude which led to sharp differences with farmers seeking credit. The appearance of building societies in the 1840's marked the first important step in the provision of adequate mortgage-loan facilities. Although in the early years these societies relied mainly on domestic funds, they were to pave the way for capital investments in Canadian agriculture from abroad. As permanent farm buildings replaced temporary structures, and improved farm equipment and drainage ventures took on new importance, these early institutions provided increasing amounts of capital for agricultural development; they encouraged the accumulation of savings, they mobilized domestic capital for investment, and they enabled farmers to obtain mortgage funds at a lower rate of interest than had formerly prevailed. Less progress was made with the provision of short-term or operating credit. The farmer continued to rely on the country storekeeper for much of his carry-over funds, although much of this store credit was provided indirectly through the banking system.

As indicated in Chapter XIX, facilities for the provision of agricultural credit in the pre-Confederation years were seldom regarded as adequate by the farming community, and there began in these years strong pressure on the banking system to serve agriculture as well as it was serving commerce. Much of the later history of agricultural credit may be traced in terms of unsuccessful attempts to modify a commercial-banking structure in the direction of a more comprehensive and systematic provision of credit for agricultural operations and expansion. Reasons for the inability of agrarian interests to create farmers' banks or to exert any significant influence on banking legislation were noted in Ch. XIX. Provision for loans on the security of bills of lading or warehouse receipts, first made in 1859, was to become of great importance to the financing of the grain and lumber trades, and later amendments were made to empower the banks to lend to farmers, lumbermen and fabricators of raw materials on the security of commodities stored awaiting marketing, or in transit, or being converted from raw materials into consumption goods. This legislation, however, so important to trade, was far from meeting farmers' demands and their attacks continued. Although these failed, the banks were important as a source of short-term and intermediate credit to farmers; a large part of this credit was supplied to those with whom the farmer did business "on time", while the rest took the form of direct bank loans renewed so frequently as to remove them from the short-term category. Farmers' complaints centred less on the volume of bank-lending than on the rate of interest and the terms on which loans were made. The financial structure was far from ideal, it is true, but a mixed pattern of store and bank credit, of mortgage loans by private individuals and building societies met the more pressing needs of the farmer, and no marked deviation from this pattern is apparent in the decades following Confederation.

In the 1870's, provision was made for the import of substantial amounts of British capital for investment on farm property. In 1874, building societies were given the right to issue debentures, and mortgage money was soon sought in London. By the close of this decade the loan companies had established a reputation for themselves abroad and the trend to lower rates of interest was becoming general. The ability of institutional lenders to tap the London money market went far to end the chronic shortage of mortgage funds for agricultural expansion. Their central position in the farm-mortgage field in Canada was not long maintained, however, for in the last decade of the century changes occurred which caused them to look to the western provinces as their principal area of operation. The most important of these was the appearance of increasing amounts of domestic capital available for investment in farm mortgages. Increasing competition among lenders, falling interest rates and lower returns led to the amalgamation of many of the loan companies into larger units. In the process these declined in importance as channels for overseas borrowing for mortgage purposes. By 1900 company operations had largely given way in eastern Canada to individuals who could lend at lower rates and on more convenient terms. Although some lending on selected farm properties was continued by the former, a more promising field of investment beckoned to the west. The time had come for a major shift in the area of operations, and mortgage-lending institutions turned to the prairies as an outlet for idle mortgage funds. They had filled a gap left by the refusal of the banks to make loans on the security of land. The strength of the banks, and their ability to withstand pressure for modifications in their lending practices in line with agricultural requirements, help to explain the importance of mortgage-lending institutions, country merchants and individual investors in the farm-credit picture. Nevertheless, bank credit was crucially important to agricultural development in its contributions to the financing of the export trade in agricultural products and of implement companies, merchants and others extending credit to farmers. When operations shifted westward, the prairie farmers were no more successful than their eastern brethren had been in their endeavours to shape banking policy in their interests, and governments were increasingly called on to supplement, even replace, private institutions in the farm-loans field.

Until the war years of the twentieth century, the role of government was that of silent partner, actively supporting agricultural development, but in the main refraining from direct intervention in agricultural problems. With respect to more permanent improvements, government measures aided development where joint efforts on the part of farmers were necessary, as with drainage, dyking and irrigation ventures. Assistance was given to agricultural associations by grants and to a lesser extent loans and guarantees of loans. Other assistance took the form of attempts to foster settlement and colonization in sparsely populated areas. Although provision was made for minor extensions of credit in some instances, the emphasis was on general support aimed at improving the position of agriculture as a field for investment. Co-operative action on the part of farmers helped to lessen the need for short-term credit, and developmental measures encouraged long-term lending in many areas. Credit advanced by governments was incidental to other purposes, and institutional lenders and private investors along with implement companies and country storekeepers functioned as the main sources of advances to farmers until the First World War brought changes which drastically altered the role of governments in farm finance.

With the beginning of rapid expansion in western Canada in the early years of the twentieth century, there was repeated a pattern of lending familiar in earlier decades in eastern Canada. Mortgage institutions, which had opened channels for the flow of investment money from Britain and Western Europe, at the turn of the century found themselves with a plethora of overseas funds which now found a welcome outlet in the prosperous areas of western agriculture. Although domestic capital was increasing in importance, British and European capital played a highly important part in frontier agricultural development. The peak years of 1909-13 witnessed a strong demand for Canadian, British, French and Netherlands capital and by 1914 more than $200 million was outstanding on farm mortgages held in large part by mortgage institutions and insurance and trust companies.

In spite of the prosperity of these boom years, complaints were directed against the level of interest rates on farm mortgages and the lack of flexibility in lending practices which failed to take into account the extreme variability of farm income. With very few exceptions there had been little change in lending policies which had evolved in a less speculative area and period of growth. Complaints sharpened as signs appeared in 1913 of a slowing down in the rate of expansion. Speculative excesses in farm lending had not been avoided and when "sail-trimming" by mortgage lenders became general, the pressure on provincial governments to intervene actively in farm-credit operations steadily increased. The proposals of the Saskatchewan Commission on Agricultural Credit (1913) provide one of the first indications of a change in governmental policies from general support of agricultural development to active government intervention in farm credit.

With the outbreak of war, the provincial legislatures of Ontario, Manitoba, Saskatchewan and British Columbia passed moratorium legislation. This protection of borrowers against foreclosure for failure to meet payments was disturbing enough to institutional lenders, but there were other equally disturbing measures to come. In 1915, when conditions of widespread drought led the federal government to vote $8 million for the purchase of seed grain, provision was made to enable the banks to make temporary loans for the purchase of seed grain supplies; these advances were given precedence over other claims in spite of the protests of mortgage lenders against this infringement of contracts already made. In 1917, government intervention entered a new stage when the Manitoba Farm Loans Association began operations.

These developments marked a decisive change to direct government intervention, but earlier indications of increased governmental participation had not been absent. Government loans and guarantees of loans had been extended to farmers' associations for a wide variety of purposes. Encouragement of livestock production, improved farming practices, the holding of fairs and exhibitions, the promotion of dairying and fruit-growing and similar measures, although at first developmental in purpose, reflect the trend to direct governmental action in farm-lending. In the pre-war years, government activities were beginning to infringe on the territory of the private lender and the events of the war period greatly strengthened this tendency. It is true that financial assistance involving credit stressed emergency advances in many instances, but the line between general support, emergency assistance and direct intervention became less clearly defined in the war and post-war periods. In addition to this growing interest of governments in farm credit, there were other developments discouraging to private investors at this time. Not only were there signs of over-expansion in wheat production but heavy losses had been taken in areas which proved to be unsuitable for cultivation. Again, with the outbreak of war, high interest rates on borrowings from foreign sources sharply reduced profit margins. And finally, the almost unlimited demand for money by the government at high rates of interest led to greater interest in government bonds and debentures. In spite of these drawbacks, the return of better conditions and the expansion of the post-war period drew institutional lenders to the better-established areas of the west and they continued to play an important part in farm-lending until world depression brought a virtual end to their activities. On the other hand, legislative action threatening the sanctity of contract and the trend to more direct action by governments led to more highly selective lending policies by private lenders and, as a result, to a growing clamour for government loans in high-risk areas.

Government action was sought by the farmers in short-term as well as mortgage lending. Although the banks had some $50 million on loan to western farmers in 1914, and although large sums were advanced from the same sources to manufacturers, implement dealers, wholesale houses, retailers and others doing business with the farmer, the difficulty of adapting a commercial form of credit to the farmers' needs remained. Amendments to the Bank Act in the war years which gave banks greater scope for loans to farmers on the security of seed grain and livestock helped matters, but provision of short-term agricultural credit by agencies established for this purpose was lacking, and pressure for more adequate financing of short-term requirements led to experiments which began before the end of the First World War.

Provincial government activities in farm-lending first became of consequence in the prairie provinces. The Manitoba Rural Credits Act of 1917 provided for short-term loans to rural credit societies formed for the purpose; a line of credit was arranged with the chartered banks, and considerable progress was made to 1923. The later history of this experiment is mainly one of committee investigation and the writing off of losses. In 1933, the remaining societies were amalgamated with the Manitoba Farm Loans Association which had also been established in 1917. Formed to make loans upon farm-mortgage security, the Association made the bulk of its loans, exceeding $8 million, over the period to 1923 when difficulties became apparent and a prolonged "cleaning-up" process began. The history of government lending in Saskatchewan displays much the same pattern. The Saskatchewan Farm Loans Board, formed in 1917, was active over a five-year period, but then its operations were curtailed and salvage operations replaced the lending function. In Alberta, although a Farm Loan Act was passed in 1917, farm-mortgage lending by the province never attained any importance. More important were short-term advances made under the Alberta Co-operative Credits Act of 1921. Conservative lending practices enabled the administration to avoid losses suffered in the neighbouring provinces. Apart from the western provinces, Ontario was most active in the farm-loans field. Under the Agricultural Development Act of 1921, mortgage loans in excess of $62 million had been made by 1934 when signs of weakness appeared and lending operations ceased.

Although government loans have received much publicity in the past, other lines of provincial action have become of greater significance over the years. These have taken the form of strong support of colonization and development, of improvements in grain and livestock production and dairying, financial aid to co-operative marketing organizations, and large sums for emergency assistance in hard-hit areas. These activities are marginal to agricultural credit but they have done much to improve the status of farming as a field for investment. Also marginal to credit but of great importance to farm-loan operations have been debt-adjustment measures both provincial and federal. The importance of these in the 1930's reflected the depression conditions of these years, and although there is no question of the necessity of some such measures at this time it is clear that their ultimate effect has been an increasingly heavy emphasis on government activities in farm-lending. And because of the unfortunate history of provincial bodies established for this purpose, this has meant reliance on federal government operations in the farm-loans field. These began in 1929 with the formation of the Canadian Farm Loans Board. Loans were made by the Board for the purchase of livestock, farm equipment and farm land, for improvements, for debt refinancing and to cover operating expenses. From the beginning of operations to March 31, 1952, more than $79,400,000 had been loaned for such purposes, and it is clear that this federal agency is now a central and permanent feature of Canadian farm finance.

To improve facilities for the provision of short-term and intermediate credit to farmers, the Farm Improvements Loans Act, 1944, was passed. The Act is administered by the Department of Finance; the banks serve as lending agencies under this legislation, operating under a government guarantee against loss up to 10 per cent of their total loans. Over the period 1945-52, loans exceeding $350 million were made; more than 77 per cent of this total was loaned in the three prairie provinces and more than one-third in Saskatchewan alone. Since these loans are made for periods and under arrangements suited to the needs of individual borrowers, this legislation has gone far to remove the more serious deficiencies of the financial structure as it affects the farmer.

Government participation in farm credit is now firmly established, but there is no indication that the day of the private lender, individual or corporate, is past. The role of the investor will be determined mainly by the attractiveness of agriculture as an area of investment and this must rest with agricultural conditions and policies which go far beyond agricultural credit. Lessons learned from the experience of the First World War period and its unhappy aftermath helped to prevent a repetition of its pattern of hectic over-expansion in the 1940's; greater stability and a high level of agricultural prosperity permitted a substantial reduction in farm indebtedness which left agriculture in a strong position to attract funds for future development. It is probable that future government action in the provision of farm credit will be directed less toward displacing private lending than toward supplementing private investment, and to adapting the existing financial structure to agricultural needs rather than introducing any radical departure from present practice.

This brief review of some of the basic problems of western agriculture reveals a heavy reliance on governmental support to strengthen the farmers' position in the economy. Much of the progress of agriculture, however, has been the result of group action, both by large-scale organizations and by strong co-operative movements in each of the prairie provinces. It is true that attempts to shape national policy in the interests of the western farmer have had only qualified success, but a combination of vigorous self-help and aggressive political tactics has done much to improve the farmers' bargaining position in the boom years and to ensure that agricultural welfare would not be overlooked as the nation became increasingly industrialized.

SUGGESTIONS FOR FURTHER READING

BASIC WORKS:

Britnell, George E., *The Wheat Economy* (Toronto, 1939)

Fowke, Vernon C., *Canadian Agricultural Policy: The Historical Pattern* (Toronto, 1946), Chapters VIII-XI, pp. 220-81.

MacGibbon, D. A., *The Canadian Grain Trade* (Toronto, 1932)

Mackintosh, A. W., *The Economic Background of Dominion-Provincial Relations: A Study Prepared for the Royal Commission on Dominion-Provincial Relations* (Appendix 3), (Ottawa, 1939)

Morton, Arthur S., and Chester Martin, *History of Prairie Settlement and "Dominion Lands" Policy* (Toronto, 1938), Part I, Chapters VI-VII, pp. 119-76; and Part II, Chapter XII, pp. 466-94

Report on the Royal Commission on Dominion-Provincial Relations, *Canada: 1867-1939*. Book I (Ottawa, 1940)

SUPPLEMENTARY WORKS:

Bank of Nova Scotia, "The Outlook for Wheat", *Monthly Review* (Toronto, March, 1954)

Bladen, V. W., *An Introduction to Political Economy* (Toronto, 1951), Chapter VI, pp. 118-61

Currie, A. W., *Economics of Canadian Transportation* (Toronto, 1954), Chapters III-V, pp. 38-152

Easterbrook, W. T., *Farm Credit in Canada* (Toronto, 1937)

Higgins, Benjamin J., and Arthur Lermer, "Trends and Structure of the Economy", in *Canada*, G. W. Brown (ed.), (Berkeley, 1950), Chapter X, pp. 222-77

McDiarmid, Orville J., *Commercial Policy in the Canadian Economy* (Cambridge, Mass., 1946), Chapters IX-XII, pp. 203-305

Murchie, R. W., *Agricultural Progress on the Prairie Frontier* (Toronto, 1936), Chapters II-III, pp. 7-34

Waines, W. J., *Prairie Population Possibilities* (Study prepared for the Royal Commission on Dominion-Provincial Relations, Ottawa, 1939; mimeographed)

CHAPTER XXI

THE NEW INDUSTRIALISM

INTRODUCTION

THROUGHOUT most of its history Canada has been an economic satellite of other more advanced nations. Its exports have been almost exclusively raw materials and foodstuffs. Its imports have been manufactured goods produced by the industries of Britain and the United States. The pace of development has been set by the rise and decline of the great staple trades: fur, fish, timber, gold, wheat, and more recently pulp and paper and the base metals.

This pattern of development depended upon the maintenance throughout the world of conditions which were sufficiently stable and orderly to permit international division of labour and a relatively free movement of goods and resources from one country to another. Under these conditions certain nations, because of their natural advantages in terms of resources and location, specialized in industrial production; other parts of the world specialized in supplying foodstuffs and materials to the industrial nations. England, for a variety of reasons which we do not need to discuss here, led the way in industrialization; other nations—the United States, Germany, France, and Japan—followed later in the nineteenth century. The decisive factors in determining which countries developed industrial economies were the availability to them of cheap coal, iron ore, and food.

By producing raw materials and foodstuffs and exporting them to Britain and the United States, inhabitants of the Canadian provinces during the nineteenth century were able to maintain, during most years, a reasonable level of material well-being, attract the immigrants and capital required for development, consolidate and extend their frontiers, build the physical and institutional framework of a commercial economy, and finally create a politically unified nation with authority extending across the entire continent north of the American boundary. The story of Canadian economic development during the nineteenth century is essentially the story of how this group of scattered colonies organized themselves into a national economy equipped to provide the industrialized areas of the world with the materials and foodstuffs they required. The rise of the great staple trades, the expansion of land settlement and agriculture, the construction of a national transportation system, the development of banking and finance—

all these special aspects of Canadian economic history fit together and acquire meaning only when seen in this general context.

This pattern of development, to be sure, was not without its disadvantages from the Canadian point of view. It compelled specialization and with specialization came instability. In the first place there was the instability which resulted from the business cycle. Primary producers are highly vulnerable to fluctuations in final demand; hence the periodic crises which have afflicted the Canadian economy throughout its history. Secondly, instability resulted from vulnerability to changes in tariff policy in other countries. Canada's weakness here was that she had no effective means of retaliation, whether the injury to her external trade came from Britain or from the United States. And thirdly there was the instability which was the unavoidable consequence of technological change. Particularly disturbing in this respect were changes in the technology of transportation. Innovations such as the steamship and the railway, however beneficial their consequences in the long run, were cyclonic in their short-run effects, upsetting established supply-and-demand relationships and bringing vast new areas into competition with one another.

Together, these sources of instability retarded Canada's economic development and to some extent prevented it from acquiring the momentum which, for instance, characterized the development of the United States. But whether the Canadian colonies had any real alternative is very doubtful. Specialization in the production of primary materials for export to the industrialized countries was the course of action which self-advantage indicated and which the economic process rewarded. The most rapid and certain way in which inhabitants of the Canadian colonies could improve their standards of living was by exporting staples to the industrially more advanced countries and importing manufactured goods from them. With the technology available at the time and with the resources which were then known to exist, industrialization was not, for Canada, an open alternative. The coming of the railway and steam power encouraged a certain amount of ancillary development in light manufacturing and mechanical engineering, but, as long as the conditions we have mentioned persisted, Canada could not become an industrial nation.

This was not to any significant extent a matter of policy—of conscious decisions taken by some person or persons to encourage development in one direction and not in another; it was, rather, a matter of resources and technology. The old industrial system—the industrialism of iron, steel, and steam, in which Britain had led the way—demanded for its existence large resources of coal and iron in reasonably close proximity to one another. The technology of production on which it was based required very great amounts of heat and power, and these could be supplied, in the quantities required and with the engineering and scientific knowledge then available, only by coal. Since coal was a weight-losing material, industrial processes using large quantities of coal tended to be located near the coal source, thus minimizing transportation costs; in the pre-industrial economy, in contrast, economic activity tended to be located near to the other major weight-losing material: food. That Canada developed as a raw-material-exporting country while Britain developed as an industrial country can be explained in large part, if not exclusively, by the fact that Britain could secure easily and relatively cheaply the energy resources which the old industrialism required.

THE NEW INDUSTRIALISM: ITS MEANING

We have mentioned two sets of conditions which were necessary for the effective functioning of the type of world economy which existed in the nineteenth century. The first set related to the maintenance of a certain minimum level of security and a certain minimum degree of order in international affairs. Without these prerequisites the specialization of function which permitted certain nations to industrialize and others to concentrate on raw-material production would have been impossible. It is clear, for instance, that a definite risk was involved when Britain, by adopting free trade, accepted dependence on imported food supplies as the price of successful industrialization. In a less secure world the risk would not have been taken. More generally, had the security conditions of the nineteenth century not been present—conditions, we may note in passing, which depended partly upon what we must now regard as a relatively primitive technology of warfare—self-sufficiency would have bulked larger as an objective of national policy, defence would have been accorded more importance and opulence less, and international specialization of function would have been much more severely circumscribed.

The second set of conditions which we have mentioned related to the forms of industrial technology. The industrialism of the nineteenth century was characterized by the use of coal as the basic source of energy, the use of iron and steel as the basic construction materials, and the use of the steam-engine as the basic form of motive power. This is the technological complex which we call "the old industrialism". By using that term we intend to contrast it (i) with a pre-industrial complex characterized by the use of wind, water, and animals as sources of energy and wood as the basic construction material, with economic activity located primarily close to food supplies, and (ii) with an emerging "new industrialism" the principal features of which, as they relate to the twentieth-century Canadian economy, it is the task of this and the following chapters to examine. Within the technological conditions of the old industrialism, no nation could develop an industrial economy unless it possessed ample and easily worked supplies of the primary source of industrial energy—coal—and of the essential metallic mineral, iron ore. This meant in practice that a relatively small number of nations came to possess a relatively large share of the world's industrial capacity. Other parts of the world supplied materials and food-stuffs to these industrialized areas and bought manufactured goods from them.

Within the last half-century important changes have taken place both in the security conditions within which the world economy functions and in the technology of industry. In the first place a breakdown in nineteenth-century patterns of political behaviour, together with advances in the tech-nology of warfare, have greatly increased the unpredictability and instability of international relations. A world economy in the nineteenth-century sense, in which the nations within certain limits accepted the strategic risks involved in mutual dependence for the sake of the economic benefits to be derived therefrom, has become impossible. Even within blocs of nations allied with one another by ties of mutual understanding and the need for co-operative defence, the movement of goods, capital, and persons is severely restricted in the interests of security and self-sufficiency. Nations whose economic life was historically organized around foreign trade, such as Canada and Britain, have found adjustment to these changed circum-stances by no means easy. At the same time the breakdown of the nine-teenth-century world economy has involved significant departures from the older pattern of specialization of function between industrial nations and primary producers. In two major world wars the productive resources of the industrialized nations have been concentrated on the manufacture of armaments; partly for this reason and partly because of large-scale destruc-tion of merchant shipping, normal trading relations have been seriously disrupted. Nations such as Canada have found, in such periods of armed conflict, that their usual sources of supply of manufactured goods were no longer available to them and have, as a result, expanded their own industrial capacity. In this sense twentieth-century warfare has played a role analogous to that of a protective tariff, in that it has excluded the competition of established low-cost industrial producers and fostered the growth of infant industries. In the case of Canada this process had received additional momentum from the adoption of policies aimed explicitly at the decentralization of war production throughout the British Commonwealth. More generally, the instability of international politics in the twentieth century and the disruption of the relatively free trading relationships of the earlier period have undermined the supremacy of the older industrial nations such as Britain and have encouraged the development of industry in other parts of the world. Policies aiming at national self-sufficiency have been encouraged and the previously sharp distinction between the industrial nations and the primary producers has become blurred.

Coincidentally with the disappearance of the security conditions which made the world economy of the nineteenth century possible, developments in the physical sciences and technology have come about to broaden the range of alternatives open to countries seeking to industrialize. In one important respect these changes may be interpreted as making possible the development of industrial capacity on an energy base other than coal. By this we refer not to very recent advances in atomic power (the economic implications of which are still highly debatable) but to the earlier technological revolution involved in the generation, transmission, and use of electricity, a convenient date-line for which might be the harnessing of Niagara Falls for the production of electricity by hydraulic turbines in 1895. Paralleling the industrial use of electricity have been a series of other technological advances, each of them of major importance for countries which, in the era of coal and iron, had found themselves ill-suited for industrialization: new fuels, such as petroleum and natural gas; new forms of motive power, such as the internal combustion engine; new means of transport, such as the aircraft, the truck, and the automobile; new structural materials, such as aluminum, the light alloys, and the alloy steels; and new industrial processes, such as the reduction of complex ores by electricity and the production of synthetic materials. These innovations have drastically modified the whole framework of possibilities within which economic development takes place. The types of industrial structure which they will make possible are still a matter for speculation. In Canada, where industrialization during the last half-century has taken place almost wholly within the context of these new technological possibilities, the main structural features are perhaps clearer than elsewhere.

It is possible to distinguish analytically between the effects on the Canadian economy of two world wars and the effects of recent innovations in industrial technology, but empirically the consequences are closely interrelated. The breakdown of the nineteenth-century world economy provided the impetus and the occasion for the growth of Canadian industry, but that growth has taken place within the framework of possibilities of the new technology. Technological change in itself can merely open up potentialities for growth; the realization of these potentialities may await the urgent pressure of events and the recognition of opportunity. Thus the First World War was directly responsible for very considerable expansion in Canadian non-ferrous metal refining, particularly for copper, zinc, and nickel. Canadian mineral production as a whole increased from just under $129 million in 1914 to $211.3 million in 1918. Wartime demand for shells and other fabricated and semi-fabricated steel products led to substantial expansion in Canada's previously insignificant steel industry, the capacity of which rose from an estimated one million ingot tons in 1914 to two and a quarter million ingot tons in 1919. The Canadian aircraft industry, born in 1917, produced some 3,000 military training planes before the end of the war, while Canadian shipyards turned out approximately 350,000 dead-weight tons of shipping. A wide range of secondary industries also felt the stimulating effect of war-time demand. The Second World War had a similar though quantitatively much greater effect, the expansion of manufacturing capacity being particularly remarkable in tool-making, electrical apparatus, chemicals, and aluminum. The aircraft and shipbuilding industries again experienced very large increases in employment and output, while several new branches of manufacturing, such as roller bearings, magnesium, synthetic rubber, optical glass, and high octane gasoline were established for the first time in Canada. Canadian steel output increased by approximately 120 per cent from 1939 to a war-time peak between 1942 and 1944, and aluminum output by about 500 per cent. Both wars, it should be added, gave considerable impetus to the discovery of new resources, particularly of metallic minerals and mineral fuels, and were responsible for significant improvements in managerial and technical skills. Without these periods of forced expansion the potentialities of the new technology would certainly have been realized much more slowly. Rapid expansion in the pulp-and-paper industry, in the automotive industry, in non-metallic minerals, and in chemicals, however, dates from the period betwen 1926 and 1929, when manufacturing investment (in volume terms) reached a level which was not surpassed even in the period after World War II.

A word of caution, however, is needed at this point. When we speak of "the new industrialism" and contrast it with more familiar types of economic structure, we are in danger of exaggerating the abruptness and extent of the changes referred to. History, of course, shows discontinuities as well as gradual development, and technological innovation is one field where change is often sudden and violent. In the case of Canada, however, the development of industry has not supplanted older patterns of staple production. Rather it has modified and supplemented them. Technological change has made possible the growth of an industrial sector in the Canadian economy and has reduced Canada's previously extreme dependence on raw-material production. But the older resources and the older patterns of trade and production are still the backbone of Canada's economic life. New resources have been discovered—oil in the western prairies, nickel and gold in Ontario, iron ore in Quebec-Labrador—and old resources have been put to new productive uses—as for instance the forests of the Precambrian Shield and the water-power of the St. Lawrence. Whole new industries have been created to exploit the possibilities and satisfy the demands of twentieth-century technology. The aluminum and the pulp-and-paper industries, to take two outstanding examples, would be inconceivable without, on the one hand, very large supplies of hydro-electric power and, on the other, the demands of the aircraft and construction industries for light metals and of the metropolitan newspapers for vast quantities of cheap newsprint. But, side by side with these striking advances, the older staples, such as wheat, fish, and lumber, continue to provide a livelihood for millions of Canadians and the bulk of Canada's earnings in international trade.

THE GROWTH OF MANUFACTURING

The relative importance of manufacturing and agriculture in the modern Canadian economy cannot be estimated merely in terms of statistics of output and employment, if only because agriculture contributes very largely to Canada's export earnings whereas Canadian manufacturing industries produce mainly for the domestic market, selling more than four-fifths of their output in Canada. Nevertheless, some idea of the relative position of the two sectors can easily be obtained. In terms of output, Canadian manufacturing had surpassed agriculture by the end of World War I; since then it has increased its lead. Of the total value of production in the nine major sectors of the Canadian economy (agriculture, forestry, fisheries, trapping, mining, electric power, manufactures, construction, and custom and repair), manufacturing contributed 44 per cent in 1919 and agriculture 32 per cent. Manufacturing's contribution increased to 46 per cent by 1929 and remained at about that level until 1939, while agriculture fell to 21 per cent in 1929 and 16 per cent in 1931, recovering to 21 per cent in 1939. In the years after World War II the share of manufacturing increased to 49 per cent in 1949 and 50 per cent in 1950, while the corresponding figures for agriculture were 19 per cent and 17 per cent respectively. Of a Canadian national income of $14.4 billion in 1950, manufacturing contributed 31 per cent and agriculture 11 per cent; this compares with a relative standing of 27 per cent and 12 per cent respectively in 1939, when the national income was $4.4 billion.

As an employer of labour, manufacturing did not surpass agriculture until the Second World War. In 1921, out of a total employed civilian labour force of just under 3 million, manufacturing employed 562,000, or roughly 19 per cent, while there were 1,107,000, or roughly 37 per cent, employed in agriculture. Both sectors suffered a relative decline, due to the expansion of "service" occupations, in the inter-war period: by 1939 manufacturing employed 710,000 or approximately 17 per cent of a total civilian labour force in employment of 4,075,000, while agriculture employed 1,364,000 or 33 per cent. By 1950 the relative positions were reversed, with agriculture employing 21 per cent (1,066,000) of a civilian labour force in employment of 4,985,000 and manufacturing 26 per cent (1,314,000).

The sectors of rapid growth in the economy can perhaps be suggested by a comparison of rates of new investment, although statistics of investment in agriculture are difficult to obtain and not altogether reliable. For the economy as a whole capital expenditures in constant (1949) dollars averaged in the years after World War II just over one-fifth of the gross national product (20.9 per cent in 1950, 21.2 per cent in 1951, 22.2 per cent in 1952, and 22.5 per cent in 1953). A declining share of new capital investment went into agriculture, fishing, forestry, and the construction industry, the proportion of the total accounted for by these sectors falling from 14.3 per cent in 1949 to 11.2 per cent in 1953. Between the same two years the share going into manufacturing (including certain industries engaged principally in primary processing) increased from 15.3 per cent to 16.8 per cent.

These quantitative measurements highlight the fact that by the middle of the twentieth century Canada had become an industrial nation. But they also make it clear that industrial development took place without adverse repercussions upon the older sectors of Canadian economic activity. Canada moved away from her former specialization in primary production and achieved a condition which might reasonably be called one of balanced growth. In manufacturing she was outranked in 1950 by only some half-a-dozen nations. In material terms the Canadian standard of living was second only to that of the United States. But at the same time Canada's prosperity and growth remained dependent on her ability to find markets in other countries for her foodstuffs and raw materials. An understanding of the state of the Canadian economy at mid-century and of its potentialities for further growth demands, therefore, both a survey of the available resources and an analysis of the changing patterns of international trade and investment in which Canada was inextricably involved.

Let us begin, then, with a brief survey of the material resources of the Canadian economy as they were known in the period roughly from 1950 to 1955. Inevitably this must be highly selective; we shall devote most space to the resources which had recently been discovered or recently brought into commercial use, and emphasize the role of modern technology in the process.

COAL

Until comparatively recently Canada's coal resources were estimated at the huge total of 1,216,770,310,000 metric tons. This estimate, originally made in 1913, included both "actual" and "probable" reserves. Subsequent investigation, both by geological surveys and by actual mining operations, has made it necessary to scale down the figure considerably, though it is still considered a reasonably close approximation to the amount of coal occurring as a geological phenomenon in Canada. Estimates made for the Royal Commission on Coal which reported in 1946 (the Carroll Commission) place the amount of mineable coal in Canada at approximately 99,000 million tons. Of this just over 49,000 million tons are classed as "recoverable". (By "recoverable" coal is meant coal which, with known techniques of mining, will probably be brought to the surface.) The three western provinces of Saskatchewan, Alberta, and British Columbia have 92 per cent of the Canadian total; there are no deposits of any commercial significance in Ontario or Quebec. In terms of output, Canada produced in 1938 just over 14¼ million tons, or roughly one per cent of total world production; this compares with 349 million tons in the United States, 397 million in Germany, and 227 million in the United Kingdom.

In the older industrialized countries, as we have mentioned, population and industry tended to concentrate around coal resources or around transportation arteries giving cheap access to coal resources. The largest coal reserves in Canada, on the other hand, are located far distant from the St. Lawrence lowlands where, for historical reasons, population has tended to cluster. Alberta and Saskatchewan coal, of course, did not become available until the construction of the transcontinental railways and the opening of the prairies for large-scale settlement. The first shipments of coal from the Lethbridge area of Alberta were made in 1886. In British Columbia the Nanaimo coal deposits were worked as early as 1852, but the Crow's Nest Pass coal-fields were opened up only in 1879. Total coal production in Canada in 1900 was only 5¾ million tons, and of this the bulk (3.6 million tons) came from the Cape Breton area of Nova Scotia. Nova Scotia has only 3 per cent of total Canadian coal reserves but, because of its proximity to Atlantic shipping and to the area of early settlement, this province has by far the longest history of continuous production, exports of coal from Cape Breton to Boston being recorded as early as 1724. Production in this area reached its peak in 1931; the increase in Canadian output from 14.5 million tons in 1912 to 17.4 million tons in 1952 was largely the result of expansion in Alberta and Saskatchewan.

The result of the geological location of coal deposits in Canada and of the fact that the principal reserves were opened to use only relatively recently has been that Canadian industrial development has had to rely principally on other sources of energy. Such industry as Canada developed during the nineteenth century grew up in the St. Lawrence lowlands. To meet its energy requirements it drew mainly on the Appalachian coal-fields of the United States, not upon Canadian coal reserves. Cape Breton coal was and still is shipped via the St. Lawrence to Quebec, but only under serious competitive handicaps. This dependence on imported coal was one reason for Canada's failure to develop heavy industry.

During the twentieth century the advent of hydro-electricity has profoundly altered the situation in so far as the energy requirements of industry in central Canada are concerned. But, as we shall have occasion to note again later, hydro-electricity cannot ordinarily compete with coal and other fuels as a source of industrial heat, whatever its advantages as a source of industrial motive power. Central Canada remains, therefore, almost entirely dependent on imports of coal from the United States to meet its requirements for industrial heat. Of the coal consumed in central Canada in 1943, 2 per cent came from the United Kingdom, 5 per cent from Canadian mines, and 93 per cent from the United States; the corresponding figures for 1937 were 6, 20, and 71 per cent, with 3 per cent coming from other foreign sources. This supply relationship has remained relatively stable, too, despite a Canadian tariff on bituminous coal and a complicated system of transportation subsidies designed to improve the competitive position of Canadian coal-producers. Nova Scotian coal, because of its high production costs, must rely on cheap water transportation to reach markets outside the Maritimes. Only the low cost of St. Lawrence shipping enabled Nova Scotian coal, before World War II, to compete with American coal in the Montreal market. As for the western provinces, coal produced there of a type suitable for domestic consumption is mostly sold locally, though a certain amount does reach the Ontario market with the help of government-subsidized freight rates. Western "steam" coal is sold mostly to the railways, but this market is declining with the increasing use of diesel locomotives.

HYDRO-ELECTRICITY

The generation of electricity from the energy provided by falling water is distinctively a twentieth-century technological development, although the crucial inventions and discoveries—the hydraulic turbine, the dynamo, the alternator, and the central power station and distribution system—were all made before 1900. For the Canadian economy hydro-electricity was an innovation of the very first importance. Canada's centres of population and industry were far distant from her coal resources, but they were conveniently close to some of her largest resources of water-power. In Ontario and Quebec, neither of which possessed any significant fuel resources of their own, as well as in British Columbia, there were available vast reserves of energy in the form of falling water which awaited only the working out of an appropriate technology to convert them into usable economic resources. This is precisely what the discovery of commercially feasible methods of generating and transmitting electricity made possible. Falling water is one of the oldest sources of energy known to man. Its major limitation is that it has to be consumed at the site: the flour or lumber or textile mill has to be built at the dam or waterfall where the power is available. Electricity does away with this limitation, or at least greatly modifies its significance. With currently available techniques, electricity can be transmitted economically up to 300 miles (costs rise sharply with greater distances) and across terrain so difficult as to make any form of surface transportation virtually impossible. Hydro-electricity, in a word, enables man to harness the energy inherent in falling water and transmit it in a convenient and easily controllable form to power-users far distant from the hydraulic site.

Canadian water-power resources, as currently recorded, are adequate to provide a turbine installation capacity of more than 51,780,000 horsepower. This figure, however, is rather deceptive, since many large water-power sites at present undeveloped are beyond effective transmission range of the main energy-using areas. This is true, for instance, of the Nelson River in Manitoba and some of the rivers flowing into James Bay. Installed turbine capacity in. 1945 totalled just over 10¼ million horsepower: of this, more than one-half (5.9 million horsepower) was in the province of Quebec and a little over a quarter (2.7 million horsepower) in Ontario. British Columbia at this date had an installed turbine capacity of 864,024 horsepower, the three prairie provinces between them 608,657 (mostly in Manitoba) and the Maritimes (including Prince Edward Island but excluding Newfoundland) a total of 269,348.

Earlier in this book the Precambrian Shield has figured mostly as an obstacle to Canadian development. Occupying as it does more than half of Canada's total land area, this huge region of glacially-eroded rock interposed a formidable barrier to transcontinental expansion and severely limited the areas in the eastern half of the country which could be made to support an agricultural or manufacturing population. It is only relatively recently, and almost entirely within the twentieth century, that the Shield has come to be recognized as one of Canada's most valuable assets—as a vast storehouse of mineral wealth and water-power. New techniques of geological surveying and new methods of transportation (in both of which the aircraft has played an indispensable role) have made possible the discovery of resources which previously were not even suspected to exist. New industrial processes and new techniques of power generation and transmission have made it possible to exploit these resources and put them to profitable use.

Ontario and Quebec between them possess more than 80 per cent of Canada's developed hydro-electric capacity primarily because they have been able to draw on the water-power of the Precambrian Shield and the St. Lawrence River. Cheap hydro-electric power, together with the mineral and forest resources of the Shield, has been the principal factor responsible for the development in these provinces of the pulp-and-paper industry and the non-ferrous metal smelting and refining industry, two of the largest industrial power-consumers. The main power sites are at Niagara Falls and on the rivers of the St. Lawrence drainage system, particularly the St. Lawrence itself, the St. Maurice, the Saguenay, and the Ottawa and its tributaries; these supply the industrial and domestic markets for electricity in the St. Lawrence lowlands and the aluminum and pulp-and-paper industries in the hinterland. There are also large installations on the rivers draining into Lake Superior and James Bay, which supply the mining districts of the northern part of the provinces. In Ontario, largely because the original development was based on the exploitation of a single very large source of power—Niagara Falls—generation and transmission are in the hands of a public body, the Hydro-Electric Power Commission of Ontario. In Quebec the industry grew up under private enterprise.

In none of the other provinces except British Columbia and possibly

Newfoundland has hydro-electricity played as large a role in industrial development as it has in Ontario and Quebec. In the Maritimes there are developed power sites on the Mersey River in Nova Scotia and on the St. John River in New Brunswick. The total hydro-power resources of the region, however, are relatively small, amounting to only about 500,000 horsepower, while the availability of locally produced coal gives an advantage to steam-generated electricity. Of the total energy consumption of the Maritimes in 1943, coal (either burned directly or in thermal electricity plants) provided almost 70 per cent and water-power only 8.5 per cent; this compares with 52.6 per cent for coal and 37.8 per cent for water-power in Ontario and Quebec. Pulp-and-paper mills at Liverpool, N.S., and at Edmundston and Dalhousie, N.B., are, however, dependent on hydro-electricity. In the prairie provinces, too, water-power resources are relatively limited, being estimated at not more than 1,800,000 horsepower. The principal power sites are located at the northeastern margin of the prairie region, where it adjoins the Precambrian Shield, and on the western margin, near the eastern range of the Rockies. There are important hydro-electric stations on the Bow River and the Winnipeg River in Manitoba, while the Saskatchewan River, the Athabasca, the Peace, and the Slave offer good prospects for future development. Natural gas and petroleum together furnish just over 30 per cent of the total energy requirements of this region, coal 58.7 per cent, and water-power only 11 per cent.

In British Columbia the impact of hydro-electric power has been no less remarkable than in central Canada. The total water-power resources of the area were estimated in 1940 at 5.2 million horsepower; of this total no more than a fraction has been harnessed for the production of electricity. The principal industrial consumers are, as in central Canada, the pulp-and-paper, light metals, and chemical industries. The large metallurgical plant at Trail, producing zinc, lead, and fertilizer, depends on hydro-electricity from the Kootenay River, and the gold-mining industry of the Yukon on power from the Klondike. The most important installations are on the Kootenay River near Nelson, on the Stave River near Vancouver, and on the North Arm of Burrard Inlet, while the Fraser River has great potential for future development. Water-power supplied 37.9 per cent of the total energy consumption of the region in 1943, as compared with 32.7 per cent from coal and 29.4 from petroleum.

The consequences of hydro-electric power are probably seen at their most dramatic in the giant new pulp-and-paper mills and aluminum smelters which have been erected at such places as La Tuque on the St. Maurice River, Arvida on the Saguenay, and Kitimat in British Columbia. By no means to be overlooked, however, is the support which cheap hydro power has given to general manufacturing development. The concentration of industry and population in the St. Lawrence lowlands, for example, would be inconceivable without hydro-electricity.

Nevertheless, the adequacy of hydro-electricity as an energy base for large-scale industrialization must not be exaggerated. Hydro power has been a *sine qua non* for the industrial development which has in fact taken place in central Canada, but, as we have already pointed out, imported coal has been no less indispensable. Of the total energy provided in Canada by water-power and mineral fuels together, coal has in recent years provided more than one-half. In Ontario and Quebec, imported coal furnished in 1943 over 50 per cent of the total energy consumed. That hydro-electricity can completely displace combustible fuels as a source of industrial energy seems doubtful—at least if we are considering the type of industrial complex with which the history of Britain, the United States, and Germany, for example, has made us familiar. Recent analyses of the type of industrial structure likely to develop on the basis of hydro-electricity have emphasized the inherent limitations of this form of power as much as its advantages. The reason for this is that almost all industrial processes require energy both for motive power and for heat. Electricity is a convenient and efficient form of energy for motive power—over 80 per cent of the power equipment installed in the mining and manufacturing industries of Canada is electrically driven—but as a source of industrial heat it is neither as efficient in the technical sense nor generally as economical as direct combustion of fuels. There are certain exceptions to this generalization: in some electro-process industries, of which the aluminum and chemical industries are outstanding examples, the use of electricity is indispensable for technical reasons; in others, such as the production of special alloy steels in electric furnaces, electricity has an advantage over fuels because it can be precisely and conveniently controlled; and in a few others, of which the pulp-and-paper industry is the best example, the availability of surplus generating capacity (when a hydro installation is operating at less than peak load) makes it advantageous to use electricity for steam-raising. In general, however, the industrial demand for heat is a demand for fuels, not for electricity.

It is theoretically conceivable that many industrial processes which at present use fuels for heat could be converted to hydro-electricity, but only at substantially higher costs. For Canada, which has to meet the industrial competition of areas having relatively cheap coal, particularly the United States, this is a decisive consideration. Industry in central Canada has to pay more for its fuels than industry in the northeastern United States, but on the other hand it has to pay less for its hydro-electricity. This tends to encourage the development in central Canada of two general types of industry: first, those in which large supplies of cheap electricity are technically indispensable, such as the pulp-and-paper and aluminum industries; and secondly, those which require relatively large amounts of energy for motive power and relatively small amounts of energy for heat. The latter type includes what are loosely called the "light manufacturing industries", or those engaged in the later stages of industrial production.

Industry in central Canada, then, has developed on a joint energy base, drawing both upon the bituminous coal deposits of the United States and upon the hydro-electric resources of the St. Lawrence drainage basin. It seems very probable that this relationship will prove stable over the long run. Petroleum and natural gas from the Alberta oil-fields may modify the situation to some extent in Ontario, and Quebec will pay less for American coal with the completion of the St. Lawrence Seaway, but it is unlikely that these developments will produce any fundamental realignment. Technological change, however, has upset similar generalizations in the past and may do so again.

Construction of hydro-electric installations entails very large investments of capital, and for this reason additions to capacity tend to take place in a series of discontinuous steps. In a period when the demand for electricity is increasing rapidly, the expansion of generating capacity can present serious problems. This was the case in central Canada in the years immediately following World War II. In Quebec several large additions to generating capacity had been made during the war years, the largest being the Shipshaw plant on the Saguenay River, providing 1.2 million horsepower for the aluminum industry. The situation in this province was less acute than in Ontario where, between 1945 and 1954, primary load requirements increased 88 per cent and an acute shortage of hydro power seemed imminent. To help meet peak-load demand the Hydro-Electric Power Commission of Ontario found it necessary to construct two steam-generating plants, one at Windsor, the other at Toronto, despite the fact that the cost of electricity generated by steam was more than twice that of hydro-electricity, and in 1954 to begin preliminary design work on a small nuclear-power generating plant. Plans were also made to increase the capacity of the generating station at Niagara Falls from 600,000 to 1,828,000 horsepower. The economic consequences of failure to keep pace with the rising demand for power would certainly have been very serious. In these circumstances the development of the last remaining water-power resource of any size in the province—the St. Lawrence River—became a matter of the utmost urgency.

Development of the power resources of the St. Lawrence was inextricably involved with the St. Lawrence Seaway project, into the long and tortuous history of which, dating back to the last years of the nineteenth century, we do not propose to enter at this point. The transportation and navigation aspects will be discussed later. As regards water-power, it is sufficient to point out that since the Great Lakes and the St. Lawrence River throughout much of its length form the international boundary between Canada and the United States, and since the diversion of water for hydraulic purposes must necessarily involve the interests of both countries, hydro-electric development inevitably depended upon the reaching of agreement between the several government authorities concerned. New York state was almost as desperate for hydro-electric power as Ontario and gave its official support to the project, but various private pressure groups in the United States— notably the coal-mining industry, certain railroad and shipping companies, and the labour organizations in those industries—offered strong opposition. Continued delays in securing congressional approval led the Canadian government in 1951 to announce its intention to proceed independently with the Seaway development, while still hoping for joint action with the United States on the power aspects. Parallel applications were submitted to the International Joint Commission by the Canadian and American federal governments and in October, 1952, the necessary permission was obtained for joint development of the hydro-power part of the project, with Canada taking sole responsibility for the construction and operation of the deep waterway. The Hydro-Electric Power Commission of Ontario and the New York State Power Authority were designated the responsible executive bodies and, after sundry legal battles had been fought and won in New York state, construction was begun on the hydro project in August, 1954. Meanwhile, in May of that year, the American Congress had finally given sanction for American participation in the Seaway development.

The St. Lawrence River between Lake Ontario and Montreal is usually divided into five sections, of which the first two—the Thousand Islands and International Rapids sections—are international, since the boundary follows the river, while the lower three—Lake St. Francis, Soulanges, and Lachine —are entirely within Canada. Within this 183-mile distance the power available has been estimated at 5.4 million horsepower. The power developments contemplated in the Seaway project were designed to raise the total horsepower produced to approximately 4 million. Of this total 2.2 million horsepower was to be developed in the International Rapids section; this would be shared equally between the Hydro-Electric Power Commission of Ontario and the New York State Power Authority. Provision was also made for enlargement of the Beauharnois plant of the Beauharnois Heat, Light and Power Company (owned and operated since 1944 by the Quebec Hydro Electric Commission) to provide an additional 600,000 horsepower, available entirely to Canada. A new power site was also proposed at Lachine, to be constructed when the navigation facilities were completed; this would provide eventually 1.2 million horsepower.

The total cost of the hydro-electric part of the project, aside from the navigation facilities, was estimated at approximately $600 million, to be shared equally between Canada and the United States. Of the physical structures involved, the largest was a dam and power-house between Barnhart Island and the Canadian mainland, combined with a dam from Barnhart Island to the American shore; the total cost of this work was estimated at just over $421 million, of which Canada would provide $72 million. The proposed development at Lachine included a dam and power-house below St. Louis Bridge, the estimated cost of which for power alone was

$213,942,000. Estimates made at the time of the probable return on these massive investments indicated that they would prove economic in the strict sense of the word: the projected secular increase in the demand for hydro-electricity in central Canada was such that the projects would pay their way. Failure to harness the power of the St. Lawrence would certainly have led to serious retardation of industrial growth.

IRON ORE

Technological change in the twentieth century has not only led to the exploitation of new forms of energy; by its effect upon techniques of exploration, geophysical surveying and transportation it has made it possible to locate and bring into production vast new mineral resources, the existence of which was previously at best vaguely suspected, at worst completely unknown. Few more dramatic examples of this can be found than the story of Canadian iron ore. Up to the end of World War II Canada's production of iron ore was insignificant. The highest production ever achieved in any one year was in 1902, when the output of Canadian mines (excluding Newfoundland) reached 400,000 tons. This figure was not again approached until 1940; in 1924 the Canadian total was 72 tons and between 1925 and 1939 no iron ore whatsoever was produced in Canada. Yet by 1952 production had reached a figure in excess of 5 million tons and was increasing at a rate of almost 1 million tons annually. By 1954 Canada, traditionally an importer of iron ore, had become one of the world's largest exporters, and this despite the rapid increase in the demands of its own steel industry. With the completion of the St. Lawrence Seaway, linking the newly developed Quebec-Labrador deposits with the centres of American steel production in the Pittsburgh area, exports of iron ore will become one of the largest credit items in Canada's balance of payments. By the mid-1960's it is forecast that Canada will rank third in world iron-ore production, outranked only by the United States and Russia.

This remarkable transformation is the result of a series of very important discoveries in Ontario and on the Quebec-Labrador boundary. Until 1938 Canadian blast furnaces at Sydney, N.S., and at Hamilton, Sault Ste. Marie, and Port Colborne, Ontario, were almost entirely dependent on imported ore, most of which came either from Newfoundland or from the Mesabi ore-field in the United States. As far as production in what is now Canada was concerned, by far the largest producing-centre was at Wabana, on Bell Island, Newfoundland. Mining operations in this area began in 1895 and from that date until 1942 some 40 million tons of ore were produced. Until the First World War the blast furnaces of the Dominion Steel and Coal Company at Sydney, N.S., absorbed fully two-thirds of the Wabana output, but after 1918, when the Nova Scotian steel industry went through a period of severe difficulties, Germany became the principal market, with Canada a close second. The orebodies at Wabana are reddish-brown hematite and are asserted to contain up to 4,000 million tons of recoverable ore, making it one of the largest deposits of its kind in the world. The ore has, however, a high silica and phosphorus content, making it unsuitable for the manufacture of Bessemer steel. For this reason British demand for Wabana ore has never been very great, as British producers prefer to draw on high-grade Spanish ore. The silica and phosphorus content also prevent Wabana ore from serving Canadian and American steel-producers in the Great Lakes area, who have up to the present relied on the Mesabi range and on Canadian deposits north of Sault Ste. Marie.

In New Brunswick and Nova Scotia there are a great number of iron deposits of various types. Some of them have been worked in the past and a few still have considerable reserves. The early history of the area shows several instances of attempts to establish an iron industry. A blast furnace was erected near Woodstock in the St. John valley in 1848 and another in 1863. More recently, quite extensive mining operations were carried on at Austin Brook, near Bathurst, N.B., in the period 1910-15, when more than 200,000 tons of ore were shipped out. This latter ore deposit was again worked in 1945, when the activities of German submarines cut off Newfoundland ore. Most of the ore occurrences in the Appalachian region, however, are very small and of interest to geologists only. In the Cordilleran region of British Columbia production is insignificant, while no iron ore has ever been mined in the Yukon. In British Columbia the known deposits are small and of minor importance, none being known to contain over ten million tons. Lack of a large market for iron ore in western Canada has retarded development and commercial exploitation of the known deposits is now only beginning, largely for export to Japan.

In Ontario and Quebec the Precambrian Shield contains many large deposits of iron ore, as indeed it does of a great variety of other metallic minerals. The industry in this area had an early start. A charcoal furnace was erected in Lyndhurst, Ontario, as early as 1800, followed within the next twenty years by several others in Hastings County and elsewhere. Most of these Ontario furnaces closed permanently after 1848, when the completion of the St. Lawrence canals cut the cost of imported iron. Later exploration has disclosed that most of the iron orebodies on the Shield are so low grade that they require "beneficiation"—that is, the grade must be raised by roasting or magnetic concentration. This is true, for example, of the ore from the Helen Mine near Michipicoten, which is siderite, an iron carbonate containing only about 35 per cent iron, and of the extensive deposits in the interior of Ungava. Relatively low-grade deposits are at present being exploited, with on-the-site concentration, by the Bethlehem Steel Corporation at Marmora, north of Lake Ontario.

The Helen Mine, north of Sault Ste. Marie, was opened up originally by Francis H. Clergue, an American promoter, in 1897; between 1924 and 1939 it was completely closed down. It is now owned by Algoma Ore Properties. The Steep Rock and Quebec-Labrador developments, in contrast, both date from the years after World War II, and in both the impetus came largely from the anticipated exhaustion of the Mesabi iron-ore range in the United States. Exploration and development were financed jointly by U.S. and Canadian capital, and American steel companies, concerned to secure a long-term source of supply, played a prominent role. The Steep Rock orebody underlies the bed of Steeprock Lake, 140 miles west of Port Arthur. Its development, which required the draining of the lake and the diversion of the Seine River, disclosed the existence of what is probably one of the largest remaining deposits of high-grade iron ore in the western hemisphere, estimated at a total of more than 1,000 million tons. The project was started in 1943 and mining began late in 1944. Operations in the area are in the hands of Steep Rock Iron Mines Limited. Other companies at one time hoped to lease ground in this area for exploration and possible development, but this hope has not so far been realized.

The existence of large iron deposits in the Quebec-Labrador region was known to Canadian geologists as early as 1893, but commercial exploration and surveying did not begin until 1938, the delay being largely explicable by the apparent impossibility of getting the ore out and delivering it to Canadian and American steel-producers at prices competitive with Mesabi and Newfoundland shipments. In 1938, however, the Hollinger interests, with capital and experience acquired originally in Ontario gold- and silver-mining, began exploration simultaneously on the Quebec and the Labrador sides of the boundary. The original objective was the discovery of gold and base metals, but between 1938 and 1939 six major deposits of iron ore were located, lying on both sides of the boundary north of Lake Petitsi-kapau. The principal deposit was estimated to contain 2.2 million tons of good hematite with a low phosphorus content. One of the other five deposits was high in silica, but the remaining four were all of high grade, one being rich in manganese. All were close to the surface. Between 1942 and 1944 further extensive surveys were carried out and a reserve proven of more than 300 million tons of high-grade ore, this being only a portion of the total probable deposits. To provide the necessary capital and organization to develop these vast deposits the Iron Ore Company of Canada was formed, representing a merger of the Hollinger group with the M. A. Hanna Company of Cleveland, a concern with wide experience in iron-ore procurement and transportation. Five leading American steel companies also participated: the Wheeling Steel Corporation, the National Steel Company, the Armco Steel Company, the Republic Steel Corporation, and the Youngstown Sheet and Tube Company. The capitalization of the Iron Ore Company of Canada was set initially at $225 million, and the greater part of the funds raised in the United States.

The first shipments of ore from this development were made on July 31, 1954. Production was geared initially to a rate of 10 million tons a year, but provision was made for increasing this output very substantially if it appeared desirable. Transportation and supply were major problems from the beginning. The deposits are located approximately 360 miles from water transportation. The construction of a railroad over this distance, through very difficult and completely undeveloped terrain, of a large hydro-electric installation, and of deep harbour facilities at Seven Islands on the Gulf of St. Lawrence, were essential parts of the project. Without techniques of supply by air-lift worked out originally during World War II the development might well have proved impossible.

Less far advanced than the Hollinger-Hanna project are plans for the development of other iron-ore deposits which have been located in Ungava, stretching from north of the Iron Ore Company of Canada's properties as far as Hudson Strait. Preliminary exploratory work has suggested the feasibility in this area of the same type of massive development as has proved successful in Quebec-Labrador. Distances to ocean transportation are appreciably shorter, but so also is the shipping season from Ungava Bay.

NICKEL, GOLD, SILVER, AND OTHER METALS

Canada's total mineral production in 1952 was valued at $1,285.3 million. Of that total gold contributed the largest share ($153.2 million), with nickel, copper, crude petroleum, asbestos, lead, and silver following in that order. By 1954 the total had climbed to $1,454 million. Petroleum, as a result of the discoveries in western Canada, had climbed to the leading position, with gold falling to fourth place; nickel and copper remained second and third respectively.

To survey within a reasonably brief compass the great variety of metallic minerals produced in Canada is out of the question. The remarkable development of the entire field of geophysics during the last quarter-century—and particularly the use of aircraft for geophysical surveying—has made it clear that Canada's mineral wealth is both very great and very diverse. Whether we think of the better-known metals, like copper, zinc, nickel, silver, and iron ore, or of the metals with less familiar names which industrial technology now demands, such as tantalum, tungsten, lithium, and titanium, it is no difficult task to demonstrate that twentieth-century Canada is in the forefront of the world's sources of supply. In nickel Canada has virtually a world monopoly; in asbestos and platinum she is the world's largest producer; in gold and zinc output she ranks second, and in copper and lead fourth. In iron-ore production Canada may soon rank third; for uranium and petroleum, if development continues at its present rate, she will certainly be among the leading sources.

In 1900 this remarkable development had barely got under way. Canadian gold-mining had its start on the gravel bars of the Fraser River in 1858, followed rapidly by the discovery of placer gold on the Thompson River and in the Cariboo country and, in the last decade of the century, by the Yukon and Klondike gold-rushes. The search for gold stimulated interest in other minerals, and important discoveries of silver, zinc, lead, and copper deposits were made. The silver-lead-zinc mines at Ainsworth and Slocan, B.C., became active in 1894; the Sullivan mine at Kimberley, a major source of lead and zinc, began shipping in the following year; and the Trail smelter went into production in 1896. During this first period of expansion British Columbia was pre-eminently the mining province. With the turn of the century the emphasis shifted to Ontario. What is often described as the most important single event in Canadian mining history —the discovery of the rich silver deposits at Cobalt in the Temiskaming district of northern Ontario—took place more or less by accident in 1903 during the construction of the National Transcontinental Railway. As had happened earlier with gold in British Columbia, the discovery of silver at Cobalt stimulated further exploration. Silver was discovered at Elk Lake, Ontario, in 1906 and at Gowganda and South Lorraine in the following year. The first gold discovery in the Porcupine area was made in 1908, a year which also saw the opening up of the Larder Lake district. The Hollinger, McIntyre, and Dome mines—all famous names in Canadian mining—date from 1909, while the important gold deposits at Kirkland Lake were discovered in 1911 and 1913. The outbreak of the First World War brought this second phase of development to a close. High war-time prices for base metals led to considerable expansion of output from mines already in production, but the pace of active prospecting was checked.

A third burst of expansion got under way after 1918, with the aircraft for the first time being used for prospecting. This innovation made it possible to extend the range of exploration very widely and into regions previously regarded as too difficult of access. Silver-lead ores were discovered at Keno Hill, in the Mayo district of the Yukon, in 1919, the first shipments of ore being made in 1921. In 1932 the important copper-gold deposits at Rouyn, in the western part of Quebec province, were staked out and in the following year lithium was discovered near Pointe du Bois in Manitoba. New gold discoveries were also made in northwestern Ontario and eastern Manitoba. In 1930 the frontier of exploration was extended still farther by the discovery of silver-radium ores at Great Bear Lake in the North West Territories. By this time the discovery and development of mineral deposits had acquired considerable momentum. An experienced cadre of prospectors had been built up, many of them with professional training, and venture capital flowed into new projects very quickly. Profits made originally in Cobalt silver sparked the development of the new Ontario and Quebec gold discoveries, just as later they accelerated the development of Quebec and Labrador iron ore.

Progress during this period was not confined to the location of new deposits of ore; no less significant was the discovery of new methods of treating and refining the various ores so as to make them suitable for commercial use. Important steps here were the discovery in 1887 of the cyanide process for gold extraction, of the Mond and Orford nickel-copper separation processes in 1892, and of electrolytic methods of refining copper and zinc in 1916. In more than one instance scientific advances of this nature were crucial in the conversion of a known deposit of complex base-metal ores into a producing mine. The extensive nickel-copper deposits of Sudbury, for example, which had been discovered as far back as 1883, did not begin producing commercially until after 1900, when the Mond Nickel Company was incorporated. Similarly the silver-lead-zinc deposits of the Kootenay district in British Columbia were not successfully developed until after 1916, when the electrolytic smelter at Trail went into production.

The onset of depression in 1929, bringing with it a serious fall in base-metal prices, curtailed the rate of development for all metals except gold which, in characteristic fashion, benefited from the extensive currency devaluations. Prospecting for gold, the development of new gold discoveries, and in some cases the reopening of older gold mines, went on apace from 1932 until the beginning of the Second World War. Production of other metals also expanded during this period, but there was little active prospecting for new orebodies. Very heavy demands followed the outbreak of World War II, the total value of mineral production increasing from $474.6 million in 1939 to a high of $566.8 million in 1942 and then falling to $498.8 million in 1945. Much of this increase, however, represented higher prices rather than greater volume; for certain strategic metals the volume of production was lower at the end of the war than at the beginning. Production of copper, for example, was 474.9 million pounds in 1945 as compared with 608.8 million pounds in 1939, while nickel registered only a moderate increase from 226.1 million pounds in 1939 to 245.1 million pounds in 1945. Beginning in 1946, however, the industry entered upon a period of very rapid growth, sparked by the opening up of the Steep Rock and Quebec-Labrador iron-ore deposits and by the discovery of the Leduc oil-field in Alberta. The circumstances were propitious: prices for base metals were rising steadily and, thanks to the backlog of demand for civilian goods and the expansion of industry in Canada and the United States, there seemed little prospect of a serious falling off within the foreseeable future. Skilled labour was once more available for prospecting and development, and refined techniques of geophysical surveying were ready to hand. The stage was set for one of the most remarkable spurts of expansion in Canada's history.

Probably the most dramatic event in the recent history of the Canadian mineral industry was the discovery of the western Canada oil-fields, beginning with the Leduc strike in 1947. This, however, we shall postpone for separate discussion. As regards metallic minerals, development was hardly less remarkable. Leaving aside petroleum and natural gas, the total value of mineral production in Canada rose from $452.2 million in 1939 to $928.4 million in 1949, $953.7 million in 1950, $1,121.7 million in 1951, and $1,130.8 million in 1952. (These figures, of course, include the effects of price changes.) Ontario retained its position as the leading mineral-producing province, with 34.3 per cent by value of the total output in 1952, but its lead was increasingly challenged as exploration revealed the presence of workable mineral deposits in other areas. At the time of writing Ontario produces all of Canada's nickel, cobalt, platinum metals, and graphite, just over half of Canada's iron ore and gold, and nearly half the copper. The most important developments in the province in the period after World War II were the opening up of the Steep Rock iron-ore deposits, to which we have already referred, the beginning of open-pit iron-ore mining at Marmora, continued expansion in the nickel, cobalt, and copper industries (stimulated by apparently insatiable demand in the United States for industrial use and for stock-piling), and the discovery of substantial deposits of uranium, tantalum, and rare earths in the Blind River and Haliburton-Bancroft areas. The gold industry continued fairly active in spite of higher operating costs and less favourable prices.

Quebec ranks second to Ontario in mineral production, with a total output valued at $267.3 million in 1952 as compared with $440.9 for Ontario. Asbestos normally contributes almost one-third of the Quebec total; the principal centres of production are at Asbestos and Thetford Mines but smaller deposits are also worked in other parts of the province. The important iron-ore developments on the Quebec-Labrador border and farther north at Knob Lake in Ungava have already been mentioned. Less spectacular but highly important developments in the post-World War II period included the commercial exploitation of large copper deposits in the Gaspé area, of ilmenite ore (from which iron and titanium are obtained) near Allard Lake, and of titanium dioxide at Sorel, while considerable expansion of production took place in cement, lead, sulphur, zinc, gold, and silver. The principal centre of base-metal production has been at Noranda in the western part of the province, where complex copper-silver-gold ores are mined and smelted. Exploration in the early 1950's disclosed the existence of copper-ore deposits at Chibougamau, 210 miles northeast of Noranda, and active development was well under way by 1955.

British Columbia, for long the home of Canadian mining, has retained its position as an important producer of lead, zinc, copper, gold, and silver. The chief source of lead, zinc, and silver has been the Sullivan mine of the Consolidated Mining and Smelting Company of Canada at Kimberley in the East Kootenay area. Copper has come mainly from mines at Allenby and Britannia Beach and is shipped to Tacoma, Washington, for smelting. Tungsten ore attracted considerable attention in the years following World War II, with four mines going into production in the Salmo and Hazelton areas, while high-quality asbestos-fibre deposits in northern British Columbia were mined commercially for the first time in 1953. Production of iron ore also increased in this period as a result of the development of deposits at Quinsam Lake and Texada Island. In the prairie provinces in the same years the metallic minerals were somewhat overshadowed by the remarkable discoveries of petroleum and natural gas. Coal, petroleum, and natural gas normally account for over 95 per cent of Alberta's mineral output. Saskatchewan and Manitoba, however, are growing in importance as producers of metallic minerals. Copper-zinc-gold deposits are mined by the Hudson Bay Mining and Smelting Company at Flin Flon, straddling the boundary between the two provinces. This company also produces cadmium, selenium, and titanium, and is engaged, through a subsidiary, in extensive exploratory and development work. Uranium mining came into prominence in Saskatchewan in the early 1950's: the Crown-owned Eldorado Mining and Refining Company owns large properties of uranium ore in the Beaverlodge area north of Lake Athabasca and brought its first mine, the Ace-Fay, into operation in April, 1953. Several private concerns are also active in this area and it appears highly probable that Saskatchewan will soon rank as one of the world's leading sources of uranium ore. In Manitoba the main centre of activity in the post-World War II period was in the Lynn Lake area, 500 miles northwest of Winnipeg, where large copper-nickel orebodies are being developed by Sherritt Gordon Mines Limited. The first shipments of nickel concentrates left Lynn Lake in January, 1954, for the Company's refinery at Fort Saskatchewan, Alberta. Copper concentrates were initially shipped to Noranda in Quebec province for smelting.

There were also several important mineral developments in this period in the maritime provinces and Newfoundland. In New Brunswick, where metal production had been insignificant in the past, extensive reserves of good-grade zinc-lead-silver-copper ores were discovered near Bathurst. One of the largest known deposits of barites in the world was discovered in the Pembroke-Walton area of Nova Scotia in 1940; a mill and smelter at Walton operated by an American firm, the Magnet Cove Barium Corporation, produces the bulk of the output, almost all of which is exported. In Newfoundland the Wabana iron mine was temporarily closed in April, 1953, to permit a radical reorganization of production. The island also produces lead, zinc, copper, gold and silver from the Buchans mine at Red Indian Lake and fluorspar from mines near St. Lawrence on the southeast coast. Extensive exploration of the island's mineral resources is being carried on by the Newfoundland and Labrador Corporation and by the British Newfoundland Corporation.

Canada's mineral resources are, of course, far from limitless, though that adjective is often applied to them. There is good reason to believe, however, that if exploration continues at the pace set in the years after World War II, new mineral deposits will be found of a size and richness at least equal to those now known. The resources of the Yukon and the North West Territories, of Ungava and Labrador and the interior of Newfoundland, are at present little known, but the information that is available suggests that they are very great. Particular interest attaches, therefore, to such pioneering developments as the Keno Hill silver mines in the Mayo district of the Yukon, the discovery of nickel-copper deposits in the Kluane Lake area, of lead and zinc at Pine Point, south of Great Slave Lake, of copper north of Port Radium, and of nickel on the west coast of Hudson Bay. These isolated mines and camp-sites, separated by vast distances from the centres of civilization, are today Canada's frontier of development.

PULP AND PAPER

The manufacture of pulp and paper had by the middle of the twentieth century securely established itself as Canada's leading industry, whether the criterion used was value of output, capital invested, wages paid, or contribution to export earnings. Canada's forest resources have, of course, figured largely in the country's economic development since the first days of European settlement. Exploitation of these resources for the manufacture of paper and allied products is, however, a comparatively recent phenomenon, dating only from the 1860's when commercial methods of manufacturing paper from wood-pulp were first evolved. The spectacular growth of the industry since then has been based on two characteristic features of the new industrial system: on the one hand, the use of hydro-electricity as a source of power, and on the other, the appearance of the huge urban centres of the present day, with their literate, news-hungry populations and mass-circulation daily newspapers. Total Canadian pulp production in 1920 was 1,960,102 tons; by 1953 it had climbed to 9,077,063 tons. Between the same two years the total circulation of daily newspapers in the United States rose from 27.8 million copies to 54.5 million with the average number of pages printed in each copy increasing from 23 to 37. The development of the industry in Canada has hinged upon the availability of large and rapidly expanding markets in the United States and upon the successful application of modern technological methods to the nation's forest resources—an achievement reflected in the fact that by 1950 Canada, with an annual output in excess of 5.2 million tons, was providing more than one-half the world's total supply of newsprint.

Canada's total forested area is currently estimated at just under 1.5 million square miles; of this, about 39 per cent (577,361 square miles) is classed as "accessible productive forest". Nine-tenths of the forest area is owned by the Crown and administered by the provincial governments, from whom the pulp-and-paper mills lease woodland areas according to their requirements—a situation which, it should be noted, contrasts sharply with that in the United States where almost all commercially exploited forest areas are privately owned. In 1954 an area of almost 183,000 square miles of Canadian forest was leased in this manner. From these leased areas the mills obtain about two-thirds of their supplies of pulpwood, the remaining one-third being purchased from farmers, settlers, and other owners and operators of woodlands. In the aggregate, the pulp-and-paper mills account for about one-fifth of the average annual consumption of wood in Canada—about two-thirds the quantity used for lumber.

There were in 1954 130 pulp-and-paper mills in Canada (2 of them asbestos paper mills), owned by some 90 companies. The location of the mills is determined by the availability of suitable forest resources and rivers, the latter often providing both hydro power and a means of transporting logs to the mills. The largest accessible stands of timber are in central and eastern Canada and in British Columbia, and it is in these areas that most of the mills are found. Quebec had 56 mills in 1954, Ontario 45, British Columbia 12, the maritime provinces 11, and Newfoundland 3. There were also 3 mills in Manitoba and 1 under construction in Alberta. The trees most used in eastern Canada are spruce, balsam fir, jack pine, and poplar. In British Columbia the trees differ in size and species from those east of the Rockies: Douglas fir, western hemlock, and Sitka spruce provide most of the supply. Differences in type and size of tree and in climate are reflected in differences in operating methods. In British Columbia, where 12 per cent of Canadian pulp-and-paper production takes place, logging operations are generally carried on throughout the year and power machinery is very widely used in logging and transportation. In eastern Canada the industry is more seasonal. Cutting and hauling are usually performed during the fall and winter months, the logs being piled on the ice until the thaw, when they are floated downstream to the mills.

The products of the industry are considerably more diversified than might be supposed. In broad categories they are: (1) pulp, manufactured for sale and for direct conversion into paper products; (2) newsprint, for daily newspapers; (3) other papers, ranging from tissue- and building-papers to fine-quality coated and rag papers; and (4) paperboard, used principally for packaging. Of the total marketed output, approximately 23 per cent (on a tonnage basis) is pulp for sale and 60 per cent is newsprint, while paperboard and other papers account for 17 per cent. On a dollar-value basis, pulp for sale contributes 24 per cent, newsprint 55 per cent, and paperboard and other papers 21 per cent. The pulp produced falls into two main categories: groundwood pulp and chemical pulp. Of the groundwood pulp, 95 per cent of the total output is converted in Canada into newsprint; the remainder is exported, chiefly to the United States. Of the chemical pulps, sulphite pulp, with an output in 1953 of almost 2.5

million tons, is the most important. Approximately one-half the total output is converted in Canada into paper while the remainder is exported. Production of sulphate or kraft pulp, used mainly for the manufacture of paperboard, is somewhat smaller, totalling 1.2 million tons in 1953; more than half the total output is exported. Small amounts of defibrated and exploded pulps are also produced. Well over 90 per cent of all pulp sold, if sales between affiliated mills in Canada are excluded, is exported to the United States.

Output of newsprint, the industry's most valuable product, reached in 1953 approximately 5.7 million tons with a market value of $633.4 million. Of this total 5.4 million tons were exported, principally to the United States, bringing in export earnings of a little over $619 million (approximately 16 per cent by value of total Canadian merchandise exports). Canada is by far the world's largest producer and exporter of newsprint. Total Canadian production of 5,984,287 tons in 1954 compared with 1,039,786 tons in Scandinavia (Norway, Sweden, and Finland), 700,000 tons in Britain, and 1,211,156 tons in the United States.

Of the industry's other products the most important are paperboard and building-board, with an annual output in excess of 900,000 tons. The greater part of this output is sold in Canada. Fine and miscellaneous papers account for an annual output of some 425,000 tons, while production of kraft paper, used for packaging, is about 200,000 tons per annum.

While there were paper mills in Canada very early in the nineteenth century—the first mill was built in St. Andrews, Quebec, between 1803 and 1805—the industry as we know it today became established only in the middle 1860's. The first chemical pulp mill in Canada—the second on the American continent—was erected at Windsor Mills, Quebec, in 1864, followed within a few years by a mechanical pulp mill at Valleyfield in the same province. The census of 1881 showed 36 paper mills and 5 pulp mills in operation, with a total output valued at $2.5 million. The majority of Canadian paper mills at this time, of course, used rags and linen, not wood-pulp, as their raw material. Sulphite pulp was first produced in Canada in the late 1880's, following experiments in Europe and the United States, and sulphate pulp in 1907. Most of the pulp output up to 1914 was made into paper in Canadian mills, and most of the paper was sold in the Canadian market. Exports of paper and paper products in 1900, for example, were confined to small quantities of hanging and wallpaper, valued at no more than $29,741. Exports of Canadian pulp to the United States, however, increased steadily, reaching 880,453 tons in 1925. The onset of depression in the 1930's brought a serious drop to a low point of 425,326 tons in 1932 but thereafter the rising trend was resumed. By 1939 Canadian pulp production had climbed to 4,166,301 tons, of which 705,516 tons was exported. The United States market in this year absorbed 637,953 tons of Canadian pulp, or a little over 90 per cent of the total quantity exported. The outbreak of World War II was followed by a period of very rapid expansion. With the German occupation of Scandinavia, exports of pulp from that area to the allied powers ceased. and the Canadian industry had to make good the deficiency. At the same time consumption of pulp for such uses as explosives, surgical dressings, containers, and special paper for war use increased very greatly. To meet these demands the Canadian industry expanded its pulp output from the 1939 level of a little over 4 million tons to a total of 5.6 million tons in 1945, and this in spite of a sharply reduced labour force and the diversion of substantial amounts of hydro-electric power to war industries in Canada and New York state. Pulp exports between 1939 and 1945 were stepped up from a little over 700,000 tons to 1.4 million tons. Exports to the United States were almost doubled while those to Great Britain were quadrupled.

While pulp has generally passed freely over international frontiers and has not been subject to serious tariff restrictions, the same is not true of the raw material, pulpwood, from which pulp is manufactured. The principal export market for Canadian pulpwood, as for pulp and newsprint, lies in the United States. Exports of Canadian pulpwood and newsprint to the United States have, since the early 1900's, been subject to a variety of export and import restrictions. These restrictions reflected, firstly, the efforts of the politically influential American newspaper-publishing industry to insure cheap supplies of newsprint; secondly, the efforts of American pulpwood and newsprint producers to secure protection against cheaper Canadian supplies; and thirdly, the efforts of Canadian governments to discourage the export of the unprocessed raw material—pulpwood—and encourage the export of the manufactured product—newsprint. From the interplay among these conflicting pressures emerged a complicated series of embargoes and retaliatory tariffs.

It was already clear by 1900 that pulpwood resources in the United States were insufficient to meet the demand for newsprint and that they would become increasingly insufficient as demand continued its secular upward trend. The cheapest and most convenient source of imports to supplement domestic supplies was Canada, where costs of production were in general somewhat lower than in the United States. Such imports, however, could in theory take several forms: pulpwood, manufactured pulp, or the final product, newsprint. The Canadian provincial governments, who controlled by far the greatest proportion of the industry's forest resources, realized at an early date that they were in a strategic position to encourage the production of newsprint within Canada, by restricting the export of the raw material and encouraging the export of the manufactured and more valuable product, newsprint. As early as 1891, British Columbia had prohibited the export of timber cut on Crown lands. Quebec in 1900 imposed what was in effect an export duty on pulpwood by reducing the fees on wood cut on Crown lands by about one-third, on

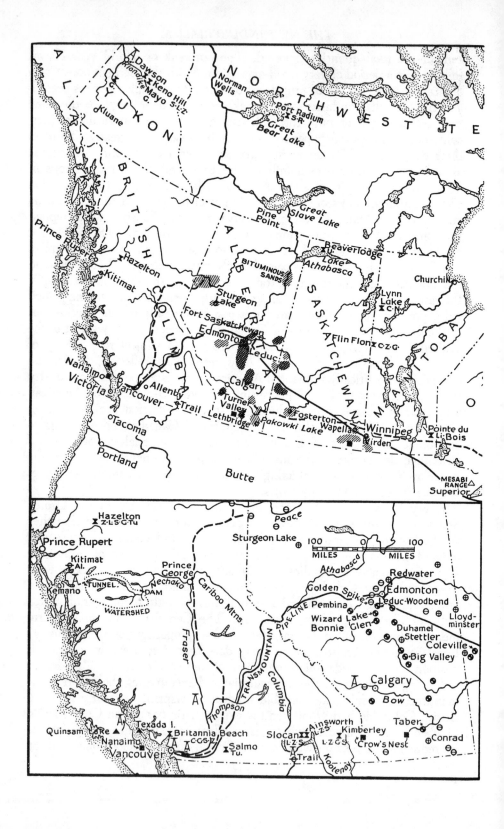

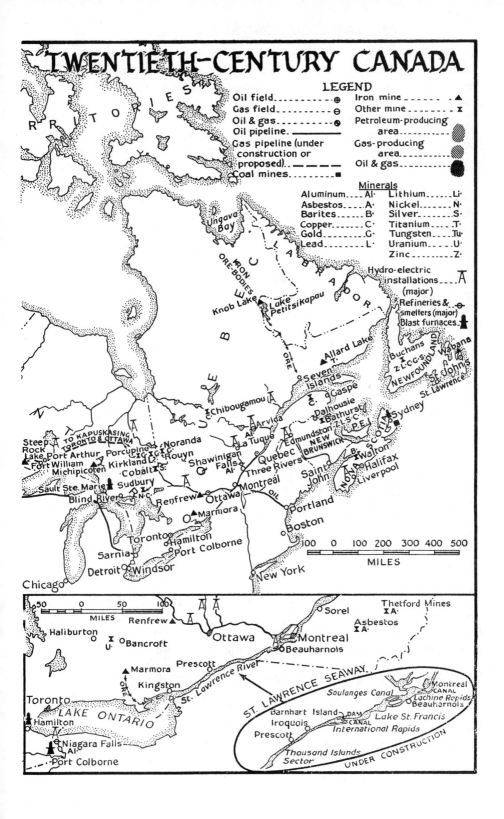

TWENTIETH-CENTURY CANADA

LEGEND

Oil field............⊕
Gas field...........⊖
Oil & gas..........⊕
Oil pipeline._____
Gas pipeline (under
construction or
proposed)._ _ _ _
Coal mines.........■

Iron mine _____ ▲
Other mine _____ x
Petroleum-producing
area.............
Gas-producing
area.............
Oil & gas...........

Minerals

Aluminum.....Al·   Lithium......Li·
Asbestos....A·   Nickel.......N·
Barites......B·   Silver.......S·
Copper.......C·   Titanium....T·
Gold.........G·   Tungsten...Tu·
Lead.........L·   Uranium.....U·
Zinc.........Z·

Hydro-electric
installations
(major)
Refineries &
smelters (major)
Blast furnaces

TERRITORIES

Ungava Bay

IRON ORE BODIES

QUEBEC

LABRADOR

Knob Lake
Lake Petitsikapau

ORE

Allard Lake ▲ T.

Buchans
Z·L·C·G·S·
Wabana

NEWFOUNDLAND

St. John's

St. Lawrence

Seven Islands

Gaspe

C.

Dalhousie
Bathurst
Z·L·S·
P.E.I.

Sydney

Chibougamou ▲

Arvida
La Tuque

Edmundston
NEW BRUNSWICK

NOVA SCOTIA

Steep Rock
TO KAPUSKASING
TORONTO & OTTAWA
Noranda
Porcupine
Rouyn

Shawinigan Falls

Quebec

Three Rivers

Saint John

Walton
B·

Halifax

Liverpool

Lake Port Arthur
Fort William
Michipicoten
Kirkland L.
Cobalt
Sault Ste. Marie
Sudbury
Blind River
N·C·

Renfrew

Ottawa

Marmora

Portland

OIL

Boston

Toronto

Hamilton
Port Colborne

Sarnia

Detroit   Windsor

New York

Chicago

100   0   100 200 300 400 500

MILES

---

50   0   50   100

MILES   Renfrew ▲

Sorel

Thetford Mines
x ▲

Asbestos
x ▲·

Haliburton
x
U·   Bancroft

Ottawa

Montreal
Beauharnois

Prescott

▲ Marmora

Kingston

ORE

St. Lawrence River

ST. LAWRENCE SEAWAY

Montreal
CANAL
Lachine Rapids
Beauharnois

Soulanges Canal

Toronto

LAKE ONTARIO

Hamilton

Niagara Falls
Al·

Port Colborne

Barnhart Island
Iroquois
Prescott

DAM
CANAL

Lake St. Francis
International Rapids

Thousand Islands
Sector

UNDER CONSTRUCTION

condition that the wood was manufactured within the province. In 1902, Ontario went even further by imposing an absolute prohibition on the export of pulpwood cut on Crown lands—an example which was followed within the next thirteen years by all the other provinces.

An American tariff on newsprint had been established in 1883 at a level of 15 per cent. In 1897 this was changed to a sliding scale, with the duty starting at three-tenths of a cent per pound for paper valued at 2 cents a pound or less and rising for higher grades. Provision was made, however, for an additional import duty if any country imposed an export duty on paper coming to the United States. Restrictions on the export of pulpwood from Canada were immediately followed by pressure for increases in the American tariff. This pressure was strongly resisted by American newspaper publishers, and the result was a compromise statute, passed by the American Congress in 1909, according to which the tariff on the lowest grade of paper was reduced to three-sixteenths of a cent, provided that the exporting country removed all prohibitions or restrictions on pulpwood exports. When the Canadian provinces refused to modify or remove their embargoes, a retaliatory duty of $2.00 per ton was imposed on Canadian paper, together with an additional tax on pulp and paper made from Crown lands timber in Quebec.

Canadian pulp and newsprint supplies, however, were by this time almost indispensable to the American newspaper-publishing industry, on whom fell most of the burden of the American duties, and the fight for a reduction in the duties was continued. Free admission of Canadian newsprint was provided for in the abortive Reciprocity Treaty of 1911 (which was rejected by Canada after having been accepted by the United States Congress), and in 1913 the advocates of free entry won a conclusive victory in the Underwood Act, according to which newsprint paper valued at not more than 2½ cents per pound, together with mechanical and chemical pulp, were admitted duty free. During the First World War the price of newsprint rose above the 2½-cent limit, and the limit was accordingly changed, first to 5 cents, then to 8, and then in 1922 back to 5 cents. Since 1913, therefore, Canadian pulp and newsprint have entered the American market free of duty.

Basic to the final success of the policies followed by the Canadian provincial governments in this period were certain important locational factors. The embargoes and restrictions on the export of pulp wood would not by themselves have been effective in attracting the newsprint industry to Canada, had it not been for the locational pull of cheap hydro-electric power and the economies of proximity to the raw material. This is clear if it is recalled that the export restriction applied only to pulpwood and not to manufactured pulp. Despite the embargoes, newsprint manufacturers in the United States were still free to import Canadian pulp and manufacture newsprint from it in plants within the United States. To some extent this was done, United States imports of pulp from Canada rising to 880,453 tons by 1925. Such imports relieved the supply situation in the United States but could not offset the advantages of manufacturing newsprint in plants closer to the raw-material and energy sources. The determination of the Canadian provincial governments to exploit to the full the strong bargaining position which control of pulpwood supplies gave them undoubtedly hastened the movement of newsprint production to Canada, but the locational factors were fundamental.

Following the removal of the American tariff, the Canadian newsprint industry entered upon a period of very rapid growth. In 1900 production of newsprint in Canada had been negligible. By 1913 output had reached 402,000 tons and Canada was already the world's leading exporter. By 1919 this output had been more than doubled, and by 1923 it had been tripled. Peak production was reached in 1929, with an output of just under 3 million tons. Newsprint prices rose sharply from 1914 to 1923 but thereafter, as production began to catch up with the increase in demand, declined irregularly until 1935; on a basis of 1926=100, the price indexes for the three years mentioned were 62.3, 160.9 and 57.1 respectively. The industry was very hard hit by the depression after 1929 and serious problems of excess capacity were encountered. As a result of the completion of new mills and machines, the construction of which had been begun before 1929, the capacity of the industry increased between 1929 and 1932 from 3,512,000 to 4,142,000 tons annually, while output between the same two years dropped by almost 30 per cent and prices (1926=100) from 88.6 to 69.0. In these circumstances the provincial governments of Quebec and Ontario adopted a pro-rating system, whereby orders for newsprint were shared among the mills, and some measure of stability was thereby restored. Prices resumed their upward trend in 1936 and output climbed gradually to just over 3 million tons in 1939. The pro-rating system remained in force until the outbreak of World War II, when the federal government assumed control of production and supply.

In many respects the pulp-and-paper industry exemplifies Canada's role in the world economy of the mid-twentieth century. On the one hand, the availability of cheap hydro-electric power, supplemented by vigorous government intervention in the control of raw material exports, has made possible the establishment in Canada of a new and powerful industry—an industry which gives seasonal or permanent employment to more than 300,000 individuals, pays out more than $370 million annually in wages, purchases more than one-quarter of all electric power purchased, and contributes by its gross value of output more than 5 per cent of the gross national product. On the other hand, the prosperity of this industry hinges upon exports and therefore upon tariff policies and fluctuations in demand in foreign countries—particularly in the United States, but also in Europe. Pulp and paper is the largest single item in Canada's external trade, accounting for approximately 24 per cent (in 1954) of all Canadian domestic exports. In trade with the United States it bulks even larger: pulp, newsprint, and other paper products contributed in 1954 33.6 per cent of all imports of Canadian produce to the United States—a figure which compares with 16.6 per cent for non-ferrous metals and their products and 9.2 per cent for agricultural and vegetable products. The advent of the new industrialism, as exemplified in the pulp-and-paper industry, has therefore done little or nothing to diminish the dependence on exports which has characterized Canadian economic history from its earliest years. In the long run, export markets for Canadian pulp and paper seem reasonably secure. Except in the Soviet Union and perhaps in the tropical forests, no large reserves of pulpwood remain to be exploited, and Canadian resources must continue to provide the bulk of the world's supply. But the possibility of serious instability in the short run remains very real. In so far as the Canadian industry is concerned, stability depends largely on the maintenance of effective demand in the United States.

ALUMINUM

Canada is currently the world's second largest producer of primary aluminum, with a production in 1957 of 557.1 thousand short tons, or 14.9 per cent of the world total. The largest producer is the United States, with 44.2 per cent of the total. The demand for the metal is distinctively a twentieth-century phenomenon, and the same is true of methods of producing it commercially (though the basic process was discovered in 1886). The industry, both as regards organization and location, is an excellent example of some of the implications of the new industrialism.

The iron and steel industry, the key sector of the older industrial structures, was located in areas where coal and iron ore were found in close proximity to each other, or in areas to which these materials could be shipped cheaply. The aluminum industry has a very different locational pattern, the determining factor in which is the indispensability of very large supplies of cheap electricity. The ore of aluminum, bauxite, although abundant in tropical or semi-tropical countries, is not found in Canada. Canada possesses a large and growing aluminum industry because it possesses cheap hydro-electricity.

The history of the industry in Canada is essentially the story of a continued search for cheap electricity. Growth and expansion of capacity have usually entailed a movement to new sources of power rather than the enlargement of existing facilities, since the development of each source of hydro-electricity has typically been followed by the appearance in the same area of other industries using comparatively smaller amounts of electricity and able to out-bid the aluminum plants for the power they do require. The typical aluminum development at the present day is found, therefore, near a large source of water-power, in a more or less isolated area where the competition of other industrial power users is not a serious threat, but within reasonably close proximity to harbour facilities where bauxite supplies can be unloaded.

The first large aluminum plant in North America was built at Niagara Falls, New York, in 1895 by the Aluminum Company of America. Rising costs for electricity compelled a search for new power sites and in 1899 the decision was made to construct a smelter in Quebec province, whose hydro-electric resources were as yet untapped. A subsidiary company (now the Aluminum Company of Canada) was formed and a large electrolytic smelter and hydro-electric installation constructed at Shawinigan Falls in 1900. Production at this plant rose from 2 million pounds in 1902 to 14½ million pounds in 1914. By 1926, when production had risen to 38.9 million pounds, rising costs for electricity made necessary the development of a new site. A suitable location was found at the head of navigation on the Saguenay River and a new smelter constructed with an initial capacity of 30,000 tons a year. Development of this site involved the building of what was in effect a completely new city, Arvida, and of a very large hydro-electric installation. The demand for aluminum continued to grow, and by 1939 Canadian output had reached 165.7 million pounds. World War II, bringing with it rapid expansion in the aircraft industry particularly, was responsible for further increases in output. By 1945 Canadian production had reached 431.4 million pounds.

In the immediate post-war years further expansion of capacity became necessary. Plans were laid to step up generating capacity in Quebec and several new hydro-electric installations were completed, that at Shipshaw being the largest. But at the same time search was made for untapped power sites in other areas, including not only other parts of Canada but also such countries as Norway, South Africa, New Zealand, and Borneo. In January, 1951, the choice finally fell on Kitimat in British Columbia, 400 miles north of Vancouver. This site offered many important advantages, not least among which was the fact that the smelter could be erected at the head of Douglas Channel, a deep-water fiord which would make it possible for supplies of bauxite or refined alumina to be brought in by sea. Development of adequate hydro-electric power, however, promised to involve very great engineering problems. What was involved essentially was the damming of the Nechako River on the eastern side of the Coast Range, so as to form a reservoir covering some 350 square miles, drilling a ten-mile tunnel through Mount DuBose, and erecting a hydro-electric generating station inside the mountain on the west side of Kemano, from where electricity could be transmitted some 50 miles across country to Kitimat. Completion of the project was certainly one of the most remarkable engineering achievements of modern times.

Production at Kitimat got under way in August, 1954. The initial capacity of 91,500 tons was raised eventually to 192,000 tons, and when market conditions warrant it the smelter can be expanded to an ultimate 500,000-ton capacity. Like the Arvida development, and like the Quebec-Labrador iron-ore project, Kitimat involved the creation of a completely new community in territory which previously was no more than wilderness. This highlights one significant difference between the way in which economic expansion took place in Canada in the nineteenth century and the way it takes place today. The typical agrarian frontier of the nineteenth century expanded more or less in a continuous wave; the frontier of development in present-day Canada expands by a series of discontinuous leaps, with the established centres of population and industry serving as no more than the spring-board for further advance.

PETROLEUM AND NATURAL GAS

It is sometimes forgotten that the first producing oil well in the American continent was drilled in Canada—in Lambton County, Ontario, in 1858 —and that the oil-fields in the southwestern peninsula of Ontario, between Lake Huron and Lake Erie, were successfully exploited throughout most of the second half of the nineteenth century. Production in this area, however, reached its peak in 1890 with an output in that year of 795,030 barrels, and thereafter declined steadily, though the wells remained important locally as a source of natural gas. The remarkable expansion of Canadian output in the early 1950's was the result of new oil discoveries in western Canada, with most of the producing wells being concentrated in Alberta.

Alberta's record as a significant source of crude petroleum dates only from the late 1920's. The Turner Valley oil-field, in the foothills of the Rockies about 35 miles southwest of Calgary, was discovered in 1914 and produced at first a wet gas from which crude naphtha and low-grade gasoline was obtained. Petroleum production was small until 1930, when output for the first time exceeded one million barrels a year, and though a number of new wells were drilled in the late 1930's, producing a heavier grade of crude, prospects for expansion seemed far from bright. During World War II, however, the rate of exploration for new supplies was stepped up substantially, partly as a result of tax concessions offered by the federal government, and several new discoveries were made in areas distant from the original Turner Valley wells. The significance of these finds was not fully appreciated at the time. Production at the Turner Valley field reached a peak of 29,000 barrels a day in 1942, but this was insufficient even to meet current demands in the western provinces, swollen as they were at the time by the requirements of the Commonwealth air-training scheme.

The outlook was completely changed by a series of very important discoveries made between 1946 and 1948. In 1946 the Conrad and Taber oil-fields near Lethbridge were brought into production, followed within the same year by the Lloydminster field, lying across the Saskatchewan and Alberta border. The boom really began, however, in 1947, with the discovery of the Leduc field near Edmonton by the Imperial Oil Company. The oil in this field was found to lie in a type of geological formation—a Devonian coral reef—very similar to the formations in the West Texas and New Mexico oil-fields, with which American oil companies were already very familiar. The significance of the new discovery and its probable extent were therefore quickly recognized and an intensive burst of exploratory drilling got under way. A series of major discoveries followed: Woodbend in 1947, across the Saskatchewan River from Leduc; Redwater in 1948, with reserves estimated at twice those of Leduc; Golden Spike, Stettler, Duhamel, Big Valley, and several others in 1949; Wizard Lake in 1951; Bonnie Glen and Pigeon Lake in 1952, and Homeglen in 1953.

Meanwhile the area of exploration expanded rapidly, covering by the end of 1953 not only prospective oil lands in the three prairie provinces but also the northeast corner of British Columbia and the North West Territories south and west of Great Slave Lake. Later discoveries disclosed the existence of oil-fields in areas far distant from Leduc and Redwater: at Coleville, Fosterton, Wapella, Forget and several other points in Saskatchewan; at Virden, Linklater, Tilston, and Waskada in Manitoba; and in Alberta at Sturgeon Lake in the Peace River area and at Pembina, seventy miles southwest of Edmonton—this last being the largest oil-field discovered up to that date in Canada. In the North West Territories the Norman Wells field, supplying oil and petroleum for local use and for mining enterprises, has been in production since 1931; exploratory drilling in the area south and west of Great Slave Lake has shown encouraging results. Perhaps the greatest promise for the future lies in the Athabasca tar sands of northern Alberta, a vast bed of bituminous sands covering an area of some 10,000 square miles, saturated with tar and heavy oil. Methods of separating the oil have already been worked out on a laboratory scale and commercial development seems only a question of time.

The speed with which the discovery and development of western Canada's oil resources took place makes it difficult to appraise objectively what the opening up of this new area of growth means for the Canadian economy as a whole and for the three prairie provinces in particular. It seems clear that the discoveries of the immediate post-war period, remarkable though they were, represented little more than a scratching of the surface. The sedimentary basin of western Canada, within which lie its reserves of oil and natural gas, covers an area three times the size of the state of Texas, an area which already has a history of over fifty years of active oil production and in which exploratory drilling is still going on apace. Estimates of potential production in western Canada are continually being stepped up as surveys and exploration proceed; at the end of 1952 the figure stood at 1,700 million barrels; by 1954 proven recoverable reserves had reached 2.5 billion barrels. These figures, however, are out of date almost as soon as published.

As a result of these discoveries production of crude petroleum in Canada as a whole rose from approximately 8.5 million barrels in 1945 to 29 million in 1950 and 60.9 million in 1952. The corresponding figures for Alberta alone are 8, 27.5, and 58.7 million barrels. Canadian production of natural gas from the oil-fields also increased greatly, from 48.4 million cubic feet in 1945 to 67.8 in 1950 and 87.6 in 1952, with over 90 per cent of the total coming from Alberta. Production figures alone, however, give a somewhat distorted picture, since the limiting factor for both crude petroleum and natural gas in the early years was not productive capacity but distribution facilities. The western Canada oil-fields lack one big advantage which the Texas fields have: cheap ocean transportation to the big consuming markets of the Atlantic seaboard. Development, once the requirements of the local market had been met, depended upon the construction of pipelines. Inadequate pipeline facilities for the western Canada oil-fields meant at first a considerable amount of "shut-in" production; the actual rate of production was very much smaller than the rate calculated to give maximum ultimate recovery.

The principal markets outside the prairie provinces which oil and gas from western Canada can expect to serve are in central Canada (Ontario and Quebec) and on the Pacific coast (British Columbia and eventually Washington, Oregon, and California). To reach the central Canada market the Interprovincial Pipeline Company, a subsidiary of Imperial Oil, began construction in 1949 of an oil pipeline from Edmonton to Superior, Wisconsin, from which point Great Lakes shipping would carry the crude to the large refinery at Sarnia, Ontario. Completed in 1950 at a cost of $90 million, the line had an initial capacity of 40,000 barrels a day and cut the cost of transporting crude from Edmonton to Superior to 55 cents a barrel, as compared with a bulk rail freight rate of $1.86. Alberta's oil production in 1951, as a direct consequence, showed a 68 per cent increase over 1950. The capacity of the pipeline, however, soon proved inadequate, while the seasonal interruption of navigation on the Great Lakes proved a serious disadvantage. During 1952, therefore, plans were announced to extend the pipeline along the south shore of Lake Superior, across the Mackinac Straits at the north end of Lake Michigan, and thence to Sarnia. This line has a capacity of 300,000 barrels a day: the capacity of the original line from Edmonton to Superior was stepped up to a corresponding figure. During 1952 an additional pipeline was put under construction to carry refined products from Sarnia to Toronto.

Construction of a pipeline across the mountains to the Pacific coast presented more serious engineering problems and would not have been justified by the demand for petroleum products in British Columbia alone, an area whose total requirements in 1955 were estimated at no more than 65,000 barrels a day. A large potential market existed, however, in Washington and Oregon, areas in which demand gave every indication of outrunning California's dwindling reserves. Construction began on the Transmountain Pipeline from Edmonton to Vancouver in 1952 and reached completion in the year following. The line had an initial capacity of 120,000 barrels a day; extensions to new refineries in the state of Washington were constructed shortly thereafter.

Construction of pipelines for natural gas proceeded at a slower pace. The provincial government of Alberta adopted a policy of prohibiting the export of gas unless and until reserves had been found adequate to provide a thirty-year supply for the province and to meet the prior needs of the Dominion. The first half of this condition was met in 1951, and in that year, at the special request of the Canadian and American federal governments, the provincial government of Alberta gave permission for the export of natural gas from the Pakowki Lake area of southern Alberta to Butte, Montana, to serve the requirements of the strategically important refinery operated by the Anaconda Copper Company in that area. In the following year approval was given to the Westcoast Transmission Company for a gas pipeline from the Peace River wells to Vancouver and thence to Portland and Seattle. Several other proposals were drawn up and submitted, but none was approved. This was in accordance with a policy stated by the Canadian federal government in March, 1953, which made it clear that permits would not be granted for the export of natural gas from Canada until the government was convinced that there could be no economic use, present or future, for that gas in Canada. This meant, in effect, that sanction would not be given for the construction of gas lines from western Canada to markets in the United States until the actual and potential needs of Ontario and Quebec had been satisfied. High priority was therefore given to the construction of a gas pipeline from Alberta to Toronto, Ottawa, and Montreal, running north of Lake Superior entirely through Canadian territory. The parallel with certain aspects of Canadian railway history is obvious.

The situation as regards gas pipelines and the natural-gas industry was, therefore, somewhat complicated by considerations of defence and national economic unity. On the one hand it was recognized that discoveries of natural gas were largely by-products of the search for oil and that, as a consequence of the rapid pace with which the search for oil had proceeded, reserves of gas had by 1953 increased to the point where export outside the prairie provinces was necessary if waste was to be avoided and if the rate of exploration was not to be seriously retarded. On the other hand, if no restrictions had been placed on the export of gas from Alberta to the United States, the construction of a gas pipeline from Alberta to the densely populated industrial areas of Ontario and Quebec might have been postponed for several years. Ontario and Quebec, as we have already emphasized, are deficient in fuels; hence their dependence on American coal. Construction of a trans-Canada gas pipeline was expected to offset this dependence, materially assist Canada's balance of payments, and reinforce the energy base on which Canada's industry has developed.

With respect to crude oil the situation was somewhat clearer. Prior to 1947 less than 10 per cent of Canada's oil requirements were met from Canadian wells. By 1953 the figure had risen to 43 per cent, despite the fact that total Canadian demand had more than doubled since 1946. In aggregate terms Canada was expected to be self-sufficient in oil by 1960. This, along with increasingly large exports of iron ore, means a fundamental improvement in Canada's trading position vis-à-vis the United States. Self-sufficiency in aggregate terms, however, does not mean a complete cessation of oil imports. By 1953 pipelines were already in existence to carry western oil from the prairies to British Columbia and Ontario. But, because of the costs and distances involved, it was expected to prove more economical for eastern Canada, particularly Quebec, to import crude from other countries and for western Canada to export part of its output to the near-by consuming centres in the Pacific northwest. Montreal refineries—one-third of total Canadian refining capacity—obtain most of their crude-oil supplies from Venezuela by means of a pipeline from Portland, Maine. It seems questionable whether oil from western Canada can be delivered at Montreal at prices lower than these imported supplies.

On the regional economy of the prairie provinces the effects of the oil and gas discoveries were remarkable. Industrial employment in Alberta increased by more than 50 per cent in the period 1946-53, and total personal incomes nearly doubled. Generally good agricultural conditions, of course, added their weight to prosperity, but these affected the three prairie provinces more or less equally. The rate of economic expansion in Alberta, where most of the oil and gas discoveries were made, was faster in the period between 1947 and 1955 than in any other province and much faster than in Saskatchewan and Manitoba. Large capital expenditures for exploration and development of oil and gas—$330 million in 1953 and more than $350 million in 1954—provided the underlying basis for expansion, but the establishment of ancillary industries also played an important role. Large and readily available supplies of natural gas, for example, attracted the petro-chemical industry and a number of plants were set up for the production of sulphur, ammonia, cellulose acetate, and various types of plastics. These developments foreshadowed important structural changes in the economy of the prairie provinces.

THE ST. LAWRENCE SEAWAY

When a country experiences a rapid surge of economic growth, along with fundamental changes in the location and organization of its economic activities, it is sometimes permissible to say that it is undergoing an economic revolution. It would be no great exaggeration to apply this term to the Canadian economy in the middle decades of the twentieth century, a period when growth proceeded at a more rapid pace and with greater momentum than probably in any previous period in the country's history. But, as with political revolutions, the impression that a completely new start was made and that there was a sharp break with the past is largely an illusion. Despite the growth of manufacturing industry, Canada as a nation in the late 1950's still paid its way in the world by exporting raw materials—the staple products of mine, field and forest. Important structural changes had certainly taken place. New resources were discovered and new industries created. The income-earning capacity of the various provinces, though still highly uneven, was brought closer to balance, and the dependence of whole regions on single staple exports significantly reduced. Nevertheless, when viewed in perspective, the process which Canada was undergoing in these years is seen not as a drastic departure from the patterns of development which had held in the past, but rather as a broadening of the base, a lessening of the degree of specialization, a matter of growth by the addition of new sectors. The pattern of Canadian development—a pattern which from the start had been determined largely by geography and geology—was modified but not erased.

The most striking example of this element of continuity was the successful conclusion of negotiations with the United States for the joint construction of the St. Lawrence Seaway. Throughout the history of Canada the St. Lawrence River has served as the major artery of commerce—the axis from which development began and around which the national economy was organized. The most important single task in the economic sphere which the Canadian colonies undertook in the first half of the nineteenth century was the building of the St. Lawrence canals between Lake Erie and tidewater at Montreal. Completed in 1848, the canals failed to satisfy some of the extravagant expectations that had inspired their building, but their continuing importance—indeed, their indispensability—to the Canadian economy was amply attested by the large sums spent to keep them in a state of first-class repair and to ensure, by successive enlargements and reconstruction, that they could accommodate the largest vessels seeking to use the waterway. The St. Lawrence Seaway, in the form finally approved in 1953 by the Canadian and American federal governments, was essentially the realization in physical form of an idea which had shaped Canadian economic development from its earliest years.

To get the Seaway built entailed unusually persistent and long-continued diplomatic pressure. As a result of the efforts of successive Canadian governments, the St. Lawrence canals by the first decade of the twentieth century had been enlarged to give a minimum depth of 14 feet throughout, while regular dredging had deepened the ship channel between Montreal and Quebec to a limiting depth of 35 feet at extreme low water. At Sault Ste. Marie an American canal had been built between 1853 and 1855; a canal on the Canadian side, giving a minimum depth of 18 feet 3 inches, had been constructed between 1887 and 1895. The Welland Canal, enlarged between 1873 and 1887 to give a minimum depth of 14 feet, was already proving inadequate to handle the tremendous volume of coal, iron ore, and wheat passing between Lake Erie and Lake Ontario, and in 1913 construction of the Welland Ship Canal got under way. Shortages of material and man-power made it necessary to suspend work in 1916, but in 1932 the Ship Canal finally reached completion, giving a depth of 25 feet in the channel but with the locks constructed so as to permit deepening to 30 feet when required. By this time Canada had spent nearly $300 million on the whole route from Sault Ste. Marie to Quebec.

Proposals to enlarge the canal system still further, to a depth adequate to permit its use by sea-going vessels, had been in the air as early as 1895, when commissions of inquiry had been appointed by both the American and the Canadian federal governments to look into the question. These early investigations, however, produced no positive action. In 1921 the International Joint Commission (a tribunal established in 1909 to arbitrate questions involving the boundary waters of Canada and the United States) recommended in favour of joint development of the upper St. Lawrence, but once again no definite agreement was reached. By this time the project had attracted wide support, not only in Ontario and Quebec, but also in certain sections of the United States, particularly the mid-western states of Minnesota, Wisconsin, Illinois, and Michigan, while several powerful American corporations, notably the Aluminum Corporation of America, General Electric, and the Du Pont company, were interested in the hydro-electric aspects. Recommendations made by investigating commissions appointed by both federal governments were brought together in the provisions of the St. Lawrence Deep Waterway Treaty. This treaty was signed in 1932, but rejected by the U.S. Senate in 1934, the opposing votes coming mostly from the states of the Atlantic seaboard. A similar fate overtook the Great Lakes-St. Lawrence Agreement of 1941.

Faced with the prospect of indefinite delay in securing American participation, the Canadian Parliament late in 1951 passed legislation creating the St. Lawrence Seaway Authority, a Crown corporation authorized to construct a deep waterway between Montreal and Lake Erie either wholly in Canada or in conjunction with the United States. Shortly thereafter the Canadian government announced its intention of proceeding with the project independently. Meanwhile agreement had been reached on joint development of the hydro-electric facilities. Early in 1953, however, bills were introduced in the United States Congress providing for American construction of the necessary Seaway facilities, and in May, 1954, after considerable pressure had been exerted by the executive branch of the American government, these bills were approved. They authorized the establishment of the St. Lawrence Seaway Development Corporation, a public body empowered to construct the facilities required for a deep waterway in the international section of the river.

This process of parallel legislative action resulted in a certain amount of duplication in the American and Canadian plans, but these were later ironed out by mutual agreement. As finally accepted the project called for the completion of a deep waterway providing a minimum depth of 27 feet throughout the entire distance from the head of Lake Superior to the sea —a total distance of more than 2,000 miles. Certain sections of this water-way were already built: the new American MacArthur locks at Sault Ste. Marie (built during World War II), the dredged channel at St. Mary's Falls opposite Detroit, and the Welland Ship Canal (in which only additional dredging was required) provided the necessary facilities from Lake Superior to Lake Ontario, while below Montreal a deep-water naviga-tion channel was already in existence. The new construction required was concentrated entirely in the St. Lawrence River between Prescott and Montreal. In this section the principal works for which Canada accepted responsibility were a canal and locks at Iroquois, locks and a bridge at Beauharnois, extensive excavations in Lake St. Francis, and a canal and locks at Lachine. The United States undertook to construct a canal and locks at Barnhart Island and to be responsible for channel dredging in the Thousand Islands section. Canada agreed not to undertake, for the time being, the construction of a canal at Barnhart Island but reserved the right to do so in the future if it seemed desirable, while the United States agreed not to construct a canal at Iroquois. The total cost of the Seaway project (leaving aside the hydro-electric development) was estimated in 1955 at $261 million, of which Canada would provide $189 million and the United States the remaining $72 million.

Early discussions of the Seaway project devoted much attention to the possibility of opening the Great Lakes to ocean-going shipping, and much ink was spilled in elaborating the benefits which the inland cities of Canada and the United States might expect to derive from being converted, in effect, into ocean ports. More realistic appraisals, however, have made it clear that the controlling depth of 27 feet effectively excludes all large, fast ocean-going freighters now in service. Of the sea-going merchant fleet of the United States in 1951 only 10 per cent of the vessels and 7 per cent of the tonnage could use the Seaway. The most important effect of the Seaway, so far as shipping is concerned, is not to open the Great Lakes to ocean-going ships but to open the St. Lawrence to large lake vessels. This eliminates the need for trans-shipment and does away with the small, shallow-draught "canallers" which the old 14-foot canals made necessary. In effect, the Seaway makes Montreal both a lake and an ocean port.

The significance of opening the St. Lawrence to large lake shipping becomes evident upon consideration of the commodities which were expected to make up the bulk of the traffic. Estimates made by the U.S. Department of Commerce shortly before construction of the Seaway began put the total potential yearly traffic between the Gulf of St. Lawrence and Lake Erie at between 57.5 and 84 million tons. The smaller of the two figures included the following categories of freight: 30 million tons of iron ore, 6.5 million tons of grain, 6 million tons of petroleum, 4 million of coal, and 11 million of other miscellaneous items. More than 50 per cent of the total expected tonnage, therefore, was iron ore from Ungava and Quebec-Labrador. This large east-to-west movement of iron ore from the new Canadian mines to the industrial centres of the United States would have been inconceivable had transportation facilities on the St. Lawrence been limited to shallow-draught canals. From the economic point of view, the availability of return cargoes of iron ore meant a more efficient use of shipping and a very significant reduction in freight costs for the west-to-east movement of coal and grain. From the strategic point of view, the importance of an inland waterway route from a major source of iron ore to the industrial heartland of the United States hardly needed emphasis. There seems, in short, little doubt that the opening up of the Quebec-Labrador iron-ore deposits was a critical factor in shaping American policy toward the Seaway.

As we have already emphasized, the improvement of the St. Lawrence waterway is one of the major continuing themes of Canadian development. The role which the Seaway actually plays in the modern Canadian economy, however, illustrates the changes which have occurred in Canada's resource position and in Canada's relations with the outside world since the project was first put forward. Traditionally the St. Lawrence River has been the channel along which exports travelled to Europe and imports were brought back. The River and the commercial system built around it have been, so to speak, the longitudinal axis of the Canadian economy, the physical counterpart of its dominant orientation toward Europe. When the pull of the United States market threatened to become so strong as to threaten national economic unity, the characteristic response of the Canadian economy was to reinforce this east-west axis, first by canals and later by railways. The creation in Canada of a transcontinental national economy was essentially the end-product of a series of forced extensions of the east-west axis until it reached the Pacific coast, the impelling motive in each case being the determination to counteract the divisive north-south pull of the United States. In a sense, the construction of the St. Lawrence Seaway is a continuation of this same national policy. But whereas formerly the St. Lawrence River carried Canada's foodstuffs and raw materials to Europe, now a large part of the traffic which passes along it consists of exports of raw material to the United States. Iron ore from Quebec and Labrador moves along it in one direction, and grain from the western prairies in the other. The St. Lawrence River, traditionally the symbol of Canada's economic orientation to Europe, now serves in part at least to strengthen Canada's ties with the United States.

SUGGESTIONS FOR FURTHER READING

BASIC WORKS:

Dales, John H., "Fuel, Power, and Industrial Development in Central Canada", *American Economic Review;* Vol. XLIII, No. 2 (May, 1953), pp. 181-98

Langford, G. B., *Out of the Earth: The Mineral Industry in Canada* (Toronto, 1954)

Royal Institute of International Affairs, *Springs of Canadian Power* (London and New York, 1953)

Van der Valk, H.M.H.A., *The Economic Future of Canada* (Toronto, 1954)

SUPPLEMENTARY WORKS:

Canada, Department of Trade and Commerce, *Private and Public Investment in Canada, 1926-1951* (Ottawa, 1951)

Canada, Dominion Bureau of Statistics, *Chronological Record of Canadian Mining Events from 1604 to 1947 and Historical Tables of Mineral Production of Canada* (Ottawa, 1948)

Canada, Dominion Bureau of Statistics and Department of Trade and Commerce, *General Review of the Manufacturing Industries of Canada, 1949* (Ottawa, 1952)

Canada, Department of Mines and Resources, *Geology and Economic Minerals of Canada* (third edition, Ottawa, 1947)

Canada Year Book, 1954, "Canada's Mineral Resources", Chapter XII, Section 1, pp. 482-506 (Ottawa, 1954)

Canada Year Book, 1952-53, "The Pulp and Paper Industry in Canada", pp. 467-75 (Ottawa, 1953)

Canadian Pulp and Paper Association, *From Watershed to Watermark: The Pulp and Paper Industry of Canada* (revised edition, Montreal, 1955)

Canadian Pulp and Paper Association, *Reference Tables* (Montreal, March, 1955)

Guthrie, John A., *The Newsprint Paper Industry, an Economic Analysis* (Cambridge, Mass., 1941)

MacKay, R. A. (ed.), *Newfoundland: Economic, Diplomatic, and Strategic Studies* (Toronto, 1946)

Report of the Royal Commission on Coal (1946), Hon. Justice W. F. Carroll, chairman (Ottawa, 1947)

CHAPTER XXII

LABOUR AND LABOUR ORGANIZATIONS

INTRODUCTION: EARLY CRAFT UNIONISM

As CANADA has moved toward the status of an industrial nation, she has had increasingly to concern herself with the problems of social welfare that characteristically accompany industrialism. Not least among these has been the problem of maintaining industrial peace and reconciling the often conflicting interests of management and labour. Some mention must therefore be made of the growth of labour organizations in the Canadian economy and of the role such organizations have come to play in the nation's affairs.

At the beginning of 1953 there were 1,219,714 labour-union members in Canada out of a total labour force in employment of approximately 5,387,000. This represented an increase of 6.4 per cent over 1952 and of more than 300 per cent over the 1939 figure, when total membership had stood at only 358,967 (as of December 31). Over most of Canadian history labour unions have included only a relatively small proportion of the labour force in employment. Expansion of membership has been limited by, among other factors, the slow growth of manufacturing, the high degree of dispersal of population, the effects of severe depressions, and the failure to achieve unity in the labour movement. The development of a unified labour movement, in its turn, has been retarded by very much the same factors that held back the development of a unified nation: regional separatism, differences in culture (particularly in religion), and inadequate communications.

In its early beginnings, Canadian trade-unionism developed under the influence of British examples and British legislation. This influence is still evident in the legislative and political programmes of the Canadian labour movement. In their economic policies, however, and in their internal organization, Canadian unions have in general followed patterns set by labour unions in the United States. This interaction between the influence of Britain and that of the United States provides one important clue to the interpretation of Canadian labour history.

The earliest unions of which we have record developed in the port towns of the St. Lawrence and the lower Lakes in the first half of the nineteenth century. Associations of workers, probably temporary in nature, are believed to have existed in Quebec as early as 1827. In 1844 a union of printers (now the International Typographical Union No. 91) was formed in Toronto and in the same year a stone-cutters' union was formed in Montreal. In the decade of the 1850's local craft unions of this type increased in numbers, particularly in Ontario. At the same time the construction of railways and the expansion of manufacturing increased the demand for skilled labour—a demand met largely by the emigration of skilled workers from England. The new local unions which these immigrant workers formed were patterned on the British model, and at least two British unions, the Amalgamated Society of Engineers and the Amalgamated Society of Carpenters and Joiners, established branches in Canada. The growing strength of the craft unions was reflected, during the inflation of the late 1850's, in strikes among the bricklayers and carpenters and successful demands for wage increases on the part of the printers.

The British influence on Canadian unionism did not long go unchallenged. After the ratification of the Reciprocity Treaty in 1854, trade with the United States expanded greatly. Closer economic ties between the two countries encouraged a constant movement of workers across the border, and it was only to be expected that labour organizations in the United States should attempt to extend their jurisdiction into Canada. The result was the appearance of "international" unionism, as it was called. Labour organizations in the United States either established branches of their own in Canadian cities or else tried to induce Canadian unions to affiliate with them. Thus the Iron Molders' Union of North America established branches in Montreal, Hamilton, Toronto, and London between 1861 and 1863, while the Toronto Typographical Society accepted affiliation with the American National (later International) Typographical Union in 1866. Canadian branches were also founded by the cigar-makers' union and the coopers, as well as by the various railway brotherhoods.

During this early period there is little evidence of co-operation between the unions, except where several locals of a trade were organized under the same American international. The unions were craft organizations, confined to skilled workers, and concerned principally with issues affecting wages and working conditions in their particular localities. Joint action within and among the craft unions dates mainly from the early 1870's, in the short-lived period of industrial expansion which followed Confederation. The Toronto Trades Assembly, the first "city central" in Canada, was founded in 1871, and the Ottawa Trades Council by 1873, while a similar organization of which little is known existed in Hamilton. These central organizations played a prominent part in the agitation for a nine-hour working day and in inducing the Canadian Parliament, following a printers' strike in Toronto, to clarify and amend the legal status of trade unions. Up to this time unions had received no legal recognition beyond what was implicit in earlier English legislation and common-law decisions.

By these criteria unions were illegal organizations since they acted "in restraint of trade". In 1871 the British Parliament had passed an Act which changed the status of trade unions, but this legislation did not affect the situation in Canada. Following the Toronto printers' strike, in the course of which several union leaders had been arrested on charges of seditious conspiracy, the Canadian unions (and particularly the Toronto Trades Assembly) exerted pressure upon Parliament to follow the example set by British legislation, and were successful in arousing public opinion on their behalf. The outcome was a statute, very closely modelled on the English Act, which was passed by the Canadian Parliament in 1872. It was laid down that trade unions were no longer to be considered unlawful merely by reason of the fact that they were in restraint of trade, and an attempt was made to define what unions could and could not legally do in such matters as strikes, picketing, and so on.

THE CANADIAN LABOUR UNION AND THE KNIGHTS OF LABOUR

This legislation provided the fundamental legal basis for the further growth of trade unions in Canada. Significant also of the growing strength of the unions and their increasing willingness to act in concert was the formation in 1873 of the Canadian Labour Union. This was the first attempt on the part of Canadian labour to bring together in a single organization all the unions in the country. The individual unions were to elect delegates to attend an annual convention, and provision was made for joint action by the unions, through the C.L.U., to assist any member union involved in a strike or lock-out, provided an attempt had been made to settle the dispute by arbitration. Political objectives, and particularly the enactment of beneficial legislation, were given a prominent place in the original constitution.

In the example it set and the possibilities it offered, the Canadian Labour Union exercised an important influence on the later history of the Canadian labour movement. Its active life, however, was very short and its concrete achievements small. The commercial panic of 1873 and the business depression which followed wiped out many of the component craft unions and, as a consequence, the central organization. The Canadian Labour Union held three annual conventions and then ceased to exist as a functioning body. Revival of union strength and the renewal of attempts to create an effective central organization awaited the return of prosperity. Moderate expansion took place in the early 1880's, with the building trades, the cigar-makers, the printers, and the coal-miners of Nova Scotia making significant additions to their strength. Rapid growth in union membership and in the formation of new locals took place during the industrial revival after 1885. With railway construction and the opening of the west to settlement, several unions established themselves in Manitoba and British Columbia. Over the whole decade of the 1880's, it has been estimated, more than one hundred new locals were formed, the majority of them being associated with the international unions.

Increases in union membership were accompanied by renewed and more determined moves in the direction of central organization. The first Canadian assembly of the Knights of Labour was held in Hamilton in 1881, and this movement, with its semi-secret ritual, its idealistic philosophy of reform, and its appeal to the agriculturist and the small business man as well as to the unskilled labourer who had been passed over by the craft unions, rapidly attained considerable popularity and influence. By the late 1880's, according to Professor Logan, it embraced not less than 250 locals, organized in seven district assemblies. Unlike most labour organizations of American origin, the Knights of Labour achieved some of their most striking successes in the province of Quebec, perhaps partly because of the guarded approval of the Catholic Church. For several years after they had sunk into insignificance in the United States, the Knights of Labour remained influential in Canada—a fact for which their strength in Quebec and their willingness to admit as members workers who were excluded from the craft unions seem to have been largely responsible. After about 1895, however, the movement seems to have lost its crusading zeal and by 1900 its constructive influence was spent.

Paralleling the rise of the Knights of Labour were attempts to organize city centrals, district councils, and a central congress along more conventional lines. As in the 1870's, the genesis of the movement was in Toronto, with the Typographical Union playing a leading role. The Toronto Trades and Labour Council was formed in 1881, followed within a few years by similar councils in the principal manufacturing cities of Ontario. Vancouver, Victoria, Winnipeg, Quebec, and Halifax all had city centrals of this type by 1898; by 1901 there were no less than 25 such bodies throughout Canada. Their principal functions were to serve as forums where the common problems of the member unions could be discussed, and to watch over (and influence where possible) municipal, provincial, and federal legislation. Efforts to secure direct labour representation in the provincial and federal legislatures met with little success.

THE TRADES AND LABOUR CONGRESS OF CANADA

During the early 1880's the Knights of Labour were a potentially serious source of competition for the craft unions and a series of attempts was made to bridge the gap between the two movements, despite the great differences in their organization and philosophy. Many members of the craft unions, in fact, were also members of the Knights of Labour. This problem of dual membership played a significant part in the negotiations leading up to the formation of a new national congress of labour. The first attempt to form such a congress was made in 1883, when the Toronto Trades and Labour Council invited all trade unions and assemblies of the Knights of Labour to send delegates to Toronto to draft a provisional programme and constitution. This convention was not followed by any concrete result. Three years later, however, a second convention was held and this time a permanent central organization was formally established which later adopted the title of the Trades and Labour Congress of Canada.

Unlike the American Federation of Labor, founded three months later, the Trades and Labour Congress of Canada did not at first confine itself to the craft unions. According to its constitution, it was to include both organizations of the Knights of Labour and trade unions, and for the first few years of its existence both these movements were approximately equally represented. The task of holding together in a single organization both the craft unions (most of whom were also affiliated with the A.F.L. and reflected its philosophy of "business unionism") and the Knights of Labour, however, caused considerable internal difficulties which finally led to crisis in 1902. In that year the Congress decided that only one union should be recognized in each trade and only one central council in each city. This entailed the abandonment of the original conception of a federation of all unions. After 1902 the T.L.C., in effect, recognized only Canadian locals of unions affiliated with the A.F.L.

The constitution of the T.L.C., as originally drafted, laid it down that the single purpose of the Congress was to "work for the passage of new laws or amendments to existing laws, in the interests of those who have to earn their living, as well as to insure at the same time the well-being of the working class". No provision was made to empower the Congress to assist member unions involved in strikes (as had been the case with the earlier Canadian Labour Union), nor was the central organization authorized to take the initiative in organizing and chartering new unions. Disappointment with the meagre results obtained through political action led in 1894 to the amendment of the constitution so as to permit the chartering of new unions in localities where local unions or assemblies of the Knights of Labour did not exist, but nothing was done to increase the effectiveness of the Congress as an instrument of direct political action. Far from evolving as the nucleus of an independent labour party, the Canadian organization seemed content to follow the policies set by the A.F.L. This was true also of its reluctance to take the initiative in organizing unskilled and semi-skilled workers.

The decision of the Trades and Labour Congress to exclude from membership assemblies of the Knights of Labour led to a serious division within the Canadian labour movement. In Quebec, where the Knights of Labour had been strong, the decline of that organization and its exclusion from the T.L.C. left a vacuum which the craft unions of the T.L.C. failed to fill. The unionized workers of this province therefore actively supported the formation of the National Trades and Labour Congress (1902), which later became the Canadian Federation of Labour. Assemblies of the Knights of Labour were encouraged to affiliate, as were all "national" unions throughout the country. This move won some support from English-speaking workers who resented the influence of the A.F.L. upon the policies of the T.L.C. and hoped for the development of a distinctively Canadian organization, free from the ties of international unionism. International unions were in fact excluded from membership in the Federation. In its early years the membership of the Federation was drawn mostly from the province of Quebec, its principal strength being among the shoe workers of Montreal and Quebec city. Later it expanded into the Maritimes, with the affiliation in 1909 of the Provincial Workmen's Association, the union of the Nova Scotian coal-miners. At this time the Federation seemed in a strong position to make good its claim to be the spokesman and primary representative of the Canadian labour movement as a whole. After 1910, however, the Federation lost support in Quebec and became for a time almost exclusively an Ontario organization; some of the ground lost in Quebec was recovered after the end of World War I and significant gains were recorded in Alberta. By 1923 total membership had risen to 17,447, but thereafter it declined steadily. By this time the anti-internationalist policies of the Federation had lost much of their appeal, while many of its most active members in Quebec were lost to the National Catholic unions.

THE WESTERN FEDERATION OF MINERS

The purge of the T.L.C. in 1902 also entailed loss of support in western Canada, particularly among the unions of mine-workers. Opposition to the T.L.C. first developed with the organizing activities of the socialist Western Federation of Miners (formed in Montana in 1893) and its affiliate, the Western Labor Union (later called the American Labor Union). The first Canadian branch of the Western Federation of Miners was established at Rossland, British Columbia, in 1895, and by the early years of the twentieth century the Federation had achieved a position of considerable strength among the miners in the eastern part of the province and on Vancouver Island. In 1903, however, it suffered serious set-backs in strikes against the Crow's Nest Pass Coal Company and the Canadian Pacific Railway and a number of locals were lost to the competing organization, the United Mineworkers of America. At this time both organizations sought to include in their membership both coal- and metal-miners, which naturally led to many jurisdictional disputes. Later an agreement was reached whereby the United Mineworkers agreed to confine itself to the coal industry and the Western Federation to metal-mining. In 1906, with the start of the mining boom in Ontario, the Western Federation expanded into that province with a branch at Cobalt, followed within a few years by others at Kirkland Lake, Sudbury, Gowganda, and Porcupine. The highest point of membership was reached in 1912, with approximately 5,000 members enrolled. The Federation retained its strength through the war years, but after 1919 it began to decline and in 1925 it ceased to function in Canada. Ten years later the organization (now entitled the International Union of Mine, Mill and Smelter Workers and affiliated with the Congress of Industrial Organizations) re-entered Canada and after an uphill fight succeeded in building up its membership in Canada to 4,000 in 1938. A strike for union recognition and wage increases at Kirkland Lake in 1941 was followed by further increases in strength and by 1944 the union claimed 39 branches throughout Canada with a total membership of 12,500.

In its early years the Western Federation of Miners held itself aloof from the A.F.L. and the Canadian Trades and Labour Congress. Its dominant philosophy was strongly socialist and its policies aimed at direct action rather than at piecemeal improvement of wages and working conditions as was typical of the A.F.L. At first these characteristics were probably a source of strength to the Federation, as were its attempts to organize labour on an industry-wide basis rather than on a craft basis on the A.F.L model. Many of the most energetic and dedicated leaders of the Federation, however, joined the Industrial Workers of the World when this organization, with a programme more revolutionary than that of the Federation, established itself in Canada in 1906. By 1911 the I.W.W. claimed a Canadian membership of 10,000, and although after 1913 it suffered a serious decline in strength its development in Canada contributed to a marked softening in the Federation's earlier ideology of militant socialism. By 1910 this process had gone so far that the Western Federation was prepared to accept affiliation with and to receive a charter from the A.F.L. and thus gain entrance to the Canadian Trades and Labour Congress. Nevertheless, conflicts in political doctrine continued to harass the organization after its return to Canada under a new name in 1935 and still do so at the present day.

THE ONE BIG UNION

During the period immediately before World War I unorganized workers in the west outside the mining industry, particularly in the metal and building trades, developed their own unions and their own forms of joint organizational campaigns. By 1914 most of these western unions, like the Western Federation of Miners, had been gathered into the fold of the Trades and Labour Congress. During the war years, with their intensive industrialization, the membership of the Congress expanded rapidly and jurisdictional boundaries between the various unions were largely ignored. The apparent harmony in the labour movement was, however, rudely shattered in 1919, when a serious split developed between the more radical members of the Congress, with their strength principally in the west, and the conservative wing, dominated by the eastern craft unions. The precipitating cause of the disruption was resentment in the west at action taken by the federal government, under war emergency powers, to ban foreign-dominated organizations and "subversive" literature and to place under arrest persons who were alleged to have been undermining the Canadian war effort. Underlying this, however, was the serious dissatisfaction which many of the leaders of the western unions felt with the cautious policies of the eastern wing of the party, particularly in regard to the alleged willingness of the leaders of the T.L.C. to co-operate with the government and thereby, as it was felt, with interests antagonistic to labour. Resolutions were introduced at the Quebec convention of the T.L.C. in 1918 condemning the government's treatment of "citizen enemies", indicating lack of confidence in the leadership of the T.L.C., and advocating the reorganization of the Canadian labour movement "by industry instead of by craft". These resolutions were defeated by narrow margins. In the following years the western unions, led by the British Columbia Federation of Labour and the Vancouver Trades and Labour Council, seceded from the T.L.C. and set up a rival organization which took the name of the One Big Union.

The One Big Union, many of whose leaders had had experience in the British labour movement before coming to Canada, adopted a programme based generally on the Marxist theory of the class struggle and looking toward the organization of workers on industry-wide rather than craft lines, so that the working class could enforce its demands by direct action rather than by parliamentary lobbying. The principal weapon to be used in this connection was the sympathetic strike. This weapon was used and severely tried in 1919, when the O.B.U. became involved in a general strike which began among the building and metal trades in Winnipeg. Demands for wage increases and union recognition by these workers were refused by the employers and negotiations broke down. The unions concerned then brought their dispute before the Winnipeg Trades and Labour Council, which in turn referred it to the O.B.U. The O.B.U., after a referendum vote of the whole membership, called a general strike in Winnipeg, announcing that its minimum demands were for union recognition, wage increases, and the reinstatement of all striking workers without prejudice. It was generally believed at the time that the unions intended to seize control of the city, and the government later alleged that the strike was in fact an attempt at political revolution. Sympathetic strikes were called in cities as far distant as Toronto and Sydney, Nova Scotia, and for a time it seemed as if the conflict might become nation-wide. Despite the fact that it was still in process of formation and as yet lacked even a formal constitution, the O.B.U. proved itself an organization of formidable strength and, if the government had not intervened, might well have succeeded in enforcing its demands. On June 17, however, the leaders of the striking unions were placed under arrest on charges of inciting revolution. Later in that month, after the metal-trades employers had announced their acceptance of the principle of collective bargaining, the unions, crippled as they were by the loss of their leaders and the government's clear intention to intervene even more decisively if necessary, called off the strike unconditionally. Despite this serious initial setback, the O.B.U. made rapid gains in membership in the period 1919-21 and appeared for a time a grave threat to the established position of the Trades and Labour Congress. In British Columbia the Vancouver Trades and Labour Council became affiliated with the O.B.U. in 1919, followed by the metal-miners in the same province and the coal-miners of British Columbia and Alberta. Similar gains were made in Manitoba and some headway was made among the members of the craft unions in the eastern provinces. By January, 1920, membership had risen to almost 50,000. Opposition gradually stiffened, however, not only among employers but also among other branches of the labour movement. The United Mineworkers of America were bitterly resentful of the inroads which the O.B.U. had made among coal-miners in British Columbia and Alberta and, backed to some extent by the employers, finally succeeded in forcing the O.B.U. to withdraw from that area at the end of 1920. In the same year the Lumber Workers' Industrial Union withdrew from the organization, and several international unions, under pressure from the T.L.C. and the A.F.L., took steps to prevent their members from belonging also to the O.B.U. By 1923 the membership of the O.B.U. had dropped to less than half its 1920 total and was drawn almost exclusively from the service trades and general workers. The organization as a whole was now little more than a minor protest movement.

The Trades and Labour Congress in the meantime was undergoing difficulties, not only from its loss of strength in the west, but also from the business depression of 1921 and an "open shop" drive on the part of employers in the early 1920's. Membership reached a peak of 173,463 in 1920 but thereafter declined to 132,071 in 1922, 117,110 in 1924, and 103,037 in 1926. Throughout this period the T.L.C. made no move toward organizing workers on an industrial basis; rather the older organizational pattern of craft unionism seems to have become more rigid than formerly. The result was that the T.L.C. came to be more and more an organization of the old-line skilled trades, with the building trades, the printers, the garment-workers, and certain classes of railway employees playing a dominant role. The new basic industries, such as pulp-and-paper and metal-mining, as well as the growing mass-employment manufacturing industries, were therefore left to form their own types of organization independently of the Trades and Labour Congress.

In the early 1930's certain of these new unions, hard hit by the depression, came together in an organization known as the Workers' Unity League, which was in effect the Canadian counterpart of the American Trade Union Unity League (a continuation of the older Trade Union Educational League). This organization, it is generally agreed, functioned as the Canadian representative of the Red International of labour unions with headquarters in Moscow. Its primary objectives were the organization of unorganized workers into unions under Communist leadership and the infiltration of established unions with a view to turning them to Communist-inspired policies. This movement had managed to get a foothold in the Canadian labour movement in the 1920's, by forming opposition unions in the needle trades and the mining industry. By 1930 the Industrial Union of Needle Trades and the Lumber and Agricultural Workers' Union were definitely affiliated with the W.U.L. Shortly thereafter the Mine Workers' Union of Canada also joined, followed within a few years by the Textile Workers' Union of Canada. Organizations were also formed among the workers in the automobile, steel, and rubber industries, as well as in sundry minor trades.

The Workers' Unity League, by its active organizing campaigns in the low-paid mass-employment industries, grew rapidly in membership during the depression years of the 1930's. By 1936, however, the central organization was in process of disbandment and most of the member unions had accepted affiliation either with the Trades and Labour Congress or with the newly formed All-Canadian Congress of Labour. The explanation for this remarkable reversal is to be found, it seems, in a change in Communist party policy. With the rise of fascism in Europe, it became official policy to cease all activities likely to cause disunity within the ranks of organized labour. Several of the Canadian leaders of the W.U.L. refused to follow this switch in tactics, but the majority accepted it without overt protest.

THE DEVELOPMENT OF INDUSTRIAL UNIONISM: THE CANADIAN CONGRESS OF LABOUR

The early success of the Workers' Unity League demonstrated that the future development of the Canadian labour movement depended upon the organizing of unskilled and semi-skilled workers on an industrial rather than a craft basis. A start had been made in this direction, independently of the Workers' Unity League, by the formation of the All-Canadian Congress of Labour in 1927, but this organization, with its strongly nationalistic philosophy, failed to make significant headway. More important in the long run were the organizing activities in Canada of unions affiliated with the American Congress of Industrial Organizations, formed in 1935. These unions conducted very active organizing campaigns in Canadian industries which, apart from the efforts of the W.U.L., had previously been almost untouched by the union movement, such as steel, automobiles, rubber, electrical manufacturing, metal-mining, and west-coast lumbering. Despite the fact that the parent organization, the C.I.O., had been expelled from the American Federation of Labour in 1935, these new Canadian industrial unions remained affiliated with the Canadian Trades and Labour Congress until 1939. In that year, however, continued pressure from the craft unions led to their expulsion. The consequence was the formation in 1940 of the Canadian Congress of Labour, a new organization formed by the amalgamation of the industrial unions expelled from the T.L.C. and the older All-Canadian Congress of Labour. This organization became in effect the Canadian counterpart of the C.I.O. in the United States, in much the same way as the Trades and Labour Congress was the counterpart of the A.F.L.

At the beginning of World War II, therefore, there were three central labour organizations in Canada: The Trades and Labour Congress; the Canadian Congress of Labour; and the Canadian and Catholic Confederation of Labour. The differences in the composition of these three organizations may be briefly summarized. The T.L.C. unions are generally craft in type, most of them being locals of the A.F.L. unions operating in Canada. Close fraternal relations are maintained with the A.F.L., but the policies of the two organizations are not always the same—as, for instance, the decision of the T.L.C. in 1946 to affiliate with the World Federation of Trade Unions. The C.C.L. unions are almost all industrial in type, being mostly locals of unions affiliated with the C.I.O. operating in Canada. The Canadian locals of C.I.O. unions have, however, been granted complete autonomy, both formally and in fact, by the American organization. There are also a few unions of the A.F.L. and the C.I.O. in Canada whose Canadian membership is not affiliated with the Canadian congresses, as well as a handful of independent unions, such as the International Railway Brotherhoods, and a few unaffiliated unions. The Canadian and Catholic Confederation of Labour operates only in the province of Quebec and is made up of local syndicates and trade or industry federations. The central organization was formed in 1921. The numerical strength of the various organizations on January 1, 1953, was as follows:

Organization	*Membership*
Trades and Labour Congress of Canada	558,722
American Federation of Labor only	10,524
Canadian Congress of Labour	352,538
Congress of Industrial Organizations only	3,000
Canadian and Catholic Confederation of Labour	104,486
International Railway Brotherhoods	41,751
Unaffiliated unions	148,693
	1,219,714

(Source: *Canada Year Book*, 1954, p. 746)

ORGANIZED LABOUR AT MID-CENTURY

The high point of union membership in Canada before World War II was reached in 1937 when the unions, with a total of 383,492 members on their books, for the first time surpassed the record of 378,047 which had been set in 1919. The total number of wage-earners in the meantime, however, had increased from just under 2 million in 1919 to more than 2.5 million in 1939, so that over the whole period the percentage of wage-earners who belonged to unions had actually declined. During the course of World War II very substantial gains in membership were made, the total rising from 358,967 in 1939 to 711,117 in 1945. These increases in strength were greatly facilitated by the passing by the federal government, on a temporary war-time basis, of collective bargaining regulations roughly parallel to those incorporated in the Wagner Act in the United States—that is, preventing employers from discriminating against workers for joining unions and forbidding employers the right to refuse to bargain collectively with their employees. Certain of the provinces had already taken action in this connection before the war but the legislation passed had not been enforced and employers had found it easy to avoid compliance. The federal government, anxious to avoid labour unrest during the war, took its first step in the direction of compulsory collective bargaining in 1940 by issuing an Order in Council (P.C. 2685) asserting the workers' right to organize and to negotiate agreements through their elected representatives. This statement of principle, however, was not at first put into practice, even in plants owned and controlled by the government itself. Growing dissatisfaction on the part of labour, accentuated by the support which the government apparently gave to the employers in the Kirkland Lake strike of November, 1941, culminated in a concerted drive, backed by both the T.L.C. and the C.C.L., for explicit enactment of collective-bargaining rights. Continued pressure upon the government led finally to the issue of an Order in Council (P.C. 1003) which granted most of labour's demands. Labour was accorded the right to bargaining representatives of its own choosing; negotiations were to be carried on in good faith; employers were forbidden to discriminate against workers for belonging to unions; union organizers were not to coerce workers to join unions nor to canvass on business premises on company time; and a War-time Labour Relations Board with equal representation from employers and labour and a neutral chairman was created to administer and enforce the regulations. Labour did not succeed, however, in its major goal, which was to have the protection afforded by this Order in Council embodied in legislation in the form of a National Labour Code.

As a consequence of this action by the federal government, taken under war-time emergency powers, collective-bargaining rights were established in almost all industries and collective agreements became the rule, whereas before the war they had been exceptional. The jurisdiction of the federal government in this matter, however, would necessarily expire, under the terms of the British North America Act, with the ending of the war emergency. This was clearly realized both by employers and by the unions. The unions therefore lost no time in instituting an aggressive campaign for union security, higher wage rates, and the "check-off" system (i.e., the deduction of union dues from pay cheques by the employer on the written authorization of the worker concerned). The employers, for their part, declining to consider the gains made by labour during the war as necessarily permanent, stiffened their resistance to union demands. The result was a succession of major strikes between September, 1945, and July, 1946, in automobiles, lumber, rubber, textiles, steel, shipping, electrical manufacturing, and mining. The number of man-working days lost as a result of strikes and lock-outs rose from a low of 490,139 in 1944 to 1,457,420 in 1945 and 4,516,393 in 1946. These strikes were supported by the labour movement as a whole with a degree of co-operation and disregard of jurisdictional boundaries that was quite unusual. They ended with acceptance of the check-off system, large increases in union membership, and a general recognition of the fact that labour's war-time gains had been consolidated.

The history of the war-time Orders in Council relating to collective bargaining, and of the subsequent reaction of labour and management, highlights one handicap under which the Canadian labour movement has developed since the formation of the Dominion in 1867. The British North America Act, passed in that year, assigned to the federal government the regulation of trade and commerce, but laid it down that all matters relating to property and civil rights (including contracts of employment) were the responsibility of the individual provinces. Subsequent decisions by the Judicial Committee of the Privy Council have tended to narrow the interpretation of the powers of the federal government and have resulted in a course of development which contrasts sharply with that in the United States, where Supreme Court decisions have in general tended to enlarge the powers of the federal government, particularly in regard to the implications of control of inter-state commerce. This has meant, in the first place, that the responsibility for legislation affecting labour in Canada has been divided among ten (now eleven) governments, instead of being centralized in one; and in the second place that the precise locus of authority for making basic changes in labour legislation has been uncertain. The result has been a diffusion and weakening of the pressure which organized labour has been able to exert on legislation. In normal peace-time conditions, for example, the federal government has no authority over such matters as minimum wages (except in the case of seamen and workers employed on federal government contracts), workmen's compensation, compulsory social insurance for old age and sickness (a constitutional amendment in 1940 made possible federal unemployment insurance) and compulsory collective bargaining. It seems clear that this division of authority has held back the development of a unified labour movement and has limited the gains which organized labour—whose interests are not limited by provincial boundaries—has been able to make. Prediction of future trends is, of course, dangerous, but it appears probable that the efforts of Canadian labour to achieve uniform legislation establishing minimum standards and basic collective-bargaining rights in all the provinces will achieve substantial success. Meanwhile the amalgamation of the T.L.C. and the C.C.L. in May, 1956, suggests that Canadian labour will in the future find its policies, economic and political, less hampered by internal disunity and separatism than has been the case in the past.

SUGGESTIONS FOR FURTHER READING

BASIC WORKS:

Forsey, Eugene, "History of the Labour Movement in Canada", *Canada Year Book, 1957-58* (Ottawa, 1958), pp. 795-802

Jamieson, Stuart, *Industrial Relations in Canada* (Toronto, 1957)

Logan, H. A., *Trade Unions in Canada: Their Development and Functioning* (Toronto, 1948)

SUPPLEMENTARY WORKS:

Forsey, Eugene, "The Influence of American Labor Organizations and Policies on Canadian Labor", *The American Economic Impact on Canada* (Durham, N.C.: Duke University Commonwealth-Studies Center, 1959), pp. 127-47

Wilson, Idele, "Labor Organization in Canada", *Annals of the American Academy of Political and Social Science*, Volume 253 (September, 1947) pp. 98-104

CHAPTER XXIII

CHANGING PATTERNS OF INVESTMENT
AND TRADE

FOREIGN CAPITAL IN CANADIAN DEVELOPMENT

REVOLUTIONARY changes in resource exploitation and use in the modern Canadian economy have been accompanied by equally striking developments in finance and trade. The financing of this twentieth-century industrial revolution drew to Canada a volume of foreign investment greater than that attracted to any other country; the increase in Canada's national production which this investment helped to bring about established her position as one of the world's leading trading nations. The magnitude of Canadian borrowings over the past three decades and the principal sources of investment funds may be noted briefly.

In 1926, foreign long-term investment in Canada amounted to slightly more than $6 billion; of this sum the United States supplied somewhat more than 53 per cent, the United Kingdom almost 44 per cent and other countries less than 3 per cent. The boom of the later twenties led to further external borrowings, and in 1930 these had reached a total of $7.6 billion, a figure not exceeded until 1949. The United States' share was now in the neighbourhood of 60 per cent, while that of the United Kingdom had dropped to 36 per cent. Until war broke out in 1939, the relative position of these two nations as investors in Canadian development displayed very little further change. War needs, however, obliged Great Britain to draw on her overseas resources. By 1946 her long-term investments in Canada had declined from the 1939 total of $2.5 billion to $1.7 billion, and her relative share from 36 per cent to little more than 23 per cent. United States investments, on the other hand, reached a total of $5.16 billion in 1946, about 72 per cent of Canadian long-term borrowings. Since 1949, foreign long-term investment in Canada has increased very rapidly and at the close of 1958 attained a high level of $19.1 billion. The United States in that year accounted for 82 per cent of new foreign investment, the United Kingdom for 15 per cent, and all other countries for 3 per cent. Estimates for 1959 indicate a further increase of about $1.4 billion in Canada's foreign borrowings in that year.

The magnitude of these borrowings is impressive, but more significant is the preponderance of United States funds in the total. The extent of that country's participation in Canadian development is even more striking if reference is made to direct investment, i.e., foreign long-term investment in branches, subsidiaries and controlled companies. In 1957, investments of this type in manufacturing, mining and smelting, utilities, merchandising, financial institutions and other enterprises totalled $10.1 billion; 84 per cent of this total was owned by the United States, 11.5 per cent by the United Kingdom, and 4.5 per cent by other countries. In that year, the United States accounted for $390 million of the net capital inflow for direct investment of $514 million; in contrast, a mere $65 million was invested by the United Kingdom and $59 million by all other countries.

Investments under this heading are of special significance because they are highly concentrated in resource development and related manufactures and because they provide a rough index of the extent of foreign ownership of selected Canadian industries. United States direct investment in the petroleum and natural-gas industry, for example, exceeded $2.3 billion in 1957. Nearly 64 per cent of this industry was owned by non-residents, while companies controlled outside Canada accounted for over 75 per cent of the total investment. Although this is an extreme case, foreign ownership of selected industries embraces over one-third of the total. In manufacturing it was as high as 50 per cent in 1957 (United States' share: 39 per cent); in mining and smelting it amounted to 56 per cent (United States' share: 46 per cent); in railways to 30 per cent (United States' share: 11 per cent). At the close of 1957, 4,449 companies in Canada were controlled in the United States, 1,121 in the United Kingdom, and 435 in other foreign countries. By concentrating on petroleum, mining (particularly iron ore and titanium), pulp and paper, and related manufacturing facilities, foreign capital has provided much of the momentum back of Canada's advance in modern industrialism.

DOMESTIC CAPITAL RESOURCES

The foregoing statistics suggest a heavy dependence on external supports to Canadian industrial expansion and a degree of foreign ownership and control which may not be entirely in the nation's best interests. The magnitude of non-resident investment in Canada (especially of direct investment) and the extent of the contributions made by the United States to her neighbour's economic progress tend, however, to obscure important offsetting factors which taken together support the conclusion that the Canadian economy is less dependent on foreign capital than it was in earlier boom periods, and that it is much stronger and more self-sufficient than the bare statistics of capital borrowing would indicate.

In the first place, Canada is herself a substantial exporter of capital. Canadian external long-term investments, including loans and advances to the United Kingdom, amounted to $4.6 billion in 1957. Of particular importance, her direct foreign investment has steadily increased in the post-war period. In 1957 $68 million was invested in this form to bring the total to just over $2 billion; $1.4 billion of this sum was invested in the United States through subsidiaries and controlled companies, and covered such activities as beverage manufacturing, farm implements, mining and petroleum development, railways and utilities. This export of capital constitutes an important item in Canada's balance of international payments, and although it is true that her net international liabilities increased by $7.6 billion in the period 1949-57, her net liabilities in 1957 were considerably smaller in relation to national income than at the end of 1930.

Secondly, in spite of the large volume of foreign long-term investment in Canadian enterprise in recent years, the proportion of Canadian capital going into the country's development has been more than maintained. The percentage of selected Canadian industries owned by non-residents was less in 1957 than in 1939. Canadians themselves have been investing heavily in their country's growth. The increasing strength of the economy is reflected in the ability of Canadians to finance a larger proportion of the nation's capital ventures. While the share of non-residents in mining and petroleum and some sectors of manufacturing has been increasing, Canadian ownership of steam railways, utilities and similar activities has shown a strong upward trend. Further, Canadian ownership of the funded debt of Canadian governments and corporations is close to 83 per cent of the total, in contrast to less than 66 per cent in 1936. And when account is taken of the very large volume of Canadian investment in farm properties, residential real estate, federal, provincial and municipal assets, items not included in statements of non-resident ownership, it is clear that Canadian ownership of Canadian wealth is substantially greater than that indicated by estimates of external participation in selected Canadian industries. These estimates are valuable for the light they throw on the extent of this participation but they understate the growing importance of Canadian domestic investment in the country's enterprises.

Thirdly, and closely related to the above, the volume of Canadian savings since World War II has been large enough to support all but a small proportion of post-war growth in the nation's productive capacity. Recent research findings support the conclusion that domestic savings in fact financed about 75 per cent of the gross capital formation in the period 1946-58, in contrast with roughly 50 per cent in the period 1929-30. In short, the economy is now generating sufficient savings to finance a very large part, if not all, of its development. They have not in fact done so for a number of reasons. Substantial amounts were invested outside the country and much went into the retirement of debts contracted abroad. Further, the scarcity of risk capital in Canada, the initiative of non-resident investors,

574

and the strength of market and financial connections with the United States has led to a continued influx of foreign capital.

In sum, the pattern of capital investment in Canada is not difficult to discern in its broad outlines. On the one hand, foreign long-term investment has increased very substantially in the post-war years; the United States has become by far the major source of investment funds; such funds have been invested very largely in Canadian resource development; this venture capital and the advanced techniques which accompanied it have strongly stimulated Canadian economic growth; this stimulus arises largely from the emphasis placed by the United States and other investors on the most dynamic and speculative sectors of Canadian enterprise. On the other hand, the volume and direction of borrowings should not be allowed to conceal the fact that the economy is now very nearly strong enough to pay its own way, that outside borrowings represent a small fraction of total investment in Canada, and that even in industry the extent of non-resident ownership is less than in earlier expansionist periods of this century.

VOLUME AND DIRECTION OF EXTERNAL TRADE

The role of Canada as both importer and exporter of long-term investment funds reflects the power and proximity of the United States economy, the increasingly close relations of Canadian and United States enterprise in an era of advanced industrialism, and the growing strength and diversity of a now highly industrialized Canada. In the pattern of investment there is clearly apparent a lessening of Canada's dependence on external capital supplies and a strengthening of complementary relationships between these two North American nations. The increasingly close economic interplay in which capital and goods move north and south across the boundary has undoubtedly accelerated the rate of advance in both countries. For Canada, this interplay has its dangers as well as its advantages. This is more easily discerned in relation to the changing pattern of Canadian trade and we turn now to this aspect of North American enterprise.

Large-scale investment in Canada's productive capacity has strengthened her position as one of the leading trading nations of the world. In the years preceding the last World War she ranked fifth or sixth among trading nations; in the post-war years she has usually occupied third place. If trade per capita is used as a basis of comparison, only New Zealand outranks Canada among the important trading nations. In value terms, Canada's total trade rose from $1.68 billion in 1939 to $5.74 billion in 1949 and exceeded $10 billion in 1958. If allowance is made for price changes these increases are less impressive, though substantial; in her import trade, volume indexes based on 1948=100 ranged from 102 in 1949 to 168.3 in 1958; export volume indexes exhibit smaller changes, attaining a high point of 130.3 in 1958. These gains are sufficient to strengthen Canada's status as a trading power, although it should be noted that in spite of her high rank as trader Canada's share of world trade is only about 5 per cent. As a consequence, prices of Canadian imports and exports are set very largely on world markets, and the nation is faced with the necessity of adjustment to frequent changes in the value as well as the volume of her foreign trade.

As with foreign investment in Canada, growth in magnitude or volume of trade has been accompanied by important changes in its direction. In the immediate post-war years, large-scale financial assistance to overseas countries helped to maintain effective demand for Canadian exports, but since 1948 the dollar shortage and related trade and exchange restrictions have greatly reduced the overseas market for Canadian goods. The result has been to reinforce tendencies strengthening Canada's trade relations with her neighbour. In the period 1948-58, the United States took approximately 57 per cent of Canada's total exports in contrast to the one-third before dollar-saving restrictions took on importance. In 1950 alone, about two-thirds of Canadian exports found a market in the United States. The United Kingdom's share has remained in the neighbourhood of 16 per cent and that of continental Europe somewhat less than 10 per cent.

The change is even more striking when we turn to Canadian imports from the United States. In 1950 slightly more than two-thirds of her imports came from her neighbour; in later years this proportion has varied between 68 and 74 per cent, in contrast to that of the United Kingdom which has fluctuated about a level of 10 per cent. Roughly two-thirds of Canada's total trade is now with the United States and it is unlikely that there will be any marked deviation from this pattern in the near future. The enormous and growing power of the United States economy, its advantages in the Canadian market, and its expanding needs for Canadian materials will probably offset any changes resulting from improvements in world trade. This is a pattern which, closely associated with capital movements, promises a steady increase in the economic interdependence of the two powers. Canada stands to benefit from this interdependence as she has done in the past, but it is not without its array of problems, some of which Canada shares with other nations.

COMMERCIAL POLICY IN THE UNITED STATES

Some of these problems have been outlined in preceding chapters. Canada's rate of progress is now closely geared to conditions in the United States market and she has become more than ever exposed to the national policies pursued by that power. In farm products and most lines of manufacturing, Canada remains a marginal supplier, one whose goods the United

States may take when convenient, or restrict or prohibit when United States supplies are abundant or low-priced. Exposure to sudden and adverse changes in United States commercial policy weakens prospects for stability in production or trade. An equally serious problem arises from the huge volume of Canada's purchases from the United States; these represent about one-fifth of the total exports of that country and make Canada her best customer. These purchases, which amounted to more than $3.4 billion in 1958, greatly exceed United States purchases from Canada. The resulting annual trade deficit commonly exceeds $0.5 billion and in 1956 went as high as $1.1 billion. If dividend returns to the United States and payments on freight, interest and tourist account are taken into consideration, Canada's total current account deficit with the United States regularly exceeds $1 billion annually. To meet her deficits, Canada must be able to sell in large volume in the United States and to other countries who can settle their accounts in United States dollars. The alternative—to reduce purchases from the United States—runs counter to the general policy of working toward greater freedom in world trade, an objective of crucial importance to Canada's future prosperity.

This problem of making ends meet in international trade is complicated by another which has taken on urgency in recent years, namely the effects of United States commercial policies on the character of Canadian economic development. These policies have significance not only for the volume and direction of Canada's export trade but also for the form in which her materials are exported. Such materials are derived mainly from her forests and mines and to a less extent from her fisheries and her farms. It is important to the rate of the country's industrial progress that a growing proportion of these products be exported in a more or less fully manufactured state, and a smaller proportion in raw or primary form. In view of Canada's industrial expansion of the past decade, a pronounced shift along these lines might be expected. Unfortunately, this shift has not taken place at the rate Canadian producers might reasonably anticipate. The principal obstacle to this shift is to be found in a United States tariff structure weighted heavily in favour of products in raw or simply processed form; materials at this stage are commonly free of duty or bear low rates of duty. On the other hand, rates on imports tend to be higher the more advanced the stage of manufacture and in some instances stand at a prohibitive level.

This policy helps to explain the fact that the bulk of Canada's mineral exports leave the country in more or less primary form; and if newsprint is omitted, this is also largely true of forest products. It has been estimated that, at best, 20 per cent of Canada's exports to the United States enter that country in manufactured form. Inability to export goods at more advanced stages of manufacture denies the Canadian producer the economies of mass production for a continental market. The necessity of concentrating

577

on her limited domestic market weakens the competitive power of industries operating under this handicap and gives strength to demands for greater protection to Canadian industry. To the effects of the weighted tariff structure must be added the uncertainties present in administrative delays which complex tariff procedures imply, and the dangers of adverse action in defence of United States price-support programmes. Such policies and procedures must inevitably slow down Canadian industrial progress and discourage the long-range planning so essential to the application of the advanced technologies of modern industrialism. The unpleasant fact must also be recognized that the United States is a major producer of most of the manufactures which Canada exports to overseas markets.

At every step, then, the state of the United States market and the nature of that country's commercial policies are matters of overwhelming importance to the rate and character of Canadian economic development. There is, however, at least one bright spot in the picture. Changes over the past few decades in the resource position of the United States appear to ensure a growing market for Canadian materials. This large and growing, if not always stable, demand reflects both the high level of economic activity in the United States and that country's increasing dependence on external sources for materials crucial to her progress and security. The future scarcity of strategic resources in the United States is suggested by the findings of the President's Material Policy Commission Report of June, 1952 (more commonly known as the Paley Report), in which an attempt is made to gauge the resource needs of the United States economy in the decade of the 1970's when its consumption of key materials and its dependence on outside sources for supplies of these materials will have substantially increased. The Canadian economy, which has felt the pull of United States demands for her resources over much of this century, is in a uniquely favourable position to meet her neighbour's expanding import needs for base metals, pulp and paper, lumber and a wide range of the new metals vitally important in the technology of modern industry. This carries with it the prospect of a continued and increasingly close relationship between the two economies. In this growing dependence of the United States on Canadian supplies, moreover, there is the likelihood of a much stronger bargaining position for the smaller country as it becomes less a marginal supplier and more a key source of the essential materials which are hers in abundance.

Much more is needed, however, than a stronger bargaining position in North America, for basically Canada's prospects for continued growth toward a more diversified and more advanced stage of economic development rest upon the restoration of multilateral world trade. This assumes the gradual removal of restrictions on trade between North America and the members of the sterling area and other non-dollar countries whose lack of dollar earnings greatly weakens their ability to purchase and pay for

Canadian products. Only the United States, with her vast domestic market and her enormous productive power, is in a position to lead the way to a new economic internationalism of expanding world trade. She alone can undertake the volume of dollar investment abroad necessary to the attainment of this objective. This aspect of the responsibility that goes with leadership appears to have been recognized. More difficult because of the strength of protectionist influences in a continental economy is the hoped-for and much-discussed revision of United States commercial policies. The competitive power of the United States is sufficiently great to support the belief that substantial progress will be made over the next few decades in freeing her trade from present restrictions, but no marked deviation from present policies is to be expected in the near future. Meanwhile, maintenance of a high level of prosperity in this key sector of the world economy, a continued flow of United States investments abroad, and strong support to underdeveloped countries provide much of the stimulus back of present world recovery. Canada, too, has her contributions to make. Her responsibilities are increasing with her growing strength, and, although overshadowed by those of her neighbour, her foreign investment and trade policies can do much to tip the scale in favour of freer world trade. No nation has a greater stake than Canada in the success of this venture.

A NEW NATIONAL POLICY?

In review, it is apparent that there will be no weakening of United States influences on Canadian trade in our time. The growing demand for Canadian materials in the United States and the strength of her marketing and financial connections in Canada are factors pulling the two economies closer together. There are indications, however, of a developing resistance to the pull of the larger economy on the smaller one. It has been pointed out earlier that Canada has shown herself to be capable of generating the larger part of the savings necessary to finance a high level of domestic investments, that her dependence on capital imports is rapidly declining, and that she herself is exporting substantial amounts of long-term capital. The new-found strength of the Canadian economy has given rise to a new confidence in the nation's ability to finance and carry through the massive undertakings of advanced industrialism. This change in attitude was reflected in the widespread demand that she proceed alone with the construction of the St. Lawrence Seaway.

It is true that United States funds have strongly supported Canada's twentieth-century economic progress; but it is also true that United States commercial policies are running directly counter to the trend of development which her foreign investments have stimulated. A nation as industrially advanced as Canada and as heavily dependent on external markets is unlikely to accept complacently a situation in which a large proportion of her exports continue to leave the country in raw or simply processed form and in which she is faced with the uncertainties of frequent and unpredictable changes in her export trade. If this situation persists, there is a strong likelihood that defensive measures will take on new importance. These will probably appear as a strengthening of existing pressures for a national policy designed to improve Canada's position as a producer of the complex and finished products of modern industry.

This nascent national policy of Canada's new industrialism is not without elements of similarity to the national policy pursued so vigorously in the half-century before 1930. The old national policy, like the new, was rooted in the necessity of erecting defences against the competitive power of the United States, and of strengthening trade and financial connections with Europe. But there are also significant elements of difference. The old policy was a staples policy; the new would hasten Canada's departure from its "staples era" into one of advanced industrial technology. Further, the United States rather than Great Britain is now the pace-setter of the world economy. Because of these differences, the new policy, if actively pursued, promises to be a more complex and arduous enterprise than that formulated in the 1870's. And it has its dangers. The close economic interplay of Canada and the United States in the twentieth century has created a mutually reinforcing network of investment and trade of great benefit to both. Increasing resort to defensive tactics by Canada must inevitably strengthen protectionist influences in this country and in the end result in a less efficient utilization of the resources of the continent. Both nations have a common interest in an expanding world economy, in a broadening and deepening of the channels of world commerce and finance. Only the United States can assume the role of leadership in this undertaking. Failing this, Canada must continue as of old her policies of adaptive, sometimes costly, response to external conditions over which she alone can exert little control.

SUGGESTIONS FOR FURTHER READING

BASIC WORKS:

Brecher, Irving, and S. S. Reisman, *Canada-United States Economic Relations* (Ottawa, 1957)

Knox, F. A., "Trade and the World Economy" in G. W. Brown (ed.), *Canada* (Berkeley, 1950), Chapter XXIII, pp. 522-40

Safarian, A. E., and E. B. Carty, "Foreign Financing of Canadian Investment in the Post-War Period", *Proceedings of the Business and Economic Statistics Section, American Statistical Association* (September 10-13, 1954, at Montreal, Canada), pp. 72-79

SUPPLEMENTARY WORKS:

Bank of Canada, *Annual Report of the Governor to the Minister of Finance and Statement of Accounts for the Year 1959* (Ottawa, 1960)

Canada, Dominion Bureau of Statistics, International Trade Division, Balance of Payments Section. *The Canadian Balance of International Payments, 1958, and International Investment Position* (Ottawa, 1959)

Canada Year Book, 1954, "Foreign Trade", Chapter XXI, Sections I-III, pp. 961-1023; and "Canada's International Investment Position", Chapter XXIV, Section 2, pp. 1115-20 (Ottawa, 1954)

The Bank of Nova Scotia, *Monthly Review* (Toronto: Feb.-March, 1953, Oct.-Nov., 1953, April, 1954)

INDEX